SACRED HISTORIES

Sacred Histories

A Festschrift for

MÁIRE HERBERT

John Carey, Kevin Murray &
Caitríona Ó Dochartaigh

EDITORS

FOUR COURTS PRESS

Set in 10.5 pt on 12.5 pt Ehrhardt for
FOUR COURTS PRESS LTD
7 Malpas Street, Dublin 8, Ireland
www.fourcourtspress.ie
and in North America for
FOUR COURTS PRESS
c/o ISBS, 920 N.E. 58th Avenue, Suite 300, Portland, OR 97213.

A catalogue record for this title
is available from the British Library.

ISBN 978-1-84682-564-4

Printed in England
by Antony Rowe Ltd, Chippenham, Wilts.

Contents

Noid / Abbreviations

ACL	*Archiv für celtische Lexikographie*, 3 vols, ed. Whitley Stokes and Kuno Meyer (Halle, 1898–1907).
AClon.	*Annals of Clonmacnoise being the Annals of Ireland from the earliest period to AD 1408*, ed. Denis Murphy (Dublin, 1896; repr. Felinfach, 1993).
ACon.	*Annála Connacht: the Annals of Connacht (AD 1224–1544)*, ed. A. Martin Freeman (Dublin, 1944).
ACott.	'The annals in Cotton MS Titus A. XXV', ed. A. Martin Freeman, *RC* 41 (1924), 301–30; 42 (1925), 283–305; 43 (1926), 358–84; 44 (1927), 336–61; repr. as a monograph (Paris, 1929).
AFM	*Annála ríoghachta Éireann: Annals of the kingdom of Ireland by the Four Masters*, 7 vols, ed. John O'Donovan (Dublin, 1848–51; 2nd ed. 1856; facs. repr. with Introduction and Appendix by Kenneth Nicholls, Dublin, 1990).
AI	*The Annals of Inisfallen (MS Rawlinson B.503)*, ed. Seán Mac Airt (Dublin, 1951).
ALC	*Annals of Loch Cé: a chronicle of Irish affairs from AD 1014 to AD 1590*, 2 vols, ed. William Maunsell Hennessy, Rolls Series (London, 1871; repr. Caisleán an Bhúrcaigh, 2000).
ALI	*Ancient laws of Ireland*, 6 vols, ed. W. Neilson Hancock, Thaddeus O'Mahony, Alexander George Richey, William Maunsell Hennessy and Robert Atkinson (Dublin, 1865–1901).
Amb.	Biblioteca Ambrosiana.
Anecd.	*Anecdota from Irish manuscripts*, 5 vols, ed. O.J. Bergin, R.I. Best, Kuno Meyer and J.G. O'Keeffe (Halle / Dublin, 1907–13).
ARÉ	Acadamh Ríoga na hÉireann.
AS	*Acta sanctorum quotquot toto orbe coluntur*, ed. Jean Bolland et al. (Antwerp / Brussels, 1643–).
ATig.	'The Annals of Tigernach', ed. Whitley Stokes, *RC* 16 (1895), 374–419; 17 (1896), 6–33, 119–263, 337–420, 18 (1897); 9–59, 150–97, 267–303; repr. 2 vols (Felinfach, 1993).
AU	*The Annals of Ulster (to AD 1131)*, ed. Seán Mac Airt and Gearóid Mac Niocaill (Dublin, 1983).
AU¹	*Annála Uladh: Annals of Ulster*, 4 vols, ed. William Maunsell Hennessy and Bartholomew Mac Carthy (Dublin, 1887–1901; facs. repr. with new Introduction by Nollaig Ó Muraíle, Dublin, 1998).

BÁC	Baile Átha Cliath.
BAR	British Archaeological Reports.
BB	The Book of Ballymote (Dublin, RIA MS 23 P 12).
BBCS	*Bulletin of the Board of Celtic Studies.*
BCC	*Betha Colaim Chille: Life of Columcille compiled by Manus O'Donnell in 1532*, ed. Andrew O'Kelleher and Gertrude Schoepperle (Illinois, 1918; repr. Dublin, 1994).
BCML	*Betha Colmáin maic Lúacháin. Life of Colmán son of Lúachán*, ed. Kuno Meyer, TLS 17 (Dublin, 1911; repr. Felinfach, 1997).
BHG	*Bibliotheca hagiographica graeca*, ed. Socii Bollandiani (Brussels, 1895–).
BHL	*Bibliotheca hagiographica latina*, 2 vols, ed. Socii Bollandiani (Brussels, 1898–1901).
BL	British Library.
BLec.	The Book of Lecan: Leabhar Mór Mhic Fhir Bhisigh Leacain (Dublin, RIA MS 23 P 2).
BLis.	The Book of Lismore: The Book of Mac Cárthaigh Riabhach (Chatsworth House, Derbyshire).
BM Cat.	*Catalogue of Irish manuscripts in the British Museum*, 3 vols, Standish Hayes O'Grady, Robin Flower and Myles Dillon (London, 1926–52; vols 1–2 repr. as *Catalogue of Irish manuscripts in the British Library [formerly British Museum]*, Dublin, 1992).
BNÉ	*Bethada náem nÉrenn. Lives of Irish saints*, 2 vols, ed. Charles Plummer (Oxford, 1922).
CCCM	Corpus Christianorum Continuatio Mediaevalis.
CCSA	Corpus Christianorum Series Apocryphorum.
CCSL	Corpus Christianorum Series Latina.
CGH	*Corpus genealogiarum Hiberniae*, I, ed. M.A. O'Brien (Dublin, 1962).
CGSH	*Corpus genealogiarum sanctorum Hiberniae*, ed. Pádraig Ó Riain (Dublin, 1985).
CIH	*Corpus iuris hibernici*, 6 vols, ed. D.A. Binchy (Dublin, 1978).
CMCS	*Cambridge Medieval Celtic Studies* (Summer 1981–Summer 1993), *Cambrian Medieval Celtic Studies* (Winter 1993–).
CS	*Chronicum Scotorum: a chronicle of Irish affairs from the earliest times to AD 1135*, ed. William Maunsell Hennessy, Rolls Series (London, 1866).
DD	*Dioghluim dána*, ed. Láimhbheartach Mac Cionnaith (Dublin, 1938).
DF	*Duanaire Finn: the book of the lays of Fionn*, 3 vols, ed. Eoin MacNeill and Gerard Murphy, ITS 7, 28, 43 (London, 1908–53).
DIAS	Dublin Institute for Advanced Studies.

DIL   *Dictionary of the Irish language based mainly on Old and Middle Irish materials*, general ed. E.G. Quin (compact edition: Dublin, 1983).

DIS   *A dictionary of Irish saints*, Pádraig Ó Riain (Dublin, 2011).

DMU   *Duanaire Mhéig Uidhir: the poembook of Cú Chonnacht Mág Uidhir, Lord of Fermanagh, 1566–1589*, ed. David Greene (Dublin, 1972).

ÉtC   *Études celtiques.*

FAI   *Fragmentary annals of Ireland*, ed. Joan Newlon Radner (Dublin, 1978).

Fél.   *Féilire Oengusso Céli Dé: the martyrology of Oengus the Culdee*, ed. Whitley Stokes, HBS 29 (London, 1905; repr. Dublin, 1984).

FGB   *Foclóir Gaedhilge agus Béarla: an Irish-English dictionary*, comp. and ed. Patrick S. Dinneen (Dublin, 1904; 2nd ed. 1927).

GOI   *A grammar of Old Irish*, Rudolf Thurneysen (Dublin, 1946).

HBS   Henry Bradshaw Society.

HDGP   *Historical dictionary of Gaelic placenames / Foclóir stairiúil áitainm- neacha na Gaeilge*, ed. Pádraig Ó Riain, Diarmuid Ó Murchadha, Kevin Murray and Emma Nic Cárthaigh (London, 2003–).

IBP   *Irish bardic poetry*, ed. Osborn Bergin, compiled and re-ed. David Greene and Fergus Kelly (Dublin, 1970).

IER   *The Irish Ecclesiastical Record.*

IGT   *Irish grammatical tracts*, ed. Osborn Bergin: I, II §§1–11, *Ériu* 8 (1916); II §§12–87, *Ériu* 9 (1921–3); II §§88–207, *Ériu* 10 (1926–8); III, IV, *Ériu* 14 (1946); V, *Ériu* 17 (1955).

IMC   Irish Manuscripts Commission.

IT   *Irische Texte mit Übersetzungen und Wörterbuch*, 4 vols, ed. Whitley Stokes and Ernst Windisch (Leipzig / Berlin, 1880–1909).

ITS   Irish Texts Society.

JCHAS   *Journal of the Cork Historical and Archaeological Society.*

JKAHS   *Journal of the Kerry Archaeological and Historical Society.*

JRSAI   *Journal of the Royal Society of Antiquaries of Ireland.*

LB   An Leabhar Breac (Dublin, RIA MS 23 P 16).

LBran.   *Leabhar Branach: the Book of the O'Byrnes*, ed. Seán Mac Airt (Dublin, 1944).

LEIA   *Lexique étymologique de l'irlandais ancien*, 7 vols (to date), ed. J. Vendryes, E. Bachellery and P.-Y. Lambert (Dublin and Paris, 1959–).

LG   *Lebor gabála Érenn: the book of the taking of Ireland*, 5 vols, ed. R.A.S. Macalister, ITS 34–5, 39, 41, 44 (Dublin and London, 1938–56); plus index vol. ed. Pádraig Ó Riain, ITS 63 (London, 2009).

LisL   *Lives of the saints from the Book of Lismore*, ed. Whitley Stokes, Anecdota Oxoniensia (Oxford, 1890).

LL	*The Book of Leinster formerly Lebar na Núachongbála*, 6 vols, ed. R.I. Best, Osborn Bergin, M.A. O'Brien and Anne O'Sullivan, (Dublin, 1954–83).
LNÉ	Leabharlann Náisiúnta na hÉireann, BÁC.
LU	*Lebor na hUidre: Book of the Dun Cow*, ed. R.I. Best and Osborn Bergin (Dublin, 1929).
LUM	Leabhar Ua Maine (Dublin, RIA Stowe MS D ii 1).
MD	*The metrical dindshenchas*, 5 vols, ed. Edward J. Gwynn, TLS 7–12 (Dublin, 1906–35; repr. 1991).
MIA	*Miscellaneous Irish annals (AD 1114–1437)*, ed. Séamus Ó hInnse (Dublin, 1947).
Ml.	The Milan glosses on the Psalms, Amb. C. 301, *Thes.* i, 7–483.
MMIS	Mediaeval and Modern Irish Series.
NLI	National Library of Ireland.
NLI Cat.	*Catalogue of Irish manuscripts in the National Library of Ireland*, 12 fasc., Nessa Ní Shéaghdha and Pádraig Ó Macháin (Dublin, 1967–1990).
NUI	National University of Ireland.
OnomG	*Onomasticon Goedelicum, locorum et tribuum Hiberniae et Scotiae: an index, with identifications, to the Gaelic names of places and tribes*, ed. Edmund Hogan (Dublin / London, 1910).
Pal. lat.	Codex palatinus latinus (Vatican Library).
PBA	*Proceedings of the British Academy.*
Pg	*Patrologia Graeca*, 161 vols, ed. Jacques Paul Migne (Paris 1857–86).
PHCC	*Proceedings of the Harvard Celtic Colloquium.*
PL	*Patrologia Latina*, 221 vols, ed. Jacques Paul Migne (Paris 1844–64).
PRIA	*Proceedings of the Royal Irish Academy.*
PRO	Public Records Office.
RC	*Revue celtique.*
RIA	Royal Irish Academy.
SC	Sources chrétiennes.
SGS	*Scottish Gaelic Studies.*
SLH	Scriptores Latini Hiberniae.
SP	State Papers.
SS	Subsidiary Series.
StC	*Studia Celtica.*
StH	*Studia Hibernica.*
TBC1	*Táin bó Cúailnge: recension 1*, ed. Cecile O'Rahilly (Dublin, 1976).
TBCL	*Táin bó Cúalnge from the Book of Leinster*, ed. Cecile O'Rahilly (Dublin, 1967).

TCD	Trinity College Dublin.
TDall	*A bhfuil againn dár chum Tadhg Dall Ó hUiginn: the bardic poems of Tadhg Dall Ó Huiginn (1550–1591)*, 2 vols, ed. Eleanor Knott, ITS 22–3 (London, 1922–6).
Thes.	*Thesaurus palæohibernicus: a collection of Old-Irish glosses, scholia and verse*, 2 vols and suppl., ed. Whitley Stokes and John Strachan (Cambridge, 1901–3, 1910; repr. Dublin, 1975).
TLS	Todd Lecture Series.
UCC	University College Cork.
UCD	University College Dublin.
UJA	*Ulster Journal of Archaeology.*
VC	*Vita Columbae.*
VSHH	*Vitae sanctorum Hiberniae e codice olim Salmanticensi*, ed. William W. Heist, Subsidia Hagiographica 28, (Brussels, 1965).
VSHP	*Vitae sanctorum Hiberniae*, 2 vols, ed. Charles Plummer (Oxford, 1910; repr. 1968).
YBL	The Yellow Book of Lecan (Dublin, TCD MS 1318 [H.2.16]).
ZCP	*Zeitschrift für celtische Philologie.*

Údair / Contributors

SEÁN HUTTON, Rúnaí, Cumann na Scríbheann Gaedhilge

ALEXANDRA BERGHOLM, Study of Religions, University of Helsinki

EDEL BHREATHNACH, The Discovery Programme, Baile Átha Cliath

ELIZABETH BOYLE, Department of Early Irish, Maynooth University

LIAM BREATNACH, Scoil an Léinn Cheiltigh, Institiúid Ard-Léinn Bhaile Átha Cliath

PÁDRAIG A. BREATNACH, Scoil an Léinn Cheiltigh, Institiúid Ard-Léinn Bhaile Átha Cliath

DAUVIT BROUN, Sgoil nan Daonnachdan, Oilthigh Ghlaschu

JOHN CAREY, Roinn na Sean- agus na Méan-Ghaeilge, Coláiste na hOllscoile Corcaigh

T.M. CHARLES-EDWARDS, Jesus College, Oxford University

PATRICIA COUGHLAN, School of English, University College Cork

PÁDRAIG DE BRÚN, Scoil an Léinn Cheiltigh, Institiúid Ard-Léinn Bhaile Átha Cliath

CLODAGH DOWNEY, Roinn na Gaeilge, Ollscoil na hÉireann, Gaillimh

JOSEPH J. FLAHIVE, Éiru Trust, Cork

MARGO GRIFFIN-WILSON, Department of Anglo-Saxon, Norse and Celtic, Cambridge University

FERGUS KELLY, Scoil an Léinn Cheiltigh, Institiúid Ard-Léinn Bhaile Átha Cliath

BRIAN LAMBKIN, Mellon Centre for Migration Studies, Ulster-American Folk Park, Omagh

MÁIRTÍN MAC CONMARA, Institiúid Bhaile an Mhuilinn, Baile Átha Cliath

MÍCHEÁL MAC CRAITH, Collegio S. Isidoro, An Róimh

GEARÓID MAC EOIN, Roinn na Sean- agus na Méan-Ghaeilge, Ollscoil na hÉireann, Gaillimh

KAY MUHR, Ulster Place-Name Society; formerly Northern Ireland Place-Names Project, Queen's University Belfast

KEVIN MURRAY, Roinn na Sean- agus na Méan-Ghaeilge, Coláiste na hOllscoile Corcaigh

PRÓINSÉAS NÍ CHATHÁIN, Roinn na Sean-Ghaeilge, An Coláiste Ollscoile, Baile Átha Cliath

MÁIRE NÍ MHAONAIGH, Department of Anglo-Saxon, Norse and Celtic, Cambridge University

EMMA NIC CÁRTHAIGH, Roinn na Sean- agus na Méan-Ghaeilge, Coláiste na hOllscoile Corcaigh

TOMÁS Ó CATHASAIGH, Department of Celtic Languages and Literatures, Harvard University

BREANDÁN Ó CONCHÚIR, Roinn na Nua-Ghaeilge, Coláiste na hOllscoile Corcaigh

CAITRÍONA Ó DOCHARTAIGH, Roinn na Sean- agus na Méan-Ghaeilge, Coláiste na hOllscoile Corcaigh

PÁDRAIG Ó MACHÁIN, Roinn na Nua-Ghaeilge, Coláiste na hOllscoile Corcaigh

PÁDRAIG Ó RIAIN, Roinn na Sean- agus na Méan-Ghaeilge, Coláiste na hOllscoile Corcaigh

†LISI OLIVER, formerly Department of English, Louisiana State University, and ANDREA ADOLPH, Department of Women's, Gender, and Sexuality Studies, Penn State University New Kensington

JENNIFER O'REILLY, School of History, University College Cork

KATJA RITARI, Collegium of Advanced Studies, University of Helsinki

KATHARINE SIMMS, School of Histories and Humanities, Trinity College Dublin

PATRICK SIMS-WILLIAMS, Adran y Gymraeg, Prifysgol Aberystwyth

Buíochas / Acknowledgements

In the first instance, we would like to thank all the contributors for their enthusiasm when approached to write for this volume, and for their commitment in producing works in honour of Professor Herbert. Tragically, Máire's old friend Lisi has not lived to see the volume published. Thanks are due to the Department of Early and Medieval Irish and to Scoil Léann na Gaeilge for assistance towards the costs of publication. As editors, we are indebted to the Honan Trust for granting us permission to reproduce Harry Clarke's stained glass triptych depicting Ireland's three patron saints, about whom Máire has written so authoritatively – particularly of course her old friend Colum Cille. We would also like to thank Virginia Teehan, Cultural Programmes and Research Support Officer, and Nancy Hawkes, Editor-in-Chief at the Office of Marketing and Communications, UCC, who advised us on the digital image of the windows and supplied other valuable assistance. Majella O'Sullivan, the College of Arts, Celtic Studies and Social Sciences College Manager, was very kind and helpful when we were attempting to locate a digital copy of the portrait of Máire by Trevor Goring (the original of which still has pride of place in the Department), which was commissioned when she was appointed to the Chair of Early and Medieval Irish. We are particularly grateful to our colleague Emma Nic Cárthaigh for her support during the final stages of preparing the volume for print. In this as in all other respects, the Department of Early and Medieval Irish cannot function without the final and essential member of the team, Ciara Ní Churnáin, who was always Máire's right-hand woman; without her unstinting support and that of Siobhán Ní Dhonghaile, preparing this work would have been much more arduous. Lastly, we would like to thank Martin Fanning and all the staff at Four Courts Press for their professionalism, courtesy and determination in seeing this project through to completion.

Brollach / Preface

The title of Máire Herbert's seminal study of the Columban monasteries centres upon the word *familia*. This is, of course, the source of the English word 'family', and is rooted in the sense of bodily kindred; but, as her usage in *Iona, Kells, and Derry* so well illustrates, its range of meanings extends well beyond this. A *familia* may unite blood relations, colleagues and co-workers, teachers and students, friends old and new. Máire's own *familia* encompasses all of these aspects: spanning not merely islands but oceans, it could be said that it is more far-flung and many-sided even than Colum Cille's. And every link in the mesh holds the same warmth, the same concern, the same sensitive and generous attention to the individual. Especially important is the care that Máire has bestowed – as mentor, teacher and supervisor – upon generations of students, many now working with her in the field, many of them contributors to this volume. We are all most thankful that we belong to her *familia*.

Is beag duine atá in ann teann dílseachta a spreagadh i measc cairde agus comhghleacaithe mar a dhéanann Máire. An chúis atá leis seo ná an cineáltas, an chneastacht agus an fhlaithiúlacht as an ngnách a léiríonn sí do chách is cuma ard nó íseal, ollamh nó mac léinn. Bhí sé seo rí-shoiléir fad is a bhí sí ina *stiúir dhírighthe* ag seoladh na Roinne trí thréimhse stoirmeach inar athraigh struchtúr na hOllscoile ó bhonn. Ceann de na tréithe is deise atá aici ná go ngabhann sí buíochas i gcónaí – le féirín beag, bosca seacláidí nó cárta álainn – fiú do ghnó beag fánach a rinneadh di.

Baineann na saintréithe seo lena hoidhreacht agus lena hoiliúint agus í ina hiníon bhunmhúinteora agus Ciarraíoch ina dteannta sin, sa tslí ina bhfuil siad ginte inti. Ach chomh maith leis seo, tá uaisleacht faoi leith a bhaineann léi; creideann sí go láidir in ionracas agus cothrom na Féinne, agus dá bharr sin sheas sí an fód go minic ar son daoine eile, fiú sa chás nach lena leas féin a bhí. Chumhdaigh Máire gach éinne a bhain léi, a daoine muinteartha agus a clann léinn, an *familia*. Cosúil le Fionnghuala lena dearthaireacha ar Shruth na Maoile, chosain Máire a muintir féin sa bhearna bhaoil le cuid acu *fóna sgiathán deas*, cuid eile *fóna sgiathán clé, ocus do dheasaigh a clúmh tarsa fá'n samhail sin*.

Throughout an extended and illustrious career, Máire's scholarship has been largely concerned with the Gaelic saints – with the realms of sanctity and belief, and especially with ways in which the imagined lives of holy men and women have found literary expression. As editor and translator, she has been particularly concerned with making texts available to her fellow scholars and to the wider world. But, for Máire, the word 'text' is rarely far removed from its sibling 'context'. Literature, no matter how remote its origins or fantastical its content, is always a part of the lived and concrete world of human society: a world of authors and scribes, of patrons and audiences, of transcription and transmission and reception, of ideology and agenda. Some of her most influential work has shown how tales of earlier times, whether secular or sacred, have carried messages of challenging relevance for the period in which they were composed. The inspiring vitality of this dialectic is encapsulated in the first two words of this Festschrift's title.

We hope that it may be a pardonable flight of fancy to see in this twofoldness an analogy with Máire as we know her: distinguished on the one hand by her commitment to the highest scholarly ideals, and to the principles of a compassionate and unhesitatingly self-sacrificing moral code; on the other, by a shrewd (and often humorous) awareness of quotidian actualities, and of the peculiarities and limitations of academics and other fellow mortals. These are traits from which our discipline has drawn abundant benefit – through her publications, through her teaching and lecturing across the world, through the services that she has rendered to such bodies as the Irish Texts Society, the Royal Irish Academy, the Irish Conference of Medievalists, the Leeds International Medieval Congress, the Apocrypha Hiberniae Project, the Irish Placenames Commission, the School of Celtic Studies of the Dublin Institute for Advanced Studies, and to her own University above all. These qualities have also bestowed on our Department a legacy of inestimable and enduring value; and in them, beyond all else, we recognize the lineaments of a treasured friend.

JOHN CAREY
KEVIN MURRAY
CAITRÍONA Ó DOCHARTAIGH

Máire Herbert:
leabharliosta / list of publications

LEABHAIR / BOOKS

(with Pádraig de Brún) *Catalogue of Irish manuscripts in Cambridge libraries* (Cambridge University Press, 1986).

Iona, Kells and Derry: the history and hagiography of the monastic familia *of Columba* (Oxford: Clarendon Press, 1988; republished Dublin: Four Courts Press, 1996).

(with Pádraig Ó Riain) *Betha Adamnáin: the Irish Life of Adamnán*, Irish Texts Society 54 (London: Irish Texts Society, 1988).

(with Martin McNamara) *Irish biblical apocrypha: selected texts in translation* (Edinburgh: T. & T. Clark, 1989).

(with John Carey and James Knowles), *Travelled tales – leabhar scéalach siúlach: the Book of Lismore at University College Cork* (Cork University Press, 2011).

LEABHAIR CURTHA IN EAGAR AICI / EDITED BOOKS

(with John Carey and Pádraig Ó Riain), *Studies in Irish hagiography: saints and scholars* (Dublin: Four Courts Press, 2001).

(with Martin McNamara, Caoimhín Breatnach, John Carey, Jean-Daniel Kaestli, Brian Ó Cuív, Pádraig Ó Fiannachta and Diarmuid Ó Laoghaire), *Apocrypha Hiberniae I: evangelia infantiae*, 2 vols, Corpus Christianorum, Series Apocryphorum vols 13 and 14 (Turnhout: Brepols, 2001).

(with Kevin Murray), *Prospect and retrospect in Celtic Studies: proceedings of the Eleventh International Congress of Celtic Studies* (Dublin: Four Courts Press, 2003).

(with John Carey and Kevin Murray), *Cín Chille Cúile: texts, saints and places: essays in honour of Pádraig Ó Riain* (Aberystwyth: Celtic Studies Publications, 2004).

CAIBIDLÍ I LEABHAIR / BOOK CHAPTERS

'Derry', *Lexikon des Mittelalters*, Band 3, Lieferung 4 (1983–).

'The Bible in early Iona' in D.F. Wright (ed.), *The Bible in Scottish life and literature* (Edinburgh: Saint Andrew Press, 1988), pp 131–9.

'The preface to *Amra Coluim Cille*' in D. Ó Corráin, L. Breatnach and K. McCone (eds), *Sages, saints, and storytellers: Celtic Studies in honour of Professor James Carney* (Maynooth: An Sagart, 1989), pp 67–75.

'Celtic heroine?: the archaeology of the Deirdre story' in T. O'Brien Johnson and D. Cairns (eds), *Gender in Irish writing* (Milton Keynes: Open University Press, 1991), pp 13–22.

'Goddess and king: the sacred marriage in early Ireland' in L.O. Fradenburg (ed.), *Women and sovereignty* (Edinburgh University Press, 1992), pp 264–75.

'The universe of male and female: a reading of the Deirdre story' in C.J. Byrne, M. Harry and P. Ó Siadhail (eds), *Celtic languages and Celtic peoples: proceedings of the Second North American Congress of Celtic Studies* (Halifax, Nova Scotia: St Mary's University, 1992), pp 53–63.

Entries on 'Columba' and 'Adomnán' in N.M. de S. Cameron (ed.), *Dictionary of Scottish church history and theology* (Edinburgh: T. & T. Clark, 1993).

'Charter material from Kells' in F. O'Mahony (ed.), *The Book of Kells: proceedings of a conference at Trinity College Dublin* (Aldershot: Scolar Press 1994), pp 60–77.

'The legacy of Colum Cille and his monastic community' in J.P. Mackey (ed.), *The cultures of Europe: the Irish contribution* (Belfast: Institute of Irish Studies, 1994), pp 9–20.

'Hagiography' in K. McCone and K. Simms (eds), *Progress in medieval Irish studies* (Maynooth: Department of Old and Middle Irish, 1996), pp 79–90.

'Transmutations of an Irish goddess' in S. Billington and M. Green (eds), *The concept of the goddess* (London & New York: Routledge, 1996), pp 141–51. (Russian translation in *Atlantika: Zametki po istoritsheskij poetike*, vol. 6, 2004.)

Entries on '*Amra Choluim Cille*', 'Colum Cille', 'Historical Cycle' in *The Oxford companion to Irish literature* (Oxford University Press, 1996).

'The death of Muirchertach Mac Erca: a twelfth-century tale' in F. Josephson (ed.), *Celts and Vikings: proceedings of the Fourth Symposium of Societas Celtologica Nordica* (Göteborgs Universitet, 1997), pp 27–39.

'Dlíthe an Domhnaigh in Éirinn 600–750' in M. Mac Conmara and E. Ní Thiarnaigh (eds), *Cothú an dúchais: aistí in omós don Ath. D. Ó Laoghaire* (Baile Átha Cliath: An Clóchomhar, 1997), pp 60–69.

'Sea-divided Gaels? Constructing relationships between Irish and Scots *c.*800–1169' in B. Smith (ed.), *Britain and Ireland, 900–1300: insular responses to medieval European change* (Cambridge University Press, 1999), pp 87–97.

'Literary sea-voyages and early Munster hagiography' in R. Black, W. Gillies and R. Ó Maolalaigh (eds), *Celtic connections: proceedings of the Tenth International Congress of Celtic Studies* (East Linton: Tuckwell, 1999), pp 182–9.

'The legacy of Columba' in T.M. Devine and J.F. McMillan (eds), *Celebrating Columba: Colm Cille a cheiliúradh. Irish-Scottish connections, 597–1887* (Edinburgh: John Donald, 1999), pp 1–14.

'Ireland and Scotland: the foundations of a relationship' in G. McCoy and M. Scott (eds), *Aithne na nGael: Gaelic identities* (Belfast: Institute of Irish Studies, 2000), pp 19–27.

'*Rí Éirenn, Rí Alban*: kingship and identity in the ninth and tenth centuries' in S. Taylor (ed.), *Kings, clerics, and chronicles in Scotland, 500–1297: essays in honour of Marjorie Ogilvie Anderson* (Dublin: Four Courts Press, 2000), pp 62–72.

'The *Liber Flavus Fergusiorum* infancy narrative: translation' (with D. Ó Laoghaire and C. Breatnach) in M. McNamara, C. Breatnach, J. Carey, M. Herbert, J.-D. Kaestli, B. Ó Cuív, P. Ó Fiannachta and D. Ó Laoghaire (eds), *Apocrypha Hiberniae I: evangelia infantiae*, Corpus Christianorum, Series Apocryphorum vol. 13 (Turnhout: Brepols, 2001), pp 148–244.

'The infancy narrative of the *Leabhar Breac* and related manuscripts: translation' (with P. Ó Fiannachta and C. Breatnach) in M. McNamara et al. (eds), *Apocrypha Hiberniae I*, pp 298–438.

'A versified narrative of the childhood deeds of the Lord Jesus: introduction' (with M. McNamara) in M. McNamara et al. (eds), *Apocrypha Hiberniae I*, pp 443–53.

'Text and translation of the Irish versified narrative of the childhood deeds of the Lord Jesus' in M. McNamara et al. (eds), *Apocrypha Hiberniae I*, pp 456–83.

'Latin and vernacular hagiography of Ireland from the origins to the sixteenth century' in G. Philippart (ed.), *Hagiographies: histoire internationale de la littérature hagiographique latine et vernaculaire en Occident des origines à 1550*, vol. 3 (Turnhout: Brepols, 2001), pp 327–60.

'The Life of Martin of Tours: a view from twelfth-century Ireland' in M. Richter and J.-M. Picard (eds), *Ogma: essays in Celtic Studies in honour of Próinséas Ní Chatháin* (Dublin: Four Courts Press, 2001), pp 76–84.

'The world of Adomnán' in T. O'Loughlin (ed.), *Adomnán at Birr AD 697: essays in commemoration of the Law of the Innocents* (Dublin: Four Courts Press, 2001), pp 33–9.

'The *Vita Columbae* and Irish hagiography: a study of *Vita Cainnechi*' in J. Carey, M. Herbert and P. Ó Riain (eds), *Studies in Irish hagiography: saints and scholars* (Dublin: Four Courts Press, 2001), pp 31–40.

'(Section III) The Irish *peregrini*', proceedings of the international conference *The city and the book I*, Florence, 30 May–1 June 2001 <www.florin.ms/aleph>; also published in Italian as 'In Irlanda: Il retaggio dei peregrini irlandesi in Toscana' in R. Stompani (ed.), *De Strata Francigena: studi e ricerche sulle vie di pellegrinaggio del Medioevo* (Florence: Firenzelibri, 2002).

'(Section III) The Celtic Otherworld and the Commedia (English and Italian translation)', proceedings of the international conference *The city and the book II*, Florence, 4–7 September 2002 <www.florin.ms/beth>.

'Society and myth, *c.*700–1300: introduction and texts' in A. Bourke, S. Kilfeather, M. Luddy, M. Mac Curtain, G. Meaney, M. Ní Dhonnchadha, M. O'Dowd and C. Wills (eds), *The Field Day anthology of Irish writing*, vol. 4 (Cork University Press, 2002), pp 250–72.

'Observations on the Life of Molaga' in J. Carey, M. Herbert and K. Murray (eds), *Cín Chille Cúile: texts, saints and places: essays in honour of Pádraig Ó Riain* (Aberystwyth: Celtic Studies Publications, 2004), pp 127–40.

'Columba', article in *Oxford dictionary of national biography* (Oxford University Press, 2004).

'Before charters? Property records in pre-Anglo-Norman Ireland' in M.-T. Flanagan and J.A. Green (eds), *Charters and charter scholarship in Britain and Ireland* (London: Palgrave Macmillan, 2005), pp 107–19.

'Becoming an exile: Colum Cille in Middle-Irish poetry' in J.F. Nagy and L.E. Jones (eds), *Heroic poets and poetic heroes in Celtic tradition: a Festschrift for Patrick K. Ford*, Celtic Studies Association of North America Yearbook 3–4 (Dublin: Four Courts Press, 2005), pp 131–40.

'The hagiographical miscellany in A 3' in P.A. Breatnach, C. Breatnach and M. Ní Úrdail (eds), *Léann lámhscríbhinní Lobháin: the Louvain manuscript heritage*, Éigse Publications 1 (Dublin: National University of Ireland, 2007), pp 112–26.

'Medieval collections of ecclesiastical and devotional materials: *Leabhar Breac, Liber Flavus Fergusiorum* and the Book of Fenagh' in B. Cunningham and S. Fitzpatrick (eds), *Treasures of the Royal Irish Academy library* (Dublin: Royal Irish Academy, 2009), pp 33–43.

'Reading recension 1 of the *Táin*' in R. Ó hUiginn and B. Ó Catháin (eds), *Ulidia 2: proceedings of the Second International Conference on the Ulster Cycle of tales* (Maigh Nuad: An Sagart, 2009), pp 208–17.

'Hagiography and holy bodies: observations on corporeal relics in pre-Viking Ireland', *L'Irlanda e gli irlandesi nell'alto medioevo* (Spoleto: Fondazione Centro Italiano di studi sull'alto medioevo, 2010), pp 239–60.

'The representation of Gregory the Great in Irish sources of the pre-Viking era' in E. Mullins and D. Scully (eds), *Listen, O isles, unto me: studies in medieval word and image in honour of Jennifer O'Reilly* (Cork University Press, 2011), pp 181–90.

'Observations on the *Vita* of Bishop Áed mac Bricc' in D. Ó Baoill, D. Ó hAodha and N. Ó Muraíle (eds), *Saltair saíochta, sanasaíochta agus seanchais: a Festschrift for Gearóid Mac Eoin* (Dublin: Four Courts Press, 2013), pp 64–74.

'Beatha Shan Tomáis Chantarbuirí i lámhscríbhinní na hochtú aoise déag: réamhfhiosrú beag' in S. Ó Coileáin, L.P. Ó Murchú and P. Riggs (eds), *Séimhfhear suairc: aistí in omós don Ollamh Breandán Ó Conchúir* (An Daingean: An Sagart, 2013), pp 86–90.

'The fleet of Inber Domnann' in J. Carey, E. Nic Cárthaigh and C. Ó Dochartaigh (eds), *The end and beyond: medieval Irish eschatology* (Aberystwyth: Celtic Studies Publications, 2014), pp 715–20.

AISTÍ IN IRISÍ / JOURNAL ARTICLES

'Some Irish prognostications', *Éigse*, 14 (1972), 303–18.

(with A. O'Sullivan) 'The provenance of Laud Misc. 615', *Celtica*, 10 (1973), 174–92.

'An grá sa tseanfhilíocht', *Léachtaí Cholm Cille*, 6 (1975), 17–31.

'Ár n-úirlisí ceóil', *Léachtaí Cholm Cille*, 7 (1976), 21–30.

'The seven journeys of the soul', *Éigse*, 17 (1977), 1–11.

'Beathaí na naomh', *Léachtaí Cholm Cille*, 8 (1977), 1–18.

'Múineadh na fiannaíochta', *Léachtaí Cholm Cille*, 9 (1978), 44–57.

'Urnaí na gCéilí Dé', *An Sagart* (Geimhreadh, 1978), 15–20.

'Beatha Mheán-Ghaeilge Cholm Cille', *Léachtaí Cholm Cille*, 15 (1984), 127–36.

'The Irish *Sex aetates mundi*: first editions', *Cambridge Medieval Celtic Studies*, 11 (Summer, 1986), 97–112.

'The text, the world, and the critic of early Irish heroic narrative', *Text and Context*, 3 (Autumn, 1988), 1–9.

'*Fled Dúin na nGéd*: a reappraisal', *Cambridge Medieval Celtic Studies*, 18 (Winter, 1989), 75–87.

Review article, 'Cummian's letter *De controversia Paschali* and the *De ratione computandi* (ed. M. Walsh and D. Ó Cróinín)', *The Innes Review*, 44, i (Spring, 1993), 109–11.

'*Caithréim Cellaig*: some literary and historical considerations', *Zeitschrift für celtische Philologie*, 49–50 (1997), 320–32.

'An infancy narrative of St Ciarán', *Proceedings of the Harvard Celtic Colloquium*, 14 (1997), 1–8.

'Gnéithe den naomhsheanchas in Éirinn sa tréimhse réamh-Lochlannach', *Léachtaí Cholm Cille*, 30 (2000), 65–74.

'The legend of St Scothíne: perspectives from early Christian Ireland', *Studia Hibernica*, 31 (2000–2001), 27–35.

'*Aislinge Meic Conglinne*: contextual considerations', *Journal of the Cork Historical and Archaeological Society*, 110 (2005), 65–72.

'Crossing literary and historical boundaries: Irish written culture around the year 1000', *Cambrian Medieval Celtic Studies*, 53/54 (2007), 87–101.

'Preliminary remarks on the content of a recently-discovered Cork manuscript', *Journal of the Cork Historical and Archaeological Society*, 113 (2008), 144–9.

'Saint Colmán of Dromore and Inchmahone', *Scottish Gaelic Studies*, 24 (2008; Festschrift for Donald Meek), 253–65.

Duine dár laochra

SEÁN HUTTON

I Harrogate an ghalántais a bhuail mé
le planda measúil ár n-aiséirí
i séasúr a fheochainte:
canbhás le hAE ar bhalla an pharlúis,
Pan adharcach ag gliúcaíocht orainn amach as cúinne,
an chloch ortha ón síbhrú sa tarraiceán i gcónaí.
Fear seo Chill Aodáin,
iarthrodaire sa Chogadh Mór, iar-Óglach
a chuidigh na gunnaí a dhíriú i mbliain a fiche dó
i gcoinne na gCeithre Cúirteanna
– seanchas an tslua sí is na laochra
á ríomh aige sa seomra sóchúil iasachta.
Las súile an tseanphágánaigh is é ag trácht
ar Ghabha Bhaile Uí Laoi is ar an gCraoibhín.
Ar sé ar ball: 'Féach mar atá an *Daily Telegraph*
ag bogadh ar Clé le deireanas'
– Oisín seo na Léine Goirme
a chuaigh ar seachrán tráth sa Chamhaoir Cheilteach
– oidhre an tí mhóir a dalladh
ag fís lóipíneach na saoirse.

Is trí mo bhaint le Cumann na Scríbheann nGaedhilge a chuir mé aithne ar
an Ollamh Máire Herbert don chéad uair. Tá sí anois ina Uachtarán ar an
gCumann. D'fhéadfá an Cumann – a d'eascair as Cumann Éireannach na
Liteardhachta (Londain) – a ainmniú i measc torthaí éagsúla na Camhaoire
Ceiltí; agus sin fáth amháin gur roghnaigh mé an dán seo don imleabhar in
ómós do Mháire Herbert. Foilsíodh an dán ar dtús i mbailiúchán liom,
Seachrán Ruairí, agus baineann sé le duine a 'chuaigh ar seachrán tráth' sa
chamhaoir stairiúil thuasluaite, An Captaen Dermot Mac Manus – údar *The
middle kingdom: the faerie world of Ireland*.

Keening in the poems of Blathmac

ALEXANDRA BERGHOLM

And I will pour out upon the house of David, and upon the inhabitants of Jerusalem, the spirit of grace, and of prayers: and they shall look upon me, whom they have pierced: and they shall mourn for him as one mourneth for an only son, and they shall grieve over him, as the manner is to grieve for the death of the firstborn. (Zech 12:10)

Blessed are they that mourn: for they shall be comforted. (Mt 5:5)[1]

Since the publication of James Carney's edition and translation of the mid-eighth-century devotional verses of Blathmac son of Cú Brettan in 1964,[2] a number of scholars have drawn attention to the significance of the theme of keening that frames his poetical account of the Passion of Christ. In the opening stanza of the first of the two poems,[3] Blathmac appeals to the Virgin Mary to come to him so that they may perform a lament together to commemorate the suffering and death of her son (§1):

> Tair cucum, a Maire boíd,
> do choíniuth frit do rochoím;
> dirsan dul fri croich dot mac
> ba mind már, ba masgérat.

> Come to me, loving Mary,
> that I may keen with you your very dear one.
> Alas that your son should go to the cross,
> he who was a great diadem, a beautiful hero.

I offer this contribution as an acknowledgement of my gratitude to Máire for all her generosity, help, and advice. The writing of this article has been funded by the Academy of Finland project number 1138310.   1 All the following biblical references in Latin are to the Vulgate, with the English translation from the Douay-Rheims version.   2 James Carney (ed. and trans.), *The poems of Blathmac son of Cú Brettan together with the Irish Gospel of Thomas and a poem on the Virgin Mary*, ITS 47 (Dublin, 1964); henceforth *Blathmac*. The translation and the numeration of the stanzas in all subsequent references follow Carney's edition. For suggested corrections to Carney's text, see the review by Gearóid S. Mac Eoin, 'The poems of Blathmac', *StH*, 7 (1967), 222–6 at 225–6.   3 In their edited form the poems have 149 and 109 stanzas respectively. The second poem is incomplete due to damage to the seventeenth-century manuscript in which the poems have been preserved. Carney suggested that both poems may have originally consisted of 150 stanzas; see *Blathmac*, p. xiii.

As Carney among others has observed, Blathmac's employment of the dramatic device of keening is of considerable interest in illustrating the 'essential "Irishness"' of his composition, and the manner in which the early Irish drew upon their own native tradition to elaborate on the teachings of Christianity.[4] In Blathmac's case, this is particularly prominent in his dependence on secular legal concepts, which he appropriates to define the relationship between the faithful and their Lord in terms of a social contract of clientship (*célsine*), but also in the way in which the structure of the composition as a whole conforms to the conventional mode of expression used in ritual lamentation.[5] While it has been convincingly argued that the effectiveness of Blathmac's poems ultimately depends on the contemporary audience's familiarity with these practices,[6] comparatively less treatment has hitherto been given to the poems' devotional nature, and to the ways in which Blathmac's treatment of the theme of keening relates to the wider context of the theology of the Passion. The aim of this contribution is therefore to draw attention to this question, by arguing that despite having been criticized for 'the distorting simplicity of the poet's account of biblical incidents and the unreserved devotion of his spirituality',[7] Blathmac's poems communicate a deep and intimate reflection of fundamental theological ideas concerning Christ's suffering and its significance in universal salvation history.

In the following, I will focus my analysis on the first poem, which constitutes the keen proper. Although the overall structure of the work supports the view that the two poems form a cohesive whole, and possibly originally

---

4 See James Carney, 'Poems of Blathmac, son of Cú Brettan' in idem (ed.), *Early Irish poetry* (Cork, 1965), pp 45–57 at p. 55; Brian Lambkin, 'The structure of the Blathmac poems', *StC*, 20/21 (1985–6), 67–77. In these terms, the Blathmac poems have been compared to the tenth-century *Saltair na Rann*; see, for example, John Carey, *King of mysteries: early Irish religious writings* (Dublin, 2000), p. 97 n. 1. 5 The literature on ritual lamentation in different historical and cultural contexts is vast. The seminal work is Margaret Alexiou, *Ritual lament in Greek tradition* (Cambridge, 1974); see also Gail Host-Warhaft, *Dangerous voices: women's laments and Greek literature* (London, 1992); Ann Suter (ed.), *Lament: studies in the ancient Mediterranean and beyond* (Oxford, 2008); Eva Harasta and Brian Brock (eds), *Evoking lament: a theological discussion* (New York, 2009). On Irish keening in particular, see Rachel Bromwich, 'The keen for Art O'Leary, its background and its place in the tradition of Irish keening', *Éigse*, 5 (1946–8), 236–52; Seán Ó Súilleabháin, *Irish wake amusements* (Dublin, 1967), pp 130–45; Seán Ó Coileáin, 'The Irish lament: an oral genre', *StH*, 24 (1984–8), 96–117; Angela Bourke, 'More in anger than in sorrow: Irish women's lament poetry' in J.N. Radner (ed.), *Feminist messages: coding in women's folk culture* (Urbana and Chicago, 1993), pp 160–81; Patricia Lysaght, '"Caoineadh os cionn coirp": the lament for the dead in Ireland', *Folklore*, 108 (1997), 65–82; Kaarina Hollo, 'Laments and lamenting in early medieval Ireland' in H. Fulton (ed.), *Medieval Celtic literature and society* (Dublin, 2005), pp 83–94; Méadhbh Nic an Airchinnigh, '*Caoineadh Airt Uí Laoghaire*: blood-drinking, Art's sister and censorship in Father Peter O'Leary's manuscripts P and Pead', *PHCC*, 30 (2011), 175–206. 6 See Lambkin, 'Structure', 67. 7 Mac Eoin, 'Poems', 223.

belonged to an even longer 'ambitious composition divided into sections',[8] a transition from the mourning of Christ's Passion to the exultant celebration of His Resurrection and Ascension is clearly indicated in the beginning of the second poem (§150), signalling a decisive shift of focus in the narrative:

> A Maire, a grian ar clainde,
> a mba moí mo chélmainde
> do mac coínsimmar – scél maith!
> sech is bithbéo, is bithflaith.

> Mary, sun of our race,
> when mine was mystic utterance
> – we keened your son – well and good;
> he lives eternally, is eternal prince.

By examining the thematic arrangement of the composition in more detail, I am hoping to illustrate how Blathmac uses the imagery of lamentation in the first poem to underscore the representation of Christ in his humanity as the sacrificial victim of the Passion, thereby inviting emotional engagement with the subject matter of the poem in order to elicit an appropriate spiritual response in its audience. This reading of the poem situates Blathmac among other authors of medieval vernacular religious lyrics, whose primary concern, as Douglas Gray notes, was not 'with the construction of an enduring object for other people to admire, but rather for other people to *use*'.[9] As will be argued in the following, Blathmac's evocative employment of the native theme of keening may also be seen as a central feature of the poem's affective mode, which enables him to draw upon the traditional setting of ritual mourning to direct the attention 'from the concrete reality of the immediate world toward the abstract and transcendent significance' of the biblical narrative.[10] The main question to be considered, then, is how the poem, by virtue of its lament form, turns the contemplative gaze from the human suffering of Christ to contrite awareness of His redemptive sacrifice, thus giving an impetus for a penitential 'spiritual sorrow growing out of love for God and hatred for one's sin'.[11]

Blathmac's choice of casting his poem as a keen places the work within the ritual context of mourning by evoking the expressive potential of lamentation in both formal and stylistic terms. Despite the limited amount of infor-

---

8 *Blathmac*, p. xiii. 9 Douglas Gray, *Themes and images in medieval English religious lyric* (London, 1972), p. 60 (emphasis original). On the nature of Blathmac's narrative lyric, see also Hildegard L.C. Tristram, 'Early modes of insular expression' in L. Breatnach, K. McCone and D. Ó Corráin (eds), *Sages, saints and storytellers: Celtic Studies in honour of Professor James Carney* (Maynooth, 1989), pp 427–48. 10 Karen Saupe, 'Introduction' in eadem (ed.), *Middle English Marian lyrics* (Kalamazoo, 1997) [electronically available at: <http://d.lib.rochester.edu/teams/text/saupe-middle-english-marian-lyrics-introduction>] (accessed 15.2.2015). 11 Ibid.

mation concerning traditional funerary practice in early Ireland, the fragmentary evidence at hand nevertheless suggests that the performance of laments
retained its significance as part of the ritual process throughout the early
medieval period. One of the earliest references comes from Tírechán's seventh-century *Collectanea* (26.16), in which he mentions the 'lament and great
keening' made by the friends of King Lóegaire's two daughters (*fecerunt ulu-
latum et planctum magnum amici earum*) as part of their funeral ceremonies.
Interestingly, Tírechán's comment regarding the performance of the burial
according to the native Irish custom (26.20: *quia sic faciebant Scotici homines
et gentiles*) is not primarily concerned with the pagan nature of the ritual as
such, but rather with the need to articulate the basic difference between the
pagan and Christian views of the girls' mortal remains, and to redefine their
status as sacred relics after the burial site was handed over to Saint Patrick.[12]
In this respect, the pragmatic outlook of Tírechán's account forms an interesting point of comparison to other, more normative sources of the early
Church, in which the traditional customs relating to death were often
regarded as problematic or harmful enough to elicit decisive actions aimed at
curbing their perceived excesses.[13] Even here, however, the attitude could
remain somewhat ambivalent, as is well illustrated by the treatment of the
topic in the early eighth-century Bigotian penitential. After listing the appropriate penances for the 'clamour aroused by grief' according to the status of
the deceased – fifty days on bread and water for a lament over a layperson,
but only fifteen for a dirge sung over an anchorite, a scribe, a bishop, or a
king – the text then continues:

> Jacob the son of Isaac was lamented for forty days in Egypt and for a
> whole week in the land of Canaan; and so was Christ in the New
> (Testament), the women wept for Him; and it is found written in the
> Canon with almost innumerable examples of the Scriptures, and for
> whom no lament is made it is reckoned as bad merit.[14]

The same notion of the importance of the lament as due public recognition
of the social status of the deceased is also evidenced in Blathmac's keen,

---

12 Ludwig Bieler (ed. and trans.), *The Patrician texts in the Book of Armagh*, SLH 10
(Dublin, 1979), pp 144–5. See also Edel Bhreathnach, 'From *fert(ae)* to *relic*: mapping
death in early sources' in C. Corlett and M. Potterton (eds), *Death and burial in early
medieval Ireland* (Dublin, 2010), pp 23–31. 13 Alexiou, *Ritual lament*, pp 28–35; Carol
Lansing, *Passion and order: restraint of grief in the medieval Italian communes* (Ithaca and
London, 2008), pp 100–4, 117–21. 14 Ludwig Bieler (ed. and trans.), *The Irish peniten-
tials*, SLH 5 (Dublin, 1975), pp 230–1: *Iacob filius Isaac xl diebus in Egypto luctatus est et
tota ebdomada in terra Canaan; et Christus in Nouo, plorauerunt eum feminae; et pene
innumerabilibus scripturarum exemplis inuenitur scriptum in canone, et pro malo merito inputatur
illi pro quo non ploratur.*

which draws extensively on the traditional lament form to elaborate on the role of Christ as hero (*gerat, galgat*), as well as lord and overking (*tigerna, ruiri*) whose honour and goodness towards his clients should be acknowledged and reciprocated in a communal lament. As noted above, this aspect is particularly prominent in the poem's legal terminology, which Brian Lambkin has previously analysed at length especially in relation to Blathmac's association with the *Céli Dé* movement.[15] The persistence of the lament form is, however, also identifiable in the overall arrangement of the first poem's episodic structure, which recounts the biblical narrative of the life and death of Christ through intricate appropriation of several conventional elements of the genre. Some of the main features that may be noted from this perspective can be outlined with reference to the relevant sections in the poem as follows:

1) Recounting the pedigree and background of the deceased
   §§2–6 Incarnation
   §§11–25 Nativity
2) Praise of His generosity and good qualities
   §§7–10 The excellence and beauty of Christ
   §§26–43 Ministry
3) Circumstances of the (violent) death
   §§44–9 Arrest and trial
   §§50–68 Crucifixion
4) Rebuking those responsible, often including a call for vengeance
   §§62–72 Annas, Caiphas and Pilate
   §§77–107, 114–18, 130 The Jews
   §§108–13 Judas
5) The acknowledgment of personal and communal loss
   §§120–9, 131–3 Universal keen
6) The expression of a variety of emotions including sorrow, love, anger, pity, compassion, loyalty and hope.

The emotional force of the lament form is made even more poignant by the presence of the Virgin Mary, the grief-stricken mother, whom Blathmac wishes to join in keening to comfort her in her loss (§§1–2, 119, 144–9). The idea of the Virgin's emotional affliction at her Son's death provides a powerful image of maternal sorrow, which effectively reinforces the poem's devotional tone and also resonates with the universal human experience of bereavement. The moving portrayal of Mary as a human mother mourning the death of her only child manifestly derives much of its affective impact

---

15 Brian Lambkin, 'Blathmac and the Céili Dé: a reappraisal', *Celtica*, 23 (1999), 132–54. Similar use of legal terminology has also been noted in the poem *Ísucán*: see E.G. Quin, 'The early Irish poem *Ísucán*', *CMCS*, 1 (Summer, 1981), 39–52.

from lived reality, as it encourages the audience to empathise with the psychological and emotional consequences of Mary's loss by gradually shifting the focus from grief to consolation. In this manner, the appropriation of the language and structure of the vernacular keen serves to evoke a referential system or 'horizon of expectations', which invites sympathetic identification with the grieving mother, and directs the feelings of pity and compassion to her as well to her Son.[16]

The emotional intensity of the keen culminates in the events surrounding the Crucifixion, which turn the attention to the contemplation of the suffering and death of Christ. Here, the image of the gentle and generous miracle-working lord of the preceding stanzas (§§26–43) is starkly contrasted with the image of Christ as captive and victim (*cimbith*), who was unjustly humiliated and killed by His mother's own kin.[17] The dramatic effect of the scene is created by a series of typological juxtapositions that point to the symbolic significance of the foregoing events as prefigurations of Christ's redemptive sacrifice, and thereby reveal the coherent order of the divine scheme. This interpretation is developed in fullest detail in a long passage drawn from Exodus (§§77–100), which temporarily suspends the Passion narrative to contrast the Old Covenant of the Israelites with the New Covenant mediated by Jesus, and explicitly articulates the role of Christ as the sacrificial Lamb of God (e.g., Ex 12:1–4; cf. 1 Pet 1:19, Jn 1:29). The bitterest sentiments, however, are evoked by the Jews' crime of kin-slaying (*fingal*), the severity of which certainly would not have escaped Blathmac's contemporary audience (§§46–7, 97–8, 100–3).[18] Envisaging

---

16 Interestingly, by emphasizing the Virgin's grief at her Son's Passion, Blathmac departs from the prevalent view of many of the early Western patristic authors, whose exegetical deliberations had tended to emphasize the Virgin's impassive acceptance of her Son's sacrifice rather than her maternal anguish. In terms of its compassionate sensibility towards the humane suffering of the Virgin, Blathmac's composition thus appears to predate the development of later religious lyrics of the twelfth and thirteenth centuries, which focused the attention fully on the affective contemplation of the figure of Mary as *Mater Dolorosa*, and contributed to the flourishing of the Marian lament as a distinctive devotional theme of medieval spirituality. See Sandro Sticca, *The planctus Mariae in the dramatic tradition of the Middle Ages* (Athens and London, 1988); M. Amelia Fraga Fuentes, 'A study of the role of the Virgin Mary in the thirteenth- and fourteenth-century English crucifixion lyrics (I)', *Atlantis*, 2, ii (1981), 10–20; Sarah McNamer, *Affective meditation and the invention of medieval compassion* (Philadelphia, 2009).   **17** Carney translates *cimbith* as 'captive' (§§3, 120, 132). According to *DIL* s.v., *cimmid* can be defined as 'captive, prisoner, condemned person (sometimes one fated to die, victim)'. In this particular context, the more specific sense of 'victim' would appear better to convey the meaning of the sacrificial nature of Christ's death (cf. §123), and to support the poem's theological understanding of Christ as both the Victim and the Victor. The same idea is communicated throughout by repeated references, especially in the second part of the composition, to His victory (*búaid*) over death and Satan (e.g., §§105, 137, 175, 178, 181, 188, 214). On this notion in Western theological thought, see further Rowan A. Greer, 'Christ the victor and the victim', *Concordia Theological Quarterly*, 59, i–ii (1995), 1–30.   **18** Lambkin, 'The structure', 76,

the punishment awaiting the Jews for this most hideous offence, Blathmac
relies on distinctively native imagery (§§117–18):

> Cenél do-rigni in sin
> atá foraib orbbadail;
> is ainces ngalair cen tráig
> a mbith cen flaith fo bithphláig.

> Dos-roidbi tengae cech bí
> co n-aír ocus escaini;
> a-taat la cách fo durnn,
> biet iar mbráth i n-ifurnn.

> The race who did that
> suffer dispersal of heritage;
> their being without a kingdom under eternal plague
> is a sickly undiminishing misery.

> The tongue of every living being has assailed them
> with satire and curse;
> they are under everybody's thumb;
> after the Last Judgment they will be in Hell.

What initially may seem to be a digression from the main narrative in fact
serves an important dual purpose in Blathmac's keen. On the one hand, it
enables him to expound on the guilt of the Jews for maximum dramatic
effect, by emphasizing their ingratitude and repeated breaches of the legally
binding 'counter-obligations' of their 'clientship' (§§103–7) in terms which
closely echo the habitual reproaches of the traditional lament. On the other
hand, the juxtaposition simultaneously functions to heighten the audience's
sense of spiritual urgency with regard to their *own* obligations towards their
Lord, arising from the acute awareness of the magnitude of Christ's redemptive suffering and every sinner's personal share in His death. From
Blathmac's perspective, the fact that the canonical Gospels make no mention
of Christ being lamented by the apostles must have been profoundly discon-
certing, as it appeared to go so starkly against the customary norms of conduct and undermine the tragedy of His violent death (cf. §§124–6).[19] In this

draws attention to Blathmac's use of *fingal* as a native term characterizing the content of
this part of the narrative; in a similar manner, the exile of the Holy Family is referred to
as *longes* (§§22–3, 25), and the death of Jesus as *aided* (§62). On the offence of *fingal* in
early Irish society, see Fergus Kelly, *A guide to early Irish law* (Dublin, 1988), pp 127–8.
19 Again, Blathmac finds the Jews to blame: not only does he deem them responsible for
preventing the followers of Jesus from mourning Him (§128), but he also accuses them for

view, the failure to mourn Christ could be seen as the foremost expression of the ungratefulness of mankind for the salvific gift bestowed upon them by their Lord: a transgression that ultimately implicates them, like the Jews, as violators of their reciprocal relationship with God.

The penitential motivation of Blathmac's poem also comes into focus against this background, as the feelings of grief and compassion prompted by the contemplation of the bloody suffering of Christ in His humanity turn into contrite compunction at the realization of the universal significance of His sacrificial death. Some of the most striking imagery of the poem is introduced in relation to this theme when Blathmac freely amplifies the scriptural account by exploiting the full symbolic potential of Christ's redeeming blood. One of these moments comes in §§56–7, where he draws upon a passage in John 19:34 to elaborate upon the emblematic significance of blood and water flowing from the pierced side of Christ, and deepens the spiritual meaning of the passage by highlighting the two momentous benefits achieved through the sacrifice of Christ: the atonement and purification of the sins of mankind.[20] The connection between the blood and the Eucharist is made clear in the depiction of the blood as wine, which recalls the celebration of the sacrament as a commemoration of the Last Supper and as a representation of the New Covenant established between God and man (cf. Mt 26:28, Mk 14:24, Lk 22:20, 1 Cor 10:16); whereas the remission of original sin and the reversal of the fall is explicitly articulated by reference to Adam's skull being baptized by His blood.[21] The salvific symbolism of Christ's blood is also reaffirmed by the

---

not allowing His people to build a tumulus on His grave (*cen fert do dul inna lecht*, §116). This latter addition to the biblical narrative is intriguing, as Blathmac undoubtedly was fully familiar with the Gospel tradition that Jesus was buried in a new tomb (*monumentum novum*, Ioh. 19:41) that was said to have been cut out of a rock (*quod erat excisum de petra*, Marc. 15:46; cf. Matth. 27:60, Luc. 23:53). The reference may plausibly be understood as yet another allusion to the poem's native secular background, as the building of a lord's funeral monument (*ferta do flatha*) is especially mentioned in early Irish law texts as an obligation of his clients; for relevant passages in the Heptads and *Senchas már*, see *CIH* 51.13–52.3, 1849.33–9, 389.9–392.3, 1693.17–1695.12.   20 Cf. Saint Augustine's commentary on the same passage (*PL* 35, 1953): 'that thereby, in a sense, the gate of life might be thrown open, from whence have flowed forth the sacraments of the Church, without which there is no entrance to the life which is the true life. That blood was shed for the remission of sins; that water it is that makes up the health-giving cup, and supplies at once the laver of baptism and water for drinking', *Homilies on the Gospel of John*, 120.2, in P. Schaff (ed.), *Nicene and post-Nicene fathers of the Christian church*, 7, First Series (New York, 1887–94), p. 879.   21 Cf. §136. Blathmac's use of this idea indicates his familiarity with a long Judaeo-Christian tradition concerning the burial of Adam on Golgotha. Jerome refers to the belief that Golgotha, 'place of the skull', took its name from the burial of Adam, noting that although this explanation 'is attractive and soothing to the ear' it is 'not true'; *Commentary on Matthew*, Book IV, 27.33, in Thomas P. Scheck (trans.), *St Jerome: commentary on Matthew*, The Fathers of the Church 117 (Washington, 2008), p. 315. One of the early examples of this notion comes from the pseudepigraphical

remarkable image of every single tree of the world being covered in blood in imitation of the Tree of the Cross (§64):[22]

> To-fich sruth folo – ro tinn! –
> combu derg snob cech oenchruinn;
> buí crú for bruinnib betho
> i mbarraib cech prímfedo.

> A stream of blood gushed forth (severe excess!)
> so that the bark of every tree was red;
> there was blood on the breasts of the world,
> in the (tree-) tops of every great forest.

Previous commentators have pointed to the close parallelism between this passage and the Crucifixion scene in Cynewulf's Old English poem *Christ III* (1174–6: 'Then many a tree wept bloody tears under its bark, ruddy, abundant tears; the sap was turned to blood'),[23] and suggested that the image may ultimately be traced back to the prophetic vision of the last days in the apocryphal IV Esdras 5:5 (*et de ligno sanguis stillabit*, 'and blood shall trickle from a tree [wood]').[24] For the present purpose, this analogue is particularly rele-

work known as the *First book of Adam and Eve*, Ch. XLII, 7–8: 'And, again, as regards the Water of Life thou seekest, it will not be granted thee this day; but on the day that I shall shed My blood upon thy head in the land of Golgotha. For My blood shall be the Water of Life unto thee, at that time, and not to thee alone, but unto all those of thy seed who shall believe in Me; that it be unto them for rest for ever': Rutherford H. Platt Jr., *The forgotten books of Eden* (Edinburgh and New York, 1926), p. 28 [electronically available at: <www.sacred-texts.com>]. The eucharistic symbolism of Blathmac's poem is briefly discussed in Neil X. O'Donoghue, *The eucharist in pre-Norman Ireland* (Notre Dame, 2011), pp 133–5. **22** Another noteworthy example of blood symbolism comes in §132, where the tears of blood brought forth by the contemplation of Christ's Passion accentuate the penitent's contrite agony. The reference could possibly be taken as an allusion to the drops of blood (*guttae sanguinis*) shed by Jesus when praying at Gethsemane; see Claire Clivaz, '"A sweat like drops of blood" (Lk 22:44): at the crossing of intertextual reading and textual criticism' (n.d.) [unpublished paper, electronically available on the Society of Biblical Literature website at: <http://www.sbl-site.org/assets/pdfs/clivaz_sweat.pdf>]. Here my reading differs from that of Lambkin ('The structure', 74–5), who proposes a more literal interpretation.   **23** Albert S. Cook (ed.), *The Christ of Cynewulf: a poem in three parts* (Boston, 1900), p. 44. The translation is from Charles W. Kennedy, *Cynewulf Christ*, In parentheses Publications, Old English Series (Cambridge, 2000), p. 22. Certain parallels between Blathmac's and Cynewulf's poetry are also discussed by Tristram, 'Early modes', pp 442–4.   **24** According to A. Lukyn Williams, the same image is also found in the writings of Pseudo-Jerome and Pseudo-Gregory of Nyssa; see his *Adversus Judaeos: a bird's-eye view of Christian apologiae until the renaissance* (Cambridge, 1935; repr. 2012), pp 25–6. The cross itself is depicted as bleeding from its side in another poem ascribed to Cynewulf; Albert S. Cook (ed.), *The dream of the rood: an Old English poem attributed to*

vant not only in terms of poetic diction, but also with regard to the overall orientation of both compositions towards the cosmic dimension of Christ's sacrifice, and their development of the eschatological vision of the Last Judgment. Indeed, in both instances the idea of the whole creation joining in universal mourning at the death of their Creator constitutes one of the most compelling reminders of the destiny awaiting those sinners who, in the words of Cynewulf, 'blind of heart, harder than stones of flint, knew not to confess that their God the Prince, the Almighty, delivered them from the torments of Hell', when even the 'lifeless things, that might not feel, still knew the Passion of our Lord'.[25] Thus in Blathmac §§65–6:

> Ba deithbir do dúilib Dé
> muir mas, nem nglas, talam cé
> ce imro-chloítis a ngné
> oc coíniud a ngalgaite.

> Corp Críst fri rinde rubae
> fo-rroelangair cruadgubae,
> cia no coíntis cruth bath má
> in fer trisa torsata.

> It would have been fitting for God's elements,
> the beautiful sea, the blue heaven, the present earth
> that they should change their aspect
> when keening their hero.

> The body of Christ pierced by points
> warranted severe lamentation;
> (it would be fitting) that they should keen in a stronger
> manner the man by whom they were created.[26]

The underlying logic of this imagery is therefore essentially biblical: just as the Egyptians bewailed their first-born (Ex 11:6) and all of Judah and

Cynewulf (Oxford, 1905), p. 2 (ll 18–20). For further analysis of both poems from a devotional viewpoint, see Christopher L. Chase, '"Christ III", "The dream of the rood", and early Christian passion piety', *Viator*, 11 (1980), 11–33. **25** Cook, *Christ*, 1178–9 (p. 45); Kennedy, *Cynewulf Christ*, p. 23. **26** Cf. §§61–3, where Blathmac treats the biblical account of the events at the moment of Christ's death (e.g., Mt 27:51–2) as expressions of the mourning and dread of the elements. Similar interpretation is presented in Cynewulf's poem: see Cook, *Christ*, 1128–62 (pp 43–4); Kennedy, *Cynewulf Christ*, p. 22. It has been noted that a direct source for this can be found in Gregory the Great's *Forty homilies on the Gospels* (Homily 10), *PL* 76, 1111; see Michael J.B. Allen and Daniel G. Calder (trans.), *Sources and analogues of Old English poetry I: the major Latin texts in translation* (Cambridge, 1976), pp 98–9.

Jerusalem lamented the death of their good king Josiah (2 Chron 35:24–5), so should all the faithful mourn even more fervently the death of Christ, who was 'the firstborn of every creature' (Col 1:15; cf. Rom 8:29), 'high above the kings of the earth' (Ps 88:28). Yet it is the anxious awareness of the imminence of the Second Coming and the prospect of one's own death which ultimately turns this mourning from an outward expression of grief to inward contemplation of sin and repentance. Hence, the final part of the composition already anticipates the theme of Christ's triumphant vengeance which predominates in the second poem, as Blathmac pleads for the Virgin's intercession to ensure the efficacy of his keen and its protective power (§§140–3):

> Cech oen diamba figel se
> fo lige ocus éirge
> ar imdídnad dianim tall
> amail lúirech co cathbarr.

> Cách nod-géba do cach deilb
> i troscud aidchi Sathairnn
> acht rob fo déraib cen meth,
> a Maire, níb ifernach.

> Fri tuidecht do maic co feirc
> cona chroich fria ais imdeirc,
> ara soírthar lat in tan
> nach carae nod-coínfedar.

> Everyone who has this as a vigil-prayer
> at lying down and at rising
> for unblemished protection in the next world
> like a breast-plate with helmet;

> Everyone, whatever he be, who shall say it
> fasting on Friday night,
> provided only that it be with copious tears,
> Mary, may he not be for Hell.

> At the angry coming of your son
> with his cross on his reddened back,
> that at that time you save any friend
> who shall have keened him.

Christian lament prayer characteristically maintains a liminal tension between 'God's self-giving love revealed in Jesus' at the Passion, and His 'defeat of death and inauguration of the new age' as revealed at the Resurrection.[27] I would propose that very same preoccupation with the 'here' and 'not yet' can be seen to underlie the manner in which Blathmac skilfully employs the conventions of the native keen to interweave the everyday reality of human bereavement into a Christological vision of God's redemptive sacrifice.[28] Instead of relying solely on the theme's 'essential "Irishness"' for its evocative power, Blathmac, even more importantly, appropriates the imagery of keening as one of several strategies by which he encourages the audience to 'internalize religious beliefs through association with personal experience and emotion', and thereby seeks to provide 'human access to the divine'.[29] With its lament form, Blathmac's poem is capable of conveying the whole array of feelings awoken by death as well as the awe, fear, and hope roused by Christ's triumphant victory over its power. Growing from the intimate and compassionate contemplation of this fundamental mystery, the feelings of sorrow and despair may thus eventually turn into joyous expectation of the promised future: 'Amen, amen I say to you, that you shall lament and weep, but the world shall rejoice; and you shall be made sorrowful, but your sorrow shall be turned into joy' (Jn 16:20).

---

27 Rebekah Ann Eklund, '"Lord, teach us how to grieve": Jesus' laments and Christian hope' (PhD, Duke University, 2012), p. 17.   28 For the Christology of the Blathmac poems, see Lisa Lawrence, 'The Irish and the incarnation: images of Christ in the Old Irish poems of Blathmac' (PhD, Harvard University, 2002). Unfortunately, I have not been able to consult Lawrence's work for this article.   29 Saupe, 'Introduction'.

Observations on the Book of Durrow memorandum

EDEL BHREATHNACH

The last folio of the early gospel book known as the Book of Durrow (248v) contains a non-contemporary memorandum that records an agreement between the monasteries of Durrow, Co. Offaly and Killeshin, Co. Laois.[1] The agreement concerns the transfer of land from Killeshin to Durrow and it is a rare example of such a text having survived from medieval Ireland. Similar memoranda were entered into the Book of Kells at various dates between $c.1114$ and 1161.[2] None of these texts have been classified as charters or deeds. In her study of the Kells memoranda, Máire Herbert described them as 'retrospective ... narrative accounts of transactions which have been performed ... evidentiary rather than dispositive, a permanent testimony that actions have taken place, that certain consequences are to follow, and that named guarantors are to oversee the fulfilment of the process'.[3] Marie Therese Flanagan has suggested that the exchange transaction between Durrow and Killeshin may have been recorded on a blank page in the Book of Durrow – a manuscript that was a relic in its own right – 'possibly because the desirability of having a written record may have been highlighted during the legal process of trying to revive a long-dormant grant'.[4] That a tradition of retrospective legal records had a long pedigree in Ireland is suggested by the evidence of earlier material. For example, a tract in the Book of Armagh known as the *Additamenta*, that probably dates to the eighth century, includes a declaration (*coibse*) and testament (*edocht / audacht*, possibly borrowed from Latin *ēdictum*) concerning the rights of a family to privileges in the church of Druim Lías (Drumlease, Co. Leitrim) along with the rights of St Patrick's community in the same church:[5]

> This is Fith Fio's declaration and his testament, (made) between the chancel and the altar two years before his death to the *familia* of Druim Lías and the nobles of Calrige: that there is no family right of inheritance to Druim Lías (for any) except the race of Fith Fio, if

1 R.I. Best, 'An early Irish monastic grant in the Book of Durrow', *Ériu*, 10 (1926–8), 135–42. 2 Gearóid Mac Niocaill (ed. and trans.), *Notitiæ as Leabhar Cheanannais 1033–1161* (Dublin, 1961); idem (ed.), 'Charters' in P. Fox (ed.), *The Book of Kells, MS 58, Trinity College Library Dublin: commentary* (Lucerne, 1990), pp 153–65. 3 Máire Herbert, 'Charter material from Kells' in F. O'Mahony (ed.), *The Book of Kells: proceedings of a conference at Trinity College Dublin, 6–9 September 1992* (Aldershot, 1994), pp 60–77 at p. 62. 4 Marie Therese Flanagan, *Irish royal charters: texts and contexts* (Oxford, 2005), p. 18. 5 Ludwig Bieler (ed. and trans.), *The Patrician texts in the Book of Armagh*, SLH 10 (Dublin, 1979), pp 173–4, §9(1).

there be one of them (available) who is good, devout, and conscientious. Should there not be, let there be an investigation whether one (such) can be obtained from among the community of Druim Lías or its church-tenants. If one be not obtained, an outlander belonging to Patrick's community is installed in it.

The import of this text is that definite legal processes existed in early Ireland and that they were secured by appropriate public ceremonies and often recorded in writing.

A further example of guarantors acting as guardians of an agreement occurs in an early eighth-century metrical legal tract on the respective rights and obligations of two major powers in the northern part of Ireland, the Uí Néill and the Airgíalla.[6] The poem ends with a list of witnesses and sureties whose obits suggest a complex legal record. The validity of the eighth-century agreement was framed in the context of earlier agreements reputed to have been concluded in the sixth century. The poem was possibly a retrospective record of a historical accord between the Uí Néill and the Airgíalla guaranteed by witnesses (*fíadain*) who bound the contract. These consisted of eminent kings and churchmen.[7] A second earlier agreement among the Airgíalla themselves is represented as having provided the framework for the eighth-century agreement. This section lists *rátha* 'paying sureties' and *aitiri* 'hostage sureties', kings of the various Airgíalla dynasties. The complexity of the legal provisions is underpinned by a historical narrative that is called upon to give authenticity to the agreement.

It is evident from such early legal texts, therefore, that there was a tradition of recording agreements in Ireland and that an essential element was its retrospective nature. It is usually argued that the administrative and legal conventions of Anglo-Saxon England and Carolingian Europe did not impinge to any great degree on Irish royal governance and legal practices. Richard Sharpe describes Ireland's perceived difference as follows:

> There was no generation of Irish kings served by scholar-bishops trained in Roman law, and there were no Romano-Irish codes ... there are virtually no documentary records of any kind of legal transaction. Though it is now accepted that the charter – in a form close to that of the British-Latin charter – enjoyed at least limited use in Ireland during the seventh century, extant sources suggest that written evidence of title to land never became widely accepted in Irish legal practice.[8]

6 Máirín O Daly, 'A poem on the Airgialla', *Ériu*, 16 (1952), 179–88; Edel Bhreathnach and Kevin Murray, 'The Airgíalla charter poem: edition' in E. Bhreathnach (ed.), *The kingship and landscape of Tara* (Dublin, 2005), pp 124–58; Thomas Charles-Edwards, 'The Airgíalla charter poem: the legal content' in ibid., pp 100–23. 7 Bhreathnach and Murray, 'The Airgíalla Charter Poem', pp 138–9. 8 Richard Sharpe, 'Dispute settlement in

Further on in his discussion of dispute settlement in medieval Ireland, Sharpe considers the Book of Durrow memorandum, along with similar material in the Book of Kells and the Book of Deer, and concludes:

> These three sources are so similar in form, and sufficiently close in date, for it to be possible that they represent a rather short-lived revival in the Gaelic areas of a form derived from the British-Latin charter. The Columban connection makes one wonder whether this revival was not even more limited.[9]

Perhaps this view of the use of written legal transactions in Ireland is somewhat minimalist? There is sufficient evidence to suggest that some form of written record provided a source for some saints' Lives. Similarly, a document such as the seventeenth-century Registry of Clonmacnoise that lists the estates of Clonmacnoise in the late medieval period is likely to reflect a number of pre-Norman donations to that church by the dominant dynasties of the midlands and Connacht.[10] Given the legalistic character of early medieval Irish society, it is inconceivable that the Uí Máil Sechnaill kings of Mide or the Uí Chonchobair kings of Connacht would have simply transferred lands to Clonmacnoise on the basis of a verbal agreement. Indeed, the Kells memoranda suggest the contrary. By the late eleventh century at least, transactions were detailed in writing. In demonstrating that such written agreements were also formulated outside the Columban churches, Flanagan points to the early twelfth-century 'charter-type' text detailing a transaction between the monastic community of Mayo and Toirdelbach Úa Conchobair, king of Connacht.[11] The Book of Durrow memorandum adds a further dimension to the conduct of legal transactions in pre-Norman Ireland in that its existence implies that written legal transactions were drawn up between churches as well as between kings and churches. While apparently unique in that it survives, it is most likely, as suggested by Charles Doherty in relation to the lives of Máedóc of Ferns and Molaise of Devenish,[12] that such material provided the basis for allusions to agreements between churches so common in the Lives of Irish saints.

If the memorandum in the Book of Durrow is a rare example of a written record that survived as a result of being incorporated into an exceptional manuscript, what does it convey to us about early medieval legal records, about agreements between churches, and about the monasteries of Durrow and

medieval Ireland: a preliminary inquiry' in W. Davies and P. Fouracre (eds), *The settlement of disputes in early medieval Europe* (Cambridge, 1986), pp 169–89 at p. 170. 9 Ibid., p. 174. 10 Annette Kehnel, *Clonmacnois – the church and lands of St Ciarán: change and continuity in an Irish monastic foundation (6th to 16th century)* (Münster, 1995), pp 202–45. 11 Flanagan, *Irish royal charters*, p. 16. 12 Charles Doherty, 'The transmission of the cult of St Máedóg' in P. Ní Chatháin and M. Richter (eds), *Ireland and Europe in the early Middle Ages: texts and transmission* (Dublin, 2002), pp 268–83 at pp 276–8.

Killeshin? It is instructive to apply the methodology of analysing medieval charters devised by Michael Gervers and Michael Margolin as part of the University of Toronto DEEDS (Documents of Early English Data Set) Research Project to the Durrow memorandum. They approached charter texts using the following premise:

> The core of our methodology is an examination of charter vocabulary in the context of other features such as origin of the scribe, topographical references, people involved in the transaction, formulae used in the text, the structure of the text, and word placement within that structure.[13]

Gervers and Margolin illustrate the structure of an English charter by analysing the diplomatic divisions of a deed pertaining to Abbot Samson of Bury St Edmunds (†1211) under a series of headings:

NOTIFICATION	Notum sit omnibus sancte matris ecclesie filiis quod
WORDS OF DISPOSITION	ego Samson dei gratia abbas sancti
PARTICULARS	Edmundi
WORDS OF DISPOSITION STANDARD PARTS	remitto et quietos clamo
GRANTEE(S) STANDARD PARTS	conuentui
GRANTEE(S) PARTICULARS	sancti Edmundi
PROPERTY PARTICULARS	lx
PROPERTY STANDARD PARTS	solidos
PROPERTY PARTICULARS	de Surreia quod alii abbates predecessores mei sibi iniuste et indebite uendicare et exigere presumpserunt
SEALING CLAUSE STANDARD PARTS	et ne ab aliquo successorum meorum de cetero exigantur presentis scripti cautione et sigilli mei appositione hoc ipsum roborare curaui ut
SEALING CLAUSE PARTICULARS	Hugo abbas memoratos lx solidos conuentui ductus penitentia remisit et remissos carte sue testimonio confirmauit
WITNESS CLAUSE STANDARD PARTS	Hiis Testibus
WITNESS CLAUSE PARTICULARS	Thoma de Hastinges Roberto de Flamuill

13 Michael Gervers and Michael Margolin, 'Application of computerized analyses in dating procedures for medieval charters': <http://res.deeds.utoronto.ca:49838/research/index.aspx> ('Publications', accessed 9 June 2013).

While the Bury St Edmunds deed is much later than the Durrow memorandum, it is instructive to consider how many of the diplomatic sections listed above can be traced in the Irish text. The Durrow text opens with the NOTIFICATION, a relatively standard invocation (*invocatio, salutatio*): *Ostende nobis domine et salutare tuum da nobis* 'Reveal to us o Lord and grant us your salvation'.[14] It is notable that only the invocation and subscription are in Latin while the rest of the text is in Irish. This might suggest that the author or scribe deliberately intended to frame the text in formulaic expressions. The brief Latin subscription at the end of the document reads: *Flannchad filius filii scientis scripsit*. Notably, none of the Kells memoranda use Latin formulaic phrases. They are entirely in Irish.

Then come the WORDS OF DISPOSITION: *Óentu mór eter Comgán 7 Colum Cille* 'A great union between Comgán and Colum Cille'. This is the subject of the document. Much can be said about the term *óentu*. It occurs initially in the Old Irish glosses on the Continent and normally is a gloss on Latin *unitas* or *fraternitas*.[15] From the tenth to the twelfth century, the conclusion of an *óentu* between major monasteries was common and these fraternal agreements are often mentioned in saints' Lives. The term had legal connotations as evidenced, for example, by the entry in the *Annals of Inisfallen* s.a. 973 when Dub dá Leithe, abbot of Armagh, went on a visitation to Munster and he and the abbot of Emly, the pre-eminent churchman in Munster, quarrelled about the collection of a levy due to Armagh. Mathgamain mac Cennétig, king of Munster (and Brian Bórama's brother) intervened and concluded a peace agreement between them, *7 a n-oentu im chert Patraicc do grés* 'and they agreed upon the perpetual right of [the coarb of] Patrick'. This agreement is unlikely to have been a verbal agreement but was probably written down in some form as the primary document that was consulted if the dispute erupted again at any later stage. That this *óentu* was successful may be inferred from an entry in the *Annals of Inisfallen* s.a. 1026 recording that the coarb of Patrick (abbot of Armagh) with a venerable entourage spent Easter with the king of Munster and aspirant king of Ireland, Donnchad mac Briain, at his royal residence of Cenn Corad (Kincora, Co. Clare).

The GRANTEE PARTICULARS: *Reclés dano dorat Comgán do Cholum Chille* 'A *reclés*, then Comgán gave to Colum Cille'. Comgán and Colum Cille are regarded as the founders of Killeshin and Durrow respectively, although Comgán's association with Killeshin was probably recent and linked to Dál Cais interference in its affairs in the early eleventh century.[16] The original founding saint of Killeshin was Diarmait who belonged to the Uí Bairrche, a dynasty who were particularly powerful in Leinster until the seventh century. No reference is made to Diarmait in the Book of Durrow memorandum.

---

14 Best, 'An early grant', p. 137.   15 Charles Doherty, 'Some aspects of hagiography as a source for Irish economic history', *Peritia*, 1 (1982), 300–28 at 326–7.   16 Edel Bhreathnach, 'Killeshin: an Irish monastery surveyed', *CMCS*, 27 (1994), 33–47.

The PROPERTY PARTICULARS: *léged fáill fair co fotta cen íarraid ó muintir Choluim Chille .i. ó muintir Darmaige* 'and it [the *reclés*] was left in neglect for a long time without being claimed by the community of Colum Cille, i.e., by the community of Durrow'. The *reclés* was probably a small complex within the landscape of Killeshin which may have consisted of a church, a settlement and enclosure for use by an eremitical community following a coenobitic rule.[17] The Durrow community's claim had been neglected for a long time and this was probably an obstacle to their reclaiming the *reclés* as in early Irish law uncontested presence on land for a period known as *rudrad* 'a long duration' (< *ro* + *dúrad*) caused legal difficulties for claim of ownership.[18] This difficulty probably accounts for the action taken by the Durrow community when the abbot, Gilla na Nóem Úa Énlúain and its priest Gilla Adamnáin Úa Cortén and many others with them visited Killeshin to claim their neglected *reclés*. By doing so, they may have been following the procedure of legal entry (*tellach*) whereby an individual took possession of land to which he believed that he was entitled, but that was alienated to someone else.[19] According to the law, certain formalities were to be adhered to, such as entering the land holding two horses and accompanied by witnesses and sureties.[20] Whatever about the horses, undoubtedly the priest and others accompanying the abbot were acting in these latter capacities. The next step in the legal procedure must have been set in train by the Killeshin community on the appearance of the delegation from Durrow. This involved coming to some settlement through arbitration. The appearance of the abbot of Durrow at the head of a delegation and acting in a legal capacity would have required a serious response. Similar scenes are alluded to elsewhere. For example, in 909, Muirenn, abbess of Kildare, 'with a large group of clergy and many relics' escorted the joint king of Munster, Flaithbertach mac Inmanéin, from Kildare to the border of Munster to negotiate a peace treaty between Munster and Leinster.[21] In 908, Flaithbertach had accompanied Cormac mac Cuilennáin, joint king of Munster with him, into battle at Belach Mugna against Flann Sinna, king of Ireland, and his allies the Leinstermen. The latter had blamed Flaithbertach for dragging the pious king-bishop, Cormac, into the battlefield against his will and after their defeat in battle, and Cormac's death, they incarcerated him in Kildare for a year before releasing him back to Munster.

The next clause in the memorandum involved a RESTITUTION to the Durrow community for the appropriated *reclés*. The Killeshin community could not hand back the *reclés* as it had been given to the Munster dynasty of

---

17 Aidan MacDonald, '*Reiclés* in the Irish annals to AD 1200', *Peritia*, 13 (1999), 259–75. 18 Fergus Kelly, *A guide to early Irish law* (Dublin, 1988), p. 109. 19 Ibid., p. 186. 20 Thomas M. Charles-Edwards, *Early Irish and Welsh kinship* (Oxford, 1993), pp 254–73. 21 *FAI* 909.

Dál Cais to whom Brian Bórama belonged. A notice in the *Annals of the Four Masters* s.a. 1024 records the slaughter of the Munstermen by Donnchad mac Áeda, king of Uí Bairrche – the local king – at Killeshin 'through the miracles of God and Comgán'.[22] It is possible that Durrow's *reclés* was handed over to Dál Cais in the early eleventh century in reparation for Donnchad mac Áeda's action or in recognition of Dál Cais authority over Killeshin at that time. Having lost the *reclés* to Dál Cais, who seem to have held onto it despite losing control over Uí Bairrche at a later stage, the Durrow community had to be given an exact equivalent. They were offered 'an equal portion of their enclosure (*airlise* 'the area around a dwelling') both length and breadth'. This *airlise* was known as Int Eidnán 'the ivy-clad place'. In her extensive study of the Kells memoranda, Máire Herbert notes that the name *eidnén* 'an ivy-clad place or church' is also used to describe churches in Kells, Clonard, possibly Clonmacnoise as well as an Eidhnén Molaga in Munster.[23] One of the Kells memoranda implies that at 'int Edhnén' there was possibly the location of a newly consecrated church associated with the *dísert* 'the locus of religious life'.[24]

One of the most interesting aspects of the Durrow memorandum is the WITNESS CLAUSE that lists the sureties on both sides. It provides a unique insight into the administrative ecclesiastical elite of a pre-Norman monastery, an elite whose careers often appear in the annals and other sources of the period. The priest Gilla Adamnáin Úa Cortén (Coirthnéin) became the abbot of Kells and was party to the settlement of a dispute in that monastery which is described in one of the Kells texts that dates to between 1117 and 1133.[25] He may have been appointed *comarba* of Colum Cille at Kells *c*.1117. Máire Herbert surmises that a member of the Durrow community may have been elected to the abbacy of Kells following the murder of the latter monastery's abbot by the Uí Briúin in 1117.[26] On the evidence of the Durrow memorandum, Gilla Adamnáin was clearly prominent in the early decades of the twelfth century and may have been an astute cleric skilled in dealing with difficult and tense situations. Máel Choluim mac Cortáin, whose name may indicate that he was related to Gilla Adamnáin (possibly his father), and Máel Choluim's brothers were sureties of the Durrow agreement. The Killeshin delegation was led by its *airchinnech* 'lay abbot', noted as Cathasach Úa Corcráin (†1045, *AFM*), although this identification may be incorrect or may suggest that that there was an original agreement in the mid-eleventh century which was renewed in the early twelfth century. The Uí Úathgaile, who are also listed as sureties, were an ecclesiastical family associated with the church from at least the late eleventh century.[27] They belonged to the same branch

---

22 Bhreathnach, 'Killeshin'.   23 Herbert, 'Charter material', p. 69.   24 Ibid.   25 Mac Niocaill, *Notitiæ*, p. 22 (VI).   26 Máire Herbert, *Iona, Kells, and Derry: the history and hagiography of the monastic* familia *of Columba* (Oxford, 1988), p. 101.   27 Bhreathnach,

of the Uí Bairrche as Diarmait, Killeshin's seventh-century founder. Dublitir Úa Úathgaile is credited with the authorship of the tract *Sex aetates mundi* and the poem beginning 'Rédig dam, a Dé, do nim', both on the biblical history of the world.[28] While his authorship of *Sex aetates mundi* is not conclusive, he is likely to have been the author of the long poem in Irish. The Durrow memorandum describes him as *fer léigind* 'lector' of Killeshin. His father was probably Conchobar, also a *fer léigind* who died in 1082 (*AFM*). Dúnchad Úa Úathgaile, possibly his brother, is also mentioned in the memorandum although he is not given any title.

The memorandum is framed within the reigns of a local king, Muiredach mac Gormáin (†1124) king of Uí Bairrche, and the aspirant king of Ireland, Muirchertach Úa Briain (†1119). It ends with the formulaic phrase 'A blessing then on the folk who gave it and to whom it was given' (*bennacht dano don lucht dosrat 7 dia tuccad*). Then there is a *subscriptio* which, as we have seen, notes the name of the scribe as *Flannchad filius filii scientis scripsit*. This may be a Latin rendering of the family name Úa Éolais, a family who were associated with Clonmacnoise. Odrán Úa Éolais died as scribe of Clonmacnoise in 995. The possible use by Flannchad of a Latin version of his family name recalls the similar action of Brian Bórama's secretary, Máel Suthain, who signed a note added to the Book of Armagh in 1005 as *Caluus Perennis*.

In conclusion, what can be seen in the Book of Durrow memorandum is a fragmentary reflection of the activities and processes of a sophisticated administrative elite who operated in the major churches of pre-Norman Ireland. This elite was legally and administratively literate; in many instances, its members were learned and not merely literate. They were present in more than one church. For example, members of the northern family of Uí Brolcháin resided in Derry, Armagh, Kildare and Lismore while the Uí Rebacháin were in Mungaret and Lismore. They held high ecclesiastical office and influenced royal rulers; and they were familiar with proper legal arrangements and the ceremonies that were appropriate to effecting them. Hence the community of Durrow came to Killeshin to make their claim and the outcome was recorded – perhaps informally at first, and then formally later on a blank page in the Book of Durrow. The presumption from the rare survival of such a memorandum has been that early medieval Ireland did not fit into the charter tradition known from elsewhere. This may not have been the case. Perhaps few texts survived simply because the manuscripts in which they were written did not survive, and the Durrow memorandum is a rare instance of the type of material that was lost.

'Killeshin', pp 44–5.   28 Dáibhí Ó Cróinín (ed. and trans.), *The Irish Sex aetates mundi* (Dublin, 1983); Máire Herbert, 'The Irish *Sex aetates mundi*: first editions', *CMCS*, 11 (1986), 96–112.

Senchas Gall Átha Clíath: aspects of the cult of St Patrick in the twelfth century

ELIZABETH BOYLE AND LIAM BREATNACH

Perhaps first among Máire Herbert's many contributions to scholarship is her exemplary work on medieval Irish hagiography. Therefore, as a token of respect, we offer here a small contribution to the study of the cult of St Patrick in the twelfth century, namely an edition, translation and analysis of *Senchas Gall Átha Clíath* ('History of the Foreigners of Dublin', henceforth *SAC*).[1] This late Middle Irish poem contains hagiographical episodes found in other texts – vernacular and Latin, Irish and Anglo-Norman – and is therefore discussed with regard to both its local and international connections. We consider the possible role of the poem in the transmission of pseudo-historical information about Patrick to his late-twelfth-century hagiographer, Jocelin of Furness, and we consider some of the wider relationships between Latin and vernacular Patrician hagiography in the twelfth century.

There has been significant scholarly attention given in recent years to the Latin literature associated more broadly with the cult of St Patrick in the eleventh, twelfth and early thirteenth centuries: we might note particularly the important editions, translations and studies by Michael Winterbottom and Rod Thomson, Robert Easting and Richard Sharpe, and Helen Birkett.[2] Other scholars have discussed literary and onomastic manifestations of the Patrician cult in eleventh- and twelfth-century Britain.[3] The Irish evidence

---

1 Introduction and source analysis by Boyle; edition, translation and notes by Breatnach (with contributions by each to the other). Liam Breatnach, whose attention was first drawn to this poem by Donnchadh Ó Corráin, read *SAC* in seminars at Trinity College Dublin in the 1990s and at the Dublin Institute for Advanced Studies in 2006–7; contributions by participants are acknowledged in the notes. We are grateful to Professor Ó Corráin for reading and commenting on an earlier version of this paper.   2 Michael Winterbottom and Rodney M. Thomson (ed. and trans.), *William of Malmesbury, saints' Lives: Lives of SS. Wulfstan, Dunstan, Patrick, Benignus and Indract*, Oxford Medieval Texts (Oxford, 2002); Robert Easting and Richard Sharpe (ed. and trans.), *Peter of Cornwall's Book of Revelations* (Toronto, 2013), ch. 3: 'Peter of Cornwall's account of St Patrick's Purgatory' (pp 116–41); Helen Birkett, *The saints' Lives of Jocelin of Furness: hagiography, patronage and ecclesiastical politics* (Woodbridge, 2010). Furthermore, Dr Ingrid Sperber has an edition of Jocelin of Furness' Life of Patrick forthcoming as part of the AHRC-funded project 'Hagiography at the Frontiers: Jocelin of Furness and Insular Politics' (University of Liverpool and University of Cambridge), and we are grateful to her for making sections of it available to us.   3 Elizabeth Boyle, 'The authorship and transmission of *De tribus habitaculis animae*', *Journal of Medieval Latin*, 22 (2012), 49–65; Fiona Edmonds, 'Personal names and the cult of Patrick in eleventh-century Strathclyde and Northumbria' in S.

from the same period has not received such sustained attention of late. However, it should be emphasized that, although the poem is primarily read here in terms of its place within the corpus of later Patrician hagiography, this is by no means the only way in which it can be read. It is simultaneously a poetic charter and a work of *dindsenchas*. We can trace the tradition of poetic charters back at least as far as the 'Airgíalla Charter Poem', which outlines the mutual obligations of the Airgíalla and the Uí Néill.[4] Of particular interest for our purposes are the poems in *Lebor na cert* (on which see p. 29 below),[5] which together form the most comprehensive collection of such poetic charter material. As a work of *dindsenchas*, *SAC* is discussed briefly below in relation to other *dindsenchas* on Dublin (see p. 30). Much more remains to be said about all aspects of this interesting and important poem, but we hope that this preliminary offering will prove useful.

SAC sets out a narrative of conversion for the Scandinavians of Dublin that excludes any outside involvement, and incorporates Dublin fully into the medieval Irish historiographical tradition in which Patrick was the sole apostle of the Irish.[6] This complete exclusion of external influence is itself likely to be a reaction to external influence, particularly that of Canterbury, and it has been argued that either *SAC*, or the poem in *Lebor na cert* to which it is closely related, was composed within the context of competition between Canterbury and Armagh for jurisdiction of Dublin.[7] Armagh and Dublin were part of a much larger jurisdictional patchwork in which major ecclesiastical centres, including York and Worcester, were using similar methods to resist Canterbury hegemony in the century or so after 1066. These methods included the production of hagiography on local pre-Conquest saints and of forged and anachronistic charter materials: *SAC* encapsulates both of these

Boardman, J.R. Davies and E. Williamson (eds), *Saints' cults in the Celtic world*, Studies in Celtic History 25 (Woodbridge, 2009), pp 42–65. After completion of the present paper, a significant collection of essays was published: Clare Downham (ed.), *Jocelin of Furness: essays from the 2011 conference* (Donington, 2013). **4** Edel Bhreathnach and Kevin Murray, 'The Airgíalla charter poem: edition' in E. Bhreathnach (ed.), *The kingship and landscape of Tara* (Dublin, 2005), pp 124–58; Máirín O Daly, 'A poem on the Airgialla', *Ériu*, 16 (1952), 179–88. For discussion of the legal obligations outlined in the poem, see Thomas Charles-Edwards, 'The Airgíalla charter poem: the legal context' in Bhreathnach (ed.), *Kingship and landscape*, pp 100–23. **5** Myles Dillon (ed. and trans.), *Lebor na cert. The Book of rights*, ITS 46 (Dublin, 1962). **6** The present study is not concerned with the historical conversion of the Scandinavians of Dublin, but rather with the late-eleventh- and twelfth-century circumstances which gave rise to the pseudo-historical account of their conversion as presented in *SAC*. On the historical evidence for conversion, see Lesley Abrams, 'The conversion of the Scandinavians of Dublin', *Anglo-Norman Studies*, 20, Proceedings of the Battle Conference (1997), 1–29, and references therein. **7** See, for example, David N. Dumville, 'St Patrick and the Scandinavians of Dublin' in his *Saint Patrick A.D. 493–1993*, Studies in Celtic History 13 (Woodbridge, 1993), pp 259–64 at pp 262–4; Martin Holland, 'Dublin and the reform of the Irish Church in the eleventh and twelfth century', *Peritia*, 14 (2000), 111–60.

processes. Indeed, one of the saints for whom Glastonbury commissioned a Life in order to 'ratchet up their local cults in the face of Canterbury's noticeable and increasing potential for hagiographical hegemony' was Benignus (Benén), to whom *SAC* is ascribed.[8] William of Malmesbury (*c.*1090 – *c.*1143) also produced a Life of Patrick for Glastonbury.[9]

During the late-eleventh and twelfth centuries, Christians in Dublin were closely involved with many interconnected spheres of ecclesiastical jurisdiction, notably those of England (particularly Canterbury, but also York); Wales (St David's); and Ireland (Armagh). As a major economic centre, with close trading connections with cities such as Chester and Bristol, and broader cultural and political ties to the Isle of Man and much of the western seaboard of Scotland and northern England (for example, Strathclyde and Cumbria), we should not be surprised that the ecclesiastical culture of Dublin was, from our earliest evidence, outward looking and subject to diverse influences. Early bishops of Dublin were frequently clerics who had trained outside Ireland, often in English reformed Benedictine communities attached to major ecclesiastical centres.[10] Many were consecrated by archbishops of Canterbury and professed obedience to them.[11] In one of these professions, Dublin was described as the *metropolis* of Ireland, namely in the profession of Patrick, preserved in the Canterbury Professions in London, BL Cotton MS Cleopatra E i:

> Quisquis aliis prẹsidet, si et ipse aliis subiaceat dedignari non debet,
> sed potius obẹdientiam, quam a subiectis suis desiderat habere, propter

---

8 Winterbottom and Thomson, *William of Malmesbury*, p. xxxii, and for an edition and translation of what survives of the Life, see pp 344–67. William of Malmesbury produced his Life of Benignus from scraps of information which he pieced together from Patrician hagiography, notably the *Vita tertia*, and local Glastonbury tradition. For the *Vita tertia*, see Ludwig Bieler (ed.), *Four Latin Lives of St Patrick*, SLH 8 (Dublin, 1971), pp 13–39, 115–90.   9 Winterbottom and Thomson, *William of Malmesbury*, pp 316–43, and see also the Life of Indract at pp 368–81. William's sources for the Life of Patrick include the *Vita tertia* and Patrick's own writings (pp xxiv–xxv). On Indract, see Michael Lapidge, 'The cult of St Indract at Glastonbury' in his *Anglo-Latin literature, 900–1066* (London, 1993), pp 419–52. 10 Marie Therese Flanagan, *The transformation of the Irish church in the twelfth century* (Woodbridge, 2010), pp 6–7. See also Martin Brett, 'Canterbury's perspective on church reform and Ireland, 1070–1115' in D. Bracken and D. Ó Riain-Raedel (eds), *Ireland and Europe in the twelfth century: reform and renewal* (Dublin, 2006), pp 13–35; Mark Philpott, 'Some interactions between the English and Irish churches', *Anglo-Norman Studies*, 20, Proceedings of the Battle Conference (1997), 187–204; Denis Bethell, 'English monks and Irish reform in the eleventh and twelfth centuries' in T.D. Williams (ed.), *Historical Studies VIII: papers read before the Irish Conference of Historians, Dublin, 27–30 May 1969* (Dublin, 1971), pp 111–35.   11 Michael Richter (ed.), *Canterbury professions*, Canterbury and York Society 67 (Torquay, 1973), pp 29 (no. 36: Patricius; 1074), 31 (no. 42: Donatus; 1085), 34 (no. 51: Samuel; 1096), and 39 (no. 69: Gregorius; 1121). See also pp 35 (no. 54: Malchus of Waterford, 1096) and 42 (Patricius of Limerick; 1140).   12 Ibid., p. 29 (no. 36).

Deum studeat prelatis sibi per omnia humiliter exhibere. Propterea ego Patricius, ad regendam Dublinam metropolem Hibernię electus antistes, tibi, reuerende pater Lanfrance, Britanniarum primas et sanctę Dorobernensis ęcclesię archiepiscope, professionis me chartam porrigo meque tibi tuisque successoribus in omnibus, quę ad Christianam religionem pertinent, obtemperaturum esse promitto.[12]

Whoever rules over others must not think it beneath him if he himself is subordinate to others; but rather let him humbly show to those who are appointed over him, in all things and for the love of God, that obedience which he wishes to receive from his own subjects. Wherefore I, Patrick, who have been chosen as bishop to rule Dublin, the *metropolis* of Ireland, do hand to you, my reverend father Lanfranc, primate of the British Isles and archbishop of the holy church of Canterbury, this charter of my profession; and I promise that I shall obey you and your successors in all things which pertain to the Christian religion.

The extraordinary wording of this profession points as much to Canterbury's tensions with York at the time, as to Dublin's own position in relation both to Canterbury and to the rest of Ireland; but this document is relatively straightforward, in the sense that it was certainly drawn up in England for the purpose of Patrick's consecration. More complicated is a letter, preserved in the same manuscript, purportedly from the clergy and people of Dublin requesting that Lanfranc consecrate Patrick as bishop. The wording of the letter is based on the *decretum quod clerus et populus firmare debet de electo episcopo* found in the Romano-Germanic Pontifical, compiled in Mainz in the tenth century, but with some additions and omissions.[13] One of the additions from the basic template of the Romano-Germanic Pontifical is the description of '"the church of Dublin which is a [or 'the'] metropolis of [or 'in'] the island of Ireland" (*aecclesia dublinensis quae hiberniae insulae metropolis est)*'.[14] This might suggest that Dublin itself was asserting its pre-eminent position within Ireland, but the letter must be treated circumspectly since, in addition to the professions of Canterbury's suffragans, Cotton MS Cleopatra E i also contains Canterbury forgeries of papal letters.[15] In his discussion of the phrase *aecclesia dublinensis quae hiberniae insulae metropolis est*, Mark Philpott has suggested that it was in the interests of Canterbury to proclaim itself as having authority over more than one metropolitan bishop, and that, in addition to proclaiming authority over York, to be able to proclaim authority over Dublin, as a metropolitan see, was politically advantageous. Therefore, we may doubt the authenticity of the letter. However, the situation might equally be viewed from the opposite direction: if we regard the letter as genuine,

13 Philpott, 'Some interactions', p. 193; Holland, 'Dublin', pp 112–13. 14 Philpott, 'Some interactions', p. 194. 15 Ibid., p. 195.

Dublin declaring itself as a metropolitan see in Ireland could be a direct response to the metropolitan claims, and aggrandizing tendencies, of Armagh. Indeed, Samuel, consecrated in 1096, also claimed archiepiscopal privileges for Dublin, even though Dublin was not recognized as a metropolitan see until the Synod of Kells–Mellifont in 1152. Further support for the idea that the letter may be genuine is the evidence adduced by Marie Therese Flanagan that Gille of Limerick drew on the Romano-Germanic Pontifical in composing his *De statu ecclesiae*, which might suggest that the Pontifical was in use in reforming circles in Ireland.[16] On balance, however, it seems most likely that the letter was produced at Canterbury, particularly given certain similarities of phrasing between it, and Bishop Patrick's profession of obedience, which was certainly drawn up at Canterbury.[17]

A letter from Lanfranc, archbishop of Canterbury, generally considered to have been addressed to Domnall úa hÉnna, bishop of Munster, and written in 1080 or 1081, is preserved in a twelfth-century Worcester manuscript, London, BL Cotton Vespasian E. IV.[18] This Worcester connection is significant, since it was the home of another text which describes Dublin in an interesting manner, namely the 'Altitonantis' charter.[19] This mid-twelfth-century fabrication purports to be a foundation charter for Worcester, recording the grant of the endowment of the see of Worcester on 28 December 964, by King Edgar. The charter has been much discussed by Anglo-Saxon historians, and is part of a wider phenomenon of anachronistic and forged charter production at Worcester,[20] but for our purposes what is significant is the description of the extent of Edgar's sovereignty. The charter states:

16 Flanagan, *Transformation*, pp 65–6.   17 Holland, 'Dublin', 115. See also the letter preserved in the twelfth-century Worcester manuscript, London, BL MS Cotton Claudius A i, f. 38r, purportedly from Gregory VII to the Irish king Toirdelbach 'Úa Briain, and the people of Ireland, which has been described by Martin Brett as a 'literary rather than a juridical fiction, since it proves nothing either way about the formal position of the Irish church' (Brett, 'Canterbury's perspective', pp 19–20 n. 14). For the letter, see Maurice P. Sheehy (ed.), *Pontificia Hibernica. Medieval papal chancery documents concerning Ireland, 640–1261*, 2 vols (Dublin, 1962), i, pp 7–8 (no. 2), beginning *Gregorius episcopus servus servorum Dei Terdelvacho inclito regi Hibernie, archiepiscopis, episcopis, abbatibus, proceribus omnibusque Christianis Hiberniam inhabitantibus salutem et apostolicam benedictionem*; H.E.J. Cowdrey (ed. and trans.), *The 'Epistolae vagantes' of Pope Gregory VII*, Oxford Medieval Texts (Oxford, 1972), no. 57. For discussion of this manuscript, see Denis Bethell, 'English black monks and episcopal elections in the 1120s', *English Historical Review*, 84 (1969), 673–98 at 694–8.   18 Helen Clover and Margaret Gibson (ed. and trans.), *The letters of Lanfranc archbishop of Canterbury* (Oxford, 1979), p. 19.   19 We are very grateful to Simon Keynes for allowing us to see his working notes on the 'Altitonantis' charter, from his paper 'The afterlife of an Anglo-Saxon charter', given at the Selden conference, Oxford, July 2010.   20 Eric John, *Land tenure in early England* (Leicester, 1964), pp 90–112; Julia Barrow, 'How the twelfth-century monks of Worcester perceived their past' in P. Magdalino (ed.), *The perception of the past in twelfth-century Europe* (London, 1992), pp 53–74; eadem, 'The chronology of forgery production at Worcester from *c.*1000 to the early twelfth century' in

Mihi autem concessit propitia divinitas cum Anglorum imperio omnia regna insularum oceani cum suis ferocissimis regibus usque Norregiam maximamque partem Hibernie cum sua nobilissima civitate Dublina Anglorum regno subiugare quos etiam omnes meis imperiis colla subdere dei favente gratia coegi.[21]

Divine favour has permitted me, along with the *imperium* of the English, to reduce all the kingdoms of the islands of the ocean as far as Norway, with their most fierce kings, and to subject the greatest part of Ireland with her chief town of Dublin to the kingdom of the English, all of whom I have constrained to bend their necks to my rule with the favourable grace of God.

The wording is interesting: as with the eleventh-century Canterbury documents which described Dublin as the *metropolis* of Ireland, the use of *nobilissimus* to describe the position of Dublin within Ireland might have come as something of a surprise to the rest of the Irish, though perhaps not nearly as surprising as the news that Edgar had managed to subjugate the greater part of the island of Ireland. Of course, this forged charter tells us more about attitudes in twelfth-century Worcester than it does about the historical reality of Edgar's reign or Dublin's self-perception; but how do we explain, even within the context of the twelfth-century Worcester community, this characterization of Dublin as Ireland's pre-eminent *civitas*? Eric John briefly explored this passage of the 'Altitonantis' charter,[22] but he accepted the hypotheses of Aubrey Gwynn regarding the Worcester connections of Patrick, bishop of Dublin, and so he set the initiation of links between Dublin and Worcester within the context of Patrick's training in Worcester and his subsequent episcopacy in Dublin.[23] Furthermore, John repeated Gwynn's suggestion that Patrick had introduced a community of monks to Dublin from Worcester; a community that was subsequently expelled in 1096. Regarding this latter point, Martin Holland has since argued that it is more likely that the community of monks was introduced from Canterbury, not Worcester, and during the episcopate of Patrick's successor, Donngus (Donatus).[24]

More generally, recent scholarship has suggested that the links between Patrick and Worcester are not as conclusive as has previously been supposed.[25] We might note, for example, another 'Patricius', who is listed as a member of the community at Coventry.[26] His name was added, along with

J.S. Barrow and N.P. Brooks (ed.), *St Wulfstan and his world*, Studies in Early Medieval Britain (Aldershot, 2005), pp 105–22 at pp 118–21. **21** John, *Land tenure*, pp 162–7 at p. 162. **22** Ibid., pp 105–7. This was repeated by Emma Mason, *St Wulfstan of Worcester c.1008–1095* (Oxford, 1990), p. 251. **23** Aubrey Gwynn, SJ, *The writings of Bishop Patrick, 1074–1084*, SLH I (Dublin, 1955). **24** Holland, 'Dublin', 120. **25** Brett, 'Canterbury's perspective', pp 33–5; Boyle, 'Authorship', passim. **26** Joan Greatrex, *Biographical register*

others of the community of Holy Trinity and St Mary, Coventry, and with
Leofric and his wife Godiva, to the mortuary roll of Vitalis, abbot of Savigny,
in or before 1122.[27] This Patricius could just as easily be Patrick of Dublin,
since the death dates of the other identifiable individuals listed in the death-
roll coincide well with the death of Patrick in 1084. During the episcopate of
Wulfstan, the sons of Harold Godwinson, earl of Wessex and briefly king of
England, took refuge in Ireland following their father's defeat at the battle of
Hastings in 1066. In 1069, Harold's sons returned from Ireland with a fleet
of ships in an attempt to recapture England from William the Conqueror. In
this unsuccessful endeavour, they were supported by Diarmait mac Maíl na
mBó (†1072), king of Leinster, whose son Murchad mac Diarmata (†1070)
was installed as king of Dublin. Perhaps it is in this political context, or in
the continuous trading links between Dublin and Bristol, rather than in connection with the episcopacy of Patrick, that we might see the initiation of
links between Dublin and Worcester, which were to endure well into the
twelfth century.[28]

    Flanagan has argued that the partial and fragmentary nature of the surviv-
ing evidence for ecclesiastical reform in Ireland leads to an over-emphasis on
the relationship between the various Irish dioceses and Canterbury; a result of
Canterbury's 'active recording strategy in support of its claims to primacy'.[29]
But we can see that it was not only Armagh that responded to Canterbury's
claims to primacy through the fabrication of anachronistic charter material and
the production of hagiographical literature about pre-Conquest saints. The circumstances within which *SAC* was produced were part of a larger, international pattern of resistance to Canterbury dominance. It is possible that Dublin
itself looked equally to both sides: its close relationship with Canterbury has
been outlined above, but we might also note that there is early evidence for
the cult of Patrick in Dublin. That an eleventh-century bishop of Dublin had
the name Patricius (Gilla Pátraic) is interesting, as is the evidence contained
in *SAC* for sites in Dublin associated with St Patrick, the dedications of which
obviously predate the poem (see below, vv 44, 47). One significant piece of
evidence which provides us with another account of a relationship of mutual

of the English cathedral priories of the province of Canterbury c.1066 to 1540 (Oxford, 1997),
p. 366.   **27** Alfred Clapham, 'Three Bede-Rolls', *Archaeological Journal*, 106 –
Supplement: Memorial Volume to Sir Alfred Clapham (1952 [for 1949]), 40–53, no. 88:
*T. sancte Trinitatis et sanctae Marie Covantrensis aecclesiae. Orate pro nostris, Leovrico comite,
Godiva comitissa, Leofwino, Rodberto episcopis, Bruningo priore, Goduino, Patricio, Thoma,
monachis et pro aliis nostris defunctis.* See also L. Delisle, *Rouleaux des morts du IXe au XVe
siècle* (Paris, 1866), pp 281–344 (for the Roll of Vitalis, abbot of Savigny); p. 313 (for the
Coventry community).   **28** On the political context for this period, see Seán Duffy,
'Irishmen and islesmen in the kingdoms of Dublin and Man, 1052–1171', *Ériu*, 43 (1992),
93–133. Duffy has suggested that, during this period, the bishopric of Dublin may have
had episcopal jurisdiction over the Isle of Man (p. 107 n. 68).   **29** Flanagan, *Transformation*, pp 6–7.

obligation between Armagh and the Hiberno-Scandinavians is found in the so-called Osraige section of the collection known as the *Fragmentary annals*. There we are told of a battle between the *Danair* and the *Lochlannaig*, in which the former were defeated. Their leader, Horm, tells them to pray to St Patrick, and make offerings to him.

> Ra freagruttur uile é, 7 eadh ra raidhsid: 'Ar comaircce', ar síad, 'antí naomh Phadraicc, 7 an Choimdhe as tigearna dhó sin fén, 7 ar ccosgar dhá eaglais 7 ar n-iondmhus'.[30]

> All answered him, and this is what they said: 'Let our protector', they said, 'be this Saint Patrick, and the Lord who is master to him, and let our spoils and our treasure be given to his church'.

The Danes were then victorious, and when messengers arrived from Máel Sechlainn, king of Tara, they found that the Danes had prepared a ditch full of gold and silver to give to Patrick. This late Middle Irish account is probably roughly contemporaneous with *SAC* and is further evidence of the retrospective projection in the twelfth century of a longstanding relationship of mutual obligation between Dublin and Armagh.[31]

SENCHAS ÁTHA CLÍATH: RELATED SOURCES AND DATING

SAC, which begins *Atá sund in senchas seng*, is an expanded version of the eighteen-quatrain poem on Dublin in *Lebor na cert*, beginning *Atá sund sean-chas suairc seang* (henceforth *LCS*).[32] Parts of both poems are related to passages in Jocelin's Life of Patrick (see below). Our poem falls into six sections, each of which is conveniently marked by a *dúnad*:[33]

> – Section I (vv 1–24) tells the story of Patrick's arrival in Dublin, his miraculous raising to life of the two children of the king, and the conversion of the Dubliners. It is an adaptation of *LCS*, with the substitution of a son and a daughter of the king for the son of *LCS*, in order to provide an account of the origin of the name Duiblinn (vv 6, 7, 10), and with the addition of four verses (12–15) on the tribute due to Patrick.[34] Both of these alterations are paralleled in Jocelin ch. 99.

30 *FAI*, pp 90–5 §235.   31 For a discussion of some economic aspects of this relationship, see Mary A. Valante, 'Taxation, tolls and tribute: the language of economics and trade in Viking-age Ireland', *PHCC*, 18/19 (2006), 243–58.   32 Dillon, *Lebor na cert*, pp 114–19.   33 Compare, for example, the use of a *dúnad* to mark off each sub-section in the *dindsenchas* of Carmun, *MD* iii, pp 2–25 at ll 80, 192, 256, 284, 296 and 324.   34 The additional verses in this section of *SAC* are then 6–7, 10 and 12–15. It also omits v. 6 of

- Section II (vv 25–33) makes the claim that Dublin's prosperity is dependent on its loyalty to Armagh, and lists the dues owed by merchants to Dublin, and the tithes to be given out of these dues to Armagh.
- Section III (vv 34–9) gives an account of the origin of the name Áth Clíath, which differs from both the prose and metrical *dindšenchas* of Áth Clíath.[35]
- Section IV (vv 40–4) tells the story of the origin of St Patrick's well, as narrated in Jocelin ch. 70, and alluded to in ch. 99.
- Section V (vv 45–50) contains an account of the churches of Dublin.
- Section VI consists of a single concluding verse.

Our poem reflects the amalgamation of Duiblinn and Áth Clíath, which were originally separate places. While it normally refers to the place as *Áth Clíath*, it uses *Duiblinn* in v. 31, and gives the origin of the name in v. 7 beside an account of the origin of Áth Clíath in section III. *LCS* uses only Áth Clíath, as does the first account in Jocelin's Life (ch. 69), while the second account has only *Dublinia* (ch. 99; see below).

The only complete copy of *SAC* known to us is found in the Book of Uí Maine 68vb52–69va5.[36] It is written in a very simple form of *deibide*, with little metrical ornamentation other than end-rhyme. Although there are some illegible letters, and a number of corrupt readings, on the whole the manuscript presents a reasonably good text.[37] Of possible relevance here is the fact that the patron of the manuscript, Muircheartach Úa Ceallaigh, spent Christmas with King Richard II in Dublin in 1394, and Úa Ceallaigh's *ollamh*, Cam Clúana Úa Dubhagáin, was killed by the king's followers in a brawl in Dublin in the same year.[38] It may well be the case that it was in the course of this stay in Dublin that a copy of our poem was made available to the compiler of the Book of Uí Maine.

The manuscript context of *SAC* requires further consideration; here, however, we are concerned with the text's place within a wider hagiographical context. The cult of St Patrick in England reached a peak during the decades following the Norman invasion of Ireland, but we have already shown above

---

LCS, and many of the remaining verses taken over from *LCS* have been modified in varying degrees.   **35** Whitley Stokes, 'The prose tales in the Rennes dindšenchas', *RC*, 15 (1894), 272–336, 418–84 at 328–9; *MD* iii, pp 100–3.   **36** On the manuscript, see William O'Sullivan, 'The Book of Uí Maine formerly the Book of Ó Dubhagáin: scripts and structure', *Éigse*, 23 (1989), 151–66; Nollaig Ó Muraíle, 'Leabhar Ua Maine *alias* Leabhar Uí Dhubhagáin', *Éigse*, 23 (1989), 167–95.   **37** Cf. Gwynn's comment on the *dindšenchas* in the Book of Uí Maine: 'The scribe of M is abominably careless. Of all texts of the Dindshenchas this has the lowest intrinsic value': *MD* v, p. 5.   **38** *AFM* 1394 (iv, p. 732); *MIA*, p. 152 §31. This is noted in O'Sullivan, 'The Book', pp 152, 161, and Ó Muraíle, 'Leabhar', p. 195 n. 79.

how this was not *sui generis*: it gained momentum during the eleventh and early twelfth centuries, with the production of William of Malmesbury's Life, and the active copying of Patrician (and related) hagiography and Patrick's own writings in English manuscripts.[39] Jocelin of Furness was commissioned by John de Courcy in the 1180s to produce his Life of Patrick, and, having a wealth of potential material on which to draw, he based it primarily on a text related to the *Vita tertia*.[40] As we have noted, there are two sections in Jocelin's Life of St Patrick which have close connections with our poem, namely chapters 69–70 and chapter 99 in the forthcoming edition by Ingrid Sperber. These correspond to chapters 69, 70 and 71 in Colgan's edition.[41] As Birkett notes, the separation of chapter 99 from the other two is found in four of the five manuscripts of the Life; in the Paris manuscript, however, it is added at the end and labelled chapter 71, and Colgan followed this.[42]

Chapter 69 tells how Patrick came to a hill near the Finglas river (*cumque iter agens deuenisset trans flumen Finglas nomine ad quendam collem a pago Athcled, qui modo dicitur Dublinia, uno ferme miliario distantem*, 'and when in the course of his journey he came across the river called Finglas to a certain hill about one mile distant from the village of Athcled, which is now called Dublinia') and prophesied the future greatness of Dublin (*Pagus iste nunc exiguus eximius erit diuiciis et dignitate dilatabitur nec crescere cessabit donec in regni solium sublimetur*, 'This village now small will be distinguished, and it will be amplified in riches and dignity, nor will it cease to grow until it is elevated to being the seat of a kingdom'). After entering Dublin, he healed the son of the lord who was on the point of death (*Domini uero loci filius unicus laborabat in extremis, ita ut iam expirasse diceretur a multis* 'The only son of the lord of the place was in his last throes, so that he was said by many to have already breathed his last'). This version is close to that in *LCS*, except that in the latter the boy had died and Patrick resuscitated him.

Chapter 70 relates how Patrick produced a freshwater well by the edge of the tidal part of a river (*Flumen namque secus uillam preterfluens ex accessu reumatis maris penitus amaricabatur nec ante recessum refluum aqua dulcis nisi de longe hausta sibi afferebatur*, 'For the river running beside the town was made thoroughly bitter from the flowing in of the sea, nor could fresh water be obtained before the ebb tide receded, unless drawn from a long way away'), which is still known as Patrick's well (*Est itaque fons ille Dublinie scaturigine*

---

39 Half of the extant manuscripts of Patrick's own writings have an English provenance: Ludwig Bieler, *Codices Patriciani Latini: a descriptive catalogue of Latin manuscripts relating to St Patrick* (Dublin, 1942), pp 2–3. 40 For a detailed analysis of Jocelin's Life of Patrick, see Birkett, *Saints' Lives*, pp 25–57, 141–70. 41 John Colgan (ed.), *Triadis thaumaturgae seu divorum Patricii, Columbæ, et Brigidæ … acta* (Louvain, 1647), pp 80–1 [*sic*: in the original the page numbers 90–2 are misprinted for 80–2]. Citations here are from Sperber's edition-in-progress. 42 Birkett, *Saints' Lives*, p. 44 n. 98. For the manuscripts of Jocelin's Life, see ibid., p. 19.

latus, profluxu peramplus, gustu sapidus, qui, ut dicunt, multis infirmantibus mede-
tur et usque in presens sancti Patricii fons recte uocatur, 'And so that is the well
of Dublin, widely gushing, abundantly flowing forth, sweet in taste, which as
is said, heals many illnesses, and up to the present day is rightly called Saint
Patrick's well'). This account is close to that in *SAC* (section IV), and it is
also alluded to briefly in chapter 99.

Chapter 99 is a separate account of Patrick's arrival in Dublin, which,
while it has some elements in common with the first account, differs in many
significant details. Thus, even the Dublin that Patrick comes to is different,
being described as a noble city, inhabited by the peoples of Norway and of
the Isles:

> Tandem uictor aduenerit urbem nobilem,[43] populo situ amenissimam,
> concurrentibus mari et flumine piscibus opulentam, commersiis
> famosam, planicie uiridante affectuosam, glandiferis nemoribus consi-
> tam, ferarum lustris circumuallatam, que postea dicta fuit Dublinia.
> Hec a conuenis Noruuagie et insularum populis exercicio peritissimis,
> omni armatura munitis, bello fortibus, dapsilibus pace, omni regno
> necessariis, in fauorem regis Hybernie sub regina filia regis Noruuagie
> iniciata in posterum per uarias rerum uices modo rebellis, modo feder-
> ata regno Hibernie consistit.

> At length he came victorious to the noble city, most pleasant in situa-
> tion and populace, rich in fish teeming in sea and river, renowned for
> commerce, gentle in green and level land, planted with acorn-bearing
> groves, surrounded by haunts of wild beasts, which afterwards was
> named Dublinia. This city, founded by the incomers from Norway and
> the peoples of the Isles, who are most skilled in exercise, fortified with
> every kind of armour, strong in warfare, bountiful in peace, and indis-
> pensable to every kingdom, in favour of the king of Ireland under the
> queen, the daughter of the king of Norway, afterwards is variously
> sometimes at war with and sometimes allied to the kingdom of Ireland.

He raised from the dead the son and daughter of the king of Dublin; she,
who had drowned, gave her name to the city (*Et rex quidem uocabatur Alpinus,
filius Eocchiad, filia Dublinia, que ciuitati nominis sui contulit uocabulum*, 'And
the king indeed was called Alpinus, the son Eochaid, the daughter Dublinia,
who bestowed on the city the appellation of her own name'). The text goes
on to say that they were baptized at a well which Patrick produced (*baptizati
sunt ad fontem beati Patricii iuxta ciuitatem ad austrum, quem ad augendam cre-
dencium fidem percuciens terram cuspide baculi Iesu pridem fecerat ebullire*, 'They

---

43 Cf. the 'Altitonantis' charter above, which describes Dublin as Ireland's *nobilissima
ciuitate*.

were baptized at the well of blessed Patrick at the southern edge of the city, which he had made bubble up long ago by striking the earth with the tip of the Staff of Jesus, in order to increase the faith of the believers') and the people vowed their allegiance to Patrick and his successors:

> Ex illa ergo die rex Alpinus et omnes Dublinie ciues uouerunt se et omnes posteros suos in seruicium et humagium beati Patricii et Ardmachanorum primatum statuentes prefatam ecclesiam iuxta fontem extra ciuitatem et aliam mansionem iuxta ecclesiam sancte trinitatis in ciuitate ad occidentem eiusdem sedis archipresulis.

> From that day king Alpinus and all the citizens of Dublin pledged themselves and all their descendants to the service and homage of blessed Patrick and the primates of Armagh, erecting the aformentioned church next to the well outside the city, and another mansion beside the church of the holy Trinity inside the city to the west of the seat of its archbishop.

The chapter ends with an account of the tribute due from Dublin to Armagh.

> Statuerunt ergo redditum suo sancto patrono Patricio, uidelicet ut de singulis nauibus mercimonialibus capam competentem Ardmachano primati aut cadum mellis seu uini aut ferri fascem siue mensuram salis, de singulis uero tabernis medonis siue seruicie metretas singulas, de omnibus officinis, curtis et uirgultis xenia donumque conueniens in sotularibus, cirothecis, cultellis, pectinibus et aliis huiusmodi rebus. Et illa quidem die rex et alii proceres singula talenta obrizi singuli optulerunt, mediocres uero optulerunt quod poterant. Que omnia collata pauper Christi Patricius pauperibus erogauit parte retenta ecclesiarum structuris.

> And they determined a render to their holy patron Patrick, namely, from each individual merchant ship a fitting cap to the primate of Armagh, or a jar of honey or of wine, or a load[44] of iron or a measure of salt; from each tavern a cask of mead or of ale [*seruicie* = *ceruisie*]; from all workshops and courtyards and yardlands, gifts and a suitable present of shoes, gloves, knives, combs, and other such things. And also on that day the king and the other nobles each offered a talent of pure gold, while the ordinary people offered what they could. Having collected all of these together, Patrick the poor in Christ bestowed them on the poor, retaining a part for the building of churches.

---

44 Taking *fascem* as the accusative of *fascis* 'bundle, burden'. However, it could be a variant spelling of *facem* 'torch'; the version in Colgan, *Triadis*, has *falcem* 'sickle'.

The parallels between this and sections I and II of *SAC* are clear, but there has been some disagreement among scholars as to the relative dating of *SAC* and Jocelin's Life of Patrick, and indeed that of *SAC* and *LCS*. As our poem is an expansion of *LCS*, it must post-date *Lebor na cert*, so it is worth briefly summarizing previous opinions on its date.

Myles Dillon argued that the pre-eminence of Cashel shows that *Lebor na cert* 'was compiled after Brian Bóramha became king of Ireland', and that the linguistic evidence is consistent 'with a date in the latter half of the eleventh century'.[45] He cited two pieces of internal evidence in support of this: a reference to Tulach Óc as the inaugural site of the Northern Uí Néill kings (not earlier than 1035x1050), and the use of the title *rí Temrach* of the king of Mide rather than of the king of Ireland.[46] F.J. Byrne, in his review of Dillon's edition, suggested that the depiction of the Uí Briúin Bréifne and the Conmaicne Maige Réin as subject to the king of the Ulaid 'reflects the situation of A.D. 1084'.[47] Anthony Candon proposed that *Lebor na cert* was 'written during the reign of Muirchertach Ua Briain, and probably, indeed, written specifically for the synod of Cashel in 1101 by an Ua Briain partisan', arguing this on the basis of the primacy given in the text to the king of Munster.[48] By contrast, David Dumville gave a date range of 1101x1152 for *LCS*, setting it in the context of ecclesiastical reform beginning with the Synod of Cashel in 1101 and Armagh's claims to jurisdiction over Dublin, not finally resolved until the Synod of Kells-Mellifont in 1152.[49]

Although the possibility of our poem deriving from Jocelin's Life has not specifically been proposed, Dillon and Joseph Szövérffy both suggested that *LCS* derived from Jocelin.[50] Szövérffy took the Dublin-Armagh conflict reflected in *LCS* to be one belonging to the immediate post-Norman period. Szövérffy also took the story of the origin of the name Dublin (*Gründungssage*) as being foreign in type in nature and origin, when in fact it is very close to that in the *dindṡenchas*. In any case, such a dating would require treating *LCS* as entirely separate from the rest of *Lebor na cert*, when in fact it is an integral part of it, and Dillon's suggestion is entirely at variance with his dating of the text as a whole. It is, as noted above, the second

45 'On the date and authorship of the *Book of rights*', *Celtica*, 4 (1958), 239–49 at 240, 246. 46 Ibid., 246–7.   47 *StH*, 5 (1965), 155–8 at 158. Cf. idem, 'The trembling sod: Ireland in 1169' in A. Cosgrove (ed.), *A new history of Ireland*, ii (Oxford, 1987), pp 1–42 at p. 14. 48 'Barefaced effrontery: secular and ecclesiastical politics in early twelfth-century Ireland', *Senchas Ard Mhacha*, 14, ii (1991), 1–25 at 12, 14–17.   49 'St Patrick and the Scandinavians', pp 259–64. Donnchadh Ó Corráin has suggested the narrow date range *c.*1121 × *c.*1129 in 'Ireland, Wales, Man and the Hebrides' in P. Sawyer (ed.), *The Oxford illustrated history of the Vikings* (Oxford, 1997), pp 83–190 at pp 107–8 (with translation of a few stanzas provided), but this is disputed by Holland, 'Dublin', 134–40, who favours an earlier date.   50 *Lebor na cert*, p. 117 n. 2; Joseph Szoverffy [sic], 'The Anglo-Norman conquest of Ireland and St Patrick: Dublin and Armagh in Jocelin's Life of St Patrick', *Repertorium Novum*, 2 (1958–60), 6–16.

account in Jocelin's Life which bears the closest relationship with our poem, and there are two strong arguments for also rejecting this as a possible source for it. The first is that since it is an alternative version of a previous episode, it is *per se* unlikely that it would have been added by Jocelin. If Jocelin had invented the story of Patrick converting the Vikings of Dublin, he surely would have provided one version, not two. The second is the clear misgivings expressed by Jocelin at the beginning of chapter 99, noted by Birkett who concludes that 'the evidence strongly indicates that Jocelin was recording a contemporary tradition which has its root in an earlier Irish narrative'.[51] Accordingly, we take the view that Jocelin's source was either *SAC* or a text very close to it. This gives us a broad date range of *c.*1100x1180: later than *Lebor na cert*, but earlier than Jocelin's Life. At present, the evidence allows us no more certainty than that.

EDITION

The text is normalized to conform broadly with Middle Irish spelling conventions. Thus MS *ea* before a broad consonant > *e*, *bh*, *dh*, *gh*, *mh* > *b*, *d*, *g*, *m*, etc. The distinction between lenited *d* and *g*, confused in the MS, is restored, for example, *robaigeadh* > *ro báided*, 7b. The letters *c*, *p*, *t* are used for the sounds /g/, /b/, /d/ after vowels, but are not standardized after consonants; thus, for example, MS *sleactfaidid* > *sléchtfaitit*, 42b, but MS *gebhdaid* > *gébdait*, 34a. In the case of *nn* vs. *nd*, as these are interchangeable in manuscripts of the Middle Irish period, we follow the MS throughout, rather than standardizing to *nn*.

The use of the hyphen is kept to a minimum, i.e., after nasalizing *n*- before vowels, before enclitics (e.g., *duit-siu*, *in déide-sin*), and after the pretonic preverb in deuterotonic verbal forms, but not after preverbal particles such as *do*, *ro* and *no*; thus, for example, *do-beir*, 43a vs. *Do hidbrad*, 11a, *ro-sía*, 33b vs. *ro leth*, 44b, *nos scérab*, 21b.

The language of the poem points to a twelfth-century date, as, for example, can be seen from the verbal system which we present here.

Present Indicative: 3sg. *díbaid* 34c, *dligid* 12ac, *sceinnid* 43b, *sloindid* 45b, *Do-beir* 43a, *do-ní* 43c. Relative: *derscnaiges* 28a, *nos ainic* 42c, *fo-geib* 42d, *thic* 14a. Dependent *ní geib* 25d. Passive *dlegar* 14c 15c 30c. Relative *dlegar* 26a 31ac.

---

51 Birkett, *Saints' Lives*, pp 46–7. Birkett discusses the possibility that Jocelin's reference to a book by Benignus may indicate that he had access to a copy of *Lebor na cert* (ibid., pp 36–7), but this may refer to a book containing *SAC* or a related text. Given the position of Furness, with its multicultural surroundings and links to its Manx daughter-house at Rushen, we should not discount the idea that Jocelin was able to read and speak Gaelic. He would certainly have had easy access to others who could.

Imperative: 3sg. *sloinded* 7c. 1pl. *insem* 24b.

Present Subjunctive: 1sg. *Dá sléchtar-sa* 42a. 2sg. *Dá nderna* 8a, *co fagba* 41c. 3sg. *Ro airchise* 50a, *co tarta* 51c, *Día tora* 17a.

Future: 1sg. *sloinnfet-sa* 36c. Dependent *ní chél* 1c 48a, *ní śléchtab* 41d, *nos scérab* 21b. 3sg. relative *i neoch ro-śia* 33b. 3pl. *sléchtfaitit* 8c 42b. Relative *In laithe gébdait* 34a. Dependent *nocho n-étfat* 17c. Passive *airgfider* 16c.

Past: 1sg. *ó tánac* 22a. 3sg. *Luid* 3a, *ro leth* 44b, *amail ro ordaig* 1d, *Ro thaith-béoaig* 10a, *i neoch do dlig* 30b, *do gab* 48bd, *Do-luid* 2a 9a, *do-rala* 36a, *do-rat* 46c, *Do-rúacht* 6a, *ruc* 5c, *tuc* 38a. Relative *do scríb* 39bc, *do-rala* 40c 44d, *do-rat* 37c, *ro lá* 50c, *In adaig ránic* 5a, *núair tháinic* 4b. Dependent *ní chreit* 2d, *díar chreit* 38e, *dár gab* 38f, *nó cor éirig* 9c, *co ráinic* 3c, *ní úair* 40e. 3pl. *Ro tuillset* 46a. Dependent *ní fetatar* 35c. Passive *amail fríth* 40b, *ro báided* 7b, *cero báided* 10b, *Do hidbrad* 11a, *do-rónad* 47b, *ro-fes* 33c. Relative *do fácbad* 16a, *do-rónad* 47b. Dependent *díar cuired* 38e.

Substantive Verb: Present Indic. 3 sg. *Atá* 1a 7d 24a 38c 45a 49bce, *mar atá* 24a 36d 39d 50d. 3 pl. *i táit* 21a. *co fuilet* 46d. Rel. *fil* 33d, *fuil* 41b. Consuetudinal Present 3 sg. *co mbí* 28c, *'ca mbí* 51d. Present Subjunctive 3 sg. rel. *bes* 25c, *Céin bes* 27a, *ní rab* 22b. 3 pl. *bet* 35b. Future 3 sg. *bíaid* 24c 27c. Rel. *bías* 15a 21d 29b. Past 3 sg. rel. *do bí* 37b, *ro bí* 39a, 3 pl. *ro bátar* 45c. Imperfect 3 sg. *ná bíth* 23a. Verbal of necessity *bedte* 36b.

Copula: Present Indic. 3 sg. *is* 5c 7d 22c 23a 31a 33d 38c 40b 45a 49f. Rel. *is* 1b 43d, *nách* 21c 48c. Conjunct *ní* 44d, *Conad hí sin* 47a, *Mása* 41a, *mana* 25c. Present Subjunctive 3 sg. *roba* 25b. Conjunct *cid* 35b. Past 3 sg. *ba mór* 6b. Rel. *Echaid ba hainm* 10d, *doba* 4a. Conjunct *nír* 37c. Future *bud hí* 21c. Conjunct *níba* 29c.

TEXT

Benén do chan in senchas-sa Gall Átha Clíath.

> 1. Atá sund in senchas seng
> is maith le Gallaib Éirenn;
> sochar Átha Clíath, ní chél,
> amail ro ordaig Benén.
>
> 2. Do-luid Pátraic ó Themraig,
> húa Deochain in órtheglaig;
> d' apstal Bretan 7 Breg
> ní chreit Láegaire lámgel.
>
> 3. Luid deisel Banba buide
> húa Deochain in degduine,
> co ráinic dún na nGall nglan
> do chobair chland Mac Míled.

4. Sé doba rí i nÁth Chlíath
núair thánic Pátraic prímthríath
Ailpín mac Aíuil fáthaig
do chlaind Domnaill dubáthaig.

5. In adaig ránic Áth Clíath
Pátraic Macha na móríath,
is ann ruc bás in bágach
áenmac Ailpín imnárach.

6. Do-rúacht dá fochainn don ríg
i n-áenló, ba mór a mbríg:
a mac d' éc aice can on
is a ingen do bádad.

7. Duiblend ingen in ríg rúaid
ro báided 'sin lind lánúair;
sloinded in senchas can meing
is de sin atá Dublinn.

8. 'Dá nderna náemdacht annois
a chléirig, ar do chubais,
sléchtfaitit duit 'na degaid
Goill Átha Clíath coirmfledaig'.

9. Do-luid 'na desel fa thrí
int apstal is int ardrí,
nó cor éirig 'na bethaid
in féndid fíal fírEchaid.

10. Ro thaithbéoaig Pátraic Breg
in ingen cero báided
ocus in mac, mór in mod,
Echaid ba hainm don úasal.

11. Do hfidbrad co sáer ónt slóg
screpall cach fir, uinge d' ór,
screpall cacha sróna íar sin,
is uinge d' ór cach áenfir.

12. Dligid lán a síthla trá
d' ublaib cumra as cach garrda;
dligid cena día flaith
corn meda as cach áendabaig.

13. Cír cacha círmaire dé,
cúarán cacha sútaire,
escra cach cerda co nglóir,
screpall ó cach monatóir.

14. Cach long cendaig thic tar sál
co Áth Clíath cétach comslán;
dlegar can fochand don chlaind
cochall ó cach stíurasluing.

15. Fat gairit bías i nÁth Chlíath
ap Ard Macha na móríath
dlegar do Gallaib can fell
a bíathad uile ar timchell.

16. Trí huingi do fácbad thall
don cháin i ngarrdaib na nGall:
airgfider fa thrí Áth Clíath
la Gaídelaib na ngelscíath.

17. 'Día tora lib cach blíadain
in cháin dam-sa co Líamain,
nocho n-étfat fir thalman
bar ndún-si do thrénfaglad.

18. Búaid ríg caidchi i nÁth Chlíath cain,
búaid nd-amais is búaid n-óclaig,
búaid cádais ara cellaib,
búaid n-árais is n-imchennaig.

19. Búaid fora Gallaib glana,
búaid n-áille ara ingena,
búaid snáma ar macaib a mban,
búaid cocaid is búaid comram.

20. Búaid cluiche cach tráth nóna,
búaid corma, búaid comóla,
búaid étaig cach datha trá,
búaid catha, búaid comrama.

21. In dún i táit co dreman
nos scérab re dubDeman;
bud hí in tres teine nách timm
bías fo dered i nnÉirind.

22. In dún ó tánac atúaid,
ní rab ara ríg robúaid;
is mór crannacht a chraide,
mo mallacht ar Láegaire'.

23. Is dé sin ná bíth síd Gall
fri ríg Midi na mórland,
etir Temair is Líamain
oc debaid cach áenblíadain.

24. Atá sund senchas Áth Clíath,
insem daíb ar cend a fíach;
bíaid i lebraib co bráth bras
mar atá sund in senchas.

25. Sacart do beith i nÁth Chlíath,
i Cill Phátraic roba líach,
mana Dún dá Lethglas bes;
ní geib a rí féin díles.

26. Déide dlegar i nÁth Chlíath
ó ré Pátraic na móríath:
escop a hArd Macha mas,
sacart ó Dún dá Lethglas.

27. Céin bes in déide-sin and,
i rígdún Gaídel is Gall,
bíaid mes fora fedaib
ocus íasc 'na n–indberaib.

28. ÁenGall derscnaiges do chách
for ágbáig is' dún co bráth,
co mbí format a ríg ris
a los meda maith milis.

29. Bríathar Phátraic la cend nGall
bías i nÁth Chlíath na comland:
níba tacha dóib co bráth
sróll ná síta ná sinnáth.

30. Cach Gall i nÉirind co becht,
i neoch do dlig cendaigecht,
dlegar cís is cáin úad dé
do muintir in rígdúine.

31. Is é cís dlegar can meing
do breith úaithib co Duiblind:
marclach bracha dlegar dé,
ocus lethmarclach saille.

32. Dá marclach connaig can ail,
cona furthain do choindlib
do Gallaib in dúin co tend
ó Gallaib cennaig Éirend.

33. Cach dechmad marclach díb sin,
i neoch ro-śía do Gallaib,
a mbeith do Phátraic ro-fes,
is ed fil isint śenchas.

34. In laithe gébdait na Goill
im cháin Pátraic meic Arploind
díbaid flaithius as cach mud
a mes is a murthorad.

35. Na filid-se Indse Fáil
cid uile bet im áendáil
ní fetatar ar bith bán
cá cenél fa dé in clíatháth.

36. Úair is and do-rala im lis
nocho bedte 'na anfis;
sloindfet-sa dáib scél can ail
mar atá i Saltair Chaisil.

37. Trí fichit gaḟid rossa
do bí i teglach Áengusa
do-rat Áengus, nír breth cam,
do ríg in dúin do Domnall.

38. Íar sin tuc Domnall dámach
dá hú Ailpín imnárach;
is dé séo atá Áth Clíath
ó ré Ailpín na móríath,
díar cuired in chlíath, díar chreit,
dár gab fo <..> Pátraic.

39. Gilla ro bí ac Pátraic bil
do scríb i Saltair Caisil;
lám Benéoin do scríb can ches
mar atá sund in senchas.

40. Senchas na tiprat can díth
is mebair lem amail fríth;
caillech do-rala isin tráig
do mac Arploind 'na chomdáil;
ní úair usce in chaillech dé
acht lán a cúaid dont śáile.

41. 'Mása thusa in Táilgenn tend
fuil ac bennachad Éirend.
co fagba dam usce nglé
ní śléchtab dot śoscéle.

42. Dá sléchtar-sa duit-siu dé,
sléchtfaitit Gaill in dúine;
a fir nos ainic cach broit
fo-geib dam uisce a Phátraic'.

43. Do-beir los na bachla is' tráig,
sceinnid in sruth 'na chomdáil;
do-ní tipra and can meing
is mó fognam i nÉirind.

44. Tipra Phátraic i nÁth Chlíath
ro leth a hainm tar cach n-íath;
súairc a huisce, sáer a blas,
ní sáeb do-rala in senchas.

45. Is dé atá Cell Mac nÁeda,
sloindid in senchas sáerda:
meic Áeda ro bátar and
meic Bric meic Echach na cland
meic Ailpín meic Aíuil úair
meic Domnaill dámaig drechrúaid.

46. Ro tuillset bennacht na meic,
taidecht fo chreitem Pátraic;
do-rat Pátraic íat íar dain
co fuilet ina náemaib.

47. Conad hí sin cétchell chain
do-rónad isin dún-sin,
ocus Cell Phátraic co mblad,
isinn áenló do-rónad.

48. Leth andes don dún, ní chél,
do gab Máel Rúain is Michél;
leth atúaid don dún nách gand
do gab Caindech is Comgall.

49. Ar certlár Átha Clíath cain
atá Cell Phóil is Petair;
atá can tríst imma lé
Cell Chríst ocus Cell Muire;
atá cell oile 'sin dún
is Cell Brigte can mírún.
50. Ro airchise Críst can chrád
do Chormac mac Cuilennán,
i Saltair Caisil ro lá
senchas in dúin mar atá. Atá sunn.

51. A Brigit i Liphe Luirc,
a Cholaim Chille, a Phátraic,
co tarta ar nem míadach mas
cach duine 'ca mbí in senchas.

Atá sund in senchas seng.

TRANSLATION

It is Benén who sang this history of the Foreigners of Dublin.

1. Here is the graceful history which is pleasing to the Foreigners of Ireland; the revenue of Dublin, I will not conceal it, as Benén ordained it.

2. Patrick, the grandson of the Deacon of the golden household, came from Tara; bright-handed Láegaire did not accept the faith from the apostle of the Britons and of Brega.

3. The grandson of the Deacon, the goodly man, went sunwise around radiant Ireland, until he reached the city of the bright Foreigners, to give assistance to the descendants of the sons of Míl.

4. The man who was king in Dublin, when Patrick the pre-eminent lord came, was Ailpín son of sagacious Aéol of the family of Domnall of the black ford.

5. On the night when Patrick of Macha of the great lands reached Dublin resolute death carried off the noble only son of Ailpín.

6. Two tribulations were visited on the king on a single day, great was their force: having his son without blemish die, and his daughter drown.

7. Duiblenn, the daughter of the ruddy king, was drowned in the entirely cold pool; let history without deceit declare, it is from that that Dublin is named.

8. 'If you perform an act of sainthood now, o cleric, by your conscience, the ale-feasting Foreigners of Dublin will submit to you afterwards'.

9. The apostle and the high-king made three circuits sunwise, so that the generous warrior, true Echaid, arose alive.

10. Patrick of Brega restored the daughter to life, although she was drowned, and the son, great the work; Echaid was the name of the noble man.

11. There were granted freely by the host a scruple for each man, an ounce of gold, a scruple for each nose then, and an ounce of gold for every single man.

12. It owes indeed the fill of his pail of fragrant apples from every garden, it owes besides to its lord a goblet of mead from every single vat.

13. A comb for every combmaker, then, a shoe for every shoemaker, a pitcher for every splendid artisan, a scruple from every moneyer.

14. Every merchant vessel which comes across the sea to populous, teeming Dublin; there is due without dispute from the crew a cowl from every cargo ship.

15. Whether for a long or a short time the abbot of Armagh of the great lands will be in Dublin, the Foreigners without treachery are all in turn obliged to provide refection for him.

16. Three ounces of the tribute were left inside in the gardens of the Foreigners: Dublin will be thrice plundered by the Gaídil of the bright shields.

17. 'If you have the tribute come to me at Líamain every year, the men of the world will not be able to powerfully despoil your city.

18. Supremacy for the king for ever in fair Dublin, supremacy for the mercenary, and supremacy for the warrior, supremacy of reverence on its churches, supremacy for dwelling-place and for commerce.

19. Supremacy on its bright Foreigners, supremacy of beauty on its girls, supremacy of swimming on the sons of their women, supremacy in war, and supremacy in conflicts.

20. Supremacy in games every afternoon, supremacy in ale-drinking, supremacy in carousing, supremacy of clothing of every hue, indeed, supremacy in battle, supremacy in conflict.

21. The city in which they fiercely are, I will deliver it from the the black Demon; that will be [the occasion of] the third unyielding fire, which will be at the end in Ireland.

22. The city to the north from which I have come, may its king not have great success; great is the stiffness of his heart, my curse on Láegaire'.

23. As a result of that the Foreigners used to give no peace to the king of Meath of the great blades, fighting every single year between Tara and Líamain.

24. Here is the history of Dublin, let us tell to you in return for its reward; the history as it is here will be in books for ever.

25. It would be grievous for a priest to be in Dublin in the Church of Patrick, unless he is from Downpatrick; its own king does not accept [him] as proper.

26. Two things are required in Dublin since the time of Patrick of the great lands: a bishop from fine Armagh, a priest from Downpatrick.

27. As long as those two things are there, in the royal city of Gaídil and Foreigners, there will be mast on its trees, and fish in its estuaries,

28. [There will be] a single Foreigner who surpasses everyone else in battling contention in the city for ever, so that their kings will be envious of him on account of good sweet mead.

29. The assurance of Patrick to the head of the Foreigners who will be in Dublin of the conflicts [is]: they will never want for satin, silk or sendal.

30. Assuredly every Foreigner in Ireland, wherever he was entitled to trade; tax and tribute is owed by him, then, to the people of the royal city.

31. The tax which is required without deceit to be brought from them to Dublin is a packhorse-load of malt which is required, then, and half a packhorse-load of salt meat.

32. Two packhorse-loads of firewood without fault, with their sufficiency of candles for the Foreigners of the city firmly from the trading Foreigners of Ireland.

33. Every tenth packhorse-load of those, wherever it will come to the Foreigners, they are to be for Patrick, it is known, it is that which is in the history.

34. The day when the Foreigners will refuse the tribute of Patrick son of Calpurnius, there will perish sovereignty, in all regards, their mast and their sea-produce.

35. These poets of the island of Ireland, though they all be together beside me, do not know at all of what kind the hurdle-ford was.

36. Since it has happened to be in my abode, one should not remain ignorant of it; I will declare to them a tale without fault as it is in the Psalter of Cashel.

37. Three score timber spear-shafts which were in the household of Áengus, Áengus gave, it was no crooked decision, to the king of the city, Domnall.

38. Then Domnall of the retinues gave [them] to his noble grandson Ailpín; as a result Áth Clíath is so named since the time of Ailpín of the great lands, when the hurdle was laid down, when he believed, when he ...

39. A servant who was with fine Patrick wrote in the Psalter of Cashel; it is the hand of Benén which wrote, without doubt, the history as it is here.

40. The history of the well without fail, I remember how it was found; an old woman happened to meet the son of Calpurnius on the strand; the old woman had got no water then, only the fill of her mug of brine.

41. 'If you are the sturdy Adzehead who is blessing Ireland; until you get for me fresh water I will not submit to your Gospel.

42. If I submit to you then, the Foreigners of the city will submit; o man who takes care of every tribulation, who gets water for me, o Patrick'.

43. He puts the butt of the crozier into the strand, the stream gushes towards him; he makes a well there without deceit, which is of the greatest service in Ireland.

44. The well of Patrick in Dublin, its name has spread over every land, its water is pleasant, its taste is noble, the history does not happen to be misleading.

45. The reason why Cell Mac nÁeda is so called, the noble history declares [it], is because in it were the sons of Áed, son of Brec, son of Echaid, with numerous descendants, son of Ailpín, son of cold Aéol, son of ruddy-faced Domnall of the retinues.

46. The sons merited a blessing – to come under the faith of Patrick; Patrick brought it about afterwards that they are saints.

47. So that that is the first fair church which was founded in Dublin, together with the renowned Church of Patrick; on the same day it was founded.

48. To the south of the city, I will not conceal it, Máel Rúain and Michael settled; to the north of the city which is not meagre, Cainnech and Comgall settled.

49. Right in the middle of fair Dublin is the Church of Paul and Peter; along with it are, without sorrow, Christchurch and St Mary's; there is [yet] another church in the city – it is the Church of Brigit without malice.

50. May Christ without destruction have pity on Cormac mac Cuilennáin, who has entered in the Psalter of Cashel the history of the city as it is.

51. O Brigit in Liphe of Lorc, o Colum Cille, o Patrick, may the history bring to noble fine heaven every person who knows it.

Here is the graceful history.

NOTES

3c dún: This clearly means 'city' in our text; cf. *DIL* s.v. at col. 449.53, and John Maas, '*Longphort, dún,* and *dúnad* in the Irish annals of the Viking period', *Peritia*, 20 (2008), 257–75.

nglan: In the corresponding verse 3 in *LCS* Dillon reads *ngeal* against the majority of the MSS, which have *nglan*. Dillon regarded the latter as a 'bad rhyme', but for this kind of rhyme in Old and Middle Irish verse cf. Liam Breatnach, '*Cinnus atá do thinnrem*: a poem to Máel Brigte on his coming of age', *Ériu*, 58 (2008), 1–35 at 7.

3d do chobair chland Mac Míled: We understand this as meaning that Patrick is assisting the Gaelic Irish by converting the Foreigners of Dublin to Christianity.

4ab: The key word in this revision of *Is hé ba rí a nÁth Chlíath chruaid / dia táinic Pádraic atuaid* in *LCS* is *prímthríath*, which provides a further allusion to the primacy of Armagh.

4c fáthaig: The MS has *athaig*. As Donnchadh Ó Corráin points out to us, rhyming a word with itself, even as the second element of a compound, is unacceptable; accordingly we take it that the MS form represents the masc. gsg. of *fáthach* with the lenited *f* omitted.

4d dubáthaig: The *LCS* version has *Dubdámaig*, while our poem has a similar epithet in *Domnall dámach*, 38a, and *meic Domnaill dámaig*, 45f. The reading here, however, is not to be taken as an error, but rather as occasioned by the author's concern with representing Dublinn and Áth Clíath as one (see above, p. 30), in that he brings together one element each from the placenames *Dublinn* and *Áth Clíath*.

5c bás in bágach: For the use of the article cf. *GOI* §472, and compare *Basilla in búadach*, *Fél.* June 11 (similarly Aug. 2, June 11).

6a dá fochainn: See *DIL* s.v. *fochonn* which notes the later by-form *fochain(n)*; the MS form *fochaing* shows confusion of unstressed *nn* and *ng*, for which see T.F. O'Rahilly, *Irish dialects past and present* (Dublin, 1972; with new indexes by Brian Ó Cuív), pp 184, 270.

7a Duiblend: The MS has *Duibleand*, with *lenn* 'cloak' as the second element. A principle in the methodology of *dindšenchas* seems to have been that a placename should be connected with the name of a person, even in cases where one might think that the elements of a placename are obvious, as in *Dublinn*, with *dub* 'black (or dark)' and *linn* 'pool'. When we consider that the prose *dindšenchas* of Dublinn (*LL* 21144) derives the placename from a woman called Dub ingen Roduib ('Dark daughter of Very Dark; the metrical *dindšenchas*, *MD* iii, p. 94, uses only *ingen Roduib*), we may conclude that the differentiated form of the personal name is deliberate.

7cd can meing (: Dublinn): The MS has *gan mheng* and *dub* with a suspension-stroke. Compare *can meing : nÉirinn*, 43cd, where the MS has *gan meang* and *aneirind*.

12a lán a síthla: The MS reading, *lan ashila*, cannot stand. There is no evidence for *u*-stem inflection of *síl*, and the regular *o*-stem gsg. *síl* would leave the line a syllable short. In any case 'the full amount of its seed' makes little sense. We adopt the emendation proposed by Caoimhín Breatnach, namely to read the gsg. of *síthal* 'bucket, pail', which makes excellent sense, and take the possessive to refer to *flaith* in 12c.

12b d' ublaib cumra: For the distinction between *ubull cumra* and *ubull fiadain*, see Fergus Kelly, *Early Irish farming: a study based mainly on the law-texts of the 7th and 8th centuries AD*, Early Irish Law Series 4 (Dublin, 1997), pp 259–61, 306–7.

13a dé: Also in 30c, 31c, 40e, 42a. See *DIL* 'D' 153, R.A. Breatnach, 'Some Welsh and Irish adverbial formations', *Celtica*, 3 (1956), 332–7 at 334, and Liam Breatnach, 'On words ending in a stressed vowel in Early Irish', *Ériu*, 53 (2003), 133–42 at 135.

13c cach cerda: Although the disyllabic form is required in the preceding two lines, here MS *gacha cearda* must be emended to *cach* for a heptasyllabic line.

13d monatóir: The three examples cited in *DIL* s.v. *monotóir* from *PH* are all from the homily *Domnach na hImrime*, with the meaning 'money-changer', and all render forms of Latin *numularius* (at LB 40b1, 41b60 and 42b46). The context here (the preceding three persons manufacture things) points to a wider meaning, to include one not only one who changes money, but also one who makes coins.

14b cétach comšlán: Lit. 'hundredfold, complete'.

14c don chlaind: This has to mean more than 'family'; with our translation 'crew' compare the example translated 'band' at *DIL* 'C' 217.64.

14d cochall ó cach stíurasluing: MS *cochall gacha sdiurasluing* cannot stand. A distributive genitive, as in lines 1–3 of verse 13, would require emending the final word to *stíurasluinge*, and even if we read *cach* for the preceding word in order to get 7 syllables, this would not rhyme. The solution adopted here is to emend *gacha* to *ó cach*, giving a phrase parallel to that in verse 13d. There is no entry for *stíuraslong* in *DIL*, and the instance in our poem is the only one so far attested. The meaning however is fairly clear; the second element has to be *long* 'ship' etc. and the first the same as in the comparatively well attested *stíurasmann* 'steersman, helmsman', a borrowing from Old Norse. While the literal meaning of the compound would be 'ruddered vessel', in our translation we follow a suggestion from Donnchadh Ó Corráin, who notes that 'laden merchantmen had to be piloted into port and to dock – unlike warships', and refers to the words of Jocelin's version *de singulis nauibus mercimonialibus*, on p. 33 above.

15a Fat gairit: MS *Fagairid* is clearly corrupt; the proposed emendation is a minimal one and makes good sense.

15b ap Ard Macha: For the non-inflexion of the first element in a name cf. *a Bretnaib Ail Clūade*, *Thes.* ii, p. 309.18, and *i tūascert Dāl Araide*, ibid. p. 25 (in Middle Irish commentary on the *Liber hymnorum*), and *senchas Áth Clíath*, 24a below.

16: Dillon, in a note on the corresponding *LCS* §10, states: 'The meaning of this quatrain is obscure to me. It appears in all four MSS. It seems to refer to a story that part of the offering to Patrick and his companion was withheld'. The only significant difference between *LCS* §10 and the version here is that our text has the future *airgfider*, where *LCS* has present *aircther*. This certainly does not make it any less obscure.

17b dam-sa co Líamain: Lit. 'to me as far as Líamain'. The MS has *guliamhain*, whereas the corresponding *LCS* §11 has *ó Liamain*.

18b búaid nd-amais: For the spelling of the nasalization here and in 21d, see Liam Breatnach, 'An Mheán-Ghaeilge', in K. McCone, D. McManus, C. Ó Háinle, N. Williams and L. Breatnach (eds), *Stair na Gaeilge in ómós do Pádraig Ó Fiannachta* (Maynooth, 1994), pp 221–333 at p. 238 §4.10.

18d n-imchennaig: *LCS* §15d has *naímchendaig* 'sacred heights'. Not only is the translation highly dubious, but the reading *naimchendaig* is found in only one of the three MSS used by Dillon in which the verse appears, namely BLec. 201va27; the other two, BLis. 104vb1 and BB 279b43, agree with our poem.

19a glana: In the corresponding verse 13 in *LCS*, Dillon again reads *geala* against *glana* in the majority of the MSS; see note on 3c above.

20c cach datha: MS *gacha datha* gives a hypermetrical line.

21b nos scérab: MS *nosgerab*; the prefixed *no* indicates that the form must contain an infixed pronoun. For the combination of long-*é* stem and *f*-future ending in *scérab*, cf. Breatnach, 'An Mheán-Ghaeilge', p. 282 §11.15.

21c in tres teine: Note MS *tine*. Dillon translates the corresponding *LCS* §12cd as 'one of the three last surviving hearths in Ireland', without comment. Apart from the fact that 'hearth' would be appropriate only to a single household, there is the matter of the qualifying *nách timm*. These issues can in our view be resolved by taking *teine* in its literal sense, and *nách timm* 'unyielding', as the equivalent of *búadach* 'victorious' and understanding the whole as a reflection of the idea of the three victories of fire, as expressed for instance in *Dic mihi tres uictorias ignis. Prima uictoria, in qua apparuit spiritus sanctus; secunda, quae eleuauit Eliam; tertia, quae comburit peccatores et terram in die iudicii* 'Tell me the three victories of fire. The first victory, in which it appeared as the Holy Spirit; the second, which raised up Elias; the third, which burns sinners and the earth on the Day of Judgement': Martha Bayless and Michael Lapidge (ed. and trans.), *Collectanea Pseudo-Bedae*, SLH 14 (Dublin, 1998), pp 130–1 (with further references in the notes). In other words, the text is presenting Patrick as saving the people of Dublin from eternal fire on the Day of Judgement.

23: This would appear to be a justification for attacks by the Dubliners on Mide. Contrast v. 16.

23c etir Temair is Líamain: The MS has *etir Liemain is Liamain*, which clearly cannot be right. Our emendation follows the corresponding verse 17 of *LCS* which has *itir Theamair is Liamain* in the third line.

24a senchas Áth Clíath: The MS has *seancas ath cliath*; see note on 15b. The only way to fit in the genitive form would be to emend to *Tá sund senchas Átha Clíath* (for the occasional elision of the first vowel of *atá* see Breatnach, 'An Mheán-Ghaeilge', p. 323 §12.190), but this seems excessive.

24b insem: For examples of the rare (and late?) syncope of the second vowel of forms of *innisid* see Gerard Murphy, *Duanaire Finn* iii, ITS 43 (Dublin, 1953), p. 284. One could, however, restore *innisem* and have a heptasyllabic line by omitting the *a* before *fiach*.

25b i Cill: The MS has *agill*. Similarly *burrthain* 32b, *iardain* 46c, and *go dardar* 51c. For comparable spellings of nasalized words in Middle Irish manuscripts, see Breatnach, 'An Mheán-Ghaeilge', p. 238 §4.10.

26cd: Cf. Holland, 'Dublin', p. 156 n. 202.

27c bíaid: Note that this scans as a disyllable. The hiatus in *Aíuil*, 4c, 45e, is a different matter, as the second syllable is a long diphthong; Liam Breatnach intends to address this issue further in a forthcoming note.

28a ÁenGall: That is, the ruler ('head of the Foreigners') referred to in 29a.
28c format a ríg: 'their kings' probably refers to *Gaídel is Gall* (gpl.) in 27b.
28d meda: That is, the mead of sovereignty.

29d sinnáth: *DIL* s.v. *sinsnáth*.

30b i neoch: MS *ineach*; in the case of the next occurrence of this conjunction (cf. *DIL* s.v. *nech* at col. 19.40), in 33b, the MS has *ineoch*.

32b cona furthain: MS *gunburrthain*. We emend *gun* to *cona* (for syllable count and sense) and adopt the suggestion by Ruairí Ó hUiginn that the spelling *burrthain* represents a nasalized *furrthain* (*DIL* s.v. *furthain*); see the note on *i Cill*, 25b above.

34c díbaid: Cf. the note in Brian Ó Cuív, 'Two items from Irish apocryphal tradition', *Celtica*, 10 (1973), 87–113 at 101 v. 16b: 'Although the coming of Antichrist belongs to the future the present tense is used in referring to him here and in most of the following quatrains'.
as cach mud: Cf. *as cach mud* 'in all regards': *MD* iv, p. 286.45.

35c ar bith bán: For this expression, see Breatnach, '*Cinnus*', p. 29.
35d: As MS *cacinel fadim cliathsa* lacks end-rhyme, it is clearly corrupt. The proposed emendation is tentative. For the spelling *cinel*, cf. MS *tine*, 21c; and for the possibility of a compound *clíatháth* compare, for example, *ar Femenmaig*, *MD* iii, p. 202.32, beside *Mag Femen* (ibid., l. 40).

36a is and: MS *isund* is clearly an error for *is and*, which anticipates *im lis*. Cf. Cecile O'Rahilly, 'Varia: 2. is ann : is amlaid', *Celtica*, 12 (1977), 188–91.
do-rala: That is, the poet has access to a copy of *Saltair Chaisil* (line d), taking this to be the referent of the subject pronoun of *do-rala*.
36b bedte: Verbal of necessity of *attá*, which could also be spelled *be(i)thte*, or, phonetically, *be(i)tte*.
36d i Saltair Chaisil Also mentioned in 39b and 50c. See Pádraig Ó Riain, 'The Psalter of Cashel: a provisional list of contents', *Éigse*, 23 (1989), 107–30, and Bart Jaski, 'The genealogical section of the Psalter of Cashel', *Peritia*, 17/18 (2003–4), 295–337.

37a Trí fichit gaḟid rossa: A compound of *gáe* and *fid*; for *fid* in the sense 'shaft', see *DIL* s.v. at col. 126.17. For another example of a *u*-stem gen. sg. of the word registered in *DIL* s.v. *1 ros* 'wood, timber', see Roisin McLaughlin, *Early Irish satire* (Dublin, 2008), p. 148 no. 39.
37d dúin: To get a heptasyllabic line, MS *duine* must be emended to the alternative *o*-stem genitive.

38f: About five letters are illegible (the final one perhaps a *b*), and it is not at all obvious what they might be.

40: The well in question here is probably that which was near St Patrick's Cathedral; see Gary Branigan, *Ancient and holy wells of Dublin* (Dublin, 2012), p. 83.

40c caillech: Compare *in domo cujusdam matrisfamilias*, at the beginning of ch. 70 of Jocelin's Life.

40d 'na chomdáil: MS *na comdail* lacks the required lenition here and in 43b.

40f acht lán a cúaid: MS *achlan a chuaid*, where the lenition of the last word is odd. For other examples of *ach* for *acht* in the Book of Uí Maine, see the note in Ó Cuív, 'Two items', p. 102 v. 26d.

41d sléchtab: The MS has *shlechtadh*; we emend to a 1sg. future form, which is required by the context, taking the final *dh* as perhaps an instance of confusion of lenited *b* and *d*, for which see Breatnach, 'An Mheán-Ghaeilge', p. 235 §3.19.

42: This partly duplicates verse 8.

42c nos ainic: See Tomás Ó Máille, 'Some cases of de-lenition in Irish', *ZCP*, 9 (1913), 341–52 at 345, for the development of the lenited *g* in Old Irish *aingid* to *c* in the later language.

45: For comments on some of the churches listed in this and the following verses, see Howard B. Clarke, 'Conversion, church and cathedral: the diocese of Dublin to 1152', in J. Kelly and D. Keogh (eds), *History of the Catholic diocese of Dublin* (Dublin, 2000), pp 19–50 at pp 45–7; idem, 'Christian cults and cult-centres in Hiberno-Norse Dublin and its hinterland', in A. Mac Shamhráin (ed.), *The island of St Patrick: church and ruling dynasties in Fingal and Meath, 400–1148* (Dublin, 2004), pp 140–58; and idem, 'Cult, church and collegiate church before *c.*1200', in J. Crawford and R. Gillespie (eds), *St Patrick's Cathedral: a history* (Dublin, 2009), pp 23–44 at pp 30–3.

45a Cell Mac nÁeda: Given the setting of the poem as a whole, it seems pointless to worry about the presentation of the sons of Áed as contemporaneous with Patrick and at the same time as the grandsons of the boy whom he raised from the dead. There may, however, be some basis to the statement in v. 47 that the church in question was the first established in Dublin, and here we may note the comments in Clarke, 'Conversion', p. 24: 'Reputedly the oldest church site in the city centre is St Audoen's (Church of Ireland) and its location in Cornmarket, at the hub of a whole network of roads, laneways and property boundaries, would support this belief despite the lack of archaeological confirmation. The dedication to St Ouen (latinized as Audoenus), who died in 684, is probably of much later date, while the hypothesis attributed to Aubrey Gwynn that this church was previously dedicated to St Colum Cille (Columba) has been dismissed' (see also Clarke, 'Christian cults', pp 154–7). Certainly the rough phonetic similarity between Áed and the first syllable of Audoenus makes a church named after *meic Áeda* a much more likely candidate for re-dedication than one named after Colum Cille.

46cd do-rat Pátraic íat ... co fuilet: For the syntax, cf. M.A. O'Brien, 'Two passages in Serglige Con Culaind', *Celtica*, 2 (1954), 346–9 at 348–9, to which can be added *doruménair curpu na esérgi comtis sēmiu ; comtis fōiliu indás aér nō gáeth*, *LU* (H) 2627 (*Scéla Laí Brátha*).

47b dún-sin: The MS has *duns* followed by no more than two illegible letters; syntax and rhyme indicated that these must be *in*, written either as two letters or as *i* with an *n*-stroke.

47c Cell Phátraic: In the vicinity of the present St Patrick's Cathedral; see Clarke, 'Cult', pp 30–3.

48b Máel Rúain: The well-known founder of the church of Tallaght (†792 *AU*).

48b Michél: This must refer to the church later known as St Michael le Pole's; see

Clarke, 'Conversion', pp 45–6, and idem, 'Christian cults', pp 149–50.

48d Caindech: This is the church of Finglas, as Colmán Etchingham points out; for its association with Cainnech, cf. *Findglas Cannig*, LL 39448; *abb Finglaisse Cainnig*, *Fél* 132.10.

48d Comgall: Colmán Etchingham suggests that if Mo Chonna is a hypocoristic form of this name, then the church in question will be St Michan's. For the difficulties in identifying Michan, see Emer Purcell, 'Michan: saint, cult and church', in J. Bradley, A.J. Fletcher and A. Simms (eds), *Dublin in the medieval world: studies in honour of Howard B. Clarke* (Dublin, 2009), pp 119–40. It is surely significant, however, that in the Irish Life of Colum Cille, Comgall and Cainnech (as well as Cíarán) are represented as studying together with Mo Bí of Glasnevin: *Celebrais iarum Colum Cille do Finnén 7 luid co Glais Noíden, uair boi coeca ic fógluimm isin dú sin ic Mo Bíí, im Chaindech 7 im Chomgall 7 im Chiarán*; 'Colum Cille then took his leave of Finnén and went to Glas Noíden (Glasnevin), since there were fifty studying in that place with Mo Bíí, including Cainnech, Comgall, and Ciarán': Máire Herbert, *Iona, Kells, and Derry: the history and hagiography of the monastic* familia *of Columba* (Oxford, 1988), pp 228, 255 §29.

49b Cell Phóil is Petair: See Clarke, 'Conversion', p. 46, and idem, 'Christian cults', p. 149.

49d Cell Muire: The location specified in the text excludes St Mary's Abbey; Clarke, 'Conversion', p. 46, suggests that it 'may reasonably be identified with the church of St Mary del Dam, due north of the later castle'.

49e 'sin dún: We emend MS *sa dun* to the expected Middle Irish form.

49f Cell Brigte: See Clarke, 'Conversion', pp 46–7, and idem, 'Christian cults', pp 151–2.

51a A Brigit i Liphe Luirc: The second word is illegible in the MS. The metre requires a disyllable and the context requires the name of a saint. The most prominent saint in the area in question is Brigit, and what makes the restoration virtually certain is the same collocation of saint and place in a line in a poem in the *Bórama*, noted by Clodagh Downey: *a Brigit i lLife Luirc*, LL 39228. For the association of the territory of Liphe with Lorc (probably Lóegaire Lorc, but see *MD* iv, p. 433 n. 15), cf. also *for Life Luirc* and *ar thír Lifi Luirc* in Kuno Meyer, 'Orthanach ūa Cōllāma cecinit', *ZCP*, 11 (1917), 107–13, vv 2d and 18b.

51c co tarta ar: As a passive form will not fit the context MS *go dardar* must be emended to a 3sg. subj. pres. (with *senchas* as the subject) followed by the preposition *ar*.

51d 'ca mbí: The MS has *gam* followed by two illegible letter-spaces. The proposed restoration makes good sense, and it is at least certain that the final letter must be a vowel to allow elision in the following *in*.

PERSONS

Áengus, 37; Áengusa, 37.

Ailpín, 5, 38 (2x) Ailpín mac Aíuil, 4, gen. 45.

Benén, 1; Benéoin, 39.

Cainnech, 48.

a Cholaim Chille, 51.

Comgall, 48.

do Chormac mac Cuilennán, 50

Críst, 50.

re dubDeman, 21.

Domnall, 38; Domnaill, 4, 45; do Domnall, 37

Duiblend, 7.

Echaid, 10; firEchaid, 9; gen. Echach, 45.

Láegaire, 2; ar Láegaire, 22.
Máel Rúain, 48.
Meic Áeda … meic Bric, 45
Michél, 48.
Pátraic, 2, 4, 10, 26, 29, 33, 38, 39, 42, 46, 46, 51; Pátraic Macha, 5; im cháin Pátraic meic
Arploind, 34; do mac Arploind, 40; in Táilgenn 41; húa Deochain, 2, 3.

PLACES

a hArd Macha, 26; ap Ard Macha, 15
Áth Clíath, 5, 16, 38, 14; i nÁth Chlíath, 4, 15, 18, 25, 26, 29, 44; gen. Átha Clíath, 1, 8,
49; Áth Clíath, 24.
Banba (gen.), 3.
Breg (gen.), 2, 10
Cell Brigte, 49
Cell Chríst, 49
Cell Mac nAeda, 45
Cell Muire, 49
Cell Phátraic, 47; i Cill Phátraic, 25.
Cell Phóil is Petair, 49
Dublinn, 7; co Duiblinn, 31.
Dún dá Lethglas (dat.), 25, 26.
i nÉirind, 21, i nÉirinn, 30, 43; gen. Éirenn, 1, 32, 41.
Inse Fáil (gen.), 35
Líamain (acc.), 17, 23.
i Liphe Luirc, 51.
Midi (gen.), 23
Temair (acc.), 23; ó Themraig, 2.
Tipra Phátraic, 44.

PEOPLES

Bretan (gen. pl.), 2.
Gaídel (gen. pl.), 27; dat. Gaídelaib, 16.
Gaill, 42, Goill, 8, 34; gen. Gall, 16, 23, 27, 29; dat. Gallaib, 1, 15, 19, 33, 32 (x2). As sg.:
Gall, 30; ÁenGall, 28.
Mac Míled (gen. pl.), 3.

OTHERS

i Saltair Caisil, 39, 50; i Saltair Chaisil, 36.

MANUSCRIPT TEXT[52]

Benen dochan in sencasa Gall Ath<.> Cliath.

1. Ata sund inseancas seang. is maith le gallaib eirenn. sochar atha cliath niceil.
amail ro ordaigh benen.

---

52 All abbreviations are italicized. In cases of illegibility, the number of dots in angle
brackets indicates the number of illegible letter spaces.

2. Doluig*h* pad*r*aig otea*m*raig*h* .h. deoc*h*ain inort*h*eglaig*h*. dabsdal breatan 7 breag*h*. nicreid lægaire lam*h*geal.

3. Luig*h* deseal banba buigi .h. deoc*h*ain i*n*degduine. gurainic du*n* nangall nglan. dacobai*r* cland m*a*c milead*h*.

4. (69ra1) Se doba rig*h* anath cliath. nuai*r* t*h*anig pad*r*aig p*r*imt*r*iath ailpin m*a*c aiuil athaig*h* doclai*n*d do*m*naill dubathaig*h*.

5. IN adaig*h* ranic ath cliath. pad*r*aig macha na moriath. isan*n* rug bas i*n*badac*h*. æn*m*ac ailpin imna*r*ach.

6. Doruac*h*t dafoc*h*aing donrig*h*. anænlo bamor ambrig*h*. am*a*c deg aigi ganon. isa ingean dobad*h*ad*h*.

7. Duibleand i*n*gean i*n*rig*h* ruaig*h*. robaigead*h* san lind lanuai*r* sloindeag*h* inseanc*us* gan m*h*eng. isdesin ata dub*l*inn.

8. Da nderna næm*h*dac*h*t annois. acleirig*h* a*r*da cubais. slectfaidit duid nadeagaig*h*. goill atha cliath coirmfleagaig*h*.

9. Doluig nadeseal fat*r*i. i*n*tabsdal isanta*r*drig*h*. nogur eirig*h* nabeataig*h*. i*n*fendig*h* fial firechaig*h*.

10. Rot*h*aithbeoaig*h* pad*r*aig breag*h*. i*n*inge*n* gerobaigead*h*. 7 i*n*mac. mor inmod*h*. eoc*h*aid*h* bahai*n*m donuasal.

11. Dohibrad*h* gusær onts*h*lod*h*. sgreaball gac*h* fir uingi d*h*or. sgreabull gac*h*a srona ia*r*sin isuingi d*h*or gac*h* ænfir.

12. Dligid*h* lan as*h*ila tra. dub*l*aib cu*m*ra asgac*h* garrd*h*a. dligid*h* ceana diafl*a*ith. corn*n* meag*h*a asgac*h* ændabaig*h*

13. Cir gac*h*a cirmaire d*h*e. cuaran gac*h*a sudai*r*e. easgra gac*h*a cearda gungloir. sgreaball ogac*h* m*h*onadoir

14. Gac*h* long ceandaig*h* t*h*ig ta*r* sal. goath cliath c*e*tach coms*h*lan. dleaga*r* gan f*h*oc*h*and donclai*n*d coc*h*all gac*h*a sdiurasluing.

15. Fagai*r*id bias anath cliat*h*. ab a*r*d mac*h*a namoriath. dleaga*r* dogallaib ganfeall abiat*h*ad*h* uili a*r*timceall

16. Tri huingi dofagbad*h* t*h*all. donc*h*ain angarrgaib*h* nagall. airgfidea*r* fat*r*i hath cl*i*ath. lagaidealaib*h* nangelsgiath.

17. Diatora lib gach bl*i*adain. ancain damsa guliam*h*ain. nocho netfad fir t*h*alma*n*. ba*r* ndhunsi dot*h*renfad*h*lad*h*.

18. Buaig*h* rig*h* caichi anat*h* cl*i*ath. cain. buaig*h* ndamuis isbuaig*h* noglaig*h*. buaig*h* cad*h*ais a*r*aceallaib*h*. buaig*h* narais is ni*m*cen*n*aig*h*.

19. Buaig*h* f*o*ragallaib glana .b. nailli a*r*a ingena. .b. snama a*r*m*a*caib*h* a mban .b. cogaig*h*. is .b. com*h*ram.

20. Buaid cluithi gach trath nona .b. corma .b. comola. b. edaig*h* gac*h*a datha tra .b. catha .b. com*h*ramh*a*

21. Andun atait gudreaman. nosgerab re dubdeman. bud*h* hi antres tine nac*h* tim. bias fad*e*read*h* a*n*neiri*n*d.

22. Andun otanag atuaig*h*. nirab ara rig*h* robuaig*h*. ismor cran*n*ac*h*t acraidi. momallac*h*t a*r*lægaire

23. IS de si*n* nabith sid*h* gall. fri rig*h* mid*h*i namorland. *etir* liemain is liamain. agdeabaig*h* gac*h* æ*n*bli*a*dai*n*

24. Ata su*n*d seancas ath cliath. in*n*seam daib a*r* cea*n*d afiac*h*. biaig*h* aleabraib*h* gobrath bras. ma*r* ata sund inseancas.

25. Saga*r*t dob*eith* anath cl*iath*. agill pad*r*aig roba liac*h*. mana dun daleathglas beas nigeb arig fein dileas.

26. Degi dlega*r* anath cl*iath*. ore pad*r*aig namoriath. easgob aha*r*dmac*h*a mas. saga*r*t odun daleathglas.

27. Gen beas indegisin and. arig*h* dun gaigeal is gall. biaig*h* (69rb1) meas f*o*ra fead*h*aib*h*. 7 iasg nani*n*db*e*raib*h*.

28. Æ*n*gall dearsgnaigis docach f*o*ragbaig*h* isdun gu brath. gumbi f*o*rmad arig*h* ris. alos mead*h*a maith milis.

29. Briat*h*ar p*adraig* laceand ngall. bias anath cl*iath*. na comland. niba tacha doib gobrath. sroll nasida nasin*n*ath

30. Gach gall aneiri*n*d gubeac*h*t. ineach dodlig*h* ceandaid*echt*. dleagar cis iscain uad*h* de. domuintir i*n*rig*h*duine.

31. ISe cis dleaga*r* gan meing. dobreith uaithib gu duiblind. ma*r*clach bracha dleaga*r* de. 7 leathma*r*clach saille.

32. Dama*r*chlach co*n*naig*h* gan ail. gu*n*burrt*h*ain docoindlib. dagallaib*h* induin goteand. ogallaib cea*n*naig*h* eiri*n*d.

33. Gach deachmad*h* ma*r*clach dibsi*n*. ineoch ro sia dogallaib*h*. ambeith dopad*r*aig rofeas. aseag*h* fil isi*n* ts*h*eancas.

34. INlaithi geb*h*daid nagoill. imcain p*adraig* m*ei*c a*r*ploind. dibad*h* flaithi*us* asgac*h* mud*h*. ameas isa murt*h*orad*h*

35. Nafilid*h* sea indsi fail. gid uili bed imæ*n*dail. nifeadada*r* a*r*bith ban. cacinel fadim cliathsa.

36. Uai*r* isund dorala i*m*lis. noc*h*o bedte na anfis.[53] sloindfeadsa daib sgel ga*n* ail. marata asailtir caisil.

37. Tri .xx.it ga fid*h* rossa dobi teaglach æ*n*gusa. dorad æng*us* nir breath cam. dorig*h* i*n*duine dodo*m*nall.

38. IA*r*sin tug do*m*nall damach. da .h. ailpin i*m*narach. isde seo ata ath cliath. ore ailpin na moriat*h*. dia*r*cuiread*h* ancliat*h* dia*r* cred da*r*gab fo <....> padraig.

39. Gilla robi ag p*adraig* bil. dosgrib asaltir caisil. la*m* beneoin dosgrib gan ceas. ma*r* ata sund inseancas.

40. Seanc*h*as natibrad gan dith. is meabai*r* leam amail frith. cailleach dorala isi*n* traig*h*. dom*a*c a*r*ploind nacomdail. ni uai*r* us*c*i incailleach de. achlan a chuaid donts*h*aile

41. Masa t*h*usa intailgean*n* teand. fuil agbean*n*achug*h* eiri*n*d. gufadb*h*a dam us*c*e ngle. ni s*h*lec*h*tad*h* dat s*h*oscele.

---

53 So altered by later hand.

42. Daslecta*r*sa duidsiu de. sleactfaidid gaill in duine. afir nos ainic gac*h* broid. fogeib da*m* us*c*e apad*r*aig.

43. Dob*eir* los na bachli astraig*h*. sgein*n*ig*h* i*n*sruth na co*m*dail. doni tipra and gan meang. ismo fognam aneiri*n*d.

44. Tipra pad*r*aig anath cl*iath*. roleath ahai*n*m ta*r*gac*h* niath. suai*r*c ahus*c*e sær ablas. nisæb dorala inseancus.

45. ISde ata ceall m*a*c næda. sloindig*h* inseancus særda. m*eic* æd*h*a robada*r* and. m*eic* bric m*eic* eachac na cland. m*eic* ailpin m*eic* aid*h*iuil uai*r*. m*eic* do*m*naill damaig*h* dreac*h*ruaig*h*.

46. Rotuillsead bean*n*ach*t* nam*eic*. taig*echt* focreide*m* pad*r*aig. dorad p*adraig* iad ia*r*dain. gufuilead inanæmaib*h*.

47. Gonad hisi*n* c*et*ceall cain. doronad*h* isi*n* du*n*s<.> 7 ceall p*adraig* gombladh isi*n* nænlo doronad*h*

48. Leath andeas dondun nicel. dogab mælruai*n* ismicel. leat*h* atuaig*h* do*n*dun nac*h*gand. do gab caindeach iscomgall.

49. Arceartlar atha cl*iath* cain. ata ceall poil is pedair. ata gan t*r*ist imale. ceall c*r*ist 7 ceall muire. ata ceall oile sa dun. is ceall brigdi gan mirun.

50. Ro aircisi (69Va1) c*r*ist gancrad*h*. docorm*a*c m*a*c cuil*ennan*. asaltai*r* caissil rola. seancus induin ma*r*ata. Ata .su*n*.

51. A<.......> alip*h*i luirc acolaim cilli apad*r*aig. go da*r*da*r* neam miadach mas. gac*h* duine gam<..> inseancus.

Ata .s. inse. se.

Comhar na mban

PÁDRAIG A. BREATNACH

(i) AN TUIRNE LÍN

Onóra Ní Dheasúna

Ní mór nach bhfuil trí bliana
ó iarras-sa túrann lín
Ar an óigfhear milisbhriathrach
is fial fairsing fionntach croí;
5   Atá eolas cliste is ciall aige
is riail lena thabhairt chum cinn,
'S is dóigh go dtiocfaidh an iarmhais
aniar anois chugham gan mhoill.

Cnoc na bPréachán, an<no?> 1833.

Lámhscríbhinn: Leabharlann Náisiúnta na hÉireann G 103, 89 (19ú haois). *Scríofa i gceithre líne; ceannscríbhinn in easnamh.* 1 fuil; bliaghna 2 iarasa 3 air 4 fíónntach croídhe 6 riaghail; chuim cínn 7 dóith; tti; iairbhis 8 mhaill. *Iarscríbhinn* Onóra ní dheasmhúna; *faoina bun tar éis spáis leanann* Cnoc na bpréachan /an/ 1833 (/ = *briseadh líne*).

An mheadaracht

$$4 \ \{(\text{-}) \smile \acute{o} \smile \ |\, i/u \smile (\text{-}) \ |\, ia \ (\text{-}) \smile \ || \smile (\text{-})|\, ia \smile \smile \ |\, \acute{u} \smile \ |\, \acute{i}\}$$

Foirm an bhailéid: dá stair sin, feic an cur síos ag Pádraig A. Breatnach, 'Die Entwicklung und Gestaltung des neuirischen rhythmischen Versmaßes' in H.L.C. Tristram (eag.), *Metrik und Medienwechsel / Metrics and media* (Tübingen, 1991), lgh 289–300 ag 294–5, 299.

Nótaí

2 *túrann* .i. turn túrn turna tuirne 'wheel'.

4 *fionntach* Cf. *FGB* s.v.: '"fair" (= *fionn*)'; for example, 'Cois abhann an tsléibhe tá an féinics fionntach' (Pádraig Ua Duinnín [eag.], *Amhráin Eoghain Ruaidh Uí Shúilleabháin* [Baile Átha Cliath, 1907], l. 707, tos. *I Sacsaibh na séad*); an litriú *fiúntach* ag Breandán Ó Conchúir (eag.), *Eoghan Rua Ó Súilleabháin* (Baile Átha Cliath, 2009), lch 43 (l. 113), ach tá *fiúntach* áirithe mar fhocal ar leithligh ag *FGB* 'worthy, generous' s.v.; cf. *fionntach* 'adj. hairy woolly' (Edward O'Reilly, *An Irish-English dictionary* [Dublin, 1821] s.v.).

7 *iarmhais* ('iairbhis' LS) 'wealth, valuables'. Tá an focal céanna (dhá shiolla) ag Seán Clárach, cf. 'Do ghoid ó Dhiarmuid mórán íarmhis as a chúiltig', ARÉ LS 23 L 24 [29],

300 (v.l. 'an iomadh iarmhis as a chuiltig' ARÉ LS 23 I 26 [413], 73). A shanasaíocht amhrasach; feic Séamus Caomhánach et al., *Hessens irisches Lexicon* H-R (Halle, 1933), s.v. *iarmaise* '(*leg.* iar maise?)'; tagairt do *ALI* iv, 356 (= *CIH* ii, 586.15: *Sai caem canoine conidh iar maisi an maith*). Feic, leis, *DIL* s.v. *?íarmaisi*.

Tá an bhanfhile ag feitheamh ar thuirne a d'iarr sí ar cheardaí a dhéanamh di.[1] Níorbh ionadh é dá mothódh mo sheanchara Máire Herbert i gcás cosúil ó am go ham ag feitheamh di ar shaothar éigin geallta do cheann de na comhthionscnaimh faoina stiúir. Mar shamhlaím, is ar éigin a bhí *óigfhear milisbhriathrach* an bhlúire bhig seo i riocht gan géilleadh don mbanfhile Onóra Ní Dheasúna ar dheiseacht agus daingneacht na teachtaireachta uaithi.

B'é Mícheál Óg Ó Longáin (1766–1837) a bhreac an téacs ar bhilleog de chnuasach ó lámha éagsúla atá in G 103. Níl scríofa ar an mbilleog ach an véarsa amháin, ainm an údair faoina bhun, agus laistíos de sin seoladh agus dáta. Ní fios cé acu an le húdar an bhlúire nó le hócáid a chóipeála a bhaineann an fhaisnéis deiridh ('Cnoc na bPréachán … 1833'). Tá Cnoc na bPréachán (Crow Hill) i bparóiste Chnoc an Bhile (Upton) i mbarúntacht Mhúscraí Thoir, agus tá a fhios againn ó fhianaise eile gur thug Mícheál Óg turas ar pharóiste Theampaill Mháirtín atá teorannach le Cnoc an Bhile sa bhliain 1833.[2] Ar an ócáid úd, tharla baint aige le Conchúr Ó Deasúna 'ar an mBruinne' (abhainn na Bruinne in aice le Teampall Máirtín) ar scríobh sé cnuasach de 'Aistí cúmha air Éirinn' dó.[3] B'fhéidir gur dhuine muinteartha don Deasúnach sin ab ea Seán Ó Deasúna, máistir scoile 'do bhí a nInnis Eóghanáin cois Banndan … agá raibh mac Mhíchíl air sgoil san mbliadhain 1818'.[4] Chum an scríobhaí véarsaí do Sheán ó am go ham,[5] agus tá freagra véarsaíochta ó Sheán ón mbliain 1818 a tháinig slán.[6] Ráineodh gurbh iníon nó deirfiúr do dhuine de na Deasúnaigh seo ab ea údar an véarsa. Níor tháinig aon déantús eile léi slán faid m'eolais.

(ii) DÁN DO SHEÁN Ó MAOLDOMHNAIGH A CHUM A INÍON

Máire iníon Sheáin Uí Mhaoldomhnaigh cct ar theacht do Sheán glé (An Saor) Ó Maoldomhnaigh gan bá thar fairrge

Fáilte is daichead ón bhfairrge choímhthigh ard
do ráib na fairsinge an faraire croímhear Seán,

1 Tá cúpla amhrán beag dar téama 'An túrna' sa chnuasach a bhailigh Seán Ó Dubhda (eag.), *Duanaire Duibhneach* (Baile Átha Cliath, 1933), §§XLV, XLVI. 2 Cf. Breandán Ó Conchúir, *Scríobhaithe Chorcaí 1700–1850* (Baile Átha Cliath, 1982), lch 129. 3 LNÉ LS G 105, lch 50 (cf. *NLI Cat.* iii, lch 111). 4 ARÉ LS 23 N 32 [259], lch 29 (cf. *RIA Cat.* lch 731). 5 23 N 32, lch 29 (cf. *RIA Cat.* lch 731); ARÉ LS 23 C 19 [726], lch 32 (cf. *RIA Cat.* lch 2198). 6 23 N 32, lch 30 (cf. *RIA Cat.* lch 731).

sáirfhear seasamhach, seabhac suilt síothmhar sámh
grásmhar greannmhar geanmnach gnaoighlan grách.

5   Ba cásmhar cathaitheach ceasnamhail cloíte cás
gach fáidh san gcathair ó sgarais-se linn, a Sheáin,
gan ábhacht gan aiteas gan gairm na dí ar clár
go fánach scaipthe, scartha le hintinn ard.

An bás dá leagfadh mo phreabaire grinn san mbád
10   dar bás ar dhearcas de charaid sa tsaol os ard –
an bás do ghreadfainn, 's do stracfainn a phíp gan spás,
an bás ní scarfadh acht marbh le claíomh óm láimh!

An ceangal
Chum Seáin gan chlaon gan bhéim Uí Mhaoldomhnaigh
ráib na féile an saorfhear le gléfhoghluim,
15   fáilteach féastach béasach caomhchabharthach
[…]

Lámhscríbhinn: UCC T 12 (b) 28 (1778). *Ceannscríbhinn*: Máire inghean Chseaghain Uí
Maoldomhna cct air theacht do Chseaghan glé an saór O Maóldhomhna gan bágha thar
fairge 1 dáfitchiod; chuibhthicc 2 croídhmhear 3 síodmhar 4 greanmhar 5 budh
cathathach ceasnamail claoidhte 6 gcaithir; chseághan 7 díghe 8 fághnach sgaipithe
10 do caraid; tsaóghal 11 greadfin; stracfin 12 cloidheamh 13 chseaghain; chlainn
14 ráibh; saoirfhear táom- le glé 15 caomh chobharthach 16 *Líne in easnamh i mbun an
leathanaigh de bharr gearradh a deineadh sular ceanglaíodh.*

An mheadaracht

(1–12) (˘) |á �’ |a ˘ ˘ |a ˘ ˘ |í ˘ |á
      Fuaim *í*: 6 linn, 10 saol.
(13–15) (˘) |á ˘ |é ˘ |é ˘ (˘) é | a ˘

D'ionad na haiste (cúig aiceann) sa traidisiún, féach Pádraig A. Breatnach,
'Múnlaí véarsaíocht rithimiúil na Nua-Ghaeilge', in P. de Brún, S. Ó Coileáin
agus P. Ó Riain (eag.), *Folia Gadelica: aistí ó iardhaltaí leis a bronnadh ar R.A.
Breatnach* (Corcaigh, 1983), lgh 54–71 ag lgh 54, 63–4; idem, 'Die
Entwicklung und Gestaltung des neuirischen rhythmischen Versmaßes', lgh
295–8.

Nótaí

1 *choímhthigh* tuis. tabh. < coimhtheach = coimhthíoch 'wild, rude'.
ard Ní oirfeadh foirm thabharthach (.i. a(o)ird) sa mheadaracht, bíodh gur léi a bheadh
   coinne ó tá an aidiacht roimhe sa tuiseal sin; cf. l. 8.

10 Aistr. 'By the death of all friends I have seen ...'
13 *chlaon* Foirm bhaininscneach thabharthach na LS ('chlainn') leasaithe ar son na
meadarachta; is ainmfh. fir. é de ghnáth.
16 An líne ar bóiléagar sa LS.

Tá an bhanfhile ag cur fáilte roimh a hathair Seán Ó Maoldomhnaigh a d'fhill
slán thar farraige.

Seán Ó Maoldomhnaigh

Gabhann véarsaí eile do Sheán Ó Maoldomhnaigh seo roimh an téacs sa
lámhscríbhinn (scríobhaí: Seaghann Ó Súilliomháinn, Ceann Tuirc, 1778),
viz. (1) dán le Tomás Ó Míocháin, *'Fhir charrthanach cháig [cháil]ghlan (sic
leg.) sa carad gan chiach* (6v), agus ag leanúint air sin, leis an údar céanna, (2)
Chum Seaghain sineanta sultmhar Uí Maoildomhna (1v).[7] Tá cóip níos sine den
dá bhlúire i lámhscríbhinn ón mbliain 1773 i Maigh Nuad, C 25 (a), 21–22
(scríobhaí: Seon Lloyd).[8]

Is le haghaidh úsáid Sheáin Uí Mhaoldomhnaigh áirithe ó Luimneach a
scríobhadh an lámhscríbhinn Egerton 150 sa bhliain 1773–4 (scríobhaithe:
Seón Lloyd, Séamas Boinbhíol, Aindrias Mac Mathghamhna, agus Diarmaid
Ó Mulchaoine).[9] Dá chomhartha gurb éinne amháin eisean agus an té ar dó
ár ndán fáilte (agus (1), (2) thuas chomh maith leis), féach go bhfuil an
leasainm ('An Saor') atá luaite i gceannscríbhinn an dáin seo againne le Ó
Maoldomhnaigh le fáil chomh maith i gceannscríbhinn curtha le véarsa dó in
Egerton 150 (f. 364b) mar leanas, .i. 'Aindrias Mac Mathghamhna chum
Cseaghain Uí Mhaoldomna ct .i. Sean saor'.[10]

---

7 Cf. Pádraig de Brún, *Clár lámhscríbhinní Gaeilge Choláiste Ollscoile Chorcaí: cnuasach
Thorna*, 2 iml. (Corcaigh, 1967), i, lch 47.   8 Cláraithe ag Pádraig Ó Fiannachta,
Lámhscríbhinní Gaeilge Choláiste Phádraig Má Nuad: clár, fascúl v (Má Nuad, 1968), lch
50. D'úsáid Diarmaid Ó Muirithe an LS seo ag cur (1) i gcló ina chnuasach *Tomás
Ó Míocháin: filíocht* (Baile Átha Cliath, 1988), lch 51, faoi theideal ón LS nach mbaineann
leis; an véarsa a mbaineann an teideal dáríribh leis, .i. (2) thuas, níl sé i leabhar
Uí Mhuirithe in aon chor; don téacs, feic laistíos (lch 61).   9 Cf. *BM Cat.* ii, lgh 395–411:
lch 395; feic cur síos ar an ngrúpa scríobhaithe seo ag Breandán Ó Madagáin, 'The Irish
tradition in Limerick' in Liam Irwin agus Gearóid Ó Tuathaigh (eag.), *Limerick: history
and society* (Dublin, 2009), lgh 357–80 ag lgh 364–5.   10 *BM Cat.* ii, lch 409. Sid é téacs
an véarsa úd (ibid.): 'A shaoi ghrinn do phrimhshíol na seabhac saor súghach / budh fior-
chaoin gan aoinbhaois a rana caomh ciuil / le siorghuidhe chum righe nimhe mo
bheanacht fein chugaibh / mar dhion dibh ar chaimmnaimhid go breatha lae an chuil'. Ag
leanúint air sa LS tá na focail seo: 'Foirchean ar na sgriobh le Aindreas Mac
Mathghamhna an 7mha la don Abran 1773'. Do chomhthéacs meadarachta an bhlúire sin,
feic Pádraig A. Breatnach, 'Roinnt amhrán ar comhfhoirm ón seachtú haois déag', *Éigse*,
23 (1989), 67–79. Tá an téacs le cur i gcomparáid le véarsaí ar comhfhoirm leis a chum
Toirrdhealbhach Mac Mathghamhna áirithe do Mhíchéal Coimín (†1760), *A Mhíchíl ó
chím sínte i gcré gach fear*, a bhfuil cóip díobh in ARÉ LS 23 M 16 (1767–76), lch 126, ó
láimh Aindriais Mhic Mhathghamhna. B'fhéidir gurbh é an blúire don Choimíneach a

Scríobh Aindrias Mac Mathghamhna sin lámhscríbhinn eile a ngabhann an dáta 1767 léi agus a bhfuil tuilleadh véarsaí dá dhéantús féin ag tagairt do Sheán Ó Maoldomhnaigh inti. Ar lgh 44, 47 na lámhscríbhinne ARÉ 23 M 51 (351) atá an tsraith téacsaí, agus ón gcuma atá orthu (mírialtacht litrithe, dréachtlínte scriosta amach agus leasuithe scríofa isteach i láimh an scríobhaí), is le linn a ndréachtaithe a breacadh iad. I measc a bhfuil le léamh ar lch 44 tá véarsa amháin slán (nó geall leis do) mar leanas:

> Chum chSeághain ui Mholdómhna
>
> Sin daorghoin sa taobh so agus tuismiugh*adh* bróin
> an raeghilt*eann* má threagion*n* mo chuid[i]úgh fós
> an saorfhear do thaotruig gan tuirsiúgh an ceol
> is leann liom a gcéin tu gan áirgh[*iú*] (?) am choair.[11]

Leanann faoina bhun sin roinnt línte a bhfuil focail scriosta amach iontu agus bearnaí fágtha eatarthu, agus, mar chríoch, an líne:

> Thar bealach annúnn o diómpaigh a[n] t-árdmhac Seón.

Is é is téama do na blúiríocha seo, mar is léir, Seán Ó Maoldomhnaigh a bheith imithe 'i gcéin'. Ní léir dom aon leide sna blúiríocha éagsúla a mhíneodh cad a chuir i gcéin é, ná cár chuaigh sé. Ach is é is dóichí gur tar éis dó filleadh abhaile (agus gan choinne leis, is cosúil) i ndiaidh na heachtra céanna a bhfuil tagairt di sna blúiríocha sin a d'fháiltigh a iníon Máire roimhe leis na véarsaí *Fáilte is daichead*. Ó na tagairtí atá don bhfarraige agus do bhád (l. 9) aici, b'fhéidir a thuiscint gur mhairnéalach a bhí ann chomh maith le bheith ina 'shaor'.[12]

Luas cheana gur i Luimneach a bhí cónaí ar Sheán Ó Maoldomhnaigh do réir Egerton LS 150. Tugann scríobhaí amháin sa leabhar cruinnfhaisnéis uaidh ar a sheoladh i gcolafan (f. 229):

> Ar na sgríobhadh lé Séamus Boinnbhíol chum uasáighde chSeághain saor súairc súaimhneach saorbheartach úa Maoldomhnaigh do chómhnuíghios a Sráid an Chaisleain a Luimneach an naomhadh lá don mhíosa June aois an tiagharrnadh an tan san 1773.[13]

spreag Aindrias chun aithrise in onóir do 'Sheán saor' thuas; ní fios an raibh gaol ag Aindrias le fear a chomhshloinne, Toirrdhealbhach.   11 'áirgh-' (scríob bhuailte i ndiaidh *h*), ag seasamh do 'airiú' = 'arú', an leicséim dhearbhaithe (béim ar an gcéad siolla anseo murab ionann agus a bheadh i ngnáthchaint), agus 'beannú' mar chiall leis sa chomhthéacs b'fhéidir?   12 Tá leid mar sin le fáil, ar a seans, in ARÉ LS 23 M 51 [351], mar a bhfuil ainm 'John Mahun (?)' áirithe scríofa isteach ar lch 1 agus nóta ag gabháil leis i dtaobh é a bheith sa Bhruiséal: cf. *RIA Cat.* 959.   13 Feic *BM Cat.* ii, lch 406.

I dtéacs 'barrántais' ón mbliain chéanna sin sa lámhscríbhinn, tá tagairt déanta do Sheán Ó Maoldomhnaigh agus don scríobhaí úd, Séamus Bóinbhíol, mar chomharsana dá chéile a bhí chun cónaithe sa cheantar ar a dtugtar Sbarr Thuamhumhan (Thomondgate), atá in oirthuaisceart na cathrach ar an dtaobh thall de dhroichead na Sionna (Droichead Tuamhan) ó Shráid an Chaisleáin.[14] Ag teacht leis an bhfaisnéis sin tá, chomh maith, a bhfuil ráite sa véarsa eile seo leanas 'chum Seagháin Uí Mhaoldomhna'. Is é véarsa é an ceann úd le Tomás Ó Míocháin a luadh thuas a bheith i lámhscríbhinn Ollscoil Chorcaí a bhfuil cóip de ag gabháil roimh *Fáilte is daichead* inti. Tá cóip de is sine ná í sa lámhscríbhinn Maigh Nuad C 25 (a) ar lch 22 i gcrot mar seo leanas (i láimh Sheoin Lloyd):

An fear céadna cct [= Tomás Ó Míodhcháin]

Chum Seagain shultmhar shoinionda Uí Maoldhomhna
ag Sparr an oinig cois Sionna na saorabhuine
do ghrádhas an sionnach gan drisle ná díol foghla
le crántuibh criosluightheach cinneadhmhear caoinchabharthach.

Cathair Luimní, más ea, is í atá i gceist sa tagairt don 'gcathair' (l. 6) mar áit a gcónaithe i ndán a iníne.

Nóta ar imeartas

Tá an leasainm 'An Saor' tugtha ar Ó Maoldomhnaigh sa lámhscríbhinn ina bhfuil an dán le Máire a iníon ag tagairt dá cheird (mar shaor loinge b'fhéidir?). Ar an gcuma chéanna, 'Seán saor' atá air ag Aindrias Mac Mathghamhna agus ag Séamas Boinbhíol fá seach i nótaí in Egerton 150 mar a chonaiceamar. Is léir dá réir sin gur imeartas ar a leasainm atá i gceist sa chaint 'an saorfhear' ag a iníon (l. 14). Tá an t-imeartas céanna ag an Mathúnach sa tríú líne den véarsa atá luaite ó lch 44 de 23 M 51 (*supra* lch 60); agus ar lch 47 den leabhar sin i measc an ábhair a thráchtann ar an bhfear céanna a bheith imithe gan tásc ná tuairisc, tarraingíonn Aindrias an focal chuige arís i ndréachtvéarsa (4 líne) a ngabhann *chorus* leis (4 líne) mar seo leanas. (Tá foirmeacha ar deacair dul amach orthu i bhfo-áit ann (1 éibhigh [?], 8 do sgíle), ach tá an patrún meadarachta ar chomhdhéanamh le samplaí eile a bhfuil an fonn ainmnithe luaite leo, .i. 'Maidin bhog aoibhinn').[15]

14 An téacs curtha in eagar ag Pádraig Ó Fiannachta, *An barrántas*, i (Má Nuad, 1978), §48, ll 181–6: 'Go *Spar* Thuamhumhan / draíocht dá scuabfadh / iad ná d'intleacht, / Bheadh a gcoirp pollta / ag Seán Ua Maoldomhnaigh / is Séamas Boínbhiol' (169).
15 Tá amhrán eile ar an bhfonn céanna ón lámhscríbhinn seo in eagar ag Risteárd Ó Foghludha (eag.), *Cois na Bríde: Liam Inglis, O.S.A. 1709–1778* (Baile Átha Cliath, 1937), uimh. 34 (lgh 48–9); cf. *Éigse*, 1, i (1939), 71n. (Gearóid Ó Murchadha). An téacs céanna in eagar ag Úna Nic Éinrí, *Canfar an dán: Uilliam English agus a chairde* (An Daingean,

Chum Chseaghain Ui Maoldomhna, fonn Maidinn Bhog Aoibhinn

A raeilt*eann* na sgéibhe nár éibh*igh* dlíghe a námhad
is tuirseach me a ngeimhin ªa néagcruithª sa ngádha
gan duine fan saoghagal san taobhso dom chamha*[i]r*
ó d'imig an sáer[fhe]ar, mo ghlébhile sámh.

ᵇChorus for (?) verse ᵇ
M'atuirse choídhthe an g<h>roídheghas seudmhar Seón
ᶜdo chalms[h]liocht Chuinn ghilᶜ a d'easgair gan cháim
ta sgamal gan sgaoile ar m'aigin*eadh* is daoir*se*
ár bhfothin do sgíle ó chail[li]*us* mo (?) phráin[n].

Fuaim *a*–: 1 námhad, 3 chamha[i]r.

ª⁻ª 'a néagcruith' *scríofa os cionn na líne*
ᵇ⁻ᵇ *Scríofa i bpeannaireacht Bhéarla san imeall ar dheis (lámh an scríobhaí)*
ᶜ⁻ᶜ 'do chlanaibh dil Mhíl*eadh*' *a scríobhadh ar dtúis mar leathlíne ach scriosadh na focail amach*

2003), uimh. 24 (lgh 142–3), agus é casta ar cheol ag an amhránaí Pádraig Ó Cearbhaill ar dhlúthdhiosca a ghabhann leis an leabhar (rian 1). Tá leagan de cheol an fhoinn i gcnuasach Bunting agus véarsa mar aon le *chorus* luaite leis; feic *Bunting's ancient music of Ireland edited from the original manuscripts by Donal O'Sullivan with Mícheál Ó Súilleabháin* (Cork, 1983), uimh. 78 (lgh 121–2).

Cethri prímchenéla Dáil Ríata revisited

DAUVIT BROUN

Máire Herbert has made several seminal contributions to our understanding of Gaelic Scotland in the early Middle Ages for which Scottish historians, now and for generations to come, will always be grateful. It seems fitting, therefore, that one of the earliest accounts of the kingdom of Dál Ríata written in Gaelic should feature in this volume, albeit that the brevity of the text and the limited nature of the discussion that follows hardly seem appropriate for the occasion.

The text in question, conveniently referred to by its opening words, *Cethri prímchenéla Dáil Ríata* ('the four chief kindreds of Dál Ríata'), is a small collection of pedigrees from sometime in the first half of the eighth century.[1] The only edition based on all manuscript witnesses is David Dumville's, published in 2000.[2] The text, at its fullest surviving extent, can be summarized as follows:

1. Introductory statement. In standardized orthography, this reads: *Cethri prímchenéla Dáil Ríata .i. Cenél nGabráin, Cenél Loairn Máir, Cenél nÓengusa, Cenél Comgaill. Gabrán ocus Comgall dá mac Domangairt ocus Fedelm Foltchain ingen Briúin meic Echach Mugmedóin a máthair*, 'The four chief *cenéla* of Dál Ríata: Cenél nGabráin, Cenél Loairn Máir, Cenél nÓengusa, Cenél Comgaill. Gabrán and Comgall, two sons of Domangart: Fedelm Foltchain daughter of Brión son of Eochu Mugmedón their mother'.

2. 'Genealogy of Cenél nGabráin'. A pedigree headed by Congus[3] mac Consamla, who is given as four generations after Áedán mac Gabráin.

I am very grateful to Dr Nicholas Evans for reading and commenting on this essay, and to Dr Nerys Ann Jones for her constant support and encouragement. **1** This is the dating offered by Marjorie O. Anderson, *Kings and kingship in early Scotland* (2nd ed.: Edinburgh, 1980), pp 161–2. John Bannerman, *Studies in the history of Dalriada* (Edinburgh, 1974), p. 110, favours the early eighth century, a view given more precision in different ways by Dumville and Fraser (see below, nn. 27, 29). A different approach to dating is discussed below, pp 69–70. **2** David N. Dumville, '*Cethri prímchenéla Dáil Riata*', *SGS*, 20 (2000), 170–91. It was edited from one manuscript in Bannerman, *Studies*, pp 65–7. William F. Skene, *Chronicles of the Picts, chronicles of the Scots and other memorials of Scottish history* (Edinburgh, 1867), pp 308–17 at pp 316–17, remains the only edition that presents it in its context in three manuscripts – BB, BLec and TCD MS 1298 (H.2.7) Bannerman's and Dumville's 'H' – as part of a larger genealogical compendium (discussed below, p. 67 and n. 22). The only translation (from BB, again in context) is Alan O. Anderson, *Early sources of Scottish history, AD 500 to 1286*, 2 vols (Edinburgh, 1922), ii, pp clv–clvii. **3** Manuscript readings vary (*Conn, Cormac, Conmhac, Congus*: the latter is

63

The pedigree is taken no further than Áedán's father, the eponymous Gabrán.[4]

3. 'Genealogy of Cenél Loairn Máir'. Two pedigrees are given. The first, headed by Ainbchellach mac Ferchair Fota (†719; king of Dál Ríata 697–8), is taken six generations back to Báetán mac Echdach, and then through Báetán's grandfather, Muiredach, to Muiredach's father, Loarn Már. Loarn Már is then presented as son of Erc and grandson of Eochu Munremar. The second is a branch headed by a name that is likely to have originally been Morgán,[5] who is taken six generations back to Báetán mac Echdach. Most manuscripts continue as far as Báetán's grandfather, Muiredach.

4. 'Genealogy of Cenél Comgaill'. A pedigree headed by Échtgach mac Nechtáin (who is otherwise unknown). He is given as six generations above the eponymous Comgall mac Domangairt. Comgall's grandfather is given as Mac Nisse, and the pedigree finishes with Mac Nisse's father, Erc, and grandfather, Eochu Munremar.

5. 'Genealogy of Cenél nÓengusa'. A pedigree headed by Óengus mac Boidb (who is also otherwise unknown). He is presented as seven generations above the eponymous Óengus, who is given as son of Erc and grandson of Eochu Munremar.

The treatment of Cenél nGabráin has particularly caught the eye of scholars.[6] Whereas the other three *prímchenéla* are taken back to Erc and his father Eochu Munremar, Cenél nGabráin reaches only as far as Gabrán. The reader has to refer to the introductory statement in order to see how this pedigree relates to the others in the collection:[7] there we are told that Gabrán was a

preferable). See Dumville, '*Cethri prímchenéla Dáil Riata*', 175–6, 184; Anderson, *Kings and kingship*, pp 183–4; Bannerman, *Studies*, pp 67, 109.   4 Richard Sharpe has suggested that a cousin of Áedán mac Gabráin was described anachronistically by Adomnán (*Vita Columbae*, ii, 22) as of the royal lineage of Cenél nGabráin (*de regio Gabrani ortus genere*): Richard Sharpe (trans.), *Adomnán of Iona: Life of St Columba* (London, 1995), p. 328. 5 The evidence is discussed inconclusively in Dumville, '*Cethri prímchenéla Dáil Riata*', pp 185–6; see also Bannerman, *Studies*, p. 37. To this can be added *Morggain* in the pedigree of Máel Snechta mac Lulaig (king of Moray, †1085) in *CGH* p. 329: all but the first five generations have been created from combining the Cenél Loairn pedigrees in *Cethri prímchenéla Dáil Ríata* (as noted in Hector M. Chadwick, *Early Scotland: the Picts, the Scots and the Welsh of southern Scotland* [Cambridge, 1949], p. 96 n. 1).   6 Anderson, *Kings and kingship*, p. 161; Dumville, '*Cethri prímchenéla Dáil Riata*', 184; see also David N. Dumville, 'Political organization in Dál Riata' in F. Edmonds and P. Russell (eds), *Tome: studies in medieval Celtic history and law in honour of Thomas Charles-Edwards* (Woodbridge, 2011), pp 41–52 at p. 48.   7 It is true that this statement is also found in *Míniugud senchusa fer nAlban* (although not exactly: for example, Fedelm's epithet is omitted): Bannerman, *Studies*, p. 41, ll 13–14; David N. Dumville, 'Ireland and north Britain in the earlier Middle Ages: contexts for *Míniugud senchasa fher nAlban*' in C. Ó Baoill and N.R. McGuire (eds), *Rannsachadh na Gàidhlig 2000* (Aberdeen, 2002), pp 185–

full brother of Comgall mac Domangairt.[8] Even more striking is that the pedigree that has been chosen to represent Cenél nGabráin is headed by a descendant of Áedán's son, Gartnait.[9] It is difficult to see why Cenél nGabráin have not been represented by a descendant of Áedán's son, Eochaid Buide – in particular Eochu mac Domangairt (†697), or his son Eochaid (†733), who were kings of Dál Ríata descended from an unbroken line of kings back to Áedán mac Gabráin. None of Gartnait mac Áedáin's offspring, by contrast, were kings of Dál Ríata.

David Dumville commented that 'unless we are to suspect textual loss, which is possible but undemonstrable, we have to allow that the author's principal interests lay elsewhere' than Cenél nGabráin.[10] Although the 'Genealogy of Cenél Loairn Máir' follows that of Cenél nGabráin, the fact that it alone is given two pedigrees caused Dumville to conclude that 'the clear implication seems to be that the author of this tractate had more knowledge of and interest in Cenél Loairn than in the other *prímchenéla*'.[11] For him, therefore, the author was 'presumptively a partisan of Cenél Loairn writing in the early eighth century'.[12] James Fraser has interpreted this as showing that the author of *Cethri prímchenéla Dáil Ríata* 'took an antagonistic line towards Cenél nGabráin',[13] and he has seen the text as providing an important alternative to the 'centrist' view of Dál Ríata in Adomnán's *Vita Columbae* and the Iona Chronicle.[14]

211 at p. 201, §8. It is difficult to see why this would have been the only interpolation into *Cethri prímchenéla Dáil Ríata* from *Míniugud senchusa fer nAlban*: at the very least, a mention of Fergus Mór might be expected. Given the manifestly composite nature of *Míniugud senchusa fer nAlban* (see Dumville, 'Ireland and north Britain', pp 204–9), it is much more likely that the statement that Gabrán and Comgall had the same mother has been added to *Míniugud senchusa fer nAlban* from *Cethri prímchenéla Dáil Ríata* (notwithstanding the opposite assumption in Bannerman, *Studies*, p. 109). This would also be consistent with Fedelm's epithet appearing only in *Cethri prímchenéla Dáil Ríata*. 8 Dumville, '*Cethri prímchenéla Dáil Riata*', 186–7, comments that 'there appears to be more than a hint here that the author was elevating the descendants of Comgall above those of Gabrán'. A more mundane explanation is offered, below n. 37. 9 James E. Fraser, *From Caledonia to Pictland: Scotland to 795*, The New Edinburgh History of Scotland 1 (Edinburgh, 2009), pp 206, 249, 293–4, takes this as evidence that this was the principal segment of Cenél nGabráin. Fraser has argued that Gartnait was, in fact, a son of 'Accidan' (*AU* 649.4), not a son of Áedán: James E. Fraser, 'The Iona Chronicle, the descendants of Áedán mac Gabráin, and the "principal kindreds of Dál Riata"', *Northern Studies*, 38 (2004), 77–96 at 87–9 (see also Fraser, *From Caledonia*, pp 204–6, 249). Although this is an attractive proposition, it is not a necessary one: Gartnait son of Áedán and Gartnait son of 'Accidan' could be separate people. Dumville, 'Political organization', pp 47–8, proposed that 'Accidan' is a misreading of *Aidán*: this would not meet Fraser's point, however, that in the annal item Gartnait is distinguished from sons of Áedán (Fraser, 'The Iona Chronicle', 88 n. 39). 10 Dumville, '*Cethri prímchenéla Dáil Riata*', 184: the textual loss considered here is the lack of descendants for Gabrán. 11 Ibid., 186. 12 Ibid., 189. 13 Fraser, *From Caledonia*, p. 249. 14 Fraser, 'The Iona Chronicle'. Another notable feature is the inclusion of Cenél Comgaill as one of the *prímchenéla*. This

In this short article the possibility of textual loss will be examined more deeply, looking particularly at the impact of the genealogical material that precedes *Cethri primchenéla Dáil Ríata* in all manuscripts (including the Book of Leinster, which has only the introductory statement). It is argued that *Cethri primchenéla Dáil Ríata* originally began with a pedigree of Eochaid son of Eochu mac Domangairt, of Cenél nGabráin, and that the text's author should not, therefore, be seen as in any way antagonistic to Cenél nGabráin or biased towards Cenél Loairn. It is not clear, indeed, that his choice of pedigrees would have been regarded as particularly controversial.[15] It may be more appropriate to read *Cethri primchenéla Dáil Ríata* as a piece of contemporary political commentary rather than a partisan declaration. As such, it has the potential to give us access to what was, at the time of writing, regarded as a standard framework for thinking about Dál Ríata. This would include the idea that the chief *cenéla* had a common ancestor in Erc son of Eochu Munremar.[16] The figure conspicuous by his absence is Fergus Mór mac Eirc.[17]

Before considering the material that precedes *Cethri primchenéla Dáil Ríata*, there are indications in the text itself that there was once another pedigree of Cenél nGabráin. It would be curious, if the author wished to advance Cenél Loairn ahead of Cenél nGabráin, that Cenél nGabráin should remain at the head of the collection. It is also curious that Cenél nGabráin, despite being given ahead of Cenél Loairn, is merely given a branch rather than the stem and branch provided for Cenél Loairn. Both the structure of the text and the fact that Cenél nGabráin only has a branch pedigree therefore sug-

---

is at variance with the insistence in *Miniugud senchusa fer nAlban* (or, rather, one strain of that composite text) that there were 'three thirds of Dál Ríata', with Cenél Comgaill's territory assigned to Cenél nGabráin. It is difficult to know what to make of this, however, without establishing which came first. James Fraser has suggested that this part of *Miniugud senchusa fer nAlban* could be later (Fraser, *From Caledonia*, p. 353), whereas Dumville, '*Cethri primchenéla Dáil Riata*', 189–90, followed Bannerman's view (Bannerman, *Studies*, p. 110) that this material belongs originally to the mid-seventh century, and that *Cethri primchenéla Dáil Ríata*, therefore, is evidence that Cenél Comgaill gained as Cenél nGabráin weakened in the early eighth century.   15 This could even extend to Congus mac Conśamla's membership of Cenél nGabráin, even if we accept Fraser's view that Congus' ancestor, Gartnait, was not in reality the son of Áedán (see n. 10, above): it depends on how long the fiction (if such it was) had been accepted as fact. 16 Bannerman, *Studies*, pp 118–32 (see esp. p. 126), saw this as an invention of a tenth-century editor of *Miniugud senchusa fer nAlban*. Descent from Erc is not discussed in Dumville, '*Cethri primchenéla Dáil Riata*'. Dumville, 'Ireland and north Britain', p. 208, regards *Miniugud senchusa fer nAlban* as we have it as essentially a tenth-century text: his view of how it was composed is different from Bannerman's.   17 Fergus first appears in Patrician material datable to late in the eighth century. See Dumville, 'Ireland and north Britain', pp 189–91, and 205–6, for indications of the ambiguity of Fergus Mór mac Eirc in *Miniugud senchusa fer nAlban*. I have discussed this further in the Morgyn Wagner Memorial Lecture at the University of Edinburgh, '*Miniugud senchusa fer nAlban* and the history of Dál Riata', 15 December 2008.

gests that the text's introductory statement was originally followed by a stem pedigree for Cenél nGabráin reaching back to Erc son of Eochu Munremar.

The reason for the disappearance of a putative stem pedigree for Cenél nGabráin is revealed by the Scottish royal pedigrees that appear immediately before it in all the manuscripts. These go under the title *Genelach fer nAlban* (or *Genelaig Albanensium*).[18] At its fullest this consisted of a pedigree of David I (1124–53), followed by a pedigree of Causantín mac Cuiléin (995–7), and another of Cináed mac Maíl Choluim (971–95) and his brother Dub (962–6).[19] David I's pedigree gives a version of the section between Eochu Munremar and Eochaid Ríata found in Scottish texts of the royal genealogy; Causantín's, in its fullest manifestation, gives a different account, and has Coirpre Rígfota rather than Eochaid Ríata.[20] It would appear that, in its earliest form, *Genelach fer nAlban* gave Causantín's pedigree as the stem, followed by a branch headed by Cináed mac Maíl Choluim (971–95) and his brother Dub (962–6); the pedigree of David I is a later addition.[21]

There is no doubt, therefore, that *Cethri prímchenéla Dáil Ríata* has come down to us from a manuscript in which it came after the pedigrees of kings of Alba.[22] The title *Genelach fer nAlban* (possibly originally Latin *Genelogia Albanensium*) may, indeed, have been intended to cover both it and the late-tenth-century pedigrees: *Cethri prímchenéla Dáil Ríata* are merely the first words in the introductory statement of the eighth-century material, rather than a title as such.[23] The significance of the tenth-century pedigrees is that they trace the ancestry of kings of Alba through their nearest common ances-

18 Bannerman, *Studies*, p. 65, gives *Genelaig Albanensium* as the reading in TCD MS 1298 (H.2.7). I have not checked all the manuscript witnesses.   19 The Book of Leinster 336b37–c21 (including pedigrees of eleventh-century rulers, Máel Snechta and Mac Bethad, that follow the material from *Cethri prímchenéla Dáil Ríata*): LL, vi, ll 1471–2. The collection is represented in Rawl. MS B. 502, albeit in much reduced form: *CGH* pp 328–30.   20 A text with Gaelic orthography originating from Scotland in the twelfth century is edited in Dauvit Broun, *The Irish identity of the kingdom of the Scots in the twelfth and thirteenth centuries* (Woodbridge, 1999), pp 175–80. In BB 148b1–149b3 and BLec 109rd8–110rb13, Causantín is the head of the stem (with one version of Eochu Munremar's immediate ancestors back to Coirpre Rígfota) and David I the head of the next pedigree (with the other version of Eochu Munremar's immediate ancestors back to Eochaid Ríata). In H.2.7, this is reduced to Causantín as the stem and Máel Coluim mac Cináeda as a branch (from Cináed mac Ailpín).   21 Not necessarily as late as David's reign: there are indications that it was added in the reign of Máel Coluim mac Cináeda, 1005–34, and was subsequently updated to David I (I have constructed a stemma of these texts which I intend to publish as part of a wider study of the Scottish royal genealogy).   22 This archetype may also have included *Míniugud senchusa fer nAlban*; it is also possible that this was added later. The statement about Gabrán and Comgall's parents suggests that whoever brought *Míniugud senchusa fer nAlban* into the form in which it survives had knowledge of *Cethri prímchenéla Dáil Ríata*: see n. 8, above.   23 This raises the question of whether the introductory statement could have been written as a link rather than being originally part of the text. It reads more convincingly as the latter.

tor, Cináed mac Ailpín (†858), back to Áed Find (†778) son of Eochaid (†733) son of Eochu (†697), and so back to Eochaid Buide son of Áedán mac Gabráin and on to Erc son of Eochu Munremar and beyond.[24] A putative stem pedigree of Cenél nGabráin in *Cethri prímchenéla Dáil Ríata* headed by an eighth-century Cenél nGabráin king of Dál Ríata would merely have repeated what was given in Causantín's pedigree. It would be perfectly under-standable if a scribe in this situation (who could have been the person who first attached *Cethri prímchenéla Dáil Ríata* to the genealogy of Causantín mac Cuiléin) avoided duplication and copied only the branch pedigree of Cenél nGabráin, which would naturally have gone no further than the point where it joined with the now excised first pedigree. The result would be exactly what now appears in *Cethri prímchenéla Dáil Ríata*.

A recognition that *Cethri prímchenéla Dáil Ríata* originally began with two pedigrees of Cenél nGabráin could also offer a solution to another puzzle.[25] It might be expected that Ainbchellach's appearance at the top of the first pedi-gree in the section on Cenél Loairn would only have occurred when he was head of the kindred – all the more so if the text was conceived as a document in favour of Cenél Loairn. Ainbchellach only held this position between the death of his father (*AU* 697.2, *ATig.* 697.2) and the advent of his brother, Selbach, as king of Dál Ríata no more than a few years later. There is no indication, indeed, that Ainbchellach recovered after he lost the kingship of Dál Ríata and was taken, bound, to Ireland (*AU* 698.4).[26] Selbach first appears in the chronicle-record in *AU* 701.8; according to the regnal lists, he reigned as king of Dál Ríata for 24 years.[27] He retired to the Church (*AU* 723.4, *ATig.* 723.4), but made an unsuccessful comeback (*AU* 727.3). His death is noted at *AU* 730.4. Ainbchellach was himself killed in battle by Selbach (*AU* 719.6, *ATig.* 719.4), presumably in an attempt to regain power. The problem that arises is that *Cethri prímchenéla Dáil Ríata* cannot be dated as early as Ainbchellach's brief period as head of Cenél Loairn. This is

---

24 This is what is found in the text with Gaelic orthography originating from Scotland in the twelfth century, edited in Broun, *The Irish identity*, pp 175–80. The regular confusion of Eochu and Eochaid made the transmission of this section of the genealogy unstable, presumably because it was assumed that father and son had the same name, which would be almost unheard of. In what follows, it is irrelevant whether Cináed mac Ailpín was genuinely a descendant of Eochaid son of Eochu mac Domangairt or not: all that is required is that, by the late tenth century, this was regarded as an established fact. 25 In what follows *AU* is taken from <http://celt.ucc.ie/published/G100001A/index.html>, and *ATig.* from <http://celt.ucc.ie/published/G100002/index.html>. The entry numbers for *AU* are the same as those in the published edition of Mac Airt and Mac Niocaill; the entry numbers for *ATig.* are an innovation of the CELT text which are utilized here for ease of reference. 26 Dumville's dating of *Cethri prímchenéla Dáil Ríata* to 697×719 (Dumville, '*Cethri prímchenéla Dáil Riata*', p. 190) implies that Ainbchellach could have recovered headship of Cenél Loairn at any point between these dates. 27 Anderson, *Kings and kingship*, p. 112.

because the extant pedigree of Cenél nGabráin, headed by Congus son of Conṡamail, must belong after Conṡamail's death (*AU* 705.4: he was slain, so it would be difficult to argue that he had retired).[28] The possibility cannot be ruled out absolutely that Ainbchellach returned to power briefly at some point after 705, but that this has not been recorded in an extant source. This seems improbable, however, given the detailed information that is available on this period, derived ultimately from the Chronicle of Iona. It cannot be disproved either that the text has been updated haphazardly by adding Congus: again, however, this lacks any intrinsic merit. Instead of invoking special pleading of this kind, another explanation should be sought for the appearance of Ainbchellach at the head of the section on Cenél Loairn and Congus heading a branch of Cenél nGabráin.

Pedigrees headed by Ainbchellach and Congus son of Conṡamail would only be incompatible if they were both alive at the time that *Cethri prímchenéla Dáil Ríata* was written. Is this assumption necessary? Ainbchellach and Congus could each stand for their descendants. Admittedly, the top of pedigrees has not attracted much scholarly attention, and as a result the conventions that were used by early medieval genealogists are not well understood.[29] It might be expected that each kind of genealogical text had distinct conventions. What kind was *Cethri prímchenéla Dáil Ríata*? Its crucial characteristic is that it is a near-minimal statement of Dál Ríata as an extended kindred: four *cenéla* descended from Erc son of Eochu Munremar are identified, and only two pedigrees (stem and branch) or a single pedigree are given for each. Only the most important lines have been chosen. It would be in keeping with this highly selective approach if the only named person alive at the time of composition was the man heading the first pedigree – the first name in the text as a whole. He was not in this position simply as head of Cenél nGabráin, but because he was the head of the extended kin-group that was defined in the text by a common ancestor. If the text was intended as a snapshot of Dál Ríata as a body, then it could have made sense to emphasize his status by making him the only contemporary head of a *cenél* who was named. If so, then the other pedigrees – the most important branches of Dál Ríata at the time – would have reached no further than the father of the current heads of kindred represented in each line.

Before returning to *Cethri prímchenéla Dáil Ríata* to investigate this hypothesis in more detail, it may be useful to look first at the pedigrees of kings of Alba that precede it. As a snapshot of the descendants of Cináed mac

28 Fraser recognizes this by dating *Cethri prímchenéla Dáil Ríata* to 'after 706' (Fraser, *After Caledonia*, pp 204, 249, 353; this implicitly becomes 'c. 706' at p. 206). 29 It is typically assumed that whoever tops a pedigree was alive at the time of writing: see, for example, Diarmuid Ó Murchadha, 'Rawlinson B. 502: dating the genealogies' in J. Carey, M. Herbert and K. Murray (eds), *Cín Chille Cúile: texts, saints and places: essays in honour of Pádraig Ó Riain* (Aberystwyth, 2004), pp 316–33.

Ailpín it is not an extended kindred. Also, it can be read as simply an account of the relationship of recent kings of Alba to each other: every king is named from Cináed's grandsons to the reigning king, Causantín mac Cuiléin (including Amlaíb mac Illuilb, *rí Alban* in his obit in *ATig.* 977.4, although he was not admitted to any extant king-list).[30] An alternative reading, however, is of Causantín mac Cuiléin as king by virtue of being head of Clann Chináeda meic Ailpín. If so, it is notable that, as head of kindred, he was the only living person named in the text. The branches extended no further than the fathers of his contemporaries, Cináed (†971) and Dub (†966), fathers of Máel Coluim mac Cináeda (†1034) and Cináed mac Duib (†1005). (No son of Amlaíb is mentioned in an extant source, however.) Again, we could have a kin-group represented in a genealogical text with the head as one pivot – the ego, as it were – and the common ancestor as the other pivot: a concise and coherent statement of a kin-group as a living body.

Returning to *Cethri prímchenéla Dáil Ríata*, this could be tested by seeing if there was a time in the first half of the eighth century, during the reign of a Cénel nGabráin king of Dál Ríata, when a son of Ainbchellach was leader of Cenél Loairn and a son of Congus was particularly prominent. An additional criterion is that the reigning Cenél nGabráin king would also need to have been an ancestor of Cináed mac Ailpin in order to have caused a scribe to omit the Cenél nGabráin stem pedigree because it coincided with that of Causantín mac Cuiléin. Such a test would only be significant if the reign of only one Cenél nGabráin king (and ancestor of Cináed mac Ailpín) fell comfortably within this period. Fortunately this is the case: he is Eochaid son of Eochu mac Domangairt. The beginning of his reign is noted at *ATig.* 726.9,[31] and he is recorded at *AU* 731.2 and *ATig.* 731.2 as taking clerical status – which implies that he ceased to reign. He was presumably the Eochaid descendant of Domnall who defeated Selbach in *AU* 727.3. His death is noted at *ATig.* 733.5. The only other member of Cenél nGabráin who can be identified in the chronicle-record between the death of Dúnchad Becc (*AU* 721.1, *ATig.* 721.1) and the defeat and death of two sons of Fíannamail (*AU* 741.6) is Talorc son of Congus, who is mentioned fighting a battle unsuccessfully against the Picts (*AU* 731.6, *ATig.* 731.5), and being drowned by them (probably as a form of execution) (*AU* 734.5, *ATig.* 734.4). Two of the criteria are therefore met if we suppose that *Cethri prímchenéla Dáil Ríata* was written *c.*730: an ancestor of Cináed mac Ailpín was king of Dál Ríata, and a son of Congus was almost certainly the next most prominent member of Cenél nGabráin. (Another son of Congus, Cú Bretan, whose death is noted

---

30 <http://celt.ucc.ie/published/G100002/index.html> (accessed 7 July 2013). In *AU* 977.4, *.i. rí Alban* is an addition: <http://celt.ucc.ie/published/G100001A/index.html> (accessed 7 July 2013). 31 See Thomas Charles-Edwards (trans.), *The chronicle of Ireland*, 2 vols (Liverpool, 2006), i, pp 18–19 for discussion.

in *AU* 740.5, has been identified by Thomas Charles-Edwards as a member of the Uí Ségáin rather than Talorc's brother.)[32]

The final criterion is that a son of Ainbchellach was king of Cenél Loairn. In *AU* 733.2 and *ATig.* 733.2 we are told that Muiredach son of Ainbchellach 'took the kingship of Cenél Loairn' – but Eochaid had apparently ceased to reign two years earlier. True, in his death notice (*ATig.* 733.5) Eochaid is given the title 'king of Dál Ríata', which could suggest that he reassumed power, just as his contemporaries Selbach (unsuccessfully) and the Pictish king Nechtán (successfully) did after entering the Church (*AU* 723.4, *ATig.* 723.4, and *AU* 727.3; *ATig.* 724.2 and *ATig.* 728.5).[33] Is it possible, on the other hand, that Muiredach son of Ainbchellach was head of Cenél Loairn a few years earlier, when Eochaid was definitely king of Dál Ríata? Muiredach's rival for the leadership of Cenél Loairn was Selbach's son, Dúngal. Dúngal 'was expelled from the kingship' (*ATig.* 726.4) – meaning the kingship of Dál Ríata: his successor was Eochaid.[34] This could also have undermined Dúngal's authority over Cenél Loairn: Selbach himself led Cenél Loairn when he was defeated by Eochaid's *familia* the following year (*AU* 727.3). Selbach's defeat could have allowed his brother's son, Muiredach, to take charge. Dúngal is next mentioned burning a stronghold in *AU* 731.4: if Muiredach's putative leadership of Cenél Loairn depended on Eochaid's victory over Selbach in 727, then perhaps his power waned when Eochaid withdrew to the clerical life in 731. Be this as it may, although there is no explicit evidence that Muiredach was king of Cenél Loairn until 733, it is conceivable that he held this position between 727 and 731. If so, all the pieces of the jigsaw would be in place, pointing to *c*.730 as the likely date of composition for *Cethri prím-chenéla Dáil Ríata*. Alternatively, the possibility remains that Eochaid had reclaimed the kingship of Dál Ríata at the time of his death in 733.[35] Talorc son of Congus was still at large, and Muiredach son of Ainbchellach king of Cenél Loairn. It is also possible, therefore, that *Cethri prímchenéla Dáil Ríata* was composed in 733. Indeed, it may have the edge on *c*.730; if Muiredach had previously been king of Cenél Loairn, then it might be expected that the

---

32 Charles-Edwards, *Chronicle of Ireland*, i, p. 212 n. 5.   33 Unfortunately Eochaid's obit is not in *AU*, so the possibility that the title is a later addition cannot be ruled out. On the other hand, the title 'king of Dál Ríata' could appear in *AU* as well as *ATig.*: instances in *AU* are listed in Dumville, 'Political organization', p. 50. Nicholas Evans, *The present and the past in medieval Irish chronicles* (Woodbridge, 2010), pp 210–13, discusses the likelihood that a Dál Ríata king-list was used by an ancestor of *ATig.*   34 Charles-Edwards, *Chronicle of Ireland*, i, pp 18–19; see also Anderson, *Kings and kingship*, pp 112, 181–2. 35 Regnal lists offer little intelligible guidance for the succession of kings in this period. For a notable attempt, see Anderson, *Kings and kingship*, p. 112, but she was unaware of Eochaid's entry into the Church in 731. Muiredach appears to have become king of Dál Ríata, assuming that he was the son of Ainbchellach who led Dál Ríata to defeat against the Picts in *AU* 736.2. His obit is given in *AFM* 771 [i, 374] (see Anderson, *Kings and kingship*, p. 185 n. 251*a*).

wording in *AU* 733.2 and *ATig.* 733.2 would reflect this, instead of saying simply *regnum generis Loairn assumit* ('he took the kingship of Cenél Loairn').[36]

Although the evidence does not provide a completely clear-cut answer, all the most puzzling features of *Cethri prímchenéla Dáil Ríata* can be resolved if it is envisaged that there was an initial Cenél nGabráin stem pedigree, now lost, headed by Eochaid son of Eochu, who was the only person in the collection who was alive at the time of writing. As such, the text would no longer bear an explicitly partisan message that is intelligible today.[37] Instead, it can be read as a snapshot of the kingdom of Dál Ríata through the eyes of an informed contemporary, capturing the balance of power in Dál Ríata in the early 730s. The top of genealogies needs to be investigated more widely, however, before the interpretation offered here can be embraced with confidence.

---

36 I am grateful to Nicholas Evans for this point.   37 The connection with Uí Briúin (see above, pp 64–5 and n. 8) catches the eye as probably a political fiction. Presumably the purpose was not so much to create a link indirectly with Uí Néill but to emphasize a bond with Uí Briúin, who were rising to prominence in Connacht in the eighth century: Thomas Charles-Edwards, *Early Christian Ireland* (Oxford, 2000), pp 39–40.

Yonec and *Tochmarc Becfola*: two female *echtrai*

JOHN CAREY

Marie de France's lay *Yonec* relates how, in the twilight of his life, the old lord of Caerwent took a young and beautiful wife in hopes of securing an heir. After seven years, however, their union remained childless. The lady was kept by her jealous husband in a tower, in a state of solitary and frustrated misery, with no companion but his widowed sister. One day, as she lamented her situation and yearned for some amorous adventure, a hawk flew through the tower window and changed into a handsome knight. After he had allayed her fears by proving that he was a Christian, she joyfully took him as her lover. He told her that he would come to her as often as she wished for him; but he urged her to be cautious, as discovery of their affair would be his death.

The lady wished for his visits as often as was possible, and her new happiness restored her spirits and good looks. Noticing the change, and suspecting that something was amiss, the husband told his sister to spy on her. When he had learned of the knight's existence, and of his means of access, he placed sharp blades on the window-sill, and when the hawk next came he was terribly wounded; predicting that he would die from his injuries, he flew away. The lady, overcome by distress, threw herself from a high window but alit on the ground unhurt. Following the trail of her lover's blood, she passed through a door in a barrow and came into another country, where she found him dying in a splendid and apparently abandoned city. He told her that she would bear his son; and he gave her a dress, a ring which would cause her husband to forget all his suspicions of her, and a sword with which their child would avenge his death when he became a man. The lady returned home and resumed her life with her husband as if nothing had happened.

When the boy Yonec had grown up and had been knighted, his mother and her husband took him on a journey, in the course of which they stayed at an abbey in which there was a splendid tomb. This proved to be the burial place of the lady's lover, who had been king of that country. She told her son the true story of his begetting and of his father's death, gave him the sword, and died of grief. Yonec immediately cut off his stepfather's head, and was made king in his father's place.[1]

This disturbing story, described by Roberta Krueger as 'one of Marie's most profound explorations of the joys and dangers of desire',[2] is among the

1 I have used the edition of Jean Rychner, *Les lais de Marie de France* (Paris, 1983), pp 102–19. All translations are my own.   2 'The wound, the knot, and the book: Marie de France and the literary tradition of love in the *Lais*' in L.E. Whalen (ed.), *A companion to*

lays for which a Celtic background has been most vehemently argued; but these arguments have also been strenuously opposed. Such proper names as the poem contains are certainly Brythonic: the toponyms are Welsh, while the only anthroponyms – the names of Yonec himself, and of his father Muldumarec (with variants in other manuscripts) – are evidently Breton in their present forms even though their etymology remains uncertain.³ But what of the story itself? Does it, in fact, have native roots, or did Marie merely use borrowed nomenclature to give local colouring to a narrative which had originated elsewhere?

The former alternative was advocated, just over a hundred years ago, by Tom Peete Cross.⁴ Cross' extensive discussion proposed Celtic, and notably Irish, counterparts for elements in *Yonec* under several headings: 'The shape-shifting fairy lover' (in particular the transformation of the lovers Étaín and Midir into swans in *Tochmarc Étaíne*; the captive Mess Búachalla's impregnation by a stranger who has come to her in bird form in *Togail Bruidne Da Derga*; and the *dindṡenchas* of Snám Dá Én, in which two men of the *síde* use their ability to become birds to seduce a woman, who then dies of grief after they have been killed by her jealous husband); 'The journey to the lover's kingdom' (where both the entrance through a hill and the splendour of the city in *Yonec* bear a general resemblance to accounts of the Otherworld of the *síde*); and 'The semi-supernatural son' (comparing the token of the ring to rings which are entrusted to women by the fathers of their unborn sons, in order to identify these children in later life, in *Cath Maige Tuired* and *Aided Oenfir Aífe*).

The first half of the twentieth century witnessed the efforts of several American medievalists to find sources for much of the 'Matter of Britain' in Irish legend: besides Cross himself, this group included A.C.L. Brown, George Lyman Kittredge, Alexander Haggerty Krappe and Roger Sherman Loomis. Their enthusiasm was sometimes intemperate, and many of their arguments were weak; it is not surprising that the approach which they advocated often exasperated their fellow scholars. In the present case, it was Marbury Bladen Ogle who rose to the bait.⁵ In an article that from the outset made no secret of its author's opposition to 'those scholars who maintain that the primary source of these early French poems is to be found in Irish liter-

---

Marie de France (Leiden and Boston, 2011), pp 55–87 at p. 76. 3 On the toponyms, see Jean-Luc Moreau, '"La citiez siet sur Duëlas": à propos des lais d'*Yonec* et de *Milon*', *Romania*, 106 (1985), 492–504. Despite Moreau's inclination to see the evidence as ambiguous, there can be no doubt that the ending -*ec* in personal names is Breton: thus Kenneth Jackson, *A historical phonology of Breton* (Dublin, 1967), pp 138–9; and cf. Charles Foulon, 'Marie de France et la Bretagne', *Annales de Bretagne*, 60, ii (1963), 243–58 at 255. 4 'The Celtic origin of the Lay of *Yonec*', *RC*, 31 (1910), 413–71 and *Studies in Philology*, 11 (1913), 26–60. My references below are to the second version. 5 'Some theories of Irish literary influence and the *Lay of Yonec*', *Romanic Review*, 10, ii (1919), 123–48.

ature', Ogle systematically addressed and then rejected all of the Irish parallels that Cross had adduced, finding most of the similarities to be either illusory or trivial. He pointed out that the Irish rings are fundamentally different
from the ring given to the lady in *Yonec* ('In the one case it is a recognition
token, in the other a magic, protective talisman');[6] and that 'in regard to the
prophecy of a son ... there are a large number of stories, certainly not Celtic,
many of which were well-known in the twelfth century, in which the father
merely assumes that the child will be a boy and on his departure leaves as
recognition token a man's weapon, usually a sword'.[7] Ogle went on to cite a
multitude of non-Celtic comparanda for the shape-shifting bird-lover, many
of them much closer to *Yonec* than anything proposed by Cross, and one –
the Russian fairytale 'The feather of Finist the bright falcon' – including such
details as the lover's coming secretly in the shape of a hawk, his being
wounded by a trap set on the window-sill by a jealous family member, and
the heroine's journey to find him again in a distant kingdom.[8]

Some decades later, R.N. Illingworth made a valiant attempt to vindicate
Cross against Ogle; but he did not bring forward any further significant evidence, nor did he address the large number of striking non-Celtic parallels
which Ogle had assembled. Once again asserting the Irish antecedents of the
figure of the bird-lover, Illingworth limited himself to recapitulating Cross'
examples and some of his arguments; and the comparanda which he cited for
Yonec's avenging of his father's death do not resemble the events in the lay,
and in some cases indeed do not even involve revenge. Only one item in his
discussion is genuinely thought-provoking, and even here it is hard to be sure
what weight to give it: he points out that the gifts of 'his sword and his
thumb-ring of gold and his garment for the assembly' (*a chlaideb 7 a
or[d]nasc [n-]óir 7 a thimthag [n-]óenaig*), given by Art son of Conn to the
girl on whom he has begotten his son Cormac on the night before his death
in battle, can be compared with the sword, ring and 'precious garment' (*chier
bliaut*) given to the lady by the dying Muldumarec.[9]

In the wake of Ogle's critique some scholars have taken the view that,
while there is no reason to doubt that Marie told the truth in claiming to

6 Ibid., 130.   7 Ibid., 133.   8 Ibid., 143, citing Pietro Toldo, 'Yonec', *Romanische
Forschungen*, 16 (1904), 609–29 at 628–9. All of the scholars who have discussed the story
of Finist in connection with *Yonec* appear to have relied on Toldo's incomplete paraphrase
of the French translation by Léon Sichler; the ultimate source is Aleksandr Afanasiev,
Narodnye russkie skazky (1858–63). In the five-volume edition published in 1999 by Terra,
in Moscow, the tale appears in vol. ii, pp 137–43; for an English translation, see, for example, Jeremiah Curtin, *Myths and folk-tales of the Russians, Western Slavs, and Magyars*
(Boston, 1903), pp 47–58.   9 'Celtic tradition and the *Lai of Yonec*', *ÉtC*, 9 (1960–61),
501–20, with mention of the gifts on p. 516. The Irish tale in which these figure is *Scéla
Eógain 7 Cormaic*; for the passage, see Máirín O Daly (ed.), *Cath Maige Mucrama: the
battle of Mag Mucrama*, ITS 50 (Dublin, 1975), p. 66 and Tomás Ó Cathasaigh, *The heroic
biography of Cormac mac Airt* (Dublin, 1978), p. 120.

have adapted this and other stories from Breton popular narratives, *Yonec* does not in fact exhibit any distinctively Celtic features – any more than, for that matter, do the bulk of the fairytales collected in the Celtic countries in more recent times. Thus J.D. Bruce, while holding that 'the nomenclature ... is Breton, and, whatever the ultimate source of the tale may be, it seems to me that the immediate source was, most likely, Breton', stressed at the same time that 'much the closest parallel that has ever been adduced is not Celtic but Russian (doubtless Oriental in the last analysis)'.[10] Writing of the lays in general, Philippe Ménard states that 'le plus simple est de croire que Marie s'inspire, comme elle le dit, des lais bretons', but remains sceptical regarding the speculations of Cross and his associates:

> Chaque fois, il y a une petite analogie, mais lointaine ... Multiplier les textes et les explications, c'est suggérer qu'aucun des exemples n'est vraiment pertinent. Mieux vaudrait reconnaître que les schémas des contes dont Marie s'est inspirée ont disparu.[11]

Remarking on the decline in Celtic interpretations of the lays since the 1960s, Emmanuel J. Mickel sees the current emphasis on other, and primarily learned, sources as reflecting a better understanding of Marie's background and concerns:

> In the last 20 years little has been done concerning the Celtic sources of Marie's work, while there is a growing amount of scholarship that has pointed to Marie's use of Ovid and other classical sources ... It is becoming clear that Marie's work – as the other works attributed to her indicate – is deeply informed by her knowledge of Latin literature and that even the motifs that seem most closely tied to Breton motifs are reshaped into a Christian and classical philosophical context.[12]

Against this unpromising background, I propose to offer for consideration another Irish comparandum for *Yonec*. My point of departure will be Marie's account of the lady's journey to her lover's mysterious kingdom, which may be translated as follows:

> ... She follows him, with a very great cry – she goes out by a window. It is a marvel that that does not kill her, for it was a good twenty feet high there where she took the leap. [340] She was naked save for her shift.

---

10 *The evolution of Arthurian romance from the beginnings down to the year 1300*, 2 vols (2nd ed.: Baltimore, 1928), ii, p. 181 and n. 3.   11 *Les lais de Marie de France* (Paris, 1979), pp 47–8.   12 'Marie de France and the learned tradition' in Whalen (ed.), *A companion*, pp 31–54 at pp 53–4.

She set herself to follow the trail of the blood, which dropped from the knight onto the way where she went. She journeyed on that path, and keeps on until she comes to a barrow. There was an entry into this barrow, which was sprinkled all over with drops of the blood; ahead, she could see nothing. Then she thought that she could well be certain [350] that her lover had entered there; she goes rapidly in. She found no light there. She journeyed so long on the straight way that she came out of the barrow into a very beautiful meadow. She found the grass soaked with the blood, which distressed her greatly. She followed its trail through the meadow. There was a city quite near, [360] entirely surrounded by a wall. There was no house, hall or tower which did not seem to be all of silver; very rich are the buildings. In the direction of the town are the marshes and the woods and the fences. On the other side, toward the castle, a river runs all around it: there the ships arrive – [370] there were more than three hundred sails.

The gate below was unfastened. The lady entered the town, always following the fresh blood through the town toward the castle. No one spoke to her; she found no man or woman. She comes to the palace, to the pavement which she finds all covered with blood. She entered a fair chamber. [380] She found a knight sleeping – she did not know him, and goes on into another, greater chamber. She finds a bed, and nothing more, with a knight sleeping upon it. She went forth from there, and came into the third chamber – she had found the bed of her lover. The bedposts are of refined gold; I do not know what price to put upon the bedclothes. [390] The candles and the candlesticks, which are lit night and day, are worth all of the gold of a city.[13]

He tells her that he is dying, and that she must flee lest his people seek to punish her for his death. He then gives her the ring, telling her that 'as long as she will keep it, her lord will have no memory of anything that has been done, and will not keep her confined' [417–20]. He also gives her the sword with which their son will avenge him, and a dress (presumably because she is wearing only underclothes). She makes her way back 'to her country', and the story proceeds as summarized above.

For some scholars there is nothing especially Celtic in any of this: thus Ogle observed rather impatiently that 'empty cities and magnificent castles are familiar to any reader of oriental tales', while Ménard cites Edina Bozóky's study of the 'château désert' as evidence that this is a standard motif in medieval French storytelling.[14] In the tales discussed by Bozóky, however, the

13 Rychner, *Lais*, pp 112–16. The bracketed numbers refer to lines in the edition.
14 Ogle, 'Some theories', 134; Ménard, *Lais*, p. 48.

empty castle is almost invariably associated with malevolent intent or with an afflicting enchantment. She notes only three exceptions:[15] *Yonec* itself; the lay of *Guingamor*, which has been variously regarded as being also a composition of Marie's, or written under her influence with the addition of 'Celtic themes independent of Marie';[16] and the Anglo-Norman version of Brendan's voyage, itself a rendering of a Hiberno-Latin source.[17]

I have departed from earlier translators in calling the hill through which the heroine passes a 'barrow', in other words a burial mound. Marie uses the rare word *hoge* (lines 346–7, 355, 452), borrowed from Norse *haugr* and (like its English cognate 'how(e)') mainly attested as a placename element in regions of Scandinavian settlement.[18] *Haugr* means not merely 'hill, mound' but also 'a cairn, over one dead',[19] and it is possible to see echoes of this sense in the usage of *hoge*: the oldest examples of it as a common noun appear to be the present case in *Yonec*; an instance in a twelfth-century translation of the biblical books of Kings, rendering *tumulus* in the Vulgate;[20] and, most appositely, an account of ninth-century Danes constructing a barrow, in the *Estorie des Engles* of Geoffrey Gaimar.[21] It is accordingly not surprising – though certainly unnerving – that the *hoge* has an entrance.[22]

Most commentators have tended to see the second part of the story, and in particular the passage through a hill, as being typically Celtic, although statements to this effect have been cast only in rather general terms.[23] That

---

15 'Roman médiéval et conte populaire: le château désert', *Ethnologie française*, 4 (1974), 349–56 at 350.   16 Matilda Tomaryn Bruckner and Glyn S. Burgess, 'Arthur in the narrative lay' in G.S. Burgess and K. Pratt (eds), *The Arthur of the French* (Cardiff, 2006), pp 186–214 at p. 205; and cf. Rachel Bromwich, 'Celtic dynastic themes and the Breton lays', *ÉtC*, 9 (1960–1), 439–74 at 460–2, 467. For the passage in question, see Alexandre Micha (ed.), *Lais féeriques des XIIe et XIIIe siècles* (Paris, 1992), pp 84–6, ll 361–96. Line 393 (*home ne fame n'i trova*) corresponds verbatim to l. 376 of *Yonec* (*humme ne femme n'i trova*).   17 Ian Short and Brian Merrilees (eds), *Benedeit: the Anglo-Norman voyage of St Brendan* (Manchester, 1979), pp 37–40; cf. Carl Selmer (ed.), *Navigatio Sancti Brendani abbatis* (Notre Dame, 1959), pp 14–16.   18 On phonological grounds, René Lepelley takes the toponymic element *hougue* to derive 'directement de l'etymon scandinave': *Noms de lieux de Normandie et des îles Anglo-Normandes* (Paris, 1999), pp 55–6; cf. pp 73–4, 178–9.   19 Richard Cleasby and Gudbrand Vigfusson, *An Icelandic-English dictionary* (Oxford, 1874), s.v.   20 In Ernst Robert Curtius (ed.), *Li Quatre Livre des Reis* (Dresden, 1911), p. 64, *el sumet de un hoge* corresponds to *in summitate tumuli unius* (2 Samuel 2:25). This is the only passage in the books of Kings where Jerome uses this word.   21 Thomas Duffus Hardy and Charles Trice Martin (eds), *Lestorie des Engles solum la translacion Meistre Geffrei Gaimar*, 2 vols (London, 1888–9), i, p. 132, ll 3150, 3153.   22 *Hoge* may, accordingly, be the closest Old French equivalent to Irish *síd*; cf. the remarks of Rychner, *Lais*, p. 267. Of the four manuscripts in which the lay survives, all save the oldest read *cave* instead of *hoge* (ibid., p. 225): testimony both to the word's unfamiliarity and to its connotations.   23 Cross, 'Celtic origin', 53; Illingworth, 'Celtic tradition', 509 n. 1; Edith Rickert, *Marie de France: seven of her lays done into English* (London, 1901), pp 185–6; Howard Rollin Patch, *The other world according to descriptions in medieval literature*

the heroine reaches Muldumarec's kingdom after a long journey through a tunnel can be paralleled in other twelfth-century works aimed at an Anglo-French audience. Walter Map's *De nugis curialium* tells the story of an ancient British ruler Herla who visited the palace of a pygmy king by entering 'a cavern in a very high cliff' and then traversing a distance in darkness;[24] and the *Itinerarium Kambriae* of Gerald of Wales relates how diminutive beings led a boy 'by a way at first subterranean and dark, into a most beautiful country, remarkable for its rivers and meadows, woods and plains'.[25]

From the time of the heroine's escape from the tower, the plot diverges sharply from the international tale-type of which 'The feather of Finist the bright falcon' is the most striking example,[26] although some details overlooked by previous commentators may reflect awareness of such a story. Thus it is striking that several Irish versions of the tale involve the heroine following her lover or husband to a supernatural underground land, which is in some cases specifically said to lie beneath or within a hill.[27] In one case it is prophesied of her son that 'he'll be the best hero in the world when of full growth', and he becomes a prince in the subterranean country.[28] It is also tempting to compare the three chambers in the Otherworld castle in *Yonec*, the first two containing sleeping men and the third the heroine's lover, with the three nights which the heroine spends in her husband's bed at the climax of many tellings of the fairy-tale: on the first two nights he lies in a drugged or enchanted sleep, but on the third he wakes and speaks to her.[29] But such potential resemblances are out-weighed by striking differences. In considering these, I believe that a hitherto overlooked Irish comparandum may be helpful.

The text which I wish to adduce in this connection is *Tochmarc Becfola*, described by its most recent editor as being 'early Middle Irish' in its earliest

---

(Cambridge MA, 1950), p. 250; Matilda Tomaryn Bruckner, 'Speaking through animals in Marie de France's *Lais*' in Whalen (ed.), *A companion*, pp 157–85 at p. 179.   **24** Walter Map, *De nugis curialium*, ed. Montague Rhodes James (Oxford, 1914), p. 14.   **25** *Itinerarium Kambriae*, i, 8, in James F. Dimock (ed.), *Giraldi Cambrensis opera*, vol. 6 (London, 1868), p. 75.   **26** For Ernest Hoepffner, *Les lais de Marie de France* (Paris, 1935), p. 75, this is the point at which 'tous les contes populaires qu'on possède sur ce sujet s'arrêtent'. See the account of type ATU 432 'The prince as bird' in Hans-Jörg Uther, *The types of international folktales: a classification and bibliography based on the system of Antti Aarne and Stith Thompson*, 3 vols (Helsinki, 2004), i, pp 258–9; Irish examples in Seán Ó Súilleabháin and Reidar Th. Christiansen, *The types of the Irish folktale* (Helsinki, 1967), p. 92. Cf. Mary H. Ferguson, 'Folklore in the *Lais* of Marie de France', *Romanic Review*, 57 (1966), 3–24 at 8, 17–18.   **27** Jeremiah Curtin, *Myths and folk-lore of Ireland* (Boston, 1891), p. 21; idem, *Irish folk-tales* (Dublin, 1943), p. 99 (Kerry); Daniel O'Fotharta, 'Cú Bán an tsléibhe', *ZCP*, 1 (1897), 146–56 at 149 (Galway); Séamus Ó Duilearga (ed.), *Leabhar Sheáin Í Conaill: sgéalta agus seanchas ó Íbh Ráthach* (Dublin, 1948), p. 110 (Kerry).   **28** Curtin, *Irish folk-tales*, pp 98, 101.   **29** This occurs in most of the Irish versions, and in the story of Finist. It is a standard element in ATU 425A 'The animal as bridegroom', with which ATU 432 is often combined: Uther, *Types*, i, p. 249.

form, and dating to 'the late ninth or early tenth century'.[30] The tale begins
by describing how a mysterious and beautiful woman becomes the wife of
Diarmait mac Áedo Sláine, king of Tara (†664/667). From the outset, it is
evident that their union is unsatisfactory: the bride-price (*tindscra*) which the
king gives her is insultingly paltry, leading his people to call her *Becfola*
('small property'); and she falls in love with his fosterson and hostage
Crimthann and persuades him to elope with her. His followers prevent
Crimthann from going to their tryst, however; and Becfola, who despite her
husband's disapproval of travelling on Sunday has found a pretext for leaving
the court accompanied only by her handmaid, loses her way while journeying
southward from Tara and falls into difficulties. The two women wander until
it is dark, wolves eat the handmaid, and Becfola takes refuge in a tree. Seeing
a light in the woods, she makes her way to a fire where a warrior, splendidly
adorned in gold and silver, is roasting a pig. He eats, taking no notice of her,
and then goes away from the fire with Becfola at his heels.

> She went after him as far as the lake. A boat of bronze in the middle
> of the lake; a chain of bronze from the boat to the land, and another
> chain to the island that was in the middle of the lake. The warrior
> pulls in the boat. She goes into the boat before him. The boat is left
> in a boathouse of bronze, in the front of the island. She goes into the
> house before him. Wondrous was that house, with its partitions and
> beds. He sat; she sat then beside him. He reaches his arm out past her,
> where she sat, and brought a platter with food to them. They both ate,
> and they drank so that neither of them became intoxicated. There was
> no one in the house. They did not speak to one another.[31]

After the meal she joins him in bed, but he does not turn to her throughout
the night. In the morning he is called forth, and she sees three other warriors,
'of the same shape, of the same age, of the same form', as well as another
group of four. Her companion and his fellows fight against this second group,
and the combatants only part after they have wounded one another.
Returning to her, he explains that he and his three brothers are contending
with their cousins for lordship of the island.

> 'What is the name of the island?' she said.
> 'The island of Fedach son of the Blind Man', he said.
> 'And what is your own name?' she said.

30 Máire Bhreathnach, 'A new edition of Tochmarc Becfhola', *Ériu*, 35 (1984), 59–91 at
68, 70.   31 Ibid., pp 73–4 §§7–8. In the description of the boathouse, I read *credumae* with
TCD MS 1337, rather than *chréda* 'of clay' with the Yellow Book of Lecan and
Bhreathnach.

'Flann, grandson of Fedach', he said. 'The grandsons of Fedach, indeed, are at strife with one another. The island, moreover, is good: provision for a hundred, both food and drink, is what it provides every afternoon, without anyone in attendance. If there are no more than two, it provides no more than it has given [last night]'.[32]

She offers to remain with him, but he refuses to accept her while he is still a landless warrior; if he ever becomes master of the island, however, he will come to claim her. She returns to Tara, accompanied by the handmaid (who has not perished after all, 'for the warriors of the island concealed (?) her'), only to find that Diarmait is just rising from bed on the same day on which she had left him: no time has elapsed at all, and no one has any idea that she had ever left the court.

One morning a year later, while Diarmait and Becfola are lying in bed, Flann appears to them, severely wounded. He and Becfola exchange cryptic verses, relating to the cousins' battle for rule over the island; then she and Flann go swiftly away together, none knows whither. Just at this point four clerics arrive, saying that they have travelled from the island monastery of Devenish. A monk there had seen a fierce fight between two groups of four warriors, with only a single warrior surviving. The bodies of the other seven were found to be loaded with gold and silver, and it is this treasure that the clerics have come to offer to the king. Diarmait decrees, however, that it shall be used to make ritual objects for the church of Devenish, and this is done.

Even if these two stories have no genetic relation to one another, I think that it is fruitful to look at them together. Both are examples, exceptional in their respective literatures, of Otherworld journeys in which the protagonist is a woman. In each case, a woman's attempts to escape from the constraints of a loveless marriage project her into a bewildering and alien parallel reality: it can be said of each heroine, as Máire Herbert has said of the fatally seductive Sín in the tale *Aided Muirchertaig Meic Erca*, that 'she appears both as a woman whose deeds fall outside those of the mortal world, and as a woman who acts outside of societal rules, who refuses to recognize clerical authority and marriage laws'.[33] In these terms alone, it seems to me that *Tochmarc Becfola* in particular deserves considerably more critical attention than it has yet received.[34] Here, I shall confine myself to considering the question of the resemblance of some of its elements to features of *Yonec*.

---

32 Ibid., p. 75 §9. For Bhreathnach's interpretation of the puzzling final word (MSS *roirthu, roirrthai*), see p. 89 n. 26 of her edition; I understand *ro ír-(a)de*, with the fem. sg. anaphoric pronoun.   33 'The death of Muirchertach Mac Erca: a twelfth-century tale' in F. Josephson (ed.), *Celts and Vikings* (Gothenburg, 1997), pp 27–39 at p. 30.   34 A feminist reading has been proposed by Máirín Ní Dhonnchadha in A. Bourke et al. (eds), *The Field Day anthology of Irish writing*, vol. 4 (Cork, 2002), p. 210; but I am not persuaded by her view that the author portrays Becfola exclusively as a personification of 'immorality'

There were great differences between the social and material culture of the Gaelic world of the ninth century, and that of the Anglo-French world of the twelfth; and Marie herself was creative, if not indeed subversive, in the use that she made of her sources.[35] Large discrepancies, while they should not be ignored, do not accordingly in themselves rule out the possibility of influence. In these terms we can juxtapose – even if only tentatively – the lake and boat in *Tochmarc Becfola* and the river with its many ships in *Yonec*; the ubiquitous use of bronze in the former and that of silver in the latter; and the uncanny emptiness of the places in which both heroines find themselves.[36] Flann is associated with three brothers who look just like him; Muldumarec lies in the last of three rooms, each of which contains a knight on a bed.[37] At their last appearance in the story, each of the Otherworld lovers is grievously wounded.

Some readers will find these parallels more striking than will others, and I am quite willing to entertain the possibility that they are coincidences. More unusual, and potentially more significant, is a shared strangeness of narrative structure. This involves anomalies of time: Becfola experiences an adventure lasting at least twenty-four hours, but returns to court to find that no time has elapsed; and when the heroine of *Yonec* goes back to her husband he too is unaware that she has been away.[38] A magic ring explains this in the lay; in the Irish story we are dealing with the bending of time which so often accompanies mortal experiences of the Otherworld.[39] But there are also anomalies of space. Wandering in the woods of Leinster, south of Tara,[40] Becfola comes to the magical island of Fedach; but at the end of the story this island is identified as Devenish, north-west of Tara in County Fermanagh, and it is here that Flann's brothers are buried. The heroine of *Yonec* reaches the evidently magical land of Muldumarec by travelling beneath the earth; but later she is told that Muldumarec had been king of the region, apparently somewhere in Wales, where she finds his splendid tomb. In both stories, in other words, a fantastic Otherworld is inexplicably 'the same' as a place in the mortal world, where a rich monastery serves as place of burial for Otherworld warriors.

and 'danger'. **35** Thus Bromwich, 'Celtic dynastic themes', 462: 'It would seem that Marie tended to substitute literary models for older popular elements in her sources'; and cf. Ferguson, 'Folklore in the *Lais*', 10: 'All of Marie's *Lais* depart from the narrative direction of folktales which have come down to us today. Whatever the sources Marie may have drawn upon ... it seems unlikely that not one has come down to us in the form in which she found it'. **36** *Ní boí duine isin tig* (§8); *Humme ne femme n'i trova* (line 376). **37** I offer this comparison for what it is worth; an alternative analogy with ATU 425A has been noted above. **38** In Rickert's reading of the story, the lady's return too takes place 'apparently the same day' as her flight from the tower (*Marie de France*, p. 186). **39** See my discussion in 'Sequence and causation in *Echtra Nerai*', *Ériu*, 39 (1988), 67–74 at 70. **40** More specifically, we are told that she reached Dubthor Laigen (near Baltinglass, Co. Wicklow) before losing her way. Clúain Dá Chailech, where she had agreed to meet Crimthann, may not really have existed; see my remarks in 'Otherworlds and verbal worlds in Middle Irish narrative', *PHCC*, 9 (1989), 32–42 at 35–7.

Not surprisingly, scholars have assessed this aspect of both tales in similarly disparaging terms. For Cross, speaking of *Yonec*, 'the lack of skill evinced in the narration of this episode is evident even to a superficial observer. The inconsistencies look like the result of an attempt to rationalize a frankly mar-vellous story in order to fit it into a tale with which it originally had no con-nection'.[41] Illingworth too held that 'the *lai* as we possess it is an imperfectly harmonized combination of two or more themes, each of which originally formed an entity in itself',[42] while Ogle went so far as to speak of 'the evil results of such confusion of stories of different types'.[43] For Edith Rickert, 'considerable confusion seems to have existed in Marie's mind'.[44] In the same spirit, James Carney called *Tochmarc Becḟola* 'a peculiar confused tale',[45] and its editor Máire Bhreathnach has characterized it as 'a composite of a number of disrupted literary themes, none of which has been carried through to its ideal thematic conclusion'.[46] In fact, as I have argued elsewhere, the treatment of space and time in *Tochmarc Becfola* can be paralleled in several other medieval Irish stories, and must be taken to reflect deliberate paradox rather than mal-adroit conflation.[47] To find the same feature in *Yonec*, without such a support-ing cultural context, is noteworthy.

These correspondences are sufficiently numerous, and sufficiently sugges-tive, to justify giving serious consideration to the hypothesis of the Irish tale's having influenced the lay. But how might such influence have been mediated? Here the work of Patrick Sims-Williams offers an intriguing possibility. In a recent article on *Tochmarc Becfola* he has made the eminently reasonable sug-gestion that the tale's 'most likely place of composition' was Devenish itself;[48] and in the H.M. Chadwick Memorial Lecture for 2006 he had already advanced an impressive array of arguments for regarding Devenish as a source of stories which reached Wales.[49] As noted above, the toponymy of *Yonec* is Welsh; might Marie have derived the latter part of her plot from a Welsh version of *Tochmarc Becfola*?

---

41 'Celtic origin', 53.   42 'Celtic tradition', 505.   43 'Some theories', 146; and cf. his ref-erence on p. 145 to 'the clumsy episode in *Yonec* of the first visit of the lady to her lover's abode'.   44 *Marie de France*, p. 185. Cf. pp 187–8: 'Although the knight's kingdom is described as fairyland, he is here treated as a mortal and his powers of transformation must be looked upon as due to magic. Probably Marie cared very little about his exact nature; the story was all in all to her'.   45 *Studies in Irish literature and history* (Dublin, 1955), p. 229.   46 'New edition', 63.   47 'Time, space, and the Otherworld', *PHCC*, 7 (1987), 1–27 at 3–4.   48 '*Tochmarc Becfhola*: A "peculiar confused tale"?' in J.F. Eska (ed.), *Narrative in Celtic tradition*, CSANA Yearbook 8/9 (Colgate NY, 2011), pp 228–34 at p. 232. The same article presents a valuable analysis of the ecclesiastical politics which may have motivated the supernatural linking of Devenish with the Baltinglass area.   49 *The iron house in Ireland*, H.M. Chadwick Memorial Lecture 16 (Cambridge, 2006). Sims-Williams has revised and expanded his discussion in *Irish influence on medieval Welsh lit-erature* (Oxford, 2011); see especially pp 257–61.

This scenario can be supplemented by further considerations. In previous publications I have called attention to two Clonmacnoise legends that migrated to England in the course of the twelfth century: a story of a visit by an aerial ship, and another of the mysterious burial of a vanishing giant.[50] Here we again find examples of monastic wonder-tales making their way to Britain in the period under consideration; but the second of these anecdotes may have even further claims on our attention. This relates how the poet Mac Coise met a woman of unsurpassed beauty (and enormous size) 'lamenting wildly' (*fuadan guil aisti*) beside a lake. She told him that her lover had been killed at the *síd* of Codal in Brega;[51] and that his body had been buried at Clonmacnoise. Mac Coise subsequently related his experience to the king, Congalach Cnogba (reigned 944–56), who proposed that they go to Clonmacnoise to investigate the matter. But when they came to the monastery they were told that no one had been buried there for months, and the king mocked the poet for having been deluded. In the night, however, a monk died, and next day a grave was dug for him 'where the Stone of the Druids is today'. Fresh blood and birch leaves were found in the earth, and Congalach commanded that digging be continued 'as long as you find the blood and the leaves'. At last the body of a giant with a single great wound was discovered, 'the fairest of the men of the world in shape and form'. It was decided to fill the grave in again until it was decided what should be done; but when it was next dug up, the body had disappeared.[52]

Some of the elements in this anecdote recall the latter part of *Yonec*, in ways that *Tochmarc Becfola* does not. There is the distraught abandon of the 'woman wailing for her demon lover'; the dead lover himself, inexplicably appearing in (but then vanishing from) a grave in a famous monastery; and even a trail of blood that leads to him. It is tempting to go on to associate the circumstances that the corpse comes from a *síd*-mound, and is buried at a spot later associated with the druids, with the *hoge* in Marie's story; but here the connection, if it exists at all, is more oblique.

There is accordingly room for the surmise that more than one story of Irish origin contributed to the Otherworld journey in *Yonec*. Whether Marie herself combined these in creating her own tale, or whether they had already

---

50 'Aerial ships and underwater monasteries: the evolution of a monastic marvel', *PHCC*, 12 (1992), 16–28, in particular the addendum on pp 24–5; 'The finding of Arthur's grave: a story from Clonmacnoise?' in J. Carey, J.T. Koch and P.-Y. Lambert (eds), *Ildánach ildírech: a Festschrift for Proinsias Mac Cana* (Andover and Aberystwyth, 1999), pp 1–14. See now Elizabeth Boyle, 'On the wonders of Ireland: translation and adaptation' in E. Boyle and D. Hayden (eds), *Authorities and adaptations: the reworking and transmission of textual sources in medieval Ireland* (Dublin, 2014), pp 233–61 at pp 251–2.   51 For references to this place, see *HDGP* vi, s.n. Codhal (1).   52 Text in Kuno Meyer, 'Mitteilungen aus irischen Handschriften', *ZCP*, 8 (1912), 102–20, 195–232, 559–65 at 559–60. I cite my own translation: 'The finding of Arthur's grave', p. 7.

fused (either in Ireland or in Britain) by the time that she encountered them, is a question which we are not in a position to answer. In any event, we are dealing with an accumulation of evidence which points, increasingly strongly, to Ireland as having been one of the sources of the *matière de Bretagne*.

This opens up intriguing possibilities for our understanding of the literary history of these islands, and indeed of medieval Europe as a whole. For the present, however, my focus remains with the two texts which have been the main subjects of this essay. In *Tochmarc Becfola*, we have the story of a woman's journey beyond the framework of time and space: it is a female *echtrae*,[53] so far as I know unique in Irish saga. In *Yonec*, we have *Tochmarc Becfola*'s French counterpart, and very possibly its offspring. Máire, among the many achievements of her versatile and distinguished career, has advanced and refined our understanding of the roles imposed upon mortal and supernatural women by medieval Irish literature,[54] and also of the ecclesiastical element in Otherworld voyage narratives.[55] In admiration, gratitude and friendship, I offer to her these reflections on tales of women whose rebellion against such roles has taken them on such a voyage.

---

53 This term is applied to Irish tales of excursions to the Otherworld. There has been considerable debate concerning the possibility of defining it more narrowly; the most recent treatment, with references to earlier scholarship, is Leonie Duignan, *The echtrae as an early Irish literary genre* (Rahden / Westfalen, 2011).   54 'Celtic heroine?: the archaeology of the Deirdre story' in T. O'Brien Johnson and D. Cairns (eds), *Gender in Irish writing* (Milton Keynes, 1991), pp 13–22; 'Goddess and king: the sacred marriage in early Ireland' in L.O. Fradenburg (ed.), *Women and sovereignty* (Edinburgh, 1992), pp 264–75; 'The universe of male and female: a reading of the Deirdre story' in C.J. Byrne, M. Harry and P. Ó Siadhail (eds), *Celtic languages and Celtic peoples: proceedings of the Second North American Congress of Celtic Studies* (Halifax, 1992), pp 53–63; 'Transmutations of an Irish goddess' in S. Billington and M. Green (eds), *The concept of the goddess* (London, 1996), pp 141–51.   55 'Literary sea-voyages and early Munster hagiography' in R. Black, W. Gillies and R. Ó Maolalaigh (eds), *Celtic connections: proceedings of the Tenth International Congress of Celtic Studies*, vol. 1 (East Linton, 1999), pp 182–9; 'The legend of St Scothíne: perspectives from early Christian Ireland', *StH*, 31 (2000–1), 27–35.

Táin bó Cúailnge, hagiography and history

T.M. CHARLES-EDWARDS

Máire Herbert has done equally distinguished work on Irish vernacular saga, hagiography, and history. This essay is offered in grateful recognition of her contribution in all three fields. It seeks to answer a question about the date of Recension 1 of *Táin bó Cúailnge*, once undoubted accretions have been set aside. By these accretions is meant, first, the text in Lebor na hUidre but not in the Yellow Book of Lecan (where the testimony of both manuscripts is available); secondly, the section called *Breslech mór Maige Muirthemne*; and, thirdly, *Comrac Fir Diad ocus Con Culaind*.[1] I accept Thurneysen's view that the Old Irish text (or texts)[2] left after these accretions have been discounted already contained material from other versions. There is every reason to think that a long tradition, both oral and written, lay behind the Old Irish text. In order to give an approximate date to the Old Irish *Táin*, it is necessary to identify elements in the text that derive from earlier strata and should not be used as direct evidence for the date of the Old Irish *Táin*. Also, as we shall see later, some scholars have tried to give a close date for the Old Irish *Táin* based on the notion that it is an allegorical text referring to particular circumstances in the history of Armagh. This paper will be less ambitious: its aim is to discover the approximate period into which the text fits most comfortably. Although some references to the Ireland of the *Táin* will belong to an imagined pre-Christian past, others will belong to contemporary Ireland.

Some Irish law tracts of the seventh and early-eighth centuries draw a distinction between two peoples within the northern half of Ireland: the Féni and the Ulaid, or Ulstermen. One of these texts, a tract on the law of bees, has a brief passage on a strange incident supposed to have occurred before the death in battle of Congal Cáech ('the One-Eyed'), king of the Ulaid, in 637. Congal had earlier been king of Tara and thus the leading king in Ireland; but to be king of Tara he had to be physically perfect; and, according to the tract, he was

A shorter version of the paper was given as a Beckett Lecture, Queen's University Belfast, 26 April 2007, and I would like to thank my hosts and my audience for their kindness on that occasion.   1 *TBCi* ll 2072–2234 and ll 2367–3142. For Thurneysen's list of accretions subsequent to the two old written versions which he posited and dated to the ninth century, see his *Die irische Helden- und Königsage bis zum 17. Jahrhundert* (Halle an der Saale, 1921), pp 102–7. It is more extensive than the list assumed here. The evolution of ideas about the transmission of the *Táin* is admirably discussed by Ruairí Ó hUiginn, 'The background and development of *Táin bó Cúailnge*' in J.P. Mallory (ed.), *Aspects of the Táin* (Belfast, 1992), pp 29–67.   2 'Texts' in the plural allows for Thurneysen's pair of Old Irish versions, A and B: *Heldensage*, pp 107–8.

blinded in one eye by a bee-sting and was therefore put out of the kingship of Tara. Congal was said to have charged the owner of the bees with the injury and by the joint judgement of the Ulaid and the Féni it was decided that the whole hive was liable for the offence of a single bee.[3] The text, by claiming that the Ulstermen participated in the legal process, even though one element of that process was the removal of Congal from the kingship of Tara, portrayed the judgement as the united decision of the Ulaid and the Féni, namely of two out of the three 'chief *cenéla* in Ireland' as the saga of Fergus mac Leiti[4] describes them: the Féni, the Ulstermen, and the Leinstermen (there called *Gailni*).[5] Admittedly, the Ulaid proper (of what is now Co. Down) may have had reason to be undisturbed by the ejection of Congal, since he was of the Cruithni, but *Bechbretha* does not mention his Cruithnian background. Congal was the last non-Uí Néill king of Tara until Brian Bórama at the end of the tenth century. In the seventh century, therefore, Ireland was moving from a period when the kingship of Tara was shared between more than one people in Ireland, including the Ulstermen, into a period when it was confined to one people, the Féni, and one great family of dynasties, Uí Néill.

Three major battles form the stages in which the Ulstermen declined in power and their province in size: the battle of Móin Dairi Lothair in 562, the battle of Mag Roth in 637, and the battle of Fochart in 735.[6] The first saw the loss of territory between the Foyle and the lower Bann; the second ended the period in which a king of Ulster might realistically hope to be king of Tara; and the third, to which I shall return later, saw the loss of control over the lands that now form the northern two-thirds of Co. Louth, from the river Dee roughly to the boundary between Co. Louth and Counties Armagh and Down. What was left was the land to the east of the Bann. Two qualifications must be made to this broad picture. First, on particular occasions old loyalties might resurface. After the battles of Móin Dairi Lothair and Mag Roth, but before the battle of Fochart, the first entry in the Chronicle of Ireland for AD 698 reveals an alliance between a king of the Airthir (in Co. Armagh and including Armagh itself and Emain Macha) and a king of Dál nAraidi (at this date referring to one of the Cruithnian peoples of Ulster). The two kings said to have been killed in this battle in Fernmag (from Clones to Monaghan Town) were Conchobor Machae, king of the Airthir, and Áed of Ardd, king of Dál nAraidi. According to the conventions of early Irish chronicling, both should have been on the defeated side in the battle and therefore allies. Conchobor Machae's

---

3 T.M. Charles-Edwards and Fergus Kelly (ed. and trans.), *Bechbretha: an Old Irish law-tract on bee-keeping* (Dublin, 1983), §§30–5. 4 For this form, see Ruairí Ó hUiginn, 'Fergus, Russ and Rudraige: a brief biography of Fergus mac Róich', *Emania*, 11 (1993), 31–49 at 35–6. 5 D.A. Binchy, 'The saga of Fergus mac Léti', *Ériu*, 16 (1952), 33–48 at 37. 6 For the significance of the first, see F.J. Byrne, 'The Ireland of St Columba' in J.L. McCracken (ed.), *Historical Studies*, 5 (London, 1965), pp 37–58; for the second and third, see idem, *Irish kings and high-kings* (London, 1973), pp 112–14, 117–18.

kingdom lay outside the Ulster of the late-seventh century; and yet his name evoked the legendary king of the Ulaid, Conchobor, and his alliance was with a king within the current Ulster. We shall see later that a similar complexity formed a crucial part of the context for *Táin bó Cúailnge*.

Yet, at the same time as this decline in the power and territorial extent of Ulster, one collection of tales in the narrative literature of the northern half of Ireland – that is, from the Liffey northwards – emerged in a dominant position, a collection that modern scholarship calls the Ulster Cycle. This name is appropriate, since the unity of the Cycle is established by a central cast of characters, most of whom are Ulstermen: Conchobor, king of the Ulaid; Cú Chulainn, his sister's son; Conall Cernach, Cú Chulainn's foster-brother; and Fergus, the Ulster hero driven into exile. Some of this central cast are, however, of the Connachta, namely the enemies of the Ulaid, ruled by Ailill and Medb from Crúachain (Rathcroghan in Co. Roscommon). If, then, we examine early Irish narrative tradition as a whole, we soon find that most provinces have their own narrative, just as one collection in a twelfth-century manuscript was called 'the narrative tradition of Leinster' (*Scélsenchas Laigen*); Connaught, however, is largely without its own early collection of tales – apart, that is, from the Ulster Cycle. One way of looking at the Ulster Cycle is thus as an Ulster-Connaught Cycle.[7] It is also paradoxical that the first surviving copy of many of the Ulster sagas is Lebor na hUidre, a manuscript written by scribes belonging to Clonmacnois, a monastery on the Meath side of the Shannon but also a church enjoying exceptional power in the province of Connaught across the river.[8] It becomes less paradoxical once one realizes that the Ulster Cycle also has a significant Connaught component.

A further problem is what churchmen made of the heroic narrative that they shaped and preserved. Two main forms of narrative survive from pre-Viking Ireland: saga and hagiography. Although hagiography eventually made its way into Irish, it began in Latin, and its subject-matter was the heroes of early Irish Christianity. Saga was from the first in Irish; and the heroes of the Ulster Cycle belonged to the centuries before St Patrick. It is full of violent death, *aided*, known in Hiberno-Latin as *iugulatio* and perceived as a characteristic phenomenon of a secular world ripe for hell-fire. Adomnán, in his Life of Columba, rebuked his monks for talking about two kings of Tara, Columba's own kinsmen: 'My dear sons, why do you gossip idly about these kings? For both of those you mention were recently killed by their enemies, and their heads cut off'.[9] By this standard, the entire Ulster Cycle was at best idle gossip,

7 So James Carney, 'Language and literature to 1169' in D. Ó Cróinín (ed.), *A new history of Ireland*, i, *Prehistoric and early Ireland* (Oxford, 2005), pp 451–510 at p. 468: 'The Ulster-Connacht tales'. The early eighth-century *Táin bó Froích* is an example of an Ulster Cycle tale attached more closely to Connaught than to Ulster.   8 Tírechán, *Collectanea*, 25.1, 47.4, in Ludwig Bieler (ed. and trans.), *The Patrician texts in the Book of Armagh* (Dublin, 1979), pp 142, 160; *CGSH* §729.2.   9 Adomnán, *Vita Sancti Columbae*, i, 12, in

unworthy of precious parchment. Yet our earliest version of the central text of the Ulster Cycle, *Táin bó Cúailnge*, goes back to a written text or texts dated not long after Adomnán wrote those words, and another, more peripheral saga, *Táin bó Froích*, was written within a few years of the Life of Columba.[10]

An editorial note throws a brief but revealing light on the transmission of the earliest version of *Táin bó Cúailnge*. One of the principal strands in the text is the relationship between the older warrior, Fergus mac Róich, and his foster-son, Cú Chulainn. Fergus was in exile among the Connachta, and was the lover of their queen, Medb. At an earlier stage, Ailill, the cuckolded husband of Medb, had sent his charioteer to spy on one of the couple's assignations, in the course of which he succeeded in removing Fergus' sword from its sheath and taking it back to Ailill. Now, however, Ailill and Medb wanted Fergus to challenge his foster-son to single combat. Fergus was naturally unwilling, but he could never refuse an offer of drink, and so they got him drunk on wine, and sent him tottering on his way. Fergus, however, was still without his sword, and Cú Chulainn was entirely aware of his predicament:

> 'It's with a guarantor [of safety] you are coming to encounter me, master Fergus', said he, 'without a sword in a sheath'.

The text then notes:

> For Ailill had stolen it away, *ut praediximus* ('as we have said').[11]

This explanatory note, referring back to an earlier point of the narrative, is partly in Irish and partly in Latin; the Irish part contains a construction more common in the eighth than in the ninth century, while the addition of the Latin tag is a sure sign of a scholarly editor.[12] Like the laws, the *Táin* appears to have been considered worthy of learned annotation almost from the beginning of its written transmission, something which is not true to the same extent of the other Ulster sagas.

A.O. Anderson and M.O. Anderson (eds), *Adomnán's Life of Columba* (Oxford, 1991), p. 36: 'O filioli, quare inaniter de hís síc confabulamini? Nam illi ambo reges de quibus nunc sermocinamini nuper ab inimicís decapitati disperierunt'; Richard Sharpe (trans.), *Adomnán of Iona: Life of St Columba* (London, 1995), p. 121. 10 For the date of *TBC1*, see below; for that of *Táin bó Froích*, see Wolfgang Meid's edition, *Táin bó Fraích* (Dublin, 1967), pp xxiv–xxv. 11 *TBC1* l. 2508: '"Is co nglinni dothéig ar mo chend-sa, a popa Fergus," ol sé, "cen claideb inna intiuch". – Ar gatsai Ailill ass ut praediximus'. The reading is confirmed by the YBL version: John Strachan and J.G. O'Keeffe (eds), *The Táin bó Cúailnge from the Yellow Book of Lecan* (Dublin, 1912), ll 2149–50. Cf. *TBC1* ll 1233–4, where the phrase 'as we have said' is in relatively late Irish, and thus probably translated at a late stage from Latin *ut praediximus*, and compare also Thurneysen's preference in his edition of *Scéla mucce Meic Dathó* (Dublin, 1935), §3 l. 5, for TCD MS H.3.18's reading *dixit* as opposed to the Book of Leinster's *ro ráid* and Harleian MS 5280's *idbert*. 12 Liam Breatnach, 'The suffixed pronouns in Early Irish', *Celtica*, 12 (1977), 75–107, esp.

There are good historical reasons for thinking that the early written version or versions of the *Táin* – versions lying behind Recension 1 – belonged to the eighth century; and that we can trace at least some materials out of which these were composed back into the seventh. The *Táin* was a cattle-raid with a difference: the occasion was a mysterious weakness that periodically beset the Ulstermen; yet their enemies could not use this weakness to attack them directly, since anyone who did so only transferred the same affliction (or worse) to themselves.[13] Instead, the plan was to carry off the great bull of Cúailnge, the small kingdom occupying the Cooley peninsula on the south side of Carlingford Lough. While the main part of her army was in Cúailnge searching for the bull, Medb with a third of her army went to look for it in the neighbouring kingdom of Cuib or Mag Coba (roughly the diocese of Dromore); she took the opportunity to make a raid northwards 'to harry the Ulaid and the Cruithni as far as Dún Sobairche'.[14] Slightly later, we are told that Dún Sobairche (Dunseverick) was 'in the territory of Dál Ríatai'.[15] The lands ravaged by Medb were the province of Ulster as it existed after the battle of Fochart in 735, when the king of Ulster was defeated and beheaded.[16] Moreover, by dividing the province between three major groups – Ulaid or Ulstermen proper, Cruithni, and Dál Ríata – the saga shows that it took for granted the standard picture of Ulster up to the end of the eighth century; after that, the term 'Cruithni' fell out of normal use.[17] This also shows that the saga had no truck with the plea made by the Cruithni that they were 'the true Ulstermen' (*fir-Ulaid*).[18] The text's use of 'Cruithni' rather than 'Dál nAraidi' makes it easier to place it before *c.*800 rather than after.

A background element in the *Táin*'s conception of Irish politics can, however, be traced back into the seventh century, to a period when dominance in the northern half of Ireland was disputed between the Ulaid and the Féni. I

102–3 (the ratios given for *TBCI* are closer to *Táin bó Froích* than to any other text in the list).   **13** *TBCI* ll 525–9; Vernam Hull, '*Noínden Ulad*: the debility of the Ulidians', *Celtica*, 8 (1968), 1–42 at 38 §§7–8.   **14** *TBCI* ll 1488–9.   **15** *TBCI* ll 1533–4.   **16** That the lands of the Ulaid, the Cruithni, and Dál Ríata constituted the province is shown by *TBCI* ll 1431–2.   **17** The last example in *AU* of someone entitled 'king of the Cruithni' is in an obit in 774; after that date, we get only kings of Dál nAraidi: *AU* 790, 792, 825 etc. See Thomas F. O'Rahilly, *Early Irish history and mythology* (Dublin, 1946), p. 344; but the reason for the obsolescence of Cruithni given by O'Rahilly (ibid. p. 345) is unlikely to be correct. What was probably important was the increasing domination, within the Cruithni, of the dynasty of Mag Line: T.M. Charles-Edwards, 'The province of Ulster in the early Middle Ages' in C.J. Lynn and J.A. McDowell (eds), *Deer Park Farms: the excavation of a raised rath in the Glenarm Valley, Co. Antrim* (Belfast, 2011), pp 40–60 at pp 42–3.   **18** *CGH* p. 275 (156b45). The origins of this claim are likely to go back to the eighth or ninth century, since the capacity of the Cruithni (especially Dál nAraidi and Uí Echach Coba) to share in the kingship of the province declined sharply after the late ninth century. A relatively early date is also indicated by *CGH* p. 154 (143a15), since this text predates the rise of Uí Briúin Bréifne from the late ninth century. For this reason, it is

have already mentioned the early saga about an Ulster king, Fergus mac Leiti, transmitted in company with legal texts. This begins by declaring that there were three 'free' or 'noble' (*sóer*) *cenéla*, 'kindreds' or 'races', in Ireland: the Féni, the Ulaid, and the Gailni or Gaileóin; the Féni were the dominant people of the midlands, the west, and most of Munster, the Ulaid were the Ulstermen, and the Gaileóin the Leinstermen. This agrees with *Bechbretha*, with which we started, except that the latter had no interest in the Leinstermen. When the host of Ailill and Medb set out from Crúachain, one contingent, that of the Leinstermen, put all the others to shame by its speed in making encampment. In terms of the late-eighth century, this should not have been a problem. For much of the text, the forces arrayed against the Ulstermen are named as 'the four (other) provinces of Ireland' or 'the men of Ireland';[19] the Leinstermen were merely the contingent from one of these four provinces. Yet, once we put the plot back into the seventh century, Medb's behaviour starts to make more sense: the other contingents came from the Féni, to whom the Gaileóin or Leinstermen did not belong; so the better discipline of the Leinstermen threatened to exacerbate a major potential split in Medb's army between Féni and Leinstermen. Some small details shown that the name Féni was still present in the background of our earliest text – although, by the second half of the eighth century, it seems not to have been a current term in the sense of one among the peoples of Ireland. In the laws, we can see it shifting to mean free Irishmen in general, thus including the Ulstermen and the Leinstermen.[20] When the army of Ailill and Medb had reached eastern Mide on their way home, Conchobor, king of the Ulaid, and Celtchair, a vassal-king based at Downpatrick, attacked them and went off with eight score heads from 'the Ford of Eastern Mide', 'and it is from that it is called the Ford of the Féni'.[21] The editors of the *Historical dictionary of Gaelic placenames* take this name to mean 'Ford of Warrior Band', in other words, as containing *féne*, genitive singular of the feminine ā-stem noun *fian*, rather than *Féne*, genitive plural of the *io*-stem plural name *Féni*.[22] As an etymology, this may be correct, but as an interpretation of the way the name is used in the *Táin* it is much less plausible. First, place-names arising out of the killing of men in the *Táin* are regularly derived from the names of the victims, not of the victors; but Conchobor

---

less attractive to consider Bangor (whose patron-saint and founder, Comgall, was a Cruithnian) as a likely place of origin for the *Táin*, which shows no sign of such views, as proposed by Ó hUiginn, 'Background and development', p. 62. **19** *Fir Érenn*: *TBC1* ll 1334, 2089, 2331, 3397, 3942, 3945 (heading), 3982. *cethair cóiced Érenn*: ll 21, 2073, 2079, 2101, 2141–2, 2295–6, 2304. **20** For example, the original introduction to the *Senchas Már* (R. Thurneysen, 'Aus dem irischen Recht IV', *ZCP*, 16 [1927], 167–230 at 174–81 §1) describes itself as the '*Senchas* of the men of Ireland', but later in the same text rules are said to be upheld *la Féniu*, 'by the Féni'. **21** 'Men of Ireland' = Féni implied by *TBC1* l. 3513 (less explicitly ll 1026, 1233). **22** *HDGP* i, p. 132. The name is probably attested at *AU* 796.6.

has just referred to his enemies as 'Men of Ireland', *Fir Érend*; and it is eight score of the men of Ireland, *alias* Féni, that he and Celtchair have decapitated at Áth Féne. Here, therefore, so the snippet of narrative implies, the Féni were the enemies of the Ulstermen. Two other examples of Féni in the *Táin* are in poems labelled as *roscada* in Lebor na hUidre; a third possible example may instead be the genitive singular of *fian*, since Conchobor is described as *rí féne* 'king of a warrior-band' (rather than 'of the Féni').[23]

Confirmation that our earliest version of the *Táin* belongs to the eighth rather than to the seventh century is given by other details of its political geography. One of the more mobile peoples of pre-Viking Ireland were the Fir Rois: in the time of Adomnán, *c.*700, they were merely a component part of the Mugdorna, settled around Carrickmacross in the south of Co. Monaghan;[24] by the time of the *Tripartite Life* of Patrick, they were an independent kingdom that claimed the lands to the south-east as far as the monastery of Land Léire (modern Dunleer), north of Drogheda.[25] In the *Táin*, Crích Rois included the land around Ardee in Co. Louth, and we are thus close to the situation depicted in the *Tripartite Life*.[26] On the other hand, elsewhere there are indications of an earlier situation, corresponding to that depicted in Muirchú's Life of Patrick at the end of the seventh century, when the Conailli Muirthemne were the northern neighbours of Brega, without any intrusive Crích Rois.[27] We are, therefore, reasonably safe in assuming a date no earlier than the second half of the eighth century for Recension 1 of the *Táin*.

Similarly, if, following Kay Muhr, we reject Thurneysen's suggestion that the passage on 'The mustering of the Ulstermen' was a later addition, it also offers some suggestive evidence, since it indicates that, on the western side of

---

23 *TBC1* ll 200 (*roscad*), 635 (Conchobor is *rí Féne*, translated 'king of the Fían' by Cecile O'Rahilly, but this seems to be anachronistic), 2436 (*roscad*).   24 Adomnán, *Vita Sancti Columbae*, i, 43 (Anderson and Anderson, *Adomnán's Life*, pp 76–8).   25 Kathleen Mulchrone (ed.), *Bethu Phátraic* (Dublin, 1939), ll 2159–60; Diarmuid Mac Íomhair, 'The boundaries of Fir Rois', *Journal of the Louth Archaeological Society*, 15, ii (1962), 144–79; idem, 'The history of Fir Rois', ibid., 15, iv (1964), 321–48.   26 Crích Rois: *TBC1* ll 2519, 3293, 3301, 3319. Fergus encounters Cú Chulainn at Áth Dá Ferta, l. 2496 (*HDGP* i, p. 126, suggests a ford over the river Fane, at Knockbridge, tl. Loughantarve, par. Louth, Co. Louth, National Grid H 98 03), after which the host goes southwards past Cú Chulainn and encamps in Crích Rois. By l. 2548, they are close to Áth Fir Diad on the river Dee (National Grid N 96 90). In l. 3301, Smirommair is ascribed to Crích Rois, and this is likely to be Smarmore, south of Ardee (*OnomG* s.n.). On this basis, both the monastery of Louth and Ardee would be within Crích Rois. This indicates a situation close to that indicated by the *Tripartite Life*. Cf. *AU* 827.7, 847.6, 851.7; obits of members of the royal line (but not entitled kings of Fir Rois or Crích Rois) are given for the years 740 and 759. A later situation is revealed by the *Tripartite Life* and a still later one by the earlier version of *Aislinge Meic Con Glinne*, ed. Kuno Meyer, *The vision of MacConglinne* (London, 1892), p. 114 (H.3.18 version), where Cremthann is between Magh Muirthemne and Crích Rois, which itself is situated (at that date) further south, just before Tailtiu.   27 In *TBC1* l. 947, the river Níth (river Dee) seems to have the Conailli to the north and Brega to the south (cf. l. 954).

Ireland, the Ulster of the *Táin* came as far south as the river Drowes and, on the eastern side, as far south as the Boyne.[28] So far as the eastern side is concerned, Ulster had not extended to the Boyne for a long time before the likely date of the text (which includes Tailtiu within Ulster).[29] But, on the west side, the Drowes was the boundary between the Connachta and 'The North' by the time of the *Tripartite Life*;[30] and much of the contents of the latter go back to the late-eighth century, as shown by the *Notulae* in the Book of Armagh, and yet another layer has reasonably been assigned to no later than *c.*830.[31] One cannot prove from the brief reference in the *Notulae* that the Drowes was already the frontier, but, in general, the *Notulae* are much closer to the *Tripartite Life* than they are to Tírechán.

The leading student of the Ulster Cycle, Rudolf Thurneysen, doubted whether the *Táin* as a single text could be taken further back.[32] In his view, this, much the longest of the Old Irish sagas, was created out of shorter narratives in the first half of the eighth century; this early version survived in oral tradition rather than in manuscript, but two new written versions were created in the ninth century; from these two, the archetype of the existing manuscript versions was compiled in the eleventh century. This history of the text allowed the uninterpolated written tradition to exhibit the state to which Irish had evolved by the ninth century, with minor updating, while allowing that the length and scope and much of the content might be a century or so older. The problem can be better appreciated when we remember that, in the Ulster Cycle, one group of tales is placed before the *Táin* and is, to a greater or lesser extent, presupposed by it. For example, a critical fact underlying the *Táin* is the exile of Fergus and other Ulster warriors, whose presence in Connaught gave Medb the confidence to challenge the honour of Ulster. We have two rival stories explaining why the exile took place.[33] Neither is itself part of the *Táin*, yet they form, with the *Táin*, parts of a single narrative

---

28 *TBC1* ll 3454–97; Kay Muhr, 'The location of the Ulster Cycle, part I: *Tóchustal Ulad*' in J.P. Mallory and G. Stockman (eds), *Ulidia: proceedings of the First International Conference on the Ulster Cycle of Tales* (Belfast, 1994), pp 149–58 at p. 150, proposes that this section represents 'the tales' own estimation of *Cóiced Conchobair* as from Drowes to the Boyne'. 29 Dáibhí Ó Cróinín, 'Ireland, 400–800' in idem (ed.), *A new history of Ireland*, i, pp 182–234 at p. 212; *TBC1* l. 3486. 30 Mulchrone, *Bethu Phátraic*, ll 1693–8, on Patrick's blessing the river Drowes, is followed by ll 1699–703, which marks the point at which the saint leaves the Connachta and then goes to Assaroe, Ess Rúaid, on the Erne, which is treated as within the lands of the Northern Uí Néill, as it is treated as within Ulster, in *TBC1* l. 3481 (cf. l. 942). The Drowes episode has its trace in the *Notulae*: Bieler, *Patrician texts*, p. 180 (5). In Tírechán, *Collectanea*, 46.4 (ibid., pp 158–60), the Drowes is also blessed but does not mark the frontier, to which Patrick does not come until 48.1. 31 F.J. Byrne and Pádraig Francis, 'Two Lives of Saint Patrick: *Vita secunda* and *Vita quarta*', *JRSAI*, 124 (1994), 5–117 at 6–7. 32 Thurneysen, *Heldensage*, pp 109–13. 33 (1) *Fochond loingse Fergusa meic Roig*, *LL* v, p. 1136; [a] ed. and trans. from the Glenmasan MS by Donald Mackinnon, *Celtic Review*, 1 (1905), 208–29; [b] ed. Vernam Hull, *ZCP*, 18 (1930), 293–8; (2) *Longes mac n-Uislenn*, ed. and trans. Vernam Hull (New York, 1949).

sequence. As this example also shows, there was not merely one version of this narrative sequence, just as the earliest text of the *Táin* itself refers to its own variant versions. Thurneysen's doubt was how far in time one could push back the situation existing by the middle of the eighth century, in which one exceptionally long text, *Táin bó Cúailnge*, was the central pillar around which other tales were arranged, so that those coming before the great cattle-raid were *remscéla* 'foretales', leading towards the *Táin*, while others, notably the death-tales, came afterwards. And one should note that, even by that stage, some sagas were not placed in this narrative sequence, but floated free.

Two poems in archaic style, *Verba Scáthaige* and *Conailla Medb míchuru*,[34] help to confirm the argument offered above, that some of the material found in the *Táin* goes back to the seventh century, but neither demonstrates that there was already a central text within the Ulster Cycle. Furthermore, if one accepts that the main substance of the Ulster Cycle was told orally before it acquired a new form as written literature,[35] it will be impossible to claim that a single very long saga dominated the rest, since it will have been up to each story-teller to choose where to place the divisions in the long narrative sequence; and he might well have done it differently on different occasions. The principal events of the *Táin* may already have been central to the sequence; but, to take one example, the 'childhood deeds', *macgnímrada*, of Cú Chulainn, might well have been told on a different night from the story of the cattle-raid itself, even though, in our written versions, they are recounted to Ailill and Medb by the Ulster exiles on the way to Cúailnge.[36]

A date for our earliest version of the *Táin* as a single written text is of considerable help in assessing the likely impact of this, the central tale of the Ulster Cycle, on contemporaries. Much of the action of the saga was on the fringes of the later province, in the neighbouring kingdoms of Cúailnge and Conailli Muirthemne, namely the part of Co. Louth north of the river Dee. What this area constituted in the seventh century was Ulster's share of the eastern plain of Ireland between the Mountains of Mourne and the Wicklow Mountains.

---

34 For the former: P.L. Henry, 'Verba Scáthaige', *Celtica*, 21 (1990), 191–207. A 'working text' of *Conailla Medb míchuru*, used in seminar by James Carney, is reproduced in David Sproule, 'Complex alliteration, full and unstressed rhyme, and the origin of *deibide*', *Ériu*, 38 (1987), 185–200 at 188–90; see subsequently, P.L. Henry, '*Conailla Medb míchuru* and the tradition of Fiacc son of Fergus' in S. Mac Mathúna and A. Ó Corráin (eds), *Miscellanea Celtica in memoriam Heinrich Wagner* (Uppsala, 1997), pp 53–70 at pp 60–9. See further James Carney, 'Early Irish literature: the state of research' in G. Mac Eoin, A. Ahlqvist and D. Ó hAodha (eds), *Proceedings of the Sixth International Congress of Celtic Studies* (Dublin, 1979), pp 113–30; Garret Olmstead, 'The earliest narrative version of the *Táin*,' *Emania*, 10 (1992), 5–17.   35 As maintained by Thurneysen, *Heldensage*, p. 112.   36 Moreover, the *macgnímrada* are the source for some of the strongest evidence noted by Thurneysen, *Heldensage*, p. 107, that the archetype was a compilation from at least two sources, since they show Conall Cernach as an Ulster exile together with Fergus: *TBCi* ll 486–7, 542, 607, as against ll 3479, 4067–71.

Muirchú's Life of St Patrick, written at the end of the seventh century, describes Patrick as sailing up the east coast of Ireland from Leinster, passing by Brega, Conailli Muirthemne, and then coming to Mag nInis, the heart of the historic Ulster in the south of Co. Down.[37]

A major change, however, followed the battle of Fochart in 735. This took place close to the church of Fochart in the northern part of Conailli territory, north of Dundalk but just to the south of the modern boundary between Co. Louth and Co. Armagh, with Co. Down not far away to the north-east. The church occupies the top of a hill giving a splendid view of the plain of Muirthemne to the south. Here a new king of Tara, Áed Allán from Cenél nEógain, defeated the king of Ulster, Áed Róin, who was hauled out of the church itself and decapitated.[38] After this battle, the Conailli, and with them the smaller client-kingdom of Cúailnge, came under the overlordship of the Uí Néill. Thus, in 756, the *Annals of Ulster* and the *Annals of Tigernach* have an entry recording that 'A hosting of the Leinstermen was summoned by Domnall against Níall, so that they were in Mag Muirthemne'.[39] Domnall was the current king of Tara and was based in Mide; Níall was his up-and-coming challenger and was the younger half-brother of the victor of 735, Áed Allán from Cenél nEógain; Níall would, indeed, be the next king of Tara; both of them, therefore, were kings from different branches of the Uí Néill. The part of Ulster in which much of the action of the *Táin* was played out was, by the middle of the eighth century, a land in contention between northern and midland branches of the Uí Néill; and the Uí Néill were in origin a branch of the Connachta, namely the very people who made the great cattle-raid to take the Brown Bull of Cúailnge. This was not forgotten: Áed Allán's great victory over the Leinstermen in 738, just three years after his victory over Ulster at Fochart, is described in the Chronicle of Ireland as a triumph for 'the descendants of Conn'.[40]

After 735, that was the situation at the level of grand politics; and yet the Conailli Muirthemne retained their own dynasty throughout this period, and in the genealogies it continued to be associated with Ulster.[41] Nor was that merely an antiquarian doctrine; in 752, eighteen years after the battle of Fochart and four years before Domnall summoned the Leinstermen to make a hosting to Muirthemne, the annals record the death of Foidmenn son of Fallach, king of Conailli Muirthemne.[42] His sister was the twelfth abbess of

---

37 Muirchú, *Vita S. Patricii*, I.11.3: Bieler, *Patrician texts*, p. 78.   38 *AU* 735.2; *ATig.* 734 (= 735); *AFM* 732 (= 735). The detail given by *AFM* that the king of Ulster was decapitated in the entrance to the church and the dative case of *durt[h]aigh* in *ATig.* suggest that the latter should read *a durt[h]aigh* 'from the church', rather than *a ndurt[h]aigh* translated by Stokes as 'into the oratory'.   39 *AU* 756.3: 'Slog*ad* Laighen la Domnall fri Niall co rabadu*r* i Maigh Muirtheimne'.   40 *AU*, *ATig.* 738.   41 *CGH* pp 324–7, where the Uí Echach Coba descend from Fothad mac Conaill maic Cruind ba druí, while the Conailli descend from Cairell mac Conaill maic Cruind ba druí, and the Book of Ballymote copy adds to Conall's name: 'Ō tāit U Conaill Murtemne sic inuenitur in Saltair Caisil'.   42 *AU* 752.7.

Killevy in the neighbouring kingdom of Mag Coba, and his daughter was the thirteenth.[43] Foidmenn's power straddled the boundary between the Conailli and the lands that still belonged unambiguously to Ulster.

The First Life of St Dar Ercae, *alias* St Monenna, the patron saint of Killevy, probably an abbreviation of one of the earlier Irish saints' Lives, explains the connection.[44] The first church occupied by St Dar Ercae was Fochart Muirthemne, the scene of the battle of 735 and of several encounters in the *Táin*;[45] moreover, she herself was, by paternal descent, of the Conailli.[46] However, she was born in Mag Coba to the north; and her main foundation, Killevy, on the slope of Slieve Gullion in the south of Co. Armagh, belonged to that kingdom. Her descent thus enabled the Conailli to claim the abbacy, but the location of the monastery made close relations between the Conailli and the Uí Echach Coba, rulers of Mag Coba, critical. Her adopted son, Luger, is said in the Life to have become bishop of the Conailli through her support, and to have founded the church of Rúscach in Cúailnge, namely what is now called 'The Priory' in Roosky just to the south of Carlingford.[47] As her death approached, she was visited by Eógan mac Conaill, described as a king ruling over three provinces, Muirthemne, Cúailnge, and Mag Coba, and as someone linked to the Conailli through his mother.[48] He was not, therefore, of the ruling dynasty of the Conailli of Muirthemne. The implication is that someone who belonged by dynasty to Mag Coba was overlord of the neighbouring kingdoms to the south, Muirthemne and Cúailnge. In the *Táin*, when the army of Ailill and Medb was approaching Cúailnge, the bull, namely the target of the expedition, removed itself from Cúailnge and hid 'in the secret places of Slieve Gullion', just as Dar Ercae herself left Fochart to settle 'in the hiding-places' of Slieve Gullion.[49] The topographies of much of the *Táin* and that of the Life of Dar Ercae are broadly the same.

Any such coincidence of local setting should not be taken too easily as evidence for the place of origin of the *Táin*. The difficulty is the mobility of those most likely to have developed the narrative sequence of the Ulster Cycle up to

43 Mario Esposito, 'The sources of Conchubranus's Life of St Monenna', *English Historical Review*, 35 (1920), 71–8 at 75–6. 44 A very early date, 600×624, was proposed by Esposito for the Life of which the extant version in the Codex Salmanticensis is an abbreviation, ibid., pp 74–6. Pádraig Ó Riain (*DIS* p. 495) sees the Salamancan Life as derived from the Life by Conchubranus, but Richard Sharpe, *Medieval Irish saints' Lives: an introduction to Vitae sanctorum Hiberniae* (Oxford, 1991), pp 396–7, regards the Salamancan Life (ed. Esposito, 'Conchubrani Vita Sanctae Monennae', *PRIA*, 28C (1910), 202–51) as independent of Conchubranus. The local topographical detail in the Salamancan Life makes Ó Riain's view difficult to accept. 45 *Vita S. Darercae* §18: *VSHH* pp 88–9. 46 Ibid., §1. 47 Ibid., §2; Lord Killanin and Michael V. Duignan, *The Shell guide to Ireland* (2nd ed.: London, 1967), p. 137 (National Grid J 190 105). 48 Ibid., §29. In Conchubranus' Life (§9, 234–5 of Esposito's ed.), Conall is king of Ireland and the Cobo of Mag Cobo is transmuted into a person. 49 *TBC1* ll 963, 998. In *Vita S. Darercae* §20, the saint is living *in latebris* at Killevy having left Fochart because of the din of worldly wedding-parties, so that she might hear the sweet conversation of her bridegroom, Christ, undisturbed by secular men (§18).

the eighth century, namely the *filid*, and those most likely to have written the earliest text of the *Táin*, churchmen. One example will be sufficient. In the west of Muirthemne, due west of Dundalk, lay the monastery of Inis Caín Dega (Inishkeen). The life of the patron saint, Daig mac Cairill, appears to be an abbreviated lectionary version of an earlier Life belonging to the eighth or ninth century.[50] It contains a story about the relationship of the saint, then a boy, to the great saint of Muirthemne, Mochta of Louth, a story intended to acknowledge the status of Mochta and his monastery, but to make it quite clear that Inishkeen was not subject to Louth, but rather to Clonmacnois.[51] The monastic rule in which he was trained was, however, said to have been that of Bangor, while his earliest ties were with Mo Laisse of Devenish. It will be helpful to bear this example in mind when considering proposals made by scholars to date and locate the writing of the early version of the *Táin*.

The first of these was made by the historian J.V. Kelleher in an article published in 1971.[52] Kelleher's theory has, more recently, been accepted without hesitation by another leading historian of early Ireland, Dáibhí Ó Cróinín, but rejected by Máire Herbert.[53] According to Kelleher, the *Táin* was 'brought forward and refurbished as a heartening political allegory for a cause in which Cuanu was deeply involved';[54] the cause in question was that of one claimant to the abbacy of Armagh, namely Artrí mac Conchobuir, against the claimant supported by the Cenél nEógain king, Níall Caille; and Cúanu was an abbot of Louth who, according to one set of annals, fell foul of Níall Caille's father, Áed Oirdnide; Cúanu himself was the compiler of a set of annals to which Kelleher ascribes two characteristics: first, that it was the text lying behind the Chronicle of Ireland, and, secondly, that it contained the pre-Patrician annals that were manipulated to assert 'the pre-eminence of the Táin'.[55] Artrí was backed in his claim to be abbot of Armagh by Cummuscach mac Cathail, king of Uí Chremthainn, whose royal seat was at Clogher, Co. Tyrone, and also by Muiredach son of Eochaid, king of Ulster; but Cummuscach was killed in the battle of Leth Cam, Níall Caille triumphed, and the king of Ulster fled.[56] Since

---

50 T.M. Charles-Edwards, 'The northern lectionary: a source for the *Codex Salmanticensis?*' in J. Cartwright (ed.), *Celtic hagiography and saints' cults* (Cardiff, 2003), pp 148–60. 51 *Vita S. Dagaei* §4: *VSHH* p. 390. 52 John V. Kelleher, 'The *Táin* and the annals', *Ériu*, 22 (1971), 107–27. 53 Dáibhí Ó Cróinín, 'Prosopographical analysis of *Táin bó Cuailnge* in a historical setting' in H.L.C. Tristram (ed.), *Neue Methoden der Epenforschung*, ScriptOralia 107 (Tübingen, 1998), pp 153–9 at pp 157–8; Máire Herbert, 'Reading recension 1 of the *Táin*' in R. Ó hUiginn and B. Ó Catháin (eds), *Ulidia 2: proceedings of the Second International Conference on the Ulster Cycle of Tales* (Maynooth, 2009), pp 208–17 at pp 208–9: 'There is no evidence to support the proposition that Irish heroic tales were to be read as allegorized narrative'. 54 Kelleher, 'The *Táin* and the annals', 122. 55 Ibid. The manipulation is supposed to be shown by the difference between *Do flaithiusaib Hérend* and *ATig.* in the treatment of the Ulster heroes; yet the former is in fact a text heavily abbreviated from the Clonmacnois Chronicle of the tenth century (which was also the source of *ATig.*). 56 T.M. Charles-Edwards (trans.), *The chronicle of Ireland* (Liverpool, 2006),

the cause in which the *Táin* was 'brought forward and refurbished' perished on the battlefield, the text of the saga ceased to have any importance. But it was taken to Clonmacnois by Áedacán of Louth, son of the Torbach, abbot of Armagh, for whom the Book of Armagh was written, when he 'went in pilgrimage' to Clonmacnois in 835.[57] There it 'lay dormant for nearly three hundred years' until it was copied into Lebor na hUidre.[58] Kelleher, indeed, goes on to suggest that the *Táin* did not have the position of the centrepiece of the Ulster Cycle until the twelfth century, and that the copy in Lebor na hUidre, coupled with the references to the Ulster heroes in the pre-Patrician annals, was responsible for its subsequent fame.

There is no doubt that Kelleher's reconstruction of the prehistory of the Lebor na hUidre copy of the *Táin* is delightfully clever in the way it ties together so many things. The Louth connection accounts for the local topographical detail; Máel Muire, one of the scribes of Lebor na hUidre, who was killed in 1106, was himself a descendant of the Áedacán of Louth who went to Clonmacnois in 835; and it was Clonmacnois that preserved the annals giving the detail about the Ulster heroes. The dispute involving Armagh, 'The Height of Macha', so close to Emain Macha, supposed seat of Conchobor's kingship, might have encouraged the use of saga to support a claimant whose father was named Conchobor.

Yet, this scenario has very little chance of being correct. For one thing, references to the Ulster Cycle in the eighth-century laws show that it had already acquired an acknowledged pre-eminence right across Ireland: the references occur in Munster texts as well as those from the North.[59] Admittedly, what these references show is the pre-eminence of the Ulster Cycle rather than the pre-eminence of the *Táin* within that cycle; they do not, for example, contain the name of Cú Chulainn. However, the difficult text, *Verba Scáthaige*, is unlikely to be later than the early-eighth century; and it gives, in the words of Cú Chulainn's teacher in the martial arts, Scáthach, a prophecy of what awaits him during the *Táin*. Another poem of similar date, *Conailla Medb míchuru*, takes the exile of Fergus for granted; yet that was the precondition for the *Táin* and would have a merely genealogical significance if it did not have that consequence. Finally, given that even such an early text as *Táin bó Froích* is explicitly a *remscél* to *Táin bó Cúailnge*, too great a burden of proof is required to show that the *Táin* did not have a central position in the Ulster Cycle before the twelfth century.[60]

Kelleher did not, perhaps, need to claim that the *Táin* was little known before the twelfth century. What was critical for his argument was that the earliest version that we still have should have been, as he put it, 'refurbished'

827; it is only in the later additions in *CS* that Artrí is said to have been mother's brother to Cummuscach.   **57** *CS* 835.   **58** Kelleher, 'The *Táin* and the annals', 122.   **59** Liam Breatnach, *A companion to the Corpus iuris Hibernici* (Dublin, 2005), pp 362–7. See now Fangzhe Qiu, 'Narratives in early Irish law: a typological study' in A. Ahlqvist and P. O'Neill (eds), *Medieval Irish law: text and context* (Sydney, 2013), pp 111–41, esp. pp 123–4 and appendix.   **60** Meid, *Táin bó Fraích*, ll 166–7, 313–13, 325–7, 385–6.

in the year before the battle of Leth Cam in 827 and should then have been taken from Louth to Clonmacnois in 835.[61] If our earliest version were best understood as a political allegory for a particular struggle over the abbacy of Armagh, he could allow that other versions not refurbished for this particular purpose were widely known. Even in this modified form, however, his proposal fails to carry conviction. First, as we have seen, the evidence is, on balance, in favour of a date for the earliest surviving version in the second half of the eighth not the first half of the ninth century. Second, it is precisely on the details of how the political allegory is supposed to work that Kelleher is least forthcoming. Ailill and Medb, king and queen of the Connachta, would have to represent Níall Caille, of Cenél nEógain, while the alliance of Artrí mac Conchobuir, king of the Airgíalla, and Muiredach mac Echdach, king of the Ulaid, would be represented by Conchobor mac Nesa and Cú Chulainn. The Brown Bull of Cúailnge would presumably represent the abbacy of Armagh. This last proposal is, I think, a little hard to credit.

In any case, it is critical to distinguish between two very different things: first, an historical situation taken to be what a given text is about, as Kelleher thought that Recension 1 of the *Táin* was about the conflict over the abbacy of Armagh in 826–7; and, second, an historical situation with which a contemporary might compare an older text. Someone might say, perhaps, that the conflict of 826–7, uniting on one side a king of Ulster and a king of Airgíalla, recreated the greater Ulster of saga; but that would be an example of the way older texts might resonate in later conditions. It would not be the genesis of the story itself or even, as Kelleher puts it, the occasion when our earliest text was 'refurbished'. We must, therefore, keep separate the creation of a new saga or of a newly refurbished version of an old saga from, on the other hand, merely seeing a new significance in an old text. The one involves new text, the other only a new interpretation.

The same distinction is vital when considering a more recent proposal to date and locate the *Táin*, made by Pádraig Ó Riain.[62] He seeks to preserve what he sees as valuable in Kelleher's argument, namely that our *Táin* came into existence as a text written on behalf of one side in a dispute over the abbacy of Armagh; however, he objects to Kelleher's particular identification that there is 'a lack of a credible threat from the west', by which he clearly means from the Connachta.[63] Ó Riain's proposal is that what he calls 'the genesis of the *Táin*' arose from the combination of a law against cattle-rustling promoted under the aegis of a Connaught saint, Dar Í, and an abbot of Armagh, Núadu, who, quite exceptionally, came himself from Connaught, not far to the north of Crúachain, the royal seat of Ailill and Medb and the starting-point of the *Táin*, and who

61 Presumably between the death of Mac Loingsig (*AU* 826.3) or Flanngus / Fergus mac Loingsig, whose obit is placed by the Clonmacnois chronicles in 823 (Charles-Edwards, *Chronicle of Ireland*, 823.13). 62 Pádraig Ó Riain, 'A clue to the *Táin*?' in Mallory and Stockman (eds), *Ulidia*, pp 31–7. 63 Ibid., p. 31. In defence of Kelleher, one might argue that Ailech could be seen, from an Armagh standpoint, as being in the west.

was opposed at Armagh by a faction that included the dependent church of Louth. His assumption is that Núadu himself and his supporters promoted the Law of Dar Í, since, in 812, 'the law of Dar Í was promulgated among the Connachta', namely Núadu's home province.[64]

There are various difficulties created by this theory. First, it is critical that Núadu should have been a major force behind the promulgation of the law of Dar Í, first in his own province and then among the Uí Néill. Yet both these promulgations occurred after his death – the first very probably and the second quite certainly. Ó Riain is entirely aware of this difficulty and therefore proposes that the groundwork for the promulgation was established during Núadu's abbacy. At first sight, such an idea is entirely plausible, though there is no direct evidence to support it. What makes it a distinctly more risky assumption is that Núadu did indeed promulgate a law in Connaught, but that law was the law of Patrick, not the law of Dar Í.[65] Moreover, since the Chronicle of Ireland was, at this period, favourable to, and interested in, Armagh, it may be significant that no Armagh figure is associated with the promulgation of the Law of Dar Í either in Connaught or among the Uí Néill.

The participation of Louth in the opposition to Núadu within the community of St Patrick is a further assumption; indeed, there is no positive evidence that there was any serious opposition to Núadu. Ó Riain's argument is that, since the previous abbot, Torbach, came from Louth, Núadu's candidacy was likely to have started during Torbach's brief abbacy, and likely also to have been resented by Torbach's supporters. Another oddity in Ó Riain's case is the double function ascribed to Medb: the rivalry was primarily over the abbacy of Armagh, represented, as in Kelleher's interpretation, by the bull; the Connachta, and Medb in particular, were being accused of double standards – of stealing the bull and at the same time of making laws against cattle-rustling. Medb was both a representation of the female saint, Dar Í, in whose name the law against cattle-rustling was promoted, and a cattle-thief herself; and yet the accusation of cattle-theft should really have been directed against the living abbot of Armagh, Núadu from Connaught, rather than the dead saint, Dar Í. Again, therefore, it is possible to think that an old saga might have a new resonance in such a situation, but hardly that opposition to Núadu as abbot of Armagh was the genesis of the text.

The best approach to the origins of the Old Irish *Táin* has two prongs: first, the probable date in the second half of the eighth century, but with material going back into the seventh century; and, second, the contrast between the *Táin* and many of the other Ulster sagas. Neither *Fled Bricrenn* ('The feast of Bricriu'), nor *Mescae Ulad* ('The drunkenness of the Ulstermen'), have the close topographical concentration on one area of Ulster shown by the *Táin*. Moreover, they do not have the allegiance to the cause of Ulster

64 *AU* 812.   65 *AU* 811.1.

implicit in the *Táin*. Nicholas Aitchison's highly stimulating paper, 'The Ulster Cycle: heroic image and historical reality', made here, I think, a crucial error: it is easy to see some other Ulster sagas as implicit criticisms of secular aristocratic society, as part of a contrast drawn between Emain Macha and Ard Macha, Navan Fort and Armagh, but this is hardly a reasonable judgement on the *Táin* taken as a whole.[66] By the eighth century, as the legal evidence indicates, the Ulster Cycle was well-known throughout Ireland. Particular Ulster sagas, therefore, might have their origins outside the province and show no allegiance to it; but, at least from the second half of the century, the central text of the Cycle was *Táin bó Cúailnge*, and that makes a considerable difference to the impact of the Ulster Cycle as a whole.

The action of the *Táin* might be very briefly characterized by saying that it falls into three unequal parts. The first is the march of the army of Ailill and Medb towards Cúailnge, guided by Fergus, the exiled Ulster warrior and lover of Medb. It is crucial that Fergus delays the march by taking the army on detours out of his sense of kinship with his people, the Ulaid. The more the army is delayed, the better the prospects that the Ulaid will emerge from their mysterious weakness and come to rescue their lone champion Cú Chulainn and defeat the raiders. The central section is played out in the overkingdom of Conailli Muirthemne, of which Cúailnge was a client territory. It was also the homeland of Cú Chulainn. Here Ailill and Medb succeeded in seizing the Brown Bull of Cúailnge, but an agreement made between Ailill and Cú Chulainn, through Fergus as intermediary, fatally delayed the return of the raiders westwards.[67] Finally, the Ulaid emerged from their weakness just in time to catch the army of Ailill and Medb as it went through Mide. There the Ulaid won the battle, in large part because Fergus' relationship with his foster-son, Cú Chulainn, ensured that his prowess was ineffective: the heart of the *Táin* lies in the conflict of allegiance felt by Fergus: between his sexual partner, Medb, and, on the other side, his foster-son, Cú Chulainn, and his native land, Ulster. The two bulls, the Connaught bull Findbennach, and the Brown Bull of Cúailnge, had their battle, too, in which the Brown Bull triumphed only to die of his wounds. Even the victors lost the symbol of male force and political power about which the entire affair revolved.

The bulk of our earliest version, then, is set in the overkingdom of Conailli Muirthemne. From 735, this was dominated by rival branches of the Uí Néill. At the time of the seventh-century sources of our version, the Uí Néill were still considered to be one branch of the Connachta. In the eighth century, two earlier senses of identity were fading: that of the Féni as only one among the three leading peoples of Ireland and that of Uí Néill as one among the dynasties known as the Connachta. Our version of the *Táin* belongs to the period

66 *Journal of Medieval History*, 13 (1987), 87–116, esp. 103–14.   67 *TBCi* ll 1280–4 (trans. p. 160).

after these have faded, but the older situation is there underlying the text. Another sense of identity, however, did not fade: after the battle of Fochart, the Conailli continued to regard themselves as belonging to the province of Ulster, even while Cland Cholmáin and Cenél nEógain, now the leading branches of the Uí Néill, contended for lordship over Muirthemne. I do not think the earliest version of the *Táin* was specifically about this tension between the territorial distribution of power and the sense of where a people belonged, but it helps to understand the particular state of Ireland in which this version of the *Táin* was written. A loving attention to the landscape of Cúailnge and of Muirthemne, in which place after place is given its nook in the glory of Cú Chulainn's heroic defiance of Four Provinces of Ireland, occupies much of the central section of the *Táin*. Within the Ulster loyalties of the *Táin*, there is a closer loyalty to Muirthemne. The *Táin* remarks, as it tells of Medb's ravaging of the eighth-century province of Ulster, that Cú Chulainn followed Medb northwards into Cuib, but then 'turned back again into Mag Muirthemne. He preferred to guard his own homeland'.[68]

This does not justify us, however, in ascribing the *Táin* to the monastery of Louth, even though it was, at the time, the leading church of the Conailli. The earliest manuscript which we know to have contained Ulster sagas, even though it does not survive, was entitled 'the Quire' or 'the Book' of Druimm Snechta, a significant monastery among the Airgíalla, but very far from being one of their leading churches. A relatively unimportant church might well be the place where the *Táin* was written; moreover, Muirthemne had other important churches, such as Fochart or Inis Caín.

Kelleher asked a valuable question about the numerous places in Co. Louth named in the *Táin* – sometimes with genuine names, sometimes with fictional ones: 'what could a Munster or Connacht man, aristocrat or not, have made out of the many short place-name stories it [the *Táin*] contains, some of very small literary merit, about how this ford or that hill or dolmen in Cuailnge or Muirthemne got its name?'[69] The answer is, in part, that these lands were of critical political importance in the eighth century; in part, that major churches, such as Armagh and Clonmacnois, had close links with the area, Armagh with Louth and Clonmacnois with Inis Caín Dega. The armies of 'the North' subject to Cenél nEógain, of the Southern Uí Néill, and even, as in 756, of the Leinstermen all encamped within Mag Muirthemne. Few places in eighth-century Ireland played host to a wider section of the island's population. But, more broadly, many of the Irish, so it seems from *dindšenchas*, took delight in knowing their island, not just their own province, through saga. The land of Ireland was present to the Irish in their imagination, even when it was not present to them in their memory.

---

68 *TBCi* ll 1527–8: 'Tintaí Cú Chulaind aitheruch i mMag Murthemne. Ba diliu laiss imdegail a mennato fessin'.   69 Kelleher, 'The *Táin* and the annals', 126.

'An t-éitheach; is an fíor? ...':
a note on two late poems by Máire Mhac an tSaoi

PATRICIA COUGHLAN

Máire Mhac an tSaoi is the author of five poetry collections, beginning with *Margadh na saoire* (1956), followed after a seventeen-year gap by *Codladh an ghaiscígh* (1973), and three others in 1980, 1987, and 1999.[1] 2011 saw the publication of a dual-language selection of her poems, *An paróiste míorúilteach / The miraculous parish*, with largely newly commissioned English translations.[2]

Her most celebrated single work has been the remarkable, short seven-poem sequence 'Ceathrúintí Mháire Ní Ógáin', which won the Oireachtas prize in 1956 and appeared in her first collection.[3] In poetic accomplishment, erotic charge and emotional intensity, the 'Ceathrúintí' have been rightly admired as breaking new ground in twentieth-century Irish literature, and not least among Mhac an tSaoi's achievements in the sequence is her compelling and complex construction of a woman's poetic voice. While other single lyrics are also familiar parts of the canon and have been anthologized and taught, little critical attention has as yet been devoted to her later love-poetry. In this short essay I discuss two powerful poems from the 1980s and 1990s that further explore the themes and material on which the 'Ceathrúintí' so intensely focus, and in a sense – both aesthetically and emotionally – resolve the painful conflicts played out there, thus further developing this poet's earlier transformative contributions both to the traditions of love poetry, and to Irish women's achievements in poetry.

In a 2000 interview, Mhac an tSaoi remarked of her poems that 'the common theme is refusal'; when pressed, she defined this as the refusal to commit herself to another person.[4] But as we shall see her poetry shows that this 'refusal' is part of a far more complex cluster of meanings than this would suggest. In fact, her work is pervaded by recurring tensions between contending impulses and forces. On the one hand is the fierce assertion of

<hr/>

1 *Margadh na saoire* (BÁC, 1956), henceforth *MnaS*; *Codladh an ghaiscígh* (BÁC, 1973), henceforth *CanG*; *An cion go dtí seo* (BÁC, 1987), the volume which collects all prior work and adds twenty new poems, henceforth *CGDS*; *Shoa agus dánta eile* (BÁC, 1999), henceforth *SDE*. 2 Ed. Louis de Paor (Dublin and Indreabhán, 2011), henceforth *PM*. 3 See the excellent discussion by Bríona Nic Dhiarmada, 'Máire Mhac an tSaoi' in R. Ní Fhrighil (eag.), *Filíocht chomhaimseartha na Gaeilge* (BÁC, 2010), pp 15–27 at p. 20. 4 Harry Kreisler, 'Conversations with history. Conversation with Maire MacEntee', Berkeley, California, April 2000. Available at: <http://globetrotter.berkeley.edu/people/MacEntee/>.

autonomy in the emotional and especially the sexual domain; on the other, impulses towards connection, attachment, and mutual recognition between self and other. Closely associated with the former, the imperative of autonomy or agency, is that resistance to norms which she has herself named as a salient personality trait. A compelling quality of her writing is the sheer intensity of its emotional investment in a struggle to claim or constitute selfhood, and how rich a vein it mines, in terms both of its material (emotional, psychological) and of the poetic techniques deployed in working on it. Her focus on this theme coexists, of course, with her impeccable skill and exact ear in grafting her work onto the inherited forms and diction of earlier poetic tradition in Irish, especially the *dánta grádha*: in these respects also, her work is of considerable importance, since it engages so accurately with inherited forms and gestures, ultimately with important innovative effect.

I have written elsewhere about a notable strand within this knot of meanings, namely the negative and sometimes disturbing writing of women's reproductive roles.[5] A darker side to the warm loving maternality of her poems about children, this recurs repeatedly in contexts of emotional and especially sexual suffering. It includes the fantasy of an incubus-infant who aggressively bites the breast, poisoning the mother; the mother's inability to nurse, her breasts dry or her milk turned salt; nurture withheld and the child dashed from the breast; the torment of erotic jealousy compared with the inescapability of the embryo growing within; the experience of unhappy love likened to a pregnant woman's constant awareness of carrying the foetus 'féna coim', always within her body; and a lover's *absence* overseas felt as a *presence* in the woman's abdomen, in the place where an infant would have nested, though in reality none ever has. All of these scenarios occur in the figurative domain of the poetry, but they are none the less arresting.[6]

In the later collections, from *Codladh an ghaiscígh* (1973) onwards, however, such expressions of bitterness and self-abasement are less frequent, and opposite impulses gain purchase: towards connection, attachment, mutual recognition between self and other, and the sense of achieved insight, transcending emotional pain. The work registers this more positive writing of attachment not only in a few love-poems, including those I discuss below, but in several well-known, charming, and eloquent lyrics celebrating parenting and in particular mothering. These poems have, however, tended to be received in a somewhat essentialist way which takes maternal love as natural to a female poet and to the feminine speakers she constructs in her poems, thereby dulling the force of the ethical and emotional quest which is dis-

5 '"For nothing can be sole or whole / That has not been rent": torn motherhood in Mhac an tSaoi's "Love has pitched his mansion"' in L. de Paor (eag.), *Míorúilt an pharóiste: aistí ar fhilíocht Mháire Mhac an tSaoi* (Indreabhán, 2014), pp 41–62.   6 The poems referred to are: 'An dá thráigh' (*CanG*, p. 9); 'Ceathrúintí Mháire Ní Ógáin' V (*MnaS*, p. 62); 'Ceangal do Cheol Pop' (*CanG*, p. 21.).

cernible in Mhac an tSaoi's work, and which awaits more extensive critical analysis. In the Kreisler interview, she somewhat drily remarked: 'The "I" is not me. They are dramatic lyrics'. The context makes it probable that she was here referring specifically to 'Ceathrúintí' and associated work; but the notorious difficulty of maintaining awareness of the performative function of poetry and the fictionality of the lyric persona, as against a quasi-voyeuristic search for the raw expression of a biographical poet's intimate experience, is a pervasive theme in the criticism and scholarship of women's writing internationally.[7] Mhac an tSaoi's own clear-sighted focus on poetry as the practice of a craft is of course evident in the precision, grace and formal decorum of the poems themselves. T.S. Eliot tried to insist that 'the progress of an artist is … a continual extinction of personality', and Yeats, similarly, distanced the poet from what he called 'the bundle of accident and incoherence that sits down to breakfast'. Both were rehearsing the creed of high modernism, and both failed, of course, in dispelling biographical interest from their readers' minds.[8] In Mhac an tSaoi's case, this relation between poet and woman remains a site of exceptional defensiveness and contradiction; this is bound up with that internalization of misogyny I have already identified. Even late in her career, reviewing the *Penguin book of women poets* for *Innti*, she bemoans the domination of the collection by love-poetry, describes the pervasiveness of this as cloying and expresses a longing for intellect, while drily remarking that from time to time 'tiocfaidh tú ar cheardaí mná' ('you will come upon a craftswoman') whose skills are manifest in her poem.[9] Her resistance to 'faoistiniúlacht' ('confessionalism') and firm emphasis on the 'neamh-phearsantacht' ('impersonalism') of the traditional Irish poet-figure are well discussed by Nic Dhiarmada. Both Nic Dhiarmada and Louis de Paor, however, further observe how Mhac an tSaoi's later work, in de Paor's words, in a marked shift from her earlier practice, 'flouts the standard conventions of authorial discretion by exploiting the overlap between her private and public personae' … thus 'allowing the intimate to infiltrate the public, to reorder and to write it from within'.[10]

These counter-currents are important as context for the two poems I discuss here. Thematically, they explore deep concerns about the possibility and the ethics of self-realization in relation to an other. Taken together, they represent the conduct of such a relation as an always-in-process, never-completed, struggle for truly creative and fulfilling attachment. This human need

7 See Vicki Bertram, *Gendering poetry: contemporary women and men poets* (London, 2005); Jan Montefiore, *Feminism and poetry: language, experience, identity in women's writing* (London, 2003). 8 T.S. Eliot, 'Tradition and the individual talent', *The sacred wood* (London, 1950), pp 52–3; W.B. Yeats, 'A general introduction for my work' in E. Larrissy (ed.), *The major works* (Oxford, 2008), p. 379. 9 *Innti*, 5 (1978), 21. 10 de Paor, 'Contemporary poetry in Irish: 1940–2000' in M. Kelleher and P. O'Leary (eds), *Cambridge history of Irish literature*, 2 vols (Cambridge, 2006), ii (1890–2000), p. 327.

for connection can be expressed in different ways; in Mhac an tSaoi's work, it is often most intensely realized, in her own vivid expression, via 'cumann rúin an tsúsa' ('the secret love under the coverlet'), that 'domhan cúng rúin teolaí', the 'narrow secret warm world' of sexual love, which her poems render with such exceptional vividness and poignancy.[11]

The two poems I shall discuss – 'Collage' (*CGDS*, p. 107 [1981]) and 'Cian á thógaint díom' (*SDE*, p. 58 [1999]) – are widely separated by date of publication and also differ significantly in style and poetic register. But they belong together in the important sense that both clearly address the same intense transgressive love-affair that earlier yielded material for the 'Ceathrúintí', and that they mark two further stages, and emotionally signifi- cant advances, in the poetic persona's reflection on and processing of this painful and intense experience. Taken together, the two poems show the evo- lution of her thought about troubled human embodiment, and the closely associated questions of bodily and emotional attachment.

'Collage', which does not appear in the 2011 dual-language selection, delivers a mild shock to the reader of her previous work by openly identify- ing this hitherto unnamed lover, now he has died. This is a highly significant breach of a taboo which in this instance is more than merely conventional, as it is in the *dánta grádha* which so influence much of Mhac an tSaoi's own earlier work. In a 2008 interview, she says that in her youth one could write about sex freely in Irish 'because', as she puts it, 'no-one understood [it]', but that the lover who had occasioned many of her poems could not possibly be named because he was married and she was an unmarried young woman.[12] Here is the poem:

COLLAGE
Do Dháithí Ó hUaithne a d'éag 13 Meitheamh 1981

Oráit duit, a David, ós duit a bhí mo chéadchais?
But that
was
    in another country …

… Beo duit, do bhínn ad' chaoineadh –
Cár mhiste dhom do threascairt?
Ar nós bheithígh an Bhíobla
Ár stádar níl ach sealad;

11 Phrases from 'Cian á thógaint díom' (*SDE*, p. 58), and 'Ceathrúintí Mháire Ní Ógáin' II (*MnaS*, p. 60) respectively. 12 'Máire Mhac an tSaoi, file, scríbhneoir: agallamh le Páraic Breatnach', Broadcast on TG4, *Soiscéal Pháraic*, 2 January 2008. Available on youtube.com.

Sa gcolainn ár muinín,
Is de réir na colla ár séathlú –
Is an phaidir ghanfhiosaíochta,
An fearr í ná leabhar éithigh?

And yet,
God rest him
all road
ever he offended!
Amen.

COLLAGE
To Dáithí Ó hUaithne, who died 13 June 1981

A prayer for you, David, since you were my first love?
But that
was
in another country...

... In life, I wept over you –
Why should I care that you are felled?
Like the beasts in the Bible
Our life's span is short;
We trust in the body
And in the body we drain away –
And is a stealthy prayer
Better than a false oath?

And yet,
God rest him
all road
ever he offended!
Amen.[13]

This text is also macaronic and intertextual, all deliberate effects, and very different from the tightly restrained courtliness of earlier work such as 'A fhir dar fhulaingeas grá fé rún' (*MnaS*, p. 50; in Biddy Jenkinson's fine version 'Man for whom I suffered love / In secret', *PM*, pp 76–7). 'Collage', by contrast, conveys its theme of emotional contradiction and self-questioning in its very fracturing of the smooth surface of the conventional love-lyric. Indeed, three of the poem's eleven lines end with a question. There is also metrical

13 My translation.

disruption: though the central stanza does set up a norm of seven-syllable lines, this is varied at l. 7 (six syllables), and ll 8 and 9 (both eight syllables). The opening line is exceptionally long, and the two borrowed English lines are not only italicized, but set off typographically in a way which, to the eye, suggests a gravestone inscription. All these might be termed modernist effects, which make further evident the poem's resistance to smooth lyric closure and consolation.

Yet, while this mixed form of 'Collage' is itself an implicit rejection of traditional conventions, its long opening line uses an allusive vocabulary invoking appropriate Irish traditions to introduce the emotional problem posed by the death of the speaker's long-ago first love. The opening word 'Oráit', from Latin *oratio*, echoes grave-stone inscriptions enjoining the viewer to pray for the dead person's soul, and clearly alludes to Ó hUaithne's work as a major scholar of the early Irish language.[14] The expression 'mo chéad-chais' has a specific antecedent in *Dánta grádha*, no. 15, l. 26: 'duit tugas mo chéadchais'. Furthermore, it exploits the ambiguity of the term 'cais', which could mean both 'love' and 'hate' according to context.[15] This allusive line is followed at line 2 by the quotation of a well-known passage which occurs in two canonical English texts, namely Marlowe's play *The Jew of Malta* and T.S. Eliot's 'Portrait of a lady', and at line 11 by a part-line from Hopkins' sonnet elegy 'Felix Randal'.[16] These two English lines – one seeming cynical, the other compassionate – are symmetrically placed so as to frame the central stanza (ll 3–10) between them. This gesture of reaching for the words of others, and, what is more, for phrases prominently inscribed in another literary tradition, is itself eloquent and powerful, since it stages a kind of aporia or state of being at a loss. Mhac an tSaoi's persona casts about for an appropriate response (a prayer, or what?) to the death of her long-ago first lover, now at last named, and ends without finding one, or at least one which can be expressed in the poem's own language, namely Irish.

The Marlowe appropriation – 'But that was in another country' – is part of a scene where two friars accuse the eponymous villain-hero Barabas of various sins:

---

14 On Ó hUaithne's personality and his scholarship, see Proinsias Mac Aonghusa agus Tomás de Bhaldraithe (eag.), *Daithí Ó hUaithne: cuimhní cairde* (BÁC, 1994).   15 I thank Seán Ó Coiléain for this information concerning both terms, and for helpful discussion of Mhac an tSaoi's work. See *DIL* s.v. *cais* and Thomas F. O'Rahilly, *Dánta grádha: an anthology of Irish love poetry, A.D. 1350–1750* (Cork, 1926).   16 Hopkins' quatrain actually ends: 'Ah well, God rest him all road ever he offended': Mhac an tSaoi's modification 'And yet' suggests that in this case there have been real offences. 'Felix Randal the farrier' in W.H. Gardner and N. Mackenzie (eds), *Poems of Gerard Manley Hopkins* (New York, 1967), pp 86–7.

FRIAR BARNARDINE. Thou hast committed –
BARABAS. Fornication: but that was in another country;
And besides, the wench is dead.[17]

With ostensible delicacy Mhac an tSaoi omits the harsh words 'fornication' and 'wench', a tactic which, of course, fails to prevent them echoing in the informed reader's mind. As spoken by Barabas, we can presumably understand the remark as an expression of outright cynicism, carelessly discounting the dead 'wench' (since she is no longer alive to accuse him). Eliot, who quotes the full three lines, uses it as the epigraph to his early poem 'Portrait of a lady', a poem about a failed relationship between an older Boston society woman, constructed as predatory and accusing, and the hesitant ineffectual male persona who is clearly relieved to escape her attentions. Eliot's disavowal of aggression on the man's part, projecting it onto the woman's, may have suggested Mhac an tSaoi's striking reversal of the genders: here it is the 'wench' who lives to tell the tale, not the 'fornicator'. The passage might, alternatively, be understood as a gesture of exculpation for that 'fornication', with 'another country' signifying 'another time', thereby conferring a palliative distance on the pain of things done so long ago; but such softening is not explicit. There may be another faint verbal echo, of the celebrated opening sentence of L.P. Hartley's 1953 novel *The Go-Between*: 'The past is a foreign country: they do things differently there'. This ghost-resonance, if present, would strengthen the passage of time as a factor in altering the significance of acts and events.[18]

If the opening line ended with a question – to pray, or not to pray, for the dead 'David', here addressed intimately by his given name, as would the lover she once was – so too do ll 3–4 and also 9–10 which end this main stanza. In her *own* voice, then, the speaker seems able to express only uncertainty, a deficit of answers or enlightenment. We may understand the closing line – in Hopkins a prayer that God may forgive Randal's injuries of anyone else – as an answer to the first of her own poem's opening questions, whether formally to mourn her first love-object now he has died. But this strategy, particularly the displacement of the prayer onto another poet's voice and into another language, hardly answers the second, harsher, question at l. 3, namely why she should now mourn his death, as distinct from her grieving ('caoineadh') over the failure, while he was alive, of their clandestine love: 'cár mhiste dhom do threascairt?'

Mhac an tSaoi regularly uses biblical allusions as a powerful intertext for her work, though often below the surface of a line; here ll 5–6 'Ar nós bheithígh an Bhíobla / Ár stádar níl ach sealad' refers explicitly to one of the Old Testament's many expressions of impermanence and mortality: 'But man,

---

17 Christopher Marlowe, *The Jew of Malta*, ed. N.W. Bawcut (Manchester, 1997), iv, 1, ll 40–2.   **18** L.P. Hartley, *The Go-Between* (1953; repr. London, 1971), p. 7.

despite his riches, does not endure; he is like the beasts that perish' (Psalms 49:12). The inevitable fate of the 'beasts', namely to be slaughtered, gives a disturbing frisson to the word 'treascairt' used in l. 3 to mean 'death', strengthening its connotations of forcible bringing low, the felling of oxen or being violently overcome as if in a battle. The equation of animal and human dead is an expression of desolation, disavowing any possibility of transcendence: we merely perish like the dumb beasts. In l. 6, 'ár stádar níl ach sealad', the word 'stádar', which belongs specifically to Corca Dhuibhne vocabulary, suggests the duty of a sentry, soldier, policeman or watchman, to patrol a given 'beat'. Its alliterative conjunction with 'sealad' gives poignancy to the sense of temporariness of the allotted span with an inevitable term (Dinneen defines the related word 'sealaidhe' as 'one that takes a turn about at work' and 'one who relieves, as a guard, one working on a shift').[19]

At the outset, the poem's title has already suggested a bringing together of heterogeneous bits and pieces, forming a palimpsest that is deliberately unintegrated, ostensibly like a child's artwork, expressing the unresolved self-questioning and refusal of closure which is this text's defining act. The poem is further enriched by the bilingual word-play between the title-word 'Collage' and ll 7–8, 'Sa gcolainn ár muinín, / Is de réir na colla ár séathlú': we can do no other than live in the body, yet its dissolution always entails our being drained away. The concrete and domestic word 'séathlú' connotes the filtering or draining away of the fleshly body, as if sieving whey from curds, while the genitive 'colla' links, across languages, this spare, economical acknowledgement of physical mortality with the poet's own countervailing activity of trying to assemble stray affects into a coherent emotional whole, and the necessary failure (draining away) of this too. The following lines (9–10) engage in a heart-searching enquiry: is such a furtive, hidden prayer as this poem indeed preferable to the keeping of silence, analogous to perjury by omission? The text offers no definite answer. But in borrowing the Hopkins original, where the priest-speaker is blessing the dead blacksmith to whom he had ministered, it does assent to the gesture of forgiveness and blessing.

I turn now to 'Cian á thógaint díom' (*SDE*, p. 58), which returns later to the same nexus of events and experiences and is one of Mhac an tSaoi's very finest poems. The deliberate jaggedness of 'Collage' contrasts sharply with 'Cian ...', which builds intricately woven sentences, used with strong and regular assonantal and syllabic patterning which plays no small part in its beauty. Remarkably, with its three quatrains and a couplet it simultaneously suggests the sonnet-form, so dominant in Renaissance love-poetry in several European languages including English.

In *An paróiste míorúilteach*, de Paor relocates 'Cian' from its chronological order of composition 'in the interest of thematic continuity', placing it instead

19 *FGB* s.v. *sealaidhe*.

at the end of the 'Ceathrúintí ...' and 'An dá thráigh', poems from at least thirty years earlier (*PM*, p. 228). This offers a biographically coherent ending to the story of the love-affair that provided material for the 1950s work, and it does offer a satisfying sense of closure to the reader of this selection. Here I approach the poem from an alternative perspective chronologically, juxtaposing it rather with 'Collage' (1991), which is not reprinted in *An paróiste míorúilteach*, and focusing as much on the – contrasting – aesthetic character of these two poems, as on that primarily biographical coherence discussed above. In terms of Mhac an tSaoi's conscious artistic design, including that of her individual collections, we should note that 'Cian' is significantly placed as the final poem in the 1999 *SDE* volume. This implicitly indicates its intended function of providing closure for both this key body of poetic material and for the emotional negotiation it has entailed over decades of the poet's life. Here is the text.

CIAN Á THÓGAINT DÍOM

Do mheabhair is mó anois a bhraithim uaim –
Ní cuí dhom feasta cumann rúin an tsúsa –
Cleamhnas na hintinne, ná téann i ndísc,
A d'fhág an t-éasc im lár, an créacht ná dúnann.   4

An mó de bhlianaibh scartha dhúinn go beacht
Roimh lasadh im cheann don láchtaint seo taibhríodh dom?
Téann díom, ach staonfad fós den gcomhaireamh seasc,
Altaím an uain is ní cheistím an faoiseamh.   8

Milse ár gcomhluadar d'fhill orm trém néall,
Cling do chuileachtan leanann tréis na físe,
Do leath ár sonas tharainn mar an t-aer,
Bheith beo in éineacht, fiú gan cnaipe 'scaoileadh.   12

Do cheannfhionn dílis seirgthe i gcré
An t-éitheach; is an fíor? An aisling ghlé.

SORROW LIFTS FROM ME[20]

More than anything, it's your mind I feel the loss of now.
The love between the sheets has had its day
But the bond of mind, which never fades
Is what tears me, is the wound that never heals.

20 Translation by Peter Sirr, *PM*, p. 99 (reprinted with the author's permission).

> How many years exactly since we parted
> Before this brightening kindled like a waking dream?
> I can't remember, and will not count them, but
> Give thanks for the moment and not question its peace.
>
> The sweetness of our company came back to me in the dream,
> The chime of your pleasure still sounds in the room,
> Our joy spread round us like the air.
> Even if no button is undone, just to be alive together.
>
> This is the lie: your fair head withered in clay.
> And the truth? The clear vision in the brightening day.

Only in the closing couplet do we learn that this long-lost lover is dead; up to the shock of this penultimate line, it just seems like a long-finished sexual relationship, from which the speaker is recouping memories of companionship and intellectual converse. Line 13 – 'your fair head withered in clay' in Sirr's phrase – brings the first-time reader up short with the shock of physical mortality.

Thematically, 'Cian' sets up a strong body-mind binary, familiar from the traditions of European love-poetry in many languages. On the one hand is the concrete bodily-fluid-exchanging business of sexual relations, rendered in 'cumann rúin an tsúsa' (l. 2), 'gan cnaipe 'scaoileadh' (l. 12), and, as noted, 'do cheannfhionn dílis seirgthe i gcré' (l. 13). On the other are all those experiences of emotional and mental union, figured as brightening light, chiming as of a bell, and even as a radiant vision: 'do mheabhair' (l. 1), 'cleamhnas na hintinne, ná téann i ndísc' (l. 3), 'láchtaint' (l. 6), 'Cling do chuileachtan' (l. 10), 'Mílse ár gcomhluadar' (l. 9), 'Bheith beo in éineacht' (l. 12), and finally 'an aisling ghlé' (l. 14). This concluding line is divided, with technically brilliant poise, into three: the physical dissolution of the lover's body is shown as sheer falsehood; and the truth is the now luminously experienced dream-vision of their shared happiness. This may, however, be a chimera, like the lovely young woman in *aisling* poetry. So, while 'Cian' is recognisably a poem acknowledging the great poetic tradition renouncing physical love, it also diverges significantly from works in that tradition, in not following their usual path through disavowal of the body to any kind of explicit Christian transcendence.

Mhac an tSaoi maintains the antinomies throughout the poem until the very end. The 'love between the sheets' is relinquished and replaced by the imperishableness of 'cleamhnas na hintinne'. But this farewell to physical love is not readily achieved, nor is it as unequivocal as this formulation suggests. Certainly, the items standing for mental and emotional consolation are more numerous than those representing the stubborn body; but there is nevertheless an abiding sense of loss. One way in which this is figured, with perhaps uncomfortable vividness, is as 'an t-éasc im lár, an créacht ná dúnann' (l. 4). This image of an open wound, together with 'éasc' – a flaw in rock or timber, or a soft vein or breaking point (*FGB*, s.v.) – makes an undertow of non-assuaged bodiliness and pain, exerting its pull against all the assertions of emotional solace. The 'éasc im lár', in particular, recalls that cluster of disturbing recurrent imagery involving pregnancy, miscarriage and a failure of physical mothering in Mhac an tSaoi's earlier work.[21] Section V of 'Ceathrúintí Mháire Ní Ógáin' is also a striking intertext for this line of 'Cian', with its characterization of the unhappy female lover as 'i bpéin', like one perpetually pregnant: 'ag iompar cuileachtan de shíor / Mar bhean gin féna coim' (*MnaS*, p. 62).

The second quatrain, indeed, dwells on the sheer difficulty of relinquishing 'cumann rúin an tsúsa', acknowledging how protracted and unproductive a process it has been to mark the years since her loss ('comhaireamh seasc', l. 7). The dawning of this new insight in her mind is a relief upon which she seizes, but only after more years have passed than she could, barrenly, count. The concrete and humble metonymies of 'súsa' and 'cnaipe' may, like Gray's paths of glory, lead but to the grave, but there is something irreducible about their persistence alongside the exaltation which must override them. They retain a poignancy recalling the most electrifying passage in the 'Ceathrúintí' decades before:

> Beagbheann ar amhras daoine,
> Beagbheann ar chros na sagart,
> Ar gach ní ach bheith sínte
> Idir tú agus falla –
> II, 1–4 (*MnaS*, p. 88)
>
> Heedless of suspicion,
> Of prohibition by priests,
> Of everything but to be lying
> Between you and the wall –[22]

Both passages refer to items contiguous to the lovers' bodies – the bed-cover, the buttons on their clothes, the wall – rather than the bodies on or under or inside or beside these things. The naked erotic body is itself thereby masked in the language of both poems, and the only body-part actually mentioned is the 'ceannfhionn dílis', now denatured in the grave.

In the final outcome of the poem's meditation on the transience of sexual passion, the brightness of the speaker's concluding vision trumps bodily delight. This brightness is repeatedly expressed in the language of dreams:

21 Discussed at more length in Coughlan "'For nothing can be sole or whole / That has not been rent'". 22 My translation.

'... an láchtaint seo *taibhríodh* dom' (l. 6), 'Mílse ár gcomhluadar d'fhill orm *trém néall* (l. 9), and '... a leanann tréis na *fise*', all leading up to the climactic '*aisling* ghlé'. This dream-motif indicates a drawing upon inner experience and the self-capacity to attain meaning through memory and reflection. In this sense, the poem is secular, constructing the human memory of the key relationship as what is permanent, rather than turning to metaphysical transcendence. Yet there are religious associations in the language of the speaker's newly achieved insight, not only in the persistent imagery of light ('láchtaint', leading to 'ghlé'), but particularly in the lovely phrase 'cling do chuileachtan', which invests the lovers' recalled unity with the persisting resonance of a church or monastery bell whose chime hangs on the air – 'leanann' – even after the vision has faded (l. 10).

I have earlier noted the conflicted and complex relationship between femininity and poetry-making in Mhac an tSaoi's thought and in her work, as well as her insistent struggle for autonomy as a separate self, and the painful attenuation of that autonomy so powerfully played out in the earlier love-poems with their powerful and innovative invention of a frank woman speaker, and their countervailing impulses of misogyny. 'Collage', as I have sought to show, constitutes a brief but intense engagement with those earlier states of mind, and it arrives at a tentative, muted expression of forgiveness and of the capacity to relinquish and pass beyond the brutal language of 'wench' and 'fornication'. 'Cian', in which she returns after some years to this same biographical material, is perhaps especially remarkable for its triumphant establishment of a poise, both aesthetic and emotional, which balances and contains the pain and conflict of all the earlier work. Finally, and not of least importance, the speaker's state of mind also indicates that the agon of gender also seems to have ceased, in the light of that 'aisling ghlé' of human loving union which ultimately displaces its rhyme-word, 'cré', as truth does falsehood. One might say that 'Cian' ends what Freud described as 'the work of mourning', uncertainly and painfully begun with 'Collage' but now at last complete. Taken together, these poems reveal the continuing power and beauty of Máire Mhac an tSaoi's poetic imagination and strengthen her claim to more, and more sustained, critical and readerly attention.

'Pé rí bheas i gcoróin':
Seán Caoch Ó Cearbhaill agus an tiarna talún

PÁDRAIG DE BRÚN

Ar an dá thaobh de bhileoig (lgh 7–8) i LS 432 (23 B 4) in Acadamh Ríoga na hÉireann atá an t-amhrán so thíos, i script an Bhéarla, i litriú leath-fhoghraíochta, gan teideal ná ainm údair ag gabháil leis. Is léir, áfach, gur leis an Ráth Tuaidh, paróiste dúchais Mháire Herbert, a bhaineann sé. Is é an t-aon déantús filíochta Gaeilge amháin é a tháinig anuas chugainn ón bparóiste sin.[1] Uilliam Gun, leanbh mic le tiarna talún na Rátha féin agus roinnt bailte eile, is abhar don aiste, in aois a bhliana dhó, Máirt Chásca bliain éigin.

Ainm coitianta ag muintir Gun ab ea William, sa tslí nach cabhair ró-mhór é sin chun dáta a chur leis an amhrán. Bhí 'Will[ielm]us Gun de Rathoe, Gent.' ina bhall de 'Grand Jury' Chiarraí sa bhliain 1679.[2] Is dócha gurbh é seo William Gun 'of Rattoo', a cailleadh timpeall na bliana 1699. William eile a tháinig i gcomharbacht air sin. Fuair sé sin bás sa bhliain 1723.[3] Bhí mac aige dárbh ainm William chomh maith, ach níorbh é sin ach mac eile, Townsend Gun, a fuair an t-eastát ina dhiaidh.

Cailleadh Townsend Gun i 1766, tar éis dó an t-eastát a thabhairt ar láimh dá mhac, William Townsend Gun, ar phósadh dhó le 'Sarah dau. of Anthony Stoughton of Ballyhorgan' (sa pharóiste céanna), 17 Deireadh Fómhair 1765, 'on condition he keeps the Church of Ratto in good repair *for ever*'.[4]

Ní fios cathain a tháinig William Townsend Gun so ar an saol, ach mhair sé go dtí 1812. Bhí mac aige, William, 'second son[5] of the late William Townsend Gun, Esq., of Rattoo, in this County, and formerly for many years a Captain in the 91st Regiment of Foot', a cailleadh i mBaile Átha Cliath, Aibreán 1829.[6] Níl teacht ar dháta a bhreithe sin ach an oiread. Ar a

---

1 Stiofán Ó hAnnracháin, *Caint an Bhaile Dhuibh* (BÁC, 1964), lgh 11–12. 2 Mary Agnes Hickson, *Selections from old Kerry records, historical and genealogical, with introductory memoir, notes and appendix* (London [1st series], 1872), lch 261. 3 Sir Bernard Burke, *A genealogical and heraldic history of the landed gentry of Ireland*, revised by A.C. Fox-Davies, 3rd ed. (London, 1912), lch 284. 4 [Rosemary ffolliott], 'Abstracts of wills', *Irish Ancestor*, 5, i (1973), 53–62 ag 57. Níor mhiste dhó féachaint chun na heaglaise, dhealródh: '... near this [*sc.* the Round Tower] is the Parish Church, patch'd up out of the old buildings' (Pádraig Ó Maidín, 'Pococke's tour of south and south-west Ireland in 1758', *JCHAS*, 63 [1958], 73–94; 64 [1959], 35–56 ag 46). Bhí sí titithe i léig um 1806: 'No Church'; 'No Glebe House' (*Papers relating to the Established Church in Ireland* [presented to the House of Commons, ordered to be printed, 29 July 1807], lch 259). 5 B'é an tríú mac é do réir Burke, *Landed gentry of Ireland*, lch 285. 6 (*Chute's*) *Western Herald* (Tralee), 13 April 1829.

dheartháir críonna, Townsend Gun, a bhí ina ardshirriam sa bhliain 1809,[7] a thit oidhreacht na Rátha Tuaidh.

William Townsend Gun eile, mac le Townsend Gun, saolaíodh é ar 28 Bealtaine 1807 agus baisteadh i dTrá Lí é an lá ina dhiaidh sin.[8] Ní réitíonn dáta a bhreithe go ró-mhaith le tagairt an fhile do Mháirt Chásca. Bhí sé ina ardshirriam ar Chiarraí sa bhliain 1834 agus cailleadh é (gan pósadh) sa bhliain 1837.[9]

Bhí an chéad William Townsend Gun ina ardshirriam ar Chiarraí sa bhliain 1768, agus ina 'Resident Justice of the Peace' i 1785,[10] nithe a thiocfadh le dóchas an fhile (línte 11–12) go bhfásfadh an leanbh atá á mhóradh aige ina chara 'chun seasamh dúinne i bhfiúntas, má castar ann sinn ciontach go brách'. B'é Col. William Townsend Gun leis é, i gceannas ('cathbhuíonach', líne 18) ar Woodford Rangers etc., 1782–90.[11] Is cosúil ná raibh sé ró-ghníomhach i gcúrsaí poiblí den tsórt san, áfach, ní hionann agus a dhaoine muinteartha, George Gun agus Thomas Stoughton, a fuair moladh i 1786, 'for their very active and spirited endeavours to suppress the tumultuous risings and outrages of those deluded people stiling themselves Whiteboys, in the neighbourhood of Listowell'.[12]

Cuireadh leagan de línte 1, 6–8, 21–4, den téacs mar atá sa lámhscríbhinn i gcló in aon véarsa amháin sa *Lóchrann*, Abrán–Bealtaine 1908. Micheál Ó Séaghdha, múinteoir fé Chonradh na Gaeilge, a sholáthraigh:[13]

Seaghan Caoch Ó Cearbhaill do cheap

Céad fáilte Máirt Cásga i naoís a bhliadna
Mo rábaire bliadhna bheith slán
Is 'na shláinte seadh airimíd Liam Gun
Na mháighistir is na thíghearna ar thighis Ráth
Sgataí dá gheal chloínn a bheith taobh leis
Na bhfairirí saothrach i stáit
Aistí ar a mhaith-ghníomhartha do dhéanfainn
Is gur mear-chroidheac do ghlaodhfainn hussá.

Do sgríobhas é seo thuas ó Bhean ní Chonchubhair 'sean-mháighistreas sgoile atá i Leach Snámhach. Abhrán fada a bhi ann, adeir sí, ach ní

7 Hickson, *Old Kerry records*, lch 262.   8 Clár na mbaistí, Eaglais na hÉireann, Trá Lí. 9 *Kerry Evening Post*, 19 April 1837; Burke, *Landed gentry of Ireland*, lch 285.   10 Hickson, *Old Kerry records*, lgh 262, 266.   11 Pádraig Ó Snodaigh, 'Notes on the Volunteers, Militia, Yeomanry and Fencibles of Kerry', *JKAHS*, 4 (1971), 48–70 ag 53, 61.   12 Rún de na rúin a ritheadh ag 'Meeting of the magistrates of the county of Kerry', i gcló, *Freeman's Journal*, 22 July 1786, agus arís go rialta go ceann leathbhliana ina dhiaidh sin.   13 Ó cheantar na Snadhma ab ea Micheál Ó Séaghdha, is cosúil. Bhailigh sé roinnt iarsmaí Gaeilge i dtuaisceart Chiarraí timpeall 1907–8, ach d'imigh a chuid páipéirí gan tuairisc (Pádraig de Brún, 'Scéal Gaeilge ón Tóchar', *JKAHS*, 8 [1975], 136–74 ag 152–3).

fhéadfadh sí cuimhneamh ar a thuille dhe. Seo mar do ceapadh é do réir mar a chualaidh sí: – Bhí fear do'n sloinne seo – Gun (Gunn) na chómhnuidhe sa tig mór i Ráth-Thuaidh (*Rattoo*) bhí leanbh mic (oidhre) aige agus bhí sé díreac bliadhain d'aois an caisg sin do tharlaig Seaghan Caoch Ó Cearbhaill an tslighe. Márt Casga agus chas sé isteach i dtig Gun. Deabhruighean an sgéal go raibh aithne mhaith agus meas mór ag Gun ar Sheaghan; mar thug sé an leanbh do na bhaclainn agus dubhairt leis cúpla bhéarsa a cheapa dhó, agus do thosnuig Seaghan mar atá luaidhte thuas.

Togha file a bheadh Seaghan Caoch Ó Cearbhaill do réir na mná so. Cheap sé mór chuid abhrán agus i nGaedhluinn agus i mBéarla agus bhi cuid d'á cheapadóireacht aici, ach d'imthigheadar as a meabhair. B'fhéidir go mbéadh rud éigin le hinnsint ag duine éigin do léightheóiribh 'An Lóchrainn' mar gheall air.

M. O. S.

Bhí de sheana-chuimhne ina pharóiste féin,[14] ní hamháin gur chum Seán Caoch Ó Cearbhaill amhrán mar gheall ar dhuine de mhuintir Gun, ach gur thagair sé ann do cheist na Coróineach,[15] mar atá sa líne dheiridh den téacs thíos. Tagairt í sin gur tógadh ceann di, mar is léir ón insint bhríomhar so ó Chorca Dhuibhne ar an gcúrsa, ina bhfuil leagan de línte 1 agus 31–2 (ach líne éagsúil a bheith rompu):

Bhí fear ann fadó 7 chuai' sé dtí an tiarna talún a' lorg spás air ach go h-áirithe. Ach bhí leanbh aige. Bhí banarthla i mbun a' linibh 7 'ios aice go raibh an fear bocht a tháinig a' lorg a' spáis filiúil. Bliain aoíse bhí an leanbh.

'Raghad-sa 'on tseómra anois,' ars-í-sin '7 nuair a bhraithfead é féin tacthuithe tiocfai' mé 'mach as a' seómra. Din rann éigin do'n leanbh,' ars-í-sin.

'Gud é'n t-aos a' leanbh?' ars-é-sin.

'Bliain aoíse,' ars-í-sin.

Chuai' sí 'on tseómra 7 le línn an tiarna talún a theacht 'on chistin do tháin' sé 'on tseómra. D'fhéach sé ar a' leanbh.

'Céud fáilte rót,' ars-é-sin, 'a shárfhir in aoís do bhliana.[']

Sé'n ainim a bhí ar an áit Rátuaig.

'Slán go raibh do shiolbhach go deó
Is go bhfaghai' tú Rátuaig mar stát ód shínsear.
Go lá'n luain pé rí bheig i gcróin'.

14 Paróiste an Tóchair, mar a bhfuil an Ráth Tuaidh (nó an Baile Dubh) agus Cill Lúirí (an Tóchar) ina gcoda den aon pharóiste Caitliceach amháin le breis mhaith agus 300 bliain anois (ach gur dealaíodh Baile Uí Thaidhg uathu sa bhliain 1857). 15 Eolas ó Éamonn Herbert, OS (†1981); cf. nótaí 31, 33, 36.

'Gud é'n rí bheach i gcróin a' lá san?' arsan *landlord*.
'Rí Seóirse,' ars-é-sin.
'Imig,' arsan tiarna, 'is go n-imí' an dial id' bhóthar'.
Fuair sé an spás.[16]

Níor mhiste don bhfile a dheimhniú don tiarna talún gurbh é Rí Seoirse a mheas sé a bheadh i gcoróin nuair a thiocfadh an mac chun inmhe. De shliocht Mrs Gun úd, an t-aon bhean i measc na 'Galway prisoners' a gabhadh agus iad ar a slí ó Mhala go Sligeach, mar a raibh díorma d'arm Rí Uilliam fé cheannas an Tiarna Kingston, i mí Márta 1689, ab ea an tiarna. B'í sin a ghríosaigh a fear céile agus athair a céile agus na huaisle eile, go mb'fhearra dhóibh, 'fight and die honourably rather than trust to the mercy of a perfidious enemy!', ach níor géilleadh di agus thugadar breis agus bliain i mbraighdeanas.[17] Bhí sí fós ina beathaidh (sa Ráth Tuaidh, is dócha) um 1756.[18] Ní fios an mbeadh a sliocht chomh himníoch i dtaobh buaine an Act of Settlement agus a bhí Muiriseach Bhaile Uí Bheagáin (thíos), ach is eol dúinn go dtarla póstaíocha idir an dá theaghlach san 18ú haois.[19]

In the will of Samuel Morris, Esq., of Ballybeggan, who died about 1700, the testator solemnly enjoins his son to repair the ruined church of Ratass, and requests his neighbour Colonel Edward Denny, of Tralee Castle, to assist in this work, as he, testator, had 'assisted to repair the church of Tralee'. Mr Morris had taken an active part against James II., and he seems to have been alarmed lest the death of Queen Anne might bring back the Stuarts, for to his directions about Ratass church he added this clause: 'if the Act of Settlement be not repealed in twenty years'...[20]

16 Cnuasach Bhéaloideas Éireann 979, lgh 153–4. Seósamh Ó Dálaigh a thóg síos ó Sheán Crithin (69), Cill Maolchéadair (mar ar saolaíodh é), Eanair 1946; óna athair a chuala. 17 Hickson, *Old Kerry records*, lgh 16–23, etc. Cuntas ar an eachtra so ag William H. Welply, 'The Galway prisoners and "Doctor" William Bromfield, being an account of some Williamites, held prisoner at Galway in 1689', *JCHAS*, 34 (1929), 76–90. 18 Charles Smith, *The antient and present state of the county of Kerry. Being a natural, civil, ecclesiastical, historical, and topographical description thereof* ... (Dublin, 1756), lch 59 n. (g). Catherine, iníon le Richard Townsend, Baile an Chaisleáin (Castletownsend), Co. Chorcaí, dob í í dar le Smith agus Miss Hickson, ach do réir Burke, *Landed gentry of Ireland*, lch 284, is i 1694, cúig bliana tar éis eachtra na Gaillimhe, a phós William Gun agus Catherine Townsend. Tá insint ábhar scaoilte ar an eachtra féin in Richard agus Dorothea Townshend (eag.), *An officer of the Long Parliament and his descendants, being some account of the life & times of Colonel Richard Townesend of Castletown (Castletownshend) & a chronicle of his family, with illustrations* (Oxford, 1892), lgh 117–19. 19 Burke, *Landed gentry of Ireland*, lgh 284–5. 20 Mary Agnes Hickson, 'Notes on Kerry topography, ancient and modern' [ar lean.], *Journal of the Royal Historical and Archaeological Association of Ireland*, 4th series, 6/58 (1884), 295–305 ag 298.

Pé scéal aige sin é, sa bhliain 1766 is ea a cuireadh deireadh le hEaspaig Caitliceacha na hÉireann a bheith a n-ainmniú ag na Stíobhartaigh, gur tugadh neamhaird ar an bPrionsa Séarlas (1720–88) sa ghnó.[21] Bhí an mhóid dílseachta do Sheoirse III go mór i dtreis go ceann blianta ina dhiaidh sin, agus an pobal Caitliceach, idir chléir agus tuath, scoiltithe dá barr.[22]

Níor dhearbhaigh an leath féin de chléir Chiarraí ar son na móide nuair a tugadh chun cinn í, 1775–6,[23] in ainneoin Easpaig na Mumhan a thoiliú léi. Sagart acu, an tAth. Muiris Ó Muircheartaigh (Muiris na Luachra), sagart paróiste Bhaile an Fheiritéaraigh 1747–81, a chum an dán dár tosach 'A fhir chalma d'fhuil Ghearaltach ó Dhún na bhFlann / Is ón bhFaiche ghil mar a gceapaidís do shinsear greann', adeir Pádraig Feiritéar le leagan de a scríobh sé ó bhéalaithris i dtreo dheireadh an 19ú haois. Ba dhoilbh agus ba dhubhach leis an údar 'Ár sagairt ag tabhairt na mionn gan iallachaibh / … / Is Cormac Stuart i ndúthaigh iasachta'.[24] Tá leagan den dán so le fáil i mblogh de lámhscríbhinn ó 1832 le príomhscríobhaí na lámhscríbhinne ina bhfuil amhrán Sheáin Chaoigh, agus an chuma air gur ó bhéalaithris nó ó chuimhne a scríobhadh é.[25]

Sagart cúnta ag an Ath. Muiris ab ea an Gearaltach do réir an Fheiritéaraigh.[26] Níl éinne den bheirt sagart ar liosta na ndaoine a thug an mhóid. Is dócha gur i gCiarraí a cumadh an dán, pé scéal é. Tá Lios Dún na bhFlann sa Bhrú Mhór Thiar i bparóiste Chill Chonla in Oireacht Uí Chonchubhair, beagán laisteas den bhFaiche, an baile fearainn ina raibh Caisleán (agus Faiche) na Lice (Leac Bhé Bhionn),[27] mar a raibh brainse de Chloinn Mhuiris a thug Mac Gearailt orthu féin.[28]

21 Rev. Cathaldus Giblin, 'The Stuart nomination of Irish bishops, 1687–1765', *IER* (Jan. 1966), 35–47 ag 47. 22 É seo pléite ag Vincent Morley, 'Catholic disaffection and the oath of allegiance of 1774' in J. Kelly, J. McCafferty and C.I. McGrath (eds), *People, politics and power: essays on Irish history 1660–1850 in honour of James I. McGuire* (Dublin, 2009), lgh 122–42. 23 *59th report of Deputy Keeper of Public Records and Keeper of State Papers, Ireland* [1964], lgh 63, 79–81. 24 In eagar ó LS G 314 sa Leabharlann Náisiúnta agus ó lámhscríbhinní eile ag an Ath. Mícheál Ó Mainín, 'A fhir chalma d'fhuil Ghearaltach' in M. Ó Ciosáin (eag.), *Céad bliain, 1871–1971* (Baile an Fheirtéaraigh, 1973), lgh 36–9. 25 Coláiste Ollscoile Chorcaí, LS 32, lgh 121–2; túslíne ' Árdfhear dfuil Ghearaltuig ó Dhunn na G(h)lann / bo ghnathaghuid do chleachtaidís do shinnsir greann'. 26 'Níl ach gur le grá d'airgead is a mhallaitheacht ar an saol gan dabht / Is dá bharra súd freagradh a n-anam súd féinig ann' [leagan den dá líne dheiridh d'eagrán an Ath. Ó Mainín], a d'fhreagair sé sin do réir mar a chuala sé (Coláiste Ollscoile Bhaile Átha Cliath, LS F 1, lch 119 [litriú cóirithe]). Tagann na dátaí le himeachtaí an Ath. Éamonn Mac Gearailt (Edmond Fitzgerald): i Nantes 1770, 'at home not beneficed' 1774, 'coadjutor parochialis' 1775, 'pastor de Brosnagh' 1777 (Pádraig de Brún, 'Some lists of Kerry priests, 1750–1835', *JKAHS*, 18 [1985 (1986)], 83–169 ag 99, 102, 105, 108); 'a distinguished Irish preacher' (Cartlann Dheoise Chiarraí, leabhar nótaí leis an Ath. James Carmody [†1 Eanair 1926]). 27 Cartlann Náisiúnta na hÉireann, Ordnance Survey Name Books, Kerry, par. Kilconly [1841], ff. 44, 30; Caroline Toal, *North Kerry archaeological survey* (Dingle, 1995), §§215, 987. Tharlódh fós an ceart a bheith ag an Ath. Ó Mainín, gurb ionann Dún na

Tá blas an 18ú haois ar an amhrán do Uilliam Gun, ach níl na tuairiscí atá againn ar Sheán Caoch ag teacht go hiomlán leis sin. Do réir chuntais amháin, is sa bhliain 1848 a cailleadh é; i gClais Maolchon (i bparóiste Chill Lúirí) a chónaigh sé; filí ab ea a athair agus a iníon chomh maith, agus – téama coitianta béaloideasa ar fuaid na Mumhan[29] – 'when it came on his daughter the gift of poetry left them'.[30]

Ón údar ba mhó ar chúrsaí staire agus seanaimsearachta an pharóiste an achoimre shlachtmhar so ar a bhfuair sé d'eolas ar an bhfile:

> Cearbhaill brought up several times for stealing. Brought before Gun, Rattoo. Sitting in the kitchen waiting for Mr Gun. Nurse suggested he make a song for the child (young Gun). Walked around the kitchen sang a lullaby and then composed verses in Irish and English. One verse said that whatever King would reign there would be a Gun in Rattoo.
>
> Old Gun understood the song, hearing it from the room. He questioned him about the reference to the King (historical reference to Jacobites). At any rate it got him off lightly and said to have given him five pounds.
>
> Doing public penance in Causeway. Ceist ag an sagart, *''Bhfuil an bárrlín ort a Sheáin?'* Seán put on the sheet in a suggestive manner with obscene remark. Priest remarked that Dromartin would be yet without a Carroll.[31]

Más le Clais Maolchon a bhain Seán Caoch, bheadh Gun ina thiarna talún aige, cé gur ar léas ó Major [Pierse] Crosbie, Baile Uí Thaidhg, a bhí an baile aige sin, sa 19ú haois ach go háirithe.[32] Más le Droim Máirtín (par. na Rátha Tuaidh), mar a raibh sráidbhaile anuas go dtí aimsir an drochshaoil nó mar sin,

---

bhFlann agus Baile (Mhic Giolla) na bhFlann i bparóiste Chill Imleach in Uíbh Ráthach (cf. An Seabhac, *Uí Ráthach: ainmneacha na mbailte fearainn sa bharúntacht* [BÁC, (1954)], lch 27). Bheadh an Fhaiche thar teorainn ó dheas uaidh sin: 'Faha' san ionad so i gcóip lámhscríofa de chuid de mhapa [1786/1800] le Henry Pelham (1749–1806) i gcartlann Suirbhéireacht Gheolaíocht na hÉireann (feic Jean B. Archer, 'Henry Pelham's lost Grand Jury map of Kerry: a newly-found derivative', *Imago Mundi*, 58, ii [2006], 183–97). Ghlac an tSuirbhéireacht Ordanáis le Clochán Ceannúigh mar bhaile fearainn agus fágadh é seo as an áireamh (eolas ón nDr Breandán Ó Cíobháin). Coinníodh 'Rathkieran and Faha' mar ainm ar cheantar stáisiún i gcóras na hEaglaise, áfach (Pádraig de Brún, 'A census of the parishes of Prior and Killemlagh, December 1834', *JKAHS*, 8 [1975], 111–35 ag 116 n. 12). **28** K.W. Nicholls, 'The FitzMaurices of Kerry', *JKAHS*, 3 (1970), 23–42 ag 34. **29** Dáithí Ó hÓgáin, *An file: staidéar ar osnádúrthacht na filíochta sa traidisiún Gaelach* (BÁC, 1982), lgh 153–63. **30** Cnuasach Bhéaloideas Éireann S 416, lgh 143–4, ó Scoil na gCailíní, Sliabh a' Mhadra (par. na Rátha Tuaidh). **31** Ó Éamonn Herbert (nóta 15): sleachta a thógas blianta ó shin as leabhar nótaí a thaispeáin sé dhom. **32** Cartlann Náisiúnta na hÉireann, Ordnance Survey Name Books, Kerry, par. Killury [1841].

a bhain sé, áfach, ní mar gheall ar chíos a bheadh sé os comhair éinne de mhuintir Gun (ná raibh aon bhaint fé leith acu leis an mbaile sin), ach mar gheall ar mhí-iompar de shórt éigin. Dá chomhartha san, is é a thuig duine de na cainteoirí deiridh Gaeilge sa cheantar (*c.*1940) gurbh é a bhí i gceist i leagan a bhí aige de línte 27–8 den amhrán, 'an appeal made by a condemned man to the landlord or to the son of the landlord at the Great House in Rattoo'.[33]

Maidir le haithrí phoiblí i leith peacaí poiblí, d'fhógair Ardeaspag Chaisil i dtosach an 19ú haois, i gcomhair a dheoisí féin, Caiseal agus Imleach, ná beadh teacht ar na Sacraimintí ag daoine a cheadódh caitheamh aimsire míchuí nó deocha meisciúla ar thórraimh, nó a dhíolfadh deocha den tsórt san ag Pátrún Dhún na Sciath, 'without first performing a course of exemplary penance', 'until they have made a public submission before the altar', nó 'without previously undergoing a public and exemplary course of penance'.[34] Ní léir, áfach, cathain a héiríodh as an mbáirlín mar chuid den bhreith aithrí. Is eol dúinn gur fhógair báicéir i gCloich na Caoilte i gCo. Chorcaí, timpeall na bliana 1805, gur tháinig sé chun an tséipéil agus báirlín bán uime le súil go saorfadh an sagart paróiste é ón gcoinnealbhá a bhí curtha aige air i dtaobh gan an táille a leagadh air mar chuid de chostas tógála an tséipéil a dhíol.[35] Ón uair gur shéan an sagart gur chuir sé an báicéir fé choinnealbhá riamh, tharlódh gur ag braith ar sheana-chuimhne éigin a bhí sé sin.

Cuimhne eile ar Sheán Caoch a mhair ná ráiteas uaidh gurbh é 'An Baile Bán' ba chóra a thabhairt ar an mBaile Dubh – ar a mbíodh de chúr ar an bpórtar ann![36] Ach arís, ní fianaise ró-láidir é sin maidir le dáta an amhráin. Tá 'Ballydove Village' marcálta ar léarscáil ó 1782/6,[37] ach ní fios cá fhaid a bhí sé ann um an dtaca san. Ar 23 Aibreán, 4 Geo. III [=1764], is ea a tugadh paitinn do Anthony Stoughton le haghaidh aontaí a thionól sa Mhín Mhór (Beenmore [Benmore]),[38] an baile fearainn ina bhfuil an tsráid. Cuid

---

33 'Guím Ráth Tuaidh mar stát buan aged sinsear i gcóir Lá an Luain'. An Canónach William O'Connor (ó Dhroim na Cora i bpar. Chill Lúirí, a chaith cuid mhaith dá shaol mar shagart sa Bhreatain Bhig) a fuair ó Tom Dunne, 'the last native speaker in the Ballyduff area' (nótaí a thógas as litreacha uaidh chuig Éamonn Herbert, Eanair–Feabhra 1965).   **34** Rev. Thomas Bray, *Statuta Synodalia unitis diœcesibus Cassel et Imelec ...* (Dublin, 1813), lch 106; idem, *Regulations, instructions, and prayers, &c. &c. in English and Irish ... for the united dioceses of Cashel and Emly* [in aon iml. leis na Statúidí], lch 233. Táim fé chomaoin ag an nDr Oirmh. Fearghus Ó Fearghail as na tagairtí seo a thabhairt dom.   **35** Revd James Coombes, 'Doctor William O'Brien of Glenanaar', *JCHAS*, 82 (1977), 115–26 ag 118–19. Mhair iarsmaí an aighnis sin go ceann i bhfad: *Gentleman's Magazine* (Jan. 1815), lch 75; (April 1815), lgh 318–19; *Baptist Magazine* (March 1815), lch 128.   **36** Ó Éamonn Herbert chomh maith.   **37** Cuid de thuaisceart Chiarraí sa 'Grand Jury map of Clare' le Henry Pelham [ordaíodh 1779; moladh maidir le 'accuracy and execution' 1782; deineadh a ghreanadh 1785/6 (*Limerick Chronicle*, 3 Oct. 1782; 26 Jan. 1786)], athchló, *Henry Pelham's map of County Clare, 1787* (Dublin, 1989).   **38** *Report of the commissioners appointed to inquire into the state of the fairs and markets in Ireland*, presented to both Houses of Parliament by Order of Her Majesty (Dublin, 1853), lch 84.

de choimín na Rátha Tuaidh ab ea an Mhín Mhór agus bailte eile go dtí 1748, nuair a deineadh 535 acra (866 d'acraí statúideacha) de thalamh an pharóiste a roinnt idir Townsend Gun agus Anthony Stoughton go ceann 900 blian.[39]

Idir 1806 agus 1815 a scríobhadh an lámhscríbhinn ina bhfuil an téacs atá in eagar anso, ach níl na bileoga ceangailte in ord a scríofa. Tomás Ó Criadáin (Thomas Needham) ab ainm don phríomhscríobhaí. Bhain sé sin le paróiste an Chluainín i ndeisceart Thiobrad Árann, agus tá fáil ar dhá bhlogh eile de lámhscríbhinn a scríobh sé 'san cClórán' sa pharóiste sin in 1832.[40] Is dócha dá réir sin gurbh é seo Thomas Needham go raibh talamh sa bhaile fearainn sin aige sa bhliain 1830,[41] nó duine muinteartha leis. Is beag amhras, ar a lámh Bhéarla a scrúdú, ná gurbh é a bhreac an t-amhrán so.[42] I dteannta nithe eile, ba bhéas leis an focal 'fáilte' a scríobh mar Ⓒ i script na Gaeilge, fé mar atá déanta i script an Bhéarla i líne 1 thíos.

Tá mír amháin (lgh 173–83) den lámhscríbhinn sínithe san Ogham Consaine ag Donac[h]adh Ó Súiliobháin, 1806. Tá an síniú céanna ar lch 26 de LS Ir. e 3 i Leabharlann Bodley in Oxford, lámhscríbhinn a bhaineann leis an dtaobh céanna tíre (le Carraig na Siúire nó lena cóngar) agus go bhfuil síniú Thomáis Uí Chriadáin inti chomh maith.[43]

Pé slí inar tharla sé, is in oirthear na Mumhan, agus ní i gCiarraí, a tháinig an t-amhrán so slán dá réir sin.

Cé gur tuigeadh gur mar amhrán a cumadh an téacs, níl aon fhianaise againn i dtaobh an cheoil a ghaibh leis. Fonn ar aon phátrún le 'Cailín deas crúite na mbó',[44] a bhí coitianta go maith,[45] a d'oirfeadh dó.

San eagrán thíos, tá téacs an amhráin i litriú cóirithe agus téacs na lámh-scríbhinne laistíos de. Chuaidh díom aon réiteach a fháil ar 'Vevus' (líne 22).[46]

39 Matthew J. Byrne, 'Rattoo' [ar lean.], *JCHAS*, 17 (1911), 17–25 ag 22–5. 40 Leabharlann Náisiúnta, LS G 582 (16 de lgh), agus Leabharlann Ollscoile Chorcaí, LS Ghaeilge 32, lgh 121–34, dhá chuid den aon lámhscríbhinn amháin, is cosúil. 41 Cartlann Náisiúnta na hÉireann, Tithe Applotment Books, Tipperary, par. Cloneen, baile fearainn Cloran. 42 Dearmad uaim ab ea a mhalairt a chur in úil in *Filíocht Sheáin Uí Bhraonáin* (BÁC, 1972), lch 63. 43 Brian Ó Cuív, *Catalogue of Irish language manuscripts in the Bodleian Library at Oxford and Oxford college libraries*, iml. i (Dublin, 2001), lgh 28–9. 44 David Cooper (ed.), *The Petrie collection of the ancient music of Ireland* (Cork, 2002, 2005), lgh 89–90, 252, mar ar léirigh Petrie an gaol idir aicmí ceoil agus aicmí meadarachta. 45 Ceithre cinn déag de línte tosaigh amhrán luaite leis an bhfonn so in *RIA Cat., Index II*, lch 640, gan dul thairis sin. 46 Gabhaim baochas leis an Ollamh Pádraig Ó Macháin agus leis an nDr Aoibheann Nic Dhonnchadha as a gcabhair agus a gcomhairle agus mé i mbun na haiste seo.

Is léir ó chuid de na tagairtí thuas gur beag de thuairisc Sheáin Chaoigh Uí Chearbhaill a bheadh fanta mura mbeadh díograis agus gnaoiúlacht Éamoinn Herbert (RIP). Tá súil agam gur cuí cloch a leagan ar charn an athar le linn scoláireacht na hiníne a chomóradh.

Céad fáilte Máirt Chásca it aois bhliana,
   roimh shárfhear na dtriatha nár stán,
an t-ardbhile dh'fhásas gan fiala
4   ach amháin le toil Dhia gheal na ngrást.
Is fearrde de an lán úd go hiarthar
   mo rábaire bliana ' bheith slán,
'na shláinte go ngáileamaoid Uilliam Gun,
8   'na mháistir ar thiarnas tíos Ráth.

Mo chara thú, mo shearca thú, mo stiúr maith,
   mo chara thú, mo dhún, mo chaisleán,
mo chara thú chun seasamh dúinne i bhfiúntas,
12   má castar ann sinn ciontach go brách.
Fearta an úirMhic freagair dhúinne 'gus umhlaigh
   an achainí ' thabhairt dúinne do ghnáth –
go maire tú go gcasair clú do dhúiche
16   's go [n]glaca tú ar do chúram tíos Ráth.

Cead (t) mairt chasga a taois Vliana
   Riov har ar na driaha nar stean
And tard vile yasas gan fiala
4   ach avain le tuil yia yal na ngrast
is fardida an lan ud go hiarher
   mo Rabura Bliana veh slan
na hlanta go ngailamaoid ulaim gun
8   na Vaistir air hiearnas ties Rah

Mo chara hu mo harka hu mo stuir mah
   mo chara hu mo yun mo caislain
mo chara hu chun sasav duna a Vuntas
12   ma castar oun sin Countach go Brach
farta an uir mic fragair yuna agus uilig
   an achanaoi hourt duna do ynach
Go mari tu go gasar Clu Do yuha
16   is go glaca tu air do churam taois rah

An tArdrí go neartaídh le *Vénus*
　　is leis an gcathbhuíonach saorbhreathach sámh,
a' fastaím ar hallaí 's a' pléireacht
　　　lena ghealchích bhreá bhéi[l]mhilis mhná,
scataí dhá dhea-chloinn a bheith taobh leis
　　'na ngaiscígh bhreá [ ] an stáit –
sin aistí ar mhaithghníomhra dhéanam,
　　　's is mear groí do ghlaofinn *huzzá*.

20

24

Beidh báid uait a' trácht cuanta ar barr taoide
　　faoina lán-ualaigh fionta 'gus beoir,
beidh dáimh uait [a'] fáil duala 'gus díolaim,
　　　beidh mná ' tuar ar innse uait fós.
Beidh t'ard-chruacha á ghnáthbhualadh 'ge saoirfhir
　　'na n-ardshluaite timpall mo leoin,
beidh Ráth Tuaidh 'na stáit bhuain agad shinsir
　　　go Lá an Luain, pé rí bheas i gcoróin.

28

32

An tard Rioy go nartaoig le Venios
　　is leis a gafaoinach saor vrahach sav
a fastaoim air halaoi 7 a pleiracht
　　　le na yal chaoich Vra Vevilis Vna
sgataoi ya yachlaoin a veh taov leis
　　na ngasgaoig vra Vevus an stait
sin astaoi air vah ynaoirah yenam
　　　sis mar graoi do [*ceartaithe ó* gó] ylaofin husza

20

24

Beig Baid Voit a tracht cuanta air bar taoida
　　faoi na lan ouylla [?] fionta 7 Beoir
Beig Daiv Vout fail doila 7 daoilim
　　　Beig mna toair air inse Voit foas
Beig tard chrocha ya ynach Volage seerir,
　　na nard hlouta timpal mo leoin
Beig Rah toug na stait Voain aig ad hinsir
　　　go la an loain pe Rioy Ves a groin

28

32

Murchadh Ó Cuindlis and
Aided Muirchertaig Meic Erca

CLODAGH DOWNEY

Among the very many contributions that she has made to the lives of her students and to the field of Celtic Studies alike, Máire Herbert has greatly advanced our understanding of how authors in the tenth to twelfth centuries revised, adapted and reconstructed traditional literary and historical materials into new narratives, for the purposes of narrativizing history, of promoting a socio-moral ethos, or of reflecting and commenting on a contemporary situation.[1] The shift of critical emphasis from those traditional materials to the accomplishments of the authors who later wielded them has revealed the complexity of these medieval Irish texts and opened up new ways to read and appreciate them. Her analysis of *Aided Muirchertaig Meic Erca* (henceforth *AMME*) demonstrates how this tale, although conspicuously evincing traditional themes and devices (such as those of the sovereignty goddess and the threefold death),[2] also involves the conscious and pointed subversion of these themes and narrativization of the present.[3] Other commentators have also highlighted the tale's complexity: Ralph O'Connor has pointed to its moral and ideological tensions and ambivalences, while Mark Williams has drawn attention to the

1 See, for example, Máire Herbert, '*Fled Dúin na nGéd*: a reappraisal', *CMCS*, 18 (Winter, 1989), 75–87; eadem, 'The universe of male and female: a reading of the Deirdre story' in C.J. Byrne, M. Harry and P. Ó Siadhail (eds), *Celtic languages and Celtic peoples: proceedings of the Second North American Congress of Celtic Studies* (Halifax, 1992), pp 53–64; eadem, 'The death of Muirchertach Mac Erca: a twelfth-century tale' in F. Josephson (ed.), *Celts and vikings: proceedings of the Fourth Symposium of Societas Celtologica Nordica* (Gothenburg, 1997), pp 27–39; eadem, '*Caithréim Cellaig*: some literary and historical considerations', *ZCP*, 49–50 (1997), 320–32; eadem, 'Observations on the Life of Molaga' in J. Carey, M. Herbert and K. Murray (eds), *Cín Chille Cúile: texts, saints and places: essays in honour of Pádraig Ó Riain* (Aberystwyth, 2004), pp 127–40. 2 The presence of the motif of the threefold death is not clear in the published editions of *AMME* (cf. note 5 below); but see Tomás Ó Concheanainn, 'The act of wounding in the death of Muirchertach Mac Erca', *Éigse*, 15 (1973), 141–4, for emendation; and see discussions in Joan N. Radner, 'The significance of the threefold death in Celtic tradition' in P.K. Ford (ed.), *Celtic folklore and Christianity: studies in memory of William W. Heist* (Santa Barbara, 1983), pp 180–200 at pp 195–8; William Sayers, '*Guin & crochad & gólad*: the earliest Irish threefold death' in Byrne et al. (eds), *Celtic languages and Celtic peoples*, pp 65–82 at pp 67–8; and Tomás Ó Cathasaigh, 'The threefold death in early Irish sources', *Studia Celtica Japonica*, 6 (1994), 53–75 at 60 – all of these contra Mark Williams' comments: '"Lady vengeance": a reading of Sín in *Aided Muirchertaig Meic Erca*', *CMCS*, 62 (Winter 2011), 1–32 at 24 n. 108. 3 Herbert, 'The death'.

author's deliberately ambiguous and allusive use of language.[4] What I propose to do here is to follow the evolution of *AMME* a little further and to consider how this twelfth-century tale was handled by a late-fourteenth-century scribe.

AMME relates the story of the unworldly punishment and destruction of Muirchertach Mac Erca, an errant and debauched but redeemable king, through the malevolent and vengeful endeavours of the fatally beautiful Sín, observed by the virtuous and admonitory saint Cairnech.[5] The story now survives in two manuscripts: the Yellow Book of Lecan (YBL) (Dublin, TCD 1318 [H.2.16], cols 310–20, henceforth Y) and Dublin, TCD 1298 [H.2.7], pp 248–54 (henceforth H). The prose parts of these copies are close enough to each other that a common exemplar at some fairly proximate stage of transmission may be posited. There is, however, one conspicuous difference between them: while Y contains thirty-one verse sections (comprising 670 lines in Lil Nic Dhonnchadha's edition), H contains only three (82 lines).[6] H was written by Uilliam Mac an Leagha, probably in the late fifteenth century.[7] Mac an Leagha has been noted by various scholars as not only a prolific and original scribe, but possibly also an author and translator;[8] yet it is in Y that we find the fullest elaboration of *AMME*. The section of YBL that contains *AMME* was written by another hard-working scribe, Murchadh Ó Cuindlis, in 1398–9.[9] Murchadh was involved in the writing of other extant manuscripts: the Book of Lecan, in which he wrote for his master, Giolla Íosa Mac Fir Bhisigh, as one of four principal hands; and the Leabhar Breac (LB),

4 Ralph O'Connor, 'Searching for the moral in *Bruiden Meic Da Réo*', *Ériu*, 56 (2006), 117–43 at 137–41; Williams, '"Lady vengeance"'.   5 *AMME* has been edited and translated by Whitley Stokes, 'The death of Muirchertach Mac Erca', *RC*, 23 (1902), 395–437; *RC*, 24 (1903), 120; *RC*, 27 (1906), 202 (omitting much of the verse content); and has been edited by Lil Nic Dhonnchadha, *Aided Muirchertaig Meic Erca*, MMIS 19 (Dublin, 1980). It has also been translated into French by Christian-J. Guyonvarc'h, 'La mort de Muirchertach, fils d'Erc. Texte irlandais du très haut Moyen Âge: la femme, le saint et le roi', *Annales. Économies, Sociétés, Civilisations*, 38, v (1983), 985–1015. References to the text will be to Nic Dhonnchadha's edition.   6 Guyonvarc'h considered the poems to be the core of the story ('La mort de Muirchertach, fils d'Erc', 986), while William Sayers suggested that the poems 'sew together' a traditional story pattern and a Christian narrative ('Deficient royal rule: the king's proxies, judges and the instruments of his fate' in D. Wiley [ed.], *Essays on the early Irish king tales* [Dublin, 2008], pp 104–26 at p. 120); I do not think that the evidence supports either of these readings.   7 Gordon Quin dated the copy of *Stair Ercuil ocus a bás*, which was also written by Mac an Leagha in the same manuscript, to the last quarter of the fifteenth century: *Stair Ercuil ocus a bás: the life and death of Hercules*, ITS 38 (Dublin, 1939), pp xxiv–xxv.   8 Quin, *Stair Ercuil*, pp xxxviii–xl; Erich Poppe, 'Narrative structure of medieval Irish adaptations: the case of *Guy* and *Beues*' in H. Fulton (ed.), *Medieval Celtic literature and society* (Dublin, 2005), pp 205–29 at p. 207, and references therein; idem, '*Stair Ercuil ocus a bás*: rewriting Hercules in Ireland' in K. Murray (ed.), *Translations from Classical literature: Imtheachta Æniasa and Stair Ercuil ocus a bás*, ITS SS 17 (London, 2006), pp 37–68.   9 Tomás Ó Concheanainn, 'The scribe of the Leabhar Breac', *Ériu*, 24 (1973), 64–79 at 67, 77; idem, 'Scríobhaithe Leacáin Mhic Fhir Bhisigh', *Celtica*, 19 (1987), 141–75 at 147.

written, as Tomás Ó Concheanainn has shown, by Murchadh alone.[10] Ó
Concheanainn has been able to trace some of the trajectory of Murchadh's
career: from apprentice working on the Book of Lecan in the years 1397–8;
to his more refined hand (in which he recorded that he was writing 'for himself') in YBL in 1398–9; to LB, the largest surviving vellum Irish manuscript
in the hand of a single scribe, which he wrote during the years 1408–11.[11]
The culmination of Murchadh's growing confidence, independence and innovatory attitude to his work can be seen in LB in various ways. On the textual
level, various commentators have noted the frequent, and sometimes radical,
deviation from archetypes observable in certain texts in LB;[12] some or many
of these deviations may have been scribal. Murchadh's confidence may not
always have been wholly justified; although he seemed often to have sought
to improve and correct his exemplars, he was not invariably successful.[13] On
the level of image, it has been suggested that the unusual drawings of the
Menorah and the Crucifixion (pp 121 and 166) may have been inspired by
foreign models.[14] This has prompted Máire Herbert to suggest that
Murchadh was familiar with Latin manuscripts of his own time and may have
been clerically trained.[15]

---

10 Ó Concheanainn, 'The scribe', 76–9 (Lecan); 64–75 (LB); idem, 'Scríobhaithe', 147–9;
Nollaig Ó Muraíle, *The celebrated antiquary: Dubhaltach Mac Fhirbhisigh (c.1600–1671)*
(Maynooth, 2002), pp 16–19.   11 See references at note 9 above, and Ó Muraíle,
Celebrated antiquary, p. 19. Murchadh's note in YBL is at col. 320.10–11: *Murchad O
Cuindlis do scrib in lebursa do fen* (see Nic Dhonnchadha, *Aided Muirchertaig*, p. 35, ll 996–
1000 and Ó Concheanainn, 'The scribe', 67 n. 21, for the full colophon). A project headed
by Professor Liam Breatnach of the School of Celtic Studies, DIAS, is working towards
an edition and comprehensive study of LB.   12 See, for example, *Fél.* pp xvii–xviii;
Vernam Hull, 'Cáin Domnaig', *Ériu*, 20 (1966), 151–77 at 151–2, 155; *CGSH*, pp xxvi–
xxvii. Kathleen Mulchrone, however, considered that the scribe of LB rarely altered his
exemplar of *Caithréim Cellaig* (*Caithréim Cellaig*, MMIS 24 [Dublin, 1978], p. xv), and
Jacopo Bisagni describes the orthography of the LB *Amrae Coluim Chille* as 'remarkably
accurate', with very few modernizations ('*Amrae Coluimb Chille*: a critical edition', unpublished PhD thesis [NUI Galway, 2008], p. 15).   13 See, for example, the observations of
Michael Herren, 'The authorship, date of composition and provenance of the so-called
Lorica Gildae', *Ériu*, 24 (1973), 35–51 at 36 n. 7; Alan Mac an Bhaird, 'Varia II. Tadhg
mac Céin and the badgers', *Ériu*, 31 (1980), 150–5 at 150; Frederic Mac Donncha, 'Páis
agus aiséirí Chríost in LB agus in LS 10', *Éigse*, 21 (1986), 170–93. Although Máire
Herbert considers the LB text of the Irish Life of Colum Cille a better reflection of the
archetype overall, she also notes certain stylistic features which set LB apart from the rest
of the witnesses, and examples of misreadings and misunderstandings by its scribe: *Iona,
Kells, and Derry: the history and hagiography of the monastic familia of Columba* (Oxford,
1988), pp 213–17.   14 Françoise Henry and Geneviève Marsh-Micheli, 'Manuscripts and
illuminations 1169–1603' in A. Cosgrove (ed.), *A new history of Ireland ii: medieval Ireland
1169–1534* (Oxford, 1987), pp 781–813 at p. 798.   15 Máire Herbert, 'Medieval collections of ecclesiastical and devotional materials: Leabhar Breac, Liber Flavus Fergusiorum and
The Book of Fenagh' in B. Cunningham and S. Fitzpatrick (eds), *Treasures of the Royal
Irish Academy library* (Dublin, 2009), pp 32–43 at p. 35.

Another place where we see this scribe making his mark on his manuscript is in the margins. Ruth Lehmann noted a *deibide* couplet written by
Murchadh on the margins of his copy of *Fled Dúin na nGéd* in YBL,[16] and
one of the notable features of LB is the abundance of marginalia it contains,
from comments on the weather or on the day or time of year, to invocations
to God and to Mary, to laments on the scribe's cold and tired state; these go
some way towards revealing Murchadh's personality to us.[17] But he also
added over ninety verse pieces in the margins, most of which share a distinctly religious character with much of the non-verse marginalia.[18] Other
verses have a gnomic or epigrammatic flavour,[19] treat of saints, biblical, historical or legendary figures,[20] or are notable for their use of natural imagery.[21]
Obviously, the physical situation of these verses indicates their extraneous or
incidental nature:[22] they do not belong to the texts that occupy the pages on
which they are found, although they sometimes have a connection to them,
such as the quatrain on the beheading of John the Baptist on p. 188, where
the Passion of John the Baptist is also found, or the quatrain on the

16 Ruth Lehmann (ed.), *Fled Dúin na nGéd*, MMIS 21 (Dublin, 1964), p. xi.   **17** See Ó
Concheanainn, 'The scribe', 64 and 71–5, where marginalia relating to the time and place
of writing are collected. The manuscript also contains marginalia from a hand or hands
other than Murchadh's.   **18** A small number of these verses have been published: Whitley
Stokes, 'On the metrical glossaries of the mediaeval Irish', *Transactions of the Philological
Society*, 22, i (1891), 1–103 at 2; Kuno Meyer, 'Anecdota from Irish manuscripts',
Irisleabhar na Gaedhilge, 4, xl (1892), 113–15, 133–4; 4, xlv (1893), 193–4; 5, vi (1894), 94;
7, viii (1896), 116–17; idem, 'Irish quatrains', *ZCP*, 1 (1897), 455–7; 2 (1899), 225; idem,
'Stories and songs from Irish manuscripts', *Otia Merseiana*, 1 (1899), 113–28 at 120 n. 3;
idem, *The triads of Ireland*, TLS 13 (Dublin, 1906), p. ix; Tomás Ua Nualláin, [no title],
The Catholic Bulletin, 3, v (May, 1913), 363; Brian Ó Cuív, 'Venite benedicti patris mei',
Éigse, 6, iv (1952), 332; idem, 'Dhá rann ar an iairmhéirghe', *Celtica*, 2, i (1952), 29;
Robert T. Meyer, 'The lonely blackbird', *Irisleabhar Ceilteach*, 2 (1954), 46; David Greene
and Frank O'Connor (trans.), *A golden treasury of Irish poetry AD 600 to 1200* (London,
1967), pp 206–7; *CGSH* §§78, 125.2, 190, 671.10; Charles D. Wright, *The Irish tradition
in Old English literature* (Cambridge, 1993), p. 140 n. 128; John Carey, 'A posthumous
quatrain', *Éigse*, 29 (1996), 172–4. Dennis King has also published and translated some of
the marginalia from LB on his website: <www.sengoidelc.com>.   **19** For example, the
verses on pp 94, 100*i* and 225 (see Meyer, *Irisleabhar na Gaedhilge*, 4, xl, pp 133–4), 176
(Meyer, *ZCP*, 1, pp 456–7), 176*i*, 223 (Meyer, *ZCP*, 2, p. 225), 225*i* / 238 (Meyer, *Triads
of Ireland*, p. ix), 226*i* (Meyer, *Irisleabhar na Gaedhilge*, 4, xlv, p. 194), 228*s*, 232.   **20** For
example, the verses on pp 16 (*CGSH* §125.2 n. ddd), 18 (*CGSH* §190 n. i), 23 (*CGSH*
§671.10 n. g–g), 60, 97 (see *Fél.* p. 186), 98*i*, 100*s*, 121, 143, 177*i*, 220, 225, 228*i*, 229, 235.
21 For example, the verses on pp 3, 36 (Meyer, *Irisleabhar na Gaedhilge*, 4, xl, 115, 134;
Meyer, 'The lonely blackbird'; Greene and O'Connor, *A golden treasury*, pp 206–7), 103,
164 (Meyer, *Irisleabhar na Gaedhilge*, 7, viii, 116), 227 (Meyer, *Irisleabhar na Gaedhilge*
4:40, 115).   **22** David Dumville has raised some important questions in relation to the
nature and function of poetry found in the margins of medieval and early modern Irish
manuscripts in 'What is mediaeval Gaelic poetry?' in D.F. Smith and H. Philsooph (eds),
Explorations in cultural history: essays for Peter Gabriel McCaffery (Aberdeen, 2010), pp 81–
153 at pp 108–14. I am very grateful to the editors for drawing my attention to this study.

Crucifixion of Jesus, found on pp 88 and 162, on the latter of which the Passion of Christ is found.[23] This quatrain is an example of a number of marginal quatrains in LB which are also found in other sources, most notably copies of *Félire Óengusso* in Rawlinson MS B 512 and in the Ó Cléirigh manuscript, Brussels, Bibliothèque royale de Belgique, 5100–4 (507).[24] A version of a quatrain on p. 89, attributed in LB to Caillech Bérri, is also found on the margin of Dublin, RIA MS D iv 2 (1223), f. 45r,[25] while other quatrains written marginally in LB may be found in the body of texts elsewhere.[26] It is likely, then, that Murchadh was using a range of sources for these marginal verses. He may even have composed some of the verses himself, though this would hardly be demonstrable. If some of the verses are contemporary with the manuscript's date, this would not make them unique among the manuscript's contents: Gearóid Mac Eoin has argued that at least one of the homilies in the collection in LB (that on the Ten Commandments) was composed in the second half of the fourteenth century.[27] The collection of marginal verses is heterogeneous, and while some contain linguistic features which would weigh against a contemporary dating, such as the frequent use of *no* with infixed pronouns, a fourteenth-century date could not be ruled out in respect to many of them.[28] But whoever their authors may have been, it seems safe to say that the man who decided to put them on the margins of his pages was interested in poetry for how it can enhance and complement a literary, learning or reading experience.

Might this interest, and Murchadh's growing confidence to act on his own initiative, offer another perspective on his copy of *AMME*, or have anything

---

23 The Crucifixion quatrain was printed and translated by Meyer, 'Irish quatrains' (*ZCP*, 2, 225), and printed by Ua Nualláin, *Catholic Bulletin*.   24 The quatrain on the Crucifixion is also in Brussels MS 5100–4 f. 90; and compare, for example, the marginal quatrains on pp 85, 88, 90, 93, 96, 97, 98, 99, 100, 102, 164 with Brussels MS 5100–4 ff 88, 89, 90, 91, 92. For quatrains on pp 96, 97, 188 also found in Rawlinson MS B 512, see *Fél.* pp 186, 190, 212.   25 See Meyer, 'Stories and songs', p. 120 n. 3.   26 For example, compare the quatrain at p. 115 with one in the story of Coirpre Crom and Máel Sechlainn's soul: Whitley Stokes, 'Three legends from the Brussels manuscript 5100–4', *RC*, 26 (1905), 360–77 at 366; or the one on p. 16 with Dublin, TCD MS 1319 (H.2.17), p. 428c. Interestingly, Máire Herbert and Pádraig Ó Riain noted that the latter manuscript shared some linguistic features with the passions and homilies of LB: *CGSH*, p. xl. 27 Gearóid Mac Eoin, 'Observations on some Middle-Irish homilies' in P. Ní Chatháin and M. Richter (eds), *Irland und Europa im früheren Mittelalter: Bildung und Literatur* (Stuttgart, 1996), pp 195–211 at pp 208–9, 210–11.   28 Examples of the use of *no* include *not gudim* (p. 14); *nos cráidend, nos ráidend* (p. 84); *nos fothraic, dianos ibe, nodus tēige* (p. 94); *nos cara* (p. 176*i*); *nos bera* (p. 228s); *nos nódra* (p. 232). The use of this preverb in relative clauses or supporting an infix was exceptional, and generally archaising, in the Early Modern Irish period, when *do* or *ro* were more usually used: Damian McManus, 'An Nua-Ghaeilge Chlasaiceach' in K. McCone, D. McManus, C. Ó Háinle, N. Williams and L. Breatnach (eds), *Stair na Gaeilge in ómós do Pádraig Ó Fiannachta* (Maigh Nuad, 1994), pp 335–445 at pp 422–3, 429–30 §§7.32, 9.2.

to do with the presence of so much verse in the Y text as against H? We can divide the verse in Y into three main groups: verse which is also found in H, verse sections for which short corresponding prose sections are found in H, and verse sections which have no parallel in H. The first group comprises lines 536–79 (§27), 668–81 (§33) and 845–68 (§47) of Nic Dhonnchadha's edition. The first of these poems consists of Muirchertach's synopsis of his life (further described in Y only as a 'fervent repentance to God' [l. 534] and a 'confession' [l. 580]): the kingships he occupied, the enemies he contended with, and his ultimate conversion to repentance and a Christian life. The texts of the poem in Y and H are fairly similar for the most part, and its presence in H indicates that Uilliam or the compiler of his exemplar was not wholly averse to including poetry in his text; if it were the case that H is an abridgement of a copy of the story closer to that in Y, this poem could presumably have been prosified along with the others if the compiler so wished.[29] An appreciation for poetry is implied elsewhere in Uilliam's work: Erich Poppe has contrasted the 'native tale' *Stair Nuadat Find Femin* in H, which is interspersed with verse, with the adaptations in H of Middle English verse tales, which are rendered wholly in prose, and has suggested that this may reflect the compiler's sense of the prosimetrum form as appropriate for native tales only.[30] The second of the verse sections common to Y and H (ll 668–81), in which Muirchertach recounts the vision he has had in his narcotized sleep of the burning of his house by Otherworldly forces, is of a slightly different nature, since it may be distinguished from the other poems in the text by its unusual metrical pattern and marked discourse. The third of these poems (ll 845–68), Cairnech's graveside eulogy of Muirchertach, involves a greater degree of difference between the two copies: Y has two quatrains not in H,

---

29 H cannot be a copy of Y, since a large blank space (corresponding to a gap in text) is left in the latter manuscript on the bottom of col. 317 and the top of col. 318 (into which a later scribe has written *is ingnad in folmuid*echt *so fūm* 'this blank beneath me is strange'), but the text continues in H. This section, now only found in H, can hardly be additional, since it includes the climax of the story, the account of Muirchertach's death. Various readings support this interpretation, for example (readings from Y are taken from Nic Dhonnchadha's edition; readings from H are taken from the MS): nom. sg. *firu* Y (l. 20), *fir* H; *ro benn a chlocc* [or *ro bennach locc*?] Y (ll 205–6), *ro bennaig log* H; *for a deis* Y (l. 309), *fora gualuind* H; acc. sg. *mnai* Y (l. 310), *ben* H; *'at-c[h]ím,' ol sē,* Muirchertach Y (l. 346), *atcíamait ar* Muirchertach H; *isin teach n-inc[h]lethi* Y (ll 647–8), *isin teach n-imtheilgthe* H; *teach Cletig 'na t[h]rom-thenid im chenn chaidche* Y (l. 672), *teach Cletig ga commaidhem fa cenn cāich* H; *trē upthaib ban* Y (l. 675), *tre upthaig ndream* H; *7 mā tā a ndán duit* Y (l. 720), *mon dūn* H; *techt* Y (l. 730), *a beith fein* H; *muig* Y (l. 737), *muir* H; *tusa do t[h]aircsin* Y (l. 738), *do flaitisa do thaircsin* H. We may also note that the name 'Sín' is not used in H until l. 157: the list of names in which it is found in Y (ll 50–1, 57–9, 72) does not occur in H, and for Y's *Sin* at lines 88, 115, H has the pronoun *si/sí*. Note also the reference in H (§16) to the *gasā[i]n sanaisi*, the sprigs of 'some plant from which armed warriors could be formed by magic' (*DIL* s.v. *sanais(e)*), not found until later in Y (ll 482 [§25], 611 [§29]). 30 Erich Poppe, 'The Early Modern Irish version of Beves of Hamtoun', *CMCS*, 23 (Summer, 1992), 77–98 at 81.

and there is significant variation in other readings. H describes Muirchertach as *rí[g] Temrach*, for example, but Y has *rí[g] Ailig*, and Ailech is mentioned in the poem a further two times in Y only.

Of the rest of the poems in Y, roughly half may be found paralleled to some extent in prose in H.[31] Of these, the question arises: which of the copies better represents the archetype? Do these poems in Y, which mostly convey dialogues, reflect subsequent versification and expansion of an earlier text, or has the version in H been condensed? A couple of factors would lead me to favour the former position. First, looking at the story as a whole, the prose of *AMME* is, by and large, of equal length in both manuscripts: if a redactor of H's version wished to condense his text, he was notably indifferent to opportunities to do so in the prose. There are only a small number of divergent prose passages, which mostly seem to reveal a slight tendency towards floridity in Y, as in the use of extra, often alliterating, descriptors.[32] Perhaps the most significant divergence may be seen at §34, the two versions of which may be read quite differently. This section as found in Y, which follows Muirchertach's account of his vision mentioned above, describes the king leaving his house to go to where the three clerics sent by Cairnech have lit a little fire, relating to them his dream, and lamenting his weakness and vulnerability, whereupon they offer counsel to him. He returns to his house and conducts a dialogue in verse with Sín (not paralleled in H), in which he inadvertently utters her name, and she foretells his destruction. In the version of this section in H, Muirchertach also rushes outside after his vision of conflagration, but does not approach the clerics; he realizes upon seeing their fire that he is doomed, perhaps because their little fire in some way represents or embodies the great fire he has seen in his vision (and which, he then realizes [§35], heralds the fulfilment of a prophecy that he will die by burning as his grandfather Loarnd did). It could be argued that the version in H is more coherent; Muirchertach's breaking of Sín's *geis* in Y seems poorly motivated, since he had already done so (see l. 631, and cf. l. 649).

Comparison of prose passages in H with poems corresponding to them in Y would also seem to suggest that H is not an abridgement of the verse. Significant verbal echoes may be found in most cases, but other verbal dif-

---

31 These are found in §§3, 4, 9, 16, 19, 20, 21, 22, 23, 25, 26, 30, 31, 49, 51.   32 For example: *maithi cloindi Néill uile co muirneach, mór-menmnach, co subach, sobrónach, ic caithem chīsa 7 conāich cach cūicid i tig comramach Cleitig ós ur na Bóinne bradánaigi, bith-āilli, 7 ós ur in Broga barr-uaine* Y (ll 84–7), *maith cloindi Néill uli ann a caithem cīsa 7 conāich Érenn a tigh Cletigh* H; *do Themair ná do Nás nā do C[h]raebruaid nā do Emain Mache nā do Aileach Néit ná do C[h]leitech teach a leithéid* Y (ll 90–2), *do C[h]leitech a nĒrind teach a leithéid* H; *do chóraig dā c[h]ath c[h]om-móra, c[h]om-nerta, chonaclacha* Y (ll 340–1), *do chóirigh Sīn dā c[h]ath c[h]omhóra* H. Cf. also the extra description in Y of Muirchertach's onrush against the illusory host as *mar tharbh ndian ndīscir ndāsachtach* (ll 407–8).

ferences between the versions weigh against the prose being secondary to the verse.[33] Reversal of phrases (such as *nā triallsa rēir na mban nā clērach* in H for *nā triallsa rēir na clēirech / 7 na mban* in Y [ll 29–30]; *ingen fhir 7 mnā* H for *ingen mnā 7 fir* Y [ll 323–4]; and *do-gēnuind ór 7 airged* H for *do-gēnaind airged is ór* Y [l. 335]) are more likely a result of prosodic requirements than of prosification. Similarly, additional details in H (such as the specification in §4 that Muirchertach will die three nights after saying Sín's name, or the reference to *gasā[i]n sanaisi* in §16) or differences in detail (such as *Ōenach Réil* in Y [l. 177], as against *Aenach Duaibsigi* in H) are unlikely to have come about if H's version was derived from one represented by Y. If H's version is not an abridgement, then, at what point were the poems in Y introduced into its version? Proinsias Mac Cana, in his study of the origins and development of the prosimetrum form in medieval Irish literature, noted that different recensions of texts can vary significantly in their use and distribution of verse sections, a disparity that often reflects 'the casual decisions of individual scribes and redactors over a period of time'.[34] Uáitéar Mac Gearailt's examination of two versions of *Cath Ruis na Ríg* shows how a comparison of poetic material can reveal important information about the methods and emphases of their respective redactors, leading him to suggest that poems were added to the intermediary archetype of the later version of that tale.[35] Mac Cana himself cited the example of *Scél Tuáin meic Cairill*, where three speech-poems have been introduced by the interpolator in *LU*, and are not found in the other versions of the tale.[36] In the latter example, we have visi-

---

33 Compare, for example, the versions in §§3, 9, 16, 20, 21, 22, 25, 26, 30, 31, 49, 51.
34 Proinsias Mac Cana, 'Prosimetrum in insular Celtic literature' in J. Harris and K. Reichl (eds), *Prosimetrum: crosscultural perspectives on narrative in prose and verse* (Cambridge, 1997), pp 99–130 at p. 109. This article is an expansion of an earlier one, 'Notes on the combination of prose and verse in early Irish narrative' in S.N. Tranter and H.L.C. Tristram (eds), *Early Irish literature: media and communication* (Tübingen, 1989), pp 125–47. For a study of poetry intended to provide corroboration or suggest authenticity in prose texts of the eleventh and twelfth centuries, see Gregory Toner, 'Authority, verse and the transmission of *senchas*', *Ériu*, 55 (2005), 59–84.   35 Uáitéar Mac Gearailt, 'Die Gedichte in *Cath Ruis na Ríg*' in E. Poppe (ed.), *Keltologie heute: Themen und Fragestellungen* (Münster, 2004), pp 211–26; idem, 'Leaganacha de *Cath Ruis na Ríg*: an deilbhíocht idir 1100 agus 1650' in P.A. Breatnach, C. Breatnach agus M. Ní Úrdail (eds), *Léann lámhscríbhinní Lobháin: the Louvain manuscript heritage* (BÁC, 2007), pp 168–97 at p. 171.   36 Mac Cana, 'Prosimetrum', pp 109–10. Mac Cana also cites the example of *Aided Con Culainn*, the earliest manuscript of which lacks almost all the poems present in other copies, which poems, he says, 'appear to have been in the archetype' (p. 110). It is not clear to me, however, that this latter has been established; although A.G. van Hamel states that 'from the outset the prose text ... was interspersed with a number of poems', and implies that the later manuscripts better represent the archetype, the only evidence he seems to offer for this view is the 'omission' itself of these poems in the oldest manuscript (*Compert Con Culainn and other stories*, MMIS 3 [Dublin, 1978], pp 69–70). Moreover, van Hamel pointed out that the poems have been preserved in *most* (not all) of the later

ble evidence of scribal contribution to the text. Could some of the poems in *AMME* have also been incorporated as late as Murchadh's own time? The linguistic evidence is equivocal, and is, in any case, more suggestive of date of composition than of integration into the text. Linguistic forms include a small number of older-looking features, such as the Old Irish / Middle Irish acc. pl. and voc. pl. ending in *clēirchiu* (ll 33, 517), past subj. 1 sg. *dá n-apraind* (l. 71), and fut. 2 sg. *fo-gēba* (l. 170), where the preverb *do-* might be expected with independent forms of this verb in Murchadh's time.[37] In general, however, forms which could accord with a composition date either in the late Middle or the Early Modern Irish period predominate, as in, for example, the use of the independent pronoun in *nī lēicfet tū* (l. 523), unnecessary for syllable count, and in *nocha trēicfed tū* (l. 926). It is by no means certain, of course, that all of the poems come from the same source or the same period: we may note, for example, that a version of one of the quatrains in the poem at §4 is found also in *ATig.*, *CS* and *LG*.[38] This quatrain in *AMME* appears to have been modernized (*is iat m'anmanna* [l. 60] as against *it é m'anmann(a)* in the other sources), which suggests that this quatrain at least had an existence prior to *AMME*.

The third poetic group mentioned above comprises poems that have no prose parallel in H.[39] Dialogue is not as prominent a feature of this verse as of the last group discussed; many of these poems are in the mouth of a single character, or of none. Within this group, there are also indications that the Y version of *AMME* has undergone a process of expansion and compilation. This process seemingly did not begin with Murchadh, however, as evidenced by a marginal note he wrote beside a poem (§28) on col. 316: *nī thuigim sin*. This poem is a meditation on the fate of the body and the soul after death, and the marginal comment is found alongside a gloss on the word *éb* (l. 595) which has been incorporated into the text: *.i. idin ele don mnaī cētna*. Nic Dhonnchadha suggests in the index that *Áeb* is a version of *Éba* 'Eve', and in the glossary that *idin* is 'perhaps for Latin *idem*'.[40] It is difficult to know exactly what Murchadh did not understand: this strange word *idin*, perhaps a corruption, or misread from an exemplar, or why another name for Sín should suddenly be introduced, when she already has so many. In any case,

---

manuscripts, and that in those that contain them, 'the same poem is not always found at the same place' (ibid., p. 70). Ruth Lehmann edited and translated poems from *Aided Con Culainn*, although not entirely satisfactorily, in 'Poems from the *Death of Cú Chulainn*', *ZCP*, 49–50 (1997), 432–9.   **37** See McManus, 'An Nua-Ghaeilge Chlasaiceach', p. 413 §7.20.   **38** *ATig.* 533; *CS* 531; *LG* v, p. 534, poem CXXIII. Six other quatrains (five in *CS*) on the death of Muirchertach are included in the *ATig.* entry but are not found in *AMME*, although one of them is found in *LG* v, p. 532, poem CXVIII.   **39** These poems are found at §§6, 7, 10, 12, 14, 18, 28, 32, 34, 44, 46, 48, 50.   **40** The Irish name for Eve is however always disyllabic, as far as I am aware (cf. gen. sg. *Ēva*, l. 324); perhaps the noun *áeb* (= *oíb*) 'beauty' is intended.

Murchadh's perplexity indicates that this poem was inherited from an exemplar or taken from some other written source. Comparison of the context of this poem in Y with the corresponding passage in H gives no reason to suggest that it may also have been in H's exemplar, however, and no direct link with the subject matter of *AMME* is evident. It may also be significant that this poem is one of only four in Y's text that is not written in *deibide* metre.

Another non-*deibide* poem, found at §48, appears to furnish evidence that Murchadh's exemplar contained more poems than does the version in H. This poem, in which Cairnech exhorts Sín to confess and repent her sins, consists of three stanzas of eight lines each (with one exception) in the metre *ochtfoclach mór* (syllabic pattern of [6^2 6^2 6^2 5^1] x 2, with rhymes between lines *abc*, *efg* and *dh*). It includes the analytic verbal form *at-bēra sinn* (l. 895) (: *ind*), and although some few examples of such forms have been found in Middle Irish texts, they are much more a feature of the Early Modern Irish period.[41] The poem also seems to betray a transcription error, since the first stanza appears to be missing a line from its second half. It refers to Sín's killing of the king of Tara (although she is not mentioned by name), and so, unlike the poem at §28 whose subject matter is not specific to the story of *AMME*, this poem seems to have been composed with Sín and Cairnech in mind. It seems likely, therefore, that this poem was also in Murchadh's exemplar.

On the other hand, there are also indications that Murchadh was doing more than just copying. Perhaps the most obvious of these is the blank space, amounting to roughly half a column, which he left in columns 317 and 318.[42] This blank begins towards the end of §37 (l. 742) in Nic Dhonnchadha's edition, after Muirchertach has realized that he is doomed to die as his grandfather did and takes to his bed again, having partaken of some more of Sín's 'false wine' (l. 727). He has another vision in his sleep, this time of being taken from a submerging ship by a griffin to its nest, only for the nest to be burned around him. When Muirchertach awakes, he asks that the dream be interpreted by his foster-brother Dub Dá Rind (Duibrenn H), a druid's son. Y's text stops before Dub Dá Rind has finished his interpretation, and the next seven paragraphs or so in Nic Dhonnchadha's edition are supplied by H. The edition picks up the Y text again in §44 with a poem (following the blank in column 318 and not in H) summarizing Muirchertach's life and career. In Nic Dhonnchadha's edition (Stokes omitted it entirely), this poem in §44 appears to come from the mouth of Cairnech, but as it stands in the manuscript it might be read as being uttered by Dub Dá Rind, since he is the previous speaker in that manuscript's text and the poem refers to the twelve years that Muirchertach spent in Dub Dá Rind's father's house (ll 792–3).

41 Liam Breatnach, 'An Mheán-Ghaeilge' in McCone et al. (eds), *Stair na Gaeilge*, pp 221–333 at pp 272–3 §10.19; McManus, 'An Nua-Ghaeilge Chlasaiceach', pp 419–21 §7.30. 42 See note 29 above.

Why did Murchadh leave this blank space? It probably corresponds fairly closely to the amount of missing text, which, moreover, includes the climax of the tale. Did he perceive some fault in his exemplar, and intend to fill in the blank later, as Nic Dhonnchadha suggests?[43] Or did he wish to modify his exemplar in some way, but miscalculated his *mise en page*? Whatever the reason was, this seems to point to some kind of unfulfilled redactorial intention on his part.

So some degree of compilation in Y is suggested by the occurrence elsewhere of an older version of the quatrain in §4, and the evidence of manuscript layout just discussed suggests that Murchadh was personally involved in the compilation process to some extent at least. Is it possible that he may have had an even more creative input into the Y text? I have mentioned above some examples of poems that were likely taken from pre-existing sources, but is it possible that he himself may have composed others? We may consider, for example, those poems which echo the prose of H particularly closely to have been freshly composed for the purposes of providing a poetic component to an existing text, although of course proving that Murchadh composed them is another matter. Compare the short poem in Y (ll 462–9) with the corresponding prose in H at §23:

> Y:
> ro t[h]uit co héneirt ar lār, co n-ebairt in lāid:
>
> Gāir trom, tairm do-níat sluaig,
> cath fer ngorm rind atuaid,
> fir cen c[h]ind fobr*es*[44] treass
> isin glind rind a-neas.
>
> Fand mo n*er*t dochum s[h]luaig,
> ba mōr fecht rugus buaid,
> mōr in sluag, tenn an dáil,
> borb a n-ainm, garb a ngāir.

H (text from MS):
do thoit f*ora* ais ina imdaigh *co* ndubair*t* is trom i*n* gāir-si ac cath*a*ibh na f*er* ngorm rin*d* atuaigh 7 i*n* gāir-si anes acna f*er*uib gan cin*n* 7 is fand mu n*er*t-sa 'na n-ag*aid*h cidh ga*r*bh in gāir.

If the arguments advanced above as to the relation of Y and H to each other are accepted, then it is difficult to escape the conclusion that this poem is based directly on an earlier version of *AMME* itself, now reflected in H, and

---

43 *Aided Muirchertaig*, p. ix.   44 Or perhaps *fōbres* (< *fōibrid* < *fúabair*)?

was composed by some later redactor of the text.[45] Since *AMME* has been argued to be a twelfth-century text on linguistic and literary-historical grounds,[46] such composition could theoretically have taken place at any point between then and the writing of the Y text, about two hundred years later. Those poems that display particularly close verbal echoes with corresponding prose passages in H (see note 45) seem linguistically of a piece with the rest of the text in general, but there are in fact very few linguistic features in them that cannot also be found paralleled in sources from Murchadh's own time. Some variants may be instructive. For example, for *nī racha doridise* 'you will not go back' (§9, l. 172) in Y, H has *nī racair tar hais*. The spread of the ending *-(a)ir* from pres. subj. 2 sg. (itself arising from analogy with pres. subj. 1 sg.) to fut. 2 sg. is a development of the Early Modern Irish period, where however it is generally restricted to non-classical prose texts.[47] So although the form *racha* in Y may seem more conservative than its counterpart in H, it would not be unexpected in verse of the Early Modern Irish period, and indeed may be found elsewhere in this context.[48] Similarly, Y's infixed pronoun in §16 (*nā rot gaba aithrechus* 'let not regret seize you', l. 326) looks older than H's independent pronoun: *nā gabadh aithreachus tusa*, but this anteriority may be more apparent than real, since infixed pronouns are quite common in Classical Irish verse, though rare in non-archaising prose texts and likely defunct in speech of that period.[49] Moreover, independent pronouns are also found in verse in Y: *nocha trēicfed tū* (§49, l. 926) 'he would not abandon you'. Anachronistic forms are sometimes used, perhaps to suit the metre, such as disyllabic *Boind* (: *lind* §6, l. 94; : *sheing* §49, l. 913; cf. monosyllabic non-rhyming *Bóinn* §16, l. 332).

The poems in Y embrace a mixture of old- and new-looking features. Independent datives are found at §12 (*techtaid giallu cāich bar lāim* 'take hold of everyone's hostages by your hand', l. 237) and §10 (*cétaib cuana* 'with hundreds of packs of hounds', l. 198); *cuana* in the latter example must be incorrect, however, both grammatically (it was declined either as an *ā-* or an *o-*stem) and because it is in rhyming position with *tulaig-si* in the previous line. A dative singular showing *u-*colouring appears in §10 (*Cletiuch*, l. 198), while accusative plurals *clēirchiu* and *giallu*, and vocative plurals *macu* and *clērchiu* are found in non-rhyming position at §3 (l. 33), §12 (l. 237), and §26 (ll 502, 517). Verbal forms like *dá n-apraind* and *nī ebēr-sa* (§4, ll 71, 80, §32 l. 658) seem more Middle than Early Modern Irish, and *nodus sāraigeb-sa* (§14, l. 298) also shows a Middle Irish future 1 sg. ending, as well as a

---

45 Similar arguments could be put forward in relation to the poems in §§9, 16, 21, 25, 49 and 51.   46 Nic Dhonnchadha, *Aided Muirchertaig*, p. xix; Herbert, 'The death'. 47 McManus, 'An Nua-Ghaeilge Chlasaiceach', pp 400 §7.6, 407 §7.14.   48 For example, Gofraidh Fionn Ó Dálaigh (†1387), *Beir eolas dúinn, a Dhomhnuill*, in *DD*, p. 232 §41d. 49 McManus, 'An Nua-Ghaeilge Chlasaiceach', pp 429–30 §9.2.

Middle Irish form of the feminine infixed pronoun.[50] In the poem from which the latter example is taken, however, we also find the 1 pl. independent pronoun *ind* (§14, l. 278) as verbal object, a form described by Damian McManus as a totally new ('úrnua') form in Early Modern Irish.[51] Other constructions found in the verse of Y which are more suggestive of Early Modern than of Middle Irish usage include the 3 sg. relative ending *-es* with a 2 pl. independent subject pronoun (*in tan maídfes sib* 'when you will boast', §12, l. 245),[52] and the impersonal use of a 3 sg. verbal form, with the subject indicated by an independent pronoun (*at-bēra sinn* 'we will say', §48, l. 895).[53] The latter example is notable for its combination of a later syntactical feature with an earlier verbal form, and is a good illustration of the eclectic and heterogeneous quality of the language of much of the verse.

As a final observation, it is interesting to note that the text preceding *AMME* in Murchadh's section of YBL, the longer version of *Cath Maige Rath*, ends with four quatrains that are not found in the other manuscripts containing this story.[54] Verbal echoes between these quatrains and some in *AMME* may be discerned; the phrase *cían bus cuman* (col. 310 l. 25), for example, is found in *AMME* at §21, l. 435 and §47, l. 867 (the latter also found in verse in H). The adjective *dingbála* (col. 310 l. 28), or the noun on which it is based, is used a number of times in *AMME* (§6, l. 110, §16, l. 325 [also in prose in H], §19, l. 373, §49, l. 922). These echoes may be no more than coincidence, but the latter example in particular occurs sufficiently frequently in *AMME* to suggest a deliberate verbal motif; its occurrence in these quatrains in *Cath Maige Rath*, then, is striking.[55]

The additional verse in YBL's *Cath Maige Rath*, the emphasis on verse that is manifest in the Y version of *AMME*, and the range and quantity of

---

50 Nic Dhonnchadha supplies a macron on the verbal ending (*nodus sāraigēbsa*), but I am not sure that this is necessary. Although *sáraigid* took an *eó-/éa-* future in Early Modern Irish, it took an *f*-future in Old and Middle Irish (see McManus, 'An Nua-Ghaeilge Chlasaiceach', p. 404 §7.10 (f), and examples in *DIL* s.v. *sáraigid*). **51** McManus, 'An Nua-Ghaeilge Chlasaiceach', p. 429 §9.1. **52** Ibid., p. 423 §7.33; cf. Breatnach, 'An Mheán-Ghaeilge', pp 287–8 §11.35. **53** McManus, 'An Nua-Ghaeilge Chlasaiceach', pp 419–20 §7.30. **54** These are Dublin, RIA MS B iv 1 (236), pp 62b–81b; RIA MS 24 P 9 (739), pp 105–44, 159–92; and RIA MS 23 K 44 (58), pp 41–130. I have not consulted the copy in Brussels mentioned by Carl Marstrander ('A new version of the battle of Mag Rath', *Ériu*, 5 [1911], 226–47 at 226) [= Brussels, Bibliothèque Royale, MS 2324–40 (3410), ff 55r–57v], but I think that it in fact contains only *Fled Dúin na nGéd* (see Lehmann, *Fled Dúin na nGéd*, pp 31–7). John O'Donovan omitted these quatrains from his edition (*The banquet of Dun na n-Gedh and the battle of Magh Rath* [Dublin, 1842]), as noted by Myles Dillon, 'A note on the texts of "Cath Maige Rath" preserved in the Yellow Book of Lecan', *Éigse*, 7 (1953–55), 199–201 at 199. **55** That one of each of these examples is paralleled in H may admittedly problematize any suggestion of common authorship of the verses, if that authorship belongs to a period subsequent to the version represented by H, as I have proposed. It may not rule such a suggestion out entirely, however.

the marginal stanzas in LB suggest a literary impulse that motivated Murchadh: to favour and endorse versions of texts in which the poetic element is prominent, or to augment and enhance his output by poetic elaboration. The evidence presented here may not allow us to go so far as to affirm that Murchadh himself composed poetry now found only in his copy of *AMME* (although this must remain a possibility, at least in some cases); it does, I think, permit the argument that he took a markedly creative and innovatory approach to his work, and had a particular interest in the power of poetry to enhance both the aesthetics and the exposition of a story. His literary sensibilities and intellectual energy make him, I hope, a fitting subject for this tribute to an outstanding teacher, colleague and scholar.

The shield of Fionn: the poem
Uchán a sciath mo rígh réigh in Leabhar Ua Maine

JOSEPH J. FLAHIVE

One of the hallmarks of Máire Herbert's approach to early Irish hagiography has been her recognition that sacred literature does not stand aloof from other literatures of its time, and she has reminded scholars that

> It is evident that many traditional disciplinary boundaries need to be transcended if hagiographical study is to achieve its full potential. Saints' Lives are not only to be viewed in their particular and collective contexts, and in tandem with other evidence relating to cult, they are also to be placed in association with other forms of contemporary writing, both in Latin and the vernacular.[1]

Just as hagiographical texts can be illuminated by comparison with secular narrative literature, on which it frequently draws in the presentation of its sanctified hero, the use of hagiographical style and motifs in secular literature has gradually received greater recognition.[2] One of the places where this has been discussed to a great extent is in regard to the importation of a framework of dialogues between an aged Fenian warrior and St Patrick into works of *fianaigheacht*. It is clear that the presence of the saint acts as a catalyst for the production – which he then proceeds to sanctify – making it an addendum to his own *acta*, but this in itself requires the elevation of the literature, which must be worthy of the blessing bestowed.[3] This is based on a common

---

1 Máire Herbert, 'Hagiography' in K. McCone and K. Simms (eds), *Progress in medieval Irish studies* (Maynooth, 1996), pp 79–90 at p. 89. This principle is fundamental to her monograph *Iona, Kells, and Derry: the history and hagiography of the monastic* familia *of Columba* (Oxford, 1988), where it is discussed in her Introduction and employed throughout. 2 The authority of the figure of the saint in the early Irish literary tradition has been explored in detail by Joseph Nagy, *Conversing with angels and ancients: literary myths of medieval Ireland* (Dublin, 1997). A recent case study of the blending of sacred and secular in medieval Irish literature is Alexandra Bergholm, *From shaman to saint: interpretative strategies in the study of Buile Suibhne*, Folklore Fellows' Communications 302 (Helsinki, 2012). 3 Ruairí Ó hUiginn, 'Duanaire Finn' in P. Ó Fiannachta (ed.), *Léachtaí Cholm Cille 25: An fhiannaíocht* (Maynooth, 1995), pp 47–68 at pp 49–50; Nagy, *Conversing with angels and ancients*, pp 317–23; Harry Roe, 'The *Acallam*: the church's eventual acceptance of the cultural inheritance of pagan Ireland' in S. Sheehan, J. Findon, and W. Follett (eds), *Gablánach in scélaigecht: Celtic Studies in honour of Ann Dooley* (Dublin, 2013), pp 103–15.

pattern of dialogue in the hagiographical corpus; the queries and recitations in hagiographical works, most especially the *Vita tripartita*, have a similar format and share aspects of their function with some Fenian texts, and Ann Dooley has recently explored the use of this Life and other hagiography in *Acallam na senórach*.[4] In my doctoral thesis, I examined a number of lays in Duanaire Finn (Dublin, UCD Archives, Franciscan MS A 20[b]),[5] arguing that a significant number of the earliest extended verse narratives in the corpus of Fenian lays share a structural model.[6] The Patrician frame-story of Caoilte or Oisín engaging Patrick and his clerics leads to an extended in-tale, introduced by the recovery or presentation of an object of particular import-ance to Fionn or one of his chief warriors, its ecphrasis, and the narration of its history and the mighty deeds associated with it; a few brief reflections of the ancients suffice to close the frame-story. The centrepiece objects are, in their most basic physical form, relics of the *fiana*, and bring with them their histories of wondrous deeds and victories; consequently, I term these poems 'relic lays'. This group of poems in DF comprises the fragment *Ceisd agam ort a Chaoílte*, describing Fionn's *corrbholg* ('crane-bag');[7] *Uchán a sgíeth mo ríogh réil* on Fionn's shield;[8] *Siothal Chaílti cía ros fuair* about Caoilte's drink-ing vessel;[9] *A chloidhimh chléircín in chluig* on a sword won by Fionn, later carried by Oscar;[10] *Iss é súd colg an laoích láin*, on Caoilte's sword.[11] In the end, the fates of the objects are various. That of the *corrbholg* is to be lost along with the end of the lay. Fionn's shield, an object associated with pagan figures, to wit, Lugh and Manannán, is burnt. Caoilte's *sitheal*, an object whose description mirrors the construction of early Irish chalices, is trans-formed by Patrick into objects that become the holy relics of the new religion:

> Níamhochthar bachla bána
> is cluig 7 ceólána
> agus soisgela sgriobhtha
> d'or is d'airgead na síthla.[12]

Oscar's sword comes into the possession of Maolchiar, one of Patrick's cler-ics, to the horror of the aged Oisín; in contrast, Caoilte's now belongs to the high-king, Diarmaid mac Cearbhaill. These relics share the travel, exaltation,

---

4 Ann Dooley, 'The deployment of some hagiographical sources in *Acallam na senórach*' in S. Arbuthnot and G. Parsons (eds), *The Gaelic Finn tradition* (Dublin, 2012), pp 97–110. 5 In this paper, a distinction will be made between the abbreviation DF (unitalicized), representing the manuscript, and *DF* (italicized), the ITS edition.   6 Joseph J. Flahive, 'The relic lays: a study in late Middle-Gaelic *fianaigheacht*' (PhD, University of Edinburgh, 2004).   7 *DF* i, pp 21–2; trans. i, pp 118–20.   8 Ibid., pp 34–8; trans. pp 134–9.   9 Ibid., pp 38–45; trans. pp 140–9.   10 Ibid., pp 49–55; trans. pp 153–62. 11 *DF* ii, pp 124–41.   12 'White croziers will be made resplendent, and bells and *ceoláns* [small bells] and gospels of writing, with the gold and silver of the urn': *DF* i, pp 45, 149.

and profanation that characterize the Christian relic in medieval history. They embody the physical past, and provide a link to the deeds of a Fenian hero, just as a crozier or chalice does to a sainted bishop.[13] Finally, these lays are characterized by their inclusion of learned lessons in history, something more than an heroic narrative. One may learn the versified lists of the hounds of the *fian* or the boars slain by Bran in the lay of Caoilte's urn; the shield of Fionn comes with a catalogue of its victories. Other learned elements appear as well, such as Fítheal's judgement of the ownership of Caoilte's sword and the trespass of Fítheal's goats in Cormac's garden, in which due legal process is followed throughout, leading to praise of a golden age of justice. Apologues and episodes incorporate and refashion literary material from the mythological and Ulster cycles, as well as references to other Fenian tales. These lays are carefully crafted fusions of the native and the Latin, secular and sacred; it is not in doubt that they are a part of the learned tradition. Nevertheless, the lays, containing a narrative element, diverged from the type of antiquarian lore preserved in *Acallam na senórach*. The lays were primarily enjoyable as tales, which opened them to the appreciation of a wider audience; in due time, function shaped their form, as Ruairí Ó hUiginn has observed in relation to the language of the poems in DF:

> Sna laoithe, áfach, don tsimplíocht agus go deimhin don tsogthuig-theacht a tugadh tús áite, agus is minic dá barr a chastar focail agus leaganacha cainte orainn sna laoithe nach mbeadh ag teacht ar aon bhealach le forálacha agus rialacha an bhairdne, ach a bhí le fada in úsáid i gcaint na ndaoine.[14]

This tendency seems to be rather more remarkable, when, as Ó hUiginn suggests, these Fenian poems could be the work of the same poets who wrote in Classical *dán díreach*. A shift away from the versified lists and obscure references that characterize Middle Irish lore poetry accompanies the change in language. At any rate, by the time one reaches the Early Modern period, the popular compositions have assumed a different literary character from their medieval predecessors.

The dates assigned to these poems by Murphy, ranging from AD 1100 to the thirteenth century, imply that at least some of them predate *Acallam na senórach* and therefore provide glimpses of the transition from Patrician hagiography to the Patrick of the *Agallamh* and of later Fenian tradition; furthermore, this period stands very close to the birth of narrative heroic verse in Irish. Nevertheless, discussion of the role of these poems in the evolution

---

13 For an account of Fenian learning as commemoration, see Máire Herbert, 'Múineadh na Fiannaíochta' in P. Ó Fiannachta (ed.), *Léachtaí Choilm Cille* 9: *An Ghaeilge á muineadh* (Maigh Nuad, 1978), pp 44–57. 14 Ó hUiginn, 'Duanaire Finn', p. 48.

of literary *fianaigheacht* has been minimal, hampered at least in part by the uncertain dates of composition assigned to poems preserved in an Early Modern manuscript.[15] Among these lays, only the one devoted to Caoilte's dipper has a wider textual tradition, being preserved also in the Reeves manuscript of *Agallamh na seanórach* and several later *duanaireadha*.[16] This was recognized by Murphy, whose commentary refers to the text in Dublin, RIA MS 24 P 5, but he was not aware of any further copies of the other relic lays in this discussion. Earlier texts of two more of these medieval poems, however, exist, though neither has been published hitherto.[17] A second copy of the lay on Fionn's shield, bearing the slightly variant opening *Uchán a sciath mo rígh réigh* ('Alas, O shield of my serene king'), along with the lay of Oscar's sword, *A cloidheam cleithrín a cluig* ('O sword of the bell-ringing clerkling'), may be found in Leabhar Ua Maine [LUM] (Dublin, RIA, Stowe MS D ii 1, ff 145ra5–va38 and 145va39–146vb25). Macalister's introduction (1942) to the collotype facsimile of LUM refers the reader to the *DF* edition of these poems.[18] In fairness to Murphy, it should be recognized that he sent

---

15 Murphy's dates for these poems, in the order cited above, are 'the 13th century, or perhaps the very late Middle Irish period' (*DF* iii, p. 30); 'the middle of the twelfth century' (ibid., p. 34); '*c.*1200' (ibid., p. 36); 'in the 13th century' (ibid., p. 44); 'the middle of the 12th century' (ibid., p. 107). John Carey gives Murphy's dating criteria a general vindication after careful re-evaluation; nevertheless, he observes that Murphy's cautiousness in interpretation caused him to assign slightly later dates to the texts than other scholars faced with similar data might have done: 'Making all due allowances for the slipperiness of the evidence, it does seem that Murphy's dates may often have been too late, sometimes by a century or more' (John Carey, 'Remarks on dating' in idem [ed.], *Duanaire Finn: reassessments*, ITS SS 13 [London, 2003], pp 1–18 at p. 18). Attention has been drawn to the implications of these conclusions for the broader understanding of the Fenian cycle by Geraldine Parsons in her review of Carey in *CMCS*, 55 (2008), 70–2 at 72. For recent evaluations of the date of *Acallam na senórach*, generally assigned to the early thirteenth century, see Anne Connon, 'The Roscommon *locus* of *Acallam na senórach* and some thoughts as to *tempus* and *persona*' in A. Doyle and K. Murray (eds), *In dialogue with the Agallamh: essays in honour of Seán Ó Coileáin* (Dublin, 2014), pp 21–59; Ann Dooley, 'The date and purpose of *Acallam na senórach*', *Éigse*, 34 (2004), 97–126; and Ann Dooley and Harry Roe (trans.), *Tales of the elders of Ireland* (Oxford, 1999), pp xx–xxviii. A valuable discussion of the gap between manuscript and textual date in the Fenian cycle is provided by Kevin Murray, 'Interpreting the evidence: problems with dating the early *Fíanaigecht* corpus' in Arbuthnot and Parsons (eds), *The Gaelic Finn tradition*, pp 31–49. 16 Dublin, RIA MS 24 P 5, published by Nessa Ní Shéaghdha (ed.), *Agallamh na seanórach*, 3 vols, Leabhair ó Láimhsgríbhnibh 7, 10, 15 (Dublin 1942–5; republished by the ITS as one volume London, 2014), with this poem appearing at iii, pp 21–42; Dublin, RIA MS 23 L 34; Dublin, RIA MS 24 M 2; and Maynooth, Russell Library, MS Renehan 69. The texts of these last three manuscripts are extremely close to that of RIA 24 P 5; they also share some few trivial common corruptions and innovations.   17 The present author has drawn attention to these poems in *An Fhianaigheacht: the Fenian cycle in Irish and Scottish Gaelic literature* (forthcoming); these remarks have been quoted in Murray, 'Interpreting the evidence', p. 38 n. 36.   18 R.A.S. Macalister (ed.), *The Book of*

his commentary to Brussels for printing in 1938, where it was held up by the war; when the ailing Murphy saw it through press so long after it was written – it was finally printed in 1953 and distributed as the annual ITS volume for 1954 – he was not in a position to update his work systematically.[19] The fascicule of the Academy's manuscript catalogue describing LUM did not appear until after his death.

The poem on Oscar's sword is lengthy, and probably of later date than the one on Fionn's shield. Any broader discussion of the relic lays will require an edition of both LUM Fenian texts. Towards this goal, the remainder of this contribution will present and discuss the text of the lay *Uchán a sciath mo rígh réigh* from this manuscript. It has already been noted that Murphy provides some linguistic discussion, on the basis of which he concludes that '[t]his poem offers few opportunities for exact dating', but he offers the linguistic and metrical judgement that it 'probably belongs to the middle of the 12th century'.[20] I have also commented on the DF text of this poem in my doctoral thesis, where I assigned it a date in the first half of the twelfth century.[21] The age of LUM is such as to confirm the medieval origin of the two Fenian poems in it: since the manuscript dates to *c*.1380, there is a great shift of the absolute *terminus ante quem*, as DF was written in 1626–7. Furthermore, it is immediately apparent that the LUM copies of these lays cannot lie behind DF as a source, even indirectly. DF contains quatrains wanting in LUM; and, in a number of textual divergences, DF readings are more conservative and metrically superior. It is clear that the textual traditions represented by the two extant witnesses must have diverged prior to the production of LUM in the late fourteenth century.

While complete analysis must wait for another occasion, some preliminary remarks on selected noteworthy features of the poem are advanced here. The lay is a recitation by a Fenian ancient in which Patrick never speaks, though his presence is implied, especially by the religious closing with a comparison of the poisoned hazel to the Tree of Knowledge in the garden of Eden. In DF, the narrator is Oisín; he mentions Caoilte as his only surviving peer in q. 8. In LUM, however, the roles reverse, and the equivalent stanza (q. 4) names Oisín as the speaker's ancient comrade: the narrator of the text must therefore be Caoilte. The origins of the shield lie in the battle of Magh Tuireadh, and the text of the lay closely reflects the dialogue between Lugh and the defeated Balor found in a variant version of this tale preserved in

Uí Maine, otherwise called 'The Book of the O'Kelly's' [sic] *with descriptive introduction and indexes*, IMC Facsimiles in Collotype of Irish Manuscripts 4 (Dublin, 1942), p. 38. **19** An account of Murphy's progress and delays is given in Pádraig Ó Riain, 'Foreword' in Carey (ed.), *Duanaire Finn: reassessments*, pp v–ix at pp vii–ix. **20** *DF* iii, p. 34. **21** Flahive, 'The relic lays', pp 94–5 (date); pp 133–41 (literary discussion); pp 241–2 (textual commentary); ideas presented in the remainder of this section are based on the discussion in pp 133–8.

RIA MS 24 P 9,[22] most especially Balor's last request, paralleled in §§7–10 (= *DF* i, pp 34–5 §§10–13) of the poem:

> 'Madh cosgrach thusa orm-sa', ar Balar, 'an tan beanfair mo cheann díom a chur ar mullach do chinn féin 7 a mhéidhe do chur red cheann ar dháigh go ndeach mo rath 7 mo rochonách, mo ghráin 7 mo ghaisgeadh sa ort-sa. Uair ní fhágbhuim dar mh'éisi neach is caradraighe dhamh iná thusa'.[23]

Here, Lugh beheads Balor and displays his head on a standing-stone, analogous to the hazel tree in the lay, §§9–10 (= *DF* i, p. 35 §§12–13):

> Beanuis Lugh a cheann de, 7 téid risin cceann iar sin, 7 cóirighis ar cholamhain chartha cloichi móire baoi a n-athfhogas dó é. Goirid do vhí ann asa h-aithle an tan do sgoilt 7 do sgaoil an cartha cruaidh coimhreamhar cloichi i cceathra leathsgoilténuibh lánmhóra go lár.[24]

This exchange does not occur in the earliest extant version of the tale, where Balor is slain instantaneously with the single stone that extinguishes his baleful eye, though there is some parallel in the mortal wounding of Indech mac Dé Domnann, who is struck by the head of the falling Balor, *co sescaind a loim foulae tara béola-side* ('so that a gush of blood sprouted from his lips').[25] Ó Cuív considers the language of the 24 P 9 version of *Cath Muighe Tuireadh* to be Early Modern Irish, but '[i]t resembles ... Lughaidh Ó Cléirigh's *Beatha Aodha Ruaidh Ui Dhomhnaill* with its stilted bombastic style and its artificially archaic language'.[26] Nevertheless, with reference to the folk versions and DF, he concludes that this tradition is probably older because 'it would seem not unlikely that our version was descended from an original compiled some centuries earlier', with infusions of alternative traditions in *Leabhar gabhála* and the *Dinnsheanchas*, allowing for the existence of 'several MS. versions in vogue between the twelfth and seventeenth centuries'.[27]

---

22 Brian Ó Cuív (ed.), *Cath Muighe Tuireadh* (Dublin, 1946). The episode discussed here appears on pp 53–5. Murphy, writing before this text was published, discusses the scene in relation to orally-collected folk tales: *DF* iii, pp xliii–xlv.   **23** 'If you would vanquish me', said Balor, 'when my head shall be cut off, place it atop your own head, and put its neck to your head in hope that my grace and good-fortune, my fearsomeness and feats-of-arms come onto you. For I do not leave behind me anyone dearer to me than you': Ó Cuív, *Cath Muighe Tuireadh*, p. 54, ll 1318–23.   **24** 'Lugh cut his head off, and he goes with the head after that, and he placed it on a pedestal of a great pillar stone that was near him. It was not long afterwards when the hard, massive pillar stone cracked and crumbled into four full fragments to the bottom': ibid., p. 54, ll 1336–40.   **25** Elizabeth Gray (ed. and trans.), *Cath Maige Tuired*, ITS 52 (London, 1983), pp 60–1 §135.   **26** Ó Cuív, *Cath Muighe Tuireadh*, p. 13.   **27** Ibid., p. 17.

From the wood, poisoned by the venom of Balor, Manannán has a marvellous shield fashioned. Manannán appears in association with origins of magical objects elsewhere in *fianaigheacht*, fashioning the *corrbholg* in *Ceisd agam ort a Chaoílte* in DF; Éanán, whose vessel becomes known as Caoilte's urn, is Manannán's son-in-law, associating that object and the accompanying fairy gifts with him also. Of note in this early section is Cairbre's composition of a *duan mholta* ('praise-poem') on the shield; he then receives it as payment for his ode. Not only does this provide a contrast with the battered ancient object of which Oisín sings, but it reflects a practice of request by praise, of which a real case from the later medieval period survives in Tadhg Dall's poem *Mo chean doit, a Ghráinne gharbh*, alongside more numerous fictional examples.[28] Most of these early claimants of the shield are shadowy figures, but one of them, Eitheor, brings the early section full circle when the Daghdha gives him the shield; the poem claims that this is the origin of his name Mac Cuill ('son of the hazel'). Mac Cuill is portrayed in the synthetic histories as killing Lugh and seizing the kingship with his brothers. When he falls at the battle of Taillte, the shield once again embarks on an untraceable progression.[29]

When the pageant of pre-Fenian pseudo-historical and mythical owners concludes, the sword comes to Tadhg mac Nuadhad; it is stolen by Cumhall in the abduction of Tadhg's daughter Muirne, Fionn's mother, and thus enters into Fenian possession. Here there is the opportunity to incorporate a list of its battles, in the style of so many of the learned versifications in *Acallam na senórach*. Within the *fian*, it comes to Criomhall after the death of Cumhall in the battle of Cnucha, and later passes to Fionn. Oisín's closing remarks compare the destruction caused by the biblical Tree of Knowledge with that of the 'fruit' of this hazel of Irish mythology. Although he laments the loss of this treasure of his father, Oisín is now a Christian; he recognizes that the heroic age has passed. The shield is burnt by a swineherd.[30]

---

28 *TDall* i, pp 242–5 (text); ii, pp 160–2 (trans.). **29** These events are documented in *Hériu ard, inis na rríg*, in Peter J. Smith (ed. and trans.), *Three historical poems ascribed to Gilla Cóemáin: a critical edition of the work of an eleventh-century Irish scholar*, Studien und Texte zur Keltologie 8 (Münster, 2007), p. 114 §§26–30 (= *LG* v, pp 492–4 §§27–31). Fuller versions are presented in *LG* iv *passim* with additional references in *LG* v (see Pádraig Ó Riain, *LG: index of names*, ITS 63 [London, 2009], s.n. Mac Cuill), the most important of which comprise his ascent in *LG* iv, pp 118–30, §§312–16 and fall at Taillte in *LG* v, p. 154 §470 (= *LG* v, p. 164 §480). Of particular note is the explanation in the list of the sons of Cearmad in *LG* iv, p. 130 §316d: *Mac Cuill .i. Sethor* (v.l. *Setheoir*) *coll a dea* ['Mac Cuill – Setheor, the hazel his god'] (= *LG* iv, p. 152 §334 with the name Ethur, and v.ll. Hethur, Heitoir, and Ethor; and *LG* iv, pp 192–4 §368 with the interesting difference of *mur a dee* ['the sea was his god'] in the Book of Lecan, though the Ballymote version retains the hazel). *AFM* AM3370–3500 (i, pp 20–6) provides a clear précis of these events. **30** Portions of this paper and text were read at *Rannsachadh na Gàidhlig* 2012, held at the University of Glasgow; Prof. Herbert was among the members of the audience who provided valuable feedback to the author, and to whom thanks is due.

EDITION

This is a semi-diplomatic edition from LUM. The quatrains are numbered, with the equivalent quatrain numbers in *DF* given in brackets. LUM contains no quatrains not paralleled in the *DF* version, and lacks six of those found there; new material is limited to occasional changes in phrasing or construction of lines and differences in proper names. Mac Neill's translation (*DF* i, pp 134–9), therefore, though stylistically dated, reasonably represents the narrative for the general reader.

The orthography of the text in the manuscript is progressive in regard to marking the lenition of voiced consonants, as well as *caol le caol agus leathan le leathan* spelling, which is therefore employed in expansions. In compressions employing superscript letters, only the omitted letters are italicized. The frequent *e*-caudata (*ȩ*) is transcribed *ea*; occasional enclitic subscript *a* and *i* are transcribed without note. The *æ* digraph has been separated. The 'lightning-bolt' stroke is expanded *–ear*. The *quia*-compendium for *ar* (and *air* with superscript *i*), the *–us* compendium, and lazy-*8* for *–ur*, which have an invariable expansion, have not been italicized. Tironian *et* (*ꝛ*) is expanded silently according to metrical requirement. The scribe hardly ever employs the mark of length, but he frequently marks *i* by a hairstroke to avoid minim confusion; this latter notation has not been reproduced. Numbers represented by Roman numerals are italicized. Further editorial introductions extend to capitalization, hyphenation, the mark of hiatus, and the apostrophe to indicate elided vowels not represented in the manuscript. Orthographical inconsistencies have not been altered or standardized. The scribal marking of the *dúnadh* by a repetition each time that it ends a quatrain has been set aside in parentheses. Rubbings-out and alterations by a contemporary or near-contemporary corrector are incorporated into the text but footnoted. There are scribal slips (e.g., nominative *Manannain* **30a**, *glach* for *glac* **39b**, and genitive *Eirind* **53d**) which are reproduced as they stand. The division of quatrains is faulty from **35–7**. **36ab** is written continuously from the previous with a small letter. *Tríath* at **36c** receives an initial, and the writing is continuous to the beginning of **38**, where the correct layout resumes. These divisions of six have been rectified here. Following the edition, this study concludes with commentary on the text and a final evaluation of the poem.

TEXT

(LUM fo. 145ra5–va38)[31]

1 (1) Uchan a sciath mo righ reigh
    insa da beith fa drochsgeimh.
doghra nach mair do triath teand
    a comhla sciath na hEir*ean*n

2 (2) Mor cosgar mor cath calma
    as tug tu do tig*hear*na
maith brig do cailc' im rennaib
    a din-bailc re beiminnaibh

3 (6) Nocho buil ar talmain tigh
    laech na faigh na fissigi
a sceith righ[a] Sigir seagtha
    neac[b] da-idir da imcechta

4 (7) Nocho[c] bhuil ar talmain taig
    neach da-idir d'fhir na mnai
cred ma buil in t-ainm a-mach
    dit 'ga[d] gairm seancoll sniäch

5 (8) Nocho fhuil ach misi fein
    agus Oissin fear gu ceill
is Finntan Duni Fearta
    neach do-fhidir t'imceacta

6 (9) Ass as tugadh sciath mo righ
    a-deirim ribh is fath fir
gan brath gan bron duni damh
    o cath mor Muigi Tuireagh[e]

7 (10) Balar da chuinigh[f] ar Lugh
    seal beg re n-a diceandugh[g]
cuir mo ceann-sa ar da ceann caein
    agus tuill mo beannachtain

31 High-resolution digital images of the manuscript are available online from the DIAS Irish Script on Screen project, <www.isos.dias.ie> in addition to the older collotype facsimile (see n. 18 above). Thanks are due to the Royal Irish Academy for access to the original manuscript. Additional thanks are due to the careful eyes of Kevin Murray and Pádraig Ó Macháin, who have made suggestions on the draft of this edition.

8 (11) In cosgair agus in grain
         do bi orm-sa ag fearaib Fail
as maith leam-sa gu praib dhe
         a beith ar m*a*c m'ingeni

9 (12) In beannacht sin ar aba
         nochor tuill Lugh Lamfada
do cuir in ceand os tuind taeir
         a ghlaic cuill ar a belaibh

10 (13) Snighi bainni nimhi annuas
         as a ceand sin gu neartcruas
do brigh 'n ailc nar beg ro
         da scailt in crand ar ceartdo

11 (14) Re re caegat bli*adh*an bil
         dan chall gan cur da cossaibh
ach a beith fa damna daer[h]
         'na agbha badhbh is branen

12 (15) Luigh Manannan in ruisg cuirr
         gu tibra Slebi Finncuill
gu fhaca in call gan falach
         a measg na crand gomhradach

13 (16) Tig Manannan luct obri
         guss in crand gu bithbuighi[i]
da thachailt a talmhun trein
         [i]do bo ghnimh[j] abul eisein.

14 (17) Eirghi deatach nimhi annis[k]
         as bun in craind sin gan scis
no gar marb fa baegal[l] de
         nonmur da loct a ob*r*i

15 (18) Do marbh nonmur eili dib
         do muinntir Manannain min
ag[m] sin scel[n] mo neall as deas dam
         is da dall in tres nonmur

16 (19) A-deirim-si rib-si dhe
         Is ass e in radh firi
fon coll adbul-so gan tar
         do-rinnigh adhbur uchain.
                              (Uchain)

17 (20) Ass e Lucridh saer do cum
    in sciath angach blaith edrum
triath Namharann dal don° muigh
    do Manannan don miligh

18 (21) Buaga do buagaibh in sceith
    a himpog a cath no cleith
gan oen oil' a m*a*c samla
    roimpi fa rian romhaghma

19 (22) Cath na Cruithin tuath nar lag
    cetcath riam do rada lat[p]
dar treath Mothla m*a*c Meirci
    ardrigh adbul Egipti

20 (23) Nocho lughu in cath eli
    tugu fa mon[q] sceili
dar traeth[r] Dubthach m*a*c Dari
    ardrigh adbul Easpani

21 (24) Toisc do-cuaigh Manannan muagh
    issan Aissia lin a sluagh
dar marb Inighdalach[s] fa miadh
    ardrig ilarmach Assiagh

22 (25) Ag sin cuid Manannain muaigh
    dod scanrathaibh teas is tuaigh
no ga tug fa dealgnas dil
    a cleamnas righ sair Sigir

23 (26) Do cum Cairbri duan moltta
    do cind in sceith sciamcorc*r*a
fear gu millsi gu n-aib sin
    do righ innsi sair-Sigir

24 (27) *Caeg*a uingi donn or dron
    tug Ola dho ar a moladh
moidi a fiaca as ard a blagh
    mar aen isin[t] sciath sciamhglan

25 (28) Do imir[u] Cairbri in fear fial
    m*a*c Eadain fa maith miagh
don triath calma ar nar cuir bron
    in sciath don Daga dreachmor

26 (29) Tug in Dadhga d'Eithoir ard
     in sciath dath-cor*c*ra donndearg
don slat gu meit gluind re radh
     do M*a*c Cuill m*a*c Cearmada

27 (30) On sciath sin tugadh M*a*c Cuill
     ar Ethoir gu ndreich min duind
flaith na glond nacar ᵛbeg blaghᵛ
     or as e coll da creideaghʷ

28 (31) Inn uair do marbhadh M*a*c Cuill
     a cath Tailltean fa mor gluind
ar fear nar beg glonnarˣ dan muig
     tarraid Scoranʸ in sciath sin

29 (32) Re re *nócha* blia*dh*an ban
     dan sciath or-buidhi imslan
crectach re gal fa sia
     da bi ag rigaibh Fear fa Niadh

30 (33) Da-cuaidh Manannain ba sia
     le sluag a tir Fear fa Niadh
da b*r*is *naoi* cath' ar tir tair
     ar muinntir Scorainᶻ sciathglain

31 (34) Da marb t*r*i catha calma
     dan sluagh edigh allmarghaᵃᵃ
ag sin sgel adbul gan tar
     fa ndernadh adbur uchan
                     (Uch)

32 (35) Caega uingi don or dearg
     *caeg*a each dualach donndearg
clar nacar t*r*itheallᵇᵇ 'n-a tith
     is fichell Scorainᶻ sciathglain

33 (36) Da-rad do comha úmo
     do Manannan nir ann ro
do cuir cliath da caegat cath
     t*r*i caegat sciath mon sciath-so

34 (37) Do bi-si ag Manannan fein
     in sciath illdealbachᶜᶜ aigmheilᵈᵈ

gun fhir langlich nir gnimh^{ee} lag
    gu tainig Tadhg^{ff} m*a*c Nughad

35 (38) Do-rad Manannan do Tadhg^{gg}
    in sciath dathcorc*r*a donndearg
do m*a*c Nugat don shaer seang
    mar aen agus in ficeall

36 (39) In laithi rug Cumull caein
    Miuirni muncaem ar eigin
tríath gaca hallaigh fhearra
    tarraidh in sciath scainfearra.

37 (40) Nuair do marbad Cumall cain
    a Cnocha os Liffe Laigne^{hh}
flaithⁱⁱ na Migall^{jj} nar beg blaidh
    tarraidh Crimall in sciath-sin

38 (41) Inn uair d'urmis Find fearrga
    ar Crimall caem catarrdha
glach gle-mor dar giall gac triath
    tug do Trenmor in caemsciath

39 (42) A tugad do cathaibh leat
    ag m*a*c Cumhaill na gel glach
a sciath ro-gel nar scaineam
    fa doili a comhaireadh

40 (43) Leat do-radad cath Cind Cluidh
    dar marbud Dubtach m*a*c Duibh
is cath Monudh Mafa gan len
    dar marbud Degeall durbeal

41 (45) Cath Loisi cath Cind Clairi
    agus cath Duni Maghi
cath Sleibi Fuait fa teand treas
    ruaig dar gaet^{kk} German garbhglas^{ll}

42 (48) Cath Ollambra fa mor gliad
    and da marbud Fatha fial
cath Éisi fa mor a gluind
    agus cath Ceisi Coraind

43 (49) Cath Cairn cath Srubhi Brain
    agus cath Beindi Edair
cath sleibi Udhi nac mall
    agus cath Muigi Maland

44 (50) Cath na Colunach calma
    agus cath Inbir Bagna
cath Atha Mogha os Leirg Luim
    cath Atha Breadh os Boïnd

45(51) Cath Mudhi Agar gan tar
    agus cath Duini Fraecain
cath Beilgi fa mor a ga
    gus^{mm} a ndernad eimhi is ucan
                     (Uchan)

46 (52) Cath Beirghi fa mor a glond
    ar tuit rig Lochland na long
Cath Uighi fa cinnti in sceil
    agus cath Insi Goibeil

47 (53) Cath Monai cath Cind Tiri
    agus cath admar hIli
cath Saxan fa borb a blaid
    cath Duni Breatain brighmair^{nn}

48 (54) Cath ar marbud Eithoir ard
    ardrigh deaglaimaibh Danmarg
cath Inbir Uigi ni ceil
    agus cath Builli boirbtrein

49 (55) Fithi cath is da cath deg
    allamuith d'Erind is ni breig
gu Tir na Finnd nar beg blaidh
    da-rad Find leat^{oo} do cathaibh

50 (56) Oct catha a lLaignibh na leand
    tugais is da triath taebhsheang
fath ratha ni breg soin
    se catha deg a nUlltaib

51 (57) Oct catha ficheat gan on
    tugais a Mugain m*h*ic Con

nocho breg mar ad-bearta
  da cath deg a Connachtaibh

52 (58) Cuig catha sa Midhi muaidh
  tugad leat a comhla cruaidh
ocht catha deg ruaig nach gand
  uaid ar Tuataibh De Danand

53 (59) A n-egmais do brugean[pp] mborb[qq]
  is da cuindsgleo fa cruaidh colg
ac sin Deis m*a*c Athi and
  do cuid da cathaibh Eirind

54 (60) Brisdi mo cradi is mo corp
  do cessais[rr] mor egonert
tu gan cosnamh ar an mhui
  arnat loscadh don muchaidh

55 (61) Tri *non*mair duinn ar Muigh Deilg
  ar eis in catha gan ceilg
fa truag ar ndail-ni re radh
  licsim tri gari uchain.

                    (Uchain)

57 (63) Gu ram saeradh Righ Nimi
  M*a*c maith Muiri ingeni
me ar iffearnd gu geri gadh
  a ndentar eimi is uchan.

                    (Uch)

56 (62) On abaill do bi a Parrthus
  fa ndernadh in t-imarbhus
nocho dealbadh crand ar lar
  is mo fan dernadh uchan

                    (Uchan)

TEXTUAL NOTES

[a] *righa*, final *a* deleted by *punctum*; [b] *e* inserted superscript with carat; [c] *a* following deleted by *punctum*; [d] inserted superscript; [e] originally *–igh*; *i* altered into tall *e* with enclitic *a*; [f] the *buailte* on *c* is added by the corrector or a later hand; [g] a *spiritus asper* on the second *d* has been incompletely scraped; [h] *a* is rubbed or worn, but this does not appear to be a correction; [i] *gh* written over *i* in the original hand without erasure, and the first *i* in *buigi*

has been re-inserted subscript; ʲ interlinear, above erroneous *Manannan* deleted by *punc-tum*; ᵏ *a* rubbed from *annias* leaving a gap; ˡ originally *baegail*; *i* deleted by expunction; ᵐ inserted superscript; ⁿ *a* rubbed out of *sceal* leaving a gap; ᵒ *n* represented by *m*-type hooked stroke; ᵖ *e* of *leat* erased, leaving a gap; �q sic; read *mór* (= DF); ʳ originally *traeith*; *i* rubbed, leaving a gap; ˢ letter (possibly *a*) rubbed after second *i*, leaving a gap; ᵗ *is* inserted superscript; ᵘ letter (possibly *r*) rubbed out leaving a gap before *–ir*; ᵛ words altered by erasure leaving gaps: *beg* altered from *beag*; something (*i* ?) has also been rubbed out after the *a* in *blagh*; ʷ altered from *creidigh* by overwriting tall *e* with enclitic *a*; ˣ sic, using *quia*-compendium; ʸ *i* of original *Scorian* rubbed; ᶻ Altered from *Scorian* by *punctum* and addition of subscript *i*; ᵃᵃ *gh* inserted superscript; ᵇᵇ *tri* inserted superscript, and *teall* has been altered from *till*; ᶜᶜ *d* inserted superscript; ᵈᵈ first *i* inserted subscript; ᵉᵉ letter rubbed out after *i*, leaving a gap; ᶠᶠ *d* written over *i* without erasure; a mark of lenition on *g* has also been rubbed out; ᵍᵍ *d* written over *i* by primary scribe; ʰʰ sic; ⁱⁱ *fl* altered by primary scribe; ʲʲ a stroke, like an *n*-stroke, stands over the *M*; it appears to be a later addition in darker ink; ᵏᵏ tall *e* by alteration from *i*; ˡˡ *a* retouched from *u*; ᵐᵐ *s* added superscript to *gᵘ*, altering it from *gur*; ⁿⁿ *gh* inserted superscript; ᵒᵒ *a* wiped after *l*, leaving a space; ᵖᵖ *ea* scraped; �qq a *punctum* is placed over the eclipsed *b*; ʳʳ *i* inserted subscript; the verb is followed by a stop and *is*, which is deleted by *punctum* and struck through as well.

COMMENTARY³²

All minor variants of phrasing, including the alternation of adjectives or phrases or sub-stitution of chevilles, with bracketed *DF* equivalents are listed here, excluding trivial changes of prepositions or preverbal particles: **1a** *reigh* (*réil*); **1b** *droch-* (*mí-*); **2c** *brig* (*dion*); **3a** *Nocho buil* (*Is úathadh*); **4c** *cred ma buil in t-ainm amach* (*in chuis fo ffuil a hainm amach, a h-* emended to *th'* by Murphy); **6a** *Ass as tugadh* (*Atá ó shoin*); **12b** *tibra* (*dithreabh*); **13b** *gu bith-buigi* (*gan loige*); **16b** *Is ass e in radh fíri* (*fiafraighther in fáisdine*); **16d** *do-rin-nigh* (*do frith mor*); **18a** *Buaga* (*Da bhúaidh*); **18b** *a himpog* (*gan gabháil ría*); **18c** *gan oen oil' a mac samla* (*terc sgieth a maca samhla*); **19c** *treath* (*gáot*); **22d** *righ sair Sigir* (*do rígh Sigir*); **24c** *moidi a fiaca as ard a blagh* (*feirrde a fiach is moide a bhladh*); **25a** *fear* (*flaith*); **27c** *flaith* (*fer*), *beg* (*clé*); **28a** *Inn uair* (*An lá*); **28b** *gluind* (*muirn*); **29ab** *nócha bliadhan ban : or buidhi im slan* (*da chét mblíadhain mbil : ordhaidhe arsaidh*); **29c** *crechtach re gal* (*a haitle sáoghail*); **30c** *ar tir tair* (*go mbloidh*); **31b** *edigh* (*aluinn*); **31c** *ag sin* (*bá hé*); **32c** *tritheall* (*critheall* emended *criteall*); **34c** *nir* (*gan*); **35c** *don* (*in*); **36a** *Miuirni mun-caem* (*Muirn mhoncaom leis*); **39c** *scaineam* (*cáineadh*); **42a** *mor* (*garp*); **43c** *nac mall* (*nar gann*); **46b** *ar tuit rig Lochland* (*iar gcath rí Lochlann*); **47c** *mor* (*borb*); **51a** *Oct* (*Deich*); **52c** *nach* (*nár*); **55a** *duinn* (*sinne*); **55b** *ar eis* (*a haithne*); **56c** *nocho* (*nochar*); **57d** *a ndentar* (*fan dearnadh*).

Variants and changes of proper names (not including the merely orthographical) are: **17c** *triath Namharannd* (*tríath na Marannmhál*), an imaginary people (see note below); **19a** *na Cruithin tuath nar lag* (*a gCruithean-thuaith nár lág*), both refer to the Cruithne (Picts), but the grammar of the phrases is different; *–thuaith* is part of the name in *DF*,

---

32 References to *DF* employ Mac Neill's text (*DF* i, pp 34–8), silently incorporating Murphy's corrigenda (*DF* iii, pp 433–4). Translations cited are based on Mac Neill (*DF* i, pp 134–9), but I have modernized and corrected as appropriate. It appears superfluous to give page references to Murphy's commentary on the poem (*DF* iii, pp 34–6) where cited, as it consists of a single summary paragraph, followed by notes organized by quatrain and line.

but in apposition in LUM; **19c** *mac Meirci* (*mac Méilge*), patronym; **21c** *Inighdalach* (?);
see commentary below (*Fiodhabhlach*), personal name; **24c** *Ola* (*Gola*), personal name;
36a *Miuirni* (*Muirn*), personal name; **37c** *Migall* (no var.) see commentary below;
41a [*Cath*] *Loisi* (*Lusga*), *DF* represents Lusk, Co. Dublin, but LUM is fanciful or
corrupt; **42b** [*Cath*] *Ollambra* (*Ollarbha*), *DF* has the Larne r., Co. Antrim, where a battle
is well-attested in Fenian literature, but LUM is simply corrupt; **44c** [*Cath*] *Átha Mogha
os Leirg Luim* (*Ata Modhuin léir linn*), Áth Mogha on the Suck in Ballymoe, Co. Galway,
is named in the *Táin* as well as in *Acallam na senórach* (see *HDGP* i, s.n.), but Leirg Luim
is unidentified, whereas *DF* has an unidentified place and a cheville; **45c** [*cath*] *Beilgi*
(*Meilge*); **47d** [*cath*] *Duni Breatain* (*Dhúine Binne*), LUM's name is Dumbarton, which
makes sense in a quatrain also containing the Scottish toponyms of Kintyre and the
Mounth, but *DF* presents an Irish place, a legendary, unidentified royal fortress in Dál
Riada, named in *LG* and subject of the tale *Forbais Dúin Binne*; **48a** *Eithoir* (*Aichil*), names
a supposed high-king of Denmark, the former doubles as the name of the owner of the
shield in qq. 26–9, and the latter Gaelicizes Achilles (as throughout *Togail Troí*; also note
DF i, p. 51 q. 41]); **48c** [*cath*] *Inbhir Uigi* (*Inbhir Buille*), the *Buill* here may be the r.
Boyle in Co. Roscommon entering Lough Key, but the vowel quantity undermines the
rhyme unless there is an etiology at work or a fanciful place has been concocted using the
noun *buille*; **48d** [*cath*] *Buille* (*Buinne*), LUM may again intend the Boyle, though it may
simply be corruption, as suggested by the presence of the same name in a different
position in *DF*, as the long *u* fails to rhyme, and *Buinne* is possibly a short form of *Buinne
an Bheithe*, or Long Island in the Shannon, tl. Raghrabeg, p. Moore, b. Moycarn, Co.
Roscommon (see *HDGP* ii, s.n.), again requiring a short-vowel rhyme; **49c** *Tir na Finnd*
(*Tír na nDionn*), fanciful countries; **52a** *sa Midhi muaidh* (*fiched go mbúaidh*), LUM places
the battles in Meath, but *DF* merely fills the line; **53c** *Deis mac Athi and* (*réd rathaibh go
tenn*), LUM introduces an unknown personal name, but the sense of *DF* is far superior;
55a *Muigh Deilg* (*Druim Deilg*), unknown places.

Forms and differences requiring comment are discussed here:
2b In addition to the analytic verb in place of the synthetic, *as tug tu* (*DF tugais*) provides
a poorer sense, requiring *do* to be read prepositionally in place of being an element of a
compound subject as in *DF*.
3ab *Nocho buil ar talmain tigh / laech na faigh na fissigi.* LUM's rhyme *tigh : fissigi* is not
only faulty, but the later form of the agent noun is required for the syllable count. *DF*'s
superior reading *Is úathadh … muna a ffuil fáidh nó fisidh* avoids both problems.
4ab The LUM text presents the faulty rhyme *taig : mnai*, which requires modern pronunciation (as with a number of other metrical faults); *DF*'s alternative, *Is terc fós ar
talmhain sin / d'fíor nó do mhnaoí do fhitir* presents an historically correct pairing.
4d *dit ga gairm sencoll sniäch* (*DF día gairm in Sencholl Snidheach*). LUM appears to have
had a metrically faulty exemplar, probably due to the loss of the article, which *DF* preserves; the corrector inserted *ga* to provide the lacking syllable.
9c *taeir*. Read *t*[*s*]*oir* rather than *t*[*s*]*aoir* (: *belaibh*; cf. *DF thsoir*).
10a *Snighi* (*DF Snighis*). LUM presents the couplet as a noun phrase, avoiding the
absolute preterite in *–is* (as elsewhere), whilst *DF* provides a verb.
10c *do brigh* is a preferable reading to *DF iar snídhe* with repetition. Read the article [*i*]*n*
with the simple loss of a minim.
13a *Tig* (*DF Cuiris*). *DF* is hypermetrical, but provides better sense.
15c *ag sin scel mo neall as deas dam* is hypermetrical with the added interlinear *ag*. *DF sgéla
on crann do fhes damh*. Possibly eliminate *as* and understand *d'*[*fh*]*eas dam*.
16bc *tar : uchain* is faulty; read *uchán* (as *DF*)
17c *triath Namharann dal don muigh. Namharann* is written continuously with *dal*; a fine

line between has been inserted to separate them. Reading it thus, so that the second phrase is taken as an aside, provides an attempted, imperfect rhyme with *Manannan* in line d. *DF*, on the other hand, rhymes properly with its alternative, *tríath na Marannmhál*.

18d *rian* should confirm Murphy's suggested emendation of *DF ráon*, *metris causa*, yet its rhyme (: *scíeth*) is not present, and the couplet lacks *aicill* in LUM.

19b *cetcath riam do rada lat*. *DF* (*in ced-cath tugadh lat*) is hypometrical.

20b LUM hypometrical; supply *lat* from *DF*.

21c The name found in *DF*, *Fiodhabhlach*, is corrupt in LUM and the line is furthermore hypermetrical. Nevertheless, *fa miadh* provides better sense than *DF fa lía*, which Murphy referred to as 'obscure and perhaps corrupt'.

22b *scanrathaibh* is correct, whereas *DF decraibh* leaves the line hypometrical (though expansion of *is* to *agus* could easily supply the syllable).

22c *dealgnas*, which is recorded in *DIL* as a *hapax legomenon* of uncertain meaning s.v. *delgnus*, can be understood in context as a substantive related to the rare adjectives ²*delgnach*, ¹*delgnaide* and its by-form ¹*delgnaid*, all meaning 'distinguished'; this is certainly a *lectio difficilior* compared with *DF degdos* (translated by MacNeill as 'goodly screen', i.e., *deagh-dhos*).

25a *do imir*. Traces of a letter, possibly *r*, after *-m-* suggest that the scribe decided to alter his verbal form whilst writing. Although the preverbal particle does not elide, generally a conservative feature, the *t*-preterite inflexion has been lost. There are a few examples of such forms from the Middle Irish period cited in *DIL* s.v. *imm-beir*. *DF* presents an alternative verb, *Bronnais*.

26cd *re radh* : *Cearmada*. Faulty rhyme requiring modern pronunciation. *DF* offers *re gleó* : *Cearmotó*, with an *eo* : *ó* rhyme that Murphy regards as indicative of post-Middle Irish (see *DF* iii, p. cxv).

28c *ar fear nar beg glonnar dan muig*. Hypermetrical, but easily repaired by deleting *ar* (which is absent in *DF*). *DF*'s reading *trom-ár* is preferable to *glonnar*; the latter compound repeats *gluind* of the previous line.

29d *ag rigaibh Fear fa Niadh* (*ag rioghaibh fFir Menía*). LUM has a fanciful people, while *DF* presents a known Gaelicization of Armenia (cf. *AUⁱ* 1299 [ii, 393]); as Murphy's index notes, the form is rare and not in *OnomG*. LUM's modern rhyme requires the silence of final *-dh* of a dental-stem. In both cases, the metre requires that the forms *Niadh* and *Menía* be read as disyllables.

30ab *fa sia* : *tir Fear fa Niad* (*na niadh* : *a ttír fFear Menía*). The same faulty rhyme type *-a* : *-adh*, (see 26cd above) but now *DF*'s alternative also pairs *-iadh* : *-ia*.

33a *úmo*. Read *búdh mó* (*DF bá mó* with emendation suggested)

33b *nir annro* (*nír bhó ro*). LUM presents the better reading in both metre and sense, though with the caution that this is one of the few places where the preterite copula takes the monosyllabic form.

33c *do cuir cliath* (*ré cuir ghlíaidh*). *Cliath* has a form that is correct as an accusative (*IGT* §39). In *DF*, *glíaidh* is the genitive singular of the later o-stem masculine noun *gliad* [< *gleo*] (cf. *IGT* §97 and earlier forms discussed by Thurneysen, 'Ir. *gleo*', *ZCP*, 20 [1936], 364–7). As Murphy notes, restoring the earlier genitive singular form in *DF* gives the required internal rhyme. See below 42ab.

33cd *cath* : *mon sciath so* (*cath* : *fan scéith sin*). The nominative is used for accusative in LUM, and both texts present faulty rhymes.

37ab *cain* : *Laigne*. If not a simple mistake, the misplaced vowel hints at a monosyllabic pronunciation of *Laighean*. Regardless, the rhyme is faulty, here and in *DF*.

37c *flaith na Migall* (*an flaith mínmall*). It seems that the scribe understood *Migall* as a fanciful tribal name, probably with a lenited *g* providing a rhyme with *Crimall* in line d.

The stroke over the *M* of *Migall* may represent a slightly misplaced *n*, perhaps intending *na Mín Gall* 'of the pastures of the Gall' (= Fine Gall?). This addition is in a different ink, and seems later; furthermore, if accepted it would destroy the rhyme. The chief evidence, however, for the correct reading is rhyme with Criomhall, a senior kinsman of Fionn who appears in many texts, and who is aptly characterized in *DF* (Mac Neill translated 'the smooth steady prince'); LUM's reading, emended or not, fails to convince.

38a *Inn uair d'urmis* (*Mar do urmais*). DF preserves unelided *do*.

38cd *dar giall gac triath : caem-sciath* (*dar diall gac glíaidh : trénsgíath*). LUM's reading is superior, with correct rhyme.

39b *glach*. Read *glac* (: *leat*)

40c *is*. The word is written thus, and the line is hypersyllabic; *DF* lacks the conjunction. The problem can be ameliorated equally by reduction to *'s* or by deletion.

41d *gaet* (*tuit*). LUM preserves the old preterite passive of *gonaid* (spelling altered from *gait* in the *prima manus*). DF clearly has the *lectio facilior*.

42ab *gliad : fial* (*DF glíaidh : fial*). This correct rhyme is again predicated on the presence of the later *o*-stem masculine noun *gliad* (< *gleo*). See above 33c.

43a *Cath Cairn* (*Cath Cairrge*). Both names are common enough, but the example in LUM renders the line hypometrical.

45cd *mor a ga : uchan* (*adbhal ágh : uchán*). LUM's rhyme is faulty.

46cd *in sceil : Innsi Goibeil* (*in sgél : Innse Gaibíel*). LUM is ungrammatical; *DF*'s form seems forced and the place is unknown.

47cd Murphy emends to *bladh : brighmar*, construing the latter with *cath*.

48c *ni ceil : boirbtrein* (*ni brég : boirbthréin*). Murphy's commentary emended *DF*'s reading to *boirbthrén*, construing the adjective as nominative with *cath* and solving *DF*'s faulty rhyme, the same type of error as in the previous quatrain. The present text is also problematic; for the nominative, one would not expect *céil* but rather *cé(a)l* (it may have been an Old Irish *u*-stem), but the word certainly presents the *lectio difficilior*. The same emendation can be applied here, *ní céal : boirb-thréan*.

49ab *deg : breig* (*dég : brég*).

49b is hypermetrical in both texts, but the reduction of *is* to *'s* easily corrects the fault.

49cd *blaidh : cathaibh* (*bladh : chathaibh*). The LUM text confirms Meyer's suggested emendation to the *DF* text, though Murphy notes the potential difficulties of this reading.

50c *fath ratha* (*fedh do ratha*). The line is hypometrical, and the phrase corrupt; the *DF* reading should probably be adopted.

51cd *mar ad-berta : a Connachtaibh* (*acht is certa : a cConnachta*). Murphy noted that *DF* was corrupt with these faulty rhymes and ungrammatical forms; it also has an introductory *is* in line d making it hypermetrical. LUM's cheville is superior, preserving a Middle Irish imperfect passive of *as-beir*, but the rhyme remains faulty and manifests additional corruption.

54b *do cessais mor egonert* (*ro ceises mor d'égcomhnart*). The LUM scribe was dissatisfied with his text. He altered his verb from first person to second, and then wrote *is* and deleted it. The word *egonert* is clearly a corruption of the reading in *DF*; the LUM scribe uncharacteristically did not dress the word according to his orthographical tendencies towards *caol le caol*, perhaps due to failure to recognize the word. Both texts present the same corruption, which Murphy suggests resolving by emendation to *ro cheiseas ar t'égcomnart*, which provides the required sense.

55b *gan ceilg* (*crói-deirg*). The *DF* reading provides an integral image and the desirable disyllabic rhyme to *Deilg*, whilst *gan ceilg* is a mere cheville.

55cd *radh : uchain*. Rhyme requires emendation to *uchán*, matching the reading in *DF*.

56a *On abaill do bhi a Parrthus* (*O crann na haithne boí a bParrthus*). *DF* is hypermetrical.
56b *fa ndernadh in t-imarbhus* (*fo ndernadh fo rior iomarbhus*). DF is hypermetrical.
57c *me* is pleonastic, and the hypermetricality of the line is repaired by its removal, which
  is verified by *DF*.

EVALUATION

Regarding content, the loss of the praise of Fionn in qq 3–5 subtracts nothing from the substance of the lay. It would not be difficult to suggest that it
was an addition, but it is worth noting that it uses *nocha raibhe* (*DF* 3a), the
disyllabic Middle Irish form of the preterite substantive with a pre-modern
negative particle, which suggests that these quatrains, even if one argue that
they have been interpolated here, are of roughly the same age as the rest of
the text. The loss of part of the *caithréim* (*DF* §§44, 46–8) is also of no narrative consequence. The lack of some items in this list in LUM appears to
reflect the later medieval trend of the lays towards action and away from the
kind of cataloguing that dominates the poetry in *Acallam na senórach*. On the
balance of probability, it appears that any hypothetical original must be
assumed to incorporate the full text as in DF. In literary terms, both manuscripts at times preserve the superior phrase; at others, it is impossible to
choose between them. The presence of a second copy allows for the restoration of some awkward phrases and minor corruptions, but whilst this satisfies
the reader's desire to repair tears and blemishes, the shape changes little.

The poem's metre is *deibhidhe*, mostly *deibhidhe scaoilte*, with *deibhidhe
ghuilbneach* in some opening couplets. *Rinn* : *airdrinn* pairs in the form x :
x+2 are found. The second couplet generally contains an internal rhyme:
some are faulty, and a few lack one altogether; it is uncertain how many
faulty attempts may be due to corruption, or whether some were original.
Alliteration provides a frequent ornament, but is not a requirement. Murphy
observed a number of rhymes suggestive of the Middle Irish period; the
LUM text offers some better or equal alternatives alongside a number of infe-
rior ones based on non-Classical modern pronunciations in which the values
of final lenited consonants are lost, but there is nothing that would give
grounds for a more general re-appraisal.

Murphy's evaluation, in which he dates the lay to 'the middle of the
twelfth century', is based mostly on vocabulary, with only a brief discussion
of other items. Among those highlighted is the sole rhymed accusative form
7cd *caein* : *beannachtain*, found in both versions, as are the verbal forms *gaet*
and *luidh*; the former of these gets an extra outing in LUM (41d). The disyllabic preterite / perfect negative copula *nocha*(*r*) is usual. To these may be
added a few other general features. The suppletive perfect of *do-beir* is regularly preserved (e.g. 33a *Da-rad*, 35a *do-rad*, 40a *do-radad*). The Middle Irish

imperfect passive *ad-berta* (51c) is also present in a rather problematic couplet in the text. The early form of the dative article before a vowel is reflected in 24a *donn* (for *dond*). Concerning vocabulary, the rare word *dealgnas* (22c), whose place is taken by a simple compound in the equivalent line in *DF*, has an early savour, as well as *ceil* (better *céal*) 48c, a word that did not survive in Modern Irish. Alongside these, there are modernisms where *DF* preserves superior readings, as noted above in the commentary. The few Middle Irish features added to those present in *DF* re-enforce rather than change Murphy's evaluation, and its basis is little affected by Carey's critique of his dating criteria.[33]

What is most striking however, is that these two manuscripts, Leabhar Ua Maine and Duanaire Finn, both literary manuscripts with firm places in a tradition of written transmission, present texts of this poem with many minor variants and rephrasings of exactly the sort that in more modern Fenian lays is usually attributed to (or blamed on) oral transmission, as paralleled in this sample quatrain with multiple variants from two versions of the popular poem 'Lá do raibh Pádraig a nDún':

> *Duanaire Finn*
> Do-níd gan ogal a ttriall
> in láochraidh far bfedmar sinn
> gluaisis in da fheindidh gheal
> go rígh Lochlann na sreath slim[34]

> *Young's Collection* (Scottish version, orally collected)
> Thog iad gu sibulte 'n triall
> 'N cloidheamh agus 'n sgiath air luing
> G'luais 'n dithist iarloch ur
> Gu riochd Lochlunn na 'n sriann sleom[35]

Both LUM and DF are manuscripts of the highest literary pedigree, yet they exhibit virtually the same type of textual evolution. Although it would be conventional to speak of the degeneration of the text, it is clear that scribes, who must have had written exemplars for such lengthy narratives, felt it appropriate to alter the poem. When they introduced modernisms, it is easy to speak of corruption; but there is also the possibility that these same scribes

33 Carey, 'Remarks on dating', pp 2–10.   34 'Those heroes about whom we were jealous set out wrathfully: the two white warriors went off to the king of Lochlainn of the smooth ranks': *DF* ii, pp 364–5 §7.   35 'They undertook their journey impudently, sword and shield on a ship: the noble young pair proceeded to the kingdom of Lochlainn of the smooth battle-lines': M. Young, 'Antient GAELIC POEMS respecting the race of the FIANS collected in the HIGHLANDS of SCOTLAND in the year 1784', *Transactions of the Royal Irish Academy*, 1 (1787), 43–119 at 85.

provided better rhymes and more satisfying phrases, which would be far harder – even impossible – to discern. Investigation of the mutability of a text, its *mouvance*, without sole focus on an hypothetical 'original', avoids the Classics-derived paradigm of corruption; this understanding is spreading through the study of medieval vernacular literatures.[36] As the Fenian lays scattered through the older manuscripts are brought into print, the understanding of them must be impoverished if they are seen simply as imperfect witnesses to an hypothetical *Urtext*; rather, the divers extant versions must be appreciated as literature in themselves. *Ní ansa*.

---

36 An excellent example of such a study, incorporating a discussion of the implications for textual studies, is provided by Bella Millett, '*Mouvance* and the medieval author: re-editing *Ancrene Wisse*' in A.J. Morris (ed.), *Late-medieval religious texts and their transmission: essays in honour of A.I. Doyle* (Cambridge, 1994), pp 9–20. The classic articulation is that of Paul Zumthor, *Essai de poétique médiévale* (Paris, 1972), pp 65–75.

St Patrick and Antaeus: two bardic apologues

MARGO GRIFFIN-WILSON

I first met Máire Herbert in Cambridge, Massachusetts, when she was a visiting professor in the Department of Celtic Languages and Literatures at Harvard University. A small group of students met weekly, in the late afternoon, to read the Old Irish text *Serglige Con Culainn*. Máire Herbert's close attention to the text, intellectual engagement and generosity during those meetings is a memory that continues to inspire, and I have been privileged to experience the same welcome and encouragement on many visits to Cork since. The poem that will be considered below is from the Classical Modern Irish period, but the bardic poet weaves medieval tales of an Irish saint and a foreign champion into a eulogy which praises his patron's fruitful lands in Co. Cork. It seems an appropriate text for a volume honouring a scholar who has contributed so much to our understanding of medieval hagiography, history and literature, and who has done so with such generosity.

This article draws attention to the eulogistic language in two prose apologues from the previously unedited bardic poem, *Teallach coisreagtha críoch Bharrach* 'The land of the Barrys is a blessed homestead', composed for Dáibhidh mac Séamais (mac Risteard) de Barra (†10 April, 1617).[1] *Teallach*, composed in a medley of verse (42½ quatrains) and prose (4 passages) known as *crosántacht*,[2] presents the notion of *fir flaithemon* 'the sovereign's truth' and the resulting fecundity of the land within the more liberal parameters of the *crosántacht* style. The fertile state of Barrymore, Co. Cork, is the result of the rightful chieftain's sacral marriage to the land, but also of St Patrick's blessing upon Munster at the baptism of Aonghus mac Nad Fraoich, king of Munster (*c.*453–89), the earliest account of which occurs in *Bethu Phátraic*.[3] The benefits of the blessing and images of *fir flaithemon* intersect, as the poet welds the two in verse and prose. In an ironic twist on the theme, *Teallach* concludes with a rare bardic apologue about the Classical figure Antaeus son

1 The opening section of this paper, with some adjustments, has been published under the title, 'Zegening van patroon gen erfgoed in "Teallach coisreagtha críoch Bharrach"', *Kelten: Mededeling van de Stichting A.G. van Hamel voor Keltische Studies*, 57 (2013), 5–9. A version was presented at Cambridge University and the University of Aberdeen (May, 2012). I thank Damian McManus and Pádraig Ó Macháin for answering several questions on the text, and I am grateful to Pádraig Breatnach for his helpful comments. Any errors are my own. 2 Alan Harrison, *An chrosántacht* (BÁC, 1979). 3 Kathleen Mulchrone (ed.), *Bethu Phátraic: the tripartite Life of Patrick* (Dublin, 1939), ll 2297–307. For some discussion, see P.A. Breatnach, *Téamaí taighde Nua-Ghaeilge* (Maigh Nuad, 1997), pp 35–6. Sources are considered below.

of Terra, or *Anteus mac Tíre*, who was born from the earth and renewed his strength by touching his body to the earth – a story narrated in the medieval Irish tale *In cath catharda*, an adaptation of Lucan's *Pharsalia*.[4] There is no connection between these two tales, but I propose that the poet of *Teallach* selects and juxtaposes motifs so as to make a connection. The land of Barrymore bears the blessing of Ireland's pre-eminent saint, and the patron's contact with the land of his birth increases his prowess and munificence.

Passages analysed here are from an edition of the poem that I am preparing for a forthcoming publication. Eleven manuscripts have been examined.[5] The text is based on the oldest of these, London, BL Additional 29614, f. 56b (A), written in 1726 by Seán Ó Murchadha na Ráithíneach. Variants are drawn from two other independent witnesses. The most important of these, Dublin, TCD MS 1411 (H.6.7), pp 48–55 (T),[6] was written in 1737 by Donnchadh Ó Conuill, whose possible connection to the Roches of Fermoy is of interest,[7] as the patron of *Teallach* was married to Ellen, daughter of David, Viscount Roche of Fermoy.[8] The third manuscript, Dublin, RIA MS 23 N 15 (490), pp 191–4 (N), is the work of Mícheál (mac Peadair) Ó Longáin (c. 1740–81). Interestingly, the final prose apologue about Antaeus is omitted from this manuscript. In the present article, variants from these manuscripts are noted sparingly.

POET, PATRON AND HISTORICAL CONTEXT

Teallach is attributed in all extant manuscripts to the poet Dáibhidh Ó Bruadair, but its early date has cast doubt upon the ascription. Ó Bruadair is thought to have lived *c.*1625–97.[9] It was the reputable scribe of the oldest manuscript, Seán Ó Murchadha na Ráithíneach, who first questioned the attribution:

4 *IT* iv, pp 220–9. For another instance of the Antaeus (*Ainntius*) episode, see Gordon Quin (ed. and trans.), *Stair Ercuil ocus a bás*, ITS 38 (Dublin, 1939), pp 122–3. The latter is very likely drawn from *In cath catharda*: Quin, ibid., pp xxvi–xxvii; cf. Eric Poppe, '*Stair Ercuil ocus a bás* – rewriting Hercules in Ireland' in K. Murray (ed.), *Translations from Classical literature: Imtheachta Aeniasa and Stair Ercuil ocus a bás*, ITS SS 17 (Dublin, 2006), pp 37–68 at pp 61–3.   5 Manuscripts are listed by P.A. Breatnach, *Téamaí taighde*, p. 33. I note two additional copies: Cork, MS 164, pp 247–54, and Cambridge, Additional MS 7089, pp 218–30.   6 See also Damian McManus and Eoghan Ó Raghallaigh (eds), *A bardic miscellany* (Dublin, 2010), pp 646–9.   7 Tomás Ó Concheanainn, 'The scribe of the Irish astronomical tract in RIA B ii 1', *Celtica*, 11 (1976), 158–67 at 166 n. 24; cf. Breandán Ó Conchúir, *Scríobhaithe Chorcaí, 1750–1850* (BÁC, 1982), pp 46, 197. 8 Vicary Gibbs (ed.), *The complete peerage of England Scotland Ireland Great Britain and the United Kingdom* (London, 1910), p. 442. She is extolled as his spouse in another poem addressed to him: *DD*, no. 87, qq 23–5 (p. 286).   9 John. C. Mac Erlean (ed. and trans.), *Duanaire Dháibhidh Uí Bhruadair: the poems of Dáibhí Ó Bruadair*, 3 vols, ITS 11, 13, 18 (London, 1910–17), i, pp xix–xx, xlvi.

Ní thuigim gurab é Dáibhídh O Bruadair do rin. Féach geineal*ach* an Bharr*aigh* san leabharsa.

I do not think that it was Dáibhídh Ó Bruadair that composed it; consult the Barry genealogy in this book.[10]

John C. Mac Erlean, the editor of Ó Bruadair's verse, was of the opinion that *Teallach* was not the poet's work,[11] and scholars remain skeptical.[12] Furthermore, *Teallach* exhibits features of *dán díreach* rarely found in Ó Bruadair's *crosántachta*; an example is its regular pattern of consonance.[13] The question of authorship, then, remains unresolved.

Teallach was composed for Dáibhídh mac Séamais (mac Risteard) de Barra, Viscount Buttevant (†10 April 1617), who ruled lands in Barrymore, Co. Cork. The poem is undated, though he is praised as *An Barrach Mór* 'the great Barry', an Irish title he presumably assumed after the death of his father, Séamas de Barra, in 1581.[14] During his father's lifetime he joined the second Desmond rebellion, but he subsequently submitted to the Crown; there is a record of his pardon on 24 August 1582.[15] In 1588 he and his wife, Ellen Roche, were living in Barryscourt Castle, near Carrigtohill.[16] A staunch Catholic, Dáibhídh de Barra nevertheless remained loyal to the Queen and refused to join the rebellion of the earl of Tyrone, Aodh Ó Néill, in 1599–1600; consequently, his lands in Barrymore were burned and plundered:

> ó chúil go cuil etir magh, 7 mothar, etir mín, 7 ainmin co ná baoí súil na saoilechtain aon duine fri a haitiucchadh, no fri a haittreabhadh go haimsir imchein.

> from one extremity to the other, both plain and wood, both level and rugged, so that no one hoped or expected that it could be inhabited for a long time afterwards.[17]

---

10 London, BL MS Additional 29614, f. 56b.   11 Lambert McKenna comments on a note from Mac Erlean: see McKenna (ed. and trans.), *Iomarbhágh na bhfileadh: the contention of the bards*, 2 vols, ITS 20–21 (London, 1918), ii, p. 228 n. 3.   12 See Breatnach, *Téamaí taighde*, p. 33 n. 104; cf. Margo Griffin-Wilson, *The wedding poems of Dáibhí Ó Bruadair* (Dublin, 2010), p. 2. Liam Ó Murchú has drawn my attention to *Do chonradh foirceadal*, dated 1648, which Ó Bruadair presents as the 'start and substance' (*tosach is toradh*) of his writing: Mac Erlean, *Duanaire Dháibhidh Uí Bhruadair*, i, p. 20 §1.   13 For some discussion, see Griffin-Wilson, *The wedding poems*, pp 199, 297.   14 'Dáibhí mac an Bharraigh Mhóir' is named among the deceased chieftains extolled in a later poem, *Maith an compánach an dán*; see P.A. Breatnach, 'A poem on the end of patronage', *Éigse*, 31 (1999), 79–88 at 84, 88 §13.   15 *The Irish fiants of the Tudor sovereigns (1543–1603)*, 4 vols (repr. Dublin, 1994), ii, p. 550 §3974. Cf. Rev. E. Barry, 'Barrymore', *JCHAS*, 6 (1900), 1–11, 65–87, 129–46, 193–209 at 145.   16 Barry, 'Barrymore', p. 194.   17 *AFM* 1600 (vi, 2150–1). See also *Calendar of state papers relating to Ireland 1600–1* (London, 1905), p. 22 §20.

He was rewarded for his fidelity to the Queen upon the accession of King James I. In another bardic poem he is addressed as *bhíocunt Barrach*, his English title, and his visits to Queen Elizabeth (†1603) and her successor King James I are mentioned.[18]

The only reference to an historical person (other than the patron) in *Teallach* is an oblique allusion to Aodh Mhág Uidhir, presumably the renowned chieftain of Fermanagh, who ruled from 1589 to 1600:

> 16 Rug a mbí do thart ar thánuibh
>   lacht ó laoghuibh:
>   Aodh Mhág Uidhir don taobh thuaidhin,
>   Aodh ós Aodhuibh.[19]

The thirst that was on herds of cattle [from the heat of the sun?] deprived calves of their milk; [he is the match of] Aodh Mhág Uidhir in the north (?), the supreme Aodh.

Aodh Mhág Uidhir is extolled, but the context is unspecific. His name may have been a by-word for a fierce raider, whose reign typifies *fír flaithemon*, with its scorching heat causing cows to stray from their young in search of water, recalling comparable images noted by Damian McManus.[20] We do know, however, that Aodh Mhág Uidhir journeyed into Munster to aid Aodh Ó Néill, earl of Tyrone, raiding and burning lands in Co. Cork in 1599–1600.[21] The poet Eochaidh Ó hEoghusa, to whom Aodh Mhág Uidhir was a special patron, and who pledged to include a quatrain to Aodh in his poems,[22] expressed anxiety over Aodh's safety in Munster in the poem *Fúar liom an adhaighsi dh'Aodh.*[23] His fears were well-founded, as Aodh died of wounds

---

18 *DD* no. 87 §§18, 21, 22 (pp 285–6).   19 *b* laedhibh N; *c* thuaigin AT, th*uidh*in (?) N; *d* Aodh is Aoduibh A, Aodh is Aodhuibh T, Aodh is Aodub N. I have taken *tuaidhin* as a variant of *tuaidheamhain* (see *DIL* s.v. *túaid, thúaid*); cf. Lambert McKenna (ed. and trans.), *Aithdioghluim dána; a miscellany of Irish bardic poetry*, 2 vols, ITS 37, 40 (London, 1939–40), ii, p. 333.   20 Compare *táinte ag loighe a leapthaibh tonn* 'herds of cattle take refuge in the sea'; *táin a n-áth sreabha 'na súan* 'cattle [are] slumbering in the river-ford': Damian McManus, '"The smallest man in Ireland can reach the tops of her trees": images of the king's peace and bounty in bardic poetry' in J.F. Nagy (ed.), *Memory and the modern in Celtic literatures*, CSANA Yearbook 5 (2006), pp 61–117 at p. 97 §§104, 105. 21 Paul Walsh (ed. and trans.), *Beatha Aodha Ruaidh Uí Dhomhnaill: the life of Aodh Ruadh O Domhnaill*, 2 vols, ITS 42, 45 (Dublin, 1948–57), i, pp 238–41 §127.   22 P.A. Breatnach, 'A covenant between Eochaidh Ó hEoghusa and Aodh Mág Uidhir', *Éigse*, 27 (1993), 59–66; idem, 'Eochaidh Ó hEódhusa (*c*.1560–1612)', *Éigse*, 27 (1993), 127–9. The presence of a quatrain to 'Aodh Mhág Uidhir' in *Teallach* is not an argument for Ó hEoghusa's authorship. Other poets sought Aodh's patronage. Tadhg Dall Ó hUiginn, for example, complains that the northern poets will not let him have access to Aodh (*TDall* i, no. 12). Cf. Pádraig Ó Macháin, 'The poetry of Tadhg Dall Ó hUiginn: themes and sources' in P. Riggs (ed.), *Tadhg Dall Ó hUiginn: his historical and literary context*, ITS SS 21 (London, 2010), pp 55–87 at p. 82 n. 83.   23 *IBP* no. 29, pp 124–7.

(† 13 March 1600), after slaying his opponent, Sir Warham St Leger, in an ambush outside of Cork city.[24] Was Mhág Uidhir still alive when the poet of *Teallach* praised him as 'the Aodh above [all] Aodhs' (*Aodh ós Aodhuibh*)? The celebratory tone suggests that he is, but it is difficult to confirm. The praise of Aodh Mhág Uidhir in this poem to a Munster chieftain is nevertheless striking, and may hint at a Maguire interest.

ST PATRICK AND ANTAEUS

The idea of linking the blessing of St Patrick to the praise of the patron's lands in *Teallach* has been drawn from the earlier bardic poem *Teallach coisreagtha clann Bhriain*, composed for Tadhg 'Caoluisce' Ó Briain (†1259), as Pádraig Breatnach has demonstrated.[25] The notion is developed in a distinctive manner in the later *Teallach*. Abundance is attributed both to Patrick's blessing (q. 3) and to the union of the rightful lord joined with the land, his spouse (q. 9). These two quatrains are the core around which the opening section is constructed:

1   Teallach coisreagtha críoch B*h*arrach,
    buaile dáimhe;
    clár beathaighthe na n-eang n-uaine
    fán seang sáile.[26]

2   Críoch B*h*arrach na mbrugh ndaithgheal
    díochur doghra;
    oirear saor na n-iongna[dh] n-iomdha,
    fionnmhagh fromhtha.[27]

3   A-tá bail beannochta Phádraig
    an phuirt aingligh
    ar an gcrích-[se] n-éachtruim n-iubhraigh
    ngéagthruim ngainmhigh.[28]

4   Ciúin a haibhne, iomdha a tortha,
    tearc a biodhbhaidh;
    ní fhuil díth teachta ar a talmhuin,
    feactha a fiodhbhaidh.[29]

24 Walsh, *Beatha Aodha Ruaidh*, i, pp 239–41 §127; cf. *AFM* vi, pp 2160–5.   25 Breatnach, *Téamaí taighde*, pp 30–6.   26 1*a* chríche Barrach AT, críche Barach N; *c* na neang nuaithne AT, naineang nuainthe N; *d* fán sheang N.   27 2*a* ndaithngheal ATN; *b* díothchur ATN; dóghradh N; *c* oiréar ATN; nionga AT, niongna N. Line 2*a* is short a syllable.   28 3*b* ainglídhe AT; *c* ccríoch N; néachttruim T, néachttruim AN; ndiubhraig A, niubhraig T, aindiubhraig N; *d* ngéagthruím T; ngainmhídhe AT, ngainbhíghe N.   29 4*c* díth teachta ar talmhuin AT, dítheachta ar a talmhuin N; *d* ag feacadh fiodhb*aidh*

The land of the Barrys is a blessed homestead; the nourishing plain of the verdant lands around which the sea is narrow is an enclosure of poets.

The land of the Barrys of the bright white halls [brings about] a banishing of sorrow; the noble region of the numerous wonders is a lustrous, [battle]-tested plain.

The prosperity of the blessing of Patrick of the angelic abode is upon the exploit-laden, yew-abounding, well-wooded, sandy land.

Calm her rivers, plentiful her produce, scarce her enemies; there is not a lack of growth upon her land; her trees are bent [with fruit].

The landscape depicted has the typical manifestations of *fir flaithemon*. The rhyming words *teachta : feactha* (4*cd*) emphasize the paradoxical upward 'growth' (*teachta*) upon the land which causes a downward bending of its trees, and the emendation of *ag feacadh* to past participle *feactha* 'bent' (4*d*), restores the required syllable count and gives internal rhyme with *teachta*.[30] Trees are 'bent' (*feactha*) not by storm or in homage to the chieftain, but by the weight of abundant fruit. One can compare another poet's praise of *Cleath Chró fa bfeacadh gach fiodh* 'the lord of Cró during whose reign the trees were bowed low', where *feacadh* similarly describes bending trees (*fiodh*).[31]

The idealized patrimony is the result of the blessing (q. 3), but the poet introduces the ancient notion of the sacral marriage of the chieftain to the land, *críoch Bharrach*, the implied sovereignty figure (q. 9).[32] The union is fundamental to *fir flaithemon*; and the quatrain conveys, structurally and semantically, a relationship of reciprocity and excellence:

9   A-tá a díol do rígh san rígh-se;
     is rádh tuilltear;
     's a-tá a dhíol-sin d'oireacht innte;
     roibheacht roinntear.[33]

In this king there is her match of a king; it is a claim which is deserved; and he [likewise] has his match of a patrimony in her [*Críoch Bharrach*]; it is precisely apportioned.

AT, ag fiachadh fiodhbha N.   **30** This emendation was proposed to me by Damian McManus.   **31** McManus, 'The smallest man in Ireland', p. 104 §133.   **32** The *hieros gamos* or sacred marriage has been discussed by many scholars, including Máire Herbert, 'Goddess and king: the sacred marriage in Early Ireland' in L.O. Fradenburg (ed.), *Women and sovereignty* (Edinburgh, 1992), pp 264–75.   **33** 9*b* tuíllthear AT, tuillthear N; *c* is atá ATN; a dhíol don oighreacht N; innt T. 9*d* róibheacht AT.

The union of patron and patrimony is reflected in the parallel repetition *a-tá a díol* (line *a*) and *a-tá a dhíol* (line *c*), with the feminine (geminating) and then masculine (leniting) possessive adjective. There is a striking juxtaposition of the prepositional phrase *do rígh* 'of a king' (9*a*), conveying the indefinite and uncertain king sought by the mateless sovereign, and *san rígh-se* 'in this king', the physically present Barry chieftain who is granted a patrimony 'in her' (*innte*).[34] The poet effectively employs the alternating long and short lines, a distinguishing feature of the syllabic metre *snéadhbhairdne*, with the eight-syllable lines setting out the terms of the union and the four-syllable lines reserved for a succinct affirmation: *is rádh tuilltear* 'it is a claim which is deserved' / *roibheacht roinntear* 'it is precisely apportioned'.

All of the images – misfortune, abundance, blessing – prepare for the prose interlude which immediately follows:

> 10 Fir Bharrach na mbleidhe[adh] gcorcra
> cuire neambocht;
> do shaor a thír ar gach tromolc
> brígh na mbeannocht.[35]

The men of the Barrys of the crimson goblets [are] a numerous company; the power of the blessings delivered his land from every grievous misfortune.

The cause of *tromolc* 'misfortune' (10*c*) or *doghra* 'sorrow' (2*b*) is not specified. One might surmise the death of the patron's father in 1581; or the death of his wife, Ellen Roche, some time after 1602;[36] or perhaps the burning of his lands in 1600 by the northern chieftain Aodh Ó Néill, in retribution for his refusal to join the Irish rising. Emphasis is on a metamorphosis, from misfortune to bounty, which is possible though *brígh na mbeannocht* 'the power of the blessings'. Here the emendation of manuscript *brugh* 'homestead' to *brígh* 'power' (10*d*) is supported by the required internal rhyme *brígh : tír* (10*cd*), and the verbal echo *brígh / bríoghmhar*, which links the final line of the verse to the opening phrase of the prose, a stylistic feature of *crosántacht*:

> **brígh** na **mbeannocht**
> *Et* **beannocht bhríoghmhar** bhuadha bhiothmharthanach bheann-
> aighthe tug an t-eapstol onóireach árdchómhachtach, 7 an t-éarlamh
> féig feochuir fíorchráibhtheach, 7 gein shochuir 7 shaoirsine

---

34 Consonance between *innte* and the rhyming pair *tuilltear : roinntear* (9*bd*) is imperfect. 35 10*a* bfléidhe N; *b* neamhbhocht N; *d* brúgh ATN; mbeanocht N.   36 She was living in 1602: see *The Irish fiants of the Tudor sovereigns*, iii, p. 583 §6700. Dáibhidh de Barra married second, Julia, daughter of Cormac Mac Carthy (Gibbs, *Complete peerage*, i, p. 442).

saorG*h*aoidheal Éirionn .i. Pádraig príomhfháidheamhuil parrathasda
mac uasal Ailpruinn do dhá chóige mhórghárgha Múmhan, iar dteacht
i gcoinne 7 i gcómhdháil Aonghus mac Nad Fraoich m*ei*c Cuirc m*ei*c
Lúigheach dá bhaisde 7 dá bhuainbheannúghadh, dá theagasg 7 dá
thréanchómhairliúghadh, do chabhair 7 do choisreagadh, do sheoladh,
do shársgaoile 7 do shaoirsheanmóir na canóinne caoimhe 7 creidimh
chogúsaigh Chatoilce an Choimhdhe dho, gur thionóladur 7 gur
thiomsuighadar saorchlanna saidhbhre soichineóil na sárMhúmhan, ider
ísiol 7 uasal, ider urra agus easurra, do shuíghe 7 do shárionnsuíghe an
tsaoireapstuil shuairc shoibhéasuigh ... gur bheanaigh iad idir fhear 7
mhnaoi, maca 7 ingeana ...

And it is a powerful, pre-eminent, ever-lasting, fortunate blessing
which the honourable, mighty apostle and keen, indomitable, truly
pious patron saint and beneficent and noble and ancient disciple [lit.
birth] of the noble Gaels of Ireland, that is, eminently wise, paradisal
Pádraig, the noble son of Alpurn, bestowed upon the two great fierce
provinces of Munster, after coming to meet and to convene with
Aonghus son of Nad Fraoich son of Corc son of Lughaidh, to baptize
and to perpetually bless him, to teach and to firmly counsel him, to
help and to consecrate, to instruct and vigorously spread and eloquently preach the precious sacred text and conscientious, Catholic
faith to him, so that the wealthy, well-born offspring of fair Munster
gathered and assembled, both low-born and noble, both the freeman
and landless man, to sit and intently seek the gentle, gracious apostle
... so that he blessed them, both man and woman and sons and daughters ...

Identifying a source precisely is difficult, as the bardic poet typically adapts a
narrative to suit his purpose.[37] The late version of *Agallamh na seanórach* is a
plausible source, as Pádraig Breatnach has proposed.[38] Another interesting version occurs in *Betha Phátraic*, from the fifteenth-century *Lebor Brecc*, where
key elements of the story are condensed into a single episode; immediately after
baptizing Aengus, St Patrick instructs the people and pronounces an effusive
verse blessing on each feature of the landscape: *Bennacht Dé for Mumain, feraib
macaib mnaib, / bennacht for in talmain do-beir tarad daib*, etc. 'God's blessing
on Munster, men children and women, / blessing on the land that gives them
fruit ...').[39] The same verses are in the older *Bethu Phátraic*, but occur several
episodes after the baptism of Óengus.[40] The poet of *Teallach* does not replicate

37 Liam Ó Caithnia, *Apalóga na bhfilí, 1200–1650* (Dublin, 1984), pp 16–17.   38 Nessa
Ní Shéaghdha (ed.), *Agallamh na seanórach*, 3 vols (Dublin, 1942–5), i, pp 58–9; cf.
Breatnach, *Téamaí taighde*, p. 35.   39 Whitley Stokes (ed. and trans.), *Three Middle-Irish
homilies* (Calcutta, 1877), pp 32–3.   40 Mulchrone, *Bethú Phátraic*, ll 2297–307, 2545–73.

the language of a particular *vita*; it is his own re-telling, and the *crosántacht* style grants considerable latitude as he formulates the analogy:

> 7 tug beannocht d'úir 7 d'uisge 7 d'fhéar na n-uasalMhuimhneach fá sgeith a dtorchair 7 a dtromthortha dá gcabhair 7 dá gcomhfhortacht i ngach n-imneadh, 7 i ngach n-aimsir budh dú 7 budh dual dóibh; agus dar linne do réir ár bhfeasa 7 ár bhfíorbharamhladh féin do thuit breath 7 buantoradh na beannochta 7 na buanghuídhe sin ar chrích mbuig mbraonaigh mbuantíodhlaicigh mBarrach Mór le linn 7 le lán-réimhios Dháibhí mheic Séamuis meic Risteard do Bárr, go bhfuil ina clár thorcharthach théachtuighthe thromchonáigh lán d'ioth 7 d'iol-torthach 7 d'iolmhaoinibh, lán d'fhéile 7 d'onóir, do ghliocus 7 do gheanmnuígheacht, lán d'uaisle, d'oineach 7 d'fhoirmidin ré gach aon-fhear, mar atáid uaisle 7 árdmhaithe chríche 7 chaomhthalmhan an Bharraigh Mhóir, 7 go speisialta an Barrach Mór féin.

> And he [St Patrick] gave a blessing to the earth and water and grass-land of the noble Munstermen on account of which bursts forth their sea-wrack and their heavy fruits to help and relieve them in every sorrow and in every season that was belonging to and natural to them; and we think, according to our wisdom and our own certain opinion, that the reward and enduring fruitfulness of that blessing and lasting prayer fell upon the gentle, dewy, perpetually abundant land of Barrymore during the reign and the full rule of Dáibhí son of Séamas son of Risteard de Barra, so that it is a plain rich in sea-wrack, firm, laden with prosperity, full of grain and many fruits and many treasures, full of generosity and honour, astute wisdom and generative power, full of nobility, honour and respect toward every single man, namely, [the] nobles and leading men of the territory and fair land of Barrymore, and especially the great Barry himself.

The poet draws on a store of images signifying *fir flaithemon*. The 'bursting forth' (*sgeith*) of 'sea-wrack' (*torchar*) recalls Tadhg (mac Dáire) Mac Bruaideadha's *Mór a-tá ar theagasg flatha*, where a just reign ensures the 'bursting forth of every full fruit' (*sgeith gach lántoraidh*).[41] Sea-waif (*tor-chairthe / turchairthe* and *torchar*) is also a witness to righteous kingship:

> An talamh gana thairthibh / 'sa[n] tonn gana torchoirthibh / ag tairn-gire ríogh o Róigh / as síon aing(h)lidhe ina onóir.

41 McManus, 'The smallest man in Ireland', p. 69. See also Emma Nic Cárthaigh, '*Mór a-tá ar theagasg flatha: Speculum principis* le Tadhg mac Dáire Mheic Bhruaideadha' in S. Ó Coileáin, L. Ó Murchú and P. Riggs (eds), *Séimhfhear suairc: Aistí in ómós don Ollamh Breandán Ó Conchúir* (An Daingean, 2013), pp 139–80 at p. 148, q. 5.

The land with its produce and the waves with their sea-waif bear witness to the king of the line of Roach, as does the angelic weather
[guaranteed] in his honour.[42]

Such images are frequent in syllabic verse, but in *Teallach* they are effectively
set into alliterative prose, a stylistic option in *crosántacht*.

It is a considerable leap from St Patrick to Antaeus, but apologues from
foreign sources become more frequent in bardic poetry during the late sixteenth century, as Katharine Simms has observed.[43] The tale of internecine
war *In cath catharda* was popular among the poets;[44] and yet *Teallach* preserves the only allusion to Antaeus in poems from the Classical Modern Irish
period (*c*.1200–1650).[45] Details are judiciously selected by the author of
Teallach, who describes only the unusual birth of Antaeus and the wondrous
manner in which he regains his courage and battle-strength: when Antaeus is
about to be vanquished by his opponent, he falls upon the earth, only to rise
up stronger when his body touches the earth, his mother. There is no mention of his single combat with the hero Hercules who, perceiving that
Antaeus' strength derives from the earth, raises him aloft and crushes him to
death between his forearms. The tale is directed at praising Barrymore and
its ruling lord.

The poet may incorporate elements of parody and caricature which, as
Pádraig Ó Macháin has demonstrated, are allowable within the liberal parameters of *crosántacht*.[46] In likening his patron to Antaeus, who shamelessly
falls to the ground to protect his form, one senses an oblique hint at the
patron's submission to the Crown.[47] If it is ironic praise, with a hint of satire,
it is praise nonetheless. Whether Dáibhidh mac Séamais bows in submission
or in battle, he rises renewed by the land of his birth. And in a poem which
praises the bounty of Barrymore, blessed by St Patrick and offering an abundance of wealth, patron and patrimony are worthy of praise. The patron
'bends' (*feac*) to guard his form, and the poet defends and praises his actions:

> 37 Mac mic Ruisdeard na ruag ndoil[i]gh
> d'fheac mur ógbhláth
> ag cosnamh a ghné ngéagm*h*aoth,
> 's é an t-óglách.[48]

42 McManus, 'The smallest man in Ireland', p. 103 §129.   43 Simms, 'Transition from
medieval to modern in the poems of Tadhg Dall Ó hUiginn' in Riggs (ed.), *Tadhg Dall Ó
hUiginn*, pp 119–34 at p. 129.   44 See, for example, *TDall* i, no. 18.17–19 (p. 134); James
Carney (ed.), *Poems on the O'Reillys* (Dublin, 1950), no. XXV, ll 2885–916 (pp 124–5). Cf.
idem, *The Irish bardic poet* (Dublin, 1948), p. 36.   45 See Bardic Poetry Database:
<www.bardic.celt.dias.ie>.   46 Ó Macháin, 'The poetry of Tadhg Dall Ó hUiginn: themes
and sources', p. 81.   47 I thank Anthony Harvey for helpful remarks on this passage
following a presentation at the University of Aberdeen.   48 37*b* dfeach AT, dféach N;

Et óglách iongantach adhuathmhar iollrachtach do bhí a gcríochaibh áille oirearmhíne na hÁfraice dár badh comhainm Anteus mhic Tíre, 7 ní ó dhúil dhaonna dhuineata mhná do geineadh an t-ársuigh ainmhín aindreannta-sin, acht a gheineamhuin go modartha míonádúrtha a tonngnúis na talmhan tromfhódúighe; 7 is amhlaidh do-níodh an tan do théigheadh do chathúghadh nó do chruadhchomhrac ré curadhaibh cródha coimseacha cleaslúithreacha colgladharthacha, ... i n-uair do bhíodh sé i n-áirc nó i n-éigion dá chlódh nó dá chómhfhorrach, ní dhéineadh acht é féin do léigean ina easglann mhór anbhail d'ionnsuíghe láir 7 lántailimh, go dtigeadh a neart 7 a bhrígh, a chalmacht 7 a churantacht féin ann ré halt na huaire sin, ó thaghall a mhátharbhunaidh .i. an talamh, go n-éirgeadh ina cholmhuin chóimhdhíreach ina chuilgsheasamh, go sloigheadh 7 go slatbhuaileadh go gcraipleadh 7 go gcruadhcheangladh, go milleadh 7 go míochóirírígheadh a lucht iomtha 7 easaonta ar an órdúghadh sin; 7 is iongna an réim 7 an obair bhí for an óglaoch sin .i. gurb ē a neartúghadh a bhuanleagadh, 7 is ionshamhluighthe sin ris an mBarrach Mór, óir fuair a choimpreadh 7 a cho[mh]fhoghluim i gcogthaibh 7 i gconghalaibh, i n-éachtaibh 7 i n-áthasaibh, i n-oineach 7 i n-e[agnomh] agus i n-árdghnīomhaibh, 7 ní bhfuil dá mhéid d'imreasan ná d'easaonta do-ghníd a fhoghluidh 7 a eascaruid dō, nách ar barr cumais 7 calmacht théid sin dō-san, 7 ní bhfuil dá mhéid a chlú 7 a chomhsgaoileadh, a bhronnta 7 a bhuantíodhlaice do lucht iarrata athchuinge 7 éadála, nách ar barr saidhbhris 7 sochonáig, ionnmhuis 7 iolmhaithis théid sin dō, do réir mar atá an cleachta 7 an cómhthaithíghe aige *et* –

> 38 A thabhairt uaidh go mór minic
> mar mhac Tíre;
> nach bí guth ag cléir 'na chuinne
> réidh do-ríne.[49]

The grandson of Richard of the grievous raids who bent like a youthful flower defending his tender-limbed form is the young warrior.

And a wondrous, terrifying, shape-shifting (?) warrior who was called Antaeus mac Tíre was in the beautiful, smooth-region of Africa, and it is not from a human woman that that rough, fierce champion was begotten, but rather, his murky, unnatural birth [was] from the surface

ogbhláth T, ogbhláith N; *d* asé ATN. Line 37*c* is short a syllable in the manuscripts. Emendation to the shorter copula form (37*d*) restores the four-syllable line. For the long vowel in the second syllable of *óglách*, compare *óglach* : *ógbhláth* (*TDall* i, p. xlii). **49** 38*a* mhaic AT; *c* guith N; ag cléir cuinne N; *d* réig ATN; do rinne N.

of the heavy-sodded earth. And this is what he used to do when he
went to battle or hard combat against fierce, strong, feat-pivoting(?),
sword-grasping champions ... when he was in difficulty or distress of
being destroyed or subdued: he just let himself fall into a large, lifeless, shameless heap to the ground and earth, so that his strength and
his power, his courage and his own warlike-action used to come in him
at that moment, from touching his own mother, that is, the earth, so
that he rose upward, as straight as a blade, until he struck and beat,
bound, tied fast, destroyed and threw his rivals and rebels into confusion in that manner; and wondrous is the manner and labour of that
warrior; that is, that it is his continual falling [upon the earth] which
causes his strengthening. And that can be compared to the Great
Barry, for he was begotten and received equal training in wars and
conflicts, in exploits and in victorious feats, in honour and in wisdom
and in noble deeds. And there is not [anything], however much strife
or chaos which his plunderer and his enemies inflict upon him, that
rivals [lit. that is not beyond] the strength and bravery which that
[falling upon the earth] gives to him, and there is not [anything], however great his fame and his yielding, his bestowing and constant sur-
rendering to those seeking a favour and wealth, which rivals the profit
and prosperity, wealth and benefits which that [yielding] gives to him,
according as he practices and performs it frequently; and –

Yielding often like the son of the Land; let not the poets have a word
[to say] against him; what he did is sensible.

I draw attention to a phrase above, which describes the source of Antaeus'
strength, *ó thaghall a mhátharbhunaidh .i. an talamh* 'from touching his own
mother, that is, the earth', which clearly echoes the text of *In cath catharda*:
co mba nert nua ar gach lo leis tre tadall a mat[h]ar bunaidh .i. in talam 'so that
on every day he had fresh vigour through touching his original mother, the
earth'.[50] The same phrasing is found in Edinburgh, Advocates MS 72.1.46 (f.
1r–v),[51] an important early copy of the Antaeus episode, written for Tomás
Óg Mág Uidhir of Fermanagh, who has been identified as either Tomás Óg
who ruled 1430–71, or his son (who ruled 1484–6).[52] It is another intriguing
hint at a Maguire interest, and its survival is of considerable importance, as

---

50 *IT* iv, 2, p. 222, ll 2911–12. Cf. *co llinta do calmatus dermair é ó mhathair bhunaidh .i. on
talmhain* 'so that he was filled with great courage by his original mother, to wit, the earth'
(ibid., ll 2898–9). For an apparent compound of gen. sg. *máthar + bunaidh* in *Teallach*,
compare *chríchfhionnMhonaidh : mhátharbhunaidh* (*DD*, no. 89.6*ab*, p. 291).   **51** Advocates
MS 72.1.46, f. 1v: *comba nert nua ar cach lo leis tre thadhull a mathar bunaidh .i. in talam.*
52 Pádraig Ó Macháin, 'Observations on the manuscript of Tadhg Ó Cianáin' in F. Ó
Fearghail (ed.), *Tadhg Ó Cianáin: an Irish scholar in Rome* (Dublin, 2011), pp 171–205 at

the Antaeus episode is missing from the two oldest manuscripts of *In cath
catharda* (TCD MS 1298 [H.2.17] and RIA MS D iv 2 [1223]) due to the
loss of a leaf.[53] I am aware of only one other instance of the Antaeus story, in
the late poem *Faoilidh Fir-mhanach a nocht* 'Fermanagh is joyous tonight',
composed for Brian Mág Uidhir, chieftain of Fermanagh (†1700).[54] Mág
Uidhir is likened to the illustrious hero Hercules, however, though Antaeus'
unnatural birth and combat with Hercules are recounted in some detail.[55] I
intend to return to these texts, which merit further comment.

The end of *Teallach* echoes and extends the theme set out at the beginning. Antaeus draws strength from touching the earth, his mother; Dáibhidh
mac Séamais gains strength from his birth and 'burnishing' in the land of
Barrymore:

> 39 Mar do coimpreadh i gclí an talmhan
> an tréan boinngheal,
> Dáibhidh iar n-uair as an ea[n]gnamh
> f[h]uair a fhoighreadh.[56]

Just as the strong, white-footed warrior [Antaeus] was born of the
land, [it is] Dáibhí in turn who got his burnishing from generosity
[and prowess].

The benefits of contact with the land extend from the chieftain to the people.
All desire to visit (*tadhall*) Barrymore, Co. Cork, and a pun on *tadhall* 'touch'
is likely, for just as Antaeus and the great Barry 'touch' the earth and rise
with renewed courage, all travel the land of Barrymore so as to partake of its
bounty:

> 43 Críoch oirbheartach airdríogh Barrach
> na mbrugh síthe;
> mian gach fhir dá dtriallann uaithe
> tadhall tríthe.[57]

pp 173–4. Ó Macháin also notes the fragmented copy of *In cath catharda* in the separated
bifolium RIA MS D i 1 (1237), part I. The Antaeus episode does not appear in this
fragment, however, as the narrative breaks off (= *IT* iv, 2, l. 2877); cf. *RIA Cat.*, p. 3427.
53 Stokes had unclear photographs of the Advocates manuscript, and drew this section of the
text from two late manuscripts (dated 1617 and 1633); see *IT* iv, 2, pp vi–vii. A digital
version of the Advocates manuscript may be viewed at Irish Script on Screen:
<www.isos.dias.ie>. 54 Ludwig Stern (ed.), 'Ueber eine Sammlung irischer Gedichte in
Kopenhagen', *ZCP*, 2 (1899), 323–72 at 361–5 §36. A passage from Advocates MS 72.1.46 is
also cited (ibid., p. 364 n. 1). 55 Antaeus is called *Antéon (: léon)*, ibid., p. 362, l. 20.
Antéon (Antheon) is the form of the name in French and English versions: Quin, *Stair
Ercuil*, p. xxvi §23. 56 39*a* Mar] Mac N; na talmhan ATN; *c* Dáibhí AT. Line *a* has an
extra syllable in the manuscripts. 57 43*a* áirdrígh AT, airdrígh N; *c* triallann AT, triallainn
N; *d* tághall A. Internal rhyme *triallann : tadhall* is imperfect and alliteration is wanting in *c*.

The accomplished land of the high-king of the Barrys of the wondrous dwellings; every one who travels away from it has a desire to travel through it.

The poem begins, and ends, with an image of *Crìoch Bharrach*, the land of the Barrys, as the idealized kingdom of delightful Otherworld dwellings, which mirrors the blessed land depicted in the opening prose apologue. The poet links the stories of saint and champion with elegance and wit, in an encomium that celebrates the courage of the chieftain and the regeneration of his patrimony.

An Early Irish category of swindler:
the *mindach méith*

FERGUS KELLY

Legal systems have great difficulty in dealing with crimes for which there is no eye-witness, and much ingenuity has been expended in trying to devise methods of fixing guilt on a suspect for crimes of this nature. The surviving early Irish legal material provides examples of various approaches to the problem. The most frequently mentioned is the use of an ordeal (*fír nDé*, lit. 'justice of God') to establish the truth. This normally involves subjecting the suspect to some form of violence – such as forcing him or her to pick up an object from a boiling cauldron or to lick a red-hot adze – and concluding from the physical effects as to his or her guilt or innocence.[1] The casting of lots may also be used to determine guilt or innocence in cases where there is no witness to an offence: this method is most frequently attested in land-law.[2]

Another approach is illustrated in a short Old Irish text with Middle Irish glosses and commentary, which lists seventeen signs of guilt. This text is to be found in London, BL MS Egerton 88, ff 33a–35d and is printed in *CIH* iv, 1359.26–1367.3. It begins: *Atait a .uii.x. doberaid anntestus do duine* 'There are seventeen things which place a person in bad legal standing'. There is an incomplete version of the text in Dublin, TCD MS 1337 (H.3.18) p. 296, which is printed at *CIH* iii, 822.6–823.10. Giolla na Naomh Mac Aodhagáin (†1309) provides a summary of the text in his 'Treatise on Irish law', which is also in H.3.18 at pp 158–9 (*CIH* ii, 692.6–20). The text on the seventeen signs of guilt has not been edited or translated.

In most of the seventeen cases listed in our text, no witness actually saw the crime being committed. There may, however, be indirect evidence that incriminates a particular individual. Thus, he may arouse the suspicion of his neighbours by very heavy sleep (*collad rothrom*) on the morning after a theft.[3] Unless he can put forward some explanation for his heavy sleep – such as being kept awake through some domestic crisis or necessity (*deithbires*) – he can be convicted of the crime by the supporting oath of thirty persons (i.e., *letharra(e)*). This only applies to a suspect who is classed as an *anteist*, i.e., one who is not in good legal standing by reason of previous criminality or low status or other impediment. By contrast, a *teist* in good legal standing cannot be convicted of a crime merely through having slept in late. The term *arra(e)*

---

1 Fergus Kelly, *A guide to early Irish law* (Dublin, 1988), pp 209–11. 2 Ibid., pp 208–9. 3 *CIH* iv, 1362.37–8.

is verbal noun of *ar-ren* 'pays on behalf of, is equivalent to', and is employed in the specialized sense of the number of oath-takers which is required to convict a suspect in the absence of direct evidence.[4] Usually, the full *arra(e)* (*lánarra(e)*) refers to the supporting oath of sixty persons, and a half *arra(e)* (*letharra(e)*) to the supporting oath of thirty persons.[5] This system obviously depended on the neighbours' assessment of the character of the suspect, and their view as to whether he was likely to have committed the offence of which he was accused. Only adult freemen of good character would be entitled to provide an oath in support of the plaintiff's accusation.

In another case, a lost personal item provides incriminating evidence. The Old Irish text has *Derm– og fuill–* which might be expanded as *Dermat og fuilliucht* 'something forgotten on the track'.[6] The Middle Irish glossator explains: *.i. a brog no lamann do fagbail don gadaige a mbel na hairbe 7 adces aigi r[o]ime* 'i.e. the leaving of his shoe or glove by the thief on the fence, and it was seen in his possession previously'. It requires a supporting oath of sixty persons (*lánarra(e)*) to convict on the basis of this evidence. Evidently, this applies whether the suspect is classed as a *teist* or an *anteist*.

Another case is described in the Old Irish text as *Cosmailus étaig* 'similarity of clothing'.[7] Here a thief has been seen in the act of stealing, but there is doubt as to his identity. If the eye-witness is prepared to swear an oath (*fír*) that the thief wore clothing of a particular colour, and that his hair was fair or red or black, and a suspect answering this description admits to having been in the area at the time of the theft, it requires the supporting oath of thirty persons (*letharra(e)*) to secure a conviction. As in the previous case, this applies whether the suspect is classed as a *teist* or an *anteist*.

In this article I examine the fifteenth of the seventeen situations discussed in this text: the case of a suspect who is classed as a *mindach* (*minnach*) *méith*, an expression which is otherwise unattested in our sources.

Here follow a transcription and tentative translation of this passage (= *CIH* iv, 1363.4–10):

TEXT AND TRANSLATION

(a) **Min*n*ach meith** .i. me*n*gac*h* é ima*n* meit*h*red, no míanec*h* (= -ach) é uma*n* meit*h*rec*h*, (b) caisi mei*nn*ic ab eo cot *est* men*n*dicus .i. bregac*h* .i. u*m* gac*h* ní; (c) .i. it*h*i 7 ni g*h*adan*n*; 7 fer dag*h*blat*h*[a], .i. dag*h*tsult*mar* 7 dot[h]eng; (d) b*eirid* (?) an gait d'it*h*i d*h*o aon*ur*: letharra <*in margin: no* lanarra> do-sli; (e) .i. do neac*h* is con*n*taba*r*t do torac*h*tain do de*n*am na gaid*e*

---

4 *DIL* s.v. *arrae* (c). **5** See discussion in D.A. Binchy, 'The Old-Irish table of penitential commutations', *Ériu*, 19 (1962), 47–72 at 51–3. **6** *CIH* iv, 1362.35. Binchy suggests expanding as 'fuill*iud* (?)'. **7** *CIH* iii, 822.39; iv, 1362.14.

risn*ar* labuirsit na coin, fasta lanfir no lanarr*a*; (f) an tuar*astal* fast*us* in*r*aic f*or* nec*h* cona faicsi*n* di budei*n*: is *ed* fast*us* g*ach* ní dib-so ma tait an*n*.

(a) **A smooth swearer**, i.e., he is guileful about the fatness, or he is desirous about the fatness; (b) as if *meinnic* from *mendicus*, i.e., lying, i.e., about every-thing; (c) i.e., he eats and does not steal; and [he is] a man of good appear-ance, i.e., of prosperous demeanour and false-tongued(?); (d) he takes the stolen [food] to eat for himself: he is convicted by the supporting oath of thirty <or sixty> persons; (e) i.e., for someone who is suspected of arriving to carry out the theft at which the dogs did not bark: a full oath or the sup-porting oath of sixty persons fixes liability; (f) the evidence which a valid wit-ness fixes on someone having seen [the crime] himself: that is what fixes liability in each of these [situations] if they (the witnesses) are there.

NOTES

(a) **Min*n*ach meit*h*.** Two Middle Irish etymological glosses are provided in explanation of the phrase *minnach méith* of the Old Irish text: *mengach é iman meithred* and *míanach (-ech* MS) *é uman meithrech.* The adjective *mengach* in the first gloss is a derivative of the fem. *ā*-stem *meng* 'wile, ruse, guile, craft', always used in a negative context (*DIL* s.vv. *meng, mengach*). The noun *méithred* (*méthrad*) is formed from the adjective *méth* (*méith*) 'fat, soft, smooth', and is used of the fat or grease of meat (*DIL* s.v. *méthrad*). In the second gloss, the adjective *míanach* echoes *minnach* of the Old Irish text. It is formed from the neut. (later masc.) *o*-stem *mían* 'wish, desire', which may be followed by the genitive of the thing desired, or by the prepositions *imm, do* or *ré* (*DIL* s.v. *mían*). The otherwise unattested noun *méithrech* is no doubt a glossator's coinage based on *méth* (*méith*), and bears the same meaning as *méithred*.

The form *mindach* (*minnach*) is a derivative of the Old Irish neuter *o*-stem *mind* 'emblem, diadem, insignia', which developed the meaning 'venerated object, halidom (especially in connection with a saint)' (*DIL* s.v. *mind* [b]). Because oaths were regularly sworn on a relic or other object associated with a saint, the word came to be used of an oath or vow (*DIL* s.v. *mind* (d); *LEIA* 'M' 53–4 s.v. *mind*). *DIL* gives no instances of the adjective *mindach* (*minnach*) but it is well attested in the later language in the meanings 'swear-ing, given to swearing'.[8] I take it that *mindach* is here used substantively, and refers to a criminal who is in the practice of swearing (false) oaths for per-sonal gain. The adjective *mé(i)th* is used here in a negative sense, and evi-dently refers to the smooth, greedy character of this type of person.

8 Niall Ó Domhnaill, *Foclóir Gaeilge-Béarla* (Dublin, 1977), s.vv. *mionnach, mionnaigh.*

(b) **caisi mei*n*nic ab eo cot est men*n*dicus .i. bregach**. This gloss provides a different explanation of the word *mindach* to those put forward in (a). The same gloss is included in Cormac's Glossary, dating from around 900AD: *Mindech quasi mendic, ob* [= *ab*] *eo quod est mendicus .i. bregach* '*Mindech* as if *mendic*, from *mendicus*, i.e., lying'.[9] Old Irish *mindech* is a borrowing from Latin *mendicus* 'needy, beggarly' (*LEIA* 'M' 54).[10] It is attested at Ml. 26b18, where it glosses Latin *tenuis* 'thin, needy, poor'. The abstract *mindchecht* glosses *mendicitas* 'beggarliness' and *adtenuatio* 'thinness, indigence' at Ml. 129c2 and 22d1 respectively. As pointed out at *DIL* s.v. *mindech*, the gloss *.i. brégach* results from confusion with Latin *mendax* 'lying'. Neither Latin *mendicus* nor *mendax* could give Old Irish *mindach*: see *GOI* 47 §75.

Note that in our version of this gloss, *.i. bregach* is followed by the further explanatory gloss *.i. um gach ní*. The *mindach méith* is thus held to be dishonest in all matters.

(c) **it*h*i 7 ni g*h*adan*n***. I take the form *ithi* to be for *ithid* 'eats', with the common omission of final lenited -*d*.

fer dag*h*blat*h*[a]. I read *fer degblátha* 'a man of good appearance' taking *blátha* to be gen. sg. of *bláth* 'bloom, appearance', which can be a masc. *u*-stem or *o*-stem (*DIL* s.v. *bláth*). Alternatively, it may be for *fer degblada* 'a man of good reputation' (*DIL* s.v. *blad*); cf. *fó degblad* 'with a good reputation' (*LU* 43.1252). However, this does not make such good sense, as the glossator is here emphasizing the convincing appearance and manner of the suspect.

dag*h*tsult*m*ar. The adjective *sultmar* is formed from the *o*-stem *sult* 'fatness, prosperity; gladness, cheerfulness' (*DIL* s.v.). In the present context, the word seems to refer to the affluent appearance of the suspect, rather than to the cheerfulness of his manner. The spelling *daghtsultmar* shows the substitution of *ts* for *s* occasionally employed in Irish manuscripts: see *DIL* 'S' 1.9–13.

dot[h]eng. My interpretation of this passage is uncertain. At *CIH* iv, 1363.6, Binchy takes 'dotengb–' of the MS to be one word, and expands it as 'dotengb*ad* (?)', evidently viewing it as a possible verbal form (perhaps a past subj. of *do-ecmaing* 'comes about, happens', with doubling of the preverb?). However, I can make no headway with this approach, and tentatively suggest that *dotheng* means 'false-tongued', perhaps echoing *mindach* '(falsely) swearing' of the Old Irish text. The spelling *dothe(i)ng* is occasionally attested, though *doithnge* and *dothenga* are more common (*DIL* s.v. *doithnge*; cf. *soithnge*). The glossator may have intended a contrast between the prefixed *dag(h)-* 'good' of *daghtsultmar* and *do-* 'bad' of *dot[h]eng*.

9 Kuno Meyer, 'Sanas Cormaic: an Old-Irish glossary compiled by Cormac Ua Cuilennáin', *Anecd.* iv (1912), p. 78 §893.   10 See also Damian McManus, 'A chronology of the Latin loan-words in early Irish', *Ériu*, 34 (1983), 23–71 at 64.

I suggest that *b–* is to be taken as an abbreviation of the verb *beirid* 'brings, takes', and belongs with the next sentence: see discussion under (d).

(d) b*eirid* (?) **an gait d'it***h***i d***h***o aonur.** Although there is only a small space between 'doteng' and 'b–' in the MS, I can see no alternative to taking them to be separate words. I tentatively suggest that *b–* is for *beirid* 'bears, takes', often used in the context of a theft or raid: see *DIL* s.v. *beirid* (IV) (a). The dat. sg. *óenur* 'alone' may be used with a preposition, for example, *m'oínur* 'on my own', *a óenur* 'on his own'. It is also commonly attested without a preposition, as in the present example: see *DIL* s.v. *oenar* 104.74–8.

letharr*a* <no lanarr*a*> do-sli. For a discussion of the *lánarra(e)* and *letharra(e)*, see Introduction above. The glossator here appears to make a distinction between two types of *mindach méith*. In the case treated in (c)–(d) the allegation of deception and theft against the suspect is upheld by the supporting oaths of thirty persons (*letharra(e)*). In the case of (e), however, the supporting oaths of sixty persons (*lánarra(e)*) are required. One could speculate that the fact that the suspect is a regular visitor or friend of the plaintiff necessitates a higher number of supporting oaths: of its nature the allegation is shocking and unusual. Note also that a later scribe clearly disagrees with the main glossator, and corrects *letharra* to *lánarra*. Presumably, his view is that in all circumstances it is necessary for the plaintiff to procure sixty oaths to convict a *mindach méith*.

The verb *do-slí* means 'earns', and is used in both the positive sense of profiting by a transaction, and in the negative sense of incurring liability for an offence. The latter is the meaning here.

(e) **do nea***ch* **is conntabar***t* **do tora***ch***tain do de***n***am na gaide.** The fem. *ā*-stem *conntabart* (*DIL* s.v. *cuntabart*) is here used of doubt or suspicion in relation to the committing of theft.

risna*r* labuirsit na coin. The form *ro labuirsit* (= *-et*) is 3rd plural perfect of *labraid* (Old Irish *labraithir*) 'speaks', which is used not only of human speech, but of a variety of other sounds, including bird-song, and the sound of the sea or of a bell (*DIL* s.vv. *labra*, *labraithir*). Here it refers to the barking of the household dogs. They do not bark in this case because they are familiar with the suspect.

fasta lanfir no lanarr*a*. The form *fasta* is Middle Irish 3rd singular present indicative of *ad-suidi*, *-asstai* 'fixes, establishes, convicts' (*DIL* s.v. *ad-suidi*). Here the glossator views a full oath (*lánfír*) as being of equal weight to the supporting oaths of sixty persons (*lánarra(e)*). In commentary preceding the H.3.18 version of the text on indirect evidence (*CIH* iii, 820.4–5), the *lánfír* in the case of a serious crime is given as the oath of fourteen persons:

six commoners and eight lords (*Cethre fir dec a lanfir: .ui. boairig 7 tri airig desa 7 tri airig tuisi 7 aire árd 7 aire forgill*).

(f) **an tuar*astal* fast*us* in*r*aic f*o*r nech**. The glossator here refers to the evidence which a witness of legal standing (*inraic*) provides in a case. The term *túarastal* (earlier *túarasndal*) is generally used of the evidence of a valid eyewitness: see *DIL* s.v. *túarastal* (I).

cona faicsi*n* di budei*n*. Compare the fragmentary text on legal procedure at *CIH* vi, 2342.12–14 which states: *is marb o neach ni nad fria suil feighe fuirmither, ar ni toing neach ni nad aici nad airdi* '[evidence] from a person is dead which has not taken place before his keen eye, for no-one swears something which he does not see or perceive'. I take *di budein* to be for *dó budéin* 'by himself' from the preposition *do* 'to, by, etc.' (*DIL* s.v. 1 *do* 171.44–5). Or perhaps read *de budéin*, from the preposition *di* 'from, by' (*DIL* s.v. 1 *de, di* 131.26–9).

is *ed* fast*us* g*a*ch ní dib-so ma tait an*n*. If the direct evidence of a valid witness may establish guilt, the use of indirect evidence is unneccessary. In the surviving early Irish legal material, the oath of a single witness is generally regarded as insufficient. Thus, the law-text *Berrad airechta* provides the general rule: *ar ni oeinfer is coir da fiadnaise, it a do no a tri* 'for one man is not proper for giving evidence, there are two or three'.[11] However, the texts also provide examples of specific situations where a single oath suffices. This applies, for instance, in the case of the evidence of a holy bishop delivered between host and chalice (i.e., between the two acts of Holy Communion), or of a woman in childbirth, or of a sick man facing death.[12] *Berrad airechta* also provides a wider category of exception: *nibi fiadha oinfer, acht mad craibdech hirisech* 'one man should not be a witness, unless he is pious and faithful'.[13] It is possible that the phrase *ma tait ann* 'if they are there' in the passage under discussion refers here to a number of witnesses in a case.

CONCLUSION

In conclusion, the offence of the *mindach méith* evidently involves the dishonest taking of an oath, by which means he deprives his victims of their

11 *CIH* ii, 596.4–5 = Rudolf Thurneysen, 'Die Bürgschaft im irischen Recht', *Abhandlungen der preussischen Akademie der Wissenschaften, Phil.-Hist. Klasse*, Nr 2 (Berlin, 1928), p. 19 §58; English translation by Robin Chapman Stacey, '*Berrad airechta*: an Old Irish tract on suretyship' in T.M. Charles-Edwards, M.E. Owen and D.B. Walters (eds), *Lawyers and laymen: studies in the history of law presented to professor Dafydd Jenkins on his seventy-fifth birthday* (Cardiff, 1986), pp 210–33 at p. 219. 12 *CIH* v, 1570.1–8. 13 *CIH* ii, 599.35–6 = Thurneysen, 'Bürgschaft', p. 31 §84; English translation by Stacey, '*Berrad airechta*', p. 219.

property. The glossator concentrates on the theft of food, but it is likely that the phrase *mindach méith* could be applied to other types of swindler. The glossator stresses the personable nature of the offender which enables him to carry out his depredations. He is of good appearance (*fer daghbláth*[*a*]) and of prosperous demeanour (*daghtsultmar*). He may not actually commit the theft himself, but gets somebody else to steal for his benefit: 'he eats and does not steal' (*ithi 7 ni ghadann*). In some cases, he has ingratiated himself with the household dogs so that they do not bark at his arrival (*risnar labuirsit na coin*), thus allowing him to make off with the family goods. Here our glossator anticipates a theme in Arthur Conan Doyle's detective story 'The adventure of Silver Blaze', where the information that the dog did not bark in the night enabled the amateur sleuth Sherlock Holmes to solve the case.

I hope that I have shed some light on this elusive category of early Irish swindler. I might add that the *mindach méith* took on a new lease of life during the recent 'Celtic Tiger' era!

Colum Cille and the *lorg bengánach*:
ritual migration from Derry

BRIAN LAMBKIN

Vita Columbae, Adomnán's Latin Life of Colum Cille, composed in the late seventh century, has only this to say about the saint's departure from Derry: 'he set sail from Ireland'.[1] The Irish Life of Colum Cille, edited and dated by Máire Herbert to about 1150, is as brief: 'he set out on the journey'.[2] By contrast, *Betha Colaim Chille*, the Irish Life composed in 1532 by Maghnus Ó Domhnaill (Manus O'Donnell), contains a detailed account, including the saint's convoy from his home in Derry to a place called Glais an Indluidh, his prophylactic lustration and circuiting of a stone there, and embarkation under the supervision of an unnamed official bearing a *lorg bengánach* ('forked staff').[3] The purpose here is to re-examine the evidence provided by Manus O'Donnell for this ritual of migrant departure from Derry in order to clarify the location of Glais an Indluidh, the identity of the office-holder, and the significance of the *lorg bengánach*.

Elsewhere an attempt has been made to reconstruct procedures of migration in the period 500–800, based mainly on applying the so-called SDO framework of migration studies (three stages, three directions, three outcomes) to the evidence of Adomnán's *Vita Columbae*.[4] Notwithstanding its lack of detail in the case of Colum Cille, Adomnán's Life contains a number of detailed stories of other pilgrims / migrants which were intended to point (both positively and negatively) to the ideal procedure of pilgrimage. This ideal was closely related to secular legal procedures governing the practice of migration (*migratio / emigratio*), defined as moving permanently or semi-permanently from one place of residence (*patria*) to another. The migration process consisted of three main

---

1 Richard Sharpe (trans.), *Adomnán of Iona: Life of Saint Columba* (London, 1995), pp 3, 118.   2 Máire Herbert, *Iona, Kells, and Derry: the history and hagiography of the monastic familia of Columba* (Oxford, 1988), pp 236, l. 401; 260 §50.   3 Andrew O'Kelleher and Gertrude Schoepperle (ed. and trans.), *Betha Colaim Chille: Life of Columcille compiled by Manus O'Donnell in 1532* (Urbana IL, 1918; repr. Dublin, 1994); Brian Lacey (ed.), *The Life of Colum Cille by Manus O'Donnell* (Dublin, 1998). This Life 'incorporates a formidable amount of material dateable to the Middle Irish period and therefore in existence before 1200': Herbert, *Iona, Kells and Derry*, p. 180. See also Brian Lacey, *Saint Columba: his life and legacy* (Dublin, 2013), pp 39–40, 43–4.   4 Brian Lambkin, '"Emigrants" and "exiles": migration in the early Irish and Scottish church' *The Innes Review*, 58, ii (2007), 133–55; Patrick Fitzgerald and Brian Lambkin, *Migration in Irish history, 1607–2007* (Basingstoke, 2008), pp 16–68. On 'ritual', see Victor Turner and Edith Turner, *Image and pilgrimage in Christian culture: anthropological perspectives* (Oxford, 1978), pp 243–4.

stages: departure (*egressus*), crossing (*transitus*) and arrival (*adventus*).[5] The 'departure' stage (*egressus*) consisted of three sub-stages or phases: obtaining permission (*permissio*); making preparations (*praeparatio*); and setting off (*exitus*).[6] Each of these is evident in the account of Colum Cille's departure in Manus O'Donnell's Irish Life, *Betha Colaim Chille* (hereafter *BCC*).

MIGRANT DEPARTURE AT GLAIS AN INDLUIDH

The account in *BCC* of Colum Cille's departure from Derry is given as follows in Brian Lacey's translation, *The Life of Colum Cille by Manus O'Donnell* (hereafter *LCC*):

> And, although that place [Derry] was dear to him, on the advice of the angel and the saints of Ireland he prepared to leave it and go on pilgrimage to Scotland.
>
> He loved that place so much that he had his boat sent up Lough Foyle to the place now called *Glais an Indluidh*, while he himself went by land to rendezvous with it.
>
> He washed his hands in that stream so that *Glais an Indluidh* ['Stream of the Preparations'] is its name since.
>
> He blessed a stone that was beside the stream and went around it right-handwise.
>
> Then from the stone he went on board the boat saying that anyone who went around it right-handwise after that, before going on a walking journey or a voyage, would be safe.
>
> And the reason he took the boat past the settlement up the lough, as we said before, was so that he would have a longer view of it going past it upwards, then coming back alongside it.
>
> When Colum Cille and his holy followers were getting into the boat, a certain person was there in the harbour (*port*) with a 'forked' or 'branching' staff (*lorg bengánach*) in his hand. He put the staff (*lorg*) against the boat to push it off from the land. When Colum Cille saw this he said: 'I leave you the "gift" of involuntary exile (*buaid ndeoraighechta*) because of the "help" you have given me in leaving Ireland as an exile, and to your successors with forked staves (*lorg benganach*) I leave the same "gift" forever'.
>
> They let the ship move off then and his own kinsmen of the Cenél Conaill and the Cenél nEógain, and of all the [neighbouring] districts, were on both sides of Lough Foyle. And, when they saw that Colum Cille was really leaving them, they raised an outcry and lament after him.[7]

5 Fitzgerald and Lambkin, *Migration*, pp 10–11.   6 Ibid., pp 140, 146, 155.   7 *LCC*, p.

The three phases of the departure stage – obtaining permission, making preparations, setting off – are now considered in turn.

Obtaining permission to migrate

When the account above opens, the first phase of Colum Cille's migration – obtaining permission – is complete. It had been initiated by 'the angel' Michael delivering the divine message that he should 'leave Ireland, never to return'. Colum Cille responded in three ways, each of which had the effect of validating the angel's message. First, he informed 'his kinsmen and his people' that 'it is necessary for me to go on pilgrimage'.[8] Second, obeying the 'advice' (*comairli*) of 'the saints of Ireland', he visited Molaisse of Devenish in order to secure his approval. Third, on his own initiative he visited 'the holy man called Cruimther Fraech', who similarly confirmed the need for him to leave Ireland.[9] Any who may have doubted the wisdom of Colum Cille's expressed intention to migrate, or the validity of the angel's order, would have been reassured by the positive outcome of referring the matter to such authorities. Colum Cille thus received approval for his migration project from the entire community, his 'kinsmen', his 'people', 'the saints of Ireland' in general (represented by Molaisse and Cruimther Fraech) and 'the saints' of Derry in particular.[10] All were now prepared to play their part in the remaining two phases of the ritual of departure.

Making preparations at Glais an Indluidh

Having taken 'advice' and obtained all the necessary permissions or approval, Colum Cille, accompanied by his 'saints' or 'holy followers', made the short journey from his home in Derry (near 'the special yew tree in front of the *Duibreigles* [Black Church]'), to the site of preparation and point of departure at Glais an Indluidh.[11] The narrative makes clear that it was important that this journey be made by land, not water. By sending his boat upstream to meet him at Glais an Indluidh, Colum Cille avoided embarkation before ritual preparation there was complete. On arrival at Glais an Indluidh, he performed two special actions of 'preparation': washing his hands in the stream, and going 'sun-wise' round the special stone nearby. The strong implication of the story is that Glais an Indluidh was a well-established site of migrant departure which Colum Cille effectively christianized, or further sanctified, by following the custom of its migrant ritual.

104; *BCC*, pp 190–92.   8 *LCC*, pp 100–1; *BCC*, p. 184.   9 *LCC*, pp 101–3. In Adomnán's Life there is the parallel case of Báetán who sought the 'permission' of Colum Cille to migrate: Lambkin, '"Emigrants" and "exiles"', 151–2.   10 *BCC*, p. 212; *LCC*, p. 104.   11 Ibid. For the site of the *Duibreigles*, see Avril Thomas, *Derry-Londonderry*, Irish Historic Towns Atlas 15 (Dublin, 2005), pp 2–3. Note the parallel case in the *Nauigatio Sancti Brendani abbatis* of St Brendan's visit to St Enda on Aran before setting off on his voyage: Peter Harbison, *Pilgrimage in Ireland* (London, 1991), p. 91.

The narrative explains that the site was given the name Glais an Indluidh ('Stream of Washing / Preparation') in memory of Colum Cille's action. What christianized or further sanctified the stream was the attachment of this piece of *dindṡenchas* ('placename lore') about Colum Cille's model action of washing his hands in it, which evidently was still widely remembered in Manus O'Donnell's day. The 'stone' (*cloch*), not named here, may similarly have had the piece of *dindṡenchas* already attached to it that 'anyone who went around it right-handwise before going on a walking journey or a voyage would be safe'. Another story elsewhere in *BCC*, concerning Colum Cille's face-to-face encounter with Christ in the guise of a poor migrant on the point of leaving Derry permanently, makes clear that the location of this stone was known as the 'Righthand-wise Turn' (*an t-impódh dessiul*). Therefore, it must have been in Termonbacca, not as Lacey suggests 'in the general area close to the *Tempull Mor*, now the precincts of the Long Tower church'.[12] Having completed the rituals of preparation, obtained all the necessary permissions, and acquired protection from the dangers of migration such as drowning and homesickness, Colum Cille and his travelling companions (who had presumably followed his example in observing the ritual) were in a state of readiness to board their boat.

Setting off from Glais an Indluidh

The third phase of departure, 'setting off' (*exitus*), lasted from embarkation to disappearance from sight, and included three further ritual actions of 'blessing', 'keening' and 'last look back'. The first action of blessing was performed on Colum Cille and his followers by 'a certain man' (*duine airidhe*). The narrative implies that this person was standing on the quayside of the harbour (*port*) where he used a special implement in the form of a 'forked staff' (*lorg bengánach*) to push the boat off. As well as giving practical assistance, this action appears also to have conferred symbolically on the intending migrants the 'gift' (*búaid*) of protection or safety, with the *lorg* functioning like a saint's *bachall* ('staff, crozier'), as if it were a 'spiritual electrode' conducting the power inherent in the stone.[13] The bearer of the *lorg bengánach* is presented as the custodian, guardian or *érlam* ('founder, patron') of the newly appropriated Columban site.[14] As well as having oversight of the special stream and stone, he appears also to have had the function of 'harbour master', authorizing and supervising the departure of migrants by boat. The *lorg bengánach*

---

12 *BCC*, p. 212; *LCC*, p. 114; Brian Lacey, *Medieval and monastic Derry: sixth century to 1600* (Dublin, 2013), p. 131.   13 A.T. Lucas, 'The social role of relics and reliquaries in ancient Ireland', *JRSAI*, 116 (1986), 5–37; Harbison, *Pilgrimage*, pp 159, 245.   14 On the pre-Christian significance of *érlam*, see Thomas Charles-Edwards, '*Érlam*: the patron saint of an Irish church' in A. Thacker and R. Sharpe (eds), *Local saints and local churches in the early medieval West* (Oxford, 2002), pp 267–90 at p. 288.

therefore was both a practical tool (boat hook) and symbol of office. Colum Cille effectively sanctified the *lorg benganách* by means of a gift exchange: in return for the practical 'help' of being pushed off in this way, he conferred the special 'gift' of 'exile' (*buaid ndeoraigechta*) on the bearer of the *lorg bengánach* and his successors.[15]

The second action of 'keening', or raising an 'outcry' (*enghair guil*) and 'lament' (*comharc*) was started as soon as the boat moved off. It was performed by Colum Cille's 'own kinsmen of the Cenél Conaill and the Cenél nEógain and of all the [neighbouring] districts', who were already assembled 'on both sides of Lough Foyle'.[16] Keening, the ritual crying appropriate at a funeral, indicates that the departure of the migrant into 'exile' (*deoraigecht*) was equated with death. One may imagine the sound effect of so many raised voices reverberating across the river in this natural amphitheatre.[17] It recalls the imagining by the eighth-century poet Blathmac of the keening that *ought* to have been given to Christ on his death; with 'cry meeting cry' (*fóid fri fóid*) raised by women, children and men 'on every hilltop' (*for cach dind*), combining in a 'great funeral lamentation' (*gubae mór*), the sound spreading like a shroud over the body.[18] The *BCC* narrative makes clear that the departing Colum Cille and his companions were accorded proper keening by the entire community. It also describes the condition of the departing migrants as one of 'homesickness' (*cumaidh*) and the appropriate behaviour, in response to the keening of the assembled community, as the shedding of tears: 'then Colum Cille shed copious tears, saying it was right that his kinsmen should lament after him; and that he would be so sad himself after-

---

15 Lacey translates *deoraigecht* by 'involuntary exile'; however, the term also comprehends 'voluntary exile'.   16 In fact, the conquest of Inishowen by the Cenél Conaill and overlordship of the east side of the Foyle was 'only a recent historical phenomenon': Darren Mac Eiteagáin, 'The renaissance and the late medieval lordship of Tír Chonaill, 1461–1555' in W. Nolan, L. Ronayne and M. Dunleavy (eds), *Donegal history and society* (Dublin, 1995), pp 203–28 at pp 219–20; Katharine Simms, 'Tír Eoghain "north of the mountain"' in G. O'Brien (ed.), *Derry and Londonderry: history and society* (Dublin, 1999), pp 149–74 at pp 167–9. An important concern of *BCC* is the political unification of 'both sides of Lough Foyle': *LCC*, p. 49. Elsewhere in *BCC*, it is made clear that the O'Donnells were promoting Cabhán an C[h]urraigh ('Slope of the Currach') on the river Roe upstream of Limavady where Colum Cille landed on his return for the Convention of Drum Ceat, as a site of migrant departure on the east side of the Foyle, complementing that on the west side upstream of Derry at Glais an Indluidh: *LCC*, p. 175. Note that Cabhán an Churraigh also complemented Port a' Churaich, the site of migrant arrival on Iona where Colum Cille first landed: Richard Sharpe, 'Iona in 1771: Gaelic tradition and visitors' experience', *The Innes Review*, 63, ii (2012), 161–259 at 226–8.   17 Máire Mac Neill observed of the custom of assembly at river sites that 'it is strange that in Ireland our information ... comes only from Meath' and that 'it seems reasonable to assume it was formerly much more widely practised': *The festival of Lughnasa* (Dublin, 1962; repr. 1982), p. 259.   18 Brian Lambkin, 'The structure of the Blathmac poems', *Studia Celtica*, 20/21 (1985–6), 67–77 at 72.

wards that there wouldn't be a day of his life that he wouldn't cry for home-sickness (*dá cumhaidh*)'.[19]

The third action, the 'last look back', required the migrants on the water and their kinsmen on the shore to 'watch' until the point they disappeared from each other's sight.[20] As the narrative explains, the advantage of the point of departure being sited upstream from Derry at Glas an Indluidh was that it enabled Colum Cille to prolong his 'last look back' at his home:

> and the reason he took the boat past the settlement (*baile*) up the lough, as we said before, was so that he would have a longer view of it (*indus co madh fhaidide do beith amhorc an baile aicce*) going past it upwards, then coming back alongside it (*dul tareis suas agus beith ag gabail ría na taebh sís arís*).[21]

So intense was the emotion induced by the mass keening of the community, who returned the gaze, that words of encouragement from Colum Cille's travelling companion, Oran, were necessary for him to maintain his composure: 'Listen, pay no attention to them. Concentrate on the reason why you left them; for the sake of Almighty God'.[22] This formulaic utterance would presumably have been appropriate in any such case of migrant departure. In the case of Derry, the 'last look back' continued to Tonna Cenanda ('white-topped waves' – a sandbank north of Magilligan known in English as 'The Tuns'), where seabirds took over the task of convoy.[23]

How then, given the lack of detail in both the Latin Life of Adomnán and the Irish Life edited by Máire Herbert, are we to account for the remarkably detailed account in the Life of Manus O'Donnell? Space does not permit extended consideration here of the serious O'Donnell ambition to promote Derry in the European pilgrimage economy as a 'second Rome'.[24] However, it is hard to resist the conclusion that Manus had in mind the departure of his own father, Aodh Dubh, on pilgrimage to Rome in 1510, and that Aodh Dubh's departure had been a full-scale re-enactment, based as closely on tradition as possible, of their ancestor Colum Cille's departure.[25] If so, the site of Aodh Dubh's departure, like that of Colum Cille in the narrative, might well have been Glais an Indluidh.

19 *LCC*, p. 105; *BCC*, p. 192. **20** Droichead na nDeor ('Bridge of Tears') on the road from Falcarragh to Derry is such a point of parting: Fitzgerald and Lambkin, *Migration*, p. 18. **21** *BCC*, 190; *LCC*, p. 104. **22** Ibid. **23** *LCC*, p. 106. On migrant 'convoy', see Fitzgerald and Lambkin, *Migration*, pp 18, 47. **24** *LCC*, p. 114. On the treatment of the theme of 'exile' in *BCC* and the political, economic and cultural context, see Bernadette Cunningham and Raymond Gillespie, 'The Uí Dhomnaill and their books in early six-teenth-century Ireland' in S. Duffy (ed.), *Princes, prelates and poets in medieval Ireland: essays in honour of Katharine Simms* (Dublin, 2013), pp 481–502 at p. 499. See also Mac Eiteagáin, 'Renaissance', p. 215; Turner and Turner, *Image and pilgrimage*, p. 125; and Harbison, *Pilgrimage*, p. 91. **25** *AU* 1510 (iii, pp 494–6); *LCC*, p. 8.

Fig. 1: A view of the hill of Derry from the west bank of the river Foyle at
Termonbacca, 28 June 2013. Photo: Brian Lambkin

LOCATING GLAIS AN INDLUIDH

Relying on the invaluable work of John Bryson, Brian Lacey identified Glais
an Indluidh with 'the area known today as the Glassaghs, about one-and-a-
half miles south-west of the ancient ecclesiastical site of Derry', where 'several small streams run down ... to the Foyle'.[26] Subsequently, Bryson
identified it more precisely as the particular stream marking the boundary
between the quarterlands of Baile Mhic Robhartaigh (Ballymagrorty) and
Baile Úi Dhaoighre (Balloughry), which is also the boundary between the
present day townlands of Ballymagowan (in Baile Mhic Robhartaigh) and
Termonbacca (in Baile Úi Dhaoighre).[27] Bryson further identified the only
other known form of the placename, 'Glesinenloe', documented in 1608.[28]

26 *LCC*, p. 234 n. 20.   27 John G. Bryson, *The streets of Derry (1625–2001)* (Derry,
2001), pp 194–5.   28 Ibid., p. 90; *Calendar of the state papers relating to Ireland of the reign
of James I, 1608–1610* (London, 1874), p. 38. 'Glesinenloe' is described as 'a little stream
of water near Digge's fort, by Derry'. Digge's fort is shown as the 'lower fort' on the contemporary sketch map of Derry dated 27 December 1600 (PRO SP 63/207 part vi, no.
84i); Thomas, *Derry-Londonderry*, Map 5.

Fig. 2: A view of the hill of Derry from the west bank of the river Foyle at
Termonbacca by John Noah Gosset, *c.*1845.[29]

This evidence suggests the existence in 1608 of a harbour at 'Glesinenloe'
that was identical with the harbour at Glais an Indluidh at which the ritual
of migrant departure was still taking place in 1532. There is some evidence
of a harbour at this location. About 100 metres upstream from where Glais
an Indluidh issues into the Foyle is a natural promontory, which is known
locally as 'The Point', 'The Wall' or 'The Second Wall', especially by the
fishermen who frequent it.[30]

This was probably the site of the harbour. It was considerably modified
1845–7 during the construction of the Londonderry Enniskillen railway line,
which passed beside it.[31] However the natural features that would have made
it an attractive harbour or quay are still evident, particularly the spread of
stones, with its distinctive grouping of three large 'flat stones', that extends
into the river and is revealed at low tide (see Fig. 1).[32]

29 Reproduced from Brian Lacey, Dermot Francis and Annesley Malley (eds), *Derry and the northwest, 1846: the paintings of John Noah Gosset* (Derry, *c.*1990), p. 5. Gossett was Barrack master for Derry, Lifford and Omagh, April 1841 to July 1846: ibid., p. 2. Railway construction commenced in October 1845 and the section between Derry and Strabane was opened 19 April 1847. **30** Fieldwork interviews with 'Gary' (13 August 2005) and 'Barney' (7 June 2013). **31** John Hume, *Derry beyond the walls* (Belfast, 2002), pp 142, 144. **32** I am grateful to Rory McNeary and the late Annesley Malley for advice on this matter. A map prepared for the construction of the railway shows a quay: 'Deposited Plans 1838: Londonderry and Enniskillen Railway', House of Lords Library HL/PO/PB/3/plan215.

A painting, made not long before construction of the railway began in October 1845, shows precisely this area at low tide (Fig. 2). The city of Derry is visible downstream in the far distance. In the middle distance is where the stream Glais an Indluidh issues into the Foyle. In the foreground is the promontory where 'The Point' wall is today. Two figures stand close by two large, distinctively upstanding stones. Could one (or both) of these stones (presumably removed in the course of railway construction) have been the special *cloch* blessed by Colum Cille?

The migrant convoy from Derry to Termonbacca commenced at the 'altar' (*ula*) located conveniently near the harbour (*port na long*), in the Shipquay area of the Plantation city.[33] Those intending to depart from Derry who possessed a boat sent it upstream to meet them at the end point of the Derry pilgrimage, the 'Righthand-wise Turn' (*an t-impódh dessiul*) in Termonbacca. All then proceeded on foot to Termonbacca, probably starting off, as Lacey has suggested, along an old routeway, indicated by the irregular line of the modern Magazine Street, which led to the *Dub Regles* (site of modern St Augustine's).[34] The promotion of Derry to the status of a 'second Rome' must have been designed to increase its attractiveness to pilgrims and hence its economic benefit to the O'Donnells.[35] There would also have been benefit to the O'Donnells' associates, not least the hereditary keeper or guardian of the *lorg bengánach* at Termonbacca.[36] Recently it has been argued by Howard Clarke that pre-Plantation Derry was not a 'monastic town', and indeed that the term should be 'excised from all archaeological and historical discourse'.[37] However, 'monastic town', or at least 'seasonal monastic town', seems an appropriate description of the complex along the 1.5 mile axis between the harbour of Derry and the harbour of Termonbacca, about which a large transient population must have been housed, in semi-permanent or temporary accommodation, during the traditional migration season between March and September.[38]

33 *BCC*, pp 212, 477; *LCC*, p. 114. No trace of this feature is known to survive. 34 Brian Lacey, 'A lost Columban turas in Derry', *Donegal Annual*, 49 (1997), 39–41 at 40–1. 35 Mac Eiteagáin, 'Renaissance', pp 203, 215, 227 n. 58; see also Darren McGettigan, 'The principality of Tír Chonaill in the early sixteenth century' in J. Mac Laughlin and S. Beattie (eds), *An historical, environmental and cultural atlas of County Donegal* (Cork, 2013), pp 135–47. 36 The succession of 'keepers' or 'guardians' at Termonbacca fits the pattern in *BCC* of Colum Cille leaving a 'successor' (*comarba*) with 'relic(s)' (*minna*) at eleven other church / pilgrimage sites that he had founded or re-founded: *LCC*, pp 34, 51, 59, 60, 63, 77, 87. On the listing of named 'successors' in the Middle Irish Life, see Herbert, *Iona, Kells, and Derry*, p. 198. 37 Howard B. Clarke, '*Quo vadis?* Mapping the Irish "monastic town"' in Duffy, *Princes, prelates and poets*, pp 261–78 at pp 267–8, 278; cf. Sharpe, *Adomnán*, pp 29, 256, and Ciarán J. Devlin, *The making of medieval Derry* (Dublin, 2013), p. 131. For an alternative view, see Turner and Turner, *Image and pilgrimage*, p. 234 and Keith Lilley, *City and cosmos: the medieval world in urban form* (London, 2009), pp 54–6. 38 Jonathan Sumption, *Pilgrimage* (London, 1975), pp

IDENTIFYING THE BEARER OF THE *LORG BENGÁNACH*

Given this identification of the ritual site of migrant departure at Glais an Indluidh, can anything further be said about the evidence of its name, or about the bearers of the *lorg bengánach* who were its hereditary custodians or guardians? Although the name Glais an Indluidh / 'Glesinenloe' is not attested after 1608, a name for the whole site does survive to the present in the townland name Termonbacca, reflecting Termon Bacach ('Sanctuary of Cripples').[39] The narrative strongly implies that the office of guardian of the 'sanctuary' (*termon*) and keeper of the *lorg bengánach* survived in unbroken succession down to the time of Manus O'Donnell. There would appear to be only one candidate for a family fulfilling this role. Termonbacca was in the quarterland of Baile Uí Dhaoighre (O'Deery's Estate), which belonged to the Columban abbey of Derry, and this suggests that the audience of *BCC* (from 1532 onwards) would have readily interpreted the identity of the 'certain man' at Glas an Indluidh in Termobacca with the *lorg bengánach* ('forked staff') as the first Ó Daoighre, *érlam* or patron of the continuing *airchinneach* ('erenagh') dynasty of the place.[40]

VISUALIZING THE *LORG BENGÁNACH*

If the *lorg bengánach* was a relic (now lost) that was central to the ritual of migrant departure from Derry, conducted by its hereditary Ó Daoighre keeper at both Glais an Indluidh ('Stream of Preparations') and An t-Iompadh Deisiul ('Right-hand Turn') in the *termon* ('sanctuary') of Termonbacca, how then may we best visualize it? The term *lorg bengánach* appears to be unique to *BCC*, which suggests that it may have been the name by which the relic was known, like the *Cathach* ('The Battler') and the *Cathbuaid* ('The Battle-victory'), Colum Cille's crozier.[41] A closely related term is *gabul-lorg*, which shares the element *lorg* ('staff') and also means 'forked staff'. It occurs

---

188–9; Fitzgerald and Lambkin, *Migration*, pp 122, 127, 138.   **39** I am grateful to Kay Muhr for advice on this matter. On 'termon', see Bryson, *Streets*, p. 164; Joseph McGuinness, *Saint Patrick's Purgatory, Lough Derg* (Dublin, 2000), pp 28, 89–90; Devlin, *Making of medieval Derry*, pp 128, 182.   **40** Bryson, *Streets*, pp 26–7; Devlin, *Making of medieval Derry*, pp 136–7. See also Raghnall Ó Floinn, 'Sandhills, silver and shrines: fine metalwork of the medieval period in Donegal' in Nolan et al. (eds), *Donegal history and society*, pp 85–148 at p. 105. On Columban relics and their keepers, see Raghnall Ó Floinn, 'Insignia Columbae I' in C. Bourke (ed.), *Studies in the cult of Saint Columba* (Dublin, 1997), pp 136–61; and Cormac Bourke, 'Insignia Columbae II' in ibid., pp 162–83.   **41** Bourke, 'Insignia', pp 173–4; Thomas Owen Clancy, 'Scottish saints and national identities in the early Middle Ages' in Thacker and Sharpe (eds), *Local saints and local churches*, pp 397–422 at p. 408. See also Ó Floinn, 'Sandhills', pp 113–16.

in a gloss on an eighth-century law-text where it is mentioned in relation to '*athlaích* (ex-laymen) who renounce their sins, i.e., going into retirement / on pilgrimage'. As Colmán Etchingham explains:

> 'forked staves' (*gabullorga*) are appropriate to such persons and the two categories ... the hospitaller and the poet. Staff-bearing symbolizes the requirement that a convert from worldly evil must abandon arms-bearing.[42]

If staff-bearing was a general requirement of the pilgrim / migrant state, this suggests that there may have been another element to the ritual of migrant departure at Termonbacca (and similar sites) in which intending migrants / pilgrims were formally presented with their own *lorg bengánach* or *gabullorg* by the Ó Daoighre bearer of the *lorg bengánach* relic. The more general term for 'staff', in both early texts such as *Críth gablach* and *Senchas már* and in later texts such as *BCC*, is *bachall*.[43] The copy of the preface to *Amrae Choluim Chille* contained in Rawlinson B 502, a twelfth-century manuscript, describes Colum Cille making an exceptional presentation of his own *bachall* to an especially nervous intending migrant, Scandlán son of the king of Ossory, with the promise that it will 'protect him on the road home'.[44]

In Europe generally, the staff was 'the most distinctive as well as the most useful part of the pilgrim's attire'.[45] From its earliest attested use by the migrant monks of Egypt in the fourth century, following the example of St Paul the Hermit and St Antony, the staff and the pouch were 'obvious and sensible accessories for any traveller on foot, not only for pilgrims'.[46] As Sumption explains:

> at the end of the eleventh century the Church began to bless the pilgrim's clothes and sanctify them as the uniform of his order. A special order of ceremony for pilgrims, as opposed to ordinary travellers, was now coming into existence. This usually took the form of blessing the pilgrim's pouch and mantle and presenting him with his staff from the altar ... indeed, the ritual presentation of the pilgrim's staff bears a striking resemblance to both the dubbing of a knight and the ordination of a priest.[47]

---

42 Colmán Etchingham, *Church organization in Ireland, AD 650 to 1000* (Maynooth, 1999), p. 296.   43 Ibid., pp 307, 388. The equivalent term in Latin texts is *virga*: ibid., p. 307. As noted, *bachall* ('walking stick') was also the symbol of office of the *briugu* ('hospitaller') who might use it, rather than a sword, as a pledge: Fergus Kelly, *A guide to early Irish law* (Dublin, 1988), pp 37, 164.   44 Joseph Falaky Nagy, *Conversing with angels and ancients: literary myths of medieval Ireland* (Dublin, 1997), p. 180.   45 Sumption, *Pilgrimage*, pp 171–2.   46 Ibid.   47 Ibid., p. 172.

There is also a striking resemblance to the Irish case referred to already of the abandonment of 'arms-bearing', where staff is substituted for weapon. Sumption further explains the staff's multi-layered practical and symbolic value:

> The pilgrim's staff is used for driving off wolves and dogs, who symbolize the snares of the Devil; the staff is the pilgrim's third leg, and three is the number of the Trinity; the staff therefore stands for the conflict of the Holy Trinity with the forces of evil, etc. This kind of imagery became very popular in the fourteenth and fifteenth centuries and it provided the themes for most of the sermons delivered to congregations of pilgrims before their departure ... the staff recalled the wood of the Cross.[48]

This would suggest that delivery of a sermon by the bearer of the *lorg bengánach*, or his representative, may have been part of the ritual of migrant / pilgrim departure at Glais an Indluidh. Thinking of the staff of the pilgrim as a 'third leg', and therefore also thinking metaphorically of the pilgrim as 'lame' or 'crippled' and in need of a spiritual 'crutch', recalls the element *bacach* ('lame one, cripple') in the name Termonbacca ('Sanctuary of Cripples'). If so, the 'cripples' of Termonbacca were for the most part physically able-bodied but spiritually 'crippled' or 'lame', and the distinguishing part of the 'forked' *lorg bengánach* may have corresponded symbolically, if not practically, with the underarm supporting cross-piece of a crutch. The pilgrim's staff in use throughout Europe in the medieval period was 'a tough wooden stick with a metal toe'.[49] If we try to visualize what the *lorg bengánach* may have looked like, its characteristic 'fork' must have been positioned either at the top or bottom end of the staff, or at both. A 'fork' at the top end, in the form of a 'T' or 'tau', would fit with the idea of a 'crutch', and a staff with a 'tau-shaped' cross-piece, suggesting its use a crutch, is in fact a common feature of representations of Saint Antony, the archetypal hermit monk.[50] References to St Antony's staff in Athanasius' *Life of Antony* and Jerome's *Life of Paul of Thebes* and *Life of Hilarion* indicate that primarily it was a 'double-pronged hoe' (*sarculum bis acutum*), which was also used as a *gnomon* for marking out land and, in old age, as a crutch.[51] There is an exam-

48 Ibid., p. 173. On the use of the pilgrim's staff in nineteenth-century Ireland, see Philip Dixon Hardy, *The holy wells of Ireland* (London, 1836), p. 14 and Turner and Turner, *Image and pilgrimage*, p. 108.   49 Sumption, *Pilgrimage*, p. 171.   50 Éamonn Ó Carragáin, 'The meeting of Saint Paul and Saint Anthony: visual and literary uses of a eucharistic motif' in G. Mac Niocaill and P. Wallace (eds), *Keimelia: studies in medieval archaeology and history in memory of Tom Delaney* (Galway, 1988), pp 1–58 at p. 7 n. 2. 51 Lilley, *City and cosmos*, p. 121. For different functions of the saint's staff, see

Fig. 3: The Worcester Pilgrim:
conjectural reconstruction of the
pilgrim whose grave was
discovered in 1986.[52]

ple of a staff 'forked' at both ends on the west face of the marigold slab at
Carndonagh, Donegal, where the figure on the left holds a staff that is T-
shaped at the top and 'pronged' at the bottom.[53]

A fork or prong at the bottom end of a staff would fit with the idea of a
'boat hook', which is the function of the *lorg bengánach* as described in

---

Carolinne White, *Early Christian lives* (London, 1998), pp 40, 78–9, 91, 105, 111. I am
grateful to Cormac Bourke for advice. Amongst the items listed in Antony's will (copy of
the Gospels, sackcloth tunic, hood and cloak), his staff was not included (ibid., p. 114).
However, when Hilarion visited Antony's tomb, he was shown the saint's 'hoe' (ibid., p.
107). On the 'double-pronged' or 'two-tined hoe' in Europe and Ireland, see W.H.
Manning, 'Mattocks, hoes, spades and related tools in Roman Britain' in A. Gailey and
A. Fenton (eds), *The spade in Northern and Atlantic Europe* (Belfast, 1970), pp 18–29;
Estyn Evans, *Irish folk ways* (London, 1957), pp 134–5; Fergus Kelly, *Early Irish farming*
(Dublin, 1997), pp 467–8.   **52** Diana Webb, *Pilgrimage in medieval England* (London,
2000), p. 210; illustration from Helen Lubin, *The Worcester pilgrim* (Worcester, 1990), p.
1. The anonymous Worcester pilgrim lived *c.*1450–1500 and his skeleton revealed 'evidence in the right hand, arm and shoulder that he had exerted a great deal of pressure on
just such a staff as the magnificent specimen of ash wood which was buried with him.
This had a double-pronged iron spike at one end and bore traces of a horn tip at the
other, to which the pierced cockle-shell which was also found in the grave may once have
been attached': Webb, *Pilgrimage in medieval England*, p. 212.

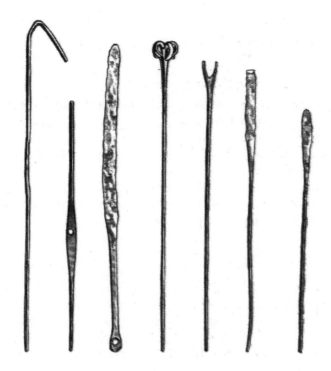

Fig. 4: Drawing from excavation report of minor objects found at Broighter,
Co. Londonderry, 1896, now in National Museum of Ireland, Dublin.

BCC, particularly for 'pushing off' the migant's boat from the harbour.
Perhaps the closest analogue in Ireland for this 'pushing off' function of the
staff is to be found in the Last Judgement scene on Muiredach's Cross at
Monasterboice, Co. Louth, in which the devil who is attempting to upset
the scales of justice is being pushed off by Michael the archangel, who has
thrust the end of his T-shaped staff into his mouth.[54] Elsewhere in Europe,

53 Michael Herity, 'Early Christian decorated slabs in Donegal: An turas and the tomb
of the founder saint' in Nolan et al. (eds), *Donegal history and society*, pp 25–50 at pp
44, 84; Harbison, *Pilgrimage*, pp 190, 192, 197; Conor Newman and Niamh Walsh,
'Iconographical analysis of the Marigold Stone, Carndonagh, Donegal' in R. Moss (ed.),
Making and meaning in Insular art (Dublin, 2007), pp 167–83.   **54** Françoise Henry,
Irish art during the Viking invasions (London, 1867), p. 106; Fig. 35b, p. 186 and Fig.
40b, p. 202. See also Turner and Turner, *Image and pilgrimage*, p. 168. Two further literary analogues may be the *geann orda* and *gabulgice*. Kelly explains *geann orda*, in the
case of the punishment of setting adrift where the culprit is pushed out to sea in a boat
with a single oar and enough gruel for a day and a night, as 'a wedge or pointed tool of
about one foot ... long, which could be used to keep the birds away from the food'
(*Early Irish farming*, p. 502). The point appears to have been 'hammer-shaped', that is

the closest analogue is the single surviving example of a pilgrim's staff, discovered in 1986 during excavations in Worcester cathedral, which has a
'forked' metal toe or shoe (see Fig. 3). The 'double-pronged iron spike' on
the end of the ash staff of the Worcester pilgrim is familiar because of its
similarity to the 'swallow-tail' type of iron shoe on the modern punt pole,
designed to prevent it from sinking into the mud. The potential use of the
pilgrim's staff as a punt pole brings to mind the three outstanding examples
of model 'forked' punt poles from Ireland which were found as part of the
Broighter hoard near the mouth of the river Roe, Co. Londonderry in 1896
(see Fig. 4).[55]

Given that the Broighter hoard represents a deliberate ritual offering,
deposited near the mouth of the river Roe in the first century BCE, could
these represent the archetype of the *lorg bengánach*?[56]

CONCLUSION

In the light of this re-examination of the sixteenth-century account by Manus
O'Donnell of Colum Cille's departure from Ireland, we may tentatively trace
broad outlines of how the ritual of migrant departure from Derry developed.
It would appear to have achieved its most developed form with the departure
of Manus O'Donnell's father, Aodh Dubh, on pilgrimage to Rome in 1510,
at a time when the O'Donnells were both extending and consolidating their
over-lordship, as if in emulation of the original Columban federation or

to say 'T-shaped': Mary E. Byrne, 'On the punishment of sending adrift', *Ériu*, 11
(1930), 97–102 at 98–9.   **55** Richard Warner, 'The Broighter hoard – a question of
ownership' in O'Brien (ed.), *Derry and Londonderry*, pp 69–90. For illustrations, see
A.T. Lucas, *Treasures of Ireland* (Dublin, 1974), p. 173; Patrick Wallace and Raghnall
Ó Floinn, *Treasures of the National Museum of Ireland: Irish antiquities* (Dublin, 2002),
pp 138–9. Sir Arthur Evans described the three implements as 'either fishing spears, or
more probably, forked barge-poles, such as are still in use': 'On a votive deposit of gold
objects from the north west coast of Ireland', *Archaeologia*, 55 (1897), 391–408 at 392;
cf. 'forked barge-poke [sic] (one of three)': A.W. Farrell, S. Penny and E.M. Jope, 'The
Broighter Boat: a reassessment', *Irish Archaeological Forum*, 2 (1975), 15–28 at 18.
56 The modern English Fenland punt pole or 'bifid quant' has a T-shaped cross piece
top and a metal shoe bottom, which indicates the possibility of the *lorg bengánach*
having been 'forked' at both ends. Thus, the *lorg bengánach* as a pilgrim / traveller /
migrant staff may have been a multi-purpose instrument, serving not only as a boat
hook or punt pole (for pushing off, fending off, propulsion, steering as a rudder, and
assisting in the re-flotation of a stranded boat), but also as a weapon for fending off
dogs or wolves or other humans, as a walking aid or crutch, and as a harpoon for catch-
ing fish or repulsing sea monsters, such as those encountered by Colum Cille in Lough
Foyle on both his outward and return voyages (*LCC*, pp 107, 175). On the Broighter
hoard and the legendary origins of Lough Foyle, see John Carey, *Ireland and the grail*
(Aberystwyth, 2007), pp 355–7.

paruchia, with Aodh Dubh cast in the role of a second Colum Cille.[57] As a re-enactment of the departure of Colum Cille, that of Aodh Dubh seems to have been on a scale not likely to have been seen before, and certainly not since. It took place, *pace* Clarke, within the setting of a 'monastic town', and at one of the lost river-side assembly sites referred to by Máire Mac Neill.[58] As practised in the early sixteenth century, the ritual was the culmination of a slow process of elaboration. Máire Herbert has explained how Derry became increasingly open to European influence in the twelfth century.[59] This would have included developments in the practice of pilgrimage, eventually with regard to the ceremonial presentation of the pilgrim's staff.[60] The *airchinnech* or hereditary guardian of the ritual site of departure at Termonbacca is likely to have been provided by the Ó Daoighre family, probably from the twelfth century, possibly earlier.[61]

There seems little reason to doubt a much greater antiquity for the main ritual elements at the site of departure – prophylactic lustration in the stream called Glais an Indluidh, circuiting of the stone called An t-Iompadh Deisiul, and embarkation and pushing off with the assistance of the forked staff known as the *lorg bengánach*. The silence of *Vita Columbae* and the Middle Irish Life is not necessarily an argument against antiquity; such a ritual may have been present but their authors may not have felt the need to refer to it. The origin of this ritual may reasonably be sought as far into the deep past as the deposition of the Broighter hoard in the first century BC. It seems that in Manus O'Donnell's account we may have a trace of 'the graft between archaic stock and historical scion'.[62]

At some stage after 1532 (when Manus O'Donnell's Life was completed), probably after the dispossession of the Ó Daoighre family and the transfer of Termonbacca as part of the quarterland of Baile Uí Dhaoighre (Balloughry) to the Protestant Bishop of Derry, the *lorg bengánach* appears, like many other similar relics, to have been lost.[63] The ritual of migrant departure at Termonbacca having been discontinued, a pale reflection of it was still to be observed in the nineteenth and twentieth centuries when it was the custom of intending migrants, like Mící Mac Gabhann of *Rotha mór*

---

57 Kim McCone, *Pagan past and Christian present in early Irish literature* (Maynooth, 1990), p. 11.   58 Mac Neill, *Festival of Lughnasa*, p. 259.   59 Herbert, *Iona, Kells, and Derry*, pp 109–23.   60 Harbison, *Pilgrimage in Ireland*, pp 238–9.   61 Devlin, *Making of medieval Derry*, pp 136–7.   62 Turner and Turner, *Image and pilgrimage*, p. 105.   63 Ó Floinn, 'Insignia Columbae I', pp 160–61; Bourke 'Insignia Columbae II', pp 173–9. Termonbacca was probably treated in a similar way to Lough Derg where the Protestant Bishop of Clogher, Spottiswoode, ordered the destruction of Station Island in May 1632: Harbison, *Pilgrimage in Ireland*, pp 60, 239. See also Raymond Gillespie, 'Relics, reliquaries and hagiography in south Ulster, 1450–1550' in R. Moss, C. Ó Clabaigh and S. Ryan (eds), *Art and devotion in late medieval Ireland* (Dublin, 2006), pp 184–202 at p. 187.

an tsaoil fame, to visit other Columban sites, such as Leac na Cumhaí ('Flagstone of Homesickness') at Gartan, in the hope of obtaining the protection of Colum Cille previously offered to migrants from Derry by the bearer of his *lorg bengánach*.[64]

64 Brian Lambkin, 'The migration story of Micí Mac Gabhann, 1865–1948' in Mac Laughlin and Beattie (eds), *An historical, environmental and cultural atlas of County Donegal*, pp 287–92 at pp 288–9. An earlier version of this paper was given at the XIV International Celtic Congress, Maynooth, August 2011. I would like to thank Cormac Bourke, John Bryson, Brian Lacey, Rory McNeary, Richard Sharpe, Andrew Sides, Patrick Fitzgerald, Johanne Devlin Trew, Kay Muhr and the editors for comments and contributions.

De initiis: Apacrafa, an Bíobla agus léann luath-eaglais na hÉireann*

MÁIRTÍN MAC CONMARA

Bhí baint lárnach ag an Ollamh Máire Herbert ó thús leis an togra *Apocrypha Hiberniae* a raibh toradh chomh fónta sin air. Sa chéad imleabhar den tsraith, cuireadh cló ar théacsanna a bhain le Soiscéal naíonachta Íosa. Tiomnaíodh an dara himleabhar do théacsanna apacailipteacha agus eascaiteolaíocha. Tarlaíonn go bhfuil a lán téacsanna Gaeilge a bhaineann le heascaiteolaíocht nach n-áiríotar iad mar apacrafúil toisc gan bhaint a bheith acu leis an mBíobla. Ina measc siúd, tá lear mór a chuireann síos i slí amháin nó i slí eile ar na críocha déanacha – *De finibus*. Ceann de mhór-thionscadail Roinn na Sean- agus na Meán-Ghaeilge i gColáiste na hOllscoile, Corcaigh, ná an togra *De finibus*, chun taighde a dhéanamh, agus eagar agus cló a chur ar na téacsanna sin.[1] Fothoradh é i slí ón togra bunaidh, *Apocrypha Hiberniae*.

Le linn bheith ag tabhairt páipéir ag seimineár *De finibus* san Ollscoil chéanna, rith sé liom go raibh áit ann anois do thogra eile dar teideal *De initiis*, 'Na céimeanna tosaigh': is é sin le rá an léann eaglasta in Éirinn sna blianta tosaigh AD 600–800. Is é a bheadh mar aidhm ag an tionscadal seo ná pictiúr iomlán den ré sin ó thaobh léann eaglasta de a chruthú ón fhianaise atá againn ó fhoinsí deimhnithe éagsúla, amhail apacrafa, téacsanna an Bhíobla, tráchtaireachtaí ar an mBíobla, cúrsaí teanga (Breatnais, Laidin agus eile), téacsanna diagachta, liotúirgeacha, agus an tseandálaíocht. Ní bheadh glacadh ach le téacsanna a bhain go cinnte leis an tréimhse sin agus bheadh dáta le socrú do chuile caipéis faoi leith.

Níl spás san aiste seo cur síos a dhéanamh ar na foinsí sin go léir. Mar sin, ní bheidh plé agam anseo ach ar na hApacrafa agus ar an mBíobla.

APACRAFA ÉIREANNACHA ÓN RÉ LUATH 600–800

Is féidir linn tosú leis na hapacrafa toisc go bhfuil lear mór díobh seo againn in Éirinn. Is é an ceann is sine díobh sin, agus dáiríre ceann dena scríbhinní is luaithe i litríocht na Gaeilge ná *Macghníomhthartha an Tiarna Íosa* (nó faoin

---

*Féach chomh maith Martin McNamara, '*De initiis*: Irish monastic learning 600–800 A.D. Irish psalm commentaries 600–800 A.D., mainly of Antiochene origin or inspiration', *Eolas: the Journal of the American Society of Irish Medieval Studies*, 6 (2013), 4–40.
1 Féach anois toradh thogra *De finibus*: John Carey, Emma Nic Cárthaigh, Caitríona Ó Dochartaigh (eag.), *The end and beyond: medieval Irish eschatology*, 2 iml. (Aberystwyth, 2014).

teideal is gnáthaí air *Soiscéal naíonachta Seoda-Thomáis*), le fáil againn i Sean-
Ghaeilge ón tréimhse timpeall AD 700. Is leagan fileata é, agus téacs Laidine
taobh thiar de, atá gaolmhar le sean-téacsanna Gréigise, Sírise, Seorsaise agus
Aetóipise. Cuireann an t-aistritheoir Gaeilge a lorg féin ar chor-ráiteas mí-
dhíscréideach sa bhuntéacs, agus déanann téacs deabhóideach de. D'fhoilsigh
James Carney eagrán criticiúil den téacs fé dhó: in 1958 agus arís in 1964.[2]
Thug Máire Herbert aistriúchán Béarla de dúinn i 1989 agus i 2001 chuir sí
eagrán nua criticiúil de ar fáil mar aon le haistriúchán Béarla agus nótaí.[3]

An dara apacrafan in Éirinn gur féidir dáta luath a chur leis ná *Transitus
Mariae*, 'Bás Mhuire', ar a dtugtar freisin an *Dormitio*, 'Suan (Mhuire)'. Díol
spéise sa luath-eaglais ab ea bás Mhuire agus cad a tharla dá corp. Bhí scríbhinní ann ar an ábhar go luath agus ní dócha go raibh aidhm ná cuspóir
chreidimh ná dheabhóide ag cuid de na scríbhínní tosaigh sin. Ach de réir a
chéile, chuir an eaglais spéis i mbás agus i bhFhreastógáil na Maighdine chun
neimhe (nó chun Parthais). Ní héasca freagra a thabhairt ar cérb í bunteanga
an traidisiúin seo (Síris nó Gréigis), nó stair a sheachadta a ríomhadh. Ar aon
chuma, tá luath-thraidisiún ann san Aetóipis-Síris-Seorsais agus Coptais ina
bhfuil saintraidisiúin eile: ina measc Críost in am bháis Mhuire ag meabhrú
eachtra na pailme di nuair a bhí siad le chéile ar an turas chun na hÉigipte,
agus cuntas faoi chuairt Mhuire ar na hanamnacha in Ifreann tar éis na
Freastógála. Tá na heachtraí sin le fáil chomh maith sna téacsanna
Éireannacha (Laidin agus Gaeilge), óna mbaineann saineolaithe san ábhar an
tátal gur luath-théacsanna iad sin, a tháinig go hÉirinn roimh 700 AD. Tá
aistriúchán Béarla déanta ar cheann de na téacsanna Gaeilge (as an Liber
Flavus Fergusiorum) ag Máire Herbert,[4] agus tá na téacsanna Éireannacha go
léir cóirithe d'eagrán criticiúil ag Caoimhín Breatnach.[5]

An tríú apacrafan a phléifimid ná na *Soiscéil Naíonachta*. Téacs fada atá
anseo, ar fáil i dhá lámhscríbhinn ón chúigiú haois déag – an Leabhar Breac
agus Liber Flavus Fergusiorum. Téann sé ar aghaidh ó ghiniúint Mhuire go
dtí an turas chun na hÉigipte. Is téacs comhcheangailte é, a raibh codanna de
neamhspleách uair amháin: mar shampla – giniúint agus óige Mhuire i
Protoevangelium Shéamais, an turas ón Nasair go Beithil agus teacht na
nDraoithe (*magi*) (ón téacs anaithnid ar a dtugtar 'An fhoinse speisialta'), agus

2 James Carney, 'Two Old Irish poems', *Ériu*, 18 (1958), 1–43; idem, *The poems of
Blathmac son of Cú Brettan together with the Irish Gospel of Thomas and a poem on the Virgin
Mary*, ITS 47 (Dublin, 1964).   3 Máire Herbert, 'Infancy Gospel of Thomas' in M.
Herbert agus M. McNamara (eag.), *Irish biblical apocrypha: selected texts in translation*
(Edinburgh, 1989), lgh 44–8; eadem (le Martin McNamara), 'A versified narrative of the
childhood deeds of the Lord Jesus' in M. McNamara, C. Breatnach, J. Carey, M. Herbert,
J.-D. Kaestli, B. Ó Cuív, P. Ó Fiannachta, agus D. Ó Laoghaire (eag.), *Apocrypha
Hiberniae I: Evangelia infantiae*, CCSA 13 (Turnhout, 2001), lgh 441–83.   4 Herbert,
'Transitus Mariae' in Herbert agus McNamara (eag.), *Irish biblical apocrypha*, lgh 119–31.
5 Le foilsiú in *Apocrypha Hiberniae* II, 2 (Turnhout, le teacht).

an turas chun na hÉigipte. Agus fiú taobh istigh den fhoinse speisialta seo, bhí stair dá chuid féin ag an mhír faoi na draoithe. I 1989, d'fhoilsigh Máire Herbert aistriúchán Béarla den chuntas faoi bhreith Chríost as an Liber Flavus Fergusiorum agus den insint faoi na draoithe as an Leabhar Breac.[6] I 1927, d'fhoilsigh M.R. James cuntas comhthreomhar Laidine leis na Soiscéil naíonachta Éireannacha san áireamh, ag dul ó ghin Mhuire ar aghaidh.[7] Gné amháin de théacs Laidine James ná go bhfuil sé go mór faoi thionchar Shoiscéal Pseudo-Matthaeus, a cumadh b'fhéidir i dtús na seachtú haoise. Cumadh 'An fhoinse speisialta' roimh AD 800, agus b'fhéidir fiú roimh AD 500. Measann saineolaithe ar an ábhar gur féidir dáta níos luaithe ná sin a chur ar an mhír faoi na draoithe, atá gaolmhar le téacs Sírise, agus go mbaineann an bunleagan leis an dara céad.[8] Maidir leis an mhír sa Soiscéal naíonachta den Leabhar Breac faoin turas chun na hÉigipte, seans go bhfuil sin an-luath chomh maith. Tá béim ann ar an mhíorúilt leis an phailm a thug bia don leanbh Íosa; i ndiaidh na heachtra sin, deireann Críost leis an phailm: 'Éirigh, a phailm, le go mbeitheá i measc crann Pharthais m'Athar'. Mar a dúradh thuas, meabhraíonn Críost an mhíorúilt chéanna seo dá mháthair Muire agus í ag fáil bháis sa chur síos atá sa sainleagan Éireannach-Aetóipise de *Transitus Mariae*.[9] Mar sin, dealraíonn sé gur traidisiún an-ársa atá anseo againn.

Ina thráchtaireacht ar Shoiscéal Mhatha, sa téacs ar na draoithe (*magi*), tugann an scríbhneoir Éireannach Sedulius Scottus (fl. 840–60) cur síos cuíosach fada fúthu tógtha, dar leis féin, as an 'Soiscéal de réir na nEabhrach', *in euangelio quod 'Secundum Ebreos' pretitulatur*, atá ag dul focal ar fhocal lena bhfuil sa bhfoinse speisialta. B'fhéidir go raibh 'An fhoinse speisialta' ar fáil faoin ainm sin, nó go raibh scríbhinn eile leis an ainm 'Soiscéal de réir na nEabhrach' ar fáil in Éirinn roimh AD 800.

Chomh maith le sin, is cosúil go raibh fáil ar scríbhinní apacrafúla in Éirinn sa luathré sin, amhail an ceann ar chomhartha an Bhrátha atá mar fhoinse ag *Blathmac*.[10] Ach is leor an méid atá cíortha againn cheana féin d'aidhm na haiste seo.

TRÁCHTAIREACHTAÍ AR AN MBÍOBLA ÓN RÉ LUATH 600–800

Cé go raibh iomrá ar Éirinn toisc an léann ar an mBíobla a bhí le fáil i scoileanna na mainistreacha sa ré luath, is tearc go deimhin an fhianaise atá

---

6 Herbert, 'Infancy Gospel' agus 'The magi' in Herbert agus McNamara (eag.), *Irish biblical apocrypha*, lgh 27–32, 36–42.   7 Montague Rhodes James, *Latin infancy Gospels. A new text, with a parallel version from the Irish* (Cambridge, 1927).   8 Faoi seo, féach Brent Landau, *Revelation of the magi: the lost tale of the wise men's journey to Bethlehem* (New York, 2010). 9 An téacs in Herbert, 'Transitus Mariae', lgh 119–20.   10 Do dhíospóireacht ar fhoinsí comharthaí an Bhrátha i mBlathmac, féach Carey, Nic Cárthaigh agus Ó Dochartaigh, *The end and beyond*, lgh 558–65; Carney, *The poems of Blathmac*, §§236–42.

againn ar na hábhair a bhí á múineadh nó ar na scríbhinní a chum an t-aos léinn a bhí iontu, seachas ar na Sailm ar a thráchtfaimid ar ball. Is eol do chách an aiste léannta a scríobh an tOllamh Bernhard Bischoff a fhreagródh an cheist seo, ach amháin nach bhfuil scoláirí na linne seo ar aon intinn gur le hÉirinn nó le hÉireannaigh a bhaineann an corpas leathan scríbhinní a sholáthair Bischoff.[11] Ach toisc go bhfuil amhras áirithe futhu, ní bhainfear úsáid astu anseo ach i gcás gur soiléir go mbaineann ceann nó cinn áirithe díobh le hÉirinn.

GLUAISEANNA 'DE RÉIR NA LITRE' AR NA SAILM IN ÉIRINN 600–800

Murab ionann agus leabhair eile an Bhíobla, tá an t-ádh linn go bhfuil ábhar cuíosach saibhir againn maidir le tuiscint ar na Sailm in Éirinn sa Luath-Mheánaois, toisc go bhfuil míniú na Salm i ngluaiseanna ar shaltracha atá tagtha slán chugainn. Míniú de réir bunbhrí na Salm den chuid is mó atá sna gluaiseanna sin, rud a nascann traidisiún na hÉireann díreach leis an traidisiún in Antíoc ar an Orontes ón gceathrú agus ón gcúigiú haois.

Rinneadh leabhar urnaithe den Saltair san Eaglais Chríostaí. Sa Tiomna Nua, tá an tuiscint ann go dtagraíonn roinnt de na Sailm do Chríost. Mar leabhar urnaithe, cuireadh níos mó béime go minic ar an tuiscint Chríostaí ná ar an mbunbhrí. Ba fhíor sin go háirithe le scoil eicsigéise Chathair Alastair, áit ar baineadh úsaid go forleathan as an míniú alagóireach, fáithchiallach. A mhalairt ar fad i scoil eicsigéise Aintíoc ar an Orontes, mar ar leagadh béim ar an mbrí liteartha, an chiall a measadh a bhí ag Salm nuair a chéadchumadh é. Bhí Diodorus (†390), Easpag Tarsus, agus Teodorus (350–428), Easpag Mopsuestia, ina máistrí ar an tuiscint seo. Mar scoláire óg, chum Teodorus tráchtaireacht ar na Sailm de réir phrionsabal a scoile, inar mhaígh sé nach raibh ach ceithre cinn díbh ina fháistine dhíreach ar Chríost (Sailm 2, 8, 44, 109 in uimhriú an LXX agus na Vulgáide). San Iodáil, bhí Iulianus (easpag ar Eclanum san Apulia, ó dheas de Napoli) fábharach don Phealagachas, agus nuair a daoradh Pealagachas sa bhliain 418 dhiúltaigh sé a ainm a chur leis an litir á dhamnú agus cuireadh as a dheoise é. Chuaigh sé soir go Teodorus agus ina dhiaidh sin d'aistrigh sé saothar Teodorus go Laidin. Ní fios cén scaipeadh a bhí air seo, ach níl le fáil de anois ach blúirí, i scríbhinní

---

11 Bernhard Bischoff, 'Wendepunkte in der Geschichte der lateinischen Exegese im Frühmittelalter', *Sacris Erudiri*, 6 (1954), 189–281; eagrán leasaithe in *Mittelalterliche Studien. Ausgewählte Aufsätze zur Schriftkunde und Literaturgeschichte*, iml. 1 (Stuttgart, 1966), lgh 205–73; aistriúchan Béarla, 'Turning-points in the history of Latin exegesis in the early Middle Ages', le Colm O'Grady, in M. McNamara (eag.), *Biblical studies: the medieval Irish contribution*, Proceedings of the Irish Biblical Association 1 (Dublin, 1976), lgh 73–160.

Éireannacha den chuid is mó. Rinneadh achoimre (*epitome*) – den iomlán de is dócha – ach ní achoimre go beacht atá ann, mar tá ábhar nach mbaineann le Iulianus inti. Ní fios cén scaipeadh a bhí ag an *Epitome* ach an oiread, ach gur dócha gur i dtuaisceart na hIodáile a scaipeadh é. Dealraíonn sé nach raibh i dtráth áirithe ach lámhscríbhinn amháin den *Epitome* fágtha, agus é lochtach, leis an tús (Salm 1:1–16:11a) in easnamh. Rinneadh an t-easnamh a cheartú i dhá shlí: le haistriú iomlán Iulianus i mbrainse amháin, agus le mír as tráchtaireacht iomlán eile ar na Sailm i dtraidisiún Aintíoc, ach go h-iomlán neamhspleách ó shaothar Teodorus agus Iulianus, sa bhrainse eile. Measaim gur rinneadh an dá iomlanú seo ar an *Epitome* i dtuaisceart na hIodáile. Cé nach bhfuil ach blúire (Salm 1:1–16:11a) de thráchtaireacht againn san iomlánú eile seo ar *Epitome* Iulianus, tá sé beagnach cinnte gur bhain sé i dtosach le tráchtaireacht iomlán ar na Sailm go léir, sa traidisiún Aintíocéanach ach é neamhspleách ar Teodorus agus Iulianus. Téann sé níos faide ná an bheirt eile maidir le tuiscint neamh-Chríosteolaíoch ar na Sailm, gan tagairt ar bith do Chríost ná an Chríostaíocht sna Sailm sin ina bhfaca Teodorus / Iulianus fáistiní faoi Chríost (Sailm 2, 8) ná in aon Salm eile (Salm 16). Agus is mar sin a bhí, gan dabht, sna Sailm tríd sios sa chuid chaillte eile den tráchtaireacht seo.

1. *An t-údar anaithnid – Sailm 1:1–16:1a: seachtú céad*

Auctor incertus nó *auctor ignotus*, an t-údar anaithnid, a thugann Luc De Coninck ar údar an tsaothair as ar tógadh na gluaiseanna ar Shailm 1:1–16:11a i Saltair Dhúbailte St-Ouen (Bibliothèque municipale Rouen, LS 24). Is cinnte gur údar le haidhm a chum an saothar seo ina bhfuil tráchtaireacht ar na Sailm sa traidisiún Aintíocéanach. Bíodh nach bhfuil fágtha againn de anois ach blúire, tá sé beagnach cinnte gur saothar iomlán a bhí ann tráth, ach is dócha nach raibh ach an blúire riamh le fáil in Éirinn. Tá taighde críochnúil ar an *auctor incertus* déanta ag De Coninck.[12] Ní fheiceann sé aon sainchomharthaí Éireannacha ann, agus ní móide gur in Éirinn a cumadh. Mar a luaigh mé cheana, is dóigh liom gur san Iodáil a cuireadh le chéile é. Measann De Coninck gur scríobhadh é faoi thionchar *Glosa in psalmos ex traditione seniorum* ag tús na seachtú haoise. Ach ba chuma le hÉireannaigh 'tír a dhéanta' agus ghlacadar chucu féin a léargas ar thuiscint áirithe ar na Sailm.

2. *Tráchtaireacht Dháibhídeach ar na Sailm: seachtú céad (caillte)*

Sa tráchtaireacht lochtach Éireannach (a thosnaíonn ag Salm 39:11) atá ar fáil i Leabharlann na Vatacáine LS Pal. lat. 68, ar a mbeidh trácht ar ball beag,

---

12 Féach go háirithe an saothar is déanaí uaidh: Luc De Coninck (eag.), *Expositiones psalmorum duae sicut in codice Rothomagensi 24 asservantur*, CCCM 256, Scriptores Celtigenae 7 (Turnhout, 2012), lgh xxv–xli: 'De incerti auctoris commentatio ex codice Rothomagensi restituendo'.

tuigtear gur do Dháibhí agus a ré don chuid is mó atá na Sailm ag tagairt, bíodh go dtógtar isteach tagairtí do Chríost agus don eaglais chomh maith. Is léir go raibh an t-údar / eagarthóir a bhreac síos an saothar seo in Pal. lat. 68 míshásta le míniú neamh-Chríosteolaíoch a bheith á thabhairt ag scoláirí na hÉireann ar an dá Shalm 44 agus 109 (Salm 'meisiasach' *par excellence*), rud a chuireann sé in iúl go soiléir. Seo mar adeir sé faoi Shalm 44: 'Tá an Salm seo go léir ag tagairt do Chríost ... bíodh go maíonn míniú staire gan éifeacht gur ag tagairt do Sholamh atá sé'. Mar an gcéanna faoi Shalm 109: 'Cantar an Salm seo go léir faoi Chríost, bíodh go bhfionn (*contexunt*) daoine eile míniú staire gan bhrí air'.[13] Tá téacsanna iomadúla i Saltair Dhúbalta St-Ouen agus i ngluaiseanna Saltrach Chaimín atá an-chosúil le téacs Pal. lat. 68. Ach thug Luc De Coninck agus Pádraig Ó Néill faoi deara go bhfuil roinnt de na gluaiseanna sin níos faide ná téacs Pal. lat. 68, rud a thacaíonn leis an tátal nach díreach ó Pal. lat. 68 a tógadh iad ach ón tráchtaireacht Dháibídeach a bhí mar fhoinse aige sin.[14] Mar sin, bhí tráchtaireacht 'Dháibhídeach' ann tráth a cumadh in Éirinn sa seachtú céad agus a raibh fáil fós uirthi i ré na Meán-Ghaeilge. Teist é seo go raibh cíoradh na Salm beo beathach in Éirinn (i scoileanna áirithe ar aon nós) sa tréimhse sin.

3. *Glosa in Psalmos na lámhscríbhinne Pal. lat. 68: tús na hochtú haoise*[15]

Cumadh an *glosa* seo (tráchtaireacht i bhfoirm gluaiseanna, le *lemma* agus míniú gonta) in Éirinn, ar Oileán Í nó i Northumbria mar tá gluaiseanna Sean-Ghaeilge agus Sean-Bhéarla ann.[16] Is dócha gur bhain an tús, atá caillte anois, le traidisiún an *Auctor ignotus* seachas leis an *Epitome*.

4. *An mhír ar na Sailm sa 'Bibelwerk' (De enigmatibus), c.750*[17]

Tráchtairecht ar an mBíobla go hiomlán, ó Genesis go dtí Apacailips Eoin, é *Das Bibelwerk / The reference Bible*, ar a dtugtar anois de ghnáth *De enigmatibus*. De réir Bernhard Bischoff, cuireadh i dtoll a chéile é ag deireadh na hochtú haoise, ar an Mhór-roinn b'fhéidir.[18] Cúis díospóireachta go fóill an de

---

13 Martin McNamara (eag.), *Glossa in psalmos: the Hiberno-Latin gloss on the psalms of Codex Palatinus latinus 68 (Psalmus 39:11–151:7)*, Studi e Testi 310 (Città del Vaticano, 1986), lgh 99, 235.   14 De Coninck, *Expositiones psalmorum duae*, lgh xli–xlii; Pádraig P. Ó Néill, 'The glosses to the Psalter of St Caimín: a preliminary investigation of their sources and function' in P.A. Breatnach, C. Breatnach agus M. Ní Úrdail (eag.), *Léann lámhscríbhinní Lobháin: the Louvain manuscript heritage*, Éigse: a Journal of Irish Studies Publications 1 (Dublin, 2007), lgh 21–31 ag lgh 29–31.   15 An saothar in eagar ag McNamara, *Glossa in psalmos*.   16 McNamara, *Glossa in psalmos*, lgh 73–4.   17 Tuilleadh eolais faoi seo ag Martin McNamara, 'Psalter text and psalter study in the early Irish church (600–1200)', *PRIA*, 73C (1973), 201–98 ag 227–9 (cf. idem, *The psalms in the early Irish church* [Sheffield, 2000], lgh 52–4).   18 Bischoff, 'Wendepunkte', 241–2; eagrán leasaithe in *Mittelalterliche Studien*, 244–5; aistriúchán Béarla, 'Turning-points', lch 88.

bhunadh Éireannach an saothar seo. I mo thuairim, ní mór breithiúnas a thabhairt ar gach mír faoi leith de. Maidir leis an mhír ar na Sailm, tá sé cinnte gur in Éirinn a cumadh. Tá brollach ag gabháil leis atá ar aon dul leis an gceann sa *Tráchtas Sean-Ghaeilge ar na Sailm*, agus atá cosúil leis an míniú ar Salm 1. Ceann de na foinsí a luaitear sa saothar féin, an teideal atá air tríd síos ná *Ios(epus)*. Ó Shalm 17 go dtí an deireadh, is é an *Epitome* atá i gceist; sa chuid roimhe sin an 't-údar anaithnid' ar aon dul le traidisiún Saltrach St-Ouen (Rouen) an fhoinse. Tá an téacs faoi thionchar *De locis sanctis* le hAdomnán chomh maith. D'oirfeadh *c.*750 mar dháta dó. Tá achoimre den saothar seo ar fáil chomh maith i dtrí lámhscríbhinní le réamhrá agus míniú cuíosach lán ar Shalm 1, ach gan ach tagairt gearr do Salm 67:14 agus 150 ina dhiaidh sin.

5. *Eglogae tractatorum in Psalterium, c.800*[19]

Sa saothar seo, a cumadh in Éirinn thart ar AD 800, tá réamhrá sa traidisiún Éireannach, agus téacsanna roghnaithe (*eglogae*) ar fáil don chuid is mó de na Sailm. Foinse amháin a úsaideadh is léir ná an *Epitome* leis an iomlánú ó théacs comhlán Iulianus atá ar aon dul le traidisiún na lámhscríbhinne Amb. C. 301.

6. *Tráchtaireacht agus gluaiseanna ar na Sailm i lámhscríbhinn Amb. C. 301 inf., c.800*

Téacs críochnúil den *Epitome* le hiomlánú déanta ar an tús ó théacs iomlán Iulianus atá anseo, mar aon le réamhráite éagsúla. Tá gluaiseanna iomadúla i Sean-Ghaeilge ar théacs na tráchtaireachta a leanann, de ghnáth, bunbhrí théacs an *Epitome* go dílis, lena mhíniú Aintíocéanach ar na Sailm. Ó mhainistir Bobbio, ar ndóigh, a tháinig an lámhscríbhinn. I measc na réamhthéacsanna ar an tráchtaireacht féin, tá réamhráite Laidine le gluaiseanna Sean-Ghaeilge ó scríbhinní Éireannacha eile, chomh maith le ceann amháin gan gluaiseanna nach bhfuil le fáil sa traidisiún Éireannach. I dteannta sin, tá blúirí suntasacha d'aistriúchán iomlán Iulianus ar Teodorus a bhfuil a macasamhail (ó Bobbio arís) ar fáil i leabharlann eile (Torino) san Iodáil. Ag cur na fianaise seo go léir le chéile, is fiú an cheist a ardú: an in Éirinn nó i mBobbio na hIodáile a cuireadh Amb. C. 301 le chéile? Is é is dóchaí ná gur cumadh an tráchtaireacht seo leis na gluaiseanna Sean-Ghaeilge d'oiliúint mhac léinn.

7. *An tráchtas Sean-Ghaeilge ar na Sailm: tús na naoú haoise*[20]

Seo é an ceann is déanaí a bhfuil againn de na tráchtaireachtaí Éireannacha ar na Sailm, nach bhfuil ann de anois ach an réamhrá agus an chuid is mó den

---

19 Féach McNamara, 'Psalter text and psalter study', 225–7 (cf. idem, *The psalms in the early Irish church*, lgh 50–2). 20 In eagar ag Kuno Meyer, *Hibernica minora, being a fragment of an Old-Irish treatise on the Psalter*, Anecdota Oxoniensa, Mediaeval and Modern Series, part VIII (Oxford, 1894); féach Pádraig Ó Néill, 'The Old-Irish treatise on the psalter and its Hiberno-Latin background', *Ériu*, 30 (1979), 148–64.

tráchtaireacht ar Shalm 1. Más rud é go raibh tráchtaireacht iomlán ar an Saltair ann tráth, leabhar mór a bheadh ann. Ach tá seans ann gur ar Shalm 1 amháin a bhí an míniú, a bheag nó a mhór, mar a bhí san achoimre ar an mhír ar na Sailm in *De enigmatibus* (a luadh thuas).

NA SAILM I LUATHRÉ NA HEAGLAISE IN ÉIRINN: FOCAIL SCOIR

Bhí scoláirí na hÉireann sa luathré gafa go cruthaitheach le gnéithe éagsúla de na Sailm. D'fhéadfaí iniúchadh faoi leith a dhéanamh ar na réamhráite Éireannacha ar na Sailm atá le fail in *De enigmatibus, Eglogae tractatorum in psalterium* agus *Tráchtas Sean-Ghaeilge ar na Sailm*, ar na saintréithe Éireannacha atá iontu, agus ar ainmneacha na n-údar anaithnide *Hilarius, Ambrosius*, agus *Hieronimus*; is dócha gur scoláirí Éireannacha a bhí iontu ar fad. D'fhéadfaí scagadh a dhéanamh ar an dtrí mion-chur síos ar Shalm 1, gaolmhar dá chéile, atá againn in *De enigmatibus*, an *Tráchtas Sean-Ghaeilge*, agus an *Catechesis Celtica* atá ciortha cheana,[21] agus staidéar a dhéanamh ar shaibhreas léann na tréimhe sin.

D'fhéadfaí staidéar na tráchtaireachtaí sin a leathnú go dtí téacsanna bíobalta na Saltrach: an Vulgáid (*Gallicanum*) agus an t-aistriú den téacs Eabhraise go Laidin ag Iaróm (an *Hebraicum*); agus an saothar critice a bhí ar siúl leis an Vulgáid a chur i gcomparáid le haistriú Iaróm. Bhí sainleaganacha Éireannacha den *Gallicanum* agus den *Hebraicum* in Éirinn sa seachtú céad agus saothar criticiúil á dhéanamh leis an *Gallicanum* a chur i gcomórtas le Iaróm mar is léir ón *Cathach*.[22] Ní beag sin mar cheangal agus conclúid don mhír seo den aiste ar an ghníomhaíocht eicsigéiticiúil ar na Sailm in Éirinn sa tréimhse 600–800.

TRÁCHTAIREACHTAÍ ÉIREANNACHA AR APACAILIPS EOIN SAN OCHTÚ CÉAD

Ceann de na tráchtaireachtaí is faide sa *Bibelwerk* (*De enigmatibus*) ná an mhír ar Apacailips Eoin, le tráchtaireacht leanúnach ar an téacs go léir. Sa mhéid seo, tá sé éagsúil leis an gcur síos ar leabhair eile an Bhíobla sa *Bibelwerk*. Cheapfá go mbeadh sé deacair argóintí faoi leith a dhéanamh i bhfabhar bunúis Éireannach don saothar seo. Tháinig athrú mór ar an gceist seo le deireanas, áfach. In 1999, chuir David Ganz san airdeall mé do thrácht-aireacht ar an Apacailips atá lán de nodanna Éireannacha i lámhscríbhinn Dd

21 Féach Martin McNamara, 'The Irish affiliations of the *Catechesis Celtica*', *Celtica*, 21 (1990), 292–334 ag 305–9; idem, *The psalms*, lgh 435–9. 22 McNamara, 'Psalter text', 266–8; idem, *The psalms*, lgh 107–10.

X 16 i Leabharlann Ollscoil Cambridge. Rinne mé staidéar ar an téacs agus ba léir dom go raibh sé gaolta leis an gceann sa *Bibelwerk*, gan a bheith díreach cosúil leis, dhá théacs iad i dtuilleamaí cinn níos sine.[23] Tharla go raibh spéis curtha ag scoláirí na Mór-roinne sa téacs agus bhí sé de mhisneach ag an Ollamh Roger Gryson an cheist a chíoradh agus na téacsanna uile a fhoilsiú.[24] Tá eagrán criticiúil de na téacsanna go léir foilsithe ag Gryson: téacs ón *Bibelwerk*,[25] ó Cambridge,[26] agus ceann eile leis i mBíobla Micy a cumadh (810) faoi stiúir Teodulph as Orléans.[27] Is finnéithe iad go léir de thráchtaireacht bhunaidh Hibearna-Laidine chaillte a cumadh sa chéad leath den ochtú haois. Bhí eolas ag údar na scríbhinne sin ar shaothar Tyconius agus bhain sé úsáid as. Tá tagairtí fós sna téacsanna atá againn ar ghéar-leanúint na hEaglaise san Aifric, i dtéacs Cambridge níos mó ná mar atá i dtéacs an *Bibelwerk*.

Tá an buntéacs céanna i dtuilleamaí an tsaothair *Commemoratorium de Apocalypsi Joannis apostoli*,[28] sraith gluaiseanna ar an Apacailips a cuireadh le chéile sa dara leath den seachtú céad. D'áirigh Bischoff an saothar seo i measc na scríbhinní Laidine a d'fhéadfadh baint a bheith acu le hÉirinn. Shéan Michael Gorman é sin, ach ní ghlacann Gryson le hargóintí Gorman. Tá Gryson cinnte go dtagann téacs Cambridge ón *milieu* intleachtúil céanna, an *milieu* as a dtáinig na scríbhinní atá scagtha ag Bischoff ina aiste '*Wendepunkte*'. Cumadh téacs Cambridge idir na blianta 750 agus 900, agus níos cóngaraí do thús ná do dheireadh na tréimhse sin is dócha.[29]

Creidim go bhfuil argóintí láidre ann gur in Éirinn seachas ar an Mhór-roinn a cumadh an bunleagan Hibearna-Laidine den tráchtaireacht ar an Apacailips. Nuair a luaigh mé an fhadhb seo le Máire Herbert tamall ó shin, mhol sí dom machnamh a dhéanamh ar an *Altus Prosator*. Scríobhadh an dán seo ar Oileán Í – idir 650 agus 700 is dócha.[30] Tá scagadh déanta ar fhoinsí an dáin ag Jane

---

23 Rinne mé cur síos air seo in 'The newly-identified Cambridge apocalypse commentary and the Reference Bible: a preliminary enquiry', *Peritia*, 15 (2001), 208–60. **24** Saineolaí é ar théacs Sean-Laidine an Apacailips, agus go mór mór ar thráchtaireacht chaillte an mhór-scoláire Afraiceánaigh, Tyconius. As na blúirí atá fágtha, tá tráchtaireacht Tyconius curtha le chéile aige agus aistriú Fraincise déanta aige uirthi. Féach Roger Gryson (eag.), *Tyconius: expositio apocalypseos*, CCSL 107A (Turnhout, 2011); idem, *Tyconius: commentaire de l'apocalypse*, Corpus Christianorum in Translation 10 (Turnhout, 2011). **25** Idem (eag.), 'De enigmatibus ex Apocalypsi Johannis' in *Variorum auctorum commentaria minora in Apocalypsin Johannis*, CCSL 107 (Turnhout, 2003), lgh 231–95. **26** Idem (eag.), *Incerti auctoris glossa in Apocalypsin e codice bibliothecae universitatis Cantabrigiensis Sd. X. 16*, CCSL 108G (Turnhout, 2013). **27** Idem (eag.), 'Commemoratorium de Apocalypsi Johannis a Theodulpho auctum' in *Variorum auctorum commentaria minora in Apocalypsin Johannis*, lgh 297–337. **28** Tá téacs an *Commemoratorium* seo foilsithe ag Gryson, 'Incerti auctoris commemoratorium de Apocalypsi Johanni Apostoli' in *Variorum auctorum commentaria minora in Apocalypsin Johannis*, lgh 159–229. **29** Idem, *Incerti auctoris glossa in Apocalypsin*, lch 36. **30** Don téacs, féach Thomas Owen Clancy agus Gilbert Márkus, *Iona: the earliest poetry of a Celtic monastery* (Edinburgh, 1995), lgh 39–68.

Stevenson, agus is iad na foinsí is tábhachtaí ná an Apacailips (17 tagairtí éagsúla), Iób (10 tagairtí) agus litreacha Phóil (14 tagairtí).[31] Chomh maith leis sin, tá fianaise lámhscríbhinní againn a léiríonn go raibh fáil ar Apacailips Eoin in Éirinn sa naoú haois, agus b'fhéidir níos luaithe. In Stiftsbibliothek St Gallen, i gCodex 728, leathanach 4, codex ó lár na naoú haoise, tá liosta againn de na lámhscríbhinní i bpeannaireacht Éireannach (*libri scottice scripti*) agus ina measc siúd tá trí lámhscríbhinn leis an Apacailips iontu.[32]

Má tá éifeacht leis na hargóintí seo, bhí machnamh domhain á dhéanamh ar an Apacailips in Éirinn sa chéad leath den ochtú haois agus tráchtaireacht léannta á chur le chéile air. Bhí teacht ag na scoláirí a chum an tráchtaireacht sin ar fhoinsí tábhachtacha, tráchtaireacht Tyconius ina measc. Ceist atá le cíoradh fós ná conas a bhain na saothair sin oileán na hÉireann amach. Bhí tionchar ag an tráchtaireacht Hibearna-Laidine seo chomh maith ar an Mhór-roinn agus rinneadh athruithe ar an mbunscríbhinn chun na trí finnéithe de atá againn inniu a chur ar fáil. Ina dteannta sin, bhí réamhstair ag an scríbhinn seo: ceann dá foinsí ná an *Commemoratorium de Apocalypsi Joannis apostoli*, 'aide mémoire' le nótaí nó gluaiseanna gearra a cumadh sa dara leath den seachtú céad. Dar le Bischoff, agus le húdair eile, saothar Hibearna-Laidne, nó saothar a cumadh faoi ionsparáid Hibearna-Laidne, é an *Commemoratorium*.[33]

IARFHOCAL

I dtosach na haiste seo, dúirt mé gurb í an aidhm a bheadh ag tionscadal mar *De initiis* ná iniúchadh a dhéanamh ar 'an léann eaglasta in Éirinn sna blianta tosaigh 600–800 AD ... [chun] ... pictiúr iomlán den ré sin ó thaobh léann eaglasta de a chruthú ón fhianaise atá againn ó fhoinsí éagsúla deimhnithe, amhail apacrafa, téacsanna an Bhíobla, tráchtaireachtaí ar an mBíobla, cúrsaí teanga (Breatnais, Laidin agus eile), téacsanna diagachta, liotúirgeacha, agus an tseandálaíocht ... [agus nach mbeadh] ... glacadh ach le téacsanna a bhain go cinnte leis an tréimhse sin'. San aiste seo, phléigh mé cúpla apacrafa ón ré sin, agus rinne mé iniúchadh níos doimhne ar thráchtaireachtaí ar na Sailm agus ar Apacailips Eoin. Léiríonn siadsan gur bhain lucht a gcumtha le traidisiún áirithe, agus gur rinneadar machnamh leanúnach ar théacsanna leabhar seo an Bhíobla. Má leantar le hiniúchadh ar na téacsanna agus ar na hábhair eile atá luaite agam, measaim go mbeidh bunús maith curtha le stair an Bhíobla in Éirinn, stair atá fós le ríomhadh.

---

31 Jane Stevenson, 'Altus Prosator', *Celtica*, 23 (1999), 326–68 ag 364.   32 Ar na *libri scottice scripti*, féach Johannes Duft agus Peter Meyer, *The Irish miniatures in the Abbey library of St Gall* (Olten, Berne and Lausanne, 1954), lgh 40–3. Tá an téacs ar fáil go digiteach agus ar líne ag: <http://www/e-codices.unifr.ch/en/csg/0728/4>.   33 Bischoff, 'Turning-points', lch 143.

Na taoisigh Ultacha agus an Veronica

MÍCHEÁL MAC CRAITH

Duine ar bith a thugann cuairt ar Bhaisleac Naomh Peadar sa Róimh, bíodh sé ina oilithreach nó ina ghnáth-thurasóir, ní féidir leis gan a bheith corraithe go mór ag ollmhéid agus ag maorgacht an fhoirgnimh. Má ghluaiseann sé ar aghaidh go dtí an ardaltóir, tógtha os cionn uaigh Pheadair aspal, déanfaidh sé iontas den *Baldacchino*, an forscáth práis os cionn na haltóra ar chaith an dealbhadóir Gianlorenzo Bernini deich mbliana i mbun a thógála, díon an fhorscátha ina shuí ar cheithre cholúin atá fiche méadar ar airde. Tá an altóir i gceartlár na baislice, díreach faoi bhun an chruinneacháin, ollsaothar ealaíonta ailtireachta a críochnaíodh sa bhliain 1590. Tá an cruinneachán féin á iompar ag ceithre ollcholún agus idir na blianta 1627 agus 1629 cheap Bernini beartas chun leas ealaíonta teagascach a bhaint as na colúin seo.

Tógadh cuas i ngach colún le haghaidh dealbh naoimh a raibh taise dá chuid sa bhaisleac, Naoimh Veronica, Helena, Longinus agus Aindrias. Ní raibh taise d'fhíorchroich Íosa le fail sa bhaisleac, ach sa bhliain 1629 thóg an Pápa Urbanus VIII giota ón taise i Santa Croce in Iarúsailéim agus rug leis go San Peadar é, taise fheiliúnach do Naomh Helena, máthair an impire Constaintín, arae is uirthi a leagtar fionnachtain na fíorchroiche i Iarúsailéim nuair a rinne sí oilithreacht chuig an Talamh Naofa sna blianta 324–6. De réir an traidisiúin, is í Veronica an bhean a chuimil aghaidh Íosa le ceirt agus é ar a bhealach chun a chéasta, gur fágadh a íomhá breactha ar an gceirt. Cé nach mór a rá ag an am céanna nach bhfuil bunús scrioptúrtha ar bith leis an eachtra seo agus gurb é an saothar *Meditationes vitae Christae* (14ú haois) a bhuanaigh an scéal san iarthar. Is é Longinus an t-ainm a thugtaí sa seanchas Críostaí riamh anall ar an saighdiúir anaithnid a pholl taobh Íosa tar éis a bháis (Eoin 19:34). Toisc go bhfuil scéal sa *Legenda aurea* gur fhuascail fuil Íosa ón daille é agus í ag sileadh anuas ar sháfach a shleá, is fearr aithne air i ndúchas na Gaeilge mar an Dall.[1] Bhí taisí naomh Aindrias á gcoiméad i gCathair Chonstaintín ó lár an cheathrú haois. Thug an forlámhaí, Tomás Palaeologos, cloigeann an naoimh don Phápa Pius II sa bhliain 1461. Mar chomhartha dea-mhéine d'Eaglais Cheartchreidmheach na Gréige, sa bhliain 1964 d'ordaigh an Pápa Pól VI go dtabharfaí na taisí ar fad a bhain le hAindrias a bhí ar coiméad sa Vatacáin ar ais go Patras, an áit ar fhulaing sé mairtíreacht.

---

1 William Granger Ryan (trans.), *Jacobus de Voragine. The golden legend: readings on the saints*, 2 vols (Princeton, New Jersey, 1993), i, lch 184.

Bhí na taisí seo á gcoimeád in áiteanna éagsúla sa bhaisleac ach mar chuid den bheartas a cheap Bernini agus Urbanus VIII, tógadh iad chuig na colúin seo agus tógadh balcóin os cionn gach deilbhe óna bhféadfaí an taise a thaispeáint ar ócáidí sollúnta. Mheabhraigh na dealbha agus na taisí seo páis Íosa don lucht féachana, íobairt na croiche agus geallúint an tslánaithe, an téama céanna a bhí á léiriú ag an *Baldacchino* ar cuireadh croich agus cruinne ar a bharr, é ag cosaint na hardaltóra mar a n-aithghníomhtar íobairt Íosa. Agus thíos faoi chuile shórt, bhí tuama Pheadair chun an dlúthbhaint idir an pháis, an slánú agus an eaglais a dhéanamh chomh soiléir agus ab fhéidir. Is é toradh a bhí ar ealaín theagascach Bernini go ndearnadh áit shacrálta ar leith den spás thíos faoin trasnú i mBaisleac Naomh Peadar. Sin mar a chuaigh sé i bhfeidhm ar na cuairteoirí tosaigh nuair a bhí na dealbha ollmhóra, cúig mhéadar ar airde gach aon cheann acu, críochnaithe sa bhliain 1640; sin mar atá sé ceaptha dul i bhfeidhm ar chuairteoirí ó shin i leith.[2]

Ní raibh aon iomrá ar an mbeartas seo, áfach, nuair a bhain Aodh Ó Néill an Róimh amach in Aibreán na bliana 1608, cé go raibh tógáil agus athchóiriú na baislice nua faoi lánseol. Sa bhliain chéanna, mar shampla, leagadh an seanaireagal laistigh de phríomhdhoras na baislice ar thaobh na láimhe deise ina gcoimeádtaí ceirt Veronica. Dhá bhliain roimhe sin, ar 25 Eanáir, rinne an Pápa Pól V an taise a thionlacan i mórshiúl sollúnta ó aireagal an Phápa Eoin VII chuig sacraistí na baislice. Ar 21 Bealtaine, cuireadh an taise ar coimeád in áit rúnda laistigh de cholún an Veronica.[3]

Tugann Tadhg Ó Cianáin, cuntas ar na taisí ba mhó tábhacht a chonaic Aodh Ó Néill agus a choimhdeachta nuair a thug siad cuairt ar Bhaisleac Naomh Peadar, 12 Meitheamh 1608. Bhí oilithreacht na seacht n-eaglais ar bun acu an lá sin agus dearbhaíonn Ó Cianáin gur ordaigh an Pápa Pól V go dtaispeánfaí na taisí ar fad sna séipéil éagsúla don bhuíon Éireannach, rud a bhronnann blas na timchuairte ríoga ar an oilithreacht: 'Ro bhuí barántas agus ughdarás an athar naomhtha leó as go bhfuighbhidís taisealbhadh uile reilicias gach aoneagailse gusa roichfidis'.[4]

Seo a leanas cuntas Uí Chianáin ar a bhfaca na hIarlaí i mBaisleac Naomh Peadar:

Iar ndéanamh turais seacht bpríomhaltór bpríviléideach theampaill Pheadair dóibh taispéantar tra ceann an apstail uasail adhamhra S. Andrias dóibh 's é ar n-a threórughadh gusan Róimh feacht n-aill le prionnsa na Múraighe i ré agus i réimheas an dara Pius do bheith i

2 Irving Lavin, 'Bernini at St. Peter's: *singularis in singulis, in omnibus unicus*' in W. Tronzo (ed.), *St Peter's in the Vatican* (Cambridge, 2005), lgh 111–243 ar lgh 137–41.   3 Ian Wilson, *Holy faces, secret places: an amazing quest for the face of Jesus* (London / New York, 1991), lch 77; Saverio Gaeta, *L'enigma del volto di Gesù* (Milano, 2010), lch 222. 4 Nollaig Ó Muraíle (ed.), *Turas na dtaoiseach nUltach as Éirinn: from Ráth Maoláin to Rome* (Rome, 2007), lch 300 §7.2.

n-a phápa agus do dheachaidh badhéin céadna i bpearsain dá mhíle ó bhallaighibh na Rómha seachtair go Ponte Molle i bproiséisión ro-onórach do ghlacadh chinn na naomhapstail uasail ón bprionnsa.[5]

Luann an Cianánach taisí eile seachas na cinn mhóra:

Ro taisealbhadh dóibh as a haithle ceann Lúcáis soiscéil, ceann Sanct Séim óig, ceann S. Sebastian, ceann S. Tomáis easpaig Cantoirbí, ceann S. Amando, lámh Steafáin mhairtír, lámh S. Cristoforus mhairtír maille fri hiliomad oile do thaisibh naomh agus firéan.[6]

Ansin téann sé ar aghaidh chun labhairt ar an dá thaise mhóra eile:

Fó phríomhaltóir mhóir na heagailse an dara leith de thaisibh Peadair agus Póil. Taibearnacul ro-onórach uas uillinn deisceartaigh na príomhaltóra móire airm i n-a bhfuil Volta Sancta .i. an aghaidh naomhtha .i. an naipcín ro chomail an ban-naomh uasal adhamhra Veronica do ghlanghnúis chréachtnaighthe an tSlánaightheóra Íosa Críost an tan ro bhaoi fó dhaoirse agus fó mhartra ag iomchar na croiche céasta. Is follas agus is éagnach do na huile dhaoinibh pioctúir agus fiodhair ghnúise agus aighthe an Tighearna dia fhuil luachmhair chróidheirg isin naipcín sin, ceann na sleighe slinnleithne dia ro ghoin an dall Longinus agus dia ro threaghd go neamhchoilgealtach combhar croidhe Críost an tan ro bhuí marbh gan anmain i gcrann na croiche.

An Turcach Mór ba hé ros-tíodhlaic na seóid adhamhra oireaghdha sin gusan bPápa .i. an t-ochtmhadh Innocentius. Atáid aniú go bhfeartaibh agus míorbhailibh éagsamhla iongantacha.[7]

Tá na sonraí a thugann an Cianánach chomh mion sin go ndealraíonn sé gur cheadaigh sé foinsí scríofa mar *aide mémoire* chun cur le fianaise a dhá shúil. Is beag idir na sonraí a bhreac sé síos agus na sonraí a bhfuil fáil orthu sa treoirleabhar comhaimseartha is iomráití don Róimh, *Le cose maravigliose dell'alma città di Roma*. D'eascair an saothar seo ó leabhar a d'fhoilsigh an t-ailtire cáiliúil Andrea Palladio sa bhliain 1554, *Descritione de le chiese, stationi, indulgenze et reliquie de Corpi Sancti, che sonno in la città di Roma*. Foilsíodh an leabhar seo arís sa bhliain 1557 gan tagairt ar bith don údar agus faoi theideal nua, *Le cose maravigliose dell'alma città di Roma*. Cuireadh atheagráin den leagan seo amach arís agus arís eile anuas go dtí an bhliain 1750, sonraí á gcur leis chun ceann a thógáil de na hathruithe ailtireachta agus meoin a bhí ag tarlú sa chathair shíoraí féin in imeacht na mblianta. Maidir le Baisleac Naomh Peadar, tá sonraí an Chianánaigh agus an t-ord ina dtugtar iad an-ghar ar fad

---

5 Ibid., lch 332 §7.56.   6 Ibid., lch 334 §7.57.   7 Ibid., lch 334 §7.58–9.

don chur síos atá le fáil in eagráin 1608 agus 1609 de na *Cose maraviglose*.[8]
D'ainneoin a dhílse a leanann Ó Cianáin an fhoinse, áfach, níl sé gan locht.
Tugann sé le fios, mar shampla, gurb é an Turcach Mór a thug an dá thaise,
an Veronica agus sleá Longinus, araon don Phápa Innocentius VIII. Is í firinne
an scéil nár thug an Sabhdán Bayezit ach sleá Longinus don phápa. Nuair a
tháinig Bayezit II (An Turcach Mór) i réim mar Shabhdán sa bhliain 1482,
d'iarr deartháir óg leis an bprionsa, Cem, cabhair ar ridirí Naomh Eoin i
Rhodes chun an Sabhdán a threascairt. Cad a rinne na ridirí ach Cem a ghabh-
áil agus a choinneáil i ngéibheann. Cheannaigh an Pápa Innocentius VIII an
cime ó Ard-Mháistir na Ridirí sa bhliain 1486 agus thug chun na Róimhe é trí
bliana ina dhiaidh sin. Mar ghníomh buíochais as an iomaitheoir ba mhó a bhí
ina choinne a chur ó mhaith, bhronn an Sabhdán sleá Longinus ar an bPápa
maraon le suim mhór airgid móide 45000 ducat in aghaidh na bliana mar
airgead fuascailte. In ionad crosáid chostasach fhuilteach a thionscnamh chun
srian a chur le dul chun cinn na dTurcach san Eoraip, d'éirigh leis an bPápa
iad a chiúnú gan foréigean ar bith agus ar bhealach ba thairbheach dó féin.[9]

Ní raibh baint ar bith ag an eachtra seo le stair an Veronica, áfach, rud a
phléifear ar ball. Ach bhí an ceart ag an gCianánach nuair a dúirt sé go raibh
an taise á coimeád i dtaibearnacal gradamach os cionn uilleann dheisceartach
na príomhaltóra, mar a dúradh thuas. Díol spéise go ndeireann eagráin 1608
agus 1609 de na *Cose maravigliose* go raibh an taise fós *a man dritto de la porta
grande*. Má cheadaigh an Cianánach foinsí scríofa, níor ghá cloí go huile is go
hiomlán leo má ba chruinne an t-eolas a bhí aige féin, cé nach mór a chur san
áireamh go ndeireann eagrán 1610 gur aistríodh an Veronica, sleá Longinus
agus cloigeann San Aindrias chuig na cuasa sa chúpóil.

Rinne an croiniceoir tagairt don Veronica agus do shleá Longinus uair
amháin eile ina shaothar. B'shin 26 Bealtaine 1608 nuair a ghluais na díll-
eachtaigh ó ospidéal an Santo Spirito in Sassia, clann an phápa, mar a thug
sé orthu, i morshiúl sollúnta chuig Baisleac Naomh Peadar mar ar taispeánadh
an dá thaise dóibh:[10]

Is gnáth Veronica (.i. naipcín uasal oirdhearc mórmhíorbhaileach ro
chomail ban-naomh an chomhanma sin do ghnúis gheildeirg ghruadh-
chorcra agus do ghlanaghaidh ghlórmhair chréachtnaighthe ar

---

8 Guglielmo Facciotte, *Le cose maravigliose dell' alma città di Roma* (Roma, 1608; eagrán
1609); Giovanni Battista Cherubini, *Le cose maravigliose dell'alma città di Roma* (Roma,
1609); Pietro Martire Felini, *Le cose maravigliose dell'alma città di Roma* (Roma, 1610;
macasamhail, Roma, 1995).   9 Eamon Duffy, *Saints and sinners: a history of the Popes*
(London, 2006), lgh 211–12.   10 Faoi réimeas an Phápa Sixtus IV (1471–84) aistríodh an
mórshiúl a thionscain Innocentius III ón gcéad Domhnach tar éis na hEipeafáine go Luan
Cincíse: féach Eunice Howe, 'Appropriating space: woman's place in confraternal life at
Santo Spirito in Sassia, Rome' in B. Wisch and D. Cole Ahl (eds), *Confraternities and the
visual arts in renaissance Italy* (Cambridge, 2000), lgh 235–58 ar lch 248.

Slánaightheóra Íosa Críost an tan ro bhuí fo dhaoirse agus dócomhal agus aimhnirte fó lámhaibh námhad n-éadtrócar ag iomchar chroiche a pháise agus a mhartra gusan gcoróin spíne um a cheann a haithle a bhfuair do phéin agus do pheannaid roimhe sin) do thaispéanadh don chloinn-se an Phápa an lá sin (é). Atá go bhfíodhair dheilbhe agus aighthe Críost iar n-a choimhlíonadh agus iar n-a uasailpheinntéaladh go míorbhaileach éagsamhail dia fhuil luachmhair badhéin. Ro taisealbhadh dóibh iar sin ceann na sleighe slinnleithne do chuir Longinus tré chompar croidhe Chríost an tan ro bhuí marbh gan anmain i gcrann na croiche.[11]

Is léir go dtagann dhá thuairisc Uí Chianáin ar an Veronica leis an leagan traidisiúnta den scéal a d'eascair ó *Meditationes vitae Christi*, ach díol spéise go dtugann sé an t-ainm Veronica ar an naipcín chomh maith leis an mbean. Níor mhiste, áfach, foinsí eile faoin taise iomráiteach seo a cheadú. Nuair a thug Giraldus Cambrensis cuairt ar an Róimh 1199–1203, d'fhág sé an cuntas seo a leanas againn ar an Veronica:

ainm a thagann ó bhean darb ainm Veronica ar theastaigh uaithi le fada an lá ina cuid paidreacha an Tiarna a fheiceáil. I ndeireadh na dála éisteadh lena guí. Uair amháin nuair a bhí sí ag fágáil an teampaill chas sí ar an Tiarna a dúirt léi, 'A Veronica féach an té ar mhian leat é a fheiceáil'. Agus nuair a d'fhéach sí air, thóg sé a clóca, chuir lena aghaidh é, agus d'fhág lorg a ghnúise breactha air. Tugtar urraim don íomhá seo ach ní féidir le héinne é a fheiceáil ach amháin trí na cúirtíní atá ar crochadh os a comhair. Tá an íomhá á coimeád i mBaisleac Naomh Peadar. Seo í an bhean a léimid ina taobh gur bhain sí le scothóg bhrat Íosa agus gur leigheasadh í ó rith fola. Deirtear faoin mbean chéanna seo, tar éis pháis Chríost, gur cuireadh iachall uirthi teacht ó Iarusailéim chun na Róimhe agus an íomhá a bhreith léi, cé gurbh fhearr léi í a fhágáil ina diaidh. Ach nuair a tugadh os comhair Tiberius Caesar í, fuasclaíodh é ó ghalar doleigheasta a bhí á fhulaingt aige. Agus áitíonn daoine áirithe, agus imeartas focal á dhéanamh acu ar an bhfocal Veronica, gur ó *vera icona*, is é sin le rá 'fíoríomhá' a eascraíonn sé.[12]

Díol spéise nach bhfuil aon tagairt anseo don traidisiún faoin mbean darbh ainm Veronica a chuimil an fhuil d'aghaidh Íosa agus é ar bhóthar na croise.

Rinne Peadar Mallius cur síos ar an mbaisleac tuairim is tríocha bliain roimh Giraldus Cambrensis ach ní raibh le rá aige sin faoin taise ach an méad seo a leanas:

11 Ó Muraíle, *Turas na dtaoiseach*, lch 280 §6.38. 12 Herbert Thurston, *The holy year of jubilee, an account of the history and ceremony of the Roman jubilee* (London, 1900), lgh 194–5. An t-údar a d'aistrigh.

Tá naipcín Chríost ar chuimil sé a aghaidh air roimh a pháis nuair a bhí a chuid allais mar bhraonacha fola ag sileadh go talamh, ar coimeád in aireagal na Maighdine Beannaithe, Máthair Dé, ar a dtugtar Veronica.[13]

Sa bhliain 1198, bhunaigh an Pápa Innocens III ospidéal cáiliúil Santo Spirito in Sassia i dtimpeallacht na Vatacáine. Naoi mbliana ina dhiaidh sin, thionscain sé searmanas bliantúil ar an gcéad Domhnach tar éis ochtáibh na hEipeafáine, mórshiúl sollúnta ó Bhaisleac Naomh Peadar go dtí an t-ospidéal, agus an Veronica féin á iompar ag canóin na baislice. Ba í buaic an tsearmanais nuair a thóg an Pápa an taise gur thaispeáin go poiblí don lucht féachana í agus bhronn loghanna speisialta ní hamháin ar a raibh i láthair ach ar dhuine ar bith, áit ar bith ar fud an domhain, a déarfadh an phaidir speisialta a chum an Pápa don ócáid.[14] Seo é an chéad taispeántas poiblí den Veronica go bhfios dúinn cé go ndealraíonn sé nach dtarlaíodh sé ach uair in aghaidh na bliana i rith an tríú haois déag. Rinne Dante tagairt sa *Vita nova* (1294) d'oilithrigh ag teacht ar cuairt chun na Róimhe chun an taise a fheiceáil ach is do mhórshiúl mhí Eanáir a bhí sé ag tagairt, is cosúil.

Ansin bunaíodh an chéad Bhliain Naofa sa bhliain 1300 cé gur dócha nach raibh mórán réamhullmhúcháin taobh thiar di. Bhailigh slua mór ag Baisleac Naomh Peadar oíche Nollag 1299. Dealraíonn sé gur cheap siad go mbeadh logha ar leith ar fáil acu siúd a thabharfadh cuairt ar thuamaí na n-aspal an bhliain dár gcionn. Ansin ar an seachtú lá déag de mhí Eanáir, lá mhórshiúl an Veronica, chas an Pápa Bonifatius VIII ar sheanóir céad is a seacht mbliana d'aois. B'ait leis an bPápa go mbeadh oilithreacht á déanamh ag duine chomh sean leis. D'fhreagair mo dhuine go raibh sé i láthair sa Róimh i dteannta a athar céad bliain roimhe sin chun logha ar leith a fháil, agus gur chomhairligh a athair dó gan dearmad a dhéanamh den logha céanna ag tús na haoise ina dhiaidh sin. Cé nár éirigh leis an bPápa fianaise ar bith a aimsiú i dtaobh an logha sin, bhí drogall air na hoilithrigh a chur ó dhoras agus is mar sin a tháinig ann don chéad bhliain naofa. Bhí loghanna ar leith le fáil acu siúd a thabharfadh cuairt ar Bhaisleaca Naoimh Peadar agus Pól agus bhí an Veronica le taispeáint uair in aghaidh na seachtaine. Tugann foinsí comhaimseartha le fios gur tháinig borradh mór faoi líon na n-oilithreach a chuaigh chun na Róimhe le linn na haoise sin agus go raibh baint mhór ag taisí Bhaisleac Naomh Peadar, an Veronica go háirithe, leis an mborradh sin. I ngeall ar dhul chun cinn na Muslamach sa Phailistín, bhí sé ag éirí i bhfad níos deacra oilithreacht a dhéanamh chun na Talún Naofa. Diaidh ar ndiaidh bhí an Róimh, an Iarúsailéim nua, ag easáitiú na Pailistíne mar ionad oilithreachta. Go dtí sin, ní fhéadfadh ach crosáidithe lánlogha peacaí a fháil, ach bhí sé le fáil feasta do dhuine ar bith a dhéanfadh oilithreacht chun na Róimhe.[15]

13 Ibid., lch 194. An t-údar a d'aistrigh.   14 Wilson, *Holy faces, secret places*, lgh 44–6.
15 Debra J. Birch, *Pilgrimage to Rome in the Middle Ages* (Woodbridge, 1998; athchló

Is léir ó fhoinsí éagsúla gurb í taispeáint an Veronica buaic na hoilithreachta. In *Paradiso*, mar shampla, a scríobh Dante idir 1314 agus 1321, cuireann an file é féin i gcomórtas le hoilithreach ó thír i gcéin atá díreach tar éis teacht chun na Róimhe chun urraim a thabhairt don Veronica:

> Qual è colui che forse di Croazia
> viene a veder la Veronica nostra,
> che per l'antica fame non sazia,
> ma dice nel pensier, fin che si mostra:
> 'Segnor mio Jesù Cristo, Dio verace,
> or fu sì fatta la sembianza vostra?'
> tal era io mirando la vivace
> carità di colui che 'n questo mondo,
> contemplando, gustò di questa pace.
>
> (Paradiso 31, ll 103–11)[16]

> Díreach ar nós an té
> atá tar éis teacht ón gCroáit, b'fhéidir,
> chun ár Veronica a fheiceáil,
> duine nach sásaítear a sheanchíocras,
> ach a deireann ina intinn, fad a thaispeántar é:
> 'Mo Thiarna, Íosa Críost, fíorDhia;
> an mar seo a bhí do dheilbh tráth?'
> Is amhlaidh a bhí mé agus mé ag breathnú
> ar bheoghrá an té sin a bhlais an tsíocháin seo
> ar bith cé sa rinnfheitheamh dó.

Measann roinnt tráchtairí go raibh Dante féin i láthair sa Róimh d'Iubhaile na bliana 1300. Dúirt an croiniceoir, Giovanni Villani, go raibh éileamh chomh mór sin ar an Veronica sa bhliain 1300 gurbh éigean é a thaispeáint gach Aoine chomh maith leis na mórfhéilte.[17] Chuaigh taispeáint na taise i bhfeidhm chomh mór sin ar Phetrarca le linn Iubhaile na bliana 1350 gur bhunaigh sé an íomhá lárnach i gceann de na soinéid is cáiliúla dá chuid ar an Veronica:

> Movesi il vecchierel canuto e biancho
> Del dolce loco ov'ha sua età fornita,
> et de la famigliuola sbigottita
> Che vede il caro padre venir manco;

2000), lgh 197–202. 16 Alessandro Vittori, 'Veronica: Dante's pilgrimage from image to vision', *Dante Studies*, 121 (2003), 43–65 ar 44–5; an t-údar a rinne an t-aistriúchán. 17 Giovanni Morello, 'La Veronica nostra' in G. Foss (ed.), *I giubilei Roma, il sogno dei pellegrini* (Roma, 1999), lgh 134–41 ar lch 135; Vittori, 'Veronica: Dante's pilgrimage', 62 n. 190.

Indi trahendo poi l'antiquo fianco
Per l'extreme giornate di sua vita,
Quanto più pò coll buon voler s'aita,
Rotto dagli anni, et del camino stanco;
et viene a Roma, seguendo 'l desio,
per mirar la sembianza di colui
ch'ancor lassù nel ciel vedere spera:
cosi, lasso, talor vo cerchand'io
donna, quanto è possibile, in altrui
la disiata vostra forma vera.[18]

Fágann an seanóir liath leicthe an áit chaoin dúchais
inar chaith sé an chuid is fearr dá shaol,
agus an teaghlaichín, alltacht orthu
ag breathnú ar a n-athair dílis ag dul as radharc.
Uaidh sin streachlaíonn sé a chliatháin sheirgthe
trí laethanta deireanacha a shaoil.
Cabhraíonn sé leis féin de réir a dhíchill agus le teann dea-thola,
Briste ag na blianta, traochta ag an mbóthar.
Agus tagann sé chun na Róimhe, mian a chroí á leanúint aige,
chun breathnú ar dheilbh an té sin
a bhfuil súil aige é a fheiceáil thuas ar neamh.
Is amhlaidh, faraor, a théim ag cuardach, a bhean uasail,
an oiread is féidir, i ndaoine eile
d'fhíordheilbhe a bhfuilim ag tnúth léi.

Teist bhreá ar an tóir a bhí ar an Veronica is ea an leas meafarach a bhain Dante agus Petrarca araon ina gcuid filíochta as dúil na n-oilithreach. Bunaíodh ceardchuallacht ar leith sa Róimh, *pictores Veronicarum*, a raibh sé de chúram uirthi pictiúir a dhéanamh den taise agus ba nós le hoilithrigh suaitheantas den Veronica a chaitheamh ar a gceannbheart. Go fiú Chaucer ag deireadh an cheathrú haois déag, thagair sé don nós seo sa chur síos a rinne sé ar an Maithiúnaí i bprológ na *Canterbury tales*: 'A Vernicle hadde he sowed upon his cappe'.[19]

Sa dara leath den chúigiú haois déag, tá greanadóireachtaí adhmaid againn a léiríonn an Veronica á thaispeáint don phobal. Baineann an léaráid seo a leanas le heagrán 1475 den treoirleabhar ba mhó tábhacht chun na Róimhe sa mheánaois, *Mirabilia urbis Romae* (Léaráid 1):

Ar 6 Bealtaine 1527, tharla ceann de na heachtraí ba thubaistí riamh i stair na Róimhe nuair a chreach *Landsknechte* nó saighdiúirí tuarastail an Impire

---

18 Vittori, 'Veronica: Dante's pilgrimage', 62; an t-údar a d'aistrigh. 19 Wilson, *Holy faces, secret places*, lch 61.

Léaráid 1: Taispeáint an Veronica le caoinchead an Bayerishe
staatsbibliothek München, Xylogr. 50, f. 1v.

Séarlas V an chathair shíoraí. Cé gur éirigh leis an bPápa Clemens VII agus
a chomhairleoirí dídean a aimsiú i gCastel Sant'Angelo, ní raibh an t-ádh
céanna ar ghnáthmhuintir na Róimhe. Maraíodh fir, mná agus páistí.
Bánaíodh agus creachadh idir pháláis agus séipéil, agus goideadh earraí
luachmhara agus taisí. Deir foinsí comhaimseartha gur goideadh agus gur
maslaíodh an dá thaise ba mhó tábhacht sa Róimh, an Veronica agus sleá
Longinus, ach deir foinsí eile a mhalairt.[20] Dealraíonn sé gur taispeánadh an
Veronica arís sna blianta 1533, 1536 agus ar feadh sé lá as a chéile le linn
Iubhailí na mblianta 1550 agus 1575. Thug Montaigne cuntas ar thaispeáint
a chonaic sé Déardaoin na Mandála 1580:

> Ce jours se montre la Véronique, qui est un visage ombrageux, et de
> couleur sombre et obscure, dans un carré comme un grand miroir; il se
> montre avec grande cérémonie du haut d'un pupitre qui a cinq ou six
> pas de large. Le prêtre qui le tient a les mains revêtues de gants rouges,

20 Ibid., lgh 72–5; André Chastel, *Il sacco di Roma* (1983; traduzione italiana, Torino,
2010), lgh 78–87; Gaeta, *L'enigma del volto di Gesù*, lgh 15–18.

et y a deux ou trois autres prêtres qui le soutiennent. Il ne se voit rien avec grande révérence, le peuple prosterné à terre, la plupart les larmes aux yeux, avec de ces cris commisération. Une femme, qu'on disait être *spiritata*, se tempêtait, voyant cette figure, criait, tendait et tordait les bras. Ces prêtres, se promenant autour de ce pupitre, la vont présentant au peuple, tantôt ici, tantôt là; et à chaque mouvement, ceux à qui on la présente s'écrient. On y montre aussi en même temps et même cérémonie, le fer de lance dans une bouteille de cristal, Plusieurs fois ce jour se fait cette montre, avec une assemblée de peuple si infinie que jusques bien loin au-dehors de l'église, autant que la vue peut arriver à ce pupitre, c'est une extrême presse d'hommes et de femmes.[21]

Ar na laethanta seo taispeánann siad an Veronica. Seo aghaidh scáthach, dath dorcha gruama uirthi, agus fráma air mar a bheadh ar scáthán. Taispeántar é ó chrannóg ard, cúig nó sé choiscéim ar leithead. Caitheann an sagart a bhíonn á thaispeáint láimhíní dearga ar a lámha agus cabhraíonn beirt nó triúr sagart eile leis chun é a thaispeáint. Ní fhéadfadh aon rud eile an oiread urraime a chothú is a chothaíonn sé seo. Sléachtann an pobal go léir go talamh, an chuid is mó acu ag sileadh na ndeor agus ag osnaíl le teann trua. Bean amháin a raibh deamhan inti, dar leis an bpobal, rinne sí gleo nuair a chonaic sí an íomhá seo agus thosaigh sí ag screadaíl agus ag únfairt agus ag fáisceadh na lámh. Na sagairt seo, gluaiseann siad ar fud na crannóige, chun an taise a thaispeáint don phobal, uaireanta ar an taobh seo, uaireanta ar an taobh eile; agus le gach gluaiseacht a dhéanann siad, screadann a mbíonn i láthair os ard. Taispeántar ceann na sleá i soitheach criostail ag an am céanna agus leis an tsollúntacht chéanna. Déantar an taispeáint seo roinnt uaireanta sa lá, agus bíonn slua chomh hollmhór sin i láthair, go fiú go ceann achair fhada lasmuigh den eaglais, áit ar bith a bhféadfaí spleáchadh a fháil ar an gcrannóg, nach mbíonn le feiceáil ach trombhrú fear agus ban.

Taispeánadh an Veronica le linn na Bliana Naofa 1600. Ansin tharla na hathruithe a luamar thuas nuair a aistríodh an Veronica go hionad nua sa bhaisleac. Dealraíonn sé nár taispeánadh an taise go poiblí ó shin i leith lasmuigh den bheannacht a thugtar don phobal tar éis easpartan ar an gcúigiú Domhnach den Charghas gach bliain. Ach tharla cor nua sa scéal le blianta beaga anuas nuair a mhaígh Heinrich Pfeiffer CÍ, iarollamh le stair na healaíne eaglasta in Ollscoil Ghréagóir sa Róimh, nach ann don Veronica i mBaisleac Naomh Peadar agus nárbh ann dó le fada an lá. Áitíonn Pfeiffer

21 Michel de Montaigne, *Journal de voyage*, in eagar ag Fausta Garavini (Éditions Gallimard, 1983), lgh 225–6. An t-údar a rinne an t-aistriuchán.

gur goideadh nó ar a laghad gur tógadh an bhuntaise ón mbaisleac le linn na hatógála, gur cuireadh ceirt eile ina háit, agus go bhfuil fáil ar an bhfiorVeronica i séipéal na gCaipisíneach i Manoppello, sráidbhaile céad ochtó ciliméadar soir ó thuaidh den Róimh. Scrúdaigh sé cáipéis a scríobh bráthair Caipisíneach idir 1640–6, Donato da Bomba. Dar leis an údar, ghoid saighdiúir darbh ainm Pancratio Petrucci an taise sa bhliain 1608. Deich mbliana ina dhiaidh sin, dhíol bean chéile Petrucci í leis an Dochtúir Antonio de Fabritiis chun a fear céile a fhuascailt as príosún. Is é De Fabritiis a thug ar na Caipisínigh teacht go Manoppello agus sa bhliain 1638 bhronn sé an Veronica orthu.[22] Cé nár scrúdaíodh an fial go heolaíochtúil go fóill, díol spéise gur forshuíodh grianghraf ardghléineachta den aghaidh atá le feiceáil ar an bhfial anuas ar ghrianghraf den aghaidh atá le feiceáil ar thaiséadach Torino, agus is í an aghaidh chéanna atá le feiceáil sa dá chás.[23] An t-aon difríocht shuntasach atá le tabhairt faoi deara eatarthu go bhfuil na súile dúnta ar an taiséadach fad is go bhfuil siad oscailte ar an aghaidh i Manoppello.

Díol suntais chomh maith gur ordaigh an Pápa Pól V sa bhliain 1617 nár cheadmhach d'éinne feasta cóipeana a dhéanamh den Veronica i mBaisleac Naomh Peadar ach do chanóin na baislice amháin. Agus sa bhliain 1628, ní hamháin gur eisigh Urbanus VIII an cosc seo arís, ach d'ordaigh sé freisin go scriosfaí cibé cóipeanna a bhí ar fail. Tá sé tugtha faoi deara ag Pfeiffer go bhfuil na súile ar oscailt sna leaganacha a rinneadh roimh 1617 agus go bhfuil na súile dúnta i gcóipeanna a rinneadh ina dhiaidh sin. An t-aon mhíniú le himní na bpápaí ná go raibh fhios acu go rímhaith nárbh é an fial fírinneach é an ceann a bhí i mBaisleac Naomh Peadar.[24]

Bhí ábhar eile imní ag Pól V. I ngeall ar an dochar ar fad ab éigean a dhéanamh don oiread sin tuamaí agus scrínte nuair a bhí an obair atógála ar siúl i mBaisleac Naomh Peadar, sa bhliain 1617 d'iarr sé ar nótaire na baislice, Jacopo Grimaldi, tuairisc a scríobh ar na nithe ba ghá a scrios nó a athlonnú. Scríobh Grimaldi cuntas cuimsitheach ar an Veronica, cáipéis céad tríocha haon leathanach. Tagraíonn Grimaldi don fhráma gloine a rinneadh don taise sa bhliain 1350, fráma atá fós ar coimeád i gciste na Vatacáine. Dhá phána gloine atá san earra agus díol spéise le Pfeiffer gur fial trédhearcach atá á thaispeáint i Manoppello. Ina theannta sin, dúirt Grimaldi go raibh gloine

22 Heinrich Pfeiffer, 'Il volto santo a Manoppello' in idem (ed.), *Il volto santo di Manoppello* (Pescara, 2000), lgh 24–31 ar lgh 24–6.   23 B. Paschalis Schlömer, 'Il velo del volto di Manoppello e la sacra sindone di Torino' in H. Pfeiffer (ed.), *Il volto santo di Manoppello*, lgh 41–65, ar lgh 56–65.   24 Pfeiffer, 'Il volto santo a Manoppello', lgh 22–7. Deir cáipéis Da Bomba gur thóg oilithreach rúndiamhrach an Veronica go Manoppello chomh fada siar le 1506, ach áitíonn Pfeiffer nach bhfuil ansin ach bréagchumadóireacht chun dallamullóg a chur ar údaráis na Vatacáine a bhí ag tóraíocht an fhéil a bhí ar iarraidh ó Bhaisleac Naomh Peadar. Ní féidir brath ar stairiúlacht na n-eachtraí a luann da Bomba ach tar éis an dáta 1618, dar le Pfeiffer.

an chumhdaigh briste agus dealraíonn sé go bhfuil mír ghloine greamaithe den fhial i Manoppello.[25]

Rinne fear darb ainm Francesco Speroni cóip de *Opusculum* Grimaldi sa bhliain 1635, cóip a leanann an bunsaothar go dlúth beacht, ach amháin go bhfuil súile Íosa dúnta i leagan Speroni fad atá siad oscailte ag Grimaldi. Mar gheall ar thoirmisc Phól V agus Urbanus VIII, agus mar gheall ar an difríocht bhunúsach idir léiriúcháin an Veronica roimh agus tar éis 1617 maidir le súile Íosa a bheith oscailte nó dúnta, tá Pfeiffer cinnte nach í an bhuntaise atá á coimeád sa Vatacáin. An dornán beag daoine a fuair cead é a ghrinnbhreithniú ó thús an fichiú haois, tá siad ar fad ar aon intinn go bhfuil an brat chomh doiléir sin nach féidir a rá céard atá breactha air.[26]

Tagann cuntas an Chianánaigh leis an leagan traidisiúnta de scéal Veronica, insint nach réitíonn le cuntas Giraldus Cambrensis. B'fhiú féachaint an bhfuil leaganacha eile den traidisiún ann roimh aimsir Cambrensis. Scríobh an staraí eaglasta, Eusebius, sa bhliain 325 gur thóg an bhean leis an rith fola sa Soiscéal dealbh in ómós Íosa mar ghníomh buíochais dá leigheas. Ní hamháin sin ach thug sé le fios go bhfaca sé féin an dealbh i Caesarea Philippi, baile dúchais na mná.[27] Taca an ama chéanna, thug *Gníomhartha Pioláit* Veronica nó Berenice ar an mbean seo.[28] Finscéal eile, *Cura sanitatis Tiberii*, a dtéann na lámhscríbhinní siar go dtí an t-ochtú haois, insíonn sé go raibh an t-impire Tiberius go dona tinn. Ar chloisteáil dó faoi mhíorúiltí Íosa, cuireann sé teachtaire go hIarúsailéim chun an leigheasóir a bhreith leis chun na Róimhe. Bhí Íosa marbh faoin am sin ach d'aimsigh an teachtaire bean darbh ainm Veronica a d'fhulaing ó rith fola ach ar leigheas Íosa í. Tharla go raibh portráid d'Íosa ina seilbh aici. Más go drogallach féin é, téann sí chun na Róimhe, leigheastar Tiberias, baistear é agus tógann an t-impire scrín don phortráid.[29] Tá mórán an scéal céanna le fáil in *Vindicta Salvatoris*, téacs a cumadh i ndeisceart na Fraince timpeall 700 agus ar eascair scéal Fraincise uaidh sa dara haois déag.[30]

Ní mór scéal eile fós a chur san áireamh, leigheas Abgar, rí Edessa, a mhair sa chéad aois tar éis Chríost. Bhí sé ag fulaingt ó ghalar doleigheasta

25 Paul Badde, *The face of God: the rediscovery of the true face of Jesus*, trans. Henry Taylor (San Francisco, 2010), lgh 90–103. 26 Paul Badde, *The true icon: from the shroud of Turin to the veil of Manoppello*, trans. Michael J. Miller (San Francisco, 2010), lgh 91–2, 282–3; Wilson, *Holy faces, secret places*, lgh 185–6. 27 Wilson, *Holy faces, secret places*, lgh 126–7. 28 Ibid. 29 Ibid.; Ewa Kuryluk, *Veronica and her shroud* (Oxford, 1991), lgh 120–2. 30 Kuryluk, *Veronica and her shroud*, lgh 120–2; John C. Iannone, *The three cloths of Christ: the emerging treasures of Christianity* (Kissimmee, Florida, 2009), lch 188; Wilson, *Holy faces, secret places*, lgh 126–7. Tá dhá leagan de leigheas Tiberius le fáil sa Ghaeilge, cé gur mó a dhíríonn siad ar dhroch-chinniúint Phíoláit ná ar Veronica (cf. Gearóid Mac Niocaill, 'Dhá leagan de Scéal Phíoláit', *Celtica*, 7 [1966], 205–13; Salvador Ryan, '"Wily women of God" in Breifne's late medieval and early modern devotional collections' in B. Scott [ed.], *Culture and society in early modern Breifne / Cavan* [Dublin, 2009], lgh 31–47 ar lgh 35–7). Dealraíonn sé go n-eascraíonn siad ón *Legenda aurea*: féach Granger Ryan, *Jacobus de Voragine*, i, lgh 212–13.

agus sheol teachtaire go Iarúsailéim agus litir aige d'Íosa ag iarraidh air teacht i gcabhair air. Ní raibh Íosa in ann dul, ach scríobh sé ar ais agus gheall deisceabal dá chuid a chur chuige i ndiaidh a bháis. Chuaigh Thaddeus nó Addai go hEdessa agus ceirt le cumraíocht Íosa breactha air. Nuair a chonaic Abgar an cheirt, leigheasadh láithreach é agus rinneadh Críostaí de. Tá an scéal luaite ag Eusebius sa cheathrú aois agus faightear leagan forbartha den chomhfhreagras idir Íosa agus Abgar i dteanga na Sirice breis agus céad bliain ina dhiaidh sin, *Teagasc Addai*.[31]

Cibé faoi ghné na finscéalaíochta de, tá fianaise againn go raibh taise anluachmhar in Edessa, go raibh sé i bhfolach i gcuas os cionn gheataí na cathrach agus gur chreid muintir na cathrach gur chosain íomhá seo aghaidh Íosa iad ar ionradh na bPeirseach sa bhliain 544.[32] Ní hamháin sin ach thug Evagrius, staraí na cathrach, *acheiropoíetos* uirthi, (íomhá) nach ndearna lámha daonna. Tógadh an taise go caithréimeach chuig Cathair Chonstaintín sa bhliain 944 agus cuireadh ionad ar fail di i séipéal Naomh Muire Blachernae, agus tugadh ainm nua uirthi, an *Mandylion* naofa. Mar gheall ar úsáid an fhocail fhíorneamhghnách Gréigise *tetradiplon*, focal a chiallaíonn fillte faoi cheathair, áitíonn Ian Wilson gurb í atá in aghaidh naofa Odessa ná taiséadach Torino fillte faoi cheathair sa chaoi nach bhfuil ach íomhá na haghaidhe le feiceáil. Nuair a chreach na crosáidithe Cathair Chonstaintín sa bhliain 1204, goideadh nó loiteadh na taisí go léir a bhí i séipéal Pharos sa phálás impiriúil ach d'éirigh leis an taiséadach teacht slán. Measann Wilson freisin gur cóip d'aghaidh naofa Edessa í an Veronica a tógadh chun na Róimhe ó Chathair Chonstaintín idir 944 agus 1009, nuair a tháinig ann i gceart don Siosma Mór idir eaglais an oirthir agus eaglais an iarthair.[33] Tharla gur saineolaí domhanda ar thaiséadeach Torino é Wilson, is olc leis gur dhiúltaigh údaráis na Vatacáine cead dó an Veronica a fhiosrú agus anailis eolaíochtúil a dhéanamh air.

Dearcadh eile ar fad, mar a chonaicemar thuas, atá ag Heinrich Pfeiffer. Áitíonn seisean go bhfuilimid ag déileáil le dhá phíosa éadaigh dhifriúla, ceann acu an taiséadach, ceann eile an *sudarium* nó an cheirt allais a cuireadh anuas ar aghaidh Íosa, os cionn an taiséadaigh. Ba chóir taiséadach Íosa a ionannú le *Mandylion* Odessa agus an Aghaidh Naofa a ionannú le híomhá Camulia. Tig le Pfieffer stair na haghaidhe naofa a rianadh ó Iarúsailéim go hEifeasas agus as sin go Camulia, ónar thóg an tImpire Justinian II í go Cathair Chonstaintín *c.*574. Baineadh leas aisti mar *palladium* no íomhá coimirce chun an chathair agus arm an impire a chosaint. D'iompraítí cóipeanna den íomhá os comhair arm an impire agus iad ag dul chun catha díreach mar a d'iompraítí an Cathach os comhair arm Uí Dhomhnaill in Éirinn fadó. I ndán comhaimseartha a chomórann an bua impiriúil i gcath na habhann Arzamon i 586,

31 Kuryluk, *Veronica and her shroud*, lgh 38–47; Wilson, *Holy faces, secret places*, lgh 127–9. 32 Wilson, *Holy faces, secret places*, lch 134; idem, *The shroud: the 2000-year old mystery solved* (London, 2010), lgh 127–33. 33 Wilson, *Holy faces, secret places*, lgh 128–9.

Léaráid 2: Freascó Pinerolo a léiríonn *sudarium* agus taiséadach Íosa.
Grianghraf le caoinchead Paul Badde.

tagraítear d'íomhá Camulia, mar íomhá 'nár péinteáladh, nár fiodh, ach a rinneadh le healaín dhiaga'.[34] Bhí conspóid na n-íolscriostóirí faoi lánseol san
oirthear san ochtú haois agus ní mór cuimhneamh nár údaraíodh urraim na
n-íomhánna go foirmeálta go dtí Comhairle Nicaea II sa bhliain 787. Is cosúil
gur thóg an Paitriarc, Germanus I, íomhá Camulia chun na Róimhe chun í a
chosaint ar shlad na n-íolscriostóirí sa bhliain 708. Cuireadh isteach i
mBaisleac Naomh Peadar í sa séipéal a thóg Eoin VII sa bhliain 705.
Dealraíonn sé gur tugadh an t-ainm Veronica ar an *sudarium* don chéad uair
sa bhliain 1143.[35]

34 Badde, *The face of God*, lgh 125–9, ar lgh 128–9; Pfeiffer, 'Il volto santo a Manoppello',
lgh 16–19; Iannone, *The three cloths of Christ*, lch 192.   35 Iannone, *The three cloths of
Christ*, lgh 193–4; Badde, *The face of God*, lch 135.

Ar 19 Márta 1578, shroich Bandiúca Yolande na Saváí baile Pinerolo i dtuaisceart na hIodáile agus taiséadach Íosa á iompar aici go Torino. D'iarr Urbano Bonnivardi, ardeaspag Vercelli, cead ar an mbandiúca an taiséadach naofa a thaispeáint don phobal i Pinerolo Aoine an Chéasta. Rinne sí rud air agus is mar sin a tharla an chéad taispeántas poiblí den taiséadach san Iodáil. Tá freascó ar cheann de na sráideanna sa bhaile a chomórann an eachtra seo, os comhair mháthairtheach Oblátaigh na Maighdine Muire. Is é an rud is spéisiúla faoin bhfreascó seo, nach amháin go dtaispeántar an taiséadach ach go bhfuil an *sudarium*, an Veronica, le feiceáil freisin.[36] Díol suntais an píosa seo ealaíne sa mhéid go mbaineann sé an fód d'argóintí Wilson agus nach bhfágann sé amhras dá laghad faoi áiteamh Pfeiffer nach mór dúinn dhá bhall éadaigh dhifriúla a chur san áireamh, an taiséadach agus an cheirt allais, agus muid ag caint ar na taisí is sine d'Íosa (Léaráid 2).

CONCLÚIDÍ

Tar éis an *excursus* thuas ar stair an Veronica ní miste breathnú ar an gCianánach an athuair.

1) Siúd is go dtugann an croiniceoir dhá chuntas ar an taise atá cosúil go maith lena chéile, ní mór idirdhealú bunúsach a dhéanamh eatarthu. An chéad taispeántas den Veronica Luan Cincíse, tharla sé mar bhuaic mhórshiúil mhórthaibhsigh, searmanas ceáfrach paraliotúirgeach a bhí ann. An dara huair, áfach, taispeántas príobháideach a bhí ann do na taoisigh Ghaelacha amháin. Rud eisceachtúil amach is amach ab ea na taispeántais phríobháideacha. Ní heol dúinn, mar shampla, ach sé thaispeántas phríobháideacha idir 1536 agus 1800 agus daoine den ghradam is airde a bhí i gceist i ngach cás: an tImpire Séarlas V (1536); Cristín, iarbhanríon na Sualainne (1656); Cosimus, ard-diúca na Toscáine (1700); Séamas III (1717); Giulio Visconti, leasrí Napoli (1733); Carlo Emanuele IV, rí na Sairdíne (1800).[37] Ní mór Aodh Ó Néill a chur leis an liosta sin anois.

2) Ba dhual don Chianánach leas a bhaint as teanga bhladhmannach, í maisithe le comhchiallaigh, athrá agus uaim, agus é ag trácht ar eachtra ar bith a bhain tocht ar leith léi. Ba dhóigh le duine gur mó a bhainfeadh sé seo le taispeáint phríobháideach an Veronica ná le searmanas Luan Cincíse, ach a mhalairt atá fíor ó thaobh na teanga a úsáideann sé. B'fhéidir nach raibh an croiniceoir i láthair ag an taispeáint phríobháideach sin, nó gur mheas sé gur leor cur síos bladhmannach amháin a dhéanamh ar an taise.

36 Badde, *The true icon*, lgh 62–7.   37 Gaeta, *L'enigma del volto di Gesù*, lch 231 n 42.

3) Díol spéise go raibh an Cianánach in ann idirdhealú a dhéanamh idir an cheirt ar a dtugtaí Veronica agus an bhean darbh ainm Veronica.

4) Is suimiúil freisin gur thug sé 'an aghaidh naofa' ar an taise siúd is nár thóg sé an Iodáilis leis go hiomlán cruinn, 'volta sancta' (recte 'volto santo').

5) Díol suntais freisin gur thug sé 'naipcín' ar an Veronica. Seo ceann de na nuafhocail iasachta a d'úsáid Tadhg Ó Cianáin don chéad uair sa Ghaeilge.[38] Ón mBéarla an iasacht seo, agus baineann dhá cheann de na trí shampla ag Ó Cianáin leis an Veronica, agus is le míorúilt a d'oibrigh Maighdean Dhubh Halle le linn léigir na gCailíneach ar an mbaile sin sa Bheilg sa bhliain 1580 a bhaineann an tríú sampla. Má d'úsáid an Cianánach nuafhocal ón mBéarla chun trácht a dhéanamh ar an taispeáint phríobháideach den Veronica a tugadh do na hIarlaí, ardaíonn sé sin an fhéidearthacht go raibh cainteoir maith Béarla i gcuideachta na dtaoiseach. Peadar Lombard, a raibh cónaí air sa Róimh ón mbliain 1598, a ceapadh ina Ardeaspag teidealach ar Ard Mhacha sa bhliain 1601 agus ina bhall de líon tí an phápa Pól V go luath ina dhiaidh sin, an té is túisce a thiocfadh chun cuimhne. D'fháiltigh sé roimh na taoisigh chun na Róimhe 29 Aibreán 1608; mar an eaglaiseach Éireannach ba ghradamúla sa Róimh ag an am, is cinnte nárbh fhearr éinne ná Lombard chun tathaint ar an bPápa na taisí ar fad bhí ar coimeád i seacht mbaisleac na Róimhe a thaispeáint do na taoisigh Ultacha.

6) Cé go dtagann cuntas Uí Chianáin ar an Veronica leis an traidisiún a bhuanaigh *Meditationes vitae Christi* agus leis an séú stáisiún ar bhóthar na croiche, díol suntais an fhoclaíocht a d'úsáid an croiniceoir: 'Atá go bhfiodhair dheilbhe agus aighthe Críost *iar n-a choimhlíonadh agus iar n-a uasailpheinnteáladh go míorbhaileach éagsamhail* dia fhuil luachmhair badhéin'.[39] Tagann sé seo chomh gar agus is féidir sa Ghaeilge don saintéarma *acheiriopoíetos* sa Ghréigis, íomhá nach ndearnadh le lámha daonna.

7) I ndeireadh na dála, táimid fágtha le ceist bhunúsach amháin: céard go díreach a dtugann an Cianánach cuntas air sa bhliain chinniúnach 1608, na tuairiscí deiridh ar an bhfíorVeronica sular aistríodh go Manoppello é, nó na chéad tuairiscí ar an Veronica tacair a lonnaíodh sa Vatacáin mar ionadaí? Ar an drochuair, toisc nach dtagraíonn an croiniceoir do staid na súl san íomhá, pé acu oscailte nó dúnta iad, ní féidir linn freagra beacht a thabhairt ar an gceist sin.

38 Ó Muraíle, *Turas na dtaoiseach*, 'Appendix 6, Selection of neologisms and words borrowed into Irish from other languages', lgh 641–6; Liam Mac Mathúna, *Béarla sa Ghaeilge: cabhair choigríche. An códmheascadh Gaeilge / Béarla i litríocht na Gaeilge, 1600–1900* (BÁC, 2007), lgh 58–63. 39 Ó Muraíle, *Turas na dtaoiseach*, lch 280 §6.38 (féach n. 11 thuas).

Maol Mhuire agus a shinsear

GEARÓID MAC EOIN

Is dóigh go bhfuil eolas ag aon duine a rinne an Ghaeilge mar ábhar céime in aon cheann de ollscoileanna na hÉireann faoin triúr scríobhaithe a ghlac páirt i soláthar na lámhscríbhinne Leabhar na hUidhre.[1] Bhí (1) an duine a cheaptar a bheith ina ab ar an mainistir, fear a dtugtar **A** air dá bharr sin; bhí (2) an duine a scríobh an chuid is mó den leabhar agus a dtugtar **M** air de bhrí go dtugann sé a ainm féin dúinn, Maol Mhuire; tháinig (3) an tríú scríobhaí tamall éigin i ndiaidh na beirte eile agus tugtar an t-idirscríobhaí **H** air mar gurbh é a scríobh na hoimilí sa lámhscríbhinn. Is ar fhadhb a bhaineann leis an dara fear acu seo, an príomhscríobhaí, a ba mhaith liom aird a dhíriú anseo.

Tugann sé a ainm faoi dhó (i b*probationes pennae* ar bharr f. 55b agus ar bharr f. 70a) i bhfoirm an ghinidigh mar *Mail Muri*. Tugtar tuilleadh eolais ina thaobh i nóta (f. 37b) a thugann ainm Sigraid Húi Chuirrndín dúinn, file agus ollamh Bhréifne a fuair bás sa bhliain 1388, mar dhuine a rinne athnuachan ar an sciamhleabhar seo. Tugann an nóta *Moelmhuiri mac Ceileachair. mac meic Cuind na mbocht ro scrib 7 ro scrút a lebraib egsamlaib in lebur sa* air. Chuaigh Heinrich Zimmer tríd Annála Ríoghachta Éireann (AFM feasta) agus léirigh sé ginealach Mhaoil Mhuire mar seo a leanas:[2]

> (1) **Maolmuire** (†1106) mac Mic Cuind na mBocht do mharbhadh ar lar doimhliacc Cluana mic Nóis lá haos aidhmhillte.
>
> Maol Muire, the grandson of Conn na mBocht was killed by marauders in the stone church of Clonmacnoise.[3]

Ba mhac é le:

> (2) **Celeachair** (†1134) mac Corbmaic Uí Chuinn na mBocht, sruith shenóir, cenn comhairle, 7 tobar eccna, senchusa, cend einigh 7 coimheda riaghla Cluana mic Nóis, décc in iomdhaidh Chiaráin iar mbuaidh naithriche i Nóin September. As dó so ro ráidh mac Macaimh Uí Cíocharáin ó Edargabhail an rannso,

---

1 ARÉ, LS 23 E 25; Richard I. Best and Osborn Bergin (eag.), *Lebor na Huidre. Book of the Dun Cow* (BÁC, 1929).   2 Heinrich Zimmer, 'Keltische Studien: über den compilatorischen Charakter der irischen Sagentexte im sogenannten Lebor na hUidre', *Zeitschrift für vergleichende Sprachforschung auf dem Gebiete der indogermanischen Sprachen*, 28 (1887), 417–689 ag 671–5.   3 Is leis an údar na haistriúcháin.

Mo ghenar duit it bhethaid,
A Mhic Cuind, a Chélechair,
A taoisi, a Chelechair Cluana,
I nglé bhethaidh gle bhuadha.

Célechair, the son of Cormac son of Conn na mBocht, a noble elder,
the head of counsel, the source of wisdom and history, the head of
honour and the observance of the rule of Clonmacnoise, died in the
Bed of Ciarán after the triumph of repentance on the Nones of
September. It was of him that the son of Macoím ua Cíocharán from
Etargabáil spoke this stanza:

Hail to you in your life,
O Son of Conn, O Célechair,
You are, o Célechair of Cluain,
In a bright life of bright victory.

Chuaigh scríobhaithe Annála Ríoghachta Éireann amú anseo, áfach, mar gur
ghlac siad le Corbmac (seachas Conn na mBocht) mar ainm ar athair
Chéileachair. Tá a mhalairt le feiceáil sa rann, áit a dtugtar 'mac Cuinn' ar
Chéileachair. Uncail do Chéileachair a ba ea Cormac mac Cuinn na mBocht
(féach AFM 1103, mar a dtugtar 'Corbmac Mac Cuinn na mBocht' air). Ach
ghlac Zimmer le Cormac mar ainm d'athair Chéileachair.[4]

(3) (i) **Conn na mBocht** (†1059) ordan 7 aireachus Cluana mic Nóis,
décc iar sendataigh.

Conn na mBocht the dignity and pre-eminence of Clonmacnoise died
after a long life.

Tá nóta eile faoi Chonn na mBocht le fáil in AFM 1031. Is cosúil gur ag
comóradh na hócáide nuair a bhunaigh Conn na mBocht áirghe dona boicht
i gCluain mhac Nóis an bhliain sin.

(ii) Conn na mBocht, cend Celedh ndhé 7 ancoiri, Cluana mic Nóis,
do chéid tionól airghe do bochtaibh Cluana i nIseal Chiaráin, 7 ro
edhbair fiche bó uaidh féin inntí. As dó do ráidheadh,
A Chuinn Chluana, atclos tú a hErind i nAlbain,
A chind ordain, nochan usa do chill dargain.

Conn na mBocht, the head of the Servants of God and an anchorite of
Cluain mac Nóis, the first to collect a herd of cattle for the poor of
Cluain in Íseal Chiaráin and he donated twenty cows to it out of his
own resources. It was of him that the following was said:

4 Zimmer, 'Keltische Studien', 672.

> O Conn of Cluain, your reputation has spread from Ireland to
> Scotland,
> O head of dignity, it is not easy to plunder your church.

Is ó Chonn na mBocht a ainmnítear baill eile dá chlann, mar shampla:

(4) Ioseph (†1022) mac Dúnchadha, anmchara Cluana mic Nóis décc.
Athair Coinn na mBocht esidhe.

Joseph son of Dúnchad, the confessor of Clonmacnoise, died. He was
the father of Conn na mBocht.

(5) Dunchadh (†1005) mac Dunadhaicch, ferleighind Cluana mic
Nóis, 7 a hangcoire iarsin, cend a riaghla, 7 a sencais, décc. Sen sil
Cuinn na mbocht esidhe

Dúnchad, son of Dunadach, lector of Clonmacnoise and its anchorite
afterwards, head of its rule and of its history, died. He was the ancestor of the people of Conn na mBocht.

(6) (i) Dúnadhach (†953) mac Eccertaigh, espucc Cluana mic Nóis ...
[décc].

Dúnadach son of Eccertach, bishop of Clonmacnoise [...] died.

(ii) AFM 898: Caenchomhrac Insi Endoimh, epscop 7 abb
Lughmaidh, aitti Aenacain, mic Eccertaigh 7 Dúnadhaigh, mic
Eccertaigh ó ttat Uí Chuinn na mbocht dég an treas lá fichet Iulí.

Caenchomrac of Inis Endoimh, bishop and abbot of Lughmaidh, the
tutor of Aenacán son of Eccertach and of Dúnadach son of Eccertach
from whom are descended the family of Conn na mBocht, died on the
23rd July.

(iii) AFM 947: Oenacán, mac Eccertaigh, aircindech Eccailsi bicce hi
cCluain mic Nóis, epscop, 7 ógh iodhan, bráthairsidhe Dúnadhaigh,
mic Eccartaigh, do Mughdornaibh Maighen a chenél, 7 a écc.

Aenacán son of Eccertach, erenagh of the Small Church in
Clonmacnoise, bishop and pure virgin, the brother of Dúnadach son of
Eccertach, of the sept of Mugdorna Maigen, died.

(7) Egertach (†893) airchinnech eccailsi bicce, athair Aenacáin 7
Dunadhaigh dég.

Eccertach erenagh of the Small Church, father of Aenacán and
Dúnadach, died.

(8) (i) **Eoghan** (†845) .i. angcoire, mac Aedhagáin, mic Torbaigh, ó Cluain mic Nóis, décc.

Eogan the anchorite, son of Aedagán son of Torbach from Cluain mac Nóis, died.

Tá nóta breise i dtaobh Eoghain in AFM 834, áit a leanann sé fógra báis Aodhagáin:

(ii) **Eoghan** mac Aedhagáin, ro ansidhe hi cCluain mic Nóis, conadh uadha ro chinset Meic Cuinn na mBocht innte.

Eogan son of Aedagán, he remained in Clonmacnoise, and it is from him that the Sons of Conn na mBocht are descended there.

(9) **Aodhagan** (†834) mac Torbaigh, abb Lucchmhaidh, décc ina ailethre i cCluain mic Nóis.

Aedacán son of Torbach, abbot of Louth, died while a pilgrim in Clonmacnoise.

(10) **Torbach** (†807) mac Gormáin, scríbhnidh, leghthóir 7 abb Arda Macha esidhe [décc]. Do Chenel Torbaigh, .i. O Ceallaigh Breagh, 7 ro ba dibhsidhe Conn na mbocht ro baí i cCluain mic Nóis, 7 as aire atbeirthi Conn na mbocht fris, ar a mhéd do bhochtaibh no biathadh do ghrés.

Torbach son of Gormán, scribe, lector, and abbot of Armagh [died]. As to the family of Torbach, i.e., Ó Ceallaigh Breagh. Conn na mBocht who lived in Clonmacnoise was one of them, and the reason why he is called Conn na mBocht is on account of the number of the poor whom he always fed.

(11) **Gorman** (†753) comharba Mochta Lughmhaigh, décc i cCluain mic Nois, ina ailithre, 7 ba heisidhe athair Torbaigh, comharba Padraicc.

Gormán, successor of Mochta of Louth, died in Clonmacnoise on his pilgrimage, and he was the father of Torbach, successor of Patrick.

Ball níos luaithe den gclann chéanna atá anseo is léir:

(12) **Gorman** (†610) do Mughdhornaib, ó ttád Meic Cuinn, asé ro boi bliadhain for uisce Tiobrait Finghin, 7 ina ailitre i cCluain mic Nóis, atbath.

Gormán of the Mughdhorna from whom are the Sons of Conn. It was he who spent a year living on the water of Tiobrat Finghin and he died on his pilgrimage in Clonmacnoise.

Feidhmeannach i gCluain Mhac Nóis a ba ea gach duine díobh seo ó Chéileachair thar n-ais go hEoghan. Níos luaithe ná Eoghan bhí Aodhagán ina ab ar mhainistir Lughmhaidh agus ba é Torbach mac Gormáin scríobhaí, léitheoir, agus ab Aird Mhacha (AFM 807). Níor cuireadh aon oifig le hainm Mhaoil Mhuire, rud a chruthaíonn, is dócha, nach raibh aon phost tábhachtach i gCluain Mhac Nóis aige. Ba í stíl na gCeithre Máistrí an post a bhí ag gach duine a d'ainmnigh siad sna hannála a lua leis. Is eisceacht é Maol Mhuire sa chás seo, sa gcaoi go gceapfainn gur duine óg a bhí i Maol Mhuire nach raibh aon ghradam speisialta bainte amach aige faoin am a maraíodh é. Fianaise eile a threoraíonn sa treo céanna muid, is ea gur mhair a athair, Céileachair, go cionn 28 mblian i ndiaidh bhás Mhaoil Mhuire. Ach níl fáil ar bith ar aon chruinneas ó thaobh a aoise ag uair a bháis.

Maidir leis an dá ainm is deireannaí ar liosta sinsear Mhaoil Mhuire, ba é seo an Torbach mac Gormáin céanna a chuir Feardhomhnach i mbun oibre ag scríobhadh Leabhair Aird Mhacha sa bhliain 807 agus an fear céanna ar scríobh Feardhomhnach a ainm sa leabhar sin.[5] Nach mór an t-ábhar mórtais dóibh go raibh beirt den phór céanna páirteach i scríobhadh an dá lámhscríbhinn ba thábhachtaí i stair na litríochta in Éirinn, Leabhar Aird Mhacha atá tiomnaithe do scéal bheatha Phádraig, aspal na nGael, agus Leabhar na hUidhre, an lámhscríbhinn is sine a bhfuil scéalta as seanchas na nGael le léamh inti. Is léir nach de chosmhuintir Chluain Mhac Nóis ná Aird Mhacha féin Maol Mhuire ach de uaisle an dá mhainistir. Is léir go raibh teagmháil idir mainistreacha ainmiúla i dtuaisceart Laighean agus deisceart Uladh agus Cluain Mhac Nóis ó thús an seachtú haois ar an gcuid is deireannaí de.

Ba de na Mughdhorna sinsear Mhaoil Mhuire. B'shin cine a bhí lonnaithe i limistéar a shín ó lár Cho. Mhuineacháin, go hiarthar Cho. Lú agus go tuaisceart Cho. na Mí. Tá cuntas fairsing ag Hogan ar na Mughdhorna agus ar na tailte a raibh siad ina gcónaí iontu.[6] Is léir go raibh nós ag an dream sin, a raibh cuid dá muintir ina n-ab ar Ard Mhacha dul ar oilithreacht go Cluain Mhac Nóis, go dtí gur fhan Eoghan go buan ann. Ba é sin sinsear a shleachta uaidh sin suas. Cé an líon sleachta léinn den chineál seo atá le haithint i measc scoláirí na meánaoise in Éirinn? Fíorbheagán, cheapfainn. Ábhar taighde do dhuine éigin eile.

5 James Kenney, *The sources for the early history of Ireland: ecclesiastical. An introduction and guide* (athchló: New York, 1966), lch 338. **6** *OnomG* s.n.

The *paruchia* of St Lúrach of Uí Thuirtre

KAY MUHR

In the mid-part of the first millennium, Ulster was divided roughly into three parts. The west was inhabited by Uí Néill, the middle by Airgíalla, descendants of the three Collas, the east by the partly-Cruithin Ulaid, the former rulers of the province. All these peoples had adopted Christianity, according to tradition, from St Patrick's mission in the century before, and according to his *Tripartite Life* several had gained a saint of their own, often royal, blood.[1] There were physical boundaries between the three groups: the river Bann and Lough Neagh in the mid-east, and the river Finn and Lough Foyle in the mid-west,[2] and also the broad range of hills which stretches from the north coast southwards to Lough Erne.[3]

Nevertheless, the Cenél nEógain branch of Uí Néill extended their power eastwards across the hill passes, gradually taking over the smaller kingdoms, and creating what became Tír Eógain, the 'land of Eógan'. In the late sixth century, the battle of Móin Daire Lothair against the Cruithin of the north gained them Aird Eólairg (Magilligan) and (Fir) Lí beside the Bann (*AU* 563). Crossing the hills further south near Ballygawley they won a decisive victory over Airgíalla at the battle of Leth Cam in AD 826,[4] and by the eleventh century they were using the inauguration site of Tullaghoge near Cookstown, in territory originally belonging to Airgíalla.[5] The Uí Néill saint Colum Cille, whose main foundation was Iona in Scotland, gained in prestige in Ireland, and became a considerable rival to the national missionary, Saint Patrick, who was claimed as patron by the Ulaid of Downpatrick and the Airgíalla (Airthir) of Armagh. The history of Colum Cille and his *paruchia* has been ably elucidated by our honorand.

However, as smaller kingdoms were overlaid, earlier cults of local churches and saints often faded away,[6] although the process was in many cases only completed by the Plantation and Protestant reformation of Ireland from England in the seventeenth century. What follows is an attempt, by means of documentary history, topography, place-names, archaeology, fieldwork and

---

1 Díchu, Domangart, Trea: Whitley Stokes (ed. and trans.), *The tripartite Life of St Patrick*, 2 vols (London, 1887), i, pp 36, 52, 168.   2 Éamonn Ó Doibhlin, 'The deanery of Tulach Óg', *Seanchas Ard Mhacha*, 6, i (1971), 141–82 at 153.   3 Now often known as 'The Sperrins' from a long-lost minor rock feature in Glenelly: Brian Lacey, 'County Derry in the early historic period' in G. O'Brien (ed.), *Derry and Londonderry: history and society* (Dublin, 1999), pp 115–48 at p. 123.   4 Kay Muhr, 'Dochiaróg, Mag Enir and Leth Cam', *JCHAS*, 113 (2008), 131–43 at 139.   5 Lacey, 'County Derry in the early historic period', p. 138.   6 Meticulously documented in *DIS*.

local tradition, to retrieve a picture over time of the royal saint and church of one polity that was overlaid, among the Airgíalla in northern central Ulster.

Lúrach was a saint of the line of Colla Úais, descended from Fíachra Tort, ancestor of the group that called itself Uí Thuirtre. Tomás Ó Fiaich identified their kingdom with the northern part of the diocese of Armagh, the plain west of Lough Neagh extending from the river Blackwater between counties Armagh and Tyrone north to the river Bior or Moyola in Co. Derry.[7] Tírechán's seventh-century Life of Saint Patrick says that saint converted Uí Thuirtre, and the later *Tripartite Life* gives the names of seven churches which he is said to have founded, some of which can be identified in the area near Lough Neagh.[8]

The Uí Thuirtre kings were titled kings of Durlas from AD 660–1216, and an earthwork in the townland of Doorless, near Tullaghoge and a little east of Cookstown in Tyrone, has been identified as their royal site.[9] Later Uí Thuirtre moved north-east to mid-Antrim, where the deanery of Turtrye was named after them.[10] The shift began via a new centre nearer the Moyola, a crannóg island on a small lough, Loughinsholin, which later gave name to a barony.[11] The name Loch Inse Uí Fhloinn represents the 'lough' of Ó Floinn, the later surname of the Uí Thuirtre ruling family.[12]

ST TREA OF ARTREA

However, the only local church foundation described in the *Tripartite Life* involves not Uí Thuirtre but a parallel lineage descended from Colla Úais, Uí Meic Caírthinn.[13] When Patrick wished to build a monastic city between Lough Neagh and Slíab Calland (Slieve Gallion), the king of the area, Caírthenn Mór, told him to leave. Instead, Patrick restored and blessed his

---

7 Thomas J. Fee, 'The kingdom of Airgialla and its subkingdoms' (MA, UCD, 1950), p. 169; Pat McKay and Kay Muhr, *Lough Neagh places: their names and origins* (Belfast, 2007), pp 86–7; Gregory Toner, 'County Derry I: The Moyola Valley', *Place-Names of Northern Ireland* v (Belfast, 1996), pp 52–3.   8 Ludwig Bieler (ed. and trans.), *The Patrician texts in the Book of Armagh*, SLH 10 (Dublin, 1979), p. 162 §50; Stokes, *The tripartite Life of St Patrick*, i, p. 168; Ó Doibhlin, 'The deanery of Tulach Óg', 157–63. 9 Diarmuid Ó Murchadha, *The Annals of Tigernach: index of names* (London, 1997), p. 138; Kay Muhr, 'Hogan's *Onomasticon* and the work of the Northern Ireland Place-name Project' in K. Murray and P. Ó Riain (eds), *Edmund Hogan's Onomasticon Goedelicum: reconsiderations*, ITS SS 23 (London, 2011), pp 47–80 at pp 61–4.   10 William Reeves, *Ecclesiastical antiquities of Down, Connor and Dromore* (Dublin, 1847), pp 82n, 292–7. 11 In the townland of Annagh and Moneysterlin, west of Desertmartin (H 8492). 12 Similarly, Maigh Inse Uí Fhloinn is 'O'Flynn's plain': see Toner, 'County Derry I: The Moyola Valley', pp 1–3, 102. The earliest bearer of the surname in the annals was Muiredach Úa Flainn who died in *AU* 1059.   13 'Húi Meic-Cārthind Locha Febail': *CGH* 334a2; see *CGH* 141a9, 333c39.

exiled brother Caírthenn Becc, and consecrated his daughter Trea, who thus became the patron saint of Artrea parish north-east of Cookstown.[14] *Ard Trea* 'The Height of St Trea', is mentioned in the annals at 1127 (*AU*), and in Archbishops' registers from 1455 to 1544. Trea is still remembered in the name of the Catholic church, although the Church of Ireland church on the early site, where earlier ruins can be traced in the graveyard, is now dedicated to St Andrew.[15]

The genealogies generally present Caírthenn, eponym of Uí Meic Caírthinn 'of Lough Foyle', and Fíachra Tort of Uí Thuirtre, as the ancestors of two separate lineages descending from Colla Úais, but the geography of the *Tripartite Life* shows them both in east Tyrone near Lough Neagh.[16] As Éamonn Ó Doibhlin noted, some dynastic dispute must lie behind the account in the *Tripartite Life*.[17]

ST COLMÁN MUCCAID OF ARBOE

A few miles east, another local saint of Caírthenn's line was Colmán Muccaid ('Colmán the swineherd') of the church of Arboe beside Lough Neagh. Colmán was again of the royal line, and dateable to the mid-seventh century, since his son Fergus was king of Uí Meic Caírthinn at his death in *AU* 668. Arboe was named, not from the saint, but from the cow which in local legend appeared from Lough Neagh and allowed her milk to be used to mix the mortar for the building of the church.[18] The abbey of Arboe (with an erenagh recorded in 1103, a burning in 1166, *AU*) has a magnificent carved stone cross from early in the second millennium, the focus of a pilgrimage in early August. In 1727, the pattern still finished with an offering 'for the use of the family descended (as they suppose) from Colman's clerk'.[19]

ST MAC LÍAG OF DRUMGLASS

A Saint Mac Líag of Drumglass parish at Dungannon was also a member of Uí Meic Caírthinn and a nephew of Colmán Muccaid,[20] but he seems totally

---

14 Stokes, *The tripartite Life of St Patrick*, p. 168; Ó Doibhlin, 'The deanery of Tulach Óg', pp 145–6. 15 Ann E. Hamlin, *The archaeology of early Christianity in the north of Ireland*, ed. Thomas Kerr, BAR British series vol. 460 (Oxford, 2008), p. 367. 16 Durlas 'Doorless' is on the boundary of Derryloran and Artrea parishes and there are other boundary references nearby. Cookstown townland was 'the boundary hill': McKay and Muhr, *Lough Neagh places*, p. 99. Desertcreat parish was 'the hermitage of two territories': *MIA* 1195, *AU¹* 1281. 17 Ó Doibhlin, 'The deanery of Tulach Óg', 147. 18 *Ard Bó* 'height of the cow(s)': McKay and Muhr, *Lough Neagh places*, pp 104–5; see references in *HDGP* i, s.n. 'Ard Bó'. 19 McKay and Muhr, *Lough Neagh places*, pp 104–5. 20 *DIS*

forgotten now and the Church of Ireland parish is dedicated to St Anne, the Catholic parish to St Patrick.

SAINTS GÚAIRE OF AGHADOWEY

Further north, we find slightly earlier saintly contemporaries of Colmán Muccaid, of the direct line of Fíachra Tort. These were two saints called Gúaire, cousins a generation apart, in the parish of Aghadowey beside the Bann, situated in Mag Lí.[21] This was the territory of Fir Lí, which extended north of the Moyola to Camus in the parish of Macosquin,[22] and was apparently a kingdom of Airgíalla following the battle of Móin Daire Lothair.[23] The church at Aghadowey was not named after its saints, but their name was preserved in the townland immediately south in the parish, Seygorry, from Suí Gúaire 'The Seat of St Gúaire'.[24] At the time of the Plantation, the name also referred to a full ballibetagh of termon land dedicated to Saint[s] Gúaire.[25] Today, the Church of Ireland parish church remains dedicated to St Gúaire, apparently in name only, while the Catholic church is dedicated to Our Lady of the Assumption.

ST LÚRACH OF MAGHERA

Apparently contemporary with Saints Gúaire was a saint with a pedigree from the Uí Thuirtre royal line, Lúrach.[26] He was a brother of Bécc, *rí Airgiall* 'king of Airgíalla', who was killed in battle in AD 598,[27] and is recorded in the secular genealogies as *Lúrech mac Cuanach ó Ráith Lúrig* 'Lúrach son of Cúanu from Lúrach's rath'.[28] Lúrach's name originally formed part of the parish name Maghera in south Derry, as Machaire Rátha Lúraigh 'the (church-)plain of Lúrach's fort', as can be seen in the study by Gregory Toner.[29]

Lúrach appears in the saints' genealogies, and two later martyrologies,[30] but there is no saint's Life. However, in the Life of St Cainnech (founder of Aghaboe and Kilkenny, whose death is noted in *AU* 599), Lúrach ('Luyrech') receives mention as the bishop who baptized that saint, who was born in Cíanachta, now the barony of Keenaght, Co. Derry, west across the hills from Maghera.[31] The pre-Viking version in the *Codex Salmanticensis*, possibly

p. 418; cf. *CGSH* §310.   21 William Reeves, *Acts of Archbishop Colton in his metropolitan visitation in the diocese of Derry, AD MCCCXCVII, with a rental of the see estates at that time* (Dublin, 1850), p. 80.   22 *Fir Lí ó Bir co Camus: CGH* 333c35.   23 Lacey, 'County Derry in the early historic period', p. 136.   24 C 8420. 'Suidhe-Guaire': Reeves, *Acts of Archbishop Colton*, p. 74 n. z (from John O'Donovan).   25 Ibid., pp 74 n. z, 116.   26 *CGSH* §79.   27 *CGH* 333c46; *AU*.   28 *CGH* 333c51.   29 Toner, 'County Derry I: The Moyola Valley', pp 168–70.   30 *CGSH* §§541, 615, 662.103; *DIS* p. 411 (Feb. 17th).   31 The spot was in Valle Pellis or Glenn Geimen, near Dungiven (Dún Geimen, 'The

adapted from an Irish original, gives more detail: the parents of 'Kannechus' were too poor to keep a cow to provide milk for their child, but on the night of his birth a cow came out of a faraway lake and was led by God to their house. Next a clergyman was lacking, but twelve cattle of bishop 'Lurech' went astray, and his search led him to Cainnech's house.[32]

Maghera was plundered by the Vikings in 832 (*AU*), and it was burned in 1135 (*AFM*). The ruins of the medieval church still stand in the townland of Largantogher, and the earliest sections belong to the twelfth century.[33] As with the cross at Arboe, the old church site contains evidence of its former importance in the probably twelfth-century carved lintel stone depicting the Crucifixion.[34]

In his discussion of the element *ráth* 'ring-fort' in the place-name, Toner suggested that Maghera could have been the centre of the kingdom held by seven descendants of Cúanu, Lúrach's father, as kings of Airgíalla:

> This same tract states that they ruled all of Airgialla from their fort (*ráth*). The editor of the genealogies is almost certainly correct in taking this to be a common noun meaning 'fort' rather than a proper name, but there is considerable circumstantial evidence to suggest that the fort was indeed situated at *Ráth Lúraigh* or Maghera. In one of the manuscripts, Lúrach mac Cuanach is said to have been from *Ráith*, which indicates a shorter, possibly earlier, form of the name (the other MSS have the longer form).[35]

Maghera was incorporated in 1111 into the diocese of Cinéal Eoghain, the seat of which was placed at Ardstraw. About 1150 under Muireadhach Ó Cobhthaigh, a native, it achieved prominence as a bishop's seat, but in 1254 the seat was transferred to Derry. Maghera decreased in importance after this date but it was still frequently mentioned in ecclesiastical documents of the 15th century.[36]

Fort of the Hide / Skin'): *VSHP* i, p. 152 §i; Pat McKay, *A dictionary of Ulster place-names* (Belfast, 1999; revised 2007), p. 64.   **32** Máire Herbert, 'The *Vita Columbae* and Irish hagiography: a study of *Vita Cainnechi*' in J. Carey, M. Herbert and P. Ó Riain (eds), *Studies in Irish hagiography: saints and scholars* (Dublin, 2001), pp 31–40 at p. 32; Charles de Smedt and Joseph Backer (eds), *Acta sanctorum Hiberniae: ex codice Salmanticensi* (Edinburgh / London, 1888), §§1–3, cols 361–2 (= *VSHH* p. 182).   **33** Hamlin, *The archaeology of early Christianity in the north of Ireland*, pp 275–8.   **34** Oliver Crilly, 'The Christ of Maghera: a preliminary study of the lintel of the old church of St Lurach at Maghera, County Derry' in H. Jefferies and C. Devlin (eds), *History of the diocese of Derry* (Dublin, 1999), pp 73–84.   **35** *CGH* 333c40–46; Toner, 'County Derry I: The Moyola Valley', p. 168: first referring to the line in verse reading *ro gabsat ónd ráith roglaiss* (*CGH* 333c41). A few lines later, MS **La** has *Lúrech m. Cuanach o Ráith* only, while other MSS include the personal name: *Ráith Lúrig*; *CGH* 333c51.   **36** Toner, 'County Derry I: The Moyola Valley', p. 168.

THE FADING OF LÚRACH IN LOCAL TRADITION

The name of Lúrach's church, attested as Ráith Lúraigh in the annals until 1320, was early anglicized as 'Rathloury' (1397), and 'Rathlory' (1435). However, the modern settlement name Machaire Rátha (Maghera) replaced it from 1609, although an Irish form including the saint's name, 'Machuire Rath Luraidh', was still being quoted in the late seventeenth century.[37]

In 1813, the Church of Ireland curate, Reverend John Graham, quoted the saint's name in English and Latin as 'St Luroc or Laurochus', 'said to have been the patron of the cathedral church of Maghera'. He continued, 'His festival or patron day was formerly observed on the 17 February, but is now neglected, as well as many other holidays more worthy of observation'.[38] In 1834, John O'Donovan described the place-name as 'the plain of Rath-Lúry', and called the saint 'St Luroch'.[39]

The earlier saint's name seems to have been kept up among the educated, since the Church of Ireland parish church is still St Lurach's today.[40] However, the fading of local memory of the saint is also attested in the *Ordnance survey memoirs*, where, in its mountainous parts and in Ballinascreen,[41] Maghera was said to be one of nine local churches founded by St Colum Cille 'though the more immediate residents of the town of Maghera would give St Laurence O'Quin or Bradley the credit of founding these institutions … some assert on tradition that St Laurence was Abbot in Maghera in the 12th century'.[42] Veneration for St Laurence, an early martyr, is attested in the Lives of St Patrick.[43] There was an Irish St Laurence in the twelfth century, in the person of St Laurence O'Toole, but perhaps more relevant is the evidence of fifteenth- and sixteenth-century devotion to the martyr Laurence in the decoration of the shrines of St Caillín and St Maodhóg in west Ulster.[44] The long-standing Co. Derry ecclesiastical family

37 Ibid., p. 169. 38 Statistical account of the parish of Maghera written by its curate Revd John Graham in 1812–13, ed. William Shaw Mason, *A statistical account, or parochial survey of Ireland: drawn up from the communications of the clergy*, 3 vols (Dublin / London / Edinburgh, 1814–19), i, pp 575–619. Reprinted as idem, *Extracts from a statistical account or parochial survey of Ireland* (Ballinascreen Historical Society, 2001), p. 21. 39 Graham Mawhinney (ed.), *John O'Donovan's letters from County Londonderry (1834)* (Ballinascreen Historical Society, 1992), p. 57. 40 Although acknowledging faith 'built on Lurach's sixth-century foundations', the Catholic church is dedicated to St Patrick: <http://www.derrydiocese.org/maghera.asp> [accessed Nov. 2013]. 41 Angélique Day and Patrick McWilliams (eds), *Ordnance survey memoirs of Ireland*, 40 vols (Belfast, 1990–98), xxxi, pp 9, 24: 'According to tradition … [Ballynascreen] is the central one of the nine churches founded by St Columbkille, viz. Ballynascreen, Desertlyn, Desertcreat, *Tarmonmcgurk, Killylagh*, Bodoney, Magherafelt, Maghera, and Dungiven'. 42 Day and McWilliams, *Ordnance survey memoirs*, xviii, p. 39. 'Lawrence Bradley' also named on p. 57. 43 Bieler, *The Patrician texts in the Book of Armagh*, p. 122 §II 3; Stokes, *The tripartite Life of St Patrick*, i, p. 238. 44 Raymond Gillespie, 'Relics, reliquaries and hagiography in south

of Ó Brolcháin, anglicized as Bradley, were well-known as priests locally, and there were priests called O'Quin ('Ó Choinne') in Tyrone.

Although the old church in Maghera had been abandoned in 1819, memory remained most vivid in the area around the church and rectory. 'St Lawrence' had the 'most ancient tomb in the graveyard', an undated slab with a much-weathered 'ringed cross'.[45] In 1829, the grave was opened and robbed by two apparent 'gentlemen' and a silver cross was found and taken away. The deposition made afterwards by a local witness called the saint 'Saint Lorny', a local abbreviation for Laurence.[46]

However, Reverend Graham recorded the original name of the parish as 'Magher-na-dra' ('The Field of Vespers'), and in 1837 the Vesper Field was used for the rector's garden where foundations of ruins had been uncovered, 'the site of an old abbey founded by St Lowrie'.[47]

TOBAR LÚRAIGH

The saint's name was not only attached to the name of the parish and early church, but also to a holy well. Further tradition said that the monks of the abbey 'applied to St Lowrie' who miraculously opened for them 'the well in the town still known by the name of Tober Lowrie'... 'a good clear spring, and emits all year round a plentiful supply'.[48] One writer recorded the re-interpreted name, but in Irish: 'that ancient Spring well which is the chief support of the town ... dedicated to his name and called in the Irish language Tobbar- nieve Lourass or "St Laurence's well"'.[49] Another writer recorded: 'St Tobberlowrie is said to have been the founder of the old church ... The town of Maghera is supplied with excellent water from Tobberlowrie's well, which is situated at the end of Miss Paterson's house nearly opposite the hotel'.[50] Here 'St Tobberlowrie' had been created out of the name of the well, in Irish Tobar Lúraigh. The well-site was marked in Largantogher townland on the 2nd edition Ordnance Survey 6-inch map as 'Toberlowry', but, as the Northern Ireland Sites and Monuments Record describes:

No precise spot is indicated. A report of 1981 located the well in an entry of[f] Main St. It was covered over, but its position well known

Ulster, 1450–1550' in R. Moss, C. Ó Clabaigh and S. Ryan (eds), *Art and devotion in later medieval Ireland* (Dublin, 2006), pp 184–201 at pp 188–94.   **45** Day and McWilliams, *Ordnance survey memoirs*, xviii, pp 9, 57; Hamlin, *The archaeology of early Christianity in the north of Ireland*, p. 277.   **46** A.K. Morrison and S.D. Lytle, 'Some notes on the parish of Maghera and neighbourhood, in the county of Derry', *UJA*, 8 (1902), 129–31 at 130–1.   **47** Shaw Mason, *Extracts from a statistical account or parochial survey of Ireland*, p. 1; Day and McWilliams, *Ordnance survey memoirs*, xviii, pp 1, 10.   **48** Day and McWilliams, *Ordnance survey memoirs*, xviii, p. 10.   **49** Ibid., p. 39.   **50** Ibid., p. 57.

and there was a tradition that whoever drank the water would have to return to Maghera. The site (at C 8528000400) is not now visible and the area is being developed.[51]

'It is a pity to obliterate such an ancient and celebrated landmark' was already the opinion in 1902, when the well, for long 'the principal water supply of the town', was threatened with being closed up and a pump placed over it.[52]

ST LOURY'S WELL IN DRUMACHOSE

St Lúrach of Maghera also appears to have been commemorated in another holy well, called on the Ordnance Survey map 'St Loury's Well', sixteen miles NNW of Maghera over the hills, in the parish of Drumachose and townland of Ballycrum. The site, high on a hillside, has a wonderful view westward to the Foyle. As described by the Northern Ireland Sites and Monuments Record: 'The well is a spring which emerges from a steep E-W slope. There is no sign of a surrounding enclosure or other early Christian feature. At the well is a large oak tree. The well itself has a modern concrete cover and sill'.[53] The author and Brian Lambkin visited the well on Whitsunday 19 May 2013, finding that several local people knew about it, some from former parish priest Fr T.P. Donnelly, but none had visited it. They warned that it was on the land of a farmer who was 'not of the same kind'. The landowner, John Oliver, was a little gruff about being bothered by people led to his well by the map, but said it was the most precious thing on the farm to him because it supplies both house and fields with water. He agreed to show us the way, across a ford in the stream above his farmhouse.

At the gate into the fields beyond, Mr Oliver asked us to pick out the well, now marked only by the stump of an ash tree. According to Mr Oliver, when the tree was young, rags used to be left on it by pilgrims, who believed that as the rag rotted away, so did the disease they were suffering from. The well, channelled into a cistern by his father or grandfather who bought the farm, lies below the stump at the top of a scatter of stones, some quite large. The water is piped all round the house and farm, including at one time to a cottage near the well and another further downhill.

Fr Donnelly used to bring groups of old men up to the well, an outing he obviously felt would benefit them. Mr Oliver had taken many believing people up himself, sometimes returning to the area from afar. One elderly

---

51 *NISMR: Northern Ireland Sites and Monuments Record*, a public database (a section of the Monuments and Buildings Record) of the Northern Ireland Environment Agency. <http://www.doeni.gov.uk/niea/built-home/recording/sites_monuments.htm Site LDY036:023>.
52 Morrison and Lytle, 'Some notes on the parish of Maghera', p. 129. **53** *NISMR* LDY 010.012 at C7415022350.

lady had come regularly and he had taken her up on his motor scooter and filled bottles of the water for her. He is unconvinced of its healing power but respectful, and we were grateful to him and his son for their courtesy, and their obvious pride in the well.

The Olivers knew the name Toberloury, but the name seems partly to have been revived. Oral tradition of the well recorded in the *Ordnance survey memoirs* retained no memory of the saint:

> In the townland of Ballycrum in the south-eastern part of the parish is a holy well called Tobar Loora. In former times people from the neighbourhood repaired to this well to be cured of all kinds of bodily diseases ... At the departure of the invalid, a rag from some part of his clothes was always left at the well, in the hopes of putting the disorder away with it.[54]

The account mentions prayers and washing the affected part, with the sighting of two trout in the well being a good omen of a cure. However, a local landlord had roasted one of the trout, after which he went blind and the other trout disappeared.

> The aforesaid practice of stations by adults was much neglected since the removal of the trouts, and the only persons who now visit the above well at May and Midsummer is back-going or sickly children. Whatever saint the above well had been anciently dedicated to is not now known. But it has been subsequently called after the first disorder it was first known to cure: Tober Loora is 'the leprosy well'.[55]

However, some tradition had clearly been maintained locally, linked with the patron of Drumachose parish, St Cainnech. Bishop Reeves noted that it had been in a union of three parishes called Termonconny or Tearmann Cainnigh, 'Cainnech's sanctuary', since Cainnech was born near Drumachose.[56] According to local tradition recorded more recently, the baptism of St Cainnech by St Lúrach in Cíanachta already quoted was in the well called Toberloury in Ballycrum.[57]

SOME COMMENT ON THE NAME LÚRACH

The sources generally omit a length mark on the *u*, and pronunciation with short *u* is common local practice today.[58] Lúrach's name is unusual; it may

54 Day and McWilliams, *Ordnance survey memoirs*, ix, pp 56–7.   55 Ibid., p. 109.   56 Reeves, *Acts of Archbishop Colton*, pp 39, 132 (cf. idem, *Ecclesiastical antiquities*, p. 374).   57 Alfred Moore Munn, *Notes on the place-names of the parishes and townlands of the county of Londonderry* (Derry, 1925; repr. Ballinascreen Historical Society, 1985), p. 141.   58 Ciarán J. Devlin, *The*

derive from the adjective *lúar* 'fierce' attested in the O'Clery and O'Mulconry glossaries, *luar .i. borb*.[59] Anglicizing Loury [lauri] from genitive 'Lúraigh' is regular if the *u* is long (compare Co. Down from Irish *dún*). Although the saint's name of the well in Drumachose was not remembered by local people in the 1830s, their re-interpretation of the name Tober Loora as 'the leprosy well' (Tobar Lobhra) also suggests a long vowel.

ST LÚARÁN OF DERRYLORAN

A saint with a very similar name, Lúarán, was formerly patron of the Tyrone church and parish of Derryloran, Doire Lúaráin ('Lúarán's oakwood'), 17 miles south of Maghera in the old Uí Thuirtre heartland now dominated by Cookstown.[60] Lúarán appears in the saints' genealogies, without reference to a father, but as one of fifteen bishop sons of his mother, St Patrick's legendary sister Dar Erca. Two brothers with alliterating names are quoted together: *Luran Duanaire o Daire Lurain et Loorn o Cill Chunnu*,[61] 'Lúrán of the poem-book from Derryloran and Loarn of Kilcoony'. 'Cill Chunnu' is likely to refer to a lost church five miles further south in Ballyclog parish, at the townland of Kilcoony, which is no longer church land.[62] However, the cult of a St Mochonna was known around Lough Neagh, including references to a woman doctor 'Coney' at Kilcoony and Coney Island in the Lough, and the church of Cill Chonna is referred to in *AFM* 732 and in a later poem on Armagh.[63] Conna may be a hypocoristic of Cainnech.[64]

The information to be gleaned about Lúarán is complementary to what is recorded of Lúrach. Lúarán's mother links him to the traditions of St Patrick and the Patrician churches in Uí Thuirtre, and his paired brother may be another attempt to make sense of his unusual name, connecting him to another local church, as well as St Loarn, bishop, succeeding Patrick, of Durlas or Bright in Co. Down.[65]

The contents of the *Dúanaire* or poem-book (cited above) are unknown, but literary activity at Derryloran is corroborated in the medieval Irish text *Auraicept na n-éces* 'The scholar's primer'. In its formal introduction, its author is named as Cend Fáelad son of Oilill, who lost his 'brain of forgetting' after sustaining a head wound in the battle of Mag Roth (*AU* 637), and its place of composition is named as Derryloran.[66]

---

making of medieval Derry (Dublin, 2013), p. 186. **59** *DIL* s.v.; Donnchadh Ó Corráin and Fidelma Maguire, *Gaelic personal names* (Dublin, 1981), p. 125. **60** Many thanks to Emma Nic Cárthaigh for showing me her place-name references from *HDGP* vii (forthcoming). The original form could be Doire Luráin or Doire Lúráin. See below, p. 241. **61** *CGSH* §722.16. **62** See McKay and Muhr, *Lough Neagh places*, p. 97; *HDGP* iii, s.n. 'Ceall Chunna'. **63** McKay and Muhr, *Lough Neagh places*, pp 86, 90, 97. **64** Alternatively, cf. *AU* 726: *Du-Chonna Craibdech episcopus Condere*. **65** Stokes, *The tripartite Life of St Patrick*, i, pp 38–40; Reeves, *Ecclesiastical antiquities*, pp 35n, 142. **66** George Calder (ed. and

Lúarán has a different commemoration day, 29 October, in the saints' calendars, but the similarity of the names and proximity of the churches of
Lúarán and Lúrach has not escaped notice. J.R. Walsh, writing on the early
church in Co. Derry, thought that 'Lurach was probably a product of
Derryloran', founding 'Maghera in Fir Lí' among relations.[67] Pádraig Ó Riain
makes the link straightforwardly, saying of Lúrach of Maghera, '[u]nder the
guise of Lúrán (Lúarán, Lúrach) [he was] patron of the Tyrone church of
Derryloran (*Doire Lúráin*)'.[68] Ciarán Devlin agreed, quoting the *Martyrology
of Donegal* which uses both forms of the name, with paternal descent:
'Lurach, of the POEMS, son of Cuana, of Doire Lurain'.[69]

Since Hogan's *Onomasticon* in 1910, Derryloran has also achieved false
fame by being confused with Móin [mór] Daire Lothair, site of the defeat of
the northern Cruithin in *AU* 563. Under the heading Móin Daire Lothair,
Hogan did not directly name Derryloran as the site, although he located the
battle at Moneymore in 'Derryloran parish'.[70] In a less-considered note on
Doire Lothuir, he suggested 'Derryloran in Ultonia'.[71] One version of the
annals (*ATig.*) attributes a poem on the battle to Cend Fáelad, which may
have strengthened the presumption. The annal entry mentions '[Fir] Lí' and
'Aird Eolairg' (Magilligan) and the poem references 'Eilne', so that Reeves
located the battle in the old kingdom of Eilne, near Coleraine.[72] Ciarán Devlin
would also place the battle nearer 'the scene of the action', suggesting
Loughermore in north-west Co. Derry.[73] Not only is Derryloran too far south
but, if the identity of Lúrán and Lúrach is correct, the place-name Daire
Lúaráin is unlikely to have existed at the time of the battle.

Many generations later, there are records of erenaghs at Derryloran in
1123 and 1136, and an attack on the church of 'Doire Loráin' is noted in
MIA 1195. Both place and saint were referred to in 1541, 'the perpetual vic-
arage of St Luran, abbot of *Dereluran*'.[74] Physically, nothing early remains at
Derryloran, where the presumed medieval church site is occupied by the
ruins of a Plantation church, abandoned in 1822, beside the Ballinderry river
in Derryloran Glebe, adjacent to the townland now renamed Kirktown or
Derryloran. However, Cend Fáelad's link to Derryloran adds focus to another

trans.), *Auraicept na n-éces: the scholars' primer* (Edinburgh, 1917; repr. Dublin, 1995), pp
67–9. For Cend Fáelad, see Proinsias Mac Cana, 'The three languages and the three laws',
StC, 5 (1970), 62–78. **67** J.R. Walsh, 'The early church' in Jefferies and Devlin, *History
of the diocese of Derry*, pp 30–48 at p. 46. **68** *DIS* p. 411. **69** Devlin, *The making of
medieval Derry*, p. 187 n. 62; James H. Todd and William Reeves (ed. and trans.), *The
martyrology of Donegal: a calendar of the saints of Ireland* (Dublin, 1864), pp 52–3.
70 *OnomG* s.n.; Moneymore is actually in Artrea parish. **71** *OnomG* s.n. **72** William
Reeves (ed. and trans.), *The Life of St Columba, founder of Hy, written by Adamnan* (Dublin
and Edinburgh, 1857), p. 32 n. c. **73** Devlin, *The making of medieval Derry*, pp 33, 84.
74 Laurence P. Murray, 'A calendar of the register of Primate George Dowdall, commonly
called the "Liber Niger" or "Black Book"', *Journal of the County Louth Archaeological
Society*, 6, ii (1926), 90–100 at 97.

early reference, in a verse attributed to him, on the death of an Uí Thuirtre king, Máel Fothartaig, a great-grandson of Bécc, who was taken in his shroud *do Dhairiu* in *AU* 669.[75] Often interpreted as 'to (London)derry', Devlin was convinced that this place must be Daire Lúaráin (Derryloran), which, if Lúarán is the royal saint Lúrach mac Cúanach, seems appropriate for the burial of a king of Uí Thuirtre.[76]

Both replacement churches, Catholic and Church of Ireland, are dedicated to St Lúarán or Luran, but the only fragment of local tradition about him was recorded by a Fr Bernard Mooney, from a local scholar Joseph Mooney who died about 1860, and now published online thanks to Monsignor Réamonn Ó Muirí.[77] When Catholic burial in the old graveyard became difficult, due to local Protestant hostility, the mourners would carry the coffin to the top of a high mound in the crossroads outside the church, and the priest would read the burial service there. The mound was surmounted by a 'giant oak tree, which tradition said was planted by St Lúaran and his monks'.[78]

THE NAME LÚARÁN

Once again the personal and place-name need to be considered together. As at Tober Loora, there is evidence of the re-interpretation of the place-name Derryloran to mean 'The Leper's Oakwood', in the reference in *AU* 1123 to the death of an erenagh: *Mael-Muire hUa Condubhán, airchinnech Daire Lubhrain* (the location confirmed by the others in the obit list all being northern). *Lubhra* is a variant of *lobhra* 'leprosy, weakness, infirmity', but only Ó Dónaill has *lobhrán* 'leper, weakling, afflicted person'. There is a Tipperary saint called *Lobhrán* 'little infirm one',[79] and this also seems to have been the interpretation here.

Alternatively, there are other words in the dictionaries, in Irish *larán* 'pretty female child', or 'stripling'; *lorán* 'weak young creature' or 'impish child';[80] while in Scottish Gaelic more positively *luran* is an endearment, 'pretty or beloved youth or boy', as in the traditional lullaby *Ho mo luran*.[81] Earlier the word *lurán* meant 'foal', a derivative of *láir* 'mare', and could be used pejoratively of feeble humans, also as *lorán* 'poor, weak or miserable person'.[82] This word seems to be the origin of another personal-name example: the poor boy Luran, *Luranus parvus puer*, who was drowned in Lough

---

75 *CGH* 141a39. Cenfaelad, *sapiens*, died in *AU* 679.   **76** Devlin, *The making of medieval Derry*, p. 151.   **77** <http://www.cookstownparish.com/2010/08/st-luarans-church/> [accessed Oct. 2013].   **78** Mound possibly still shown on the 6-inch OS map (1859). **79** *DIS* p. 399: also later interpreted as 'Lawrence'.   **80** See entries in *FGB*; Niall Ó Dónaill, *Foclóir Gaeilge-Béarla* (Baile Átha Cliath, 1998).   **81** See entry in Edward Dwelly, *The illustrated Gaelic-English dictionary* (6th ed. Glasgow, 1967), p. 610; words at: <http://www.bbc.co.uk/alba/oran/orain/ho_mo_luran/> [accessed August 2013].   **82** *DIL* s.vv.

Erne and revived by St Molaise, and who could possibly be the 'Luran mac Conan' mentioned in the notes to *Félire Óengusso*.[83] In a Scottish Gaelic folktale, Luran was the name the fairies used for a man whose cow they were carrying off and who could not catch them up to retrieve her.[84]

Association of the personal names Lúrach and Lúarán with sickness and feebleness may have contributed to the fading of the saint's significance in later times. However, his earlier importance is attested by further place-names, not all surviving to the present: Dounlaran, Seyloran, Lislooran, and Killoran.

DOUNLARAN / DERRYLORAN

Within the parish of Derryloran, there seems to have been another land unit, now obsolete, named after Lúarán. This was 'Dounlaran' (*Dún Lúaráin* 'Lúarán's hillfort') among the nine church lands held by the Ó Mealláin erenagh family, forming the district or termon called Meallánacht ('Melanaght'), at the north end of Cookstown. As shown on the Escheated Counties map in 1609, Dounlaran lies adjacent to the townlands of 'Corucrigagh' (Cookstown townland), 'neLongie' (Loy), 'b:molune' (Maloon), 'keiluama' (Killymam), and 'Contreagh' (Coolreaghs).[85] This links it geographically with the north-western part of Cookstown townland in the north of the town, while the list of 'bishopp lands' of Derryloran held by planter Dr Allan Cooke in 1654 still included 'Dunlorin'.[86] However, the 'high-status' fort after which it was named cannot now be identified, although some earthworks survive in the area.[87]

SEYLORAN, CLONFEACLE

Thirteen miles further south, beyond Dungannon, is Seyloran townland, on the northern edge of the parish of Clonfeacle, between Grange, a church townland on the Escheated Counties map, and the church lands of the parish of Killyman.[88] Although the status of 'Sillawran' was unclear on the 1609 map, Seyloran was owned in 1654 by Sir Toby Caulfield who had been granted the church lands of Clonfeacle in 1619.[89] Nollaig Ó Muraíle agreed with Liam Ó Ceallaigh in saying, 'Is é atá sa dara cuid den ainm an t-ainm

---

83 *VSHP* ii, p. 137 §xxv (see index, p. 324); *Fél.* p. 144 (2 June).   84 Told by Calum Johnston (Barra), recorded by Donald Archie MacDonald in 1965, and printed in *Tocher*, 13 (1974), 172–4, with translation by Alan Bruford.   85 *Barony maps of the escheated counties in Ireland, AD 1609*, 28 maps, PRO London. Published as *The Irish historical atlas*, Sir Henry James, Ordnance Survey (Southampton, 1861), map 13: part near Dungannon. 86 Robert C. Simington (ed.), *The civil survey A.D. 1654–1656*, 10 vols, Irish Manuscripts Commission (Dublin, 1931–61), iii: counties of Donegal, Londonderry and Tyrone, p. 290. 87 Deirdre Flanagan, 'Settlement terms in Irish place-names', *Onoma*, 17 (1972–3), 157–69 at 159. Cf. *NISMR* TYR 029:004: forts forming part of a 'wider early Christian landscape'. 88 *Barony maps of the escheated counties*, map 13. 89 Simington, *The civil survey*, iii, p. 272.

pearsanta céanna atá le fáil in ainm an pharóiste, *Doire Lúráin*, in oirthuaisceart Thír Eoghain. *Suí Luaráin* "(St) Loran's seat or dwelling" atá ag L O
C'.[90] The element *suí* 'seat' in place-names usually refers to a small hill with
a view, and there is one here, at H 8459, at a bend of the river Rhone.

LISLOORAN, BALLYCLOG?

Moving northwards again, another lost local place-name seems to refer to the
saint. This is 'Lislooran' in the contents of the grange of 'Ardaghearan alias
Ballinleah near Ballicloige', belonging to the abbey of Saints Peter and Paul in
Armagh, which follows the grange of Tullaghoge in the sources.[91] The identification of church lands is often difficult, but the Peter and Paul lands are particularly tricky to situate, as many of the names listed refer to subdivisions of
townlands.[92] This grange is hard to locate, but it seems likely that the name
'Ballinleah' refers to the church townland now called Leck in the parish of
Ballyclog, which was referred to as 'Balleleck al. Ballineleagh' in 1633.[93] The
part of the grange called Lislooran must be Lios Lúaráin, 'Lúarán's Ringfort'.

KILLORAN, BODONEY

Finally, 13 miles north-west of Cookstown and 12 miles south-west of
Maghera, is an enigmatic upland site at the top of the Glenelly valley, which
provides a routeway into west Tyrone. Killoran is sited on the valley floor, at
a bend of the Glenelly river where it is joined by the stream from Altaloran
Glen (H 6693). The confluence is the townland boundary between three
townlands. The hill of Carnanelly (height 562m) at the top of Altaloran Glen
is 'little cairn of the lookout point', Carnán Aichle.[94] It indeed provides a
magnificent view, north-east over the hills across the Bann plain to Slemish
and the Antrim hills, north past Sawel to the hills of north Derry, west down
the Glenelly routeway to Donegal, and south east past Slieve Gallion to
Lough Neagh and the hills of south Armagh. Carnanelly has given name to
the whole Glenelly valley, 'glen of the lookout point'.[95] The ancient importance of the area is shown by the megalithic monument known as the Goles
stone row, beside the present road through Glenelly, which points to the

90 Nollaig Ó Muraíle, 'Ainmneacha na mbailte fearainn i seanpharóiste Chluain Fiacla: notes
on the townland names of the old parish of Clonfeacle', *Dúiche Néill*, 4 (1989), 32–40 at 38.
91 James Hardiman (ed.), *Inquisitionum in officio rotulorum cancellariae Hiberniae asservatorum
repertorium*, vol. ii: Ulster (Dublin, 1829), Tyrone §1 (Jac. I, 1614).   **92** See the comment
on names in the Peter and Paul granges of Navan and Creeveroe, Armagh, in Kay Muhr,
'The early place-names of Co. Armagh', *Seanchas Ard Mhacha*, 19, i (2002), 1–54 at 14–16.
93 Hardiman, *Inquisitionum in officio rotulorum*, ii, Tyrone (§40 Car. I).   **94** McKay, *A
dictionary of Ulster place-names*, p. 75.   **95** Ibid.: *Gleann Aichle; AU* 856: *i nGlinn Foichle*.

crescent-shaped depression on the summit of Carnanelly, although the actual cairn on the mountain is a little way to the east.

Killoran is included because of its name, which corroborates local tradition that it is a saint's grave, while the Northern Ireland Sites and Monuments Record describes it as the remains of a cairn, in an area liable to flooding used for grazing: 'The site consists of a roughly polygonal, flat-topped & grass covered mound ... There is no apparent structure visible, but some large stones were noted in the adjacent field banks'.[96] The site was marked with its name on the Ordnance Survey 6-inch map in 1859, and again in 1908, but it is not marked now and the name Killoran has been forgotten in the vicinity. Local tradition in English now calls the site St Cormack's Grave, or the Saint's Cook's Grave after the same early cleric. This reflects the story in the *Tripartite Life* of the Airgíalla saint Cormac left by Saint Patrick in Bodoney.[97]

Visiting the spot on 31 August 2013, the author and Brian Lambkin found a gated track down to good level pasture across a modernized ford in the Glenelly river. Prominent beside the confluence is a tall steep mound, but this, containing little stone, is probably a natural feature, possibly part of a hill spur cut off by floods. Within the river bend surrounded by pasture fields are the ruins of a three-room stone cottage and outbuildings. A stone wall partly tumbled and earth-covered encloses the ruins and most of the land in the bend, with the bank also strengthened with stone. The wall crosses from the cottage to the east bank of the river, but a grassy bank encloses more grazing land north of the cottage within the bend. At the west corner of this is what looks at first like a small three-cornered field, with a tree and bushes growing on its banks, but in fact is the potential archaeological site.

Glenelly suffered a great flood on 26 June 1680, as described in a collection of reports in the British Library:

> It hath not only tore up a mountain of near 200 acres, but the cloud breaking thereon hath carried away several houses and families inasmuch that of men, women and children already above thirty [?corpses] are found ... All fish for several miles up the river is destroyed by the blackness and muddiness of the waters which the surface of the mountain made.[98]

This was quoted in an article in a local newspaper, at another time of destructive flooding in 1965. The author also reported that:

> According to tradition only one spot in the Glenelly valley escaped. It appears that ... the floodwaters by-passed 'The Wee Kill' or 'The Saint's Grave' located at Alt-a-Loraan in Upper Badoney, the reputed burial place of St. Patrick's cook St. Aitchen, alias St Cormac.[99]

96 *NISMR* TYR 013:002, 'Giant's Grave, Killoran' at H6656094570.   97 Stokes, *The tripartite Life of St Patrick*, i, p. 264.   98 British Library System number 002253468. 99 G.M. McNamara in the *Ulster Herald*, 31 July, 1965.

It seems possible that the small raised field represents a cairn denuded both by flood waters and removal of some of the stone. Returning from our inspection, we met sheep-farmer Anne Mulholland who has inherited the land. She told us the cottage had been lived in by a Mr Brown, later ident-ified as Barney Brown, a traditional singer.[100]

Barney Brown might have remembered the name Killoran, no doubt anglicized from *cill* 'church' plus a saint's name beginning with either a vowel or *L*. There is a far-away Killoran in Sligo belonging to a woman saint Lúaithrinn.[101] Other possibilities are Cill Odhráin, 'Oran's Church', from a companion of St Colum Cille, or Cill Lúaráin, from the saint of Derryloran, east of the hills. Cill Odhráin seems unlikely since the parish church of Bodoney in the lower Glenelly valley was said to be founded by St Patrick.[102] I would suggest we have a Cill Lúaráin ('Lúarán's Church') and Alt Chille Lúaráin ('Steep Glen of Lúarán's Church') here, just over the watershed on the routeway west from Uí Thuirtre. Killoran is some distance from the church of Bodoney parish, and might represent a refuge for travellers, or an upland hermitage connected with the saint of Derryloran, away from the royal centre of Durlas near Cookstown; just as Toberloury at Ballycrum was linked with the saint, there called Lúrach, of the royal centre of Maghera.

CONCLUSION

The place-names Maghera / Rathloury (Machaire Rátha Lúraigh), Toberloury, Derryloran, Seyloran, 'Dunlorin' and 'Lislooran' (now obsolete), and Killoran record an important early seventh-century saint, a member of the contemporary ruling family of Uí Thuirtre, the memory of whom has now been overlaid by traditions of saints cultivated by, or who retained the devotion of, those with political influence later. These place-names reveal the extent of his cult across the mid-Ulster plain, west of Lough Neagh and the Lower Bann, with two outliers near routes across the hills to the west. Centred on what are now the two towns of Maghera and Cookstown, the area stretched north to south for some forty miles, across the hills to Keady Mountain in the north-west, Bodoney in the west, and to Clonfeacle parish in the south.

The compiled dossier of St Lúrach or Lúarán emphasizes the significance of Maghera, Derryloran and Doorless within the first-millennium Uí Thuirtre kingdom, and corrects the notion that Daire Lúaráin named from the saint *c.*600 is connected with the site of the battle of Móin Daire Lothair further north a generation earlier. Likewise, it becomes clear that the simplex place-name Daire in the first millennium need not always refer to Derry on the Foyle.[103] Local

---

100 Thanks to Rose Mary Murphy, Michael McCormack, Pat O'Donnell and Claire Lawlor Kilgallen. 101 *DIS* p. 406. 102 Stokes, *The tripartite Life of St Patrick*, i, pp 154, 264. 103 Other examples are Molua Daire and Mochonna Daire, an epithet which may link these saints with Ballinderry in Co. Antrim: McKay and Muhr, *Lough Neagh*

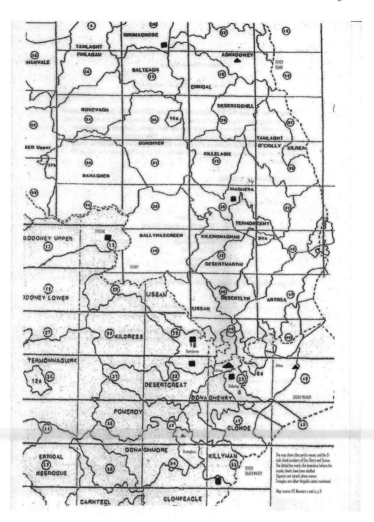

Fig. 1: The 'paruchia of St Lúrach', west and north of Lough Neagh

investigation to fill out academic research on early texts is still productive, largely thanks to the endurance and mnemonic significance of names.[104]

The map shows relevant parishes and their names with 6-inch sheet numbers for Cos Derry and Tyrone. The dotted line marks the boundary where the county sheets have been abutted. Squares locate Lúrach place-names mentioned, triangles locate place-names referring to other related saints of Airgialla. The source of the map is Day and McWilliams, *Ordnance survey memoirs* v and xi, p. 6.

---

places, p. 36.   **104** Work for 'a gleaner rather than a reaper': Hamlin, *The archaeology of early Christianity in the north of Ireland*, pp 3, 5.

The dating of *Branwen*: the 'Irish question' revisited

KEVIN MURRAY

The most recent translator of the *Mabinogi* remarks that 'although the general consensus is that the tales were first committed to writing between *c.*1060 and 1120, nothing is certain'.[1] The 'general consensus' that gives *c.*1060 as the *terminus post quem* for the writing of the tales is based primarily on the arguments presented by Thomas Charles-Edwards in an appendix to his influential article on the dating of the *Mabinogi* penned in 1970.[2] Although not accepting the earlier case made by Ifor Williams, the dating proposed by Charles-Edwards accords with that put forward by Williams who saw in the *Mabinogi* the harmonization by a scholar from Dyfed of older stories from 'Gwent, Dyfed and Gwynedd around 1060 when the three kingdoms had been united'.[3]

Charles-Edwards' dating for *Branwen*, and consequently for the compilation of the *Mabinogi* as a whole, was advanced in response to an article on *Branwen* by Saunders Lewis who argued therein for a date of composition between 1172 and 1174.[4] In rejecting the arguments of Saunders Lewis, Charles-Edwards puts great weight on the Irish custom of one king entering another's house as a symbol of submission. It is argued that the existence of this custom helps to explain the importance of the house that is built for Bendigeidfran in *Branwen* so that Matholwch and the Irish might come to submit to him there. Charles-Edwards points to the attestation of this practice in the Irish annals from 1059 onwards,[5] and argues that entering another's house (*dul i tech*) as a mark of submission was a recent development; the traditional terminology for articulating submission was to say that one king had taken the hostages of another.[6] He believes that the new custom,

---

1 Sioned Davies (trans.), *The Mabinogion* (Oxford, 2007), pp xxvi–xxvii. See Brynley F. Roberts, 'Where were the Four Branches of the Mabinogi written?' in J.F. Nagy (ed.), *The individual in Celtic literatures*, CSANA Yearbook 1 (Dublin, 2001), pp 61–73 at pp 71–2, who though believing that the date of the *Mabinogi* remains an 'open question', articulates the possibility that 'we are being led to consider, once again, a twelfth-century date'. 2 Thomas Charles-Edwards, 'The date of the Four Branches of the Mabinogi', *Transactions of the Honourable Society of Cymmrodorion* (1970, part 2), 263–98 esp. 289–98; cf. discussion by Eric P. Hamp, 'Mabinogi and archaism', *Celtica*, 23 (1999), 96–110. For a succint discussion of many of the issues involved in dating the *Mabinogi*, see now Simon Rodway, *Dating medieval Welsh literature: evidence from the verbal system* (Aberystwyth, 2013), esp. Chapter 1 (and references therein). 3 Ibid., 263; see Ifor Williams (ed.), *Pedeir Keinc y Mabinogi* (2nd ed., Cardiff, 1951), p. xli. 4 Saunders Lewis, 'Branwen', *Ysgrifau Beirniadol*, 5 (1970), 30–43. 5 The first two such references are *AI* 1059 and *CS* 1057 (recte 1059). 6 However, as Katharine Simms reminds us 'hostages are handed over to

and consequently the terminology, may have originated with kings submitting to Brian Bóraime at his residence in Cenn Corad and may thus date up to half a century before its first attestation in the annals.[7] Notwithstanding this earlier postulated date, Charles-Edwards argues that it was 'likely that the Four Branches belong to sometime between about 1050 and 1120'.[8]

Because of the importance of this argument for the dating of the *Mabinogi*, the attestation and dating of the phrase *dul i tech* have assumed a special significance.[9] The arguments concerning its usage and date have recently been re-examined in detail by Patrick Sims-Williams who concludes:

> the Irish custom of submission by entering the overlord's house was probably much earlier than the annal of 1059, which cannot give *c.*1050 as the *terminus post quem* for the invention of the story of Bendigeidfran's house. Besides it is doubtful whether the Welsh story has anything to do with the annalistic formula and the custom that lay behind it.[10]

There are two issues here. It is not my intention to address the second of these, i.e., whether *Branwen* reflects knowledge of the Irish custom of submitting to a king by entering his house. However, the date of the recording of this practice in the written record might be revisited with profit. To date, no-one has suggested a date prior to the beginning of the eleventh century for this custom. However, there is a medieval Irish legal text which contains a record of the practice and which is dated by Meyer to 'the period of transition from Old to Middle Irish', a dating accepted by Charles-Edwards and by myself although it would seem that it was 'quite possibly based (at least in part) on an earlier original'.[11] I quote the relevant text and translation here:

guarantee a contract; their transfer is primarily a sign that a formal treaty between leaders has been agreed upon' and thus that 'handing over hostages did not in itself constitute the essence of submission': *From kings to warlords: the changing political structure of Gaelic Ireland in the later Middle Ages* (Woodbridge, 1987), pp 99–100. 7 Charles-Edwards, 'The date', pp 296–7. This is also the position of Marie Therese Flanagan, *Irish society, Anglo-Norman settlers, Angevin kingship: interaction in Ireland in the late twelfth century* (Oxford, 1989), p. 177. 8 Charles-Edwards, 'The date', p. 298. 9 See now Thomas Charles-Edwards, '*Lebor na cert* and clientship' in K. Murray (ed.), *Lebor na cert: reassessments*, ITS SS 25 (London, 2013), pp 13–33 at pp 27–30. 10 Patrick Sims-Williams, *Irish influence on medieval Welsh literature* (Oxford, 2011), p. 229. The central arguments are contained in pp 188–91 and in pp 208–29 (Chapter 8: 'The submission of Irish kings in fact and fiction'). This is a reworking of his earlier article: 'The submission of Irish kings in fact and fiction: Henry II, Bendigeidfran, and the dating of *The Four Branches of the Mabinogi*', *CMCS*, 22 (Winter, 1991), 31–61. 11 Kuno Meyer, 'A collation of *Crith gablach* and a treatise on *cró* and *díbad*', *Ériu*, 1 (1904), 209–15 at 209; Thomas Charles-Edwards, *Early Irish and Welsh kinship* (Oxford, 1993), pp 491, 506; Kevin Murray, 'A Middle Irish tract on *cró* and *díbad*' in A.P. Smyth (ed.), *Seanchas: essays in early and medieval archaeology,*

§3 Ran*n* ó bun cé*tamus* .i. té*t* rí(g) in c[h]óicidh nó na mórt*húaithe* i tech rí[g] *Érenn*. Ma[d] rí(gh) cóicid ma[d] rí(gh) mórt*húaithe*, té*t* i tegh rígh in c[h]óicid *nó* ind ardrígh cena 7 gaibid gíall n-an*n* im c[h]i*n*aigh ind-í marb*us* a *fer co n*-éirre*n* fris a cró 7 ran*n*tair íaram in cró. *Secht*mad as cé*tamus* do gíall frisi tobong*ar*.

A division from the bottom first, i.e., the king of the province or of the major *túath* goes into the house of (that is, submits to) the king of Ireland. Whether provincial king or king of a major *túath* he goes into the house of (that is, submits to) the king of the province or the high-king on the other hand and he takes a hostage there for the crime of the one who kills their man, until he pays him their *cró* and this is then divided. One seventh of it in the first place for the hostage who is taken for it.[12]

This obviously does not reflect fully what seems to become the standard practice later, i.e., the entering by one king into another king's house specifically to acknowledge overlordship. Here, the submission is made as part of a wider act (including taking a hostage) to help acquire *cró* 'wergild' on behalf of the subordinate king and his *túath*.[13] If successful, the levying overking receives $\frac{2}{7}$ of the wergild as payment and the hostage receives $\frac{1}{7}$ of the *cró* for his part in the proceedings.

It is interesting here to note the central part that hostages play in this example as the later practice of *dul i tech* displaced the well-attested early procedure whereby provision of hostages by a subordinate was the method by which overlordship was acknowledged.[14] Notwithstanding the fact that the hostage here is taken rather than given, perhaps this early example of 'going into the house' of the overking reflects the emergence of the new practice of submission alongside the traditional system of hostageship which was to remain important for so many centuries afterwards.

A final note of caution must be struck, however. This legal text is composite in nature and the absolute dating of its constituent elements is not entirely secure. Although drawing in part on Old Irish sources, it survives in only one composite manuscript of the sixteenth century: Dublin TCD 1337

history and literature in honour of Francis J. Byrne (Dublin, 2000), pp 251–60 at pp 251–2. See now Neil McLeod, 'The distribution of the body-fine: AD 650–1150' in A. Ahlqvist and P. O'Neill (eds), *Medieval Irish law: text and context* (Sydney, 2013), pp 65–109 at pp 72–5.   **12** Murray, 'A Middle Irish tract', pp 252–3. The text is also printed (without translation) in Meyer, 'A collation of *Críth gablach*', 214–15, and in *CIH* ii, 600.1–601.11 at 600.11–14.   **13** See Fergus Kelly, *A guide to early Irish law* (Dublin, 1988), p. 23. Philip Healy suggests to me that the hostage taken may be drawn from among those previously submitted to the overking by the king of the offending *túath*. I wish to thank Philip for his comments on the final draft of this contribution.   **14** For discussion, see Simms, *From kings to warlords*, pp 96–9.

(H.3.18).[15] Consequently, we cannot say for sure that the section on going into the house of the overking dates categorically to the tenth century, after the death of Cormac mac Cuilennáin (†908) who is mentioned in the text; however, that still remains the most likely possibility.

15 For the most recent discussion of this manuscript, see Liam Breatnach, *A companion to Corpus iuris hibernici* (Dublin, 2005), pp 4–5.

The bells of the saints

PRÓINSÉAS NÍ CHATHÁIN

The monastic bell had a central role in religious life in medieval Ireland. Consequently, it comes as no surprise to find that medieval Irish hagiographical texts consistently emphasize the importance of the bell among the possessions regularly associated with saints, particularly St Patrick. As Kenney has noted, the saint's '*bacall* [sic] and bell are his instruments of supernatural power'.[1] For example, in *Baile Fínnachta* 'The Vision of Fínnachta', the saint uses his staff and bell to call forth the stream necessary for the founding of his church at Formáel:

> Faillsigthir dō techt co Formāil co mbad and nobeth a annōit ... An tan rosīacht som sin lenaid a c[h]osa don talmain 7 inn eō ōsa chind .i. cluicīn .i. mind bec 7 loigis in cloc for lār 7 adnaid for bēm nigh [sic] co tarnic in trāth do bēim. Sāidhigh Fīndachta a lorg isin talmain. Genid buindi asin talmain 7 tēid dar in cloc 7 glasais hē, conid de rāitir Glassán fris.[2]

> It was revealed to him to go to Formáel for it was there his founding church would be ... When he reached that place his feet adhered to the ground and the bell over his head, i.e., a little bell, i.e., a small treasure and the bell lay on the ground and he began striking it until the time for striking came to an end. Fínnachta planted his staff in the ground. A stream came forth from the ground, and went across the bell and made it green; because of that it was called Glassán.

Similarly, in *Betha Beraig*, we see the saint confronting Uí Briúin Sinna and their king, Cú Chathfaid, who were threatening the peoples under his protection. Berach strikes his bell (*an glasán*) against them and the bog swallows them up and the terrain becomes a lake instantly.[3] Similar maledictory acts are attributed to other clerics and saints, and bells play a prominent role in such ritual practices.[4]

---

1 James F. Kenney, *The sources for the early history of Ireland: ecclesiastical: an introduction and guide* (New York, 1929; 2nd ed. repr. Dublin, 1993), p. 303.   2 Kuno Meyer, 'Baile Fíndachta ríg Condacht', *ZCP*, 13 (1921), 25–7 at 26 §4. A new edition and translation are forthcoming from Kevin Murray.   3 *BNÉ* i, pp 40–1; ii, p. 40 §82.   4 See Lisa M. Bitel, 'Tools and scripts for cursing in medieval Ireland', *Memoirs of the American Academy in Rome*, 51–2 (2006–7), 5–27 at 7–13; Dan M. Wiley, 'The maledictory psalms', *Peritia*, 15 (2001), 261–79 at 270.

Alongside investigation of individual bells, general studies of these artefacts have been published, by Cormac Bourke in particular.[5] Furthermore, repeated attention has been drawn to the importance of the saint's bell in Pádraig Ó Riain's recent *Dictionary*.[6] The purpose of this short article is to draw additional attention to the native names for the bells associated with particular saints. As well as the common Irish generic *cloc(c)* and its diminutives *cloc(c)án* / *cluic(c)ín(e)*, and the Latin terms *cac(c)abulus*, *campana*, *clocca* (> Irish *cloc(c)*),[7] *cymbalum* (> Irish *cimbal*), *nola* and *tintin(n)abulum*, a number of different Irish words are commonly used in the sources as bell-names associated with different saints.[8] These are briefly enumerated and discussed here (in alphabetical order).[9]

1. *Bardán (Ciaráin)*

This diminutive, perhaps to be derived from *bard* '(lower grade of) poet, rhymester', is used in three different versions of his Life as the name of St Ciarán's bell, a bell which is given to him by St Patrick. The forms are not identical throughout, however. In the earlier Irish life, it is called *an bardan Ciarain*; the Latinized form is rendered *barthanus Kyarani*; and in the later Irish life it is referred to as *barcán Chiaráin*, with *barcán* most likely a misrendering of *bardán*.[10] In other sources, there are references to Ciarán striking his bell when prophesying about the coming of the Danes to Ireland, though in these texts the specific name of the bell is not given.[11]

---

5 Cormac Bourke, 'Early Irish hand-bells', *JRSAI*, 110 (1980), 52–66; idem, 'Early Irish bells', *Journal of the Dromore Historical Society*, 4 (1986), 27–38. Cf. also idem, 'The hand-bells of the early Scottish church', *Proceedings of the Antiquaries of Scotland*, 113 (1983), 463–8; idem, 'The hand-bells of the early western church' in C. Laurent and H. Davis (ed.), *Irlande et Bretagne: vingt siècles d'histoire* (Rennes, 1994), pp 77–82. All studies are also indebted to the works of T.L. Cooke, 'On ancient Irish bells', *Transactions of the Kilkenny Archaeological Society*, 2, i (1852), 47–63 and William Reeves, 'On certain Irish ecclesiastical bells in the collection of the Lord Primate', *PRIA*, 8 (1861–4), 441–50. I would like to thank Cormac Bourke for generous assistance.   6 See the 'index of subjects' in *DIS* pp 646–7.   7 The generic *clocc* / *clog* and associated forms are regularly followed by specific qualifiers. For example, Clocc an Deilcc, Clocc na Tráth ('An Fionn-clocc'), Clocc Pátraic, Clocán Óir, Clog an Udhachta (see Udachta Pátraic below), Clog na Rígh, and Cluicc na Cléire. These are not treated in this discussion.   8 It is suggested in *DIL* that the word *cairche* 'a stringed musical instrument' may be used to refer to a bell in *In cath catharda*: Whitley Stokes (ed.), 'In cath catharda: the civil war of the Romans. An Irish version of Lucan's Pharsalia', *IT* iv, 2, ll 4704–11.   9 See *DIL* s.vv. for individual entries.   10 *BNÉ* i, p. 113; ii, p. 109 §1 (cf. i, p. 103; ii, p. 99 §4); *VSHP* i, p. 218 §iv; Standish Hayes O'Grady (ed. and trans.), *Silva gadelica (I–XXXI)*, 2 vols (London, 1892), i, p. 3; ii, p. 3.   11 James Henthorn Todd (ed. and trans.), *Cogadh Gaedhel re Gallaibh: the war of the Gaedhil with the Gaill*, Rolls Series 48 (London, 1867), p. 225; Eleanor Knott, 'A poem of prophecies', *Ériu*, 17 (1958), 66–84 at 60–1.

2. *Bernán*

This word, meaning 'the little gapped one', seems to be used either of tongue-less bells or of bells which became broken (or 'gapped'). In *Betha Colmáin maic Lúacháin*, some new members of Mo Chuta's community, who were originally warriors of Motura (son of the king of Corco Baiscinn), are despatched from Lismore by an angel as God requires them to serve elsewhere. They receive a *clocc ... cen tengaid* 'a tongue-less bell' and wander Ireland for seven years until the bell sounds at Lann Ela: *conid desin ata Bernán Moturu ic Laind 7 bernán Mochutu ē iar fír* 'And hence is the gapped bell of Motura at Land, and it is really the gapped bell of Mochuta'. It is further claimed:

> mind cotaig isin bale hē 7 īcaid galra 7 tedmand imda for dæinib 7 cethraib .i. dīnnech ass 7 a bēim impu fo trí.

> It is a relic of covenant in the place, and it cures many diseases and plagues on men and cattle, viz. by their washing from it, and by its being struck three times around them.[12]

It seems that the damaging of bells was commonplace. For example, it is stated in the Life of Rúadán: *Luidh Ruadhan iarsin sechnon na cathrach oc sirbeim a cluicc, co ro ghortaigh a chlocc* 'After this Ruadan went through the city continually sounding his bell, so that he damaged it'.[13] With regard to the bell associated with St Brigit, we read that St Patrick threw it at a flock of birds 'so that its gap broke from it so that that is the *bernán* of Brigit' (*co mmebaid ass a bernd, conid hé sin Bernán Brigte*).[14] *Bernán* is one of the more common terms used for a bell and is associated with saints such as Ailbe,[15] Cíarán,[16] Conall,[17] Éimín,[18] and, as noted, Patrick.[19]

3. *Bethechán*

This is only attested once (see *DIL* s.v.) as the name of a 'small iron bell' (*cluccene becc íairnd*) associated with St Patrick. Deriving from *beithe* 'birch', it is so called because 'a birch grows through its handle' (*Ássaid bethe tría doirnn*).[20]

---

12 *BCML* pp 26–7 §27.   **13** *BNÉ* i, p. 310; ii, p. 309 §10.   **14** Kathleen Mulchrone (ed.), *Bethu Phátraic. The tripartite Life of Patrick* (Dublin and London, 1939), ll 1304–5; Whitley Stokes (ed. and trans.), *The tripartite Life of St Patrick with other documents relating to that saint*, 2 vols, Rolls Series 89 (London, 1887), i, p. 114.   **15** *AU* 1123.2; *AFM* 1123 (ii, 1016–18).   **16** *ATig.* 1043 (*RC* 17, 383).   **17** See Raghnall Ó Floinn, *Irish shrines and reliquaries of the middle ages* (Dublin, 1994), p. 41 and Plate 16.   **18** J.G. O'Keeffe, 'Four saints' in J. Fraser, P. Grosjean and J.G. O'Keeffe (eds), *Irish texts*, 5 vols (London, 1931–4), iii, pp 1–8 at p. 2.   **19** *BCC* pp 114–15 §120.   **20** Mulchrone, *Bethu Phátraic*, ll 2927–9; Stokes, *The tripartite Life of St Patrick*, i, p. 248.

4. *Bóbán*

This word, which commonly means 'calf', is utilized as a bell-name associated with Saints Molaga and Kevin. In his Life, we are told that Molaga receives the bell from St David of Mynyw in Wales.[21] In the Life of Cíarán, St Kevin receives the *bóbán* from the spirit of St Cíarán *post mortem* as payment for communion given: *dorat Quiarán a clog do Cœimgen ... As eiside Boban Coeimhgin inniu* 'Ciarán gave his bell to Coimgen ... "This is to-day Coimgen's *Bobán*"';[22] it is also mentioned in the annals among the 'relics and guarantees of Ireland'.[23]

5. *Ceólán*

A diminutive of *ceól* 'music', this may be best translated as 'little musical one' or 'little sweet-sounding one' and seems to refer to a small bell, perhaps a hand bell (see *DIL* and *FGB* s.v.).[24] It is mentioned as the name of a bell associated with Lasair in her Life, with a drink from it said to contain great healing powers.[25] The bell associated with Berach, known as Clog Bearaigh, is described as a *ceólán* in his Irish Life.[26]

Ceólán is a commonly used generic word for a bell. For example, it is the type of bell struck by Brénainn and Rúadán against Díarmait mac Cerbaill when he refuses them protection: *Ro triallsat a cclucca 7 a cceolana do bein for Diarmait, go ros gortaighset aga mbein* 'They proceeded to ring their bells, both large and small, against Diarmait (so violently) that they damaged the bells in ringing them'.[27] Other references abound: for example, this generic term is used with reference to St Máedóc, while a cleric in *Buile Śuibne* is referred to as *a fhir an cheóláin* 'O man of the bell'.[28] Furthermore, it is found twice compounded with the adjective *find* 'fair, blessed' in *Acallam na senórach*.[29]

6. *Dub Dúaibsech*

In Maghnus Ó Domhnaill's late Life of the saint, we read of the name of a bell belonging to St Colum Cille: *Acus fos adubairt an t-aingeal ris a cloc fen do caitheamh riv mar an cedna .i. an dub duaibsech* 'And the angel bade him to throw his bell Dub Duaibsech at them in like wise'.[30] This is an unusual name for a bell, perhaps translating as 'black gloomy one'.[31]

21 J.G. O'Keeffe, 'Betha Molaga' in Fraser, Grosjean and O'Keeffe (eds), *Irish texts*, iii, pp 11–22 at p. 21 §19.   22 *LisL* ll 4470–1.   23 *AFM* 1144 (ii, 1072).   24 See discussion of this term in Eugene O'Curry, *On the manners and customs of the ancient Irish*, ed. W.K. Sullivan, 3 vols (London, 1873), iii, pp 331–2.   25 Lucius Gwynn, 'The Life of St Lasair', *Ériu*, 5 (1911), 73–109 at 80, 88, 96.   26 *BNÉ* i, p. 27; ii, p. 26 §24 (for possible identification and size, see Reeves, 'On certain Irish ecclesiastical bells', 444).   27 *BNÉ* i, p. 323; ii, p. 314 §36.   28 Ibid., i, p. 236; ii, p. 229 §160; J.G. O'Keeffe (ed. and trans.), *Buile Suibhne (The Frenzy of Suibhne)*, ITS 12 (London, 1913), pp 134–5.   29 Whitley Stokes (ed. and partial trans.), 'Acallamh na senórach', *IT* iv, 1, ll 327, 2610.   30 *BCC* pp 130–1 §132.   31 For a discussion of the bells associated with St Colum Cille, see Cormac

7. *Dub Díglach*

The bell regularly associated with St Caillín is known as Clog na Rígh 'The bell of the kings'.[32] However, in the *Book of Fenagh* another bell is mentioned once with regard to him: *Mo dub diglach degfertach ... Bind a guth* 'My wondrous, good *Dubh-diglach* ... Sweet its tone'.[33] The name translates as 'black vengeful one', perhaps alluding to the bell's power which Caillín offers to Adomnán to keep the lords of Uí Fíachrach, Uí Amalgaid and Cenél Conaill in check.

8. *Finnfaídech*

Perhaps meaning 'fair sounding one' (see *DIL* s.v. *faídech*), this is the name of a bell associated with St Patrick.[34] The bell is mentioned a couple of times in the annals: as a measure of the amount of silver given by Cenél nEógain to Armagh and as the cause of a raid on Conaille for its violation (alongside the breaking of St Patrick's crozier).[35] A well called 'tipra Patraicc' in a Life of Finnian is also referred to as 'tipra in Findfadaigh'.[36]

This term is also used for bells associated with other saints: in *Betha Colmáin maic Lúacháin*, Colmán and Mocholmóc of Clonard swap their bells, both of which are called *finnfaídech*; while in his Life, Mac Creiche (< Mac Reithe) along with his fosterling Mainchín is said to have obtained his *finn-faídech* from the high altar at Rome.[37]

9. *Glasán*

As suggested in *DIL* (s.v.), this word, meaning 'the little green one', may refer to a bell's 'silvery or coppery sheen', presumably to the verdigris common to weathered copper and its alloys.[38] This is the name used for bells associated with Saints Fínnachta, Berach, Columba and Mo Chuta.[39]

10. *Glúnán*

This word, a diminutive of *glún* 'knee', is the name given to bells associated with St Domangart and St Senach.[40] It is suggested in *DIL* (s.v.) that *glúnán* may take its name from its shape.

Bourke, 'Insignia Columbae II' in idem (ed.), *Studies in the cult of Saint Columba* (Dublin, 1997), pp 162–83 at pp 168–73.   **32** See W.M. Hennessy and D.H. Kelly (ed. and trans.), *The Book of Fenagh* (Dublin, 1875; repr. Dublin, 1939), pp 140–41; Reeves, 'On certain Irish ecclesiastical bells', 444–5.   **33** Hennessy and Kelly, *The Book of Fenagh*, pp 412–13.   **34** Mulchrone, *Bethu Phátraic*, ll 3138–9; Stokes, *The tripartite Life of St Patrick*, i, p. 266.   **35** *AU* 947.2, 1013.1.   **36** See discussion in Kathleen Hughes, 'The historical value of the Lives of St Finnian of Clonard', *English Historical Review*, 69 (1954), 353–72 at 357 and n. 5.   **37** *BCML* p. 92 §90 (cf. pp 46 §48, 64 §61); Charles Plummer (ed. and trans.), *Miscellanea hagiographica Hiberniae* (Brussels, 1925), pp 16, 56 §12.   **38** A play on the homonymous word *glasán* 'stream' is also evident in some of these texts; see for example the text from *Baile Fínnachta* (cited at n. 2 above).   **39** See above, notes 2–3; *BCC* pp 156–7 §154; *BCML* p. 20 n. 1.   **40** John Colgan (ed.), *Acta sanctorum veteris et majoris*

11. *Udachta Pátraic*

This famous bell ('the testimony / bequest of Patrick'), also referred to as
Cloc in Aidechta 'the bell of testimony', was believed to have been a relic of
St Patrick which was later bequeathed to Armagh; it has been discussed in
detail by Reeves.[41] The taking of prisoners and cattle as restitution for its violation is mentioned in the annals, as is the death of an Ó Mealláin keeper of
the bell.[42] A further famous annalistic reference to the bell is to the unlawful
death of the clerics responsible for the bell on the occasion of the killing of
Muirchertach mac Néill Mac Lochlainn, 'airdri Erenn'.[43] This reference may
underpin the deliberate citing of the bell in *Aided Muirchertaig Meic Erca* (*co
rabat trí mergi acu .i. in Chathach 7 in Clog .i. in udachta Pádraic 7 in Mísach
C(h)airnig*),[44] and adds further support to the convincing argument advanced
by our honorand that this text should be read as an exemplary text focused
on the life of Muirchertach Mac Lochlainn.[45]

As can be seen from the above, there are many commonalities (as one might
expect) in the presentation of saints' bells in the literary sources. They are
regularly given wondrous origins, are seen as the source of preternatural
powers and are associated with the finding of water, particularly at the founding of ecclesiastical sites. The multiplicity of names reflects the importance of
bells in medieval Irish religious life. Different terms are used interchangeably
for bells associated with certain saints while the bells themselves generally
seem to have been named from their appearance, colour and sound. Some of
the terms used to refer to bells are uncommon and their meaning unclear,
and some are attested only as glossary words.[46] A listing of families associated
with surviving reliquaries (including bells) is provided by Raghnall Ó

Scotiae seu Hiberniae ... sanctorum insulae, i (Louvain, 1645; repr. Dublin, 1947), col. 743b;
idem (ed.), *Triadis thaumaturgae seu divorum Patricii, Columbae et Brigidae, trium veteris et
maioris Scotiae seu Hiberniae, sanctorum insulae, communium patronorum acta* (Louvain 1647;
repr. Dublin 1997), col. 431a §III.   41 *AU* 553.3; William Reeves, 'On the bell of St.
Patrick, called Clog an Edachta', *Transactions of the Royal Irish Academy*, 27 (1877–86), 1–
30.   42 *AU* 1044.4; *AFM* 1356 (iii, 608).   43 *ATig.* 1166 (*RC* 18, 268).   44 Lil Nic
Dhonnchadha (ed.), *Aided Muirchertaig Meic Erca*, MMIS 19 (Dublin, 1964), l. 217.
45 Máire Herbert, 'The death of Muirechertach Mac Erca: a twelfth-century tale' in F.
Josephson (ed.), *Celts and vikings: proceedings of the Fourth Symposium of Societas Celtologica
Nordica* (Göteborg, 1997), pp 27–39.   46 For example, the word *eó* is a *bérla na filed* term
for a bell attested in Kuno Meyer, 'Three poems in *bérla na filed*', *ZCP*, 5 (1905), 482–94
at 486 §8: *cada (.i. guth) na n-eo (.i. cloc)*. It is also found in Meyer, 'Baile Fíndachta', 26
§4 (see above n. 2). Similarly, the word *íath* (see *DIL* s.v.) is found in glossaries with the
meaning 'bell': see Whitley Stokes (ed.), *Three Irish glossaries: Cormac's glossary ...
O'Davoren's glossary ... a glossary to the calendar of Oingus the culdee* (London and
Edinburgh, 1862; repr. Felinfach, 2000), p. 6 (s.v. *Bachall*): *Iath ainm dochlug conafáeid*;
idem, 'On the metrical glossaries of the medieval Irish', *Transactions of the Philological
Society*, 22, i (November, 1891), 1–103 at 3: *'iat[h]' cloc ocus 'íath' cochall*.

Floinn.[47] We have much post-medieval evidence of the use of such artefacts in administering oaths and in the collection of dues. Enough is known with regard to the bells of the saints – names, sources and artefacts – to confirm their centrality to medieval Irish ecclesiastical culture.[48]

47 Ó Floinn, *Irish shrines and reliquaries of the middle ages*, p. 45. **48** Recently, Tomás Ó Carragáin, 'The archaeology of ecclesiastical estates in early medieval Ireland: a case study of the kingdom of Fir Maige', *Peritia*, 24–5 (2013–14), 266–312 at 281–4, has focused on the importance of ironworking and bell production at Gortnahown, near Brigown in N. Cork, which has provided the earliest evidence thus far for bell production in Ireland. I would like to thank Kevin Murray for his assistance and advice with this article.

The Hectors of Ireland and the Western World

MÁIRE NÍ MHAONAIGH

INTRODUCTION

In modern discussions of medieval Irish literature, Achilles is the Classical hero with whom its warriors have been most frequently compared. Parallels noted, specifically between the Greek fighter and Cú Chulainn, protector of the Ulaid, have been explained in a variety of ways.[1] Viewed as independent manifestations of universal themes common to texts dealing with similar issues, they cannot be taken as evidence for literary borrowing. When understood as specific echoes, ultimately of Homer, analogous episodes in the two literary traditions have been accorded greater significance, bearing witness to a direct relationship between Middle Irish narratives and Classical stories upon which they may have drawn in various forms. Cú Chulainn's depiction as an 'Irish Achilles' has personified the connections, the label being sufficiently adaptable to denote many different types of link.[2] The identification itself is modern, however, and medieval Irish scholars perceived Cú Chulainn in other terms. For them he was comparable not with Achilles but with his youthful Trojan opponent, Troilus, youngest son of King Priam who sought in vain to avenge the death of his brother, Hector, at the Greek hero's hands: *Coimfhedma Treóil is Cú Chulainn / im chomlonn, im ré is im rath*, 'Troilus and Cú Chulainn are equivalent in their combats, their lifespan and their fortune'.[3] This well-known passage from a twelfth-century poem, *Clann Ollaman úaisle Emna* ('The children of Ollam are the nobles of Emain'), forms part of a more sustained comparison of the warriors of Troy with the Ulaid who are

1 Michael Clarke summarizes past scholarship on the theme in 'An Irish Achilles and a Greek Cú Chulainn' in R. Ó hUiginn and B. Ó Catháin (eds), *Ulidia 2: proceedings of the Second International Congress on the Ulster Cycle of Tales* (Maynooth, 2009), pp 238–51 at pp 238–40. See also his 'Achilles, Byrhtnoth, Cú Chulainn: continuity and analogy from Homer to the medieval north' in M.J. Clarke, B.G.F. Currie and R.O.A.M. Lyne (eds), *Epic interactions: perspectives on Homer, Virgil, and the epic tradition presented to Jasper Griffin by former pupils* (Oxford, 2006), pp 243–71. 2 Illustrative of the differences are the following: Alfred Nutt, *Cuchulainn: the Irish Achilles* (London, 1900); Myles Dillon, *Early Irish literature* (Chicago and London, 1948), pp 1, 3; Michael Enright, 'Fires of knowledge: a theory of warband education in medieval Ireland and Homeric Greece' in P. Ní Chatháin and M. Richter (eds), *Ireland and Europe in the early Middle Ages: texts and transmission / Irland und Europa im früheren Mittelalter: Texte und Überlieferung* (Dublin, 2002), pp 342–67; Brent Miles, *Heroic saga and Classical epic in medieval Ireland*, Studies in Celtic History 30 (Woodbridge, 2011), pp 155–6, 166–7, 197–9. 3 Francis John Byrne, 'Clann Ollaman uaisle Emna', *StH*, 4 (1964), 54–94 at 61, 76 (stanza 5).

termed *Tro-fhian fhír na hÉirenn*, 'the true Trojan band of Ireland'.[4] In associating themselves with the legend of Troy, the Irish were similar to other
medieval European peoples and while, unlike many of these, they did not
trace their origins to the Trojans, the Classical tale informed their history and
image of themselves in important ways.

Its interest for the Irish is evidenced most clearly in the fact that the popular, fifth-century Latin account of the Trojan war, *De excidio Troiae historia*
(attributed to Dares Phrygius, who was allegedly an eye-witness to the events
he recounts), was cast early and often in Ireland into vernacular form. A significantly expanded version of Dares' description is preserved in the twelfth-
century codex, the Book of Leinster,[5] while an earlier recension survives only
in non-contemporary manuscripts.[6] A later third prose recension is also
extant; furthermore, a poetic rendering of the Troy tale beginning *Luid Iasōn
[i]na luing lóir* ('Jason went into his spacious ship'), which was perhaps composed in the first quarter of the twelfth century, has come down to us.[7]
Linguistic evidence suggests that the first Irish adaptation of Dares may have
been made in the eleventh century or earlier.[8] Moreover, reference to some
version of the story as *Togail Troí* ('The destruction of Troy') is found in the
list of tales embedded in the tenth-century narrative, *Airec menman Uraird
meic Coisse* ('The stratagem of Urard mac Coisse').[9] Nestling in this catalogue
alongside titles alluding to Irish events, the Troy legend had swiftly secured
an established place in the literary landscape of Ireland.

Togail Troí, the skilful vernacular retelling of that legend, in its many
forms, was to become a significant feature of that learned landscape. As a pivotal event of world history and of crucial relevance to the origin-myth of Rome,
knowledge of the Trojan War was essential to Irish scholars who sought to
construct an elaborate, historiographical narrative linking their own history with
that of other nations of the world, as has recently been shown.[10] That the Irish
should choose to associate themselves with the fallen heroes of Troy upon

---

4 Ibid., 61, 76 (stanza 1). 5 *LL* iv, pp 1063–117; Whitley Stokes (ed. and trans.), *Togail
Troí: the destruction of Troy from the facsimile of the Book of Leinster* (Calcutta, 1881).
6 Whitley Stokes, 'The destruction of Troy, aus H.2.17, mit englischer Übersetzung', *IT*,
ii, 1, pp 1–142. On the relationship between the two versions, see Gearóid Mac Eoin, 'Das
Verbalsystem von *Togail Troí* (H.2.17)', *ZCP*, 28 (1960–1), 73–136, 149–223 at 76–7, 196–
7 and Miles, *Heroic saga*, p. 54. 7 Miles, *Heroic saga*, p. 54 n. 6; Gearóid Mac Eoin, 'Dán
ar chogadh na Traoi', *StH*, 1 (1961), 19–55. 8 Mac Eoin, 'Das Verbalsystem', 201–2;
Uáitéar Mac Gearailt, 'Change and innovation in eleventh-century prose narrative in Irish'
in H.L.C. Tristram (ed.), *(Re)oralisierung*, ScriptOralia 84 (Tübingen, 1996), pp 443–96 at
pp 459–62, 466, 476, and his 'Zur literarischen Sprache des 11. Jahrhunderts' in S. Zimmer,
R. Ködderitzsch and A. Wigger (eds), *Akten des zweiten deutschen Keltologen-Symposiums
(Bonn, 2.–4. April 1997)* (Tübingen, 1999), pp 105–20 at pp 111–18; but see also Clarke,
'An Irish Achilles', pp 242–3. 9 Proinsias Mac Cana, *The learned tales of medieval Ireland*
(Dublin, 1980), pp 54, 84. 10 Clarke, 'An Irish Achilles'; Erich Poppe and Dagmar
Schlüter, 'Greece, Ireland, Ulster and Troy: of hybrid origins and heroes' in W.M.

whose defeat the supremacy of Rome was based is unsurprising; within a biblical framework they similarly aligned themselves with the Israelites, God's chosen people, who had been led out of exile into the Promised Land.[11] As a window on a relevant, parallel universe, the events at Troy were thus intrinsically interesting in their own right and were cultivated and expanded with considerable artistry and skill. Comparable expertise was applied to the development of their own foundation history, as related in narratives such as *Táin bó Cúailnge* ('The cattle raid of Cúailnge') and its sequel *Cath Ruis na Ríg* ('The battle of Ross na Ríg').[12] These creative compositions, all emanating from the same intellectual milieu and forming part of what Clarke has termed 'a single historiographical project',[13] influenced each other across various recensions. Their interrelationships are highlighted by their placement on adjacent manuscript pages, their very physical proximity inviting textual comparisons to be drawn. In this regard, the thematic, structural and conceptual parallels between *Togail Troí* and the *Táin* to which Clarke has drawn attention would have been apparent to a medieval audience.[14] Moreover, the many correspondences between two defining, ancient wars should also have been clear.[15]

Against this interpretative background, the act of equating Cú Chulainn with Troilus acquires an added resonance, the deeds of the one bringing those of the other to mind.[16] Pre-eminent Trojan warrior after the death of his brother Hector, Troilus was considered by many to be the premier champion of Troy. Dares Phrygius celebrated his greatness, deeming him to have surpassed his older sibling on one occasion, and in this he is followed by the author(s) of *Togail Troí*: *treissi immurro indás Hechtoir ar imguin 7 áni 7 forneurt*, 'moreover, he was mightier than Hector, in fighting, nobility and excessive strength'.[17] Elsewhere, however, the relative merits of the siblings are said to have been contested by their opponents. Helen's husband, Menelaus, is made to comment that there was no longer a hero of Hector's ilk (*láech mar Hectoir*) to defend Troy, to which Ulysses and Diomedes responded: *narbad treisse Hectoir indás Troil i ngnimaib gaiscid 7 engnama*, 'that Hector was not mightier than Troilus in deeds of valour and prowess'.[18]

Hoofnagle and W.R. Keller (eds), *Other nations: the hybridization of medieval insular mythology and identity*, Brittanica et Americana 3, xxvii (Heidelberg, 2011), pp 127–43. 11 For discussion of this theme, see, for example, Mark Scowcroft, '*Leabhar gabhála* – part II: the growth of the tradition', *Ériu*, 36 (1988), 1–66, and John Carey, '*Lebor gabála* and the legendary history of Ireland' in H. Fulton (ed.), *Medieval Celtic literature and society* (Dublin, 2005), pp 32–48. 12 *TBCI* and *TBCL*; Edmund Hogan (ed. and trans.), *Cath Ruis na Ríg for Bóinn*, TLS 4 (Dublin, 1902). 13 'An Irish Achilles', p. 244. 14 Ibid. 15 Ibid.; Poppe and Schlüter, 'Greece'. 16 Significant parallels in the portrayal of both have been discussed by Leslie Diane Myrick, *From the* De excidio Troiae historia *to the* Togail Troí: *literary-cultural synthesis in a medieval Irish adaptation of Dares' Troy tale* (Heidelberg, 1993), pp 141–57; Clarke, 'An Irish Achilles', pp 247–50; Poppe and Schlüter, 'Greece', pp 137–9. 17 Stokes, 'Destruction', pp 14, 77, ll 391–2; Ferdinand Meister (ed.), *Daretis Phrygii de excidio Troiae historia* (Leipzig, 1873), chapter 7. 18 Stokes, 'Destruction', pp 44–5, ll

HECTOR'S PORTRAYAL IN THE NARRATIVES OF TROY

Notwithstanding such expressions of the younger Trojan's skill, or accounts of his frenzied fighting and heroic death in single combat against Achilles, his brother's slayer, *De excidio Troiae historia* and its dependent vernacular narratives focus on Hector to a far greater degree than his would-be avenger. In addition, the exceptional qualities of the older brother are underlined throughout the text. Even in the prelude to war, Hector is set apart.[19] He dismisses a prophecy of death by countering that hosts will fall and Greece will be cast into sorrow on his account.[20] Priam acknowledges his pre-eminence by appointing him battle-leader,[21] and is rewarded by displays of unparalleled strength on the part of his military commander.[22] Hector slays multitudes before being killed by Achilles. He outshines the world's heroes and is lamented by all in death.[23]

Furthermore, the authors of the different recensions of *Togail Troí* enhance Hector's role, accommodating additional details not derived from Dares' text. A minute description of Hector's appearance and general demeanour, termed *tuarascbáil Hectoir* in a marginal note, forms a unique part of the account of the first day's fighting in the Book of Leinster version of the text.[24] Moreover, his actions are comparable with those of Cú Chulainn in the *Táin*. Like the champion of the Ulaid, he too had supernatural weaponry; and a story recounting how he came to possess the wondrous *sigen Satuirn* ('standard of Saturn') is found in the Book of Leinster and in the later Recension III of *Togail Troí* alone.[25] As Recension I has a lacuna at this point in the narrative, whether it once contained this episode cannot be ascertained.[26] Elsewhere, however, this version too enhances the portrayal of Hector. A panegyric of him of a different kind augments the record of a truce in fighting in Recension I alone, noting the extent of his fame and likening his ferocity to that of a lion (*co luinde leoman*) and his wildness to that of a wolf (*co n-ainbthinche onchon*).[27] He is said to have filled the fields before Troy

---

1405–6; Meister, *De excidio*, chapter 31. **19** Stokes, 'Destruction', pp 12, 74, ll 311–12; Meister, *De excidio*, chapter 6. **20** Stokes, 'Destruction', pp 25, 90, ll 758–64; Meister, *De excidio*, chapter 17. **21** Stokes, 'Destruction', pp 27, 92, ll 800–1; Meister, *De excidio*, chapter 19. **22** Stokes, 'Destruction', pp 31, 33–4, 97, 100, ll 947–9, 1038–40; Meister, *De excidio*, chapters 21, 22. **23** Stokes, 'Destruction', pp 37–8, 104–6, ll 1167–98; Meister, *De excidio*, chapter 24. **24** *LL* iv, pp 1103–4. **25** Ibid., p. 1088, ll 31761–91; for the unpublished version in Recension III, see Miles, *Heroic saga*, pp 64–5. See also Rudolf Thurneysen, 'Irische Miscellen I: Die *Sigen Satuirn* in Togail Troí', *RC*, 6 (1883), 91–3; Mac Gearailt, 'Change', p. 473 and 'Zur literarischen Sprache', pp 113–14; Myrick, *From the* De excidio, pp 155–7 (though correspondences cited in the latter do not appear to be particularly close). **26** There was clearly a gap in the source text drawn on by the scribe of Dublin, TCD MS 1319 (H.2.17) at this point who remarks *esbaid so ar in l(a)ebar* 'there is a gap here in the book': Stokes, 'Destruction', p. 30, l. 921; Miles, *Heroic saga*, pp 65–6 and n. 72. **27** Stokes, 'Destruction', pp 34–5, 101, ll 1067–72.

with corpses (*rolin na maige do chollaib arbélaib na Trói*), causing Greece to lament (*robói dano óengáir guil 7 éighme for fut na Gréce*).[28] Nonetheless, its women love him having heard of his exploits (*ara herscélaib*) and kings' sons and noblemen journey to Troy to gaze upon his form (*do décain Hectoir*).[29] No skilled military man could defeat him; the Greeks failed to overcome him (*nocor-[fh]etsatar éim Gréic ... techt airi*), despite their superior knowledge and wisdom.[30] Similarly, a list of names of warriors killed by Hector in Dares is transformed into a series of dramatic encounters in the same version of *Togail Troí*;[31] in this case, the Book of Leinster version retains the brief format of the Latin text.[32]

It is in death that the preoccupation of Irish authors with Hector is particularly clear and three different versions of his demise are preserved in the extant recensions of *Togail Troí*.[33] According to Dares, in his final encounter with Achilles, Hector wounded his Greek opponent in the right thigh but was subsequently killed by a furious Achilles and this record of events is also found in the Book of Leinster, as well as in the twelfth-century poetic retelling of the Trojan War.[34] As Hector was struck in the back, the implication of cowardice this could imply, should the injury have been sustained while he was running away, is immediately refuted:

> Gē ra-goinedh ina druim,
> gē ra-thuit ar talmain truim
> ni thānic laech dār ghíall gail
> bidh chomhchalma re hEchtair.

> Though he was wounded in his back, though he fell on the mighty earth, there has not come [into the world] a hero whom valour serves, who was as brave as Hector.[35]

It is to the Greeks that negative actions are ascribed in an alternative account of Hector's death also preserved in the Book of Leinster, directly following on from the first account.[36] Attributed to Fergil ('Virgil') therein,[37] it links the

---

28 Ibid., pp 35, 101–2, ll 1074–84.   **29** Ibid., pp 35, 101–2, ll 1088–95.   **30** Ibid., pp 35, 101–2, ll 1097–102.   **31** Ibid., p. 32, ll 975–82. This section of the text is discussed in Miles, *Heroic saga*, pp 122–4; see also Myrick, *From the* De excidio, p. 120.   **32** *LL* iv, pp 1110–1, ll 32641–5.   **33** For a discussion of Hector's death, see Mac Eoin, 'Dán', p. 20 and Miles, *Heroic saga*, pp 64–6.   **34** *LL* iv, pp 1115–6, ll 32804–41; Mac Eoin, 'Dán', pp 40, 54 (stanza 84).   **35** Mac Eoin, 'Dán', pp 40, 54 (stanza 85). According to the Book of Leinster, Achilles was facing Hector when he cast at him the spear that the infernal smith, Ulcán, had wrought on his behalf, so that it pierced through Hector's protective armour and broke his back in two: *LL* iv, pp 1115–16, ll 32826–33.   **36** *LL* iv, p. 1116, ll 32842–7.   **37** Miles suggests that Fergil was originally an illustrious Irishman who was later merged with Virgil: *Heroic saga*, p. 66.

Trojan's death to deceit on the part of his opponents who hid Achilles in a pile of clothes (*daringset Gréic duma dá n-etaigib im Achíl*). Arising unbeknownst to Hector from the mound, the Greek hero wounded his rival dishonourably in the back (*coro guin fo chommus ina druim*).[38] This tale of treachery is the only version of Hector's slaying included in Recension I of *Togail Troí*.[39] The Book of Leinster adds a third twist, claiming that the Trojan champion only ever made one thrust at a battle opponent. Having failed to kill Achilles with that single blow, his enemy came upon him again after the encounter (*i ndiaid in madma*). Far from being a fair fight in battle, Achilles is said to have wounded him surreptitiously (*cen fhiss dó*), implying that an underhand method was involved. This is underlined by the final sentence relating to the killing: *Is tria cheilg tra amlaidsein darochair Hectoir co fír*, 'Thus, it was because of treachery that Hector really fell'.[40] Reference to their champion's extraordinary exploits,[41] and to the despondency of the Trojans as a result of his death,[42] concludes this episode in the Book of Leinster since the manuscript breaks off at this point. Thus it is with *Aided Hectoir* 'Hector's death-tale', which is designated as such in the text,[43] that this version of the Troy tale now ends. The subsequent actions of Troilus are considered in other extant versions of *Togail Troí*. He is not made to overshadow his sibling, however, and Hector's heroism remains undiminished in all the Irish narratives of Troy.

CONALL CERNACH *ALIAS* HECTOR

In Hector, therefore, the medieval Irish had an heroic type against whom their own champions could be measured. Moreover, since his exploits were allegedly witnessed by Dares, as emphasized in the Book of Leinster version of *Togail Troí*, they had been authenticated.[44] Direct testimony conveyed authority in an intellectual culture concerned with the construction of a narrative of history. Thus, Hector's value as a yardstick was immeasurable: his actions appear tangible and, best of all, were 'true'. He is accorded a place in the pre-Christian chronological scheme surviving in interrelated annalistic compilations in which

---

38 For discussion, see Miles, *Heroic saga*, p. 65; he cites the equivalent passage from another manuscript copy of Recension II (National Library of Scotland MS 71.1.15, fo. 19r), where some doubt is cast on the veracity of Fergil's account.   39 Stokes, 'Destruction', pp 37–8, ll 1167–98; Miles, *Heroic saga*, p. 65.   40 Mac Eoin, 'Dán', p. 20; Miles, *Heroic saga*, pp 64–6.   41 *LL* iv, p. 1116, ll 32863–4.   42 Ibid., p. 1117, ll 32872–4.   43 Ibid., p. 1113, l. 32740: *Aided Hectoir so sís*, 'Here follows "The death-tale of Hector"'.   44 Ibid., p. 1008, ll 32552–5. For discussion, see Dagmar Schlüter, *History or fable? The Book of Leinster as a document of cultural memory in twelfth-century Ireland*, Studien und Texte zur Keltologie 9 (Münster, 2010), p. 47; and Poppe and Schlüter, 'Greece', pp 141–2.

his slaying by Achilles, together with Helen's abduction and Achilles' own death, is recorded in the midst of Old Testament events.[45] His Irish heroic counterparts occupy a later place in the same timeline around the birth of Christ. Cú Chulainn, for example, as well as his wife, Emer, are said to have died in the very year Christ was born; a short time later, in the reign of Emperor Tiberius, Irél Glúnmár, son of Conall Cernach, reigned.[46]

In the case of Conall Cernach, specifically, a particular affinity with Hector was cultivated. In *Clann Ollaman úaisle Emna*, the two heroes are linked in the parallel list of Trojan and Irish warriors with which the poem commences: *Echtair mar Chonal cert Cernach / nert ro-garb re hernach n-áig*, 'Hector is like just Conall Cernach, a fierce strength against the iron of conflict'.[47] This reference proves pivotal since it is Hector who is again recalled when the poet turns to a depiction of the contemporary ruler of the Ulaid, Eochaid mac Duinnśléibe, having catalogued his sixty-six predecessors in the main body of his work.[48] Celebrated for military exploits – *ro-sia ler comrumach cliarach, / fer forburach fianach finn*, 'he will reach the sea triumphant with his retinues, the fair eager hero of war-bands'[49] – Eochaid is cast in the image of Hector, superior battle-leader, rather than that of King Priam.[50] Circumstances require royal warriors; hence *súil re hEchtair d'Éirinn aird*, 'noble Ireland looks to him as her Hector'.[51] As in the case of the Trojan champion, the affection of his kinsmen for him is famous (*is airrdeirc báid Ulad ann*) and he is the subject of women's talk (*comrád ban*).[52] Most importantly, like Hector he is a daring hero (*láech laimthenach*),[53] under whose leadership the Ulaid will emerge victorious.[54] What they need is a king who will combine justice (*cert*) with military strength (*nert ro-garb re hernach n-áig*). The significance of the opening stanzas, which culminate deliberately in the diptych of Hector and Conall Cernach, is thus skilfully revealed. The unifying image of Hector, counterpart of Conall Cernach in the past as he will be the equivalent of Eochaid in the future, provides the interpretative key.

We may speculate that in recalling Hector, the poet deliberately aligned his patron with a hero confronted by a superior host. Eochaid's rule was dominated by his struggle against his powerful Cenél nEógain contemporary, Muirchertach Mac Lochlainn.[55] In 1165, he led the Ulaid in a futile uprising

45 *ACott.*, p. 307.   46 Ibid., p. 314; *ATig.* (*RC* 16), p. 411.   47 Byrne, 'Clann Ollaman', pp 62, 76 (stanza 5), where *cert* is translated 'honest' rather than 'just'.   48 The mathematical calculation is the poet's own: ibid., pp 74, 80 (stanza 73).   49 Ibid., pp 75, 80 (stanza 79).   50 Priam is coupled with Conchobar mac Nessa: ibid., pp 61, 76 (stanza 3).   51 Ibid., pp 74, 80 (stanza 75).   52 Ibid., pp 74, 80 (stanzas 74, 75); Stokes, 'Destruction', pp 35, 102, ll 1085–92.   53 Byrne, 'Clann Ollaman', pp 75, 80 (stanza 78).   54 Ibid., stanza 80.   55 For his career, see Máire Herbert, 'The death of Muirchertach Mac Erca: a twelfth-century tale' in F. Josephson (ed.), *Celts and Vikings: proceedings of the Fourth Symposium of Societas Celtologica Nordica* (Göteborg, 1997), pp 27–40; and Donnchadh Ó Corráin, 'Muirchertach Mac Lochlainn and the "Circuit of Ireland"' in

against Mac Lochlainn and was expelled from the kingship as a result. Through the intercession of the king of Airgíalla, Donnchad Úa Cerbaill, who was Eochaid's foster-father, he was restored as ruler; the hostages of the Ulaid being pledged to his opponent as part of the contract (*tar cenn giall Uladh uile*).[56] The agreement did not remain in place for long, since he was blinded by Mac Lochlainn the following year.[57] This treacherous act was to prove Muirchertach's downfall: enraged, Úa Cerbaill gathered allies and marched against him and he was slain in the ensuing battle.[58]

Hector's heroism would have served Eochaid well at many stages during his chequered career.[59] The poem may have been written during a period of 'comparative prosperity' during his reign, as Francis John Byrne has suggested.[60] Alternatively, reminding the Ulaid that Eochaid was their Hector (*súil re hEchtair d'Éirinn aird*) could have served as a rallying cry of sorts during more troubled times. In its opening stanzas recalling ancient heroes, the poem echoes a composition of roughly the same date, that beginning *A Mhuirchertaigh mhic Néill náir* ('O noble Muirchertach mac Néill'), also known as *Mórthimchell Érenn uile*, the 'Circuit of Ireland'.[61] The subject of the poem, the tenth-century king of Ailech, Muirchertach mac Néill, is compared favourably with Cú Chulainn and Fergus mac Róich, who also appear in *Clann Ollaman*, as well as with the Munster hero, Cú Roí mac Dáire, who is not mentioned in the poem on the Ulaid.[62] Donnchadh Ó Corráin has demonstrated that the 'Circuit of Ireland' is in fact dynastic propaganda in favour of Muirchertach's twelfth-century namesake and successor, Muirchertach Mac Lochlainn, Eochaid mac Duinnshléibe's nemesis.[63] In their parallel preludes, therefore, one learned author may be deliberately responding to another in a skilful exchange. As a third comparative layer in the form of Trojan heroes is included in *Clann Ollaman*, it is tempting to see this as the later poem and to read it in part as a sophisticated response to a work cel-

---

A.P. Smyth (ed.), *Seanchas: studies in early and medieval archaeology, history and literature in honour of Francis J. Byrne* (Dublin, 2000), pp 238–50 at pp 246–7.   **56** *AU¹* 1165.   **57** *AU¹* 1166.   **58** The fragmentary annalistic compilation, Mac Cárthaigh's Book, preserves a particularly detailed account of the event: *gur marbhadh Muircheartach mac Neil h. Lochlainn, ri Oiligh, ann 7 do beanadh a ceann de a n-eanach Isa 7 Padraic 7 Hi Cearrbuill*, 'Muirchertach son of Niall Ó Lochlainn, king of Oileach, was killed and his head cut off for the [outraged] honour of Jesus, Patrick, and Ó Cearbhaill': *MIA*, pp 46–7.   **59** Byrne terms him 'unfortunate', noting that he 'scarcely lived up to the fulsome panegyric with which this poem concludes': 'Clann Ollaman', p. 93.   **60** He places the composition either in the years between 1158 and 1164 or during the short period after his restoration to the kingship in 1165 and before he was blinded at Easter of the following year: ibid., pp 54, 59.   **61** John O'Donovan (ed. and trans.), *The circuit of Ireland by Muircheartach mac Néill, prince of Aileach*, Tracts Relating to Ireland 1 (Dublin, 1841); Edmund Hogan (ed. and trans.), *Móirthimchell Éirenn uile dorigne Muirchertach mac Néill: the circuit of Ireland by Muirchertach son of Niall, A.D. 941* (Dublin, 1941).   **62** O'Donovan, *Circuit*, pp 26–9 (stanzas 3, 4, 5).   **63** Ó Corráin, 'Muirchertach Mac Lochlainn'.

ebrating a rival ruler. Like Muirchertach, Eochaid too is on a par with past Irish heroes, but he is the equivalent of their Trojan counterparts as well, being specifically a Hector for Ireland. In this connection, it is significant that Muirchertach mac Néill is termed 'Hector of the Western World' (*Echtoir iarthair beatha*) in his annalistic obit of 943.[64] The author of *Clann Ollaman* drew expertly on a diverse range of annalistic and other sources in his composition,[65] and may thus have been familiar with the earlier designation. If so, his portrayal of Eochaid as Hector could have served as a subtle link between this Ulaid ruler and the exalted leader in whose achievements Eochaid's archenemy, Muirchertach Mac Lochlainn, sought to bask.

In depicting Eochaid as Hector, the poet was also comparing him with the Trojan's Irish alter ego, Conall Cernach, as we have seen. The same pairing is employed in a late Middle Irish version (Recension III) of *Togail bruidne Da Derga* ('The destruction of Da Derga's hostel').[66] As part of an extended formulaic sequence in which Ingcél, a British brigand, describes a series of Irish heroes who are then identified for him by their kinsmen, a depiction of Conall Cernach's chamber (*imda Conaill Chernaig*) is given. In an elaboration not found in the corresponding passage of the earlier Recension II of the tale, Fer Rogain, one of the foster-brothers of King Conaire Mór, around whose destruction (*togail*) in the hostel (*bruiden*) the story revolves, provides additional information on Conall Cernach comparing him with Lug in the process.[67] His brother, Lomna Drúth, responds, beginning with his usual refrain: *mairg iuras in orgain, cid fodáig ind [fh]ir sin a óenur*, 'woe to him that shall wreak the Destruction, even because of this man alone!'.[68] An augmented description of the Irish warrior follows in which Lomna Drúth compares him specifically with Hector:

> ar is é sin óenlaech na fuilnget laich .i. is é in léo lond letartach látir lamthenach infuilech forderg fíchda forránach fir[f]eochair ardairsid Eorpa, oen inthamail Hechtair maic Priaím i n-iarthar in betha, in caur créchtaidi coscrach commáidmech sin Conall caem Cernach.
>
> for he is the one hero that heroes endure not: he is the savage, fierce, rending, strong, daring, bloody, crimson, warlike, destructive, truly-

---

64 *AU*[1] 943.2.   65 Byrne, 'Clann Ollaman', p. 59.   66 Recension III is preserved in London, BL MS Egerton 1782 and in a later direct copy of it: see Máire West, 'Leabhar na hUidhre's position in the manuscript history of *Togail bruidne Da Derga* and *Orgain brudne Uí Dergae*', *CMCS*, 20 (Winter 1990), 61–98 at 64 and her 'The genesis of *Togail bruidne Da Derga*: a re-appraisal of the "two source" theory', *Celtica*, 23 (1999), 413–35 at 413–14.   67 *Ar ni ro shaltair for féor Erenn dar n-éis Logha maicc Eithlenn gaiscedach a aiesa ro sosed for in fer sin*, 'For never since Lugh mac Eithlenn has there trodden the grass of Erin a champion of his age that would attain to this man': Whitley Stokes, 'The destruction of Da Derga's hostel', *RC*, 22 (1901), 9–61, 165–215, 282–329, 390–437 at 396–7.   68 Ibid.; cf. pp 200–1 and Eleanor Knott (ed.), *Togail bruidne Da Derga*, MMIS 8 (Dublin, 1936), p. 29.

fierce, Europe's high veteran, the one resembler of Hector son of Priam in the west of the world, that wound-inflicting, triumphant, praiseworthy hero, dear Conall Cernach.[69]

As one of a pair of right-hand protectors of King Conaire in this tale, Conall Cernach's role is pivotal in this version, as well as in the closely related, somewhat shorter Recension II which dates from earlier in the Middle Irish period. Conall Cernach is the antithesis in appearance of his partner-in-defence, Mac Cécht, both of whom 'embody opposite but complementary aspects of the martial hero's identity' in Ralph O'Connor's words.[70] Significantly, questions are raised about the heroism of both men in the story's powerful ending preserved in both versions.[71] In Conall Cernach's case his father, Amairgen, imputes cowardly motives to him on his return home alive, though wounded, after the *togail*.[72] On beholding his son's badly maimed arm, Amairgen acknowledges that Conall had in fact fought bravely.[73] In O'Connor's words, 'Conall becomes a true hero deserving of an audience's sympathy by virtue of his wounds'.[74] In this context, it is tempting to recall the implication of cowardice contained in the account of Hector's death, which is vigorously denied in the Irish retelling of the event.[75] While the parallel is in no way specific, the resonance may have chimed with some more learned members of the audience of *Togail bruidne Da Derga*. In specifying the link with Hector in the expanded description of Conall in Recension III of the tale, its author was alluding to an identity which appears by his time to have been well-known. This late Middle Irish version of the *Togail* may be roughly contemporary with *Clann Ollaman* in which the comparison is explicitly drawn, as we have seen.

The specific comparison is not drawn, however, in the detailed account of Conall Cernach's exploits in *Cath Ruis na Ríg*.[76] The version of this tale which survives in the Book of Leinster was also written about the same time as *Togail*

---

69 Stokes, 'Destruction of Da Derga's hostel', pp 396–7 §97; cf. 198–201 and Knott, *Togail*, p. 29. **70** *The destruction of Da Derga's hostel: kingship and narrative artistry in a mediaeval Irish saga* (Oxford, 2013), p. 197. I am grateful to Prof. O'Connor for fruitful discussion of this passage. **71** O'Connor, *Destruction*, pp 220–7, 326–8, provides an insightful, perceptive analysis of the tale's ending. See also Thomas Owen Clancy, 'Court, king and justice in the Ulster Cycle' in H. Fulton (ed.), *Medieval Celtic literature and society* (Dublin, 2005), 163–82. **72** *Tonga do dia tongthi mo thúath, is midlachdo dond fir do-deachaid a mbeathaid as iar fácbáil a thigernai lia a námtiu i mbás*, 'I swear by the god my people swear by, it is cowardly of the man who has come away alive having left his lord dead among his foes': Knott, *Togail*, p. 46; Stokes, 'Destruction of Da Derga's hostel', p. 328; O'Connor, *Destruction*, p. 221 (translation). **73** *'Ro fich ind lám sin indnocht for cách, a maccáin, 7 ro fiched furri'* ol *Amairgin*, '"That arm beat everybody down tonight, little son, and it was beaten down", said Amairgin': Knott, *Togail*, p. 46; Stokes, 'Destruction of Da Derga's hostel', p. 328; O'Connor, *Destruction*, p. 326 (translation). See also Amy C. Eichorn-Mulligan, '*Togail bruidne Da Derga* and the politics of anatomy', *CMCS*, 49 (Summer, 2005), 1–19 at 18. **74** *Destruction*, p. 327. **75** See above, p. 262. **76** Hogan, *Cath Ruis na Ríg*.

bruidne Da Derga's Recension III.[77] Moreover, stylistic similarities between this battle-tale and *Togail Troí* have been noted by Mac Gearailt who highlights the common intellectual milieu in which both compositions took form. Notwithstanding the obvious potential for parallels between Conall's heroic exploits as recounted in this story and Hector's deeds as related in accounts of Troy, the connection between both warriors is not made in this particular *cath*-narrative. Conall's valour is therein eloquently expressed in other ways.

CONCLUSION

In general, however, appropriating Hector's image to adorn an Irish hero formed part of the literary currency of the day and Conall Cernach in particular was most frequently so described.[78] In *Clann Ollaman úaisle Emna*, the identification of the two warriors forms the cornerstone of the poem, as the author skilfully admits his subject, Eochaid mac Duinnshléibe, to their company also. In so doing, I suggest, he was responding subtly and effectively to propaganda written on behalf of his patron's main opponent, Muirchertach Mac Lochlainn, in which it was implied that, like his tenth-century predecessor, Muirchertach mac Néill, he was the 'Hector of the Western World'. The counter-claim that noble Ireland looks rather to Eochaid as Hector (*súil re hEchtair d'Éirinn aird*) acquires the added resonance that the ruler of the Ulaid embodies the justice and strength of Conall Cernach, since an equivalence between him and Hector had already been noted (*Echtair mar Chonal cert Cernach / nert ro-garb re hernach n-áig*). In connecting these two heroes, the poet most likely had recourse to earlier texts in which Conall was Ireland's Hector, as well as accounts of the Trojan War. In this way, the story of Troy coloured the constructed record of Ireland's remote and more recent history, as local characters and events were made to resonate with those of a wider world stage. In this important learned enterprise, the Hectors of Ireland and the Western World are accorded a central place.[79]

---

77 Uáitéar Mac Gearailt, '*Cath Ruis na Ríg* and twelfth-century literary and oral tradition', *ZCP*, 44 (1991), 128–53 at 148.   78 The most extended comparison of an Irish hero with Hector, however, is that of Murchad son of Brían Bórama, written early in the twelfth century: James Henthorn Todd (ed. and trans.), *Cogadh Gaedhel re Gallaibh: the war of the Gaedhil with the Gaill, or the invasions of Ireland by the Danes and other Norsemen* (London, 1867), pp 166–7, 186–7; see Máire Ní Mhaonaigh, '"The metaphorical Hector": the literary portrayal of Murchad mac Bríain' in R. O'Connor (ed.), *Classical literature and learning in medieval Irish narrative*, Studies in Celtic History 34 (Woodbridge, 2014), pp 140–61.   79 Máire Herbert's research has revolutionized our understanding of this 'learned enterprise' and of the intellectual world of medieval Ireland in general. This contribution owes much to her analysis of twelfth-century texts in particular, and more to her support, guidance and friendship through very many years.

Tús na heagna omhan Dé:
penance and retribution in a poem by
Aonghus Fionn Ó Dálaigh

EMMA NIC CÁRTHAIGH

Quid prius dicam solitis parentis
Laudibus? qui res hominum ac deorum,
Qui mare ac terras, variisque mundum
Temperat horis (Horatius, Liber I, Carmen xii)[1]

The poem beginning *Tús na heagna omhan Dé* was transcribed from Dublin, RIA MS 23 G 23 (259) and translated by Lambert McKenna in the volume of fifty-four poems by Aonghus Fionn Ó Dálaigh that he compiled in 1919.[2] In light of McKenna's statement in his preface to this volume that '[t]he lyrics of Aonghus Ó Dálaigh and his fellows are as untranslatable as those of Horace',[3] and considering the theme of *Tús na heagna omhan Dé*, the above verse would seem to be a fitting epigraph for a study of the poem.[4] While Ó Dálaigh's composition is not intended to be a traditional eulogy, he appropriated its *initium* from a well-known praise poem of the Christian tradition, Psalm 110, a connection that will be discussed later in the course of this introduction.

The following edition and translation of the poem are based on the oldest extant copy of the text which is preserved in the Book of the O'Conor Don. This poem survives in full or in part in twenty-eight manuscripts of the seventeenth, eighteenth and nineteenth centuries. The edition is supplemented with variant readings from seven other manuscripts including the only other extant seventeenth-century copy of the poem and the six complete

---

I dedicate this article to Professor Máire Herbert whose unparalleled wisdom, generosity, humour and constant encouragement have been an invaluable part of my life and work since I first became her student more than twenty years ago.
1 'What should come first in my song but the honor due to the Father, ruler of men and gods, whose realm is the earth and the sea and the sky in all its seasons?' Text from H.H. Milman (ed.), *Quinti Horatii Flacci opera* (London, 1868), p. 17. Translation from Joseph P. Clancy, *The odes and epodes of Horace: a modern English verse translation* (Chicago and London, 1960), p. 38. 2 Lambert McKenna (ed. and trans.), *Dánta do chum Aonghus Fionn Ó Dálaigh* (Dublin and London, 1919), pp 50–1. This collection first appeared in print in instalments in *The Irish Monthly*, 45, dxxiii–dxxxxiv and 46, dxxxv–dxliii (1917–18); *Tús na heagna omhan Dé* is found in 46, dxxxviii–dxxix (1918), pp 215, 288. See also a partial transcript of the poem in Úna Ní Ógáin and Riobard Ó Duibhir (eds), *Dánta Dé idir sean agus nuadh* (Dublin, 1928), p. 124. 3 Ibid., p. iv. 4 I am most grateful to Dr Aidan Doyle for reading a draft of this article and for his corrections, suggestions and comments.

eighteenth-century copies. The following seven manuscripts were consulted for the *apparatus criticus*:

1	Dublin, RIA MS 24 L 6 (8)	1679	L
2	Maynooth, St Patrick's College MS C 88	1704	C
3	Maynooth, St Patrick's College MS M 84	1738–47	M
4	Dublin, RIA MS 24 B 26 (242)	1760–1	B
5	Dublin, RIA MS 23 G 27 (492)	1785	R
6	Dublin, RIA MS 23 G 23 (256)	1794–5	G
7	Dublin, NLI MS G 40	18th c.	N

Of the twenty-eight surviving copies of the poem, twenty-one provide a full text (twelve / thirteen quatrains), one provides a four-quatrain text, one a three-quatrain text, while five provide merely the first quatrain of the poem.[5]

The twenty-one full copies of the poem generally provide the same text with little variation. However, those in Fermoy, St Colman's College MS CF 5; Dublin, RIA MS 23 B 26 (500) and Maynooth, St Patrick's College MS M 72, all comprising thirteen quatrains, also include an additional quatrain after the poem's *dúnadh*. This verse is clearly meant to be read in connection with the poem even though it is not directly related to it. The verse reads as follows in MS CF 5 (*vel sim.* in MS 23 B 26 (500) and MS M 72):

> A fhir na heagna diaraidh
> bheith ria as obair éigchialladh
> gan grádh is eagla an Athar
> mádh áil teagna dullmhachadh. etc.

> O man who is searching for wisdom,
> it is meaningless work to have it –
> if you desire to prepare your wisdom –
> without love and fear of the Father. etc.

This verse is, in fact, the opening of a short religious poem, five quatrains in length, that is extant in five manuscripts, one of which, Maynooth, St Patrick's College MS M 84, also preserves a copy of *Tús na heagna omhan Dé*.[6] This poem is in print in *Measgra dánta* and the first two quatrains were also included by T.F. O'Rahilly in *Dánfhocail*, his anthology of epigrammatic verse collected from modern Irish manuscripts.[7] While the quatrain beginning *A fhir*

---

5 Details of the manuscripts containing copies of the poem may be found in the appendix to this edition. 6 The five manuscripts are as follows: London, BL MS Egerton 136; Dublin, RIA MS 23 O 78 (1387); Dublin, NLI MS G 140; Maynooth, St Patrick's College MS M 84 and Dublin, RIA MS 24 L 13 (7). This information was gleaned from the Bardic Poetry Database of the Dublin Institute for Advanced Studies. 7 Thomas F.

na heagna d'iarraidh evidently belongs to a separate poem, there is no denying that its content mirrors some of the same core sentiments as those expressed in general in *Tús na heagna omhan Dé*; it also displays a similar cautionary tone to that expressed in the latter poem. The first scribe to append the initial quatrain of *A fhir na heagna d'iarraidh* to his transcript of *Tús na heagna omhan Dé* – and indeed subsequent copyists who also appended the quatrain to their own transcripts – may have intended to include it as a hint or reminder to the reader of the existence of the full text of this companion piece of advice, the perusal of which would undoubtedly complement a reading of the longer poem.

We may consider the contents of the incomplete copies before examining the poem in full. The four-quatrain copy may be found in Dublin, RIA MS 23 N 20 (465) and consists of the first four quatrains of the poem (including that beginning *A dhuine bhoicht*) written by Mícheál Óg Ó Longáin in *ogham órdha* (golden ogham), a late development of traditional *ogam* script.[8] In this manuscript, the cipher is designed to represent vowel-sounds and comprises symbols that denote the five vowels followed by five digraphs, i.e., *ao, ea, ia, ua* and *oi*. Two exceptions are symbols that represent *ng* and *h*; other consonants are rendered according to the Roman alphabet.

The three-quatrain copy is in Dublin, RIA MS 3 B 5 (226) and consists of the first three quatrains of the poem introduced as *deirbhshiúr // don // eagna // 7c.* (The sister to wisdom, etc.). The text concludes abruptly at the end of a page and is immediately followed by another poem. It is possible that the scribe included the fragment merely as a means to fill a page that was half-empty. This poem with its popular *initium* would be a suitable filler in such a case.

Five manuscripts contain the first quatrain only of *Tús na heagna omhan Dé*:

(1)   In London, BL MS Egerton 165, Seán Ó Neachtain inscribed the verse in the middle of the first folio and in the absence of any other text. Here, it seems to serve as a talisman of sorts at the opening of the manuscript.

(2)   Similarly, in London, BL MS Egerton 147, this quatrain is found at the beginning of a new section of the manuscript where it is accompanied by a four-line Irish text, two lines of Latin and the name of the scribe 'James Naghten', which is written twice in English even though the manuscript was compiled by Tadhg and Seán Ó Neachtain.[9] Robin Flower has commented on Seán Ó Neachtain's

O'Rahilly (ed.), *Measgra dánta. Miscellaneous Irish poems*, part II (Dublin, 1977), pp 178–9 §68; idem (ed.), *Dánfhocail: Irish epigrams in verse* (Dublin, 1921), p. 28 §139.   8 Cf. Meidhbhín Ní Úrdail, '*Ogham órdha* in den späteren irisch-gälischen Handschriften' in R. Ködderitzsch, A. Wigger and S. Zimmer (eds), *Akten des zweiten deutschen Keltologen-Symposiums* (Tübingen, 1999), pp 149–62.   9 *BM Cat.* ii, p. 370.

propensity to give this cautionary verse prominence. In his catalogue of Irish manuscripts in the British Museum, he notes in his description of MS Egerton 147 that, 'On f. 59 b among other scribbles in the hand of Seán Ó Neachtain is the quatrain: "Tús na heagna uamhain Dé", a favourite with him (cf. Eg. 165, art. 1)'.[10]

(3–4) In Dublin, RIA MS 23 M 7 (287) the quatrain is slotted in between two unrelated texts, while in Cork, UCC MS Torna 28, it occurs among a short series of proverbs, the first of which is *Is geal leis a bhfiach-dubh a ghearcacach* (sic) *fhéin* ('the raven thinks his own chick is beautiful').

(5) The most interesting occurrence of this single quatrain is in London, BL Egerton MS 146, which contains a list of 'Seanráidhte Eireannacha' (old Irish sayings or proverbs) in alphabetical order. *Tús na heagna omhan Dé* occurs at the end of the section of phrases beginning with T. Unlike the other proverbs which consist of one line or sentence, this one begins with 'Tos eagnadh uathmuin Dé' and is followed by the rest of the quatrain: 'ni'l eagnadh mar í / maith an gne don é / eagladh Dé gi ar a mbi'. In a more modern context, the proverb 'Túis na heagna uamhan Dé' is also included by T.F. O'Rahilly in his miscellany of Irish proverbs.[11]

The origin of this proverb lies in the Bible, where it appears in four places: Ecclesiasticus 1:16 (*initium sapientiae timor Domini*), Proverbs 1:7 (*timor Domini principium scientiae sapientiam atque doctrinam stulti despiciunt*), Proverbs 9:10 (*principium sapientiae timor Domini et scientia sanctorum prudentia*),[12] and Psalm 110:10 (according to the numbering of the Vulgate) which begins, *Alleluia. Confitebor tibi, Domine*. The last verse of this psalm states: *initium sapientiae timor Domini, intellectus bonus omnibus facientibus eum. Laudatio eius manet in saeculum saeculi* ('The fear of the Lord is the beginning of wisdom. A good understanding to all that do it: his praise continueth for ever and ever').[13] The latter text would appear to have given rise to the Irish proverb. This verse from Psalm 110 was widely known and commonly

---

10 *BM Cat.* ii, p. 372.   11 T.F. O'Rahilly (ed.), *A miscellany of Irish proverbs* (Dublin, 1922), p. 45 §163.   12 Considering that the Irish translation of this extract entered into common parlance as a proverb in early modern Ireland, it is worth noting that certain resonances exist between the opening quatrain of Ó Dálaigh's poem and the Irish translation of the above-mentioned extracts from Proverbs: *Asé eagla an* TIGHEARNA *tosach a néoluis: acht dísbeaguid na hamadáin eagna agus teagasg*, Proverbs 1:7; *Isé eagla an* TIGHEARNA *tosach na heagna: agus éolus na náomh is tuigse sin*, Proverbs 9:10 (from William Bedell, *An Biobla Naomhtha*, London, 1817).   13 All extracts quoted in Latin from the Bible are from the Vulgate. This translation, like that of Psalm 110 in its entirety below, is taken from the 1899 edition of the Douay-Rheims Bible.

employed in daily discourse in early modern Ireland and continental Europe and the Irish proverb is a direct translation of the opening statement of the same verse. The popularity of this verse may even be inferred from Aonghus Fionn Ó Dálaigh's appropriation of the saying as an apt *initium* for the composition edited below which concerns penance, retribution and remorse for sin in the face both of Christ's wounds and of Judgement Day.

While this Irish proverb, which derives from the psalter, forms the *initium* of Ó Dálaigh's poem, it is noteworthy that it is also intrinsically connected with Tadhg mac Dáire Mac Bruaideadha's address to the fourth earl of Thomond, Donnchadh Ó Briain, written close to the end of the sixteenth century and beginning *Mór a-tá ar theagasc flatha*.[14] Quatrain 26 reads as follows:

> Ná tréig choidhche ceachtar dhíobh:
> searc is omhan an Airdríogh;
> tús gach fíreagna is sé sin:
> síreagla Dé ar na daoinibh.

Never forsake either of them: love and fear of the High-King; that is the beginning of all true wisdom: people's constant fear of God.[15]

This quatrain occurs, in turn, as part of an inscription over a doorway in a cloister of the Irish College of Saint Isidore in Rome.[16] The inscription is prefaced by the above-mentioned extract from Psalm 110 as follows: *Initivm Sapientiæ, timor Domini*. Incidentally, the same extract appears over the main entrance to *Archiginnasio della Sapienza*, the former site of the modern *Università di Roma 'La Sapienza'*, whose nickname clearly derives from the inscription. The existence of these two inscriptions and the occurrence of quatrain 26 of Mac Bruaideadha's poem next to that in the College of Saint Isidore indicate the popularity both in Ireland and continental Europe of this aphorism from the psalter, whose unveiled admonition constitutes one of the central tenets of the Christian message.

Unlike Ó Dálaigh, Mac Bruaideadha does not translate the extract from Psalm 110 directly into his poem; nor does he refer to the extract *per se* or to the psalm from which it is taken in any marginal notes connected to quatrain 26. However, this quatrain is clearly influenced by Psalm 110:10. It would appear that Mac Bruaideadha is deliberately paraphrasing this well-known warning in the course of these four lines for the purpose of advising

---

14 For the most recent edition and translation of this poem, see Emma Nic Cárthaigh, '*Mór a-tá ar theagasc flatha*: *Speculum principis* le Tadhg mac Dáire Mheic Bhruaideadha' in S. Ó Coileáin, L.P. Ó Murchú and P. Riggs (eds), *Séimhfhear suairc: aistí in ómós don Ollamh Breandán Ó Conchúir* (An Daingean, 2013), pp 139–80. 15 Ibid., pp 155, 168; see also note 26, pp 172–3. 16 Ibid., p. 180, where a photograph of the inscription has been reproduced.

Donnchadh Ó Briain concerning the essential attributes of a good and successful prince.

There is possibly an even deeper connection between Mac Bruaideadha's
poem and Psalm 110. While *Mór a-tá ar theagasc flatha* is ostensibly a metrical *speculum principis*, in which Mac Bruaidheadha, according to the preroga-
tive of the traditional *ollamh flatha*, assumes the role of advisor and instructor
to his prince and patron, the composition also serves indirectly and somewhat
tentatively as a praise poem. The first forty-four quatrains are chiefly concerned with the kind of advice that we may expect in a *speculum principis* that
is directed at a new leader. For example, Donnchadh Ó Briain is advised not
to go into battle without just cause (q. 40) and is warned to deal fiercely with
plunderers but compassionately with men of art (q. 38). The poet is explicit
at times in expressing the positive outcomes that may be expected should Ó
Briain fulfil his traditional duties (q. 5):

> Ag leanmhuin ríogh don reacht cháir,
> tig a-rís – ríoghdha an éadáil –
> sgeith gach lántoraidh re a linn
> 's gach leith d'fhántolaigh Fhéilim.

> By a king adhering to correct law, there comes again – princely the
> gain – a pouring forth of every plentiful fruit during his reign against
> every part of Féilim's sloping hill (Ireland).[17]

The implication is that should Ó Briain imbibe his chief poet's advice and
follow his instructions, then his country and his people will prosper and he,
as *taoiseach*, will deserve high praise. We understand from the tone of the text
that this has not happened yet; Ó Briain (q. 45) has only recently assumed his
role as *taoiseach* or *iarla*:

> Ní mholabh, a mheic mh'ochta,
> tusa, gé a-taoi ionmholta,
> dod dheirc ghoirmríogha a-tú im thosd
> go gcoimhlíona tú ar dteagasg.

> I will not praise you, dear son, although you are praiseworthy; regarding
> your eye of princely blue I remain quiet until you carry out our teaching.[18]

It is at this point in the poem that the tone changes and Mac Bruaideadha
employs a trope of the traditional praise poem, spending fifteen quatrains
saying in various ways that he will *not* praise Ó Briain and his various praiseworthy attributes until he follows his chief poet's advice, for example:

17 Ibid., pp 148, 166.   18 Ibid., pp 161, 170.

> Ní mholabh, go dtí ar mo thal,
> géaga an chnis nó an cneas donnghlan,
> niamhchroinn is neamhchumhgha fiodh
> d'fhialchoill ghealchubhra Gaoidheal.

Until you follow me, I will not praise the limbs of your body or your swarthy clear complexion, bright trees and unnarrow wood of the noble, vivid, fragrant forest of the Gaels. (q. 46)[19]

He thus indirectly lauds Ó Briain while simultaneously withholding his praise until it will have been earned well.

Psalm 110 is also a traditional praise poem, but it has no need to employ such literary devices. The king to whom the praise is directed in this psalm has already fulfilled his traditional duties as king and is afforded all the tributes deserving of a good and noble lord:

1 I will praise thee, O Lord, with my whole heart; in the council of the just: and in the congregation.

2 Great are the works of the Lord: sought out according to all his wills.

3 His work is praise and magnificence: and his justice continueth for ever and ever.

4 He hath made a remembrance of his wonderful works, being a merciful and gracious Lord:

5 He hath given food to them that fear him. He will be mindful for ever of his covenant:

6 He will shew forth to his people the power of his works.

7 That he may give them the inheritance of the Gentiles: the works of his hands are truth and judgement.

8 All his commandments are faithful: confirmed for ever and ever, made in truth and equity.

9 He hath sent redemption to his people: he hath commanded his covenant for ever. Holy and terrible is his name:

10 The fear of the Lord is the beginning of wisdom. A good understanding to all that do it: his praise continueth for ever and ever.

In including a paraphrase of the key verse of the psalm in his own poem, which is directed at a callow lord who has yet to fulfil his traditional role, Mac Bruaideadha is perhaps drawing the mind of his *taoiseach* and his general audience to this devotional text, the author of which is in a position to offer fulsome praise to a long-established, just, generous, wise and merciful lord who is an example to all.

19 Ibid., pp 162, 170.

Let us return now to the first quatrain of *Tús na heagna omhan Dé*, whose opening is a translation of the same key verse of Psalm 110.[20] Its occurrence unaccompanied by any related text in five manuscripts, two of which place it among a list of commonly used proverbs or sayings, is not surprising in the context of a devout Christian setting, considering, not only its derivation from Psalm 110:10, but also the message that this verse conveys alongside its general popularity. It is perhaps no surprise that Aonghus Fionn Ó Dálaigh, referred to as 'Aonghus na Diadhachta' ('the Aonghus of Piety') in some manuscripts,[21] and whose name is synonymous with bardic poems of a religious nature, should have selected the popular Psalm 110:10 for attention and chosen to elaborate on its core sentiments in the form of a full poem.

As mentioned at the outset, this edition is based on the earliest extant copy of the poem, which is found in the Book of the O'Conor Don, and is supplemented by variant readings from the seven next earliest extant copies. A full diplomatic transcript of the text from the Book of the O'Conor Don accompanies the edited text for the convenience of the reader who may wish to consult the manuscript readings. Italics have been used both in the semi-diplomatic transcript and in the *apparatus criticus* to indicate expansions of all scribal contractions (excluding the *punctum delens* and *spiritus asper*), except where two or more copies share the same reading but employ contractions differently. In cases such as these, the reading is left in Roman script. *Vel sim.* (i.e., *vel similia*) is used for groups of readings that are more or less identical except for inclusion or absence of lenition and length-marks, and for minor orthographical variation. The text of the edition has been normalised and emended where necessary, either for metrical or semantic reasons, in accordance with the standards of Classical Modern Irish. Punctuation, capital letters and length-marks have been either supplied or standardised throughout the text.

A minor but somewhat interesting point to note in relation to the transmission of the text is that only one of the twenty-seven other copies of the

---

20 It is interesting to note that the last line of this opening quatrain, which reads *eagla Dé gidh bé ar a mbí*, echoes the exact wording of part of a verse concerning love and fear in the Irish translation of 1 John 4:18: *Ní bhfuil eagla sa ngrádh; achd cuiridh an grádh diongmhálta eagla amach úadh: óir atá pían aig an neagla. Uime sin gidh bé ar a mbí eagla ní bhfuil sé diongmhálta a ngrádh* [my emphasis] ('There is no fear in love; but perfect love casteth out fear: because fear hath torment. He that feareth is not made perfect in love'.) The Irish text is taken from William Bedell, *An Biobla naomhtha* (London, 1817); the English is taken from the King James Version.   **21** For example, in Dublin, NLI MS G 312, p. 482, a poem by Ó Dálaigh is introduced as follows: 'Ó Dálaigh Fionn .i. Aongus na Diadhachta cc do Mhuire'. The same introduction is found in Dublin, NLI MS G 429, p. 219: 'Ó Dála Fionn .i. Aongus na Diadhachta cc. do Mhuire'. In Cork, UCC MS Murphy 63, p. 731, he is described as 'Aongus na Diadhachta O Dálaigh' and in Kilkenny, St Kieran's College MS CC 6, pp 97 and 143, he is referred to as 'Aongus Ó Dála na Diadhachta'.

poem displays an unmistakeable similarity to that preserved in the Book of the O'Conor Don. This is Kilkenny, St Kieran's College MS CC 1, which was compiled by Eugene O'Curry for the priest and scholar Mathghamhain Ó Caolaighe in St Patrick's College, Maynooth in 1846. O'Curry outlines the details of his commission in the following colophon on page 634:

> Orait ar Eóghan Ó Chómhraidhe do scríbh, agus thionóil as leabhraibh éagsamhlaibh, an duanaire diadha so; do Mhathghamhain ua Chaolaighe, sacart agus saoi léighinn a ccolláiste Maighe Nuadhat. A n-Áth Cliath. 1846.

> Pray for Eoghan Ó Comhraidhe who wrote, and collected from various books, this devotional anthology; for Mathghamhain Ua Caolaighe, a priest and man of letters in the college of Maynooth. In Dublin. 1846.

One of the 'leabhair éagsamhla' was doubtless the Book of the O'Conor Don. Pádraig Ó Macháin has observed that, in 1848, O'Curry 'made an important two-volume transcript of much of its contents, which was used as a surrogate by scholars over the years'.[22] The copies of *Tús na heagna omhan Dé* in the Book of the O'Conor Don and in CC 1 are the only two to omit the quatrain beginning 'A dhuine bhoicht as claon cúis' which occurs after q. 3 in the complete copies of the text. These two manuscripts are also the only ones to provide the metrically faulty reading *aisléin* and the semantically faulty reading *uaín*, both of which occur in q. 5.

Turning now to metrical matters, the poem was composed according to the exigencies of *rannaigheacht mhór* ($7^1,7^1,7^1,7^1$). The Book of the O'Conor Don copy fulfils the requirements of this metre to a large degree, including a relatively small amount of metrical faults, as may be expected. In the edition, I have emended these faults where emendation is feasible while interfering as little as possible with the integrity of the text.

The demands of the metre as well as the metrical faults that the poem exhibits may be observed as follows. There are three instances of faulty syllable-count in lines 2d, 3a, 5b, all of which were emended without much intervention. All end-rhyme between *b* and *d* is perfect except for *leís : cnis* in q. 9; this may be emended to *leis : cneis* in order to render the rhyme perfect. There is perfect consonance between *bd* and *ac* in all quatrains. Of the forty-eight required internal rhymes, six are absent, all omissions being from first couplets; twenty-eight of the forty-two extant internal rhymes are perfect and fourteen are faulty; it was possible to emend fully or partially three of these: *mfaludh : omhan* → *m'fholudh : omhan* 3cd; *aithmeile : aisléin* →

22 Pádraig Ó Macháin, 'An introduction to the Book of the O'Conor Don' in idem (ed.), *The Book of the O'Conor Don: essays on an Irish manuscript* (Dublin, 2010), pp 1–31 at pp 2–3.

aithmhéile : aisléine 5ab; *chionta : iompu* → *chionnta : iompu* 5cd. One perfect rhyme had to be rendered imperfect for semantic reasons: *dhearg : leanb* → *dhearg : leanbh* 9cd. *Aicill* rhyme between the final stressed word of *c* and a stressed word in the interior of *d* is faulty in quatrains 2 and 10; it was possible to emend one of these rhymes successfully: *cruaíd : lúan* → *cruadh : luan* 10cd. Alliteration is present between two words in every line, the final word of *d* alliterating with the preceding stressed word. The only exception is in 4c where alliteration is absent. The poem ends with the stressed word *tú*, a perfect *dúnadh* with the opening word of the text *tús*.

Turning to an examination of the text itself, even the most cursory of readings reveals Ó Dálaigh's explicit purpose in composing this poem as well as the simultaneous subtlety and force of his style and turn of phrase. There is a number of familiar signs embedded in the text that leave us in no doubt as to the authorship of the poem. Lambert McKenna, in the introduction to his compilation of Ó Dálaigh's *opus*, comments on the poet's frequent devotion to the Virgin Mary in his work: 'Some seventeen of the poems of Aonghus are devoted to the Blessed Virgin. Some of these are simply eulogies of the personal beauty of Our Lady'.[23] There are three references to the Virgin in *Tús na heagna omhan Dé* (qq 8, 9, 11), two of which are intended particularly to encourage the reader to take notice of the exhortations of the poem as a whole: 'think of Mary and her women around the stone' (q. 8) and 'Mary's breast and the redness of her tears serve as a restraint on the anger of the King of Kings' (q. 11). Ó Dálaigh does not doubt the power that the image of the Virgin's grief, suffering and influence over God will have over the Christian reader who may suffer from self-doubt and dread the fate of his own soul after death. In quatrain 8, the poet employs an image of the tableau of the Virgin and her attendants suffused with grief at the mouth of Christ's tomb, in order to wring repentance and humility from his reader. He probes the reader's conscience using as a tool to do so the suffering of the Virgin as a mother whose son has been killed before her eyes. He continues, in quatrain 11, to coax the reader to repentance in light of the Virgin's power to mitigate the anger of God himself. In quatrain 9, Ó Dálaigh conjures up a sweeping cosmic image of the Virgin as Christ's closest companion standing beside the devout Christian hosts together with the Cross, which will reveal itself alongside Christ in Judgement on Doomsday. In doing so, he expresses his own devotion to the Virgin, while exalting her position as mother, as bereaved one, as merciful one and as intercessor on behalf of any Christian sinner who lives in fear of his fate.

The poem provides us with a second sign that points to Ó Dálaigh as the author of the text, a sign that McKenna also refers to in the introduction to his compilation of the former's work: 'A characteristic of the poems of

23 McKenna, *Dánta*, pp ix–x.

Aonghus is the frequency with which the Archangel Michael is prayed to'.[24] Meidhbhín Ní Urdail has also drawn attention to this feature of Ó Dálaigh's poetry:

> The poet in question is probably Aonghus (mac Amhlaoibh) *al.* Aonghus 'na Diadhachta' Ó Dálaigh ... This is particularly likely in light of the poem's *iargomharc* which is an invocation to the Archangel Michael. Aonghus Fionn's poetry, in fact, is characterised by the frequency with which the Archangel Michael is prayed to.[25]

The concluding verse, or *iargomharc*, of *Tús na heagna omhan Dé* consists of an invocation to the Archangel Michael, in which the poet relinquishes his role as advisor to his general readership and expresses a deeply personal and meaningful association with the Archangel, which, we are given to understand, is a source of continual and enduring solace to the poet, who appears to maintain the highest and harshest standards imaginable for himself.

Amid the layers of public exhortation and personal struggle, certain aspects of Ó Dálaigh's style are so strong, bold and deliberate that they set this short poem apart. The text is littered with epithets, metaphors, conceits, and a powerful appropriation of official terms pertaining to medieval Irish law. It is worth paying some attention to each of these aspects of Ó Dálaigh's style in turn.

God is referred to through use of epithets such as 'the King of Kings' (qq 3, 4, 11) and 'the God of Creation' (q. 4). Ó Dálaigh uses two different terms to describe God as the King of Kings: *Rí na Ríogh* (qq 3 and 4) and *Ruire na Ríogh* (q. 11). The latter epithet is commonly used in religious poetry to describe God and is a borrowing of the native Irish term for a higher grade of king. The Archangel Michael is addressed as *a Ríoghmhaoir bheo* 'o living Royal-steward' (q. 12). As in the case of *ruire*, the term *maor* is an official term used in royal contexts and refers specifically to the steward of an Irish king. Such epithets drawn directly from the particular Irish experience of royalty enliven the text and heighten the rhetoric, undoubtedly with a view to striking true fear and remorse into the hearts of the susceptible reader.

If fear of God is the beginning of wisdom, then quatrain 3 would have it that fear and love of God together constitute metaphorical shelter that is adequate for the protection of the essence of the poet's self. Here, Ó Dálaigh emphasizes the power of love and fear of God in order to give force to his point. The essence or substance of his self, which is unfree and blemished by

---

24 Ibid., p. xiii.   **25** Meidhbhín Ní Urdail, 'A poem addressed to Donnchadh Ó Briain, fourth earl of Thomond' in J. Carey, M. Herbert and K. Murray (eds), *Cín Chille Cúile: texts, saints and places: essays in honour of Pádraig Ó Riain* (Aberystwyth, 2004), pp 193–207 at p. 194.

sin, is indirectly portrayed as an unworthy, fragile, vulnerable thing requiring shelter, which ultimately need not consist of more than love and respect for God. This frailty implies the weakness and imperfection of man in contrast with the steadfast love and mercy of God. The sinner need not feel under threat of eternal damnation, although he might deserve it, as long as he has true love for and fear of his spiritual King.

In the same quatrain, the poet employs a conceit that is reminiscent of metaphysical poetry: he speaks longingly of being possessed by his God, of being rendered unfree by such possession. This 'unfreedom' is a subjugation to be desired and to be aspired to. This is not unlike the passionate exhortations of the metaphysical poet John Donne in his sonnet beginning 'Batter my heart' where he exclaims that God's possession of him will make him simultaneously free and unfree: 'Take mee to you, imprison mee, for I / Except you'enthrall mee, never shall be free, / nor ever chast, except you ravish mee'.[26]

Quatrain 9 employs a moving conceit, 'skin-companion', to describe Christ's cross. This conceit strikes at the very nature and character of the cross' relationship with Christ. There is a contradiction at the heart of this relationship: the cross tortures Christ, the beloved lord of all Christians, whose hearts break to think of Christ's passion; however, without the cross to assist him, Christ cannot fulfil his role of Saviour. The cross is to be maligned and cherished simultaneously. The conceit in quatrain 9 encapsulates this contradiction: the cross is Christ's companion, his intimate friend, his aide, who will help him to discharge his duty and the sacrifice that is demanded of him and that is simultaneously his birth-right and his torment; the cross is not only his companion in this regard, but is more specifically his 'skin-companion', implying not only the intimate relationship between Christ and his cross, but also his humiliation in having been stripped bare as well as his physical suffering in having the harsh unyielding wood of the cross pressed against his skin.

Quatrain 11 employs the conceit of the redness of the Virgin's tears in a burst of gratitude, admiration and exaltation of the mother of Christ as intercessor for the poet, and as a powerful voice in the heavenly realm that has the ear of God himself. The conceit does not explicitly refer to the cause of the redness of the Virgin's tears; the implication is that they are blood-stained, which in itself is reminiscent of the blood that her son shed on the cross. The poet blends the fire and boldness of the conceit with a poignant metaphor: the Virgin's reddened tears pain God so much that they serve as a restraint on the full outpouring of his justified anger towards the disobedience and sinfulness of his children on earth. Thus the Virgin is associated, as is so often the case in Ó Dálaigh's poetry, with a pure and unwarranted mercy that can

---

26 Herbert J.C. Grierson (ed.), *Metaphysical lyrics and poems of the seventeenth century: Donne to Butler* (Oxford, 1921), p. 88.

be seen as nothing less than miraculous in the face of the wickedness and perversity of humankind.

Yet another striking feature of Ó Dálaigh's writing style in this poem is his adoption of Irish legal terms to describe both the relationship between Christ and humankind and the compensation that will be paid by the latter on Doomsday. The term *foludh* in quatrain 3 certainly has legal connotations. *DIL* paraphrases Thurneysen's definition of the word as follows:

> *folad* can hardly be described as a single word. It denotes that which constitutes the essence of a thing; in the case of words, the idea they denote; in contracts, the objects or liabilities to which they refer; in the case of lords and clients the essence of their relationship, the correct discharge of their reciprocal obligations ... in Laws also used to denote, of contracts, the objects or undertakings to which they refer; of lords and clients, that which constitutes their mutual relation, their correct conduct towards each other in their respective capacities.[27]

However, in this quatrain, *foludh* does not occur in a legal context, but is employed by the poet in its more general sense to express the very essence of the sinner who is defined by his misdemeanours. Ó Dálaigh asserts that having love and fear of God is enough to protect this essence however flawed it may be (see *DIL* s.v. *dín* for the usage here). In light of two legal terms that Ó Dálaigh uses later in the poem, however, an echo of the legal connotations associated with the word may be felt in quatrain 3.

The first of these two other legal terms employed by the poet is *sochar*, which occurs in quatrains 4 and 8. *DIL* defines *sochar* as '(a) Legal *a good or valid contract* ... (b) *privileges, rights, dues, revenues* ... (c) *profit, advantage, benefit* (in abstract sense)'.[28] In both quatrains, the word is used in the sense of advantage or benefit, as we see in *DIL* under (c). In quatrain 4, spontaneous and sincere lamentation is classed as a blessing that transcends every kind of *sochar* that exists; quatrain 8 refers directly to Christ's crucifixion as a *sochar* for those who came after him.

The last legal term to appear in the poem is *éiric* in quatrain 10. *Éiric* is defined in *DIL* as: '(a) *paying out, disbursing* ... (b) *paying an equivalent for,*

---

27 *DIL* s.v. *folud*; Rudolf Thurneysen, 'Aus dem irischen Recht I:1. Das Unfrei-Lehen', *ZCP*, 14 (1923), 335–94 at 374. For detailed definitions of *folud*, see D.A. Binchy, 'Irish history and Irish law', *StH*, 16 (1976), 1–45 at 26–31; the glossary to T.M. Charles-Edwards, Morfydd E. Owen and D.B Walters (eds), *Lawyers and laymen: studies in the history of law presented to Professor Dafydd Jenkins on his seventy-fifth birthday* (Cardiff, 1986), pp 346–7; and T.M. Charles-Edwards, 'A contract between king and people in medieval Ireland? *Críth gablach* on kingship', *Peritia*, 8 (1994), 107–19 at 111–12. **28** *DIL* s.v. *sochar*. For a discussion of *sochar*, see Rudolf Thurneysen, 'Sochor' in E. Ua Riain (ed.), *Féil-sgríbhinn Eóin Mhic Néill* (Dublin, 1940), pp 158–9.

compensation (for an injury) ... (c) as a legal term, *eric-fine, mulct, damages* imposed acc. to loss inflicted ... (d) in general *compensation, return* (for something done or suffered)'.[29] Ó Dálaigh uses the term towards the end of the poem as the text moves towards the chief reason that humankind must do penance and fear retribution; the impetus for the poet's exhortations in the main body of the text is Doomsday itself, an event that could be visited upon us at any time, a day on which those who have not repented will have cause to regret such an omission. In his vision of Doomsday, Ó Dálaigh moves away from his litany of cautionary appeals and presents the reader with an overwhelming image of Christ in Judgement, accompanied by his mother, whose grief will bring shame to repentant sinners, and his cross, which will remind all present of his passion and sacrifice. Once again, the poet selects a well-known Irish legal term to describe one of the torments in store for the damned. It would appear that he employs such terminology because it is familiar to him and creates a potent image. Ó Dálaigh also knows that his audience will be in no doubt as to the kind of consequences they face when judgement will be meted out to them and that by using terms like *éiric* in relation to Christ, the poet brings Christ and his lamentable wounds closer to this audience.

Ó Dálaigh is not the first Irish poet to employ native terminology pertaining to status, law and other matters in his work in order to lend force to his argument and to assist him in reaching deep into the hearts of his audience. The early Irish poem *Ísúcán* and the eighth-century poems attributed to Blathmac son of Cú Brettan are littered with similar references which lend comparable dynamism to these texts.[30] A few examples will suffice in order to show the resonances between the latter work and *Tús na heagna omhan Dé*. Blathmac refers to the slaying of Christ by the Jews as *fingal* (q. 103), or 'kin-slaying', a great taboo in medieval Irish society. Shortly after this, Blathmac deplores Judas Iscariot's betrayal of Christ by setting the thirty pieces of silver against an unfavourable *comparandum* which is drawn from the familiar terms of the Irish *lóg n-enech* or honour-price: *cid clár nderccóir bithbalc buan / ar Chríst mac nDé ba bbecluag*, 'even a strong, enduring board of red gold were a poor price for Christ, son of God' (q. 109). In quatrain 194, he expresses God's abundant wealth and generosity by describing him as a *briugu*, or 'hospitaller', a term with specific resonance in a legal context.[31]

The most interesting thing about Ó Dálaigh's usage of legal vocabulary pertaining to the sphere that he and his acquaintance occupy is that it

29 *DIL* s.v. *éric, éraic*.   30 E.G. Quin, 'The early Irish poem *Ísucán*', *CMCS*, 1 (Summer, 1981), 39–52; James Carney (ed. and trans.), *The poems of Blathmac son of Cú Brettan* (Dublin, 1964) [the legal aspect of this poetry was the subject of Prof. Liam Breatnach's contribution to the 2014 UCC / ITS seminar to be published in the proceedings later this year].   31 Gearóid Mac Eoin, 'Old Irish *briugu* "hospitaller" and connected words', *Celtica*, 23 (1999), 169–73.

appears, on one level, to be an attempt to help his fellow countrymen to understand their relationship with God (*foludh*) as well as Christ's passion and sacrifice (*sochar*) in the most precise and enlightening way possible. In addition, his appropriation of the term *éiric* enables the poet to emphasise the need for penance in order to mitigate the appalling consequences due to be faced on Doomsday. Ó Dálaigh's audience knew that *éiric* demanded compensation for wrong-doing and that failure to fulfil the defined terms of that compensation would bring about harsh, but not unwarranted, retribution. Ó Dálaigh employs *foludh*, *sochar* and *éiric* as tropes in order to impress on his audience the gravity of their situation in relation to sin, repentance and the shadow of retribution ever-darkening on the horizon.

CLONALIS HOUSE, BOOK OF THE O'CONOR DON, FF. 79V–80R
EDITION

Ó Dálaigh .i. Aonghus cecinit

Tús na heagna omhan Dé,
ní fhaghthar eagna mur í;
maith an ghné don eagna é
eagla Dé gidh bé ar a mbí.

Lór duit-se, a dhuine gan neart
ar leighius na n-uile olc;
tús na heagna é ann gach eacht
searc Dé is a eagla ort.

Dá mbeinn aige, im' dhuine dhaor,
re hainimh na n-uile gníomh,
lór do dhín m'fholudh – madh ál –
grádh is omhan Rígh na Ríogh.

Guil fa ghonuibh Rígh na Ríogh
dá dtí dot rosgaibh fa rún,
tar gach sochar as é an séan,
déar fa crochadh Dé na nDúl.

Variant readings from RIA MS 24.L.6 [L]; NUI Maynooth MS C 88 [C]; NUI Maynooth
MS M 84 [M]; RIA MS 24.B.26 [B]; RIA MS 23.G.27 [R]; RIA MS 23.G.23 [G]; and
NLI MS G 40 [N].

Headings: An *fear* céadna cc. (*vel sim.*) LCMBGN; A léightheóir bhig ionmhuin aig siu
duit an eagna fhíre, 7 fós an duain d*o* chan ó dála fi*ón*n *air* an eagna so, m*ur* lean*us* – H.
lala cct R (*lala* is a playful scribal contraction for Dálaigh which is commonly pronounced
Dála'. *Lala* consists of two '*las*', which, expressed in Irish, may be rendered as 'dá la').

1*a* Túis BRG   omhain B   1*b* faghthar R   2*a* Leór GN   neart] lo*cht* LCB lo*cht erased*
neart (*superscript*) M   2*b* na n-uile] gach uile MBRG   2*c* túis BRGN   head*h*na RG
2*d* is a] *agus* MBRGN   3*b* ghníomh LCMBRGN   3*c* dhíden M   dhídhean BG
dhígh*ead*n R   dhíon N   mfala MRG   mfaladh BN   áil LCMBRGN   3*d* gras N
omhain BRG   Ríogh N.

Additional quatrain which occurs after q. 3 in the complete copies of the poem: A duine
bhoi*cht* as claon cúis. nár aomh fán uile olc sgíos. fiú tf*air*bhríogh go hu*air* an bháis.
smuain *ar* pháis háirdríogh a rís LCMBRG (*vel sim.*).

4*a* Gul N   4*c* sochar] son*us* RG   4*d* chrocha MRG   Dé] ~~righ~~ Dé M   rígh B.

DIPLOMATIC TEXT

O dal*aigh* .i. Aong*us* c*e*c*init*

1. Tús na heagna omhan dé. ní fhaght*har* eagna m*ur* í. maith an ghné don eagna é. eagla dé gidh bé ar a mbí.

2. Lór d*ui*tsi a dhuine gan n*ea*rt. ar leighi*us* na nuile olc. t*ús* na heagna é an*n* g*a*ch ea*cht*. se*a*rc dé sa eagla ort

3. Da mbein*n* aige mo dhuine dháor. re haini*m* na nuile gniomh. lór do dhin mfaludh m*a*dh ál. gradh as omhan rígh na ríogh

4. Guil fa gonuibh rígh na ríogh. da ttí dot rosgaibh fa rún. tur gach soch*ar* asé an sén. dér fa c*r*och*adh* dé na ndul

TRANSLATION

Ó Dálaigh, i.e., Aonghus sang[32]

1. The beginning of wisdom is fear of God, no wisdom like it may be found; a worthy aspect of this wisdom is fear of God, on whomever it may be.

2. It is enough for you, o fellow who does not have the capacity to remedy every wrongdoing; love of God is the beginning of wisdom every time, as well as fear of him.

3. If I were in his possession, an unfree person, bearing the blemish of every wrongdoing, should [I] desire it, love and fear of the King of Kings would be enough to protect my essence.

4. If lamentation for the wounds of the King of Kings were to come to your eyes secretly, that is the blessing beyond every advantage, a tear for the crucifying of the God of Creation.

Additional verse found in LCMBRG after quatrain 3:

O unfortunate one of iniquitous cause, who never grew tired of every evil, it is worth your while to engage in thinking beyond measure; think again on the passion of the High-King.

32 Translation of headings in LCMBGNR: The same man sang LCMBGN; O dear little reader, the wisdom of truth is for you here, and in addition the poem that Ó Dála Fionn sang about this wisdom, as follows – Ó Dálaigh sang.

Smuain an aithmhéile an uair chóir,
smuain an aisléine san uaigh,
smuain i gclí do chionnta féin,
ná bí réidh iompu le huaill.

Smuain gach fíorghoin dhomhain dhlúith
dá bhfuair Íosa ag cobhair cháich;
smuain ar thaobhghoin chruaidh an chích,
smuain ar chrích mbaoghlaigh an Bhráith.

Smuain ar leathadh na lámh dtinn,
a pheacaidh a-tá ar an tuinn;
féuch, nach baoghlach cneadha an chinn
is rinn fhaobhrach beara an bhuinn?

Tiucfaidh crochadh an Ríogh rú
dá shíol 'na shochar gé a-tá;
smuain san uaidh, a dhuine, ar Dhia,
smuain fan lia Muire 's a mná.

Beidh sluaigh na cruinne re chois
agus Muire sa Luan leis;
biaidh an daorchroch dhearg re ais,
leanbh nach ba tais caomhthach cneis.

5a aithmhéala (*vel sim.*) LCMBRG   thaithmhéile N   **5b** aisléine] eisléine MBG   uaig LCG   **5d** réig R   **6a** dhomhain] doimhin (*vel sim.*) MBR   domhain N   domhainn G   dlúth BN   dlúith RG   **6b** ag] om. MBRG   a N   cáich CN   **6c** chích] chígh MBRG   cígh N   **6d** chríth B   bhaoghlaigh (*vel sim.*) MR   bhaoghalaigh B   baoghlaigh N   Bhráith] bháis B.   **7a** leatha B   dtinn] tteinn (*vel sim.*) LCB   tteinn (*vel sim.*) MRNG   **7b** a pheacaicc C   a pheacaig B   athá R   ttuinn (*vel sim.*) MBR   TToinn N   **7c** cneadh R   chéinn RG   **7d** bheara B   bearra R   **8a** Tiocfa (*vel sim.*) MRG   Tiocfadh BN   crocha MBRG   croch N   rígh BRN   rú] riú MBRNG (*vel sim.*)   **8b** shíol] Pholl N   sochar C   shocar R   **8c** san B   uaig MRG   úaig B   san uaidh] gach uair N   **9a** Beid B   Biaidh RG   ré] ré a MBRGN (*vel sim.*)   **9b** Muire] mise B   sa] san MBR   **9c** biaidh] beadh R   diaidh N   dearg N   ré] rén MB   rean RG.

5. Smúain an aithmeile an uaín chóir. smúain an aisléin san úaigh. smúain a cclí do chionta feín. na bí réidh iompu lé huaill

6. Smúain *gach* fíorghoin dhomhain dhlúith. da bfhúa*ir* iosa ag cobh*air* cháich. smúain ar thaobhghoin c*r*uaídh an chích. smúain *ar* chrích mbáoghl*aig*h an b*r*aith

7. Smúain *ar* leatha*d*h na lámh ttin*n*. as peacad ata *ar* an tuinn. féuch nach báoghl*ac*h cneadha an chin*n*. as rin*n* fháobr*ac*h beara an bhuin*n*

8. Tiucfai*d*h croch*adh* an ríogh rú. da shiol na soch*ar* ge atá. smúain sa núaidh a dhuine *ar* dhía. smúain fan lía m*ur*e sa m*nn*á

9. Beídh slúaigh na c*ruinn*e ré chois. ag*us* muire sa lúan leís. biaidh an daorc*r*och dh*earg* ré ais. leanb na ba tais caom*h*thach cnis

5. Think of regret at the fitting hour, think of the shroud in the grave, think of your own misdemeanours in your heart, do not be ready to turn away on account of arrogance.

6. Think of every true wound, deep and intense, that Jesus received while coming to the aid of all mankind; think of the harsh side-wound of his breast, think of the fearful outcome of the Judgement.

7. Think of the stretching of the aching arms, o sinner who is on the earth; look, are the wounds of the head not fearful and the keen point of the spike in the foot?

8. The crucifixion of the Lord will come against them, although it is a benefit for his descendants; think, fellow, of God in the grave, think of Mary and her women around the stone.

9. The hosts of the world will be beside him, and Mary also, on Doomsday; the reddened harsh cross will be on his back, the young man whose skin-companion was not soft.

Iarrfaidh éiric a ghon ngéar
's an fhuil nach éidir do dhíol;
Mac Dé dá chneasghoin go cruadh
measfuidh sa Luan é, far-íor.

Comairce mh'anma as í an Ógh
ar an Rígh ó tharla tréan;
cosg feirge Ruire na Ríogh
cíogh Muire is deirge a déar.

Bím id' rann, a Ríoghmhaoir bheo,
a Mhichíl nár chaill a chlú;
ó táid cionta im' chionn fad chló
is liom as mó tiocfa tú

TÚS NA

10*a* Iarrfaidh] Íocfuidh (*vel sim.*) LCMBRG Iarrsuidh N   10*b* éidir] féidear (*vel sim.*) MBRG   10*c* cruaidh (*vel sim.*) MBRGN   10*d* sa] san MRG   11*a* Coimeirc MB Comairc RG Comhairc N as í] ó sí N   11*b* tharluidh B   11*c* na Ríogh] an Rígh MBRG   11*d* Mhuire MBRG a] om. MBRG   12*a* a rí=mhaoir N béo N   12*b* a Mícheal N   12*c* cionnta (*vel sim.*) MBRGN fad chló] fán ccló (*vel sim.*) MBRGN thiocfa MBRGN.

Scríbal colophon in B: *air* na sgriobhadh re Uilliam ó Cleire an 15 la déag don Mheathamh ann sa mbliadhain *da* aois an tíghearna 1762.

10. Iarrfai*d*h éruic a gon ng*ear*. sa nfuil nach eidir do díol. m*a*c dé da chneasgoin go c*r*uaíd. measfuidh sa lúan é fa ríor

11. Com*air*ce mhanma as í an ogh. ar an rígh ó tharla trén. cosg feírge ruire na ríogh. cíogh muire 7 deírge a dér

12. Bim ad ran*n* a ríogh mhaoir bheó. a michil nár caill a chlú. ó táid cion*n*ta am cion*n* fad chló. is liom as mó tiucfá tú

... TUS NA .

10. He will seek an *éiric* for his sharp wounds and for the blood that cannot be atoned for; alas, on Doomsday, the Son of God will judge his harsh skin-wounding.

11. The guardian of my soul is the Virgin, from whom came power over the King; Mary's breast and the redness of her tears serve as a restraint on the anger of the King of Kings.

12. Let me be at your side, o living Royal-steward, o Michael who never lost his good name; since offences attributed to me are turned against [me], all the more will you come to my aid.

THE BEGINNING OF

APPENDIX: MANUSCRIPT COPIES OF *TÚS NA HEAGNA OMHAN DÉ*[33]

Dublin, RIA MS 24 L 6 (8), p. 18, 13qq. (1679)
Dublin, RIA MS 23 N 34 (209), p. 8, 13qq. (1846)
Dublin, RIA MS 3 B 5 (226), f. 27v, 3qq. (1829)
Dublin, RIA MS 24 B 26 (242), p. 126, 13+1qq. (1760–61)
Dublin, RIA MS F vi 1 (252), f. 20v [p. 36], 13qq. (1820)
Dublin, RIA MS F ii 2 (254), p. 72, 13qq. (1820)
Dublin, RIA MS 23 G 23 (256), p. 242, 13qq. (1794–5)
Dublin, RIA MS F i 2 (263), p. 176, 13qq. (1820)
Dublin, RIA MS 23 M 7 (287), p. 209, 1q. (1818–19)
Dublin, RIA MS 23 N 20 (465), p. 6, 4qq. (18th cent.)
Dublin, RIA MS 23 G 27 (492), p. 126, 13qq. (1785)
Dublin, RIA MS 23 B 26 (500), p. 362, 13+1qq. (1819)
Maynooth, St Patrick's College MS Murphy 70, p. 264, 13qq. (1820)
Maynooth, St Patrick's College MS Murphy 72, p. 25, 13+1qq. (1822)
Maynooth, St Patrick's College MS Murphy 84, p. 55, 13qq. (1738–47)
Maynooth, St Patrick's College MS Murphy 96, p. 101, 13qq. (1817)
    Donnchadh Mór Ó Dála
Maynooth, St Patrick's College MS O'Curry 88, f. 22v, 13qq. (1704) Fionn
    Ó Dálaigh
London, BL Egerton MS 142, f. 88b, 13qq. (1821)
London, BL Egerton MS 146, f. 107a [p. 211], 1q. (18th–19th cent.)
London, BL Egerton MS 147, f. 59b, 1q. (early 18th cent.)
London, BL Egerton MS 165, f. 1b, 1q. (1719–97)
Kilkenny, St Kieran's College MS CC 1, p. 354, 12qq. (1846)
Kilkenny, St Kieran's College MS CC 6, p. 8, 13qq. (1846)[34]
Book of the O'Conor Don, ff. 79v–80r, 12qq. (1631)
Cork, UCC MS Torna 28, p. 162, 1q. (1868)
Cork, UCC MS Murphy 4, pp 166–7, 13qq (1874)
Fermoy, St Colman's College MS CF 5, p. 83, 13+1qq. (1842)
Dublin, NLI MS G 40, p. 7, 13qq. (18th cent.)

33 For information concerning the manuscripts, see *RIA Cat.*; *BM Cat.*; Paul Walsh et al.,
Lámhscríbhinní Gaeilge Choláiste Phádraig Má Nuad, 8 fascicles (Maynooth, 1943–73); *NLI
Cat.*; Pádraig Ó Fiannachta, *Clár lámhscríbhinní Gaeilge. Leabharlanna na cléire agus na
mionchnuasaigh* (Dublin, 1978); Pádraig de Brún, *Clár lámhscríbhinní Gaeilge Choláiste
Ollscoile Chorcaí: Cnuasach Thorna*, 2 vols (Dublin, 1967).   34 I am most grateful to John
Kirwan, consultant archivist, and Dr Fearghas Ó Fearghail, both of St Kieran's College,
Kilkenny for arranging for me to consult the Gaelic manuscripts housed in the library of
the college, for showing me their library's valuable collections and for generously sharing
with me their time, knowledge and advice.

On the genealogical preamble to *Vita Sancti Declani*

TOMÁS Ó CATHASAIGH

St Déclán is traditionally credited with evangelizing the Déisi of Munster, and establishing in their territory the ecclesiastical centre at Ardmore, where his cult survived robustly into modern times; much of his Life, *Vita Sancti Declani* (VSD),[1] is devoted to his conversion of the Déisi and the miracles he performed. There are conflicting statements of Déclán's descent:[2] in the oldest version of the corpus of saint's pedigrees he is assigned to the Fothairt, but in the Life he is said to descend from Eógan son of Fíachu Suidge, eponymous ancestor of Dál Fíachach, rulers of the Déisi.[3] (We shall see, however, that even in VSD, there are two very different versions of his descent from Fíachu.) His father, Erc, was *dux* of the Déisi; having been baptized by St Colmán, he studied the scriptures. After a long course of studies, he set out for Rome, where he was ordained bishop by the Pope. With the Pope's blessing and permission, he set out to preach the Gospel, and on his homeward journey met St Patrick who was on his way to Rome to receive the Pope's blessing. In this way, Déclán is accorded what Pádraig Ó Riain has called 'a spurious so called pre-Patrician status'.[4]

Kenney characterized VSD as 'a composite production: the final redaction cannot be much older than the twelfth century, but there seem to be various *strata* of older material of which it is a loose amalgamation'.[5] There is also an

---

1 *VSHP* ii, 32–59. Translation by Liam de Paor, *Saint Patrick's world* (Dublin, 1993), pp 244–71. In the present article, personal names are normalized except for the forms cited from pedigrees. Quotations are from de Paor's translation; references are to the paragraphs of Plummer's edition, and to the pages of the translation. There is a summary of the Life, and other sources of information about the saint, in *DIS* pp 258–60. 2 *CGSH*, pp 18, 67 (§§107, 470, 483). Cf. David Thornton, *Kings, chronologies and genealogies: studies in the political history of early medieval Ireland and Wales* (Oxford, 2003), p. 136, and *DIS* p. 258. 3 Thornton, *Kings*, p. 136 and *DIS* p. 258, point out that one line of descent attaches him to Dál Meicon (emended by Thornton to Dál Meic Chon, for which read Dál Meic Con). On the possible significance of this, see below, p. 300, and n. 37. 4 *DIS* p. 259. The supposed pre-Patrician status of Déclán, and of Ailbe, Ciarán and Ibar, has proved to be of perennial interest. See Richard Sharpe, 'Quatuor sanctissimi episcopi: Irish saints before St Patrick' in D. Ó Corráin, L. Breatnach and K. McCone (eds), *Sages, saints, and storytellers: Celtic Studies in honour of Professor James Carney* (Maynooth, 1989), pp 376–99; and Dagmar Ó Riain-Raedel, 'The question of the "pre-Patrician" saints of Munster' in M.A. Monk and J. Sheehan (eds), *Early medieval Munster: archaeology, history and society* (Cork, 1998), pp 17–22. 5 James F. Kenney, *The sources for the early history of Ireland: ecclesiastical. An introduction and guide* (New York, 1929; reprinted with addenda by Ludwig Bieler, New York, 1966), p. 313.

Irish Life,[6] which is based on VSD. Richard Sharpe tentatively proposes a date in the later twelfth century for VSD,[7] while Pádraig Ó Riain suggests that the author was probably at work towards the end of the twelfth or early in the thirteenth century.[8] In proposing their dating, Sharpe and Ó Riain are mindful of the author's clear interest in promoting Ardmore's case for diocesan status in the organizational reform of the Irish church which was being carried out in the twelfth century: at the end of the official list of the dioceses approved at the Synod of Kells in the year 1152, Ardmore is added as claiming the right to a bishopric.[9] Ardmore evidently did enjoy diocesan status throughout the second half of the twelfth century; sometime after 1210 it was absorbed into the diocese of Lismore.[10]

A bishop of Ardmore whose name is known to us is Eugenius; Sharpe notes that he had hagiographical and historical interests and suggests that 'a case could be made' for attributing VSD to him.[11] In any case, the Life is quite explicit in its claim, which is set out at length, that the Déisi should belong to Déclán's episcopal diocese, and that the Déisi should serve him just as the Irish in other parts served St Patrick (VSD §21; de Paor, p. 259). But of course the case is also made indirectly by glorifying Déclán and showing him to be eminently worthy of high office. One feature of VSD is particularly noteworthy in this regard. There is a long genealogical preamble, including an account of the expulsion of the Déisi from Tara, and their settlement in east Munster. Occupying four pages before Déclán's birth among the Déisi, it 'offers the longest and most elaborate narrative of this kind in Hiberno-Latin hagiography'.[12] What I propose to do is to examine the genealogical preamble, with a view to understanding the ways in which Déclán's biographer uses it to glorify his subject, and through him his foundation at Ardmore.

'The Expulsion of the Déisi' (ED) tells of the expulsion of the Dál Fiachach from Tara, their sojourn in Leinster, and their settlement in Munster. The version of this story included in VSD is doubtless intended to provide a quasi-historical backdrop to Déclán's labours among the Déisi: he is given a highly respectable pedigree as a descendant of the rulers of the Déisi, and further exalted by virtue of his supposed historical kinship with the kings of Tara. When we compare VSD with ED, we shall see that there are some important innovations in the biographer's version of the story. (We will further note that BD has a version of the preamble which differs from VSD in its account of the events leading to the expulsion from Tara.)[13]

---

6 Patrick Power (ed. and trans.), *Life of St Declan of Ardmore and Life of St Mochuda of Lismore*, ITS 16 (London, 1914), pp 2–73. I shall refer to the Irish life as BD (= *Betha Décláin*); reference is to the pages of Power's edition.   7 Richard Sharpe, *Medieval Irish saints' Lives: an introduction to Vitae sanctorum Hiberniae* (Oxford, 1991), p. 349.   8 *DIS* p. 258.   9 Aubrey Gwynn, *The Irish church in the eleventh and twelfth centuries* (Dublin, 1992), p. 241.   10 Ibid.   11 Sharpe, *Medieval Irish saints' Lives*, p. 32.   12 Ibid., p. 140 n. 25.   13 See n. 26, below.

Among the various manuscript texts of ED, it has been usual to distinguish an early and a later version.[14] The relationship among the surviving texts is rather complicated, as there are two recensions of the early version, one of them represented in Oxford, Bodleian Library, Rawlinson B 502 (= R),[15] and the other in Oxford, Bodleian Library, Laud Misc. 610 (= L).[16] In all of them, however, there is a common core, which may be summarized as follows: The rulers of the Déisi, Dál Fíachach, are said to have been descended from Fíachu Suidge, a brother of Conn Cétchathach, king of Tara, and to have lived in the Tara district. Their troubles begin when a son of Cormac mac Airt, variously called Conn or Cellach, abducts a daughter of a member of Dál Fíachach. The task of avenging this insult falls to the girl's uncle, the formidable Óengus Gaíbúafnech. Óengus goes to Tara, kills Cormac's son, and inadvertently half-blinds Cormac and kills his *rechtaire*. Óengus escapes from Tara, but the Déisi are opposed and defeated in battle by Cormac, so that they leave the Tara district. The Déisi go into Leinster where they spend some years. (They are also said to have gone to south-west Ireland.) They finally settle down following an alliance with Óengus mac Nad-Fraích, king of Cashel, who marries Ethne Úathach, a fosterling of the Déisi. This leads to their displacement of the Osraige from the plain of Cashel, and to the settlement of the Déisi in their Tipperary territories.

In VSD as well, the expulsion of the Dál Fíachach from Tara is the culmination of a series of events arising from an offence committed by Cormac mac Airt's son, Cellach. But before we reach that point, Déclán's biographer gives the story greater generational depth by tracing the saint's descent to the legendary king of Ireland, Echaid Feidlech, whom he credits with extending his realm over the whole of Ireland. There follows a list of Echaid's descendants who ruled at Tara down to Feidlimid Rechtaid, whose three sons were Conn Cétchathach, Echaid Finn and Fíachu Suidge. The length of each reign is given, and in some cases the location or manner of the king's death. The soubriquets of Túathal Techtmar and his son Feidlimid Rechtaid are explained: Túathal is said to have been a powerful ruler of different regions, and Feidlimid to have passed laws in his reign. Of his three sons, Conn is

---

14 For details, see Tomás Ó Cathasaigh, "'The Expulsion of the Déisi'", *JCHAS*, 110 (2005), 13–20 at 13–15. 15 Kuno Meyer, 'The Expulsion of the Dessi', *Y Cymmrodor*, 14 (1901), 101–35. 16 Kuno Meyer, 'The Expulsion of the Déssi', *Ériu*, 3 (1907), 135–42. This recension is represented fragmentarily in the Book of Uí Maine and *Liber Flavus Fergusiorum*, for which see Séamus Pender (ed.), 'Two unpublished versions of the Expulsion of the Déssi' in idem (ed.), *Féilscríbhinn Torna* (Cork, 1947), pp 209–17. A comparison of some parallel passages in R and L suggests that in some cases at least, L has replaced original readings which are preserved in R; see Tomás Ó Cathasaigh, 'Textual transmission and variation: a medieval Irish case study' in F. Josephson (ed.), *Celtic language, law and letters: proceedings of the Tenth Symposium of Societas Celtologica Nordica* (Gothenburg, 2010), pp 169–79 (at p. 174, line 28, for *innocht* read *and*).

said to have earned eternal fame because of the fertility, peace and goodness
that marked his twenty-year reign; Echaid to have achieved power in
Leinster; and Fíachu to have held the region around Tara, but not to have
acceded to the kingship of Ireland. Pride of place, however, is given to
Lugaid Reóderg, who was begotten by Echaid Feidlech's sons, Bres, Nár and
Lothar, otherwise known as the three Finns of Emain. Each of them slept
with their sister, Clothra, and she gave birth to a beautiful son, in whom his
triple conception was represented in the division of his body into three parts.
Traditional heroes, in Ireland as elsewhere, were frequently depicted as
having been conceived in an anomalous manner, but none of them is more
remarkable than the triple incest that led to Lugaid Reóderg's birth.

The sequence of kings in VSD evidently derives from a source related to
the prehistoric portion of the annals, as represented in the *Annals of
Tigernach*,[17] from which it sometimes differs in the regnal lengths. There are
two more significant innovations in this part of VSD. One of them is the
substantive character of the story of Lugaid Reóderg, the second is the syn-
chronizing of the beginning and end of Lugaid's reign with external events.

Lugaid Reóderg has a singularly important role in Irish synthetic history.
Prior to his reign, the Tara kingship had been vacant, following the cata-
strophic downfall of Conaire Mór: this was the period of the Pentarchy,
during which Ireland was ruled by the provincial kings. As Joan Radner has
observed, the significance of the Pentarchy is that 'it is actually a metaphorical time-out-of-time, a liminal period of chaos. Its immediate theme is defect-
ive sovereignty'.[18] Lugaid restored the kingship of Tara. John Kelleher has
suggested that the tale of Lugaid's begetting makes him 'a sort of ultimate
ancestor of Dál Cuinn' and that 'the result of the three-fold incest is meant
to symbolize the union of the Uí Néill, Connachta, and Airgialla in a federation'.[19] While this is obviously quite speculative, it is perhaps worth noting
that if Déclán's biographer was given to this kind of thinking, the union he
would have in mind would probably comprise the descendants respectively of
Conn Cétchathach, Echaid Finn and Déclán's supposed ancestor, Fíachu
Suidge. In his descent from Lugaid, Déclán shares some of the glory surrounding Conn and Echaid Finn, and their descendants.

VSD presents a rather more detailed account of Lugaid's conception than
we find elsewhere in the early sources. Plummer suggests that this 'horrible
story' is taken over bodily from the secular sagas, especially *Aided Meidbe* and

---

17 *ATig.*, the relevant material being at *RC*, 16 (1895), 405–19, and *RC*, 17 (1896), 6–8.
Unlike the corresponding parts of *Do flathiusaib Hérend* (*LL* i, 90–2, ll 2880–962) and of
the tract on *Ríg Érenn* (*CGH*, pp 120–1), kings who were not descended from Echaid
Feidlech are not mentioned.   18 Joan M. Radner, '"Fury destroys the world": historical
strategy in Ireland's Ulster epic', *Mankind Quarterly*, 23 (1982), 41–60 at 53.   19 John V.
Kelleher, 'The Táin and the annals', *Ériu*, 22 (1971), 107–27 at 120–1. See further Radner,
'"Fury destroys the world"', 54.

Ferchuitred Medba.[20] In *Ferchuitred Medba*, otherwise known as *Cath Bóinde*,[21] the incestuous conception is mentioned, but not with sufficient detail to suggest that Déclán's biographer had recourse to it. The notion that Lugaid Reóderg was the incestuous offspring of Echaid Feidlech's sons, the three Finns of Emain, and their sister Clothra had entered the learned and pseudo-historical tradition by the twelfth century.[22] The most circumstantial account is given in *Aided Meidbe*,[23] but it does not offer all of the detail that we find in VSD. Moreover, the two accounts differ in one important respect. In *Aided Meidbe*, Clothra, using the second person plural imperative, invites her brothers to sleep with her, and each of them does so in turn. In VSD, however, the narrator informs us that none of the brothers knew that either of the others had slept with Clothra, and that she did not tell them. It is of course possible that Déclán's biographer deliberately changed this detail in the story as he had it before him. It is noteworthy also that VSD does not record the statement that Lugaid incestuously begot his son Crimthann on his mother Clothra.[24] Déclán's biographer depicts Lugaid Reóderg as a hero: 'he was handsome in appearance and manly in his strength, and from his infancy great things were expected of him' (§1, p. 244).

In one of the boldest acts of aggrandisement in VSD, the beginning of Lugaid Reóderg's reign is synchronized with the death of Gaius Caesar, and Lugaid's death at the hands of Leinstermen is synchronized with the killing of Peter and Paul by Nero. These events are noted in the prehistoric Irish annals, but do not coincide there with events in the life of Lugaid Reóderg. Their appropriation by Déclán's biographer burnishes the saint's Roman credentials, and the coincidence of the death of Déclán's ancestor with the killing of Peter and Paul is especially significant in this respect.

In ED, as we have seen, the events leading to the expulsion of Dál Fíachach from the Tara district begin with an offence against them committed by a son of Cormac mac Airt's. Óengus Gaíbúafnech takes revenge,[25] and this in turn leads to the expulsion of Dál Fíachach from the Tara district. The same basic pattern is found in VSD, but the offence committed by Cormac mac Airt's son is different. In ED, the king's son abducts a niece of

20 *VSHP* i, p. lxii.   **21** The text of Rawlinson MS B. 512 bears the title *Ferchuitred Medba* and is ed. by Kuno Meyer, 'Ferchuitred Medba', *Anecd.* v (1913), pp 17–22; in the Book of Lecan the title is *Cath Boinde*: its text is ed. and trans., with variants from Rawlinson, by Joseph O'Neill, 'Cath Boinde', *Ériu*, 2 (1905), 173–85.   **22** *LL* i, 91, ll 2895–97 (*Do flathiusaib Hérend*). Cf. *MD* iv, 44, ll 33–4, where the incest is recounted, but no mention is made of Lugaid; and Sharon Arbuthnot (ed. and trans.), *Cóir anmann: a late Middle Irish treatise on Irish personal names*, 2 vols, ITS 59–60 (London, 2005, 2007), i, 110 §139; ii, 29 §105.   **23** Vernam Hull, '*Aided Meidbe*: the violent death of Medb', *Speculum*, 13 (1938), 52–61 at 55.   **24** *LL* i, 91, ll 2897–8.   **25** On the role of the avenging hero, as exemplified by Óengus, see Neil McLeod, 'The lord of slaughter' in P. O'Neill (ed.), *The land beneath the sea: essays in honour of Anders Ahlqvist's contribution to Celtic Studies in Australia* (Sydney, 2013), pp 101–14.

Óengus'. In VSD, Cormac makes peace with an (unnamed) enemy of his, and
Óengus is assigned to the man as guarantor. But some days later, and without authority from the king, Cormac's son Cellach seizes the man and puts
out his eyes. This is of course an affront to Óengus' honour: he goes in great
rage to Tara, and demands that the king's son be surrendered to him, so that
he might kill him. Cellach, however, stands in front of the king, whereupon
the king's 'governor' (*comes*) places himself between the king and his son. But,
as in ED, Óengus kills the king's son, and in doing so inadvertently kills the
'governor' and pierces the king's eye. In this variation on the original tale,
Óengus' vengeance has to an extent become a case of 'an eye for an eye'.
There is a further innovation in VSD at this point: when Óengus decides to
kill the king, Cormac appeals to him in the name of their gods and their kinship to spare him, and Óengus does so.[26]

In VSD, as in ED, Cormac expels Óengus and his brothers from the Tara
district, and they go into Leinster. In ED, there is a chronological inconsis-
tency that bears upon the duration of the sojourn of the Dál Fíachach in
Leinster. In ED generally, Óengus Gaíbúaifnech is son of Art Corb and
grandson of Fíachu Suidge.[27] In the oldest extant version of the pedigree, four
further generations separate Óengus from Fíachu Suidge: Art Corb is son of
Mes Corb s. of Mes Gegra s. of Corb s. of Cairbre Rígrón s. of Fíachu
Suidge.[28] There are traces of this pedigree in the early version of ED. But it
is the foreshortening of the pedigree that allows for the presentation of
Cormac (Fíachu Suidge's great-grandson) and Óengus (Fíachu's grandson) as
contemporaries, and thus makes possible the tale of the expulsion of Dál
Fíachach from Tara. And the main account of the sojourn of the Dál
Fíachach in Leinster requires a lapse of four generations between their arrival
in the province and the reign of Crimthann of the Uí Chennselaig, after
whose death the Dál Fíachach are driven out of Leinster; but there are clear
indications of an alternative tradition that the Leinster sojourn lasted for
thirty-three years.

In VSD, the Leinster sojourn of Dál Fíachach is brief: they go into
Leinster, and a year later they arrive in Munster, having been attacked along
the way by the Osraige. The leaders of Dál Fíachach upon their entry into
Munster are Óengus, Ross and Eógan. But in VSD there are two conflicting
versions of the pedigree. The first of them is given in the genealogical introduction to the expulsion episode. There is no mention of Art Corb: Óengus
– shorn of his epithet – is one of three *sons* of Fíachu Suidge. The others are

---

26 BD (pp 4–5) does not have the innovations of VSD in this episode. On the other hand,
Keating draws on the Latin Life for his account: *FFÉ*, ii, 312.   27 On what follows in
this paragraph, see Tomás Ó Cathasaigh, 'The Déisi and Dyfed', *Éigse*, 20 (1984), 1–33 at
11–14. There is an invaluable discussion of the Déisi genealogies in Thornton, *Kings*, pp
126–42.   28 *CGH*, p. 394.

Ross and Eógan, who in ED are the sons of Óengus' brother Brecc. The second version of the pedigree is given at the end of the account of the settlement in Munster of Ross, Eógan and Óengus. It is here that Déclán's descent from Fíachu Suidge is given. The ancestors of the rulers of the Déisi down the ages are said to descend from Fíachu's son Eógan, father of *Carbri Rigruad*, father of *Conra Cathbuadach*, father of *Cuano Cambretach*, father of *Mess Fore*, father of *Moscegrai*, father of *Moss Corp*, father of *Ard Corp*, whose son was the second Eógan, father of Brian, father of *Niath*, father of Lugaid, father of *Tren*, father of Erc, who was St Déclán's father. This extended pedigree is clearly an (unsuccessful) attempt to accommodate both Eógan son of Art Corb, and a much earlier namesake, Eógan son of Fíachu. If the pedigree is to make any chronological sense in the context of the expulsion and settlement of the Dál Fíachach, the Eógan who set out from Tara and settled in Munster would have to be the son of Art Corb.

In the early version of ED, the settlement of the Déisi in their east Munster territories is made possible by a marriage alliance between Óengus mac Nad-Fraích, Eóganacht king of Cashel, and Ethne Úathach, a daughter of Crimthann of the Uí Chennselaig. Ethne, whose maternal grandfather was Ernbrand of Dál Fíachach, had been fostered by her maternal kin: it was on their behalf that she negotiated the terms of her marriage alliance with Óengus mac Nad-Fraích. She was to be granted the meadow land from Cashel to Lúasc for her maternal kin to occupy; they would have the right to drive out the Osraige and take possession of their lands; and they would have the status of a free people. The Osraige defeated them in seven battles. It is remarkable that in ED no male leaders of Dál Fíachach are named in connection with the alliance with Óengus mac Nad-Fraích, the campaign against the Osraige, or the settlement of the east Munster territories. When the Dál Fíachach ranks are seriously depleted, Ethne procures the assistance of the Corcu Loígde, and gathers every 'exiled band' that she knew of in Ireland. Dál Fíachach then defeat the Osraige whom they drive first of all to the river Anner, and then as far the river Lingaun. In ED(L), as well as in the later version, it is said that the Lingaun was consequently to be the boundary between the Déisi and the Osraige until the end of time.[29]

In VSD, the Eóganacht king with whom the Déisi make an alliance is Ailill Aulomm, whose wife Sadb was daughter of their kinsman, Conn Cétchathach. Ailill offers them a variety of opportunities to acquire land, and they elect to wage war on the Osraige, to avenge their mistreatment of the Dál Fíachach in Leinster. We are then told that they fought four battles for land on the borders of Munster and Leinster – two against the Osraige, and two against the

---

29 In the later version, Lúasc is not mentioned; the Déisi neither seek nor receive the help of the Corcu Loígde, and there is no mention of the Anner in the description of the rout of the Osraige to the Lingaun.

Munstermen, in all of which Óengus prevailed. In describing the offensive against the Osraige, however, VSD simply says that the Déisi drove them from the plain of Femen to the Lingaun, which 'is subsequently the boundary of Munster and Leinster in that area, dividing the land of the Déisi from that of the Osraige' (§2, p. 247). As it stands, this is not self-evidently a description of two battles. Perhaps there is a dim reflection here of the testimony of the early version of ED that the Déisi's campaign against the Osraige was conducted in two stages, the second of which – after they had enlisted the Corcu Loígde and the assorted migratory bands – was successful. Or perhaps – though this seems less likely – what lies behind the 'two battles' is the twofold rout of the Osraige first to the Anner, and second to the Lingaun.

The inclusion in VSD of two battles against the Munstermen is highly significant. ED, as we have seen, recounts the appropriation from the Osraige of the Tipperary portion of Déisi Muman. VSD, as David Thornton has noted, offers a fuller account of the establishment of the Déisi territories. In describing the two battles of the Déisi against the Munstermen, Déclán's biographer says that they drove the Fir Maige Féne as far as Brí Gobann (Brigown in Co. Cork), and the Uí Líatháin from the Munster Blackwater to the unidentified Cell Chobthaig, 'which is now on the border of the Dési and Uí Líatháin' (§2, p. 247).

In ED, the newly conquered land is divided up, and twenty-five of the 'exiled bands' recruited by Ethne receive a share.[30] In VSD, the three brothers, Ross, Eógan and Óengus amicably divide the territory among themselves; it is to Ross and Eógan in particular that the early historical rulers of the Déisi trace their descent.[31]

While Óengus mac Nad-Fraích is not connected with the settlement of the Déisi in VSD, he looms large in Déclán's life. As presented in VSD, the saint's relationship with Óengus has three phases. At the behest of a uterine brother of Déclán's, who was a son of Óengus', the king allows the saint to preach at Cashel. Although he finds no fault with the saint's teaching, he accepts neither faith nor baptism from him. In explaining Óengus' motivation, VSD departs radically from the depiction in ED of his alliance with Dál Fíachach:

> Some say that the reason the king didn't wish to be baptized by St Declan was that St Declan was of the blood of the Dési, a people which was always at enmity with the king's people, the Eóganacht, by whom Munster was ruled. He was not willing to have a patron from that people (§14, p. 252).

St Patrick the Briton, meanwhile, was on his way to Cashel, and Óengus was happy to receive baptism from him, since he had nothing against the British

---

30 Ó Cathasaigh, "'The Expulsion'", p. 18.   31 Thornton, *Kings*, p. 141.

people. Having spread the Gospel in Cashel, St Déclán returned to his mission among the Déisi.

VSD is consistent here with other sources in claiming that Óengus mac Nad-Fraích received the faith at Cashel from Patrick. Tírechán tells us that Patrick baptized the sons of Nad-Fraích on the rock of Cothrige in Cashel:[32] how much more (if anything) Tírechán might have had to say about this episode we do not know, for the extant text is incomplete, and breaks off at this very point. Various tentative explanations have been offered for this:[33] Bieler suggests that 'perhaps Armagh's claims to sovereignty did not yet extend beyond Cashel when Tírechán wrote, and the Tripartite Life, with its long Munster section [...] testifies to a further stage of Armagh policies'.[34] The *Tripartite Life* gives a more substantive account of Patrick's conversion of Óengus mac Nad-Fraích, and provides Patrick with a considerable Munster itinerary, but one which apparently did not include Déisi Muman.[35] St Patrick's conversion and blessing of Óengus and the men of all Munster is elaborately narrated in *Senchas fagbála Caisil*.[36]

The next phase in Déclán's relationship with Óengus follows a meeting at which Déclán accepted the superior authority of St Patrick. The two saints went together to Cashel, and it was while they were there that Óengus, Patrick and the people said that St Ailbe should be archbishop of Munster, and Déclán bishop of the Déisi (§21, p. 259). In the final phase, Óengus beseeches Déclán to assist him in a time of great difficulty; he does so in the name of Christ, in whom, as he claims, he believes thanks to Déclán's preaching. Déclán exercises his miraculous power on behalf of Óengus and the people of Munster, and is rewarded by the king with a fort beside Cashel, tribute for him and his successors, and the freedom of Cashel and its diocese (§§23–4, pp 260–1).

The reward that Déclán finally receives from Óengus is reminiscent of that which Ethne Úathach receives for Dál Fíachach in ED: they are given the status of a free people. There remains the puzzle of Óengus' implacable hostility to the Déisi, which is spelt out in the context of Déclán's first encounter with Óengus at Cashel. A possible explanation of this lies in the ambivalence of 'Déisi', which can refer to their rulers, Dál Fíachach, or to the

---

32 Ludwig Bieler (ed. and trans.), *The Patrician texts in the Book of Armagh*, SLH 10 (Dublin, 2000), pp 162–3. Anthony Harvey, 'The significance of *Cothraige*', *Ériu*, 36 (1985), 1–9 at 7, suggests that Tírechán's *Petra(m) Coithrigi* is a name for the Rock of Cashel. But see now Pádraig Ó Riain, 'When and why Cothraige was first equated with Patricius?', *ZCP*, 49–50 (1997), 698–711. 33 See Bieler, *The Patrician texts*, p. 38 n. 2. 34 Ibid. 35 *VT*, pp 118–29, ll 2286–573. He went to In Déis Deiscirt, which at one point is called *crích na nDéisi* (l. 2444), but this is hardly a reference to Déisi Muman. 36 Myles Dillon, 'The story of the finding of Cashel', *Ériu*, 16 (1952), 61–73 at 67–8. Cf. Clodagh Downey, 'Medieval literature about Conall Corc', *JCHAS*, 110 (2005), 21–32 at 27.

inhabitants of the territory of Déisi Muman. In ED, Óengus makes an alliance with Dál Fíachach, who acquire the Tipperary territories of Déisi Muman. It is possible that the hostility attributed to Óengus in VSD is to be understood as being directed at the people of the broader region of Déisi Muman, rather than at their Dál Fíachach rulers.[37]

The origin legend of the Déisi recounted in VSD differs in many details from that in ED, and adds much to it as well. Chronology is not the author's strong suit: he evidently sees no reason to allow chronological nicety to get in the way of a good story. His aim is to confer prestige upon St Déclán and his foundation at Ardmore, and in doing so he not only uses the conventional stuff of hagiography, but also shows an impressive capacity to exploit traditional Irish narrative.

37 The affiliation of St Déclán to the Dál Meicon (n. 3, above) may reflect a tradition that he is descended from the leader of one the 'exiled bands' recruited by Ethne. In the early version of ED, one of them is named as Mechain (R, p. 124), which corresponds to Dal Maic Con in L (p. 138, l. 110.) There is also a Dál Mechon in L (p. 139, l. 147), corresponding to Dál Michol in R (p. 128).

Véarsaí ó oirthear Chorcaí ar an ngorta a lean sioc mór an gheimhridh 1739–40[1]

BREANDÁN Ó CONCHÚIR

AN TÚDAR

Tá na véarsaí seo ar ghorta 1740–41 tagtha anuas i bhfoirm dhá aiste. Tá an chéad aiste acu (uimh. 1 anseo) le fáil ina hiomláine i dtrí cinn de lámhscríbhinní ón 19ú haois agus na véarsaí déanacha di i lámhscríbhinn ón 18ú haois, gan ainm an údair luaite in aon lámhscríbhinn acu. Ag leanúint ar an aiste seo sna lámhscríbhinní céanna is ea a gheibhtear an dara haiste (uimh. 2 anseo), agus arís gan ainm údair luaite léi, ach cuireann an scríobhaí, Seán Ó Conaire (Cluain Uamha, 1757), in úil, áfach, i gceannscríbhinn na lámhscríbhinne aigesean gurb é an file céanna a chum an dá aiste acu ('An fear céanna cct chum na críche céanna'). Is léir ar na tagairtí do na pearsain (uimh. 1, l 31; uimh. 2, ll 45–6, 51) agus do na háiteanna (uimh. 1, ll 30, 34; uimh. 2, l 56) gur file in oirthear Chorcaí (barúntachtaí an Bharraigh Mhóir, Cine Tolamhan agus Uíbh Mac Coille) a chum iad.

Tá ar a laghad cúig cinn d'aistí a chum Séamas Mac Coitir ón gceantar céanna so sna blianta 1739–41 tagtha anuas, ceann acu, ná fuil ach trí cinn de véarsaí ann, ar ábhar na n-aistí seo againne,[2] ceann eile a bhfuil trí cinn is fiche de véarsaí ann, ag tromaíocht ar mhinistir de dheasca deachú a bhaint de shagart paróiste na háite,[3] an tríú ceann, agus seacht gcinn de véarsaí ann,

---

1 Ar 29 Nollaig 1739 a thit an sioc mór so a mhair go tús mhí na Feabhra, ach do lean drochaimsir neamhghnách in Éirinn é go ceann bliain go leith eile, ar shlí gur mhair an drochshaol isteach go maith sa bhliain 1741 ('bliain an áir'). Rug an sioc ar na prátaí láithreach agus in imeacht laethanta scriosadh ar fad iad, an príomhbhia a mbíodh formhór de mhuintir na tuaithe ag brath air i gcaitheamh an gheimhridh. Feic David Dickson, *Arctic Ireland: the extraordinary story of the great frost and forgotten famine of 1740–41* (Dublin, 1997). Tá tuairiscí comhaimseartha i bprós ina chuid lámhscríbhinní ag Tadhg Ó Neachtain (1671–*c*.1752) i mBaile Átha Cliath ar an sioc so agus ar ghnéithe den drochshaol a lean é (Neil Buttimer, 'The Great Famine in Gaelic manuscripts' in J. Crowley, W.J. Smyth agus M. Murphy [eag.], *Atlas of the Great Irish Famine, 1845–52* [Cork, 2012], lgh 460–72 ag lgh 461–2). Tá roinnt véarsaí leis (i mBéarla agus i nGaeilge) ar an ábhar seo ag Ó Neachtain i LNÉ LS G 135, lgh 23–4, 27: féach *NLI Cat.*, iv, lch 71. 2 *Ní cogadh ná cargaill fhada idir airdríthibh* (in eagar ag Pádraig A. Breatnach, 'Togha na héigse 1700–1800', *Éigse*, 27 [1993], 120–1). Feic leis Buttimer, 'The Great Famine in Gaelic manuscripts', lch 462 mar a bhfuil gearrathrácht ar ábhar na haiste seo. 3 *Is mé an chrínbhean bheag chnaoidhte gan aird* (feic *RIA Cat.*, Index I, lch 364). Luaite ag Dickson, *Arctic Ireland*, lch 82 n. 62 agus ag Buttimer, 'The Great Famine in Gaelic manuscripts', lch 463. 4 *An mearughadh fada so ar fhearaibh mo dhúthasa* (feic *RIA Cat.*,

---

'do phrócadóir do bhain deachú as leathacra cruithneachta do bhí ag sagart maith'[4], an ceathrú ceann, agus sé cinn déag de véarsaí ann, 'ag caoineadh éagomhlainn Éireann', agus an file 'san 17ú bliain dá aois',[5] agus an cúigiú ceann, a bhfuil seacht gcinn de véarsaí ann, 'do Sheán mac Risteird Coipinéar le linn dulta don Fhrainc dó'.[6] Ní miste a cheapadh, dar liom, gurb é Séamas Mac Coitir leis a chum an dá aiste (1740–41) atá in eagar anseo. Bhí an dá Shéamas Mac Coitir, Séamas (Mór) Mac Coitir agus Séamas (Beag) Mac Coitir, athair agus mac, ag cumadh filíochta ag an am, agus an-mhinic sna lámhscríbhinní ní dhealaítear saothar an athar agus an mhic ó chéile.

   Is beag ar fad an t-eolas atá againn ar bheatha Shéamais Mhóir, ach gur deartháir é do Uilliam Rua (*c*.1675–1738);[7] go raibh sé chun cónaithe i gCurrach Diarmada,[8] i ngiorracht trí mhíle slí do Chaisleán Ó Liatháin, sa tigh céanna le hUilliam Rua, b'fhéidir; gur dhein sé beagán saothair mar scríobhaí sna daichidí i bpáirt le Seán Ó Murchú na Ráithíneach; go raibh meas air lena linn féin mar fhile,[9] agus go bhfuil na blianta 1720, 1731 agus 1736 luaite le trí cinn dá chuid aistí filíochta.[10] Timpeall na bliana 1721, a saolaíodh Séamas Beag.[11] Is é is dóichí go raibh sé fostaithe fén mbliain 1768 mar mhaor ('land-agent') ag Iarla an Bharraigh Mhóir, a bhí an uair sin chun cónaithe sa chaisleán i gCaisleán Ó Liatháin agus bhí an post céanna san ag a mhac, Séamas, a fuair bás sa bhliain 1786 in aois a ocht mbliana fichead.[12] Tá

Index I, lch 107). **5** *Mo léansa an galar so shearg me i sírghéibheann* (LNÉ LS G 430, lch 64; feic *NLI Cat.*, ix, lch 85). Leagtha go héagórach ar Shéamas Óg Mac Coitir (†1720) i gcuid de na lámhscríbhinní agus i gcatalóg an Acadaimh (feic *RIA Cat., Index II*, lch 884), nuair is é Séamas Beag Mac Coitir, dar liom, a chum. **6** *Chúig achainí táid agam duit, a Sheáin, chum siúil* (ARÉ LS 24 A 6, lch 365; feic *RIA Cat.*, lch 2882). **7** Bhí deartháir eile ag Uilliam Rua agus ag Séamas Mór darbh ainm Éamann a cailleadh uair éigin roimh éag do Uilliam Rua (†1738). Chuir Uilliam Rua cuntas ar a bhás go dtí an tAthair Domhnall Ó Duinnín a bhí i gColáiste na nÉireannach i dToulouse chomh luath leis an mbliain 1732 agus ina uachtarán ann 1738–51. Feic Risteárd Ó Foghludha ['Fiachra Éilgeach'] (eag.), *Cois na Cora* (BÁC, 1937), lgh 15, 28; T.C. Cunningham, 'The Irish College at Toulouse', *JCHAS*, 74 (1969), 88–9; Laurence W.B. Brockliss agus Patrick Ferte, 'Prosopography of Irish clerics in the universities of Paris and Toulouse, 1573–1792', *Archivium Hibernicum*, 58 (2004), 7–166 ag 66. Mo bhuíochas do Dhiarmaid Ó Catháin as na tuairiscí ar an Ath. Ó Duinnín a chur ar mo shúile dhom. **8** I bparóiste Bhriach (par. Cait. Chaisleáin Ó Liatháin), i mbarúntacht an Bharraigh Mhóir. **9** Pádraig A. Breatnach, 'Dhá dhuain leanbaíochta', *Éigse*, 22 (1987), 111–23 ag 112. **10** *Cia hí an bhean nó an eol díbh* (1720, in eagar ag Ó Foghludha, *Cois na Cora*, lgh 24–5; níl aon deimhniú, áfach, ar dháta cumtha na haiste seo); *Tarla gné dhaoldatha d'fhoiligh gach rian* (1731, feic Breatnach, 'Dhá dhuain leanbaíochta', 111 agus n. 3); *Fáilte óm chroí le báb na milse* (1736, in eagar ag Breatnach, 'Dhá dhuain leanbaíochta', 111–17). I ndearmad is ea a luaigh mé féin (Breandán Ó Conchúir, 'Comhfhreagras sa deibhidhe ón mbliain 1762' in M. Ó Briain agus P. Ó Héalaí [eag.], *Téada dúchais: aistí in ómós don Ollamh Breandán Ó Madagáin* [Conamara, 2002], lgh 273–93 ag lch 292 n. 2) gurb é Séamas Mór leis a chum *Ní cogadh ná cargaill fhada idir airdríthibh* sa bhliain 1741 (feic n. 2 thuas). **11** Feic an mhairbhne a dhein sé sa bhliain 1738, in aois a sheacht mbliana déag, ar bhás dhearthár a athar, Uilliam Rua (Ó Foghludha, *Cois na Cora*, lch 75). **12** Ó Conchúir, 'Comhfhreagras

teistiméireacht ar Shéamas Beag ón gceathrú deiridh den 18ú haois a thugann ardmholadh dhó mar dhuine foghlamtha sa Ghaeilge agus mar fhile.[13] Ar fhianaise na lámhscríbhinní is féidir 1738 (nuair a chum sé tuireamh ar bhás dhearthár a athar, Uilliam Rua), agus 1762 (nuair a bhí comhfhreagras i bhfoirm filíochta aige le Conchubhar Bán Ó Dála i mBaile Mhistéala) a lua le dhá aiste leis.[14]

Más é Séamas Mac Coitir a chum an dá aiste seo againne, ní féidir a rá, ar fhianaise na lámhscríbhinní, cé acu arbh é Séamas Mór nó Séamas Beag é. Ach le saolré na beirte a chur san áireamh, fara dátaí cumtha na n-aistí, bheadh fonn orm a thuairimiú gurbh é Séamas Beag é.[15]

TÉACSAÍ[16]

1. Tuireamh na bhfataí bliain an tseaca mhóir *anno Domini* 1739

> Créad an fhuaim seo ar fuaid na dtíortha
> tug na táinte cráite cloíte,
> tug an Mhumhain fá chumha i ndaoirse
> 's do neartaigh tráth na gártha caointe.　　　4
>
> Is trua liom féin mar scéal le hinsint
> an cruatan géar so scéidh ar chríoch Luirc,
> guais trér creachadh gan aiseag na daoine,
> ruaig lér scaipeadh ár mbeatha gan saoirse.　　　8
>
> Díth na beatha do chleachtadar roímhe sin
> tug ár bhflatha go fatuirseach scíosmhar,

sa deibhidhe', lch 276. Bhí mac darbh ainm Séamas (1784–1867) aige seo chomh maith a dheineadh léamh ar ghinealaigh agus ar cháipéisí dlíthiúla sa Laidin do mhuintir Choipinéar agus do Bharraigh an cheantair (Liam Ó Buachalla agus Richard Henchion, 'Gravestones of historical interest at Britway, Co. Cork', *JCHAS*, 68 [1963], 102–3 ag 102 agus n. 5). An t-eolas ar ghinealaigh agus ar Laidin leis, de dhealramh, dob é a chuir ar chumas an teaghlaigh seo na gCoitireach feidhmiú mar mhaoir ag Tiarnaí an Bharraigh Mhóir sa dara leath den ochtú haois déag. Ba mhinic na tiarnaí féin thar lear nó tugtha don charbhas agus don scléip, agus thairis sin ní bheidís inniúil go minic ar an saghas san oibre a dhéanamh (feic David O'Riordan, *Castlelyons* [(Castlelyons), 1976], lgh 27–8). **13** Ó Conchúir, 'Comhfhreagras sa deibhidhe', lgh 275–6. **14** *Mo ghearán glacaidh is measaidh ar mhéad mo liach* (1738, in eagar ag Ó Foghludha, *Cois na Cora*, lch 75); *Bímse suirgheach le saoithibh* (1762, in eagar ag Ó Conchúir, 'Comhfhreagras sa deibhidhe', lgh 279–84). Is é is dóichí gurb é leis a chum *Mo léansa an galar so shearg me i sírghéibheann*, c.1738, 'san 17ú bliain dá aois' (feic n. 4 thuas). **15** Tá dearmad ar Dickson (*Arctic Ireland*, lgh 12, 39) agus é ag tagairt d'uimh. 2 anseo nuair a deir sé gurbh é an tAth. Seán Ó Conaire (scríobhaí ARÉ LS 23 C 12) a chum. **16** Gabhaim mo mhórbhuíochas leis an Ollamh Máirtín Ó Murchú a léigh na téacsaí agus a réitigh na ceisteanna teanga dom.

suim a dtortha, lón a dtaoiseach,
an bheatha d'fhóirfeadh d'óg 's do chríonna.   12

Is iomdha maith fairis san aicme gan chuibhdheas,
le braon na bó ba leor a milseacht,
ba rómhaith iad le hiasc 's le him glan
's níor hitheadh riamh bia ba shaoire.   16

Dá mbeith cóisir mhór ag muintir,
fíon is feoil is ól go hoíche,
na seacht soird i gcóir 'na dtimpeall,
níor bhia gan potátaí, an sás ba mhilse.   20

Níl cruit dá gléas, níl spéis acu inti,
níl éin ag cantain mar chleachta*dh* ar choilltibh,
níl céir níl meas níl rath ar ní ar bith,
acht pléasca*dh* bas ag gach neach dá gcaoine*adh*.   24

Tá an spéir fá smúit le dúnas caointe
's an ghrian ní thabhair an lonradh díreach,
géim na n-eas a' teacht in aoirde
's do scéidh an bhóchna mhór tar líne.   28

Tá saoi oirirc fhoirtil ba dhíonmhar
i Lios na gCárr is fearr i gcríoch Luirc,
an Barrach is sine is cirte 's is dísle
do phrímhshliocht iníon Riobaird Mhic Stiabhna.   32

Is é rinn déirc is daonnacht timpeall,
cois an tsléibhe 's gach taobh don Bhríd ghil,
ar díon Dé don laoch ná stríocadh
do churaíbh tána i mbeárnain bhaogail.   36

A Dhia láidir na ngrás 's na soillse,
níor iaidhis bearna gan bearna 'scaoileadh,
fortaigh an tórmach bróin seo ar chrích Luirc
's in am an bháis déin scáth is díon dom.   40

Lámhscríbhinní

Boston Public Library q Eng. 484, lch 58 (*Pádraig Ó Mathamhna*, 1824) [A]
UCC 85, lch 103 (d) (*Seán Breatnach*, Port Láirge, 1850) [B]
ARÉ LS 24 M 5, lch 93 (*Sean Ó Dálaigh*, Baile Átha Cliath, 1857) [C]
ARÉ LS 23 C 12, lch 83 [ll 25–40] (*Seán Ó Conaire*, Cluain Uamha, Co. Chorcaí,
    1757) [D]

Malairtí

Ceannscríbhinní Tuireamh na ffataoi bliadhain an tseaca mhóir Anno Domini 1739 A
Tuireamh na bhfataoi bliadhain an tseaca móir noch do thosaig cromdu 24 la 1739 B
Tuireamh na bhfataoi bliadhain an tseaca mhóir .i. 1739 C

1 an úaim so B an fhuaimsi C **2** tug] (a)tá AB **4** tráct B **5** ninnsint C **6** sgeith a
ccrioch B sgéitheadh a gClár Luirc C **7** guas A gurta árr gcreacha B **8** leir A **9** dioth
A **10** tug] tre B **11** suidheam A **12** air óg 's air chriona A **13** maith] meath A;
gan chuibhthios A gan cuíbhteacht B gan chuibhtheas C **17** dá mbiadh B **19** suird A
sórt B sóirt C **22** mar budh chleachta A a canta mar chleachta BC **23** meas] mil B
25 le cumha(dh) a ccaointe ABC **26** ní thabhradh B ní thúir D; lúnradh D **27** géim]
geo(i)n AC; le teacht A **28** do sgeadhaig A do sgéith C **29** taoi C atá D; fhoirtile
dhíonmhur D **30** a lios na gcárth D agus laighios na ngá(r)rtha ABC **31** an *ar lár* BC
32 phréimhshliocht oinig mac ABC; Stiabhain A mic Stíobhard B Stébhin D **33** as sé
D **34** is gach déighbheart timpchioll na tíre B; na sléibhe D; is *ar lár* AC; do Brighid
A don mBrighid C **35** stríocadh] na striocfach A ná stríocfa C **36** tána] dána AC bo
dhána B; a mbearrna an bhaog(h)uil BC bhaoguil A a mbeárnuin bhaoíguil D **37** a dhé
AC; na ngrása is BD **38** iadhais riamh bearna ABC íadhbhuis D **39** fortacht don tórmach mórsa ABC; a ccrí(o)ch Luirc AC **40** is *ar lár* D; dom] dúin(n) ABC

Nótaí téacsa

Ceannscríbhinn *fataí*, ní bheadh coinne leis an bhfoirm seo i dtéacsaí Muimhneacha, ach
thug an scríobhaí, Pádraig Ó Mathamhna (ó iarthar Chorcaí) tamall éigin ag obair i
gCill Chainnigh agus i Londain leis, b'fhéidir (feic Pádraig de Brún, *Scriptural instruction in the vernacular. The Irish Society and its teachers 1818–1827* [Dublin, 2009], lgh
368–9). Agus gan amhras ní bheadh Seán Ó Dálaigh dall ar an bhfoirm ach oiread. Feic
leis uimh. 2, ll 26, 31, 37 sna malairtí.

11 *suim a dtortha*, a gcuid tortha ar fad; *a dtórtha* a theastaíonn ar mhaithe leis an
meadaracht.

13 *san aicme*, sna prátaí.

25 *dúnas*, foirm ná fuil inaitheanta, maran truailliú í. Bheadh an mheadaracht lochtach ag
an leagan sna malairtí, *cumha a gcaointe*.

30–31 *Lios na gCárr*, Lisnagar Demesne (par. Rathcormack, bar. Barrymore), mar a raibh
Tigh Mór ag an am ag brainse de na Barraigh, agus níos déanaí, i dtreo dheireadh na
haoise, ag an Tiarna Riversdale (feic Samuel Lewis, *A topographical dictionary of Ireland*
[London, 1837], ii, lch 494; Diarmuid Ó Murchadha, *Family names of County Cork*
[Dún Laoghaire, 1985], lch 31). Bhí Barraigh Lios na gCárr 'ar an dream ba
Ghaedhlaighe de shliocht an Bharraigh Mhóir', dar le Torna. Ní foláir nó sé an Barrach
atá i gceist anseo an bhfile ná an Coirnéal Réamonn de Barra a bhí 'na ardshiriam ar
Cho. Chorcaí, 1721, agus a bhí 'na cheann ar fhoireann Chorcaí sa chluiche
iománaíochta ('báire mór Ghleann na nGall') i gcoinne Thiobrad Árann sa bhliain 1741
(feic Torna [Tadhg Ó Donnchadha], *Seán na Ráithíneach* [Baile Átha Cliath, 1954], lgh
187, 446–7). Sid í an teistiméireacht a thug óstóir ón gceantar dó beagán blianta ina dhiaidh sin: 'he was the life of the country round him, and in the late hard times … supported numbers that must have otherwise perished' (William R. Chetwood, *A tour
through Ireland in several entertaining letters … by two English gentlemen* [2nd ed., Dublin,
1748], lch 128; luaite ag Dickson, *Arctic Ireland*, lgh 39–40). Ar an láimh eile, ceapadh
véarsaí dó dar tús *A leoghain nach tim i dtreas*, 'when he endeavoured to persecute the
Roman Catholic clergy A.D. 1733' (ARÉ LS 23 M 14, lch 36; feic *RIA Cat.*, lch 869).

32 *Riobard Mac Stiabhna* (Robert fitz Stephen), an chéad cheannaire ar na hAngla-
Normannaigh a tháinig i dtír in Éirinn sa bhliain 1169. Fuair sé tailte ar ball i ndeisceart

na Mumhan, in oirthear Chorcaí san áireamh, ó Annraí II. Dar le Seán Ó Conaire
(scríobhaí ARÉ LS 23 C 12), bhí dul amú ar an bhfile nuair a mhaígh sé an Barrach a
bheith *do phrímhshliocht iníon Riobaird Mhic Stiabhna*. Tugann Ó Conaire le tuiscint leis
an gceartú a dheineann sé ar imeall an leathanaigh ar an bhfocal *inigion* ('potius
deirbhshiúr') gur de shliocht *dheirféar* Mhic Stiabhna [.i. Pilib de Barra, mac a dheir-
féar] na Barraigh in oirthear Chorcaí. Bhí an ceart ag Ó Conaire. Feic Rev. Edmond
Barry, *Barrymore: records of the Barrys of County Cork, from the earliest to the present
time, with pedigrees* (Cork, 1902), lch 15 (athchló ón *JCHAS*).
34 *gach taobh don Bhríd ghil*, sníonn abha na Bríde soir trí bharúntacht an Bharraigh
Mhóir (mar a bhfuil Ráth Chormaic agus Caisleán Ó Liatháin) agus trí Chine
Tolamhan.

2. Caoineadh na bpotátaí bliain an tseaca mhóir *anno Domini* 1739

M'atuirse ghéar mo phéin monuar mo bhroid
flatha na nGael i ngéibhinn chruaidh anois,
a mbeatha go léir gur léirscrios uatha an sioc
's gan carthanacht Dé níl gaor a bhfuascalta.   4

Fuascailse, 'Uain dhil 's a chara mo chléibh,
an ghuasacht so buaileadh ar Bhanba an tséin,
dá luainn liot a gcruatan 's a n-easpa go léir
sé an t-Uan ag múin' uaille dá bhanaltrain é.   8

Éighim is aicim ar Athair na nguí 's a Mhac
's an réilteann mhaidne tá 'n-aici sa diacht ar neamh
go léigid eatarthu ár n-anamna suí 'na measc
's go réidhid gach easpa tá ag cealgadh ár gcroí 's ár gcreat.   12

Creat locartha atá orainne le cian 'na smáilc,
creach dhochrach do bhochtanaigh, mo chiach, an dáimh,
neart borbchon 'na conchlann a hiathaibh námhad
's níor chogadh san go hocras, a Dhia na ngrás.   16

Grása an Athar go dtagaidh 'nár ndáil anuas
go dtála a mhaitheas, a rachmas, a ghrá 's a chnuas
in áit gach easpa, gach galair, gach plá 's gach cruas
's ná táidhfeadh armas Aicill ár gcneá-na uait.   20

Uaitse ling na saighde groda géara,
cruatan bídh is dí is gorta 'n éineacht,
uaill is caoi aige daoine i gcrothaibh éaga;
'Uain dhil, scaoilse dhínn na crosa daora.   24

Daor na heaspaithe cachtaithe in ardchrích Mogha,
glaoch ar airgead fearainn 's potátaí a' lobhadh;
do thraoch an galar seo an ghasra bhán bhíth-mhodhail,
tá fraoch ar fhearaibh gan beatha 's na mná tí lom.   28

Is lom an golfhairt do chloisim ag mná tí ar siúl,
gan chabhair gan chothrom dá stolladh 'dir pháistíbh dubha,
más trom nó torrach ní locaid na potátaí a bhrú
's mar dheabhadh ar ár ndonas gur bhrostaigh na báilí chughainn.   32

Chughainn, mo ghreadadh croí, leagtar síos lúmpa ar clár,
crústa seacairí 's dá fhichead stríoc dhubha 'na lár,
is dubhach mo dhealbh roímhe, is fada bhíonn blúire im láimh,
cumha do mhairfidh fíor againne í i dtionsc' mo bháis.   36

Bás na [b]potátaí chráigh tinn dubhach na fir,
d'fhág na páistí fá scíos cumha 'gus goil,
gláimh ag mná tí 's scoláirí ag lúbarnaigh,
níl náid le fáil díbh ardaíodh fúibh bhur gcrios.   40

Cros cruatain is trua liom le n-aithris díbhse,
cros tuaiscirt do buaileadh ar Chlannaibh Míle,
cith crua sioca ruaigeadh a rannaibh nimhe Styx
an cith d'fhuadaigh tar chuantaibh ár mbeatha dhíleas.   44

Is díleas na gníomhartha rinn Barraigh aosta,
saoithe na críche 'gus maithe Paorach,
do scaoileadar daoirse 'gus glasa daora
don mhuintear do chímtear ar easpa béile.   48

Béile bé bhéarfadh don dealbh uasal,
réidhfidh an tAonmhac a cheasta i nguasacht,
– tá déirc agus daonnacht in Easpag Chluana –
's glaofaidh go haerach i bhflaitheas tuas air.   52

'S air scríobhtar gur bríomhar gach téacs thig uaidh
's gur chríochnaigh go fínis an léann go suairc,
maífead ar dhraoithibh 's ar éigsibh duan
gur fírinneach díntear an déirc i gCluain.   56

I gCluain, ní chanaim le bladar i ríomh bréige
an cruas so ar bhailtibh, ní chaithid acht aoinbhéile,
uaisle 's eaglais caraid an fhíoréigin,
seo an uair do braithfear a maitheas do chrích Éibhir.   60

Ó Éibhear do théarnaigh na fiorfhlatha
ba thréine ba fhéile do níodh maitheas,
Gréagaigh dá ndéis sin is Gaill Sacsan,
do réidhfid na daorghlais seo a' luí ar lagaibh.   64

'S níor lagadh go léir na Gaeil in iathaibh Luirc
gur caitheadh le spéir na gaotha dian anoir,
's gan againn do ghréithe an tsaogail iachtagaigh
acht atuirse ghéar is péin is fiacha 's broid.   68

Ceangal

Guímse an tAthair 's a bhanaltra naofa ar dtúis,
's na trí ceathrair do scaipeadh le scéaltaibh chughainn,
dár ndíon ar pheaca 's ar chleasaibh an tsaogail chiúin,
's ná bíonn againn acht sealad beag éagosúil.   72

Lámhscríbhinní

ARÉ LS 23 C 12, lch 83 (*Seán Ó Conaire*, Cluain Uamha, Co. Chorcaí, 1757) [A]
Boston Public Library q Eng. 484, lch 59 [ll 1–44, 69–72] (*Pádraig Ó Mathamhna*, 1824) [B]
UCC 85, lch 103 (e) (*Seán Breatnach*, Port Láirge, 1850) [C]
ARÉ LS 24 M 5, lch 94 (*Sean Ó Dálaigh*, Baile Átha Cliath, 1857) (D)

Malairtí

Ceannscríbhinní An fear céadhna cct chum na críche ceadhna A Caoine na ppotataoi bliadhain an tseaca mhóir Anno Domini 1739 B Ar an adhbar céadna CD
1 monuar] mo bhrón BCD   2 a ngéibhionn A   7 liot] leatsa BCD; an crúatan C   8 asé
A dob é BCD   9 éighim is *ar lár* A; na g(h)uidhe BCD   10 's air an BCD; mhaidne]
Mhuire C; (a)ta naice AD (a)ta an aice BC; sa] san D   11 nanama B nanmanna D; is
suighe BCD   12 atá cealg A; 's ár gcreat] ar fad BCD   13 creat] creach D   14 do
bhrostana(igh) BCD; na dáimh A   15 na ccon(n)achlann BD na cconachladh C
16 sníor cogadh sin gus a torannuibh A; a Dhé BCD   17 an tathair A; go ttagadh BC
18 ttáile(adh) ACD; reachmas A   19 pláig(h) BCD 20 ná taidhfioch A ná tárfa(dh) BCD;
ár ccnámh(a) BCD 21 líon BCD; síoda A saoigheada B soigheadh C soigheada D
22 cruaghtain B; gorta] coda BCD; a naoinfheacht BD   23 caoi a(i)g BCD   24 is (a)
uain(n) BCD; ár(r) ccrosa BCD   25 is daor na heasbuighe chleachtaoid BCD   26 fearann A; fataoi BCD; lógha(dh) ABCD   27 do] o BCD; seo] sa BCD; ban B; bhíg
mhómhuil A bhi m(h)odhamhuil BC bhí modhuil D   28 atá A; gan beatha *ar lár* A; tí
lom] thig liomm C   29 an galtairt A an ghólfhuirt seo B an gholphortsa C an golfartsa
D; do chluinimsi ag A chloinim ag D; piastaoibh dúbha BCD   30 dá stolladh ... dubha]
mo dheacair na mná tighe dúbhach BCD 31 nó] más BCD; na fataoi BD na prátaoi C
32 's *ar lár* BCD; ár] a(n) BCD; gur] do BCD   33 ghreadadh] dheacair C; leacar A
léigthear C; lúmpa] iompa D   34 crúsca D; seacuirídhe A seacairighe BD seacraidhe
C; is aist(i)righe dubha BCD   35 is dubhach ... roímhe] mo bhruth mo dhealbh-
bhighe B mo bhrúgha mo dhealbh bhríghe D   36 's as cubha do mhairbh sinn againn

í a ttionnsgnadh bháis BD ationns mo bháis A **37** na bhfataoi BD na brataoi C; (dfag) san dubhach na fir BCD **38** is d'fhág BCD **39** mnáibh BC; lubairne B lubarnach C **40** nád BD nídh C; gcrios] ccros C **41** cros] crios BCD; nairthis A **42** crios BCD; chlana B **43** cith ruaidhseach B crios ruaidhtheacha C cith ruaidh-sheaca D; do ruagabh B do ruagadh CD; ó ranaibh BC; nídh A nimhe *ar lár* C **44** an *ar lár* BCD; cith] crios C; dhíolas A dílis C **45** díolas A dílis A; an gniomh do CD **47** sgaoil-fighear CD **48** mhuintir noch chidhfear CD **49** bé] gibé CD; béarthach A bhéarfa C **50** an taonmhac a cceasna CD **51** atá A; Chlua(dh)nach CD **52** agus glaodhfad D; tsúas A s(h)uas CD **53** do sgribeadair go firineach C do sgríbhfidhear go fireannach D; téx A text CD **55** maoid(h)feadsa CD; 'sair éigsibh suaigh CD **56** do ghnít(h)ear CD **57** as Chluain ní chanfadsa ... a rainn bhréige CD **58** san ccruadhacht so ... na caithid CD **59** is fir éigin CD **60** uair braithfar A uair do bhrai(th)tear ... a ccríoch Eibhir CD **61** ó Éimhir ... fiorflatha A d'Eibhir do thar(r)aing na sao(i)rfhlaithe CD **62** ba t(h)éarnach ba saoghaltach do ghníodh CD **63** na ndéig s(i)ud CD; is *ar lár* A; saxon AC Sagsann D **64** do *ar lár* CD; na géarghlais(e) ag CD **65** O lagaig CD **66** 'sgur caithe D; diana CD; ansoir A **67** 's *ar lár* CD; de ghreit(h)ribh CD; an táoguil íacht-aguig A an tsaoghail íasachtach C an tsaoghail iasachtaicc D **68** fa(d)tuirse CD; is diachair bhruid CD **69** an bhanaltra BC **70** do sgaireadh C; sgéalaibh BCD **71** ár ndíon BCD; chiúin] úd BCD **72** air nach beidh B úair na beig C ar nach bíodh D; éagasamhuil A eagsamhuil BD sealaid beig eiginn ann C.

Nótaí téacsa

(Aistriúchán Béarla ag Nessa Doran i gcló in R. McKay [ed.], *An anthology of the potato* [Dublin, 1961], lgh 43–5)

8 cf. an seanfhocal, *an t-uan ag múineadh méilí dá mháthair*; *dá bhanaltrain*, don Mhaighdin Mhuire.

10 *an réilteann mhaidne*, An Mhaighdean Mhuire; *tá 'n-aici sa diacht* = tá 'na n-aici sa diacht, 'next to them in divine nature'.

15 *'na conchlann*, 'compared to it'. *Neart borbchon ... a hiathaibh námhad* á chur i gcomparáid leis an *creach dhochrach*.

20 *táidhfeadh*, feic *DIL* s.v. *táidid*, 'steals', 'thieves'.

25 *cachtaithe*, feic *DIL* s.v. *cachtaid*, 'shackles', 'fetters' 7rl.

34 *seacairí* (*seacuirídhe* A *seacairíghe* BD *seacraidhe* C), iol. *seacaire* atá ag Dinn. san fhoirm *siocaide*, *al. seacaide*, agus 'a frost-bitten potato' ar na bríonna atá aige leis. Maidir le malartaíocht idir *d* caol agus *r* caol, is tréith í ná fuil neamhchoitianta, cf. *dréimide / dréimire*, *leidhcide / leidhcire*, *sceachóid / sceachóir* 7rl. Mo bhuíochas do Mháirtín Ó Murchú as an réiteach seo a sholáthar dom.

43 *Styx*, abha a raibh a cuid uiscí nimhiúil i miotaseolaíocht na Gréige.

45–6 *Barraigh ... maithe Paorach*, ar na teaghlaigh acmhainneacha i mbarúntacht an Bharraigh Mhóir ar éirigh leo greim a choimeád ar chuid éigin dá dtailte sa chéad leath den 18ú haois, agus a dhein pátrúnacht ar scríobhaithe agus ar fhilí na Gaeilge, bhí Barraigh Dhún Dolraic agus Léim Lára agus Paoraigh Chluain Molt. Dá chomhartha san tá mórán aistí molta ag na filí ar bhaill de na teaghlaigh sin (feic, mar shampla, an tuairisc ag Richard Henchion, 'The gravestone inscriptions of Co. Cork, xi: Clonmult burial ground', *JCHAS*, 81 [1976], 115–17). Tagairt do na línte seo agus do líne 51 ag Dickson, *Arctic Ireland*, lgh 39–40 agus ag Buttimer, 'The Great Famine in Gaelic manuscripts', lgh 462–3.

48 *chímtear* = chimtear < cimim.

51 *déirc agus daonnacht in Easpag Chluana*, George Berkeley (1685–1753), an fealsamh mórchlú agus an t-easpag de chuid Eaglais na hÉireann i gCluain (1734–53), is é atá i gceist anseo. Le linn dó bheith ina easpag i gCluain i mbar. Uíbh Mic Coille, fiche éigin míle laisteas de Chaisleán Ó Liatháin (atá i ndeoise Chluana) bhí gorta agus galar go for-leathan mórthimpeall air agus chaith sé mórán duaidh ag freastal ar ghantar na mbochtán, d'iarraidh a gcás a leigheas. Is mó scéim, mar shampla, a chuir sé ar bun chun feabhas a chur ar thionscal agus ar thalmhaíocht an cheantair, agus i gcaitheamh an gheimhridh 1739–40 agus le linn an ghorta a lean é thugadh sé fiche punt in aghaidh na seachtaine mar dhéirc do na bochtáin i gCluain. Feic *The dictionary of Irish biography* (Cambridge, 2009), s.n.

53 *gach téacs thig uaidh*, dob fhéidir nach tagairt í seo dá chuid leabhar ar an bhfealsúnacht go luath ina shaol, ach do na tráchtais ar chúrsaí eacnamaíochta a scríobh sé le linn dó bheith i gCluain, mar shampla, *The Querist* (1735–7), agus go háirithe a chuid scríbhinní ar fhadhbanna an phobail sa cheantar áitiúil. Feic *The dictionary of Irish biography*, s.n.

67 *iachtagaigh*, gin. *iachtagach* < *iacht*, 'sigh', 'lament'. Níl aon sampla eile dá leithéid d'fhocal le fáil. Dob fhéidir gur foirm í a shíolraigh go hearráideach i seachadadh an téacsa ó fhoirm mar *iachtasach, .i. iacht + as + ach*. Ní thabharfadh *iachtach* an trí shi-olla atá ag teastáil ón meadaracht. Mo bhuíochas do Mháirtín Ó Murchú as an dtuairim seo a léiriú dom.

70 *na trí ceathrair*, An Dáréag (Aspal).

A cult of Saint Thecla in early medieval Ireland?

CAITRÍONA Ó DOCHARTAIGH

In a short article entitled 'Notes on apocrypha in Ireland' published in 1926, St John Seymour affirmed that the apocryphal *Acts of Paul and Thecla* were known in medieval Ireland.[1] This non-canonical text, part of a larger work entitled simply the *Acts of Paul*,[2] was already well-established in certain circles by the end of the second century AD despite the disapproval of writers such as Tertullian who condemned it in *De baptismo*[3] as supplying false encouragement to women who wished to teach and baptise on the model of Thecla.[4] Notwithstanding criticism by Tertullian, amongst others,[5] and ultimate condemnation in the Gelasian Decree,[6] the story of the courageous young woman from Iconium who, inspired by Saint Paul's teaching, takes up the life of a wandering Christian missionary and survives multiple attempts on her life, by fire, wild beasts and dismemberment, continued to have considerable appeal.[7]

Seymour's assertion that the *Acts of Paul* was known in medieval Ireland was based on two pieces of evidence: a reference to the early Christian protomartyr in the medieval Irish versified martyrology *Félire Óengusso*,[8] and a brief remark by Douglas Hyde in his preface to a modern Irish version of the *Visio S. Pauli*.[9] In the course of discussing parallels to the vision text, Hyde referred to a further, unidentified source containing a physical description of the apostle:

---

1 St John D. Seymour, 'Notes on apocrypha in Ireland', *PRIA*, 37C (1926), 107–17 at 113. 2 Wilhelm Schneemelcher (ed.; Eng. ed. R. McL. Wilson), *New Testament apocrypha*, 2 vols (Tübingen, 1989; Cambridge, 1992), ii, pp 213–47; François Bovon and Pierre Geoltrain (eds), *Écrits apocryphes chrétiens*, 2 vols (Paris, 1997), i, pp 1117–77. The *Acts of Paul* was thought to be lost until the University of Heidelberg acquired a collection of papyrus fragments in 1896 containing the full account which was subsequently published by Carl Schmidt, *Acta Pauli aus der Heidelberger koptischen Papyrushandschrift Nr. 1* (Leipzig, 1904). 3 *De baptismo* 17, 5 (CCSL 1, pp 291–2). 4 Willy Rordorf has argued that the text of the *Acts of Paul* to which Tertullian refers in late second- or early third-century Carthage was already a Latin translation of the original Greek: 'Sainte Thècle dans la tradition hagiographique occidentale', *Augustinianum*, 24 (1984), 73–81 at 75. 5 Léon Vouaux examined in detail references to Thecla by early Christian writers such as Origen, Eusebius, Athanasius, Gregory of Nyssa, Ambrose of Milan, Jerome, Augustine, etc.: *Les Actes de Paul et ses lettres apocryphes* (Paris, 1913), pp 24–69. Although many of these authors condemned the *Acts*, they do not doubt that Thecla was a genuine historical figure, and their disapproval of the apocryphal work is often accompanied by admiration for Thecla as a model of Christian chastity. 6 Ernst von Dobschütz (ed.), *Das Decretum Gelasianum de libris recipiendis et non recipiendis* (Leipzig, 1912), p. 52. 7 On the growth of her cult, see Stephen J. Davis, *The cult of St Thecla: a tradition of women's piety in late Antiquity* (Oxford, 2001). 8 Whitley Stokes (ed. and trans.), *Félire Óengusso Céli Dé: the martyrology of Oengus the Culdee*, HBS 29 (London, 1905). 9 Charles D. Wright has described this text as 'a

I found an account of St Paul in another Irish MS., probably taken from some lost source. 'A small, miserable-looking person was the apostle Paul. Broad shoulders he had; a white face with a sedate demeanour. His head small. Pleasant bright eyes he had. Long brows, a projecting (?) nose and a long beard with a little grey hair'.[10]

Hyde was, unfortunately, unaware of the significance of this description, but Seymour recognized its importance and declared that it 'is evidently based on the well-known description given of that Saint in the Greek and Syriac versions of those *Acts*'.[11] The account of the apostle is found at the opening of the *Acts of Paul* when Paul is approaching Iconium for the first time, the place where Thecla will subsequently hear him preaching and be inspired to abandon her family and fiancé. A man named Onesiphorus and his family are awaiting Paul's arrival at the approach to the city in order to welcome him into their home, but because they have never seen him before they are dependent upon a physical description of the apostle recounted to them by a third party. The description is, however, adequate because Onesiphorus immediately recognizes the apostle as he approaches:

And he saw Paul coming, a man small of stature, with a bald head and crooked legs, in a good state of body, with eyebrows meeting and nose somewhat hooked, full of friendliness; for now he appeared like a man, and now he had the face of an angel.[12]

The Irish account is significant in that it shares with the *Acts of Paul* an emphasis on Paul's short stature, long eyebrows and prominent nose. Hyde's Irish text also makes reference to Paul's long beard, a feature which is not included in the apocryphon but which dominates a collection of unrelated descriptions of Paul in Irish manuscripts, which were also discussed by Seymour in another context.[13] Whitley Stokes was the first to draw attention to the latter series of physical descriptions of the apostles, some of which survive in verse form, such as the poem he edited from the Harleian manuscript 1802 (f. 9b): *Pól apstal aláind a drech / gofolt ercháin ussinech / áes cúmtha gor dochotta / ulcha póil bafirfotta* ('Paul the apostle, delightful his visage, with hair very beautiful, fawn-coloured. Until his comrades cut it short Paul's beard was truly long').[14] Stokes unearthed three further such descriptions of

strikingly divergent Irish version of the *Visio Sancti Pauli*': 'Next-to-last things: the interim state of souls in early Irish literature' in J. Carey, E. Nic Cárthaigh and C. Ó Dochartaigh (eds), *The end and beyond: medieval Irish eschatology*, 2 vols (Aberystwyth, 2014), i, pp 309–96 at p. 340.   10 Douglas Hyde, *Legends of saints and sinners* (London, 1915), p. 96.   11 Seymour, 'Notes on apocrypha', 113.   12 Schneemelcher, *New Testament apocrypha*, ii, p. 239.   13 St John D. Seymour, 'Irish descriptions of St Paul's personal appearance', *Church of Ireland Gazette*, August 20 (1920), p. 548.   14 Whitley Stokes, 'The Irish verses,

the apostles, two of which refer to Paul's long fawn-coloured beard.[15] Another such description in the Book of Uí Maine (f. 132d), also emphasizing Paul's long fair beard, was edited by Tomás Ó Máille.[16] More recently, Dáibhí Ó Cróinín has signalled the existence of three further texts in this genre and argued that they may all ultimately derive from a Latin text ascribed to Cummianus Longus.[17] Margaret Stokes, in her investigation of the motifs of medieval Irish art, suggested that these descriptions may have been excerpted from medieval painters' manuals outlining the standard depictions of the apostles.[18] Another possible source is a genre of Latin text often extant under the title *Notitia de locis apostolorum* in which the apostles are listed along with associated details such as their feastdays, the places where they were martyred and brief biographical details.[19] Whatever their origins, the Irish lists detailing the physical appearance of the apostles are evidently unconnected to the description of Saint Paul supplied in the *Acts of Paul*; the only feature of the apostle which they share is his reputed baldness.

Conversely, the passage quoted by Hyde is clearly related to the apocryphon. However, the description of the apostle from the opening of the *Acts of Paul* circulated widely, without necessarily being connected to the rest of the account; due to the antiquity of the apocryphon, the description was thought to have considerable authority which only added to its popularity.[20] The adaptation of the *Acts of Paul* into discrete, independent episodes, or narratives is a process which seems to have begun quite early, especially in the case of Thecla. Her cult grew rapidly in the late antique period and she

notes and glosses in Harl. 1802', *RC*, 8 (1887), 346–69 at 350. **15** Ibid., p. 362, where Stokes supplies two further texts, one from the Book of Ballymote (p. 14b facs.) and the other from the Leabhar Breac (p. 180, col. 2). Furthermore, in a 'Note on the personal appearance and death of Christ, his apostles and others', *RC*, 9 (1888), 364, he supplies another description of the apostles from YBL (col. 332). **16** Tomás Ó Máille, 'Críst rocrochad', *Ériu*, 3 (1907), 194–9 at 194 §3. **17** Dáibhí Ó Cróinín, 'Cummianus Longus and the iconography of Christ and the apostles in early Irish literature' in L. Breatnach, K. McCone and D. Ó Corráin (eds), *Sages, saints and storytellers: Celtic Studies in honour of Professor James Carney*, Maynooth Monographs 2 (Maynooth, 1989), pp 268–79: Dublin, NLI MS G 3, ff 21vb–22ra; Oxford, Bodleian Library, MS Laud Misc 610, f. 42rd; Dublin, RIA, MS 23 P 2, ff 166vd–167ra. The earliest text cited by Ó Cróinín from the Irish Reference Bible does not, however, include a description of Saint Paul. **18** Margaret Stokes, *Early Christian art in Ireland* (Dublin, 1887; repr. 1911, 1927, 1932), pp 111–13 (original edition) or vol. ii, pp 10–13 (reprint). This also appears to be the conclusion arrived at tentatively by Ó Cróinín: 'Cummianus Longus and the iconography', p. 276. **19** *BHL* 648; *PL* 30, 435–7. Cf. Frederick M. Biggs (ed.), *Sources of Anglo-Saxon literary culture: the apocrypha*, Instrumenta Anglistica Mediaevalia 1 (Kalamazoo, 2007), p. 78. Ó Cróinín in his article alludes to the fact that some of the texts he discusses combine physical descriptions of the apostles with details of the place and manner of their deaths ('Cummianus Longus and the iconography', p. 271); therefore, these texts may represent a merger of two, once discrete, genres. **20** Abraham J. Malherbe, 'A physical description of St Paul', *Harvard Theological Review*, 79 (1986), 170–5.

was widely venerated in the Near and Middle East. There is evidence of regular pilgrimages to her supposed resting place at a site called Meriamlik outside ancient Seleucia (in what is now Turkey) as early as the fourth century. It was here, in order to cement her status as an important saint, that the *Life and miracles of Thecla* was redacted in the fifth century, the first part of which is heavily reliant on the *Acts of Paul*.[21] This account of Thecla's persecution during her lifetime and her (largely) post-mortem miracles reached the Latin West where it was known under the hagiographic title *Passio sanctae Theclae*[22] to distinguish it from the now heretical *Acta Pauli*. Unfortunately, given that the description of the physical appearance of Saint Paul circulated independently of the apocryphon and the passion, evidence of this description in isolation does not necessarily prove that the *Acts of Paul* or the *Passio sanctae Theclae* in their entirety were known in medieval Ireland. Without the manuscript context in which Hyde's passage occurs, or any other information concerning the source, this tantalizing reference to Saint Paul is therefore evidentially insignificant for the time being. Consequently, the second pillar of Seymour's argument, the reference in *Félire Óengusso*, is of greater interest.[23]

The litany to which Seymour refers is included in the epilogue to the verse martyrology, where Thecla is cited (between Isaac and Jacob) in a long sequence of verses where scriptural examples of divine intervention are invoked in order that the supplicant may also be saved:

> Rom-śóerae, á Íssu,
> lat nóebu tan tíastae,
> amail sóersai Teclam[24]
> de ginol na bíastae.[25]

21 For the Greek hagiographic tradition, see Michel Aubineau, 'Le panégyrique de Thècle, attribué à Jean Chrysostome (BHG 1720): la fin retrouvée d'un texte mutilé', *Analecta Bollandiana*, 93 (1975), 349–62; Gilbert Dagron (ed. and trans.) *Vie et miracles de sainte Thècle. Texte grec, traduction et commentaire*, Subsidia Hagiographica 62 (Brussels, 1978). **22** Oscar von Gebhardt, *Passio s. Theclae virginis. Die lateinischen Übersetzungen der Acta Pauli et Theclae*, Texte und Untersuchungen 22, ii (Leipzig, 1902); Hippolyte Delehaye, 'Les recueils antiques des miracles des saints', *Analecta Bollandiana*, 43 (1925), 49–57; BHL 8020–5; AS Sept. vi, 546–68. For the development of Thecla's cult, cf. Carl Holzhey, *Die Thekla-Akten. Ihre Verbreitung und Beurteilung in der Kirche* (Munich, 1905); Vouaux, *Les Actes de Paul*; Rordorf, 'Sainte Thècle dans la tradition hagiographique occidentale'; Ruth Albrecht, *Das Leben der heiligen Makrina auf dem Hintergrund der Thekla-Traditionen: Studien zu den Ursprüngen des weiblichen Mönchtums im 4. Jahrhundert in Kleinasien* (Göttingen, 1986); Sever J. Voicu, 'Thecla in the Christian East' in J.W. Barrier, J.N. Bremmer, T. Nicklas, and A. Puig i Tàrrech (eds), *Thecla: Paul's disciple and saint in the east and west* (Leuven, 2015), pp 56–82. **23** *Fél.* p. 285, ll 469–72. **24** Most manuscripts of the martyrology supply the accusative form *Teclam* here, but one manuscript supplies *Tecla* and another *Declam*: see *Fél.* p. 285. **25** Cf. Stokes' translation: 'Mayst Thou save me, O Jesus, with Thy saints when they come, as Thou savedst Thecla from the maw of the monster': *Fél.* p. 285, ll 469–72.

> May you save me, Jesus,
> with your saints when you come,
> as you saved Thecla
> from the jaws of the beast.

The litany does not respect biblical order and the majority of the incidents of divine salvation evoked come from the Old Testament (20 out of 28). At the end of the litany, three saints who were miraculously saved are grouped together: Saint Martin of Tours,[26] Saint Patrick,[27] and Saint Kevin of Glendalough.[28] In the New Testament scriptural examples cited in the text, the emphasis placed on the deeds of the apostles is noteworthy: even the sole New Testament reference is to the apostle Peter being saved from the waves of the sea (Mt 14:22–33). There are four examples of divine salvation in the litany pertaining to the missionary activities of the apostles; but only the reference to Paul and Peter being saved from 'the punishment of the prison' (Acts 16:19–34 and 12:1–12) is canonical. The other three are all from the apocryphal Acts or legends of the Apostles: Thecla being saved from a beast, John saved from poisoning,[29] and also John being delivered from a fiery cauldron.[30] In the epilogue, therefore, Thecla is not placed at the close of the sequence with the saints, but in the main section of the litany as a scriptural, quasi-biblical example of divine intervention.

This invocation of Thecla being saved from a beast is presumably a reference to the climax of the narrative when she avoids martyrdom in the

---

26 *Fél.* p. 288, ll 547–8: *amail sóersai Mártain / ar sacart ind ídail* ('as you saved Martin from the priest of the idol'). Cf. Jacques Fontaine (ed.), *Sulpice Sévère. Vie de saint Martin*, 3 vols, SC 133–5 (Paris, 1967–9), i, pp 284–6. Saint Martin of Tours is commemorated in the main body of the *Félire* on 11 November, as *slíab óir íarthair domuin* ('the mountain of gold of the western world'). His translation is commemorated on 4 June and his ordination on 4 July: *Fél.* pp 234, 138, 160. Moreover, in the section of the epilogue which enumerates the companies of the blessed, he is described as foremost of the world's saints: ibid., p. 276. 27 *Fél.* p. 288, ll 551–2: *amal sóersai Pátric / de thonnud hi Temraig* ('as you saved Patrick from poison in Tara'). Cf. Ludwig Bieler (ed. and trans.), *The Patrician texts in the Book of Armagh*, SLH 10 (Dublin, 1979), p. 92; Whitley Stokes (ed. and trans.), *The tripartite life of St Patrick*, 2 vols (London, 1887), i, p. 55; *LisL* p. 52. 28 *Fél.* p. 288, ll 555–6: *amal sóersai Cóemgein / de chutaim in tslébe* ('as you delivered Cóemgein from the falling mountain'). Cf. *VSHP* i, p. 244 §xx. 29 *Fél.* p. 285, ll 479–80: *amail sóersai Ióain / de neim inna nathrach* ('as you saved John from the poison of the serpent'). Cf. James K. Elliott (trans.), *The apocryphal New Testament: a collection of apocryphal Christian literature in an English translation based on M.R. James* (Oxford, 1993), 'The Acts of John', pp 303–49 at pp 343–5; Martin McNamara, *The apocrypha of the Irish church* (Dublin, 1984), pp 95–9. 30 *Fél.* p. 287, ll 539–40: *amail sóersai Ióain / assin dabaig thened* ('as you saved John from the fiery cauldron'). This episode is not attested in the apocryphal Acts of John but rather appears to have circulated as an independent legend first alluded to by Tertullian in an enumeration of significant events involving the apostles in Rome: *De praescriptione haereticorum* 36.3 (CCSL 1, pp 185–224). Cf. Montague R. James, *The apocryphal New Testament* (Oxford, 1924), p. 265.

amphitheatre of Antioch (§33–6). Thecla's life begins in Iconium where she
lives with her mother and is betrothed to Thamyris, a local aristocrat.
However, while sitting at the window of her house, Thecla hears the words
of Saint Paul who is preaching nearby. She is so enthralled that she refuses
to leave the window and does not react either to her mother or to her fiancé.
Thamyris is so enraged by the effect that Paul is having on his betrothed that
he seeks him out and denounces him as a danger to the city, depriving men
of their wives by preaching a doctrine of chastity.[31] Paul is then imprisoned
but Thecla bribes the guards and manages to visit him in prison. When
Thecla's mother discovers where she is, she is brought in front of the governor and is condemned to be burnt at the stake, but the Lord sends rain and
hail which extinguish the flames. Thecla is then freed and resolves to follow
Paul. He initially refuses to baptize her or allow her to follow him, but she
perserveres and continues with him to Antioch. There, the beauty of Thecla
attracts the unwanted attentions of Alexander, an eminent citizen of Antioch.
When she pushes him away as he attempts to seize her in the street, thereby
tearing his coat and knocking off his crown, he condemns her and she is sen-
tenced to death in the amphitheatre. While awaiting her fate, she is placed in
the care of a local noblewoman called Tryphanea. The day before the games
she is paraded in the street along with the wild animals who are supposed to
kill her, but a fierce lioness licks her feet instead. When Thecla subsequently
appears in the arena, the lioness protects her from the other lions and bears,
and dies defending her. Thecla, thinking that death is at hand, throws herself
into a nearby pit full of water to baptize herself. The fierce sea-lions that are
in the water are killed by lightning and fire. Fire also encircles Thecla to protect her from further attacks from wild animals. Finally, Thecla's feet are tied
to bulls goaded with red–hot irons but the fire surrounding her burns through
the ropes. After all these torments, Thecla is released and finds Paul, who,
having listened to her, encourages her to teach the word of God, after which
she returns to Iconium. Following failure in her attempt to convert her
mother, she continues to Seleucia where she takes up residence in a cave and
enlightens many in the vicinity. At the end of the narrative she dies there at
an advanced age.

During her torment in the arena, accordingly, Thecla was saved from
many beasts, including lions, bears, bulls and some man-eating seals.
Catherine Franc has demonstrated that the most common images associated
with the protomartyr are the fiancé, fire, and animals that 'appear all together
or separately in a third of all Greek and Latin texts referrring to Thecla'.[32] In

---

31 For the emphasis on chastity in the non-canonical Acts, see Stevan L. Davies, *The
revolt of the widows: the social world of the apocryphal Acts* (Carbondale, 1980).
32 Catherine Franc, 'The cult of Saint Thecla in Anglo-Saxon England: the problem of
Aldhelm's sources', *Bulletin of the John Rylands Library*, 86, ii (2004), 39–54 at 46.

the corpus of patristic authors and in the iconography of eastern Christianity, the beasts that threaten Thecla in the arena are often identified specifically as lions and particular emphasis is placed on the lioness who protects her. Saint Methodius of Olympus, writing at the beginning of the fourth century, praised Thecla in a text belonging to a genre in which she will figure prominently in later centuries: a tract in praise of virginity. He describes how this virgin renounced both nobility and marriage and was ready to suffer by abandoning her body, so to speak, to both flames and beasts.[33] At the end of his work, Methodius describes Thecla as foremost of the choir of virgins eternally singing couplets in honour of chastity. Vouaux, who published a significant edition of the *Acts of Paul* at the beginning of the twentieth century, was of the opinion that the status which Methodius afforded Thecla is evidence that already by the early fourth century, the story of Thecla had detached itself from the apocryphal Acts.[34] Saint Gregory of Nazianzus, writing in AD 363, praises her for voluntarily accepting the struggle against fire, wild beasts and tyrants.[35] In later writings, he exhorts all virgins to follow the example of Thecla whom God protected from the fire and the fury of the beasts.[36] In western Christendom, Saint Ambrose of Milan invoked Thecla on a number of occasions,[37] particularly in his influential *De virginibus ad Marcellinam* (*c.*AD 377)[38] where an extended passage refers to her ordeal in the arena. Ambrose first alludes to the wild animals (*fera*) to which she was offered, then to her act of abandoning her body to the cruel lion (*leo*), and then how this same beast (*bestia*) was seen to lie on the ground licking her feet. In this case, the terms *bestia* and *leo* are interchangeable. Willy Rordorf asserted that the devotion to Saint Thecla demonstrated by Ambrose is evidence that a Latin version of the *Acts of Paul and Thecla* was known in fourth-century Northern Italy.[39] Some patristic sources even suggest extensions of the legend which are no longer extant, such as the highly critical comment by Jerome in his *De viris illustribus* (ch. 7) where he stated that the peregrinations of Paul and Thecla and 'all the fable of the baptized lion' (*et totam baptizati leonis fabulam*) should be considered apocrypha.[40]

The beasts in the arena are also the element most referenced by Anglo-Saxon writers. Aldhelm in his prose *De virginitate*,[41] a work modeled on the earlier patristic treatises in praise of virginity, describes 'the fierce roaring

33 *PG* 18, 140. **34** Vouaux, *Les Actes de Paul*, p. 34. **35** *PG* 35, 589. **36** *PG* 37, 593. **37** *Ad Vercellensem ecclesiam*, ep. lxiii, 34 (*PL* 16, 199); *Ad Simplicianum*, xxxvii, 36 (*PL* 16, 370). **38** Bk 2, ch. 3, 19–21 (*PL* 16, 211). **39** Rordorf, 'Sainte Thècle dans la tradition hagiographique occidentale', p. 77. **40** *PL* 23, 619. **41** Michael Lapidge and Michael Herren (trans.), *Aldhelm: the prose works* (Ipswich and Cambridge, 1979), pp 59–132 at p. 113 (§xlvi); Rudolf Ehwald (ed.), *Aldhelmi opera*, Monumenta Germaniae Historica, Auctores Antiquissimi 15 (Berlin, 1919), pp 226–323; Scott Gwara (ed.), *Aldhelmi Malmesbiriensis Prosa de virginitate cum glosa latina atque anglosaxonica*, CCSL 124, 124A, 2 vols (Turnhout, 2001), ii, p. 312, l. 61.

lions and the ferocious jaws of hungry bears' which threatened Thecla.[42] Bede also singled out the beasts in the arena as the critical element of Thecla's narrative in his poem in praise of virginity for Queen Aethelthryth, later abbess of Ely, included as part of his *Historia ecclesiastica*.[43] In praising Aethelthryth's chastity, Bede invoked the example of prominent virgin saints of the early Church. He opens this sequence with verses in praise of the Virgin Mary and then proceeds to list six illustrious virgins according to the form of their martyrdom or persecution: Agatha and Eulalia who were scorched by flames; Agnes and Cecilia who laughed at swords. In the middle of this sequence is a verse in praise of Thecla and Euphemia who overcame wild beasts: *Casta feras superat mentis pro culmine Tecla, / Euphemia sacra casta feras superat* ('The lofty soul of chaste Thecla overcomes the wild beasts, chaste holy Euphemia overcomes the wild beasts'). This was not the only detail of Thecla's ordeals with which Bede was acquainted, however, for in his martyrology he supplied a synopsis of her life:

> Natale Sanctae Theclae virginis, in Oriente, de Iconio civitate: quae a Paulo Apostolo instructa in confessione Christi, ignes et bestias devicit: et post multa certamina ac doctrinam multorum veniens Seleuciam, requievit in pace.[44]

> Feastday of Saint Thecla the virgin, in the East, from the city of Iconium: she was instructed in the faith of Christ by Paul the Apostle, she overcame fire and wild beasts: and after many trials and the teaching of many people coming to Seleucia, she rested in peace.

Although Bede here alludes to other critical events in Thecla's life, her subduing of the beasts remains one of the central motifs of her persecution. In Bede's martyrology, these lines are included with the commemorations for 23 September, her traditional feastday in the Western Church. In the Eastern Church her feast falls on 24 September.

The evidence from Anglo-Saxon sources, coupled with the patristic evidence, serves to reinforce the impression that the allusion to a beast in the stanza from *Félire Óengusso*, quoted above, must refer to one of the beasts of the arena, most probably a lion.[45] The invocation of Thecla in the epilogue of

---

42 Franc, 'The cult of Saint Thecla', pp 50–1.   43 Bertram Colgrave and R.A.B. Mynors (ed. and trans.), *Bede: Historia ecclesiastica gentis Anglorum*, Oxford Medieval Texts (Oxford, 1969), Bk 4, ch. 20. I would like to express my gratitude to Máirín Mac Carron for her advice on Bede's corpus and to Jennifer O'Reilly for initially highlighting the significance of this reference at a meeting of the Irish Patristic Symposium.   44 Henri Quentin, *Les martyrologes historiques du moyen âge: étude sur la formation du martyrologe romain* (Aalen, 1969), p. 93; cf. *PL* 94, 1052.   45 This was also the opinion of Stokes: *Fél.* p. 446.

the calendar is, however, not the only reference to the protomartyr in *Félire Óengusso*. Significantly, she is also commemorated at least twice in the main body of the text, on dates which coincide with two of her feastdays in the *Martyrologium Hieronymianum*.[46] On the first of these, 22 February, she is mentioned after Saints Peter and Laurence in the last line of the stanza without auxiliary details: *la féil tóidlig Teclae* ('with Thecla's radiant feast').[47] Subsequently, on 17 November, the first half stanza for that day is devoted to Thecla:[48]

> Celebair féil Teclae,
> is íar mbúaid dorochair
>
> Celebrate Thecla's feast:
> after triumph she has fallen

The last words of this couplet are curious, since reference to triumph in a context such as this usually implies martyrdom, whereas the whole force of Thecla's narrative in the apocryphal Acts is that she consistently avoided that honour. Glossators in two manuscripts,[49] who deemed it necessary to add a short explanatory note beside her name, also seemed to be under the impression that she died a martyr: *.i. uirgo et martir*.[50] However, confusion with regard to Thecla's status as a protomartyr and not an actual martyr is not unknown in medieval sources. For instance, Aldhelm's treatise referred to above, *De virginitate*, is an *opus geminatum* containing a prose and verse account; in the latter no mention is made of her end but in the poetic *Carmina de virginitate* Thecla dies in the arena.[51] The circumstances of her death were not the only matters which caused confusion for medieval commentators as well as modern hagiographers. Due in no small part to the popularity of Saint Thecla of Iconium, and the wide dissemination of the *Acts of Paul* in the late antique period, the Christian name Thecla grew quite common, especially in the Near East. Therefore, there are many Saint Theclas recorded in patristic and medieval sources: some are spurious, a few are historically verifiable, while others may be founded on localized veneration of the virgin of Iconium.[52] One possible example of this type of local

---

46 Thecla of Iconium is celebrated in the *Martyrologium Hieronymianum* on 22 February, 12, 23, 24 September, 17 November, and 20, 21 December. She is first in the entry for 23 September; a primacy which usually indicates the main feastday: Giovanni B. de Rossi and L. Duchesne (eds), *Martyrologium Hieronymianum* in *Acta Sanctorum* LXXXII November, part II (Brussels 1894; reprint 1971). Cf. also Hippolyte Delehaye, *Commentarius perpetuus in Martyrologium Hieronymianum ad recensionem H. Quenti* in *Acta Sanctorum* XXIV November 11, part II (Brussels, 1931). 47 *Fél.* p. 62. 48 Ibid., p. 235. 49 Oxford, Bodleian Library, MSS Rawlinson B 505 and Laud 610. 50 *Fél.* p. 242. 51 Franc, 'The cult of Saint Thecla', p. 45. 52 The *Bibliotheca sanctorum* identifies at least three further Theclas: Thecla of Adrumeto (Lat. Hadrumetum, modern Sousse, Tunisia; feastday 30

appropriation is Saint Thecla of Antioch. The *Martyrologium Hieronymianum* refers to a Thecla among a group of saints martyred at Antioch who are commemorated together on 1 June. As no other details with regard to this other possible Saint Thecla survive, it is impossible to assess whether a distinct hagiographic tradition existed for the putative Antiochian martyr or whether this is a localization of Saint Thecla of Iconium's cult, especially as the latter suffered her travails with the beasts in the arena at Antioch. In addition, even if it could be proven that a separate saint Thecla of Antioch was venerated, it is unclear if Western medieval writers were aware of the distinction; and this in part may explain the confusion with regard to Saint Thecla of Iconium's status as a protomartyr. Accordingly, we have no means of ascertaining whether the author of *Félire Óengusso* was aware that the saint commemorated on 1 June was a separate figure to the Thecla to whom he refers elsewhere:[53]

> Oid menmain féil Teclae
> ardlig dínn a cétol,
> co slóg adbul úasal
> i calne Iúin éton.

> Give heed to Thecla's feast,
> which has a right for us to sing it,
> with a vast noble host
> in front of the calends of June.

An explanatory gloss in the Franciscan manuscript[54] above the name in this verse may point to Thecla of Antioch rather than Iconium: *.i. uirgo fuit et martyrio coronata est*.[55] However, as discussed above, some medieval sources record that the more famous Thecla was also martyred. The final reference to Thecla in the *Félire Óengusso* glosses occurs in another manuscript[56] within a note with regard to Saint Agnes on 21 January: *Agna et Tecla et Maria mater Domini, tres uirgines ex[c]elsisimae sunt inter uirgines Scribturae*. Once again it is unclear which Thecla is intended and it could be argued that the

August), Thecla of Aquileia (3 September) and Thecla of Rome (26 March). References are also extant to a Thecla of Gaza, a Thecla of Alexandria, and a couple of further African Theclas, *inter alias*. In addition, there are many later medieval Theclas named after their illustrious predecessors, among them an English-born Thecla of Kitzingen and Wimborne (†790), Thecla of Roubaix (†897) and a Welsh Tegla Forwyn of Llandegla. The editors of the *Bibliotheca* could be accused of understatment when they describe the problem of the multiple Saint Theclas as 'molto difficile a chiarire': Filippo Caraffa and Giuseppe Morelli (eds), *Bibliotheca sanctorum*, 13 vols (Rome 1961–1970; repr. 1998), xii, col. 174. In this regard, I would like to express my sincerest gratitude to Professor Pádraig Ó Riain for his astute guidance through the *tortae radices* of references to Thecla(s) in martyrologies and liturgical calendars. **53** *Fél*. p. 138. **54** Dublin, University College Dublin Library, MS A7. **55** *Fél*. p. 144. **56** Oxford, Bodleian Library, MS Rawlinson B 512.

reference to Saint Agnes implies that the Roman Thecla[57] is being invoked. However, this triple association does occur in other contexts where the reference is clearly to Saint Thecla of Iconium.[58]

Notwithstanding the ambiguity with regard to the entry for 1 June, the references above demonstrate that Thecla of Iconium was a considerable figure in the original early ninth-century text of *Félire Óengusso*. The fact that the *Félire* is in metrical form means that, unlike other medieval martyrologies, the entries are necessarily restricted to one rhyming verse per day. Therefore, instead of the extensive lists extant in many medieval calendars, the *Félire* can only accomodate four saints per day at the most. When choice is limited to this extent, the decision to include or exclude certain names must logically reflect the strength of devotion to that saint at the time of compilation. Martyrologies are not mere reference works but reflect contemporary religious practice at a specific place and time. In the *Féilire*'s case, this is made particularly explicit in the Prologue and Epilogue, as well as in the vivid poetic diction employed throughout. The inclusion of two, or possibly three, references to Thecla of Iconium in the main body of the *Félire*, in addition to the highly significant reference in the Epilogue, point to a not insignificant cult of the virgin protomartyr in ninth-century Ireland.[59] It would appear, however, from the confusion evident in the later glosses added to the text, that her cult may have waned by the twelfth century when the majority of the commentary was compiled.[60] Pádraig Ó Riain has demonstrated that both *Félire Óengusso* and

---

57 The issue of a Roman martyr called Thecla is a complicated one. A number of early medieval itineraries of the graves of Roman martyrs refer to a catacomb of Saint Thecla not far from the burial place of Saint Paul. It is also thought that a church was constructed at the site. However, the proximity of the supposed burial place of the putative Roman Thecla to the resting place of Saint Paul, coupled with the fact that some of the later passions or Lives of Saint Thecla of Iconium relate that after disappearing into the depths of the cave in Seleucia, she reappears in Rome, have led some to question whether the Roman cult is simply an attempt to supply a burial place for the Eastern saint: see Kate Cooper, 'A saint in exile: the early medieval Thecla at Rome and Meriamlick', *Hagiographica*, 2 (1995), 1–24. **58** *Fél.* p. 50. The association of Thecla with Agnes and the Virgin Mary is not unique to this glossator. Sulpicius Severus in his dialogues on the Life of Saint Martin recounts how these three appeared together on a number of occasions to Saint Martin: see *PL* 20, 210. Cf. Franc, 'The cult of Saint Thecla', p. 44 and Vouaux, *Les Actes de Paul*, p. 54. Bishop Maximus of Turin in a fifth-century sermon on the feast of Saint Agnes also makes a connection between the manner in which both Agnes and Thecla were miraculously saved from flames, cf. *PL* 17, 704. Note also that Bede in the poem on virginity discussed above refers to both Agnes and Thecla of Iconium. **59** Other early female saints are also included in the *Félire*: Agatha (5 February, 5 June?), Euphemia (11 July, 17 September), Agnes (21 January), Cecilia (1 September, 22 November), Juliana (16 February), Lucy (6 February), Perpetua (7 March). But none are given the quasi-biblical status afforded to Thecla in the Epilogue. **60** Thecla is commemorated only once in Gorman's martyrology (1166–74AD) on 23 September: *Tecla oengel alimm / for oebnemh co hebhinn* ('white Tecla whom I entreat [and who dwells]

its sister text *The martyrology of Tallaght*[61] were compiled between the years 829 and 833 at the Tallaght monastery.[62] Despite the fact that both texts were drawing on the same sources and were composed in the same place, *The martyrology of Tallaght* curiously does not share any dates for Saint Thecla with *Félire Óengusso*. The former, which is in Latin, not versified and more expansive, supplies an abundant alternative sequence of dates, with reference to a Thecla in nine separate entries.[63] As is typical of this type of abbreviated martyrology, the name is supplied without further comment with the exception of 20 December *Teclae uirginis* and 23 September *Teclae uirginis Euasnit*. The last word in this clause is curious; in the Book of Leinster copy, it is at the beginning of a line with a large initial letter as if it were a proper noun.[64] The editors of the Tallaght text, however, point to the *Martyrologium Wissenburgense* (AD 772) which includes the line *Tecle que aroma igne deposita euasit* which suggests that *euasit* ('goes forth') is the correct reading here.[65] As discussed above, 23 September is Thecla's principal feastday in the Western calendar and perhaps it is for this reason that extra details are added to her name on that day. It is curious, however, that the compilers of *The martyrology of Tallaght* should be aware of the significance of the date and yet the author of *Félire Óengusso* chose not to refer to her on 23 September. One possible explanation is that this is also the feast of Saint Adomnán of Iona, who has a verse dedicated to himself alone in the *Félire* on that day. Perhaps it was felt that his reputation demanded primacy of devotion on 23 September. The other date relating to a Thecla including something other than a bare name is 20 December, a date which *The martyrology of Tallaght* shares with the Hieronymian martyrology, although there are a further five dates which are unique to Tallaght and are not found in the earlier work.[66]

This profusion of Thecla feastdays may be explained by the rather idiosyncratic methodology employed by the compiler of the Tallaght calendar. As demonstrated by Pádraig Ó Riain, the redactor of *The martyrology of Tallaght* deliberately enhanced his lists of holy names by repeating certain biblical or early Christian entries.[67] For instance, the name of John the Evangelist occurs

delightfully in beautiful heaven'): Whitley Stokes (ed. and trans.), *Félire hUí Gormáin: the martyrology of Gorman*, HBS 9 (London, 1895), p. 182. 61 Richard I. Best and Hugh J. Lawlor (eds), *The martyrology of Tallaght from the Book of Leinster and MS 5100–4 in the Royal Library, Brussels*, HBS 68 (London, 1931). 62 Pádraig Ó Riain, 'The Tallaght martyrologies, redated', *CMCS*, 20 (Winter 1990), 21–38; *Feastdays of the saints: a history of Irish martyrologies*, Subsidia Hagiographica 86 (Brussels, 2006), p. 97. 63 11 April, 10 May, 11 August, 1 September, 12 September, 23 September, 18 October, 20 December, 21 December. 64 TCD MS 1339, p. 363. 65 Cf. Best and Lawlor, *The martyrology of Tallaght*, p. 168. 66 11 April, 10 May, 11 August, 1 September, 18 October. *The martyrology of Tallaght* and the *Martyrologium Hieronymianum* share the following dates for Thecla: 12 September (this entry appears to be a doublet of 17 November, one of the dates included in *Félire Óengusso*), 23 September, 20 December, 21 December. 67 Ó Riain, *Feastdays of the saints*, p. 15.

more than 40 times, and Saint Paul is cited an impressive 53 times. This form of distinction is reserved particularly for Gospel figures, and Thecla's unique position as a saint but also as a figure connected with the apostles may explain her multiple entries in the martyrology. The references to Thecla in *Félire Óengusso* and *The martyrology of Tallaght* certainly demonstrate that a cult of the protomartyr existed in ninth-century Ireland, but do not tell us how much of her narrative was known to the communities who celebrated her feastdays. One does not commemorate a saint without some acquaintance, however superficial, with their life and miracles; but how much of Thecla's passion or the *Acts of Paul* were familiar to the Irish calendar compilers? The allusion to a beast in the epilogue of *Félire Óengusso* suggests some familiarity with the events in the arena in Antioch but it is difficult to assess the extent of that familiarity.

When Seymour published the paper referred to at the beginning of this article, he was unaware of a further reference to Saint Thecla which would have served to strengthen his argument. *Saltair na rann* is a late tenth-century versified adaptation of the Bible narrative from creation to doomsday, including much apocryphal material.[68] The text consists of 162 poems, although the original composition is thought to have contained only 150 in order to mirror the structure of the Psalter. The Old Testament narrative concludes with the historical books at poem 134, after which comes a poem on the Lord's great deeds with some reference to the major prophets. Following this are two poems (136, 137) on the wonders of creation, with particular emphasis on the natural world, animals and plants. Poem 138 is structured in a litany-like sequence in which examples of divine aid to the faithful are invoked. The majority of the episodes cited come from the Old Testament; towards the end of the poem, however, we find the following verse (ll 7409–12):

> Rí saer Teclai ndíascaig ndil
> ona bíastaib béldergaib,
> isint anfabrocht for ruth
> ba hadbalbocht dind fuatluch.

> King who saved dear, blameless Thecla
> from the animals with bloody mouths,
> and the paralytic, immediately,
> who was very miserable, from the bed.[69]

68 Whitley Stokes (ed.), *The Saltair na rann: a collection of early Middle Irish poems*, Mediaeval and Modern Series 1, iii (Oxford, 1883). 69 Caitríona Ó Dochartaigh, 'Poems 138–41 in *Saltair na rann*' in D. Ó Baoill, D. Ó hAodha and N. Ó Muraíle (eds), *Saltair saíochta, sanasaíochta agus seanchais: a Festschrift for Gearóid Mac Eoin* (Dublin, 2013), pp 297–310 at p. 307. An alternative translation by David Greene ('The King saved dear

As in *Félire Óengusso*, the reference is evidently to the events in the arena at Antioch, the significant difference being that the beasts are plural here rather than singular. The plurality of animals may be referring not simply to the lions but to the bears, seals, etc. Therefore, the verse in the *Félire* is not an isolated witness and the allusion to red-mouthed beasts above reinforces the hypothesis that some details of the *Acts of Paul and Thecla* were familiar to a medieval Irish audience.

The second half of this stanza appears to refer to the miracle in which Christ heals the paralytic in Saint Matthew's Gospel (Mt 9:2–7), with the poorly attested *fúatlach* corresponding to *lectus* ('couch, bed') in the Vulgate.[70] If this is the case, however, it disturbs the biblical chronology which Poem 138 follows relatively faithfully (but with some exceptions) in recalling incidents in which the following were saved: Abel, Noah, Abraham, Lot, Isaac, Jacob, Joseph, Moses, Israelites, Joshua, Rahab, Oeth (Othniel?), Samson, Susanna, Elijah and Enoch, David, Hezekiah, Daniel, Naaman, Micaiah, Jonah, Ninevites, Tobit, Three boys, Peter, John, Mary Magdalene, Thecla, Paul and Silas. The uneven ratio of Old to New Testament in Poem 138 reflects that of the *Saltair* as a whole, with significant emphasis on the heroes of the Pentateuch and the historical books. Surprisingly, there are only two Gospel episodes cited: Peter being saved from drowning while walking on water,[71] and a vague reference to Mary Magdalene not falling again into sin.[72] The remaining four incidents cited all come from the Acts of the Apostles, both canonical and apocryphal. Remarkably, this is the only instance in the whole work of 8392 lines in which the Acts of the Apostles figure. Equally significant is the fact that the apostolic examples of divine intervention invoked are exactly the same as in *Félire Óengusso* discussed above. The canonical examples of divine aid are Peter being freed from prison (Acts 12:6–11), and Paul and Silas also being liberated (Acts 16:25–7).[73] The apocryphal episodes are John being saved from poisoning and the cauldron full of oil,[74] along with Thecla in the arena as cited above. As with *Félire Óengusso*, Thecla is included in a scriptural and not an hagiographic context,

blameless Thecla from the red-mouthed beasts, and (saved) the paralysed man, who was very miserable, immediately from his couch') can be found at <http://www.dias.ie/images/stories/celtics/pubs/saltairnarann/canto131–140.pdf>.   **70** This is only one of three attestations supplied by *DIL*, in one of which *fúatlach* glosses the Latin word *grabatus* ('couch, camp-bed, pallet').   **71** Mt 14:28–31. Stokes, *Saltair na rann*, p. 108 (ll 7393–6).   **72** Stokes, ibid., p. 109 (ll 7405–8). This may be a reference to the penitent woman washing Christ's feet, Lk 7:36–50. These lines are the only mention of Mary Magdalene in *Saltair na rann*.   **73** Paul only figures twice in *Saltair na rann*, here and in a list of the apostles at line 7585.   **74** Cf. nn 29 and 30 above. Ó Dochartaigh, 'Poems 138–41', p. 306: *Rí ro sáer Eoin bai tan / triana gnim ngleóir ngleglan, / di gae gona ind nemi glais / ocus dind olai amnais* ('King who saved John once by his pure, luminous deed, from the piercing spear of the green poison and from the cruel oil'). See Stokes, *Saltair na rann*, p. 109 (ll 7401–4).

suggesting that the Irish compilers of these texts were drawing on sources in which she was treated as a quasi-biblical figure and not simply an early saint.

Moreover, it could be argued that the paralytic who shares the verse with Thecla is slightly out of place here. He is somewhat different to the significant biblical figures who are routinely invoked in this genre of prayer. The word *anfabrocht* is not widely attested other than in glossary entries.[75] For example, *Sanas Cormaic* defines it as a name for one who is suffering from a disease that leaves him with no fat in his body.[76] The closely related *anfabrachta*, which is an adjective applied to one so afflicted rather than a term for the sufferer himself (but can also be used as a substantive designating the disease), has slightly more attestations and in particular is associated with healing miracles in saints' Lives. Of the five episodes listed in *DIL*, three attestations of the word survive in a series of closely connected healing miracles performed by Saint Brigit.[77] In the first instance she heals a group of four sick people,[78] in the second a boy,[79] and in the third a man brings his mother to be healed.[80] In all of these cases, the Latin version of the text supplies the word *paralyticus* for their condition.[81] In common with Saint Brigit, Thecla also enjoyed a considerable reputation for healing, particularly at her shrine at Seleucia.[82] As outlined above, it is believed that the end of the original Thecla narrative, while her legend was still an integral part of the *Acts of Paul*, simply stated that she died in Seleucia having enlightened many. With the growth of her cult, however, her story developed into the Life and Miracles or the Passion of Saint Thecla and further material was added. Much of this additional narrative concentrates on the post-mortem miracles of Thecla but there are also extra texts dealing with the end of Thecla's life. These additional texts have recently been edited and analysed by Jean-Daniel Kaestli.[83] Among them is what seems to have originally been a letter

---

75 The usual orthography of the word is *anfobracht* since it derives from *bracht* (cf. *DIL* s.v., where this word is said to mean 'juice, grease, fat'), but the form here is doubtlessly for internal rhyme with *adbalbocht*.　76 Whitley Stokes and John O'Donovan (ed. and trans.), *Sanas Cormaic: Cormac's glossary*, Irish Archaeological and Celtic Society (Calcutta, 1868), p. 42. Cf. *DIL* s.v., with the translation 'person suffering from some kind of wasting illness'; and J. Vendryes, É. Bachellery and P.-Y. Lambert, *Lexique étymologique de l'irlandais ancien*, 7 vols [to date] (Paris and Dublin, 1959–96), vol. B, p. 75: 'personne atteinte d'un mal qui la ronge'.　77 The other two miracle accounts are from the Life of Saint Martin: Edmund Hogan, *The Latin Lives of the saints*, TLS 5 (Dublin, 1894), p. 95, l. 4, and the life of Mochua Balla: *LisL* p. 144, l. 4851.　78 *LisL* p. 43, l. 1440: *anbhfabrachta*; Hogan, *The Latin Lives*, p. 76, l. 6: *una paralytica*.　79 *LisL* p. 43, l. 1444: *aenghilla bec anbhfhabracta 7 se balbh*; Hogan, *The Latin Lives*, p. 76, l. 9: *cum solo puero muto et paralytico*.　80 *LisL* p. 44, l. 1468: *a mháthair … ba hanfhabrachta*; Hogan, *The Latin Lives*, p. 78, ll 4–5: *matrem suam paralyticam*.　81 I would agree with Hogan's assessment when he said '*anbfabracta* (Lism.) means "paralysed" in paragraphs 69, 70, 71, not "consumptive" as Mr Stokes renders it': Hogan, *The Latin Lives*, p. 76 n. 2.　82 Dagron, *Vie et miracles de sainte Thècle*, p. 281.　83 I wish to express my sincerest gratitude to Prof. Kaestli for supplying me with a pre-

addressed to the Byzantine emperors witnessing to the authenticity of an icon image of the saint apostle (Thecla). Within the letter is an account of a miracle performed by Thecla when she healed a paralytic child.[84] The miracle story became relatively popular and also circulated separately from the account of the icon. In light of such evidence, the association of Thecla with the healing of a paralytic in the same verse cited above may have been suggested by some acquaintance with Thecla's reputation for healing and in particular the miraculous cure of the paralytic child. If one could prove such an association, it would follow that some account of the miracles of Thecla was known in medieval Ireland. However, it is near impossible to determine if the example of the paralytic is included here because of a perceived connection between Thecla and such a healing miracle (perhaps in a source text), or is simply a random insertion of an episode from Matthew's Gospel.

In addition to the reference to a beast or beasts threatening Thecla, the other striking similarity between the verses in *Saltair na rann* and *Félire Óengusso* is the formula which they employ. Each text is framed as a prayer-like litany in which the supplicant asks to be saved in the manner in which figures of the past, including Thecla, were saved. This ancient devotional genre, often referred to under the Latin title *Libera me … sicut liberasti* ('Save me … as you saved') or the 'Help of God' prayer, found its most famous manifestation as part of the *Commendatio animae*, the Roman Catholic rite for the commendation of the soul of the dying. During the sixteenth- and seventeenth-century process of liturgical regularization, Thecla was included in the 'Help of God' exhortations in the body of the *Commendatio animae*.[85] There she held sway for four centuries, until the liturgical reforms of the 1960s meant that she was no longer invoked in the liturgy for the dying.[86] However, it is a testament to the strength of her cult in the sixteenth century that her name was included in the *Commendatio animae*, because reference to her is otherwise quite rare in the history of the *Libera* prayer.[87] The only extant

publication copy of the new editions and translations, and indeed to all the members of the *Association pour l'étude de la littérature apocryphe chrétienne* for their helpful comments and encouragement when I gave an embryonic version of this paper at their annual colloquium in June 2013.   84 Jean-Daniel Kaestli and Willy Rordorf, 'La fin de la vie de Thècle dans les manuscrits des *Actes de Paul et Thècle*. Édition des textes additionnels', *Apocrypha*, 25 (2014), 9–101 at 60–5, Text V. Also François Halkin, *Bibliotheca hagiographica graeca*, 3rd ed., Subsidia Hagiographica 8a, 3 vols (Brussels, 1957), ii, pp 267–9, 1718m; *Novum auctarium bibliothecae hagiographicae graecae*, Subsidia Hagiographica 65 (Brussels, 1984), pp 200–1; Dagron, *Vie et miracles de sainte Thècle*, pp 414–15 and 419. In addition, cf. François Bovon and Bertrand Bouvier, 'Miracles additionnels de Thècle dans le manuscrit de Rome, *Angelicus graecus 108*', *Apocrypha*, 24 (2013), 91–110.   85 John Hennig, 'Quelques notes sur la mention de sainte Thècle dans la *Commendatio animae*', *Nuovo Didaskaleion*, 14 (1964), 21–7.   86 Albert Schönfelder (ed.), *Liturgische Bibliothek* (Paderborn, 1904), i, pp 38–41.   87 There are only three extant references to Thecla in this prayer genre in the medieval period. Besides the Rheinau Sacramentary and the *Oratio*

medieval example of Thecla being included in a funerary rite which employs this liturgical formula is the Rheinau Sacramentary.[88] The Rheinau manuscript[89] is part of a group of eighth-century sacramentaries in which an important development in the final rites first occurs.[90] The rites for the sick, which in earlier sacramentaries were found among prayers for clerical visits, are now placed before the rite for the dying in order to create a continuous sequence from illness and death to burial. The emphasis in the rites for the sick has moved away from healing and physical health to a purification of the soul and a penitential preparation for death.[91] The most significant innovation and the defining characteristic of these rituals, however, is the development of a separation rite. This new rite takes the form of a communal aid to the dying focussed on prayer which would later become part of the early modern *Commendatio animae*. Within this newly developed ritual, there is a series of *Libera ... sicut liberasti* invocations prefixed by another prayer and therefore the text is often referred to as the *Proficiscere*:

> Proficiscere anima christiana de hoc mundo in nomine dei patris omnipotentis, qui te creauit ... Libera domine animam serui tui illius, sicut liberasti petrum et paulum de carceribus. Libera animam serui tui illius, sicut liberasti theglam de tribus tormentis, sic liberare digneris animam hominis istius et tecum habitare in bonis caelestibus concede.[92]

> Depart Christian soul from this world in the name of God the almighty Father, who created you. Lord, free the soul of this your servant, as you freed Peter and Paul from prison. Free the soul of this your servant, as you saved Thecla from the three torments; thus may you deign to free the soul of this man and grant that it may reside with you in the heavenly good.

It will be noted that Thecla is closely associated with Saints Peter and Paul's incarceration here, as was the case in *Saltair na rann* and *Félire Óengusso*. The three saints are the only New Testament era figures invoked in the Rheinau

Cypriani discussed here, an eleventh-century manuscript also contains a prayer invoking her in this manner: Marco Magistretti, *Manuale Ambrosianum: ex codice saec. XI olim in usum canonicae Vallis Travaliae*, 3 vols (Milan, 1905), i, pp 83–93.   88 Anton Hänggi and Alfons Schönherr (eds), *Sacramentarium Rhenaugiense*, Spicilegium Friburgense 15 (Freiburg, 1970).   89 Zürich, Zentralbibliothek, MS Rh. 30 (795–800AD); see Klaus Gamber, *Codices liturgici latini antiquiores*, Spicilegii Friburgensis Subsidia 1, 2 vols (Fribourg, 1968), §802.   90 Bernard Moreton, *The eighth-century Gelasian sacramentary* (Oxford, 1976); cf. Emmanuel Bourque, *Étude sur les sacramentaires romains*, 3 vols (Laval and Vatican City, 1949–58). The eighth-century Gelasian sacramentaries are also sometimes referred to as the *Gelasiana mixta* or the *Junggelasiana*.   91 Frederick S. Paxton, *Christianizing death: the creation of a ritual process in early medieval Europe* (Ithaca, 1990), p. 109.   92 Hänggi and Schönherr, *Sacramentarium Rhenaugiense*, p. 272.

ritual and follow a long list of Old Testament patriarchs and prophets. The reference to Thecla is unusual because her tribulations are not specified, but the three torments presumably refer to the attempt to burn her at the stake, the beasts in the arena and possibly also the bulls. The Gellone Sacramentary,[93] which is very closely related to the Rheinau text, does not include Saint Thecla but rather finishes the list with Peter and Paul. The place of compilation of the Rheinau sacramentary is uncertain. A number of Frankish saints are named in the martyrology, including two references to Nivelles in present-day Belgium; and this led earlier scholars to suggest a Belgian provenance for the work. Modern researchers, however, tend to take the view that this simply points to northern influence in the text and that it was most probably compiled in Switzerland. The editors of the sacramentary laid particular emphasis on the Irish elements in the text and on Irish influence in the area of Lake Constance in the early medieval period. The strongest Irish influence is discernible in the sacramentary's calendar which appears to have a local Irish-influenced abbreviated martyrology at its core.[94] The editors also believed that the manuscript was compiled within the sphere of the St Gallen and Reichenau *scriptoria*, two monasteries which had Irish associations.[95] They argued that of these two centres, Reichenau is the most likely home of the Rheinau sacramentary. It must have been transferred to Rheinau soon after its foundation in the ninth century where it remained until the dissolution of the monastery in 1862.

At much the same period as the Rheinau sacramentary was being compiled two very long Latin prayers, with no funerary associations but rather ascribed to Saint Cyprian of Antioch, were in circulation. Cyprian of Antioch was supposedly a magician who converted to Christianity, but the accounts of his life appear to be wholly legendary and there is reason to believe that he is an invention based on the model of Saint Cyprian of Carthage.[96] Moreover, the two prayers that are ascribed to him, the *Orationes Cypriani*, demonstrate strong exorcism characteristics.[97] The earliest manuscripts in which the Latin text of the *Orationes Cypriani* survives date from the eighth century,[98] but Harnack, the first editor of the prayers, demonstrated that these manuscripts derive from

93 Paris, Bibliothèque Nationale Française, MS latinus 12048 (790–800AD).   94 Hänggi and Schönherr, *Sacramentarium Rhenaugiense*, p. 49.   95 Ibid., p. 58. Cf. also Moreton, *The eighth-century Gelasian sacramentary*, p. 186.   96 Fernand Cabrol and Henri Leclercq (eds), *Dictionnaire d'archéologie chrétienne et de liturgie* (Paris, 1907–53), s.v. 'Oratio Cypriani', cols 2326–7; G. Hartel (ed.), *S. Thasci Caecili Cypriani opera omnia*, Corpus Scriptorum Ecclesiasticorum Latinorum 3, iii (Vienna, 1868).   97 Cabrol and Leclercq, *Dictionnaire d'archéologie*, s.v. 'Oratio Cypriani', col. 2331; Cf. also Joseph Ntedika, *L'évocation de l'au-delà dans la prière pour les morts*, Recherches Africaines de Théologie 2 (Louvain, 1971), p. 76.   98 Cabrol and Leclercq, *Dictionnaire d'archéologie*, s.v. 'Défunts', cols 430–40; Per Lundberg, *La typologie baptismale dans l'ancienne Église* (Uppsala, 1942), pp 59–60; Ntedika, *L'évocation de l'au-delà*, p. 76.

a common archetype of the seventh century or earlier.[99] In addition, there are certain linguistic and stylistic features in the texts that indicate a Gallican origin.[100] Having considered these factors in conjunction, Harnack concluded that the Latin version of the prayers was written in the early fifth century in Southern Gaul, and suggested that the author may have been the Gallican Cyprian who composed a poetic version of the Heptateuch.[101] After this Cyprian's death, his prayers may have been attributed to the legendary magician from Antioch on the basis of confusion between the names. It cannot be proved definitively that it was the Gallican Cyprian who compiled the *Orationes Cypriani*, since very little is known of his life; but it is at any rate widely accepted that the prayers, in their Latin form, were written in fifth-century Gaul.[102] Whoever the compiler was, it is certain that he was modeling his Latin prayers on a Greek exemplar as Greek versions of the *Orationes Cypriani* are extant.[103] The Greek archetype is believed to date from about the year 300,[104] and was probably composed in Eastern Christian circles since late medieval versions of the prayers exist in Arabic, Ethiopic and Syriac.[105]

Towards the end of the first of the Latin prayers ascribed to Cyprian, we find the following exhortation:

> Assiste nobis, sicut apostolis in vinculis, Theclae in ignibus, Paulo in persecutionibus, Petro in fluctibus. Qui sedes super septem thronos ad dexteram Patris, respice nos et libera nos de aeternae mortis interitu.[106]

> Help us, as (you helped) the apostles in chains, Thecla in the flames, Paul in persecutions, Peter in the waves. You who sit over the seven thrones at the right hand of the Father, look upon us and free us from the destruction of eternal death.

Here Thecla is once more referred to in close association with the imprisonment of the apostles, and with Paul and Peter. The middle of the second Pseudo-Cyprian prayer also includes an invocation of Thecla: *Liberes me de medio saeculi huius, sicut liberasti Teclam de medio amphitheatro* ('Save me from

99 Adolf Harnack, *Drei wenig beachtete cyprianische Schriften und die Acta Pauli*, Texte und Untersuchungen 19, n.F. 4, iii (Leipzig, 1899), p. 30. **100** Ibid., p. 29. **101** Ibid., p. 23. **102** Ntedika, *L'évocation de l'au-delà*, p. 76; Pierre Salmon, Charles Coebergh and Pierre de Puniet (eds), *Testimonia orationis christianae antiquioris*, CCCM 47 (Turnhout, 1977), pp xvi–xvii. But see Aimé-Georges Martimort, 'L'ordo commendationis animae', *La Maison Dieu*, 15 (1948), 143–60 at 150 n. 8, who proposes a fourth-century date for the Latin texts. **103** Cf. Theodor Schermann, 'Die griechischen Kyprianosgebete', *Oriens Christianus*, 3 (1903), 303–23. **104** Ntedika, *L'évocation de l'au-delà*, p. 76. **105** Cabrol and Leclercq, *Dictionnaire d'archéologie*, s.v. 'Oratio Cypriani', cols 2331–2; René Basset, *Les prières de S. Cyprien et de Théophile*, Les Apocryphes Éthiopiens 6 (Paris, 1896). **106** Cabrol and Leclercq, *Dictionnaire d'archéologie*, s.v. 'Oratio Cypriani', col. 2332; Hartel, *Cypriani opera*, p. 145.

the midst of this age, as you saved Thecla from the midst of the amphitheatre').[107] On this occasion, it is her ordeal in the amphitheatre and not the fire which is recalled. Significantly, in the second prayer, notwithstanding the length of the *oratio*, she is the only non-Old Testament figure included in the list of 'Save me' invocations, underlining the special status she is afforded in these texts. The *Orationes Cypriani* are the most widely disseminated of any early medieval text which employs the *Libera me* formula, and they represent a significant development in the history of the genre. No other prayer of this genre is found in so many languages and in so many medieval manuscripts; and wherever the *Orationes Cypriani* were copied or translated, Thecla travelled with them. In medieval Western Europe, the second prayer with the reference to Thecla in the amphitheatre proved to be more popular than the first and was particularly widespread in Carolingian *Libelli precum*,[108] including the Pseudo-Alcuin *Officia per ferias*.[109] There is also evidence that Aldhelm was influenced by the works of the Gallican Cyprian.[110] Moreover, there is a poem in the margin of the *Martyrology of Tallaght* which refers to the feastday of Saint Cyprian[111] and a Cyprian is commemorated in the main body of the martyrology on 15 April; but it does not specify which Cyprian is intended.[112] The reference in the poem indicates a devotion to a Saint Cyprian in early ninth-century Tallaght but it does not follow that either of the *Orationes Cypriani* were known in medieval Ireland. Nevertheless, the close similarity in the formula employed in *Félire Óengusso*, *Saltair na rann*, the Rheinau sacramentary and the *Orationes Cypriani*, in conjunction with the coincidence of apostolic figures and episodes grouped together, must mean that a prayer similar to the Latin examples cited above is the source underlying the Irish texts.

There is, however, a third text, ascribed to Saint Cyprian of Antioch, closely associated both geographically and chronologically with the two prayers and probably also the work of the Gaulish Cyprian. It is often preserved in medieval manuscripts alongside the *Orationes Cypriani*, and is particularly closely connected to the second prayer. The *Caena Cypriani* is a long and curious text, best described as a litany crossed with a banquet guest-list, with an exhaustive versified enumeration of biblical figures and scriptural allusions. Included in this list are no less than eleven references to Thecla, each of which refers to a different episode in the account of her life. The events referred to are not simply the standard images of the arena or the attempt to burn her alive, although these are included; but there is also ref-

---

107 Cabrol and Leclercq, *Dictionnaire d'archéologie*, s.v. 'Oratio Cypriani', cols 2332–4; Hartel, *Cypriani opera*, pp 146–8; *PL* 101, 567–9.   108 Salmon, *Testimonia orationis*, p. xvii n. 8.   109 *PL* 101, 567–9.   110 Cf. Ehwald, *Aldhelmi opera*, p. 544 and Franc, 'The cult of Saint Thecla', p. 44.   111 Best and Lawlor, *The martyrology of Tallaght*, p. x. 112 Saint Cyprians are commemorated in two other places in the martyrology, 12 April and 14 September, but in these cases it is clear that they are not Saint Cyprian of Antioch.

erence *inter alia* to her listening to Paul at the window, Tryphanea crying and, in relation to the beginning of this article, Onesiphorus waiting attentively for Paul.[113] Moreover, there are also four allusions to episodes in the ancient *Acts of Paul* which are not connected with Thecla and which do not make their way into the later medieval narratives about her. Therefore, the author of the *Caena* knew many details from the apocryphal Acts, making this eccentric text a unique witness for the existence of some version of the *Acts of Paul* in fifth-century Western Europe. In addition, this long versified creation makes no reference to any other episode or figure from the Acts of the Apostles, whether apocryphal or otherwise; and, as has been highlighted by a number of scholars, the author treated the *Acts of Paul* as canonical.[114] The editor of the *Orationes Cypriani* also argued that the influence of the apocryphal *Acts of Paul* is discernible in the prayers.[115]

Returning to Seymour's assertion that the *Acts of Paul* (and Thecla) were known in medieval Ireland, if one were attempting to identify a likely route of transmission then the *Caena Cypriani*, the *Orationes Cypriani* and the Rheinau sacramentary make promising candidates. There can be no doubt, based on the evidence from *Félire Óengusso*, the *Martyrology of Tallaght* and *Saltair na rann*, that there was a cult of Saint Thecla in medieval Ireland. However, proving that Thecla was venerated as a saint in any one place and time does not prove that the *Acts of Paul* were known in that place also; unless one can demonstrate that references to dramatic episodes involving Thecla come from the Acts and not from another source. As Martin McNamara put it rather succinctly in relation to Seymour's assertion: 'One would like to have stronger evidence before concluding that these Acts were known in Ireland. Their influence may well have been indirect, rather than direct, i.e., through prior influence on Church or hagiographic tradition'.[116] It may very well be that the devotional references alone served to spread and strengthen her cult but a supplicant does not invoke a saint in a prayer without some further knowledge of the deeds of the holy figure, otherwise there is no guarantee of the efficacy of the petition. Unfortunately, insufficient evidence has survived to assess how much, or which redaction of her narrative was known. Perhaps nothing more was known of her other than the story of the beasts in the arena, which could have been transmitted orally or in some partial version of her *Passio*. It certainly appears unlikely that the *Acts of Paul* were known in their entirety, otherwise we might expect to find more allusions to the work. On the other hand, the references to Thecla in the 'Save me' sections of *Saltair na rann* and *Félire Óengusso* place her in a biblical con-

113 Vouaux, *Les Actes de Paul*, pp 51–2. 114 Rordorf, 'Sainte Thècle dans la tradition hagiographique occidentale', p. 78; Harnack, *Drei wenig beachtete cyprianische Schriften*, p. 18; Vouaux, *Les Actes de Paul*, pp 51–2. 115 Harnack, *Drei wenig beachtete cyprianische Schriften*, p. 33. 116 McNamara, *The apocrypha in the Irish church*, p. 113 §92.

text, demonstrating that she was commemorated as something more than a saint. There was evidently a reason for affording her this quasi-apostolic status. Devotional texts such as the *Orationes Cypriani* or the Rheinau invocations, with cursory allusions to the *Acts of Paul*, could not be the source of either the physical description of Saint Paul quoted by Hyde or of the possible reference to the healing of the paralytic child. The former would require only some knowledge of the opening of the Acts, most likely divorced from the rest of the work. For the latter, acquaintance with a more expansive account of Thecla's miracles such as the *Passio S. Theclae* or the Life and Miracles of Thecla would have to be postulated.

'Ceasta Fhíthil': buaine agus ilghnéitheacht na gaoise i litríocht na Gaeilge

PÁDRAIG Ó MACHÁIN

Ar na breithiúntais a thug an Dr Vivien Law ar údar an tseachtú haois, Virgilius Grammaticus, bhí an méid seo:

> Wisdom mattered to Virgilius, just as it mattered to the many ancient and medieval authors and compilers of the vast and as yet hardly studied corpus of post-biblical wisdom literature. Alien to our flippant age, this preoccupation with wisdom baffles and embarrasses us. We see pretentiousness and platitude where Virgilius' contemporaries found profundity and humility. But to ignore it, to fail to come to terms with its concerns and conventions, is to cut ourselves off from a zone of their mental universe to which they ascribed far greater significance than they did to mere grammar. Wisdom was the ultimate goal to which grammar and all other studies led.[1]

Tá litríocht na gaoise ar an gcatagóir is fadshaolaí de litríocht an domhain agus de litríocht na Gaeilge. Cúlra doimhin atá aici, agus bonn an-leathan atá fúithi.[2] Is féidir teacht ar phréamhacha cuid dá sáintéamaí sa Sean-Tiomna:[3] comhairle an tseanduine i Leabhar na Seanfhocal ('Éist, a mhic, le teagasc d'athar' 1:8), nó an teagasc rí i Leabhar na hEagna ('A rialtóirí an domhain, bíodh grá agaibh don fhíréantacht' 1:1). Mar is léir ar thaighde Law, i saothrú na Gael-Laidne tá ábhar an *sapientia* le rianú go ré na luath-Chríostaíochta.[4]

---

1 Vivien Law, *Wisdom, authority and grammar in the seventh century: decoding Virgilius Maro Grammaticus* (Cambridge, 1995), lgh 22–3. Iarracht atá san alt seo ar shúil a chaitheamh ar ghné de litríocht na Gaeilge a samhlaímse leithne agus leanúnachas thar an ngnáth léi. Tá sé á thiomnadh agam le buíochas d'iarmhúinteoir agus do chomhleacaí a bhfuil breis agus a cion déanta aici i gcaitheamh na mblianta maidir le léann na Gaeilge de.   2 Féach, mar shampla, Maxim Fomin, *Instructions for kings: secular and clerical images of kingship in early Ireland and ancient India* (Heidelberg, 2013).   3 Cf. Kim McCone, *Pagan past and Christian present in Early Irish literature* (Maigh Nuad, 1990), lch 31. Sa deichiú haois dhein scríobhaí Gaelach (meastar) treascríobh ar a bhfuil de leabhair ghaoise sa Sean-Tiomna, chomh maith le cuid de thráchtaireacht Iaróim orthu: St Gallen, Stiftsbibliothek, LS 10 (<http://www.e-codices.unifr.ch/en/list/one/csg/0010>); James F. Kenney, *The sources for the early history of Ireland: ecclesiastical: an introduction and guide* (Nua-Eabhrac, 1929), lch 650. Chomh maith leis sin, tá iarsma de thionchar leabhar gaoise an Bhíobla le sonrú i scéalaíocht na Sean-Ghaeilge, mar a léirigh Pádraig Ó Fiannachta agus Kim McCone, *Scéalaíocht ár sinsear*, Dán agus Tallann 3 (Maigh Nuad, 1992), lgh 5–9, 65–70.   4 Féach chomh maith Damian Bracken, 'Virgilius Grammaticus and the earliest Hiberno-

Sa Ghaeilge féin, ceann de na blúiríocha próis is luaithe dá bhfuil againn, más fíor, is ea an *Apgitir chrábaid*,[5] agus tarlaíonn gur ceann de na téacsaí gaoise is sine dá bhfuil againn is ea é chomh maith. Bhí an teagasc gaoise mar bhunchuid de rialacha na naomh i gcónaí;[6] leis an dlúthbhaint a bhí ann idir an tuath agus an mhainistir ní haon ionadh é go bhfuil lorg an teagaisc rí le feiscint ar cheann ar a laghad de na rialacha sin chomh maith, 'Regula Mucuta'.[7] Ní nach ionadh é ach oiread, agus an bunús comónta a bhí le cúrsaí dlí agus cúrsaí creidimh sa luath-thréimhse,[8] go mbeadh sean-cheangal idir an dlí agus an ghaois in Éirinn, mar deir Fergus Kelly: 'Different in tone, content and date as these wisdom texts are, they all have connections with the law texts, and medieval Irish scholars regarded them as an extension of the legal canon'.[9]

Bíonn idir léann diaga agus léann tuata i gceist i litríocht seo na gaoise mar sin, agus gabhann scata stíleanna reacaireachta léi, i véarsaíocht nó i bprós: an t-agallamh, an ceistiú, an tomhas, an tseanmóir, an fháistine, an tré nó an seachta, an teagasc lom, an aforaise agus an seanfhocal.[10] Meascán de na stíleanna sin a bhíonn i gceist go minic, agus mar shnáithín coiteann tríothu go léir, geall leis, bíonn comhairle leasa agus seachadadh na bunfhírinne. Is suaithinseach an ní é gur féidir comharthaí sóirt na litríochta seo a leanúint anuas go deisbhéalaíocht na ngnáthdhaoine sa Nua-Ghaeilge féin i bhfoirm seanfhocal nó seanráite. Cuimsíonn an tsaolré fhada seo tús agus deireadh thraidisiún na Gaeilge dá réir sin: ábhar roinnt de na lámhscríbhinní Gaeilge is luaithe dá maireann, agus litríocht bhéil agus scríte an fhichiú haois. Cosúil leis an Dinnsheanchas nó leis an bhFhianaigheacht, cineál litríochta é an ghaois ar cuma leis gabháil thar críochaibh ó *genre* go chéile, agus nach mbíonn beann rómhór aige ar theorannacha idir uasal agus íseal, ná idir modhanna craolta na béalaithrise nó an phinn. Ó cheann ceann an traidisiúin bhí glacadh sa Ghaeilge le gaois ó fhoinse ar bith, pé acu moch nó déanach,

Latin literature' in J.-M. Picard agus M. Richter (eag.), *Ogma: essays in Celtic Studies in honour of Próinséas Ní Chatháin* (Baile Átha Cliath, 2002), lgh 251–61.   5 Vernam Hull, 'Apgitir chrábaid: the alphabet of piety', *Celtica*, 8 (1968), 44–89; Pádraig P. Ó Néill, 'The date and authorship of *Apgitir chrábaid*: some internal evidence' in P. Ní Chatháin agus M. Richter (eag.), *Irland und die Christenheit: Bibelstudien und Mission / Ireland and Christendom: the Bible and the missions* (Stuttgart, 1987), lgh 203–15.   6 Liam Breatnach, '*Cinnus atá do thinnrem*: a poem to Máel Brigte on his coming of age', *Ériu*, 58 (2008), 1–35 ag 1.   7 Kuno Meyer, 'A medley of Irish texts X', *ACL*, 3 (1905), 312–21 ag 314–15. Féach Westley Follett, *Céli Dé in Ireland: monastic writing and identity in the early Middle Ages*, Studies in Celtic History 23 (Woodbridge, 2006), lgh 121–4.   8 Donnchadh Ó Corráin, Liam Breatnach agus Aidan Breen, 'The laws of the Irish', *Peritia*, 3 (1984), 382–438.   9 Fergus Kelly, 'Thinking in threes: the triad in Early Irish literature', *PBA*, 125 (2003), 1–18 ag 17.   10 Ceann de na samplaí is luaithe den téarma 'seanfhocal' agus an tsainchiall seo leis is i *Cáin Adomnáin* atá (Kelly, 'Thinking in threes', 9). Tá an ceangal idir an seanfhocal agus an teagasc cíortha i gcás sean-litríocht na gaoise in P.L. Henry, *Saoithiúlacht na Sean-Ghaeilge: bunú an traidisiúin* (BÁC, 1978), lgh 95–116.

ón dúchas nó ón iasacht di: tomhaiseanna Finn nó 'Cesta Gréga',[11] 'Briathar-theagasc Con Culainn' nó *Colloquia* Erasmus.[12]

Léiríonn na leabhair Ghaeilge is sine dá bhfuil againn gur aithin lucht an léinn dúchais an ghaois ina téama faoi leith chomh fada siar leis an dara haois déag. I Leabhar Laighean, cuirim i gcás, dhein Aodh mac meic Criomhthainn téacsaí gaolmhara gaoise a chnuasach agus a bhreacadh i dteannta a chéile mar aonad amháin, agus iad a nascadh, ó thaobh suíomh a scríte de, le comhthéacs a thugann míniú níos leithne orthu. Bhreac sé *Tecosca Cormaic, Senbriathra Fíthil,* agus *Briathra Moraind* as diaidh a chéile ar leathanaigh 343–6, i dtús sleachta ginealaigh na sean-ríthe.[13] Breis agus céad blian ina dhiaidh sin, is mar chrobhaing téacsaí arís a leagtar amach cuid de na saothair ghaoise seo i lámhscríbhinní na haimsire sin, ach na tréanna agus téacsaí eile dá leithéid a bheith curtha leo. Is mar sin atá i Leabhar Ua Maine, i Leabhar Bhaile an Mhóta agus i Leabhar Leacáin,[14] agus i dtreo dheireadh an tséú haois déag táid le fáil sa lámhscríbhinn thábhachtach, ARÉ LS 967 (23 N 10).[15]

Ón aimsir sin i leith, a fhaid is a mhair déanamh na lámhscríbhinní, do mhair chomh maith bailiúcháin de théacsaí gaoise le chéile ar leathanaigh na leabhar Gaeilge anuas go deireadh an traidisiúin féin, mar a chífimíd ar ball. Léiriú ar an síorchaitheamh a bhíodh ag na Gaeil i ndiaidh an tsaghais seo ábhair is ea fianaise na lámhscríbhinní mar sin, agus léiriú breise is ea an leas a baineadh as sa litríocht féin. Gheibhtear tagairtí do na sean-téacsaí gaoise i bhfilíocht an dara haois déag.[16] Sa tríú haois déag, mhol Giolla na Naomh Mac Aodhagáin go gcuirfeadh mac léinn le dlí na téacsaí gaoise seo de ghlanmheabhair.[17] Sa cheathrú haos déag baineadh earraíocht as cur chuige chomhairle an athar dá mhac, i slí atá greannmhar agus an-shuimiúil, i ndán dár tús 'Geabh

---

11 Brian Ó Cuív, 'Agallamh Fhinn agus Ailbhe', *Celtica*, 18 (1986), 111–15; *BM Cat.* ii, lgh 520–2.   12 Myles Dillon (eag.), *Serglige Con Culainn* (BÁC, 1953), lgh 9–10; James Stewart, 'Párliament na mban', *Celtica*, 7 (1966), 135–41. Mar le tionchar Erasmus ar an spéis a chuirtí sa seanfhocal go háirithe, féach Archer Taylor, *The proverb* (Harvard, 1931), lch 31.   13 Coláiste na Tríonóide (TCD feasta) LS 1339: *LL* vi, ll 45713–46489. Mar leis an scríobhaí, féach Elizabeth Duncan, 'Turning over a new leaf: the manuscript context of *Leabhar na Nuachongbhála*, commonly known as the Book of Leinster', *Ossory, Laois and Leinster*, 5 (2012), 146–86 ag 151; scríobhaí eile a bhreac an dara cóip den *Audacht* sa lámhscríbhinn, lgh 293–4 (ibid., lch 155). Mar le téacsaí gaoise na Sean-Ghaeilge, féach Fergus Kelly, *A guide to Early Irish law* (BÁC, 1988), lgh 284–6.   14 Acadamh Ríoga na hÉireann (ARÉ feasta) LS 1225 (D ii 1), duil. 130–33; LS 536 (23 P 12) duil. 39v–41; LS 535 (23 P 2) duil. 145v–148. Ba cheart a áireamh chomh maith cuid Ádhaimh Í Chuirnín (duine de scríobhaithe Leabhar Leacáin) de Leabharlann Náisiúnta na hAlban LS Adv. 72.1.1, mar a bhfuil *Tecosca Cormaic, Senbriathra Fíthil, Briathra Flainn Fhína* agus na Tréanna le chéile ar duil. 11–12; agus leabhar Cuirníneach eile, TCD LS 1319/2 (H.2.17) mar a bhfuil na téacsaí gaoise cnuasaithe ar lgh 179–93.   15 ARÉ LS 967 (23 N 10), lgh 1–10, 49–52.   16 Tadhg O'Donoghue, 'Advice to a prince', *Ériu*, 9 (1921–3), 43–54.   17 Máirín Ní Dhonnchadha, 'An address to a student of law' in D. Ó Corráin, L. Breatnach agus K. McCone (eag.), *Sages, saints and storytellers: Celtic studies in honour of Professor James Carney* (Maigh Nuad, 1989), lgh 159–77 ag lch 165 §§8, 10–11.

do mhúnudh a mheic bhaoith' a chum Ádhamh Ó Fialáin do Thomás Mág Shamhradháin (†1343), ina lúbann an file nósanna na dteacsaí gaoise chun dán réitigh a chur i láthair le hardéirim.[18] Níos déanaí anonn, tá tagairtí do na téacsaí gaoise le fáil i saothair eile de chuid Fhilí na Scol: mar shampla i rann cáiliúil tosaigh an dáin do Thomaltach Mac Diarmada (†1458): 'Tosach féile fairsinge / d'fhuighlibh Fíthil an focal'.[19] Samplaí eile ná na buntagairtí do *Tecosca* go háirithe ag Fearghal Óg Mac an Bhaird sa dán do Chú Chonnacht Mág Uidhir dár tús 'Cia re bhfuil Éiri ac anmhuin',[20] agus ag Tadhg mac Dáire Mac Bhruaideadha sa dán do Dhonnchadh Ó Briain dár tús 'Mór atá ar theagasg flatha'[21] ina bhfuil tarraingt ag an bhfile ar na trí téacsaí a luadh thuas le Leabhar Laighean.[22] Ní nach ionadh na tagairtí sin agus a mhinicí is a bhíonn na seanfhocail mar thosnú reitriciúil leis an saghas san filíochta, nós atá le fáil chomh déanach leis an ochtú haois déag.[23]

Lean tionchar *Tecosca* isteach sa nua-ré, agus, fé mar a d'aithin an Rathailleach, tá sé le feiscint go háirithe sa déantús dár teideal 'Comhairle na Bardscolóige', a bhfuil iliomad cóipeanna de le fáil sna lámhscríbhinní déanacha, agus ar glacadh leis sa traidisiún béil chomh maith.[24] *Genre* ann féin is ea dánta comhairle dá leithéid, go háirithe i dtraidisiún na Nua-Ghaeilge Moiche agus níos déanaí,[25] *genre* a raibh aithris air i réimsí eile – sa

---

18 Lambert McKenna (eag.), *The Book of Magauran: Leabhar Méig Shamhradháin* (BÁC, 1947), dán XIX.　19 *DD*, dán 120; féach Roland M. Smith, 'The *senbriathra Fíthail* and related texts', *RC*, 45 (1928), 1–92 ag 6 §8. Maidir le nathanna fadshaolacha, cf. Thomas F. O'Rahilly, *A miscellany of Irish proverbs* (BÁC, 1922), §§279, 281; Tomás de Bhaldraithe, 'Sean-nath a mhair', *Ériu*, 42 (1991), 147.　20 *DMU*, dán II; cf. Eleanor Knott, *An introduction to Irish syllabic poetry of the period 1200–1600* (BÁC, 1957; athchló 1981), lgh 39–40.　21 Emma Nic Cárthaigh, '*Mór a-tá ar theagasg flatha*: *speculum principis* le Tadhg mac Dáire Mheic Bhruaideadha' in S. Ó Coileáin, L.P. Ó Murchú agus P. Riggs (eag.), *Séimhfhear suairc: aistí in ómós don Ollamh Breandán Ó Conchúir* (An Daingean, 2013), lgh 139–80.　22 Fergus Kelly (eag. agus aistr.), *Audacht Morainn* (BÁC, 1976), lch xiv.　23 An dán dár tús *Treisi dúthchas ná oileamhain*, mar shampla, arbh fhéidir gurbh é Seán Ó Neachtain a chum: Nessa Ní Shéaghdha, 'Diomoladh Phádraig Naofa', *Celtica*, 15 (1983), 67–8. Maidir le feidhm an nóis féin, féach na ranna tosaigh in Lambert Mac Kenna, 'A poem by Gofraidh Fionn Ó Dálaigh', *Ériu*, 16 (1952), 131–9.　24 Thomas F. O'Rahilly, *Dánfhocail: Irish epigrams in verse* (BÁC, 1921), lgh 36–7, 83–8.　25 Mar shampla, cf. 'Comhairle an bhráthair bhoicht' (*Gabh a Chéin go séimh mo theagasg uaim-se*) in Cuthbert Mhág Craith (eag.), *Dán na mbráthar mionúr*, i–ii (BÁC, 1967, 1980), dán 89; Tomás Ó Rathile, 'Comhairle do scoláire óg', *Gadelica*, 1 (1912–13), 260–62; an díolaim de dhánta gaoise in Tomás Ua Nualláin, 'Anecdota from Maynooth MSS', *IER*, 25 (Eanair go Meitheamh 1919), 154–7. Ina theannta sin, is minic a tharlaíonn díolaimí beaga agus móra d'aforaisí gaoise sna foinsí, chomh maith le go leor aistí filíochta dár tús *A mhic*, *A ghiolla*, *A mhacaoimh*, *Gabh mo chomhairle* nó *Gabh mo theagasc* (e.g., Nicholas Williams [eag.], *Dánta Mhuiris mhic Dháibhí Dhuibh Mhic Gearailt* [BÁC, 1979], dán 10). Leanadh don aithris ar na dánta seo isteach sa Nua-Ghaeilge: cf. *Ná tréig mo theagasc a mhic* (Maigh Nuad LS C 88, duil. 7v, agus áiteanna eile), agus an déantús déanach i *rannaigheacht* anscaoilte le Dáibhí de Barra dár tús *Ná tréig mo theagasc a mhic na dísle* (Coláiste na hOllscoile Corcaigh, LS Torna T.14 (90), lgh 18–19); nó 'Teagasc Phiaruis Há da

bhFianaigheacht mar shampla[26] – agus ar deineadh scigaithris ar ball air i leithéidí 'A mheic ná meabhraigh éigse' agus 'Comhairle Mhic Clamha'.[27] Ní ceart mar sin féin go n-imeodh gan fhios orainn an cóngas idir na dánta sin agus téacsaí eile dob fhéidir a áireamh ar theaghlach na gaoise chomh maith. Mar tá sé soiléir gur teaghlach agus cineál uilí idirnáisiúnta litríochta is ea litríocht na gaoise,[28] gur mó ábhar a gheibheann fothain féna scáth.

Ba sa chreideamh, nó sa mhoráltacht diaga, is mó a tharla táirgeadh i gcúrsaí gaoise sa mheánaois, maidir leis na seanráite go háirithe. Is beag lámh-scríbhinn diaga Ghaelach ón aimsir sin nach bhfaightear tagairtí inti – i bhoirm *florilegia* go minic – do ráitisí morálta duine éigin de na hAithreacha nó de na sean-fhealsaimh chlasaiceacha; ar fhianaise na lámhscríbhinní sin, bhí éileamh faoi leith i ré na meánaoise ar leagan Gaeilge de *florilegium* áirithe ar a dtugtar an *Liber scintillarum*, díolaim de sheanráite an Bhíobla agus na nAithreacha agus iad eagraithe do réir ábhair (an fhoighne, an charthannacht etc.).[29] Is minic chomh maith ráite clasaiceacha agus ráite diaga buailte suas le chéile nó meascaithe trína chéile. I ngiorracht achair an-ghairid sa chéad chuid den Liber Flavus, mar shampla, gheofar ráite leagtha ar Seneca, Auguisdín agus Tomás de Quino.[30] Mar atá luaite thuas, an comhshuíomhú nó an meascán nádúrtha seo idir gaois tuata agus gaois na hEaglaise, tá sé le fáil sna téacsaí gaoise is sine sa Ghaeilge – tá, mar shampla, 'adrad Dé móir' luaite i *Tecosca*[31] – agus comhartha is ea é ar an gcomhbhunús atá leis an saghas seo litríochta.

Comhartha is ea é chomh maith gur dócha nár dhein lucht cnuasaithe na dtéacsaí gaoise oiread san idirdhealaithe idir gaois an Bhíobla agus a mhaca-samhail ó fhoinsí eile, pé acu foinsí dúchais nó deoranta iad. Ba chúng an domhan inar lonnaigh fear na meánaoise, aon saol intleachtúil amháin ab ea é, agus níl léiriú is fearr ar mheon – ar shiceolaíocht – an fhir sin ná an bolg an tsoláthair a chuir Pilib Bacach Ó Duibhgheannáin le chéile dó féin i ndeireadh an tséú haois déag, Leabharlann Náisiúnta na hÉireann LS G I. Scáthán is ea é ar an dearcadh comhordaithe i leith an tsaoil agus ar an meascán ábhair

chomhráduighe Mícheaghal Ó Sé, *Gabh a Mhicheaghail go caomh mo teagasg uaimse'* (Séamus Ó Mórdha, 'Irish manuscripts in St Macarten's seminary, Monaghan', *Celtica*, 4 [1958], 279–87 ag 284). **26** 'Comhairle Fhinn mhic Cumhaill do Mhac Lughach' in An Seabhac [Pádraig Ó Siochfhradha] (eag.), *Laoithe na féinne* (BÁC, 1941), lgh 284–5; cf. O'Rahilly, *Dánfhocail*, lch 86. **27** *BM Cat.* i, lgh 392–3; Seosamh Ó Dubhthaigh agus Brian E. Rainey, *Comhairle Mhic Clamha ó Achadh na Muilleann* (Lille, 1981). **28** Féach an réamhrá le Colin A. Ireland, *Old Irish wisdom attributed to Aldfrith of Northumbria: an edition of Bríathra Flainn Fhína maic Ossu* (Tempe, Arizona, 1999). **29** Mar shampla, Rawlinson LS B 513, duil. 7–8; Leabharlann Náisiúnta na hAlban LS Adv. 72.1.1, duil. 7r; TCD LS 1699, duil. 171–174r (féach thíos); Leabharlann na Breataine LS Add. 11809, duil. 32–3; Georges Dottin, 'Notice du manuscrit irlandais de la Bibliothèque de Rennes', *RC*, 15 (1994), 79–91 ag 85–6. **30** ARÉ LS 476 (23 O 48), (a) duil. 36v–37r. **31** Kuno Meyer (eag. agus aistr.), *The instructions of King Cormac mac Airt*, TLS 15 (BÁC, 1909), lch 2.

a mbíodh suim ag an bhfear léinn ann sa tréimhse seo, agus ar a raibh ar fáil san am sin chun a chuid suime a shásamh. Cnuasach is ea é de mhiontéacsaí seanchais, ranna fáin, blúiríocha gearra eolais ar mhíorúiltí agus iontaisí an tsaoil: seanráite Auguisdín agus fáistine Bhig mheic Dé taobh le taobh, orthaí agus oidisí á leanúint sin arís, an saghas ábhair a bheadh in úsáid sna lámh-scríbhinní móra chun línte folmha ag bun leathanaigh a líonadh.[32] A leithéid seo, mar shampla:

> Is mur so dhligheas rí .7. laithe na seachtmaine do chaitheam .i. breatha agus uraghaill gac luain. cluiche agus ealadha gaca mairt. Sealg agus aircheas gaca ceadaoine. Suirghe agus comdhála fri mnaibh gaca dardaoin. Aonaighe agus coimleanga ar eachaibh gaca haoine. Foilcthe agus fothruicthe agus ionnsma sleagh gaca sathairnd. Fleaghugad agus ceol agus oirmidin gaca domnach.[33]

Bíodh is go mb'fhéidir go bhfuil cuma neafaiseach gan aird ar an díolaim sin Philib, is meascán mearaí stuama é den saol mar a taibhsíodh do dhuine éirimiúil de chuid na haimsire sin é, inarbh aon aonad amháin an ghaois agus an seanchas, an stair agus an finnscéal.

Lean an ghaois ina hábhar suime agus staidéir isteach i ré na Nua-Ghaeilge. Solaoid mhaith dhéanach ar an ilghnéitheacht i gcúrsaí gaoise is ea an díolaim ar thug Einrí Mac an tSaoir 'Comhairleachaibh ó ughdaraibh maithe' air i lámhscríbhinn a bhreac sé i mBaile Átha Cliath, 1787–8.[34] Formhór na 'comhairleacha' seo, leagtar ar Sholamh iad, agus iad á dtarraingt as Leabhar na Seanfhocal. Sa chuid tosaigh den téacs, áfach, léirítear conas ab fhéidir ábhar clasaiceach, dúchasach agus bíobalta a shuíomhú taobh le taobh i saothar gaoise:

> Ná déan én ní do cheilfeá ar na daoinibh, óir gidh folaightheach do níthear an drochní, do gheibhthior a fhios fa dheoigh. Na neithe ba misde leat do chur ort, ná habair a measg morán do dhaoinibh é. Adeir Seneca, ge bé do nach eól dho thocht, nach eól dó cionnas a laibh-

---

32 Mar a tharlaíonn sa Leabhar Breac (ARÉ LS 1230 [23 P 16]), lgh 12b ['Fland Fína'] agus 185b [Gregorius agus Auguisdín]); nó an dá ghearrthéacs in Leabharlann na Breataine LS Add. 30512, duil. 35vb27–36, a bhfuil cúlra fada suimiúil leo (*BM Cat.* ii, 487–9).
33 LNÉ LS G 1, duil. 65v3–10; an téacs tugtha mar atá sa bhfoinse ach scaoileadh déanta ar nodanna. Tá samplaí de ghearrthéacsaí eile ó G 1 le fáil i saothar Mháire Herbert – 'Some Irish prognostications', *Éigse*, 14 (1972), 303–18 ag 306–7, agus 'The seven journeys of the soul', *Éigse*, 17 (1977), 1–12 ag 6–8 – agus John Carey, 'The names of the plains beneath the lakes of Ireland' in J. Carey, M. Herbert agus K. Murray (eag.), *Cín Chille Cúile: texts, saints and places. Essays in honour of Pádraig Ó Riain* (Aberystwyth, 2004), lgh 43–7. 34 ARÉ LS 37 (G vi 1), lgh 227–33; tá cóip chiorraithe den téacs céanna le fáil i lámhscríbhinn le Labhrás Mhac an Allaidh (c. 1765), ARÉ LS 59 (23 K 24), lch 144.

eórus. Ná bí maith fa ní dhuine eile, agus gan a bheith maith fa do ní féin. Má do gheall duine ní dhuit, ná geallsa do dhuine eile é, nó go ttí ar do láimh. Gach uile ní atá toirmiosgaithe dona mnáibh, atá siad ullamh dochum a dhéanta. Tairg a bheith a n-anbhfios do mhná, agus ná tairg a bheith na heolas ar Aristotel ag teagasg Alasdruinn Uaibhridh. Cia as ionruic dona mnáibh? ar Fionn. An méd nach guidhthear dhíobh ar Ailbhe. A dhuine dána léir ancháidhe bheag ar dhuine eile (ar Matha) as iongnadh nach léir dhuit ancháidh [*sic*] mhór ort féin.[35]

Tá leagan céad blian níos luaithe den téacs céanna le fáil sa lámhscríbhinn ar a dtugtaí 'Lámhscríbhinn Chuinn Í Néill' roimhe seo, ach atá anois i gcnuasach Leabharlann Náisiúnta na hÉireann, LS G 1304.[36] Conchubhar Mág Aoidh a scrígh sa mbliain 1681, agus tá an téacs seo ar dhuilleoga 125–128r. Cé go bhfuil an dá leagan gairid go maith dá chéile, díol suime is ea é nach bhfuil an tagairt do 'Agallamh Fhinn agus Ailbhe' (féach n. 11) le fáil in G 1304, ach go bhfuil an 'Agallamh' sin féin buailte suas leis chun tosaigh ina iomláine (duil. 124) ar shlí a thugann le fios go mb'fhéidir nár tuigeadh don scríobhaí go raibh aon ródheifir idir an 'Agallamh' agus an díolaim aforaisí. Is fiú a lua gur tharla an díolaimiú agus an athnuachaint déanach seo in aontráth le spéis a bheith á cur ag lucht léinn i seanfhocail ar fuaid na hEorpa.[37] Níor thaise é do lucht ársaíochta in Éirinn san am. Fé mar a léirigh Gordon Quin agus James Stewart, deineadh leaganacha Gaeilge comhaimseartha de bhailiúcháin dá leithéid a foilsíodh i mBéarla i ndeireadh an tséú haois déag agus go luath sa seachtú haois déag.[38]

Dála comhshuíomh na dtéacsaí seo, tá a leithéid chéanna le tabhairt fé ndeara i lámhscríbhinn Einrí Mhic an tSaoir. Díreach roimh na 'Comhairleacha' sa lámhscríbhinn sin, tá díolaim eile de sheanráite go bhfuil an teideal 'Comhairle Chato' curtha aige leis.[39] Cnuasach suimiúil é seo, agus is suimiúla fós gur leagan is ea é de théacs meánaoiseach ar chuir Carl Marstrander eagar air ó lámhscríbhinn ón séú haois déag a luadh cheana thuas, ARÉ LS 967 (23 N 10).[40] Caithfidh gur mheas na scríobhaithe

---

35 ARÉ LS 37, lch 227; uaimse na sínte fada, an phoncaíocht, na cinnlitreacha agus scaoileadh na nod.   36 Brian Ó Cuív, 'A seventeenth-century Irish manuscript,' *Éigse*, 13, ii (1969), 143–52. Cheannaigh an Leabharlann Náisiúnta an lámhscríbhinn nuair a ceantáladh i dtigh Sotheby é, mí na Nollag 2001 (*Sotheby's: valuable printed books and manuscripts, 13 December 2001*, lot 227); tá an lámhscríbhinn le fáil ar ISOS anois (<www.isos.dias.ie>).   37 F.P. Wilson, 'The proverbial wisdom of Shakespeare' in W. Mieder agus A. Dundes (eag.), *The wisdom of many: essays on the proverb* (Madison, WI, 1994), lgh 174–89 ag lch 178.   38 Bodleian LS Talbot g.5. E.G. Quin, 'A book of proverbs', *Éigse*, 10, ii (1962), 127–43; idem agus James Stewart, 'Supplement to "A book of proverbs"', *Éigse*, 11, ii (1965), 117–18.   39 ARÉ LS 37, lgh 217–26.   40 'Bídh crínna', *Ériu*, 5 (1911), 126–41.

déanacha gur leagan ab ea na seanráite seo de 'Disticha Catonis',[41] rud nach fíor. Is é an tábhacht atá leis an téacs seo, mar sin, ná go gcaitheann sé solas ar ilfhoinseacht litríocht na gaoise i dtraidisiún na Gaeilge, agus ar lean-únachas an traidisiúin chomh maith ón mheánaois isteach sa nua-aois, ar athchúrsáil an tsean-ábhair i gcruth leathnua. Chífimíd sampla eile den ngné seo ar ball.

Ó thaobh na litríochta agus ó thaobh an teagaisc de, ba mhóide éifeacht chraoladh na gaoise agus cur i láthair na deisbhéalaíochta iad a bheith i riocht agallamh, an-mhinic idir sinsear agus sóisear: Cú Chulainn agus Lugaid Réoderg, Cormac agus Cairbre, Fítheal agus Flaithrí. Ó's bunús scolaíochta atá le húsáid *sententiae* sa mheánaois,[42] tharlódh gur sa 'mhodh Socráiteach' atá bunús cuid de ghné an agallaimh le haimsiú leis, ráite go bhfuil córas na ceastóireachta ginte agus sean-bhunaithe sa tsean-litríocht, i dtráchtaisí diaga, sna dlíthe, sna tráchtaisí meadarachta, agus sa seanchas trí chéile, an teagasc rí go háirithe.[43] Ach pé ar domhan de, lean bunstruchtúr an agallaimh, nó an cheist agus freagra, do chuid den nuachumadóireacht déanach leis. Saothar is ea *Eólas ar an domhan* le Tadhg Ó Neachtain, cuirim i gcás, atá ag braith cuid mhaith ar théacsleabhair Bhéarla maidir le buneolas de, ach a bhfuil struchtúr an chomhráidh leagtha air ag an údar féin, comhrá idir Tadhg agus a athair Seán.[44] Ba é an Tadhg céanna, agus cnuasach seanfhocal á scríobh aige d'Antaine Réamainn, a chaomhnaigh sraith de cheisteanna agus freagraí i modh véarsaíochta ina bhfuil meascán de sheanráite morálta, ar an gcuma seo (mar shampla):

c. Grádh a íocaibh . do rígh bhus dídion
f. tá grádh neamhbhuan . ag díscearsluagh
......

c. Trosgadh fíre . bhus sódh naomhtha
f. a tteasghrádh Dé . má níthear é[45]

41 Féach *BM Cat.* ii, lgh 357–8. 42 Ernst Robert Curtius, *European literature and the Latin Middle Ages*, aistr. Willard R. Trask (Londain, 1953), lgh 58–9. 43 Mar shampla: Kuno Meyer (eag.), *Hibernica minora being a fragment of an Old-Irish treatise on the Psalter* (Oxford, 1894), lgh 82–3; 'Bretha éitgid' (Liam Breatnach, *A companion to the Corpus iuris Hibernici* [BÁC, 2005], lgh 176–82, 378–464); Rudolf Thurneysen, 'Mittelirische Verslehren I', *IT* iii, 1 (1891), 5–7, 23 etc.; Lambert McKenna, 'A poem by Gofraidh Fionn Ó Dálaigh' in S. Pender (eag.), *Féilsgríbhinn Torna* (Corcaigh, 1947), lgh 66–76; Kuno Meyer, 'Dúan in chóicat cest', *ZCP*, 4 (1903), 234–7; Daniel A. Binchy, 'An archaic legal poem', *Celtica*, 9 (1971), 152–68. Maidir le foirm an agallaimh sa luathlitríocht, féach Pádraig Ó Macháin, 'Aonghus Ó Callanáin, Leabhar Leasa Móir agus an *Agallamh bheag*' in A. Doyle agus K. Murray (eag.), *In dialogue with the Agallamh: essays in honour of Seán Ó Coileáin* (BÁC, 2014), lgh 144–63. 44 Meadhbh Ní Chléirigh (eag.), *Eólas ar an domhan: i bhfuirm chomhráidh idir Sheán Ó Neachtain agus a mhac Tadhg* (BÁC, 1944). 45 ARÉ LS 1404 (24 P 41), lgh 318 (302) – 320 (304), ag lch 318; uaimse na sínte fada.

Sa bhfichiú haois féin, níor dheacair, im thuairimse, ginealach an agallaimh agus na deisbhéalaíochta a mholadh do na saothair neamhchoitianta úd *Cainnt an tsean-shaoghail* agus *Cúrsaí an tsean-shaoghail*. Arland Ussher, fealsamh, a chuir le chéile iad ó chaint agus ó chumadóireacht sclábhaí gan léamh ná scríobh de bhunadh Shliabh gCua, Tomás Ó Muirthe.[46] B'fhéidir gurb é lámh an fhealsaimh sa dá leabhar a d'fhág blas na sean-ghaoise orthu ach, pé rud é, tá an ghaois agus an greann, an chomhairle agus na seanráite, fite le chéile sna comhráite atá leagtha amach in *Cúrsaí an tsean-shaoghail* go háirithe, mar a dtráchtar ar obair thís agus ar obair na feirme mí ar mhí. Ní miste a lua leis go bhfuil sampla níos cruinne ón bhfichiú haois de mhodh an agallaimh i múineadh cúrsaí tís le fáil i sraith de cheachtanna le Seán Ó Ciarghusa, údar a bhain leis an dúthaigh chéanna, a cuireadh i gcló i 1960 agus teagasc do dhaoine óga iontu ar bheacha, ar éin agus ar éisc, agus an teagasc sin go léir á léiriú i bhfoirm chomhrá idir 'an tOllamh' agus an 'garsún'.[47]

I dtraidisiún mheánaois na hEorpa, *genre* a raibh sinsearacht fhada leis ab ea tráchtaisí tís. Sa léann Clasaiceach, leagtar saothair dár teideal *Oeconomica* ar Arastotal, *Oeconomicus* ar Xenophon (agus é i bhfoirm chomhráidh), *Rerum rusticarum* ar Varro, *De agri cultura* ar Cato agus *Opus agriculturae* ar Palladius. Tógadh ar na saothair sin, agus ar shaothair nach iad, agus sa mheánaois dhéanach tharla bláthú ar théacsleabhair a phléigh cúrsaí tís agus talmhaíochta.[48] Solaoid amháin is ea saothar cáiliúil Angla-Normannach ón tríú haois déag le Walter de Henley ar an talmhaíocht, *Le dite de hosebondrie*. Taispeánann tosach an tsaothair seo go soiléir an ceangal idir an tráchtas tís agus litríocht chanónach na gaoise. Ar chuma Leabhar na Seanfhocal, tosnaíonn *Le dite* le hathair ag cur comhairle ar a mhac i gcúrsaí diagachta sa chéad áit, sara gcromann ar thráchtas feirmeoireachta ina dhiaidh sin:

> Le pere set en sa veylesse e dyt a son fytz beu fiz uiuet sagement solom deu e solom de secle. En uers deu pensez souent de sa passion e de la mort ke ihesu crist suffry pur nus e lamet sur tote renz e ly dotet e ses comandemens tenet e gardet.[49]

An t-athair, a bhí tar éis titim sa sean-aois, dúirt lena mhac: a mhic ionúin, déan do shaol a chaitheamh go tomhaiste maidir le Dia agus

---

46 Arland Ussher, *Cainnt an tsean-shaoghail* (BÁC, 1942); *Cúrsaí an tsean-shaoghail* (BÁC, 1948). Mar le cúlra agus déanamh na leabhar seo, féach Diarmuid Ó Hairt, 'Arland Ussher agus an sean-shaol Gaelach', *An Linn Bhuí: Iris Ghaeltacht na nDéise*, 12 (2008), 11–26. 47 Seán Ó Ciarghusa, *Gearrscoil .i. léachta don aos óg* (BÁC, 1960).   48 Lynn Staley, 'Translating "communitas"' in K. Lavezzo (eag.), *Imagining a medieval English nation* (Minneapolis, 2004), lgh 261–303 ag lgh 270–71. Maidir leis an gcúlra ginearálta féach, mar shampla, Roy C. Cave agus Herbert H. Coulson, *A source book for medieval economic history* (Milwaukee, 1936).   49 Elizabeth Lamond (eag.), *Walter of Henley's husbandry together with an anonymous husbandry, seneschaucie and Robert Grosseteste's rules* (Londain, 1890), lch 2.

maidir leis an saol. Maidir le Dia de, cuimhnigh go minic ar an bpáis agus ar an mbás a d'fhulaing Íosa Críost ar ár son, agus tabhair grá dó thar gach éinní, agus bíodh eagla ort roimhe, agus sealbhaigh agus coimeád a chuid aitheanta.

Ní nach ionadh is ea é go mbeadh plé ann i measc scoláirí i dtaobh pé acu an mbaineann nó nach mbaineann an *Dite* le gnás na seanmóireachta.[50] Ba chúntaí go mór é, ba dhóigh liom, é a thagairt do litríocht na gaoise.

Taobh amuigh de chomharthaí sóirt na deisbhéalaíochta, carnadh na seanfhocal, agus mar sin de, baineann mealltacht an chineáil seo litríochta le bunfhírinní so-aitheanta a leagan amach i bhfoirm theagaisc nó chomhairle dob fhéidir a thagairt d'aicmí éagsúla sóisialta. Cé go mbainfeadh a leithéid de sheanrá agus 'Tosach féile fairsinge' le teagasc rí sa chéad áit, mar shampla, ní deacair a shamhlú go bhféadfaí é a thagairt do ghnáthchúrsaí tís chomh maith. Is fíor, leis, go mbíonn trácht ar *trebad* go minic sna sean-téacsaí: 'Nírba úallach minba trebthach … ar is col i ndálaib in domain úall cen trebad' (*Tecosca Cormaic*),[51] mar shampla; nó an trácht ar thréithe na deaghmhná i *Senbriathra Fíthil*, mar atá i Leabhar Laighean (lch 346a) agus a thosnaíonn 'Cid imma ngéb trebad ol a mac fri Fíthal',[52] téacs a fhaightear i lámhscríbhinní níos déanaí ná Leabhar Laighean chomh maith.[53] Comhairle ar chúrsaí tís (*trebad*) is bun le cuid de thréanna na Sean-Ghaeilge,[54] agus is é is cúlra bunaidh d'an-chuid de na tagairtí do mhná chomh maith, agus iad ag eascairt ó bhunús bíobalta de shaghas 'Seanfhocail' 31.10–31 ('Bean chéile gan cháim'), cé go dtéann chun áiféise, ar an nós meánaoiseach, le himeacht aimsire. Bíodh is go mb'fhéidir nach dtiocfadh le dearcadh na laethanta seo againne, aithnítear an bhean mhaith mar 'ind indéoin trebtha' ('the keystone of husbandry') i *Senbríathra Fíthil*.[55] Ar fhianaise na dtréanna, deir Fergus Kelly: 'Reticence, virtue and industry seem to be the qualities most admired in a woman',[56] cé gur déine i bhfad orthu a bhí údar *Tecosca Cormaic*.[57] Ginealach fada a bhí laistiar de Dháibhí de Barra, mar sin, agus *Female policy detected* á aistriú go Gaeilge aige i dtreo dheireadh an ochtú haois déag.[58]

Is í an leithne seo a ghabhann le litríocht na gaoise a mheabhraíonn dúinn sainmhíniú Vivien Law ar an litríocht sin: 'It is not a genre but a content-based category, a class to which texts in a large number of genres may be

50 Alexander Falileyev, *Welsh Walter of Henley* (BÁC, 2006), lgh xvii–xxii, mar a dtagraítear chomh maith don lipéad a leag Morfydd Owen air, 'functional prose' (lch xxi). 51 Meyer, *Instructions*, lgh 18–20. 52 *LL* vi, l. 46397; Smith, 'The *senbriathra*', 52–60. 53 Kuno Meyer, 'Fíthels Ratschläge an seinen Sohn', *ZCP*, 8 (1912), 112–13. 54 Féach Kuno Meyer (eag. agus aistr.), *The triads of Ireland*, TLS 13 (Londain agus Baile Átha Cliath, 1906), §§65, 70, 72, 73, 97–9, 134, 140, 180–1. 55 Smith, 'The *senbriathra*', 52. 56 Kelly, *A guide to early Irish law*, lch 69. 57 Kelly, 'Thinking in threes', lch 17. 58 Breandán Ó Conchúir (eag.), *Corraghliocas na mban le Dáibhí de Barra* (BÁC, 1991).

assigned'.[59] I gcás litríocht na hÉireann sa mheánaois dhéanach, ní fheadar an bhfuil aon fhoinse amháin eile is fearr a thugann an leithne sin léi, agus a thugann le chéile formhór na dtéamaí a luadh thuas, ná lámhscríbhinn a bhaineann le lár an chúigiú haois déag agus ar thug Dáithí Ó hUaithne 'that great compendium of medieval literature' uirthi.[60] Is í lámhscríbhinn í TCD LS 667 (F.5.3): lámhscríbhinn mheamraim agus 254 de leathanaigh inti, seacht gcinn déag acu (165–181a15: tugtar LS 1699 orthu seo) agus ábhar Gaeilge orthu, an chuid eile i Laidin.[61] Lámhscríbhinn bheag shnasta í seo i mionscríbhinn Shasanach an chúigiú haois déag (ach amháin an chuid Ghaelach di), agus na téacsaí leagtha amach go cáiréiseach in dhá cholún, na príomhlitreacha daite agus iad maisithe go minic leis. Bolg an tsoláthair de sheanchas cráifeach na meánaoise atá ann. Is é an chéad téacs ann ná an *Elucidarium*, saothar cáiliúil ar nithe diaga ón aonú haois déag le Honorius Augustodunensis i bhfoirm agallaimh idir oide agus dalta.

Ar bhonn tagairtí do Bhrianaigh i scata beag annálacha ar lch 66,[62] thuairimigh Robin Flower gur i dtigh Proinsiascánach i gCo. an Chláir a scríodh an leabhar.[63] Pé ní i dtaobh an log a aimsiú chomh beacht sin, is áirithe gur foinse an-tábhachtach í seo ar mhórán slite. Ní gá, mar shampla, ach cuid de na mórthéacsaí atá ann a lua chun go dtuigfimís, mar a dúirt Flower, conas a nochtann an lámhscríbhinn seo na comhthéacsanna agus na foinsí téacsúla ónar fhás na haistriúcháin Ghaeilge sa mheánaois.[64] Téacsaí iad seo a bhfaightear a macasamhla Gaeilge i lámhscríbhinní eile ón aois chéanna, mar shampla an Liber Flavus, Egerton 1781, Leabhar na Rátha agus Leabhar Leasa Móir; téacsaí ar nós 'De Inuentione Sanctae Crucis', 'Visio Sancti Pauli', 'Fierabras', 'Historia Karoli Magni', 'Historia Septem Sapientum'[65] agus 'De Morte Mariae'. I dteannta na mórthéacsaí in LS 667, tá nithe eile ar nós seanmóintí agus lear mór *exempla*, agus, in áit amháin, cuid de *Disticha Catonis* (lch 158). Mar a bheadh luinneog eatarthu seo go léir, go mion minic – líonann breis agus an cúigiú cuid den leabhar san iomlán – tá sraitheanna de bhunshleachta: seanráite na nAithreacha agus na n-údar diaga.

I lár LS 667, tá an stua ina bhfuil an t-ábhar Gaeilge a luadh thuas. Ábhar diaga agus morálta atá anseo don gcuid is mó, a bhfuil cuid de le fáil chomh

59 Law, *Wisdom*, lch 23. 60 David Greene, 'A Gaelic version of *The seven wise masters*', *Béaloideas*, 14 (1944), 219–36 ag 220. 61 Marvin L. Colker, *Trinity College Library Dublin: descriptive catalogue of the mediaeval and renaissance Latin manuscripts*, i–ii (Aldershot, 1991), ii, lgh 1123–64; T.K. Abbott agus E.J. Gwynn, *Catalogue of the Irish manuscripts in the library of Trinity College, Dublin* (Baile Átha Cliath, 1921), lgh 323–5. 62 Colker, *Descriptive catalogue*, lgh 1132–3. 63 Robin Flower, *The Irish tradition* (Oxford, 1947), lgh 122–5. 64 Ibid., lch 125; ní mar a chéile é seo, áfach, is a cheapadh gurbh í LS 667 go baileach foinse na n-aistriúchán sin (Colmán N. Ó Clabaigh, *The Franciscans in Ireland, 1400–1534: from reform to reformation* [BÁC, 2002], lch 139). 65 Marab ionann agus na téacsaí eile, ní mhaireann ach cóip ón seachtú haois déag de leagan Gaeilge an téacs seo: Leabharlann Náisiúnta na hAlban LS 72.1.39, duil. 1–22r.

maith sa Liber Flavus: tráchtaisí ar an bhfaoistin, airtigil an chreidimh, cuid
d'aistriú ar an *Liber scintillarum*, ráiteas ó Arastotal, téacs ag caitheamh anuas
ar na mná, aforaisí ó *Tecosca Cormaic*, agus seanmóin ar an umhla. Ní haon
bholg an tsoláthair é seo, ach díolaim de chineálacha eagsúla téacsaí gaoise,
idir théacsaí dúchasacha agus théacsaí deoranta, idir théacsaí bunaidh agus
aistriúcháin. Taispeánann sé seo an bonn an-leathan a tuigeadh do lucht léinn
na haimsire seo a bheith faoin saghas seo litríochta. I gceartlár an ábhair seo
go léir (lgh 174b–176a) tá téacs arb é cúrsaí tís a bhun agus a bharr. 'Fearus
tighe' a tugtar air agus tá sé in eagar, agus é aistrithe go Fraincis, ag Gearóid
Mac Niocaill.[66] I bhfoirm cheist agus freagra a chuirtear an téacs seo i láthair,
agus cé go raibh áitithe ag Abbott agus Gwynn go raibh sé le fáil i bhfoinsí
eile, agus ainm Fíthil leis, dúirt Mac Niocaill nach raibh aon bhaint ag an
dtéacs le *Senbriathra Fíthil*, agus, ina theannta sin, nach raibh tagtha aige ar
chóip ar bith eile de.[67]

Bhí an ceart ag Mac Niocaill sa chéad ráiteas mar is fíor nach bhfuil an
téacs le fáil sna *Senbriathra*. Maidir le 'Fearus tighe' gan a bheith le fáil in
aon áit eile, bhí dul amú air áfach. Is amhlaidh a fhaightear é i ndornán beag
lámhscríbhinní a saothraíodh i gCúige Mumhan, i gCo. Chorcaí go háirithe,
breis agus trí chéad blian níos déanaí ná an fhoinse a bhí aige, teistiméireacht
eile, cosúil le 'Comhairle Chato' thuas, ar bhuaine théacsaí na gaoise i stair na
Gaeilge. An chóip is luaithe atá aimsithe agam go dtí seo, is é Eoghan
[Ruadh] Ó Súilleabháin a bhreac sa mbliain 1773: i gColáiste na hOllscoile,
Corcaigh, LS 124, lgh 23–4. 'Cómhairle an mhic ón athair' an teideal atá air
seo, ach gan aon léiriú déanta ann, lasmuigh den teideal sin, ar na cainteoirí
atá i gceist. Is giorra an cóngas idir an téacs seo LS 124 agus téacs TCD LS
667 ná na cóipeanna eile – gan mhír §[11] a bheith le fáil ach sa dá fhoinse
sin amháin, mar shampla – ach go bhfuil gaol gairid idir cóip Eoghain Ruaidh
agus na leaganacha déanacha sin chomh maith. An chuid is mó de na lámhscríbhinní eile sin, baineann siad le Mícheál Óg Ó Longáin, agus tugtar
'Ceasta Fhíthil' nó 'Comhagallamh idir F(h)ítheal agus a mhac Flaithrígh' air
ina bhformhór, teideal nach mbréagnaíonn Abbott agus Gwynn sa méid a bhí
le rá ina gcatalóg acu.

Duine a raibh an-suim go deo i gcúrsaí gaoise aige ab ea Mícheál Óg. Ar
chnuasach seanfhocal dá chuid (ARÉ LS 211 [23 G 20]) a bhunaigh an
Rathailleach a bhunleabhar ar an ábhar sin, *A miscellany of Irish proverbs*.[68]
Lámhscríbhinn eile le Mícheál Óg agus í ina heiseamláir ar ilghnéitheacht
agus leanúnachas litríocht na gaoise is ea ARÉ LS 492 (23 G 27), ar scríodh

66 'A propos du vocabulaire social irlandais du bas moyen âge', *ÉtC*, 12 (1968–71), 512–
46 ag 538–46. Maidir le bunús agus brí an fhocail *fearas*, féach David Greene, 'Varia iv:
1. Feras, banas, and some related abstracts', *Ériu*, 28 (1977), 155–61.   67 Abbott agus
Gwynn, *Catalogue*, lch 323; Mac Niocaill, 'A propos', 538.   68 Tuairisc ar an gcnuasach
seo in Meidhbhín Ní Úrdail, *The scribe in eighteenth- and nineteenth-century Ireland*
(Münster, 2000), lgh 157–60.

a formhór thart ar an mbliain 1795. Ar an ábhar atá sa leabhar seo tá, ón tseanaimsir, *florilegium* mór de sheanráite an Bhíobla agus na nAithreacha (lgh 51–8, 208–12), agus ón aimsir nua tá cóip de *An eagna fhíre*, aistriú go Gaeilge a deineadh ar *La vera sapienza* thart ar an mbliain 1739 (lgh 73–126). Is sa lámhscríbhinn seo atá an chóip Chorcaíoch is sine de théacs 'Fearus tighe'.

Is mar seo atá na foinsí déanacha dá réir sin:

Coláiste na hOllscoile, Corcaigh, LS 124, lgh 23–4 (U). Eoghan [Ruadh] Ó Súilleabháin a scrígh, 1773.

ARÉ LS 492 (23 G 27) lgh 65–6 (A). Cé go bhfuil dataí éagsúla leis an leabhar seo, baineann an téacs le cuid den leabhar a bhfuil an dáta 1795 le fáil ann. Mícheál Óg Ó Longáin a scrígh.

ARÉ LS 258 (23 G 25), lgh 32–4 (B). Mícheál Óg Ó Longáin a scrígh, *c.*1815.

Maigh Nuad, LS Uí Mhurchú 10, lgh 403–6 . Pól Ó Longáin a scrígh, *c.*1817. Cóip de (U) atá anseo.

ARÉ LS 226 (3 B 5) duil. 28–30r (lgh 181–5) (C). Mícheál Óg Ó Longáin a scrígh, 1829.

ARÉ LS 382 (24 B 12), lgh 66–8. Pádraig Ó Giobúin a scrígh, 1859.[69]

ARÉ LS 384 (24 B 31), lch 233–5. Séamus Ua Caoindealbháin a scrígh, 1822–4.[70]

ARÉ LS 693 (23 P 18), lgh 16–17. Uilliam Ó hÓgáin a scrígh, 1825–9.[71]

ARÉ LS 941 (23 C 10), lgh 39–41. Mícheál Óg Ó Longáin a scrígh, *c.*1819.

ARÉ LS 1009 (24 A 6), lgh [306]–9 (D). Éamonn Ó Mathghamhna a scrígh, 1845.[72]

Maigh Nuad, LS Uí Mhurchú 49, lgh 386–90. Mícheál Óg Ó Longáin a scrígh, 1818–20.

Coláiste Cholmáin, LS 17, lgh 219–20 (E). Tadhg Ó Conaill a scrígh, 1821.[73]

Coláiste na hOllscoile, Corcaigh, LS Torna 5A, lgh 3–6. Seán Ó Donnabháin a scrígh, gan aon dáta tugtha aige.

Aon dlúth-thraidisiún téacsúil amháin atá le tabhairt fé ndeara sa saothar mar a fhaightear sna foinsí seo é. Mar sin féin, sna téacsaí nach bhfuil de theideal orthu ach 'Ceasta Fhíthil', is gnách nach dtugtar le fios cé tá ag caint, cé gur

---

69 Féach Breandán Ó Conchúir, *Scríobhaithe Chorcaí, 1700–1850* (BÁC, 1982), lgh 79–80; Pádraig Ó Macháin, '"A llebraib imdaib": cleachtadh agus pátrúnacht an léinn, agus déanamh na lámhscríbhinní' in R. Ó hUiginn (eag.), *Léachtaí Cholm Cille 34: Oidhreacht na lámhscríbhinní* (Maigh Nuad, 2004), lgh 148–78 ag lgh 167–8.   70 Féach Breandán Ó Madagáin, *An Ghaeilge i Luimneach, 1700–1900* (BÁC, 1974), lgh 81–4.   71 Féach Ó Conchúir, *Scríobhaithe Chorcaí*, lch 85.   72 *Ibid.*, lgh 159–62.   73 *Ibid.*, lgh 48–9.

léir go maith gur agallamh is ea é. Na leaganacha a bhfuil 'Comhagallamh' sa teideal acu, deintear iarracht éigin ar an téacs a leagan amach i bhfoirm agallaimh, agus a thabhairt le fios go mbaineann ar a laghad an chéad cheist agus freagra le Flaithrí agus le Fítheal fé seach. Lasmuigh de sin, áfach, is beag idir na leaganacha go léir.

Níl teideal ná cainteoirí curtha in úil sa téacs atá foilsithe ag Mac Niocaill. Dá ainneoin sin, lasmuigh de chursaí litrithe, ord na bhfocal agus mar sin de, is é móran mór an téacs céanna atá i gceist agus atá le fáil sna foinsí déanacha trí chéad blian níos déanaí, gur féidir a bhformhór, taobh amuigh de chóip Eoghain Ruaidh, a thagairt do 'scoil' na Longánach. Aithneofar sa téacs cuid de ghnéithe agus de chomharthaí sóirt an téacs ghaoise: seanfhocail (§§[13] agus [20]), minicíocht na dtréanna (§§[9], [10], [15], [18]–[20], [27]), úsáid an dara pearsa uathu (§§[17] (T) agus [20]); is fiú leis ceann a thógaint de na tagairtí do na pearsana eaglasta i §§[13] agus [30], agus den macalla bíobalta, más ea, i §[27]. Tá nuaíocht sa téacs chomh maith, go háirithe an bhéim ar fad ar thíos, ar mhuintir an tí, agus ar an gcaidreamh feodach idir an óglach agus an tiarna. Thuairimigh Mac Niocaill gur leis an gceathrú haois déag a bhain an téacs.

Toisc a thábhachtaí is atá an téacs seo i gcomhthéacs na gaoise, im thuairimse, agus chun léiriú a dhéanamh ar an táirgeadh a deineadh air sa traidisiún déanach, is fiú dar liom téacs na bhfoinsí déanacha sin a chur i gcló anseo, móide aistriú i mBéarla, agus comparáid idir é agus an leagan luath a léiriú sna *variae* agus sna nótaí. Chuige sin, as na trí cinn déag d'fhoinsí déanacha atá luaite thuas, tá rogha de sé cinn déanta agam chun ionadaíocht a dhéanamh ar an traidisiún sin, LSS A–E agus U, agus A mar lámhscríbhinn bhunaidh. Tugaim T ar eagrán Mhic Niocaill (marab ionann agus an lámhscríbhinn ar a bhfuil sé bunaithe). Níl aon iarracht déanta agam ar litriú na scríobhaithe déanacha a thabhairt chun rialtachta: scaoilim na nodanna ós íseal, agus léirím 7 mar *agus*; uaimse an phoncaíocht; cuirim comharthaí faid isteach nuair a bhíonn siad in easnamh, agus ní bhacaim le comharthaí místairiúla faid sa lámhscríbhinn a léiriú; cuirim isteach séimhiú na hortagrafaíochta ós íseal ach ní bhacaim le séimhiú gramadúil a léiriú mara bhfuil in aon fhoinse díobh siúd atá roghnaithe agam. Leanaim d'uimhriú na n-alt mar atá ag Mac Niocaill.[74]

CEASTA FHÍTHIL SONN

[1] Créad[a] [b]na cheithre nidhthe[b] chongbhas teagh [c]ionna sheasamh[c]? [d]Bean thiagurtha[d] agus giolla treabhaigh[e] tairisi, láir bheiriotuis agus cráin fá arcuibh.

74 Táim fíorbhuíoch den Dr Pádraig de Brún as dréacht den alt seo a léamh agus as leasuithe áirithe a mholadh.

What four things keep a house standing? A resourceful woman and a faithful ploughboy, a brood mare and a sow carrying young.

[2] [a]Aig seo mar an ccéadna[a] na cheithre nidhthe threasgurus teach .i. bean [b]ainmhiannach íotamhuil[b] agus clann duibhthir[c] dothógbhála[d], capall fann fógurthach[e] agus giolla gann gallraightheach.[f]

Here likewise are the four things that tumble a house: a greedy, avaricious woman, and sullen children, impossible to rear; a useless, threatening horse, and an emaciated, diseased servant.

[3] [a]Aig si[a] an taonnídh[b] chongmhus teagh[c] síothchánta[d] .i. muinnter umhal uathadh.

Here is the one thing that keeps a house peaceful: an obedient small-sized household.

[4] Agus[a] an nídh do mhilleas gach teagh .i. muinntear mhór mhuiriorach[b] mhíothairbheach[c].

And the thing that ruins every house: a large, numerous, useless household.

[5] [a]Trí díogha[a] gacha tighe .i. laoígh[b], leinibh, agus [c]seandaoine seanga[c] slána.

The three worst things of every house: calves, children and slender healthy elderly people.

[6] An[a] aoncheard is treise ná gach ealadha .i. an treabhaireacht[b].

The only craft stronger than every art: husbandry.

[7] [a]Créad an[a] duine[b] dárab fearr[c] tairbhe a chloinne? [d].i. an macóglach, óir[d] dá mbeirthear[e] clann go hóg dó agus iad ag éirghe[f] [g]an aoinfheacht[g] ris féin[h], is fearr [i]dó iad[i] ná muinntear choimhightheach.

Who is the person who best reaps the benefit of his children? The young vassal, since if his children are born to him while he is young, and growing up as he is growing, they are better for him than a household of strangers.

[8] [a]Agus as é[a] duine dárab[b] measa tairbhe a chlainne [c].i. an duine[c] ealadhan, [d]óir bídh[d] biadh agus éadach a chlainne air [e]gurb áosmhar[e] íad, agus ann sin as dóibh féin do ghníd a ttiagar[f] agus ní dá n-athair.

And the person who least reaps the benefit of his children is the artisan, since on him rests the responsibility for feeding and clothing them until they are of age, and then it is for themselves that they make provision and not for their father.

[9] ^aAg so^a trí chómharthaoi^b thighe an deghdhuine .i. tine mhór, muinntear fhial, agus foirgneamh^c fairsiong.

Here are the three tokens of a good man's house: a great fire, a hospitable household, and a spacious building.

[10] Agus^a trí chomharthaoi tighe an^b drochdhuine .i. madra^c gearr^d foiléimneach, cailleach cheasachtach^e re hoíghibh^f, agus úrlár fá arcaibh.

And the three signs of a bad man's house: a small bounding dog, an old woman who grumbles at guests, and a floor covered in piglets.

[11] ^aCá haenní^a as measa fuair fear tighe riamh? ^bTighearna anbh[f]onn áilghisech^b.

What is the worst thing that a householder ever received? A weak, demanding lord.

[12] ^aAn taoinnídh^a ^bis fearr a^b fuair fear tighe riamh .i. tighearna teann tairisi.

The single best thing that a householder ever received: a strong, faithful lord.

[13] ^aIs amhlaidh dleaghthar^a an t-óglách as ^bdo dhéanamh^b .i.^c go tláth^d agus go toirbheartach, óir ní gnáith^e troid ^fle haba^f agus luighe ina^g leabaidh, agus^h ní gnáith óglachⁱ as treise ná 'n^j tighearna acht^k giolla daill agus bean mheathuigh^l.

Thus should vassalage be performed, deferentially and generously, since is it is not usual to fight with an abbot and lie in his bed; and it is not usual for a vassal to be stronger than the lord, save for the servant of a blind man and the wife of a weakling.

[14] ^aIs amhlaidh^a aithintear^b aigne^c fir tighe, air a fhoirgneamh^d; óir má^e cumhang a fhoirgneamh^f badh cumhang ^ga aigne^g.

Thus is the mind of a householder recognized: by his building; since if his building is narrow his mind will be narrow.

[15] ^aAg so na^a trí nidhthe óna fuinnmhighe^b fear tighe agus óna fearr a shaláthar .i. a athair agus a mháthair do dhul ^cd'éag go hóg uaidh^c, agus a ionarbadh as a ^dthír féin^d agus a leigean inti^e arís.

Here are the three things that most energize a householder and by which his productivity is enhanced: his father and mother dying young, he being expelled from his own land and being allowed to return to it again.

[16] [a]Ag so mur an ccéadna na cheithre nithe[a] óna measa a luaghuill[b] agus [c]a shaláthar[c] agus a fhuinniomh .i. muirn[d] mhór [e]ag an athair[e] air ar ttús[f], agus bean chonáigh[g] do phósa ris[h] agus a tabhairt ris[h] go tigh a[i] athar, agus [j]bheith ag feithiomh air oighreacht a[k] athar[j] nó [l]go mbadh críonna[l] an t-athair;[m] agus is mairg[n] nach[o] as[p] óige ghabhus tigheas chuige[q], óir an tan[r] [s]mhaolus[t] an rosg agus chasaid[u] na glúine[s], agus luathuigheas an anál agus líonas codla agus casachtach[v] agus miann sádhaile[w] an seanduine ní hintighis[x] é [y]ann sin[y], acht muna raibh[z] a charaid aga chomhfhortacht .

Here likewise are the four things most detrimental to his advancement, his productivity and his energy: his father bestowing great wealth on him at first, and a prosperous woman marrying him and he bringing her with him to his father's house, and waiting [then] for his father's inheritance until his father is aged. And alas for him who does not attain husbandry in his youth, because when the eye dims, and the knees grow twisted, and the breathing grows rapid, and sleep and coughing and desire for comfort consume the old man he is not able for husbandry then, unless his friends combine to help him.

[17] Agas[a] an tan [b]rachus neach ag iarraidh[b] fearuinn, gabhadh[c] fearann agus coill[d] [e]umá[f] mhagh[e] et a shliabh [g]umá choill[g], agus a thráigh air a chúl, agus a innbher air a bhéal.[h]

And when a person shall go in search of land, let him take land where woodland surrounds its level ground, and high ground surrounds the wood, and it has a shore to the rear and an estuary to the front.

[18] [a]Ag so[a] na trí nidhthe airgios[b] teach dhuine[c] [d]fá ar agus fá chrodh[d] .i. buachaill boghar beagnáireach, agus fear fartha[e] cáoch codaltach, agus síoladóir tanuíghe[f].

Here are the three things that despoil a man's house of its tillage and its stock: a deaf shameless cowherd, and a poor-sighted sleepy watchman, and an emaciated seedsman.

[19] [a]Ag so[a] trí díotha an air .i. tónoiriomh anbhfann[b] éagcuibheach[c], agus céacht[d] [e]sanntach dolámhaigh[e], agus capall [f]fann foghlach[f].

Here are the three ruinations of tillage: a weak, unsuitable rear-ploughman, and a thrusting, uncontrollable plough, and a weak, thieving horse.

[20] ^aAg so^a na trí^b nidhthe líonas na hiothlanna .i. tnúith agus saláthar agus síorchaithis^c, óir ^dmuna mbeir^d ina chaithis beir ina aithis^e.

Here are the three things that fill the granaries: striving and providing and eternal vigilance, because if you are not vigilant concerning it, you will be disgraced on account of it.

[21–3 (*T amháin*)] Ca tnuth is fearr ar bith? .i. tnuth treabaire.

What is the best striving in the world? That of a householder.

Ca tnuth is measa ar bith? .i. tnuth da tigerna uma thir nduthaigh.

What is the worst striving in the world? The striving of two lords over hereditary land.

Ca muinnter darab ainnis daighe ar bith? .i. a[n] mu[innter … (*Téacs doiléir: féach an nóta téacsúil thíos*)]

[24] ^aAs amhlaidh do^a ^bdhligheas an^b fear tighe do dhéanamh:^c amhuil do ghnídh^d an bheach, ag^e cnuasach a samhra agus a bhfóghmhar, agus ag^f caithiomh a ngeimhre et a n-earrach.

Thus should the man of the house do: as the bee does, gathering in summer and autumn, and expending in winter and spring.

[25] ^aAgus as amhlaidh^a ^bdo dhligheas^b an bhean tighe ^cdo dhéanamh^c: amhuil ^dlochaigh^e air leasughadh^d agus amhuil Céile nDé^f ar^g dhearbh-ionnracas, et amhuil ^hmnaoí ndrúith^h air dheaghoineach.

And the woman of the house should be thus: like a mouse in provisioning, like a Céile Dé for true integrity, and like the wife of a learned man for goodly hospitality.

[26] ^aAs é an duine^a aga mbí^b an mhuinntear uile ^cair a iocht^c .i. fear coigealta na tine.

The person on whom the entire household depends is the man who keeps the fire.

[27] ^aAgus as é^a duine as measa do dhaoinibh .i. duine^b ^cgan bháidh^c gan diadhacht gan daonacht^d.

And the worst of people is the one without love, holiness or charity.

[28] Agus^a an^b duine as fearr ^cdo dhaoinibh^c, an té ^daga mbíd sin a dtriúr^d.

And the best of people is the one who possesses those three [qualities].

[29] Duine^a as measa rún air bith .i. bean air meisge.

The person who is worst to keep any secret: a drunken woman.

[30] Duine^a as fearr rún ^bair bith^b .i. Sagart air fhaoisdin^c.

The best person to keep any secret: a priest in confession.

[31] Duine^a is^b luaithe^c air bith .i. duine diannocht^d droichéadaig.

[The] swiftest person in the world: a poorly dressed person who is practically naked.

[32 *T amháin* (§30)] Ca duine as maille ar bith .i. righan ro[imh] mhnaibh.

Who is the slowest person in the world? A queen at the head of [a procession of] women.

[33] Duine^a is measa oineach air bith .i. ^bcorr chíocrach chomhrann^b.

The person worst in the world for generosity: [one who is like] a heron hungry for meals.

[34] ^aAgus duine^a as^b fearr oineach^c, deighbhean drúith^d. Finit.

The person best for hospitality: the wife of a learned man.

VARIAE

Teideal: Fearus tighe andso T, Comhairle an mhic ón athair U, Ceas(s)ta Fhíthil(l) sonn AB, Ceasta Fhíthil. Cómhagallamh idir Fhíthiol agus a mhac Flaithrígh C, Comhagallamh idir Fíthil .i. breitheamh Chormaic Mac Airt (mic Cuinn.c.ch. D) agus a Mhac Flaithrigh et cetera DE

[1] a: cad iad T, Ag so U; b-b: na neithe U; c-c: ana shuighe TU; d-d: bean tighe tegurtach T; e: treabair T. [2] a-a: Cad iat T, Créad C; b-b: anbhand itheamar T; c: duithir T, dearóill U; d: doitheagaisg C; e: foburthach T, foghlach CU; f: gallaidtech T, galarach U. [3] §§3 agus 4 malairtithe U; a-a: Cad e T; Cread C; b: is mó *add*. T; c: teagh duine U; d: ana suighi T. [4] a: Cad e T, Cread C; b: mhuiriorach *om*. T; c: mhíodhthabharthach U. [5] a-a: Cad iat tri ditugad bidh T Cread iad trí díotha C; b: naidhe T; c-c seinbhean (LS seinmeadhan) seng T. [6] a: Ca T, Cread an C; b: an treabaire T. [7] a-a: Cad e in T; b: taenduine TU; c: tosach a chloinne, nó *add*. DE; d-d: Ni annsa in mac oglaigh T; e: mbeirthí B; f: suas *add*. C; g: ar fhanacht T; h: agus *add*. T; i: *om*. T. [8] a-a: Ca T; a-b: agus an taonduine dar ab U; b: dara T; c-c: ni annsa fear T; d-d: .i. T, oir bíon C, oir biaidh DE; e-e: *om*. U; f-f: gumaedh (gomadh U) haesach T; g: tteagar sin suas T. [9] a-a: Cad iat T, Cread iad C; b: deaghcomhartha T, comhartha BCD; c: fiadhugad T. [10] a: Cad iat T, Cread iad C, ag so mar an ccheana U; b: *om*. T; c: gadur (inadur LS) T; d: *om*.

T, gear A; e: cháinteach *add.* C; f: coindimh T, aoighibh B, aidhibh D haídhibh E; re
hoíghibh] dhoithchilleach U. [11] T agus U amháin. a-a: An taon nidh U; b-b: tigherna
sanntach sarlag do chaithfeadh é agus ná coiseónach U. [12] a-a: Ca tigerna T, Cread an
taoinnídh C; b-b: is fearra do B; c-c: duine T; d: tren T. [13] a-a: Cinnus dlegar T; b-b:
don tighearna T; c: Ni annsa T; d: agus go húmhal *add.* U; e: roghnáith C; f-f: re habaigh
T; g: ara T; h: óir U; i: óglachus *agus an* us *cealaithe* AB, ógláchus CDE; j: *om.* T, a U;
k: da oglach *add.* T; l: agus is treise iat sin ná é *add.* C. [14] a-a: Ci(o)nnas TC; b: aith-
nighter T, aitheantar BDEU, aitheanntar C; c: gach *add.* T; d: fhoirghneamh A, agus ar a
usgar *add.* T; e: madh T; f: nusgair T; g-g: cumang n-aicinnta T. [15] a-a: Ca T, Cread
iat na C; b: fuinnmidhi T, fuinniomhuidhe U, fuinneamhla C; c-c: uadha go hog T; d-d:
duithi T; e: and T. [16] a-a: Cad iat na neithe T, Cread iad na neithe C, ag so mur an
ccéanna na neither U; b: luaighill T; luadhuil BC luadhuill D; c-c: a shaláthar *om.* T; d:
muirrnn A, muirrinn BD, muirnn agus macnais U; e-e: ga mathair agus ga athair TU; f:
ttúis B; g: conaith D, tsaidhbhir U; h: ris *om.* T, leis BC; i: *om.* ABC; j-j: agus oighreacht
a athar ar a comus T; k: *om.* AB; l-l: gur chrín T; m: óir as minic fuair neach saidhbhrios
nách marfadh dhó ar feadh a ré agus go bhfaghann fein bás ina bhochtán *add.* U; n: neach
add. TU; o: nach ní D; p: as a T; q: *om.* T; r: uair T, tan *om.* B; s-s: mhaolas an tsúil agus
chasuid an rosg no na glúine C; t: mhaoluigheas DE, mhaoluigheann U; u: chrapaid agus
chruadhaid U; v: casachtacht E; w: saghaile T, saidhle ADE, seasgaireachta U; x:
hinntigheas DE; y-y: o sin suas T; z: bia T; : fhortacht DE, comluaighill T. [17] a: *om.*
U; b-b: rachair diaraigh T; c: gabh T; d: a choill U; e-e: ina medh[on] T; f: ós a C; g-g:
umá mhagh C; h: agus a eacreigh agus a moiner ar a bealaibh. Da rabair re treabaire na
deana treabaire beag ingar agus gidheadh is fearr na beith gan treabaire *add.* T. [18] Cad
iat T, Cread iat C; b: airgis in T, a áirgeas E; c: dhuine *om.* T; d-d: ma ar agus ma
innilibh T, fa eallach agus fa arbhar U; e: faire T; f: nach tulcoitceand *add.* T. [19] a-a:
Cad iat (e LS) T, Cread iad C; b: fann U; c: egubhaidh T, éagchuibhseach BDE,
faillightheach U; d: céachta B; e-e: dealam dibhalach T, sanntach solamha U; f-f:
eagcruaidh aimreigh T. [20] a-a: Cad iat (e LS) T, Cread iad C; b: *om.* T; c: sircaithais
con [*léamh doiléir* Mac Niocaill] T; d-d: muna robhair T, muna rabhair U; d-e: oir mun
mbeir ina aithis D. [24] a-a: Cionnas TC; b-b: dlighthear don U; c: .i. *add.* T; d: do
ghniodh U; e: *om.* T; f: a TCD. [25] a-a: Cionnus T; b-b: dlighidh U; c-c: bheith T; d-
d: amhuil luch air losaid C; e: loch*rann* T; f: ceile dé U g: *om.* ADE; h-h: deaghbhean
draoigh U. [26] a-a: Ca haen duine T, asé an taonduine U, Cia air a mbi C; b: mbid T;
c-c: ar a coimedh T, air a chumas no air a iocht C. [27] a-a: Ca T, Cia an C; b: an te
bhias E; c-c: gan chreidiomh U, gan bhía BDE, *om.* C; d: trocaire T. [28] a: Ce T, Cia C;
b: *om.* B; c-c: ann .i. T, ar bith U, *om.* C; d-d: na mbeid sin na triar T, aga mbíd sin a
ttriar U, aga mbeidís sin uile aige C. [29] = §31 TU; a: Ca duine T. [30] = §32 T; a: Ca
duine T, agus duine BC; b-b: is fearr ar rún do choimeád C; c: fhaisidin T, faoisidin
UDE. [31] = §29 T; a: Ca duine T, Cia an duine C; b: *om.* U; c: luaithe TUB, luatha
ACDE; d: dedla T. [33] a: Ca duine T, Cia an duine C; b-b: bean agus inghean bodaigh
U. [34] Ca duine T, Cia is ferr oineach air bith C; b: as as A; c: ar bith *add.* TU; d:
draoigh U

NÓTAÍ

[1] 'Une ménagère économe et un serviteur diligent et fidèle' (Mac Niocaill). Cf. 'A pru-
    dent wife, a ploughboy' (Eoghan Ó Comhraí, ARÉ 'Betham Collection Catalogue', i,
    duil. 180–81). Bunaithe ar an míniú ar *téagar / tiagur* mar atá in §[8] thíos atá an
    t-aistriú agamsa.

[2] *duibhthir / duithir* cf. *DIL* s.v. *doithir* 'dark, gloomy, ugly (?)'; 'daoithe duifir' (Seón Ua hUaithnín) luaite in *Corpas na Gaeilge 1600–1682* (BÁC, 2004), s.v.; 'indisciplinés' (Mac Niocaill).

[5] Tugann léamh T léiriú ar cén saghas *díogha* atá i gceist, is é sin díthiú bia. Glacaim leis gur peata lao atá i gceist le téacs an Longánaigh; 'naidhe' (léamh T).

[6] Ionann seo agus §[7] in T.

[7] *macóglach* (*mac óglaigh* T) Tá mionchíoradh déanta ag Mac Niocaill ar an dtéarma seo sa phríomhalt ('A propos', 524–35), agus féach na tagairtí chomh maith in Katharine Simms, *From kings to warlords: the changing political structure of Gaelic Ireland in the later Middle Ages* (Woodbridge, 1987), lch 176. Deir Kenneth Nicholls an méid seo: 'The little Irish tract on husbandry and housekeeping edited and translated by Dr. MacNiocaill seems to visualise the cultivator as a man of substance belonging to the class of *óglaigh*, the 'gentlemen' of sixteenth-century English sources, and with many dependants' (K.W. Nicholls, *Land, law and society in sixteenth-century Ireland* [BÁC, 1978], lch 13). Is léir ar an gcontrárthacht idir an *macóglach* agus an *duine ealadhan* gur saothrú talún seachas saothrú ceirde cúram an óglaigh.

muinntear choimhightheach Muintir (lucht oibre) an tí ina ndream deoranta, marab ionann agus clann an óglaigh féin.

[9] An t-alt seo agus §[10] i malairt ionaid in BCDE; *fiadhugad fairsing* (T) 'un accueil abondant' (Mac Niocaill). Cf. Meyer, *Triads*, §97: 'Trí fuiric thige degduni : cuirm, fothrucud, tene mór'.

[10] Aistríonn Mac Niocaill téacs T (féach v.l.) mar '"une vieille femme grognonne pour la tenir", ou peut-être "à entretenir"'. Cf. Meyer, *Triads*, §98: 'Trí fuiric thige drochduni: debuid ar do chinn, athchosan frit, a chú dot gabáil'. B'fhéidir gur leagan éigin de *casachtach* a bhí anseo i dtosach báire: cf. ibid. §114: 'Trí hamaite bít[e] i ndrochthig óiged .i. sentrichem senchaillige, roschaullach ingine móile, sirite gillai' ('... the chronic cough of an old hag ...').

[11–12] Cf. Meyer, *Triads*, §§72–3 ('Trí dotcaid threbairi ... Trí búada trebairi'): '... fognam do drochfhlaith ... fognamh do degfhlaith ...'.

[13] Níor éirigh liom fós teacht ar shampla eile den seanfhocal a luaitear anseo.

[14] Cf. §[9] thuas.

[16] Breis shuimiúil ag U anseo, arbh fhéidir é a aistriú mar seo: 'since it is often that a person received wealth that would not last him his lifetime and that he dies a pauper'.

[17] Cuireann úsáid fhoirmeacha an dara pearsa uatha cuma théacs chomhairle ar leagan T, a bhfuil breis curtha leis nach bhfuil le fáil in aon fhoinse eile.

[18] *beagnáireach* Molann Mac Niocaill, ach ní gan cheist, é seo a leasú go *beagaireach*.

[19] *tónoireamh* Féach Fergus Kelly, *Early Irish farming* (BÁC, 1997), lch 476.

[20] An chéad chuid den alt seo ina sheanfhocal ag Micheál Óg ina chnuasach mór: féach O'Rahilly, *Miscellany*, §257 ('The three things that fill a haggard – ambition, industry and constant vigilance'). Tagraíonn an Rathailleach do *Irisleabhar na Gaedhilge* 55 [5/7 (1 Deireadh Fómhair, 1894)], lch 104; is ansin a thug Domhnall Mac Cába, ón mBántír, liosta seanfhocal ó Cho. Chorcaí agus an ceann seo againne ina measc (§[9]): 'Na trí neithe líonas iothlainn, tnúth agus soláthar agus síor-chaithis, óir mara (muna) mbeidhir i n-a chaithis beidhir i n-a aithis' ('The three things that fill a haggard – longing, industry, and constant attention, for if you are not in attendance, you will be in shame').

muna rabhair (TU) / *muna mbeir* (A etc.) Leagan neamh-Chlasaiceach den mbriathar substainteach, foshuíteach láithreach 2ú uatha, spleách, in T agus U, agus é athraithe go dtí an fháistineach i dtéacsaí na Longánach; bhí an fhoirm *beir* nó *béir* le fáil mar fháistineach, 2ú uathu, neamhspleách i dtéacsaí na Nua-Ghaeilge Moiche neamh-Chlasaicí (Tomás Ó Máille, 'Contributions to the history of the verbs of existence in Irish', *Ériu*, 6 (1912), 1–102 ag 40; Mhág Craith, *Dán na mbráthar mionúr*, dán 48.39a, etc.).

[23] Mac Niocaill: 'Quelle est la "familia" pour laquelle n'importe quel (?) est miséreux?' Níl fail ar an mblúire seo ach in LS 667 amháin, agus é doiléir go maith. Arbh fhéidir gur leagan éigin de *banas taighe* (cf. Greene, 'Feras, banas', 159) 'woman's housework' atá i gceist?

[25] *leasughadh* Is mó brí a ghabhann leis an bhfocal seo, agus orthu sin tá cúram a dhéanamh de rud éigin, go háirithe i gcúrsaí bia (*DIL* 'L', 122.79–86). Maidir leis sin a bheith ar thréithe na luiche (is dóichí gur earráid atá i 'loch*rann*' Mhic Niocaill), b'fhéidir go mbaineann le teist an chíocrais a bheith uirthi sa mheánaois, nó fiú an cúnamh a thug an luch don leon i scéal Aesop (Warren R. Dawson, 'The mouse in fable and folklore', *Folklore*, 36, iii (1925), 227–48 ag 229–30, 242–3).

deaghbhean drúith An tréith chéanna luaite léi i §[34] thíos. An ghnáthbhrí a ghabhann le *bean drú(i)th* ná stríopach mhná (Lambert McKenna, *Aithdioghluim dána*, i–ii (Baile Átha Cliath, 1939–40), dán 74.17; *DIL* 'D', 416.9–14). Cé nach maífeadh éinne nach bhféadfadh imirt ar fhocal a bheith i gceist anseo, fós féin is dócha go mb'fhéidir gur cheart géilleadh do thuiscint Mhic Niocaill, is é sin gurb é an t-ainmfhocal *drúth* atá i gceist agus gurb é 'un savant' is brí leis, agus bríonna *draoi* agus *drúth* meascaithe ar a chéile (cf. *DIL* 'D', 416.45–9).

[27] Macalla anseo, b'fhéidir de 1 Corantaigh 13:13: 'fides, spes et caritas'.

[33] *corr* Thuairimigh Mac Niocaill gur mhíléamh gan bhrí a bhí in T, ach ós é an léamh céanna a fhaightear sna foinsí go léir, ach amháin U, caithfidh go bhfuil bunús leis, agus go mb'fhéidir gur duine ar déanamh na cuirre atá i gceist: duine tanaí ocrach?

[34] Féach §[25] thuas.

Saint Cataldo of Taranto:
the Irish element in the Life of an Italian saint

PÁDRAIG Ó RIAIN

In his *Acta sanctorum Hiberniae*, John Colgan devoted almost twenty pages to Cataldo, patron of the southern Italian city of Taranto.[1] Beginning with an extract from Book IV of *Catalogus sanctorum et gestorum eorum*, compiled by Pietro Natali (Petrus de Natalibus) in the fourteenth century, Colgan went on to edit a full Life of the saint – originally written by Bartolomeo Morone in 1614, allegedly from very old Tarantese manuscripts – and a short Office Life, previously printed in Rome in 1607. To these, he added detailed accounts of the saint's feastday, floruit, country of origin and writings. In his discussion of the saint's *patria*, Colgan was mainly concerned with refuting the opinion put forward by Thomas Dempster that Cataldo was born in Knapdale in the Scottish Highlands and was therefore a Scot.[2] In detailed notes to the various texts, however, Colgan discussed the places in Ireland allegedly associated with the saint, beginning with 'Baile Cathail' in Co. Tipperary, which he took to represent the *oppidum* named *Cataldus* by Pietro Natali.[3] Now anglicized Ballycahill, and used to refer to a parish in the Tipperary barony of Eliogarty, historically this place has nothing to do with the name Cathal. Despite Colgan and local opinion, which can also be traced to the seventeenth century, the name derives from Bealach Achaille, 'Way of Achall'.[4] Possibly under the influence of Colgan's comments, the alleged association of the place with the story of Cataldo of Taranto proved popular; when the local parish church was consecrated in the early nineteenth century, it was called after St Cathal, alias Cataldus.[5]

This contribution is based on a lecture given in Taranto, Italy, in May 2003, an Italian synopsis of which was published in *Casa Italia III: Gemellaggi tra Italia e Irlanda* (Dublin, 2004), pp 108–12. Christian Úa Conairche, one of the possible sources of the Irish element in Cataldo's Life, lies buried in Kyrie Eleison abbey, Abbeydorney, Co. Kerry, close to Máire Herbert's homeplace.
1 John Colgan, *Acta sanctorum veteris et majoris Scotiae seu Hiberniae ... sanctorum insulae*, i (Louvain, 1645; repr. Dublin, 1947), pp 544–62. 2 Thomas Dempster, *Historia ecclesiastica gentis Scotorum libri XIX* (Bologna, 1627), p. 163; cf. Annibale Ilari, 'L'agiografia di S. Cataldo, vescovo di Taranto. Apporti della cultura benedettina e canonicale. Testi inediti di Fra Pietro Da Chioggia (†1348) e del Vat. Lat. 5492 (*c*.1450)' in G. Giammaria (ed.), *Scritti in onore di Filippo Caraffa*, Biblioteca di Latium 2 (Anagni, 1986), pp 105–86 at pp 169–70. 3 Colgan, *Acta sanctorum*, p. 544 §2. 4 Thomas F. O'Rahilly, 'Notes on Irish place-names', *Hermathena*, 48 (1933), 196–220 at 205–6; *HDGP* ii, p. 100. 5 William J. Hayes and Joseph Kennedy, *The parish churches of north Tipperary: commem-*

Colgan went on to mention three other possible equivalents of the *oppidum* named *Cataldus*: a site called 'Kill Cathuil' in Munster; 'Dun-canaind'; and 'Callaind' on the borders of Munster and Leinster.[6] Neither Duncannon in the Wexford parish of St James and Dunbrody nor Callan in the Kilkenny barony of Kells, the latter two places mentioned by him, has any known association with the saint or with the name Cathal. As for 'Kill Cathuil', Colgan probably had in mind the place mistakenly so named in the vernacular Life of Finbarr, more correctly Ceall Mhic Cathail, now Kilmacahill in the barony of Gowran, Co. Kilkenny.[7]

The assertion in Morone's version of the Life that many held 'Rachau' in Munster to be Cataldo's *patria* led Colgan to put forward various other possible locations.[8] Having proposed that '*Rathan Ratha vel Rathach*' be read, he mentioned places that included Rahan in Co. Offaly, Rathgormack in Co. Waterford, and Rathronan in Co. Tipperary. He was inclined, however, to favour 'Sen-Rathen', now the townland and parish of Shanrahan in the Tipperary barony of Iffa and Offa West, within the kingdom of the Déise and diocese of Waterford and Lismore.[9] As at Ballycahill, however, there is no early trace of a cult of the saint in Shanrahan.[10]

In 1680, the Bollandist Gottfried Henschen, who edited Berlingerio Tarentino's account of the discovery of Cataldo's remains, placed little faith in the genuineness of the saint's Irish associations.[11] While prepared to accept that the saint bore an Irish name, he suggested that the detail of the Irish element of the Life may have come from a *vagus Hibernus*, a wandering Irishman of the kind that was well known on the Continent in medieval times.[12] Colgan's nineteenth-century successor, John Canon O'Hanlon, who devoted over twenty pages to the saint, had nothing to add to the earlier conjectures concerning the saint's native place.[13]

Modern continental, mostly Italian, commentators, beginning with Giuseppe Blandamura (†1957), whose influential writings inaugurated a more

orating a two-hundred year heritage (Roscrea, 2007), pp 313–16.   6 Colgan, *Acta sanctorum*, p. 544 §2.   7 Pádraig Ó Riain (ed.), *Beatha Bharra: Saint Finbarr of Cork. The complete Life*, ITS 57 (Dublin, 1994), p. 206 §11: *go Bealach Gabhráin áit a bhfuil Cill Chathail aniu*; cf. *HDGP* iv, p. 20.   8 Colgan, *Acta sanctorum*, pp 545, 555: *Patriam eius nonnulli Rachau fuisse affirmant, in Momoniae partibus quondam non obscure nominis urbem.*   9 Patrick Power, *Waterford and Lismore: a compendious history of the united dioceses* (Dublin and Cork, 1937), pp 132–7.   10 Under the influence of Colgan's comments, some later ecclesiastical historians accepted the identification, which John Lanigan (*An ecclesiastical history of Ireland*, 4 vols [Dublin, 1822], iii, p. 125) deemed to be 'really probable'. The espousal of the saint in Shanrahan itself appears, however, to date to no earlier than the twentieth century (Power, *Waterford and Lismore*, p. 136). Canice Mooney ('St Cathaldus of Taranto' in John Ryan [ed.], *Irish monks in the golden age* [Dublin, 1963], pp 86–99 at p. 97), proposed 'Ráth Chua', the name of an old fort, near Shanrahan.   11 *AS* Maii ii, 569–78.   12 Ibid., 577.   13 John O'Hanlon, *The Lives of the Irish saints*, 10 vols (Dublin, 1875–1903), v, pp 185–207.

critical approach to Cataldo's record, were, as might be expected, slow to discuss the Irish names contained within it.[14] Blandamura arranged to have a series of questions in Latin concerning the names of the saint's parents and his place of birth submitted to the Catholic bishop of Waterford and Lismore, Richard A. Sheehan, in 1913.[15] Sheehan's detailed reply, also in Latin, included the comment that there were no memorials of the saint in the area about Lismore.[16] Since then, Annibale Ilari, in the course of his thorough investigation of the sources bearing on the saint, has also given brief consideration to the Irish topography of Cataldo's Life, of which, however, only Lismore made any sense to him.[17]

Blandamura and most other Italian commentators, who by now have created an extensive literature on the saint and his church in Taranto, have tended to accept the view that Cataldo was of Irish origin.[18] Recently, however, the saint's name has become the focus of critical commentary, spearheaded by Alberto Carducci, and the question of his origins has become a source of controversy.[19] Carducci's discussion of the name Cataldo, carried out with the assistance of Maria Giovanna Arcamone of Pisa University, led to the conclusion that it was Lombardian in origin, the original being the Germanic form *Gaidoaldus*.[20]

Even if the saint's name were Lombardian in origin, the question would still remain as to where the Irish element of the saint's Life originated. The earliest manuscript evidence for the assumption that Cataldo was Irish dates

---

14 For an account of the historiography of Taranto and its saint, see Cosimo Damiano Fonseca, 'Introduzione alla storiografia ecclesiastica tarantina' in idem (ed.), *La chiesa di Taranto*, i, *Dalle origini all'avvento dei Normanni: Studi storici in onore di Mons. Guglielmo Motolese arcivescovo di Taranto nel 25 anniversario del suo episcopato* (Lecce, 1977), pp 5–20. 15 Fonseca, 'Introduzione', pp 17–20. Cf. Giuseppe Blandamura, *Un cimelio del secolo VII esistente nel Duomo di Taranto* (Lecce, 1917). 16 Fonseca, 'Introduzione', p. 20: *Memoriae de Sto. Cataldo apud Lismore non videntur haberi*. 17 Ilari, 'L'agiografia di S. Cataldo', pp 119–24 at p. 123; *di tutti questi elementi ... no sono riuscito ad identificare nemmeno la topografia della Lismore cataldiana*. 18 See Fonseca, 'Introduzione'; Francesco Lanzoni, *Le diocesi d'Italia dalle origini al principio del sec. VII (a. 601)*, Studi e Testi 35 (Faenza, 1927), pp 79, 315–6; Anselmo M. Tommasini, *Irish saints in Italy* (London, 1937), pp 401–32; Giuseppe Carata, 'Cataldo', *Bibliotheca sanctorum* iii (Rome, 1962), cols 950–52. 19 Alberto Carducci, 'La cripta e la leggenda agiografica di San Cataldo' in C. D'Angela (ed.), *La cripta della cattedrale di Taranto* (Taranto, 1986), pp 83–98; idem, 'L'agiografia tarantina' in C.D. Fonseca (ed.), *La chiesa e le chiese* (Taranto, 1992), pp 177–227. 20 Alberto Carducci, 'Sull'origine longobarda del nome Cataldo', *Annali di Storia-Facoltà di Lettere e Filosofia, Università degli Studi di Lecce*, i (1980), 7–15; idem, 'L'agiografia tarantina', p. 196; Maria Giovanna Arcamone, 'Nomi medievali di santi e demoni' in *Santi e demoni nell'alto medioevo occidentale*, Settimane di studio del centro Italiano di studi sull'alto medioevo 36, 2 vols (Spoleto, 1989), ii, pp 759–82 at pp 767–8; eadem, 'L'onomastica personale nell'Europa occidentale fra IV e VIII secolo' in *Morfologie sociali e culturali in Europa fra tarda antichità e alto medioevo*, Settimane di studio del centro Italiano di studi sull'alto medioevo 45 (Spoleto, 1998), pp 585–617 at p. 615n.

to the first half of the fourteenth century, when a legendary – as yet unpublished – compiled by the Dominican Pietro Calò (hereafter PC) included a brief account of the saint, based on a previous *historia*.[21] This was followed by a similar account, apparently based on Calò, in the previously mentioned work of Pietro Natali (hereafter PN), compiled between 1369 and 1372.[22] Giovanni Iuvene (hereafter GI) published a longer version of the saint's Life in 1589, which claimed that Cataldo's brother, Donatus, was elected first bishop of Lecce in southern Italy.[23] Several Office Lives of the saint are also extant, of which two are considered here: one, a manuscript breviary of *c.*1450 (hereafter BET), was formerly kept in Taranto; the other, published in Rome in 1607 (hereafter OC), was republished, as already stated, with annotations by John Colgan.[24] A longer Life, which includes the previously mentioned extensive account of the saint's time in Ireland, was drawn up by Bartolomeo Morone (hereafter BM) in 1614 from what he described as 'most ancient manuscript codices' of the church in Taranto, and also republished with annotations by John Colgan in 1645.[25]

Of modern scholars working on the Irish tradition – if we except the brief comments on the saint's Irish backgound by James F. Kenney, Felim Ó Briain, Canice Mooney, Simon Young and Aidan Breen – only John Hennig has re-assessed in any detail the local element of the Life.[26] Drawing attention to the description of the saint as an archbishop to whom twelve other bishops were subject, a claim preserved in most versions of the Life, Hennig took this to reflect ecclesiastical conditions in Ireland in the period between 1100 and 1150. As is well known, the Irish diocesan system was first introduced on a national scale during this period, following a model devised for

---

21 Ilari, 'L'agiografia di S. Cataldo', pp 171–6; cf. Albert Poncelet, 'Le légendier de Pierre Calo', *Analecta Bollandiana*, 29 (1910), 5–116.   22 See Colgan, *Acta sanctorum*, p. 544. 23 Giovanni Iuvene, *De antiquitate et varia Tarentinorum fortuna libri octo* (Naples, 1589), pp 201–6 at pp 205–6; cf. Ferdinando Ughelli, *Italia sacra sive de episcopis Italiae, et insularum adjacentium*, 2nd ed., ed. N. Coleti, 10 vols (Venice, 1721), viii, col. 124; Colgan, *Acta sanctorum*, pp 547, 556 (13); Lanigan, *An ecclesiastical history*, iii, p. 128.   24 Colgan, *Acta sanctorum*, pp 556–9; Ilari, 'L'agiografia di S. Cataldo', pp 177–86.   25 Colgan, *Acta sanctorum*, pp 545–56. Drawing on this work and on a volume published by Morone's brother Bonaventura, John Lynch gave an extended account of Cataldo in his *De praesulibus Hiberniae* (J.F. O'Doherty [ed.], *De praesulibus Hiberniae … authore Joanne Linchaeo*, 2 vols [Dublin, 1944], ii, pp 125–8).   26 James F. Kenney, *The sources for the early history of Ireland: ecclesiastical: an introduction and guide* (New York, 1929; repr. Dublin, 1979), p. 185; Felim Ó Briain, 'Catalde', *Dictionnaire d'histoire et de géographie ecclesiastique*, xi (Paris, 1949), cols 1490–1; Mooney, 'St Cathaldus of Taranto'; Simon Young, 'On the Irish *peregrini* in Italy', *Peritia*, 16 (2002), 250–55 at 253; Aidan Breen, 'Cathaldus' in J. McGuire and J. Quinn (eds), *Dictionary of Irish biography from the earliest times to the year 2002*, 9 vols (Cambridge, 2009), ii, p. 428; John Hennig, 'Cataldus Rachau. A study in the early history of diocesan episcopacy in Ireland', *Medieval Studies*, 8 (1946), 217–44. Kenney, Ó Briain, and Young placed little faith in the tradition that Cataldo was Irish, whereas Mooney saw no reason to doubt it.

the English church which favoured the establishment of two metropolitan centres, each with its own archbishop, and twelve suffragan bishops subject to him.[27] Using evidence of this kind, Hennig concluded that the saint's Life, as first published by Morone, is datable to the twelfth century: more precisely, to shortly after 1151 when, as is known from other sources, the final translation of the saint's remains took place in Taranto.[28]

To set the scene for my own discussion of the Irish element in the Life, the relevant onomastic content is here set out in accordance with the above-mentioned sources, arranged chronologically:

PLACE OF BIRTH: *Catandus* (PC); *Cataldus* (PN); *Rachau ... Numenie in partibus* (BET); *oppido Numeniae Cataldo* (GI); *oppido Numeniae Catando* (OC); *Rachau ... in Momoniae / Cathandum* (BM).

PARENTS: *Ehuca ... Athle* (PC); *Eucho ... Athena* (PN/GI); *Euchu ... Aclena* (BET); *Euchus ... Achlena siue Athena* (BM).

BIRTH FORETOLD BY: *Dichus magus* (PC); *a mago Dicho* (BET); *vir eximiae virtutis ... Dichus* (GI); *sapientissimus vir nomine Dichus* (BM).

EDUCATED AT: *Losmeniam civitatem ... Lesmoniam* (PC); *Lesmoriam civitatem* (BET); *Lesmoria* (OC/BM).

TAUGHT IN: *Lesmoria vel Catandum ... breuissimum ... spatium interiectum* (BM).

FALSELY ACCUSED BY CHIEFTAIN NAMED: *Malatridus* (PC); *Meltridis* (GI/BM/OC).

APPOINTED BISHOP / ARCHBISHOP OF: *Rachau Archiepiscopo* (GI); *ducatus Meltridis / Rachuensis Ecclesiae Praesul ab urbe Rachau, cognomen accepit* (BM); *Rachau* (OC).

The orthography of the Irish names cited in the text, although based on a very limited number of items, supports the view taken by Hennig. The spelling of *Eucho / Euchus*, the saint's father; *Dichus*, the wise man; and *Lesmoria*, the monastery in which the saint received his ecclesiastical formation, reflects Middle Irish orthography. After 1200, the two personal names would normally have been written as *Eacha* and *Díocha* and the placename as *Lios Mór*.[29] Moreover, as John Hennig pointed out, the spelling *Numenia* (recte *Mumenia*) / *Momonia* for the name of the province of Munster is

---

27 Aubrey Gwynn, *The twelfth-century reform*, A History of Irish Catholicism 2 (Dublin, 1968), pp 30–1. **28** Hennig, 'Cataldus Rachau', p. 243; idem, 'A note on the traditions of St. Frediano and St. Silao of Lucca', *Medieval Studies*, 13 (1951), 234–42 at 235. Patrick S. Dinneen and David Comyn (ed. and trans.), *Foras feasa ar Éirinn: the history of Ireland by Geoffrey Keating D.D.*, 4 vols, ITS 4, 8, 9, 15 (London, 1902–14), iii, pp 298–307. John MacErlean, 'Synod of Ráith Breasail: boundaries of the dioceses of Ireland', *Archivium Hibernicum*, 3 (1914), 1–33. **29** All attestations of the placename prior to 1200 in the *Annals of Inisfallen*, in nominative and accusative positions, read *Les Mór*.

common in twelfth-century Irish hagiography.[30] The spellings of the name of
the chieftain who conspired against the saint, *Malatridus / Meltridis*, while
undatable in their corrupt forms, are nonetheless in harmony with the topographical context in which they appear. Their Irish equivalent, Máel
Ochtraig, was the name of a king of the Déise who died in 645 (*AI*). Lismore
was located in this territory and, according to the traditions surrounding
Mochuta, patron of the monastery, its site was granted by a king of the Déise
of this name.[31] The internal consistency of the Irish names in the text implies,
therefore, a reasonably good acquaintance on the part of their author with
Ireland, and especially with that part of it in which Cataldo is said to have
been born and brought up.

On the face of it, a Tarantese author is unlikely to have been entirely
responsible for a text that includes names of Irish persons and places, which
would surely have seemed very strange if not barbaric to him. Accordingly,
John Hennig joined Henschen, the Bollandist editor of the text, in assuming
that a *vagus Hibernus*, who found himself in Taranto, was the likely author.[32]
Alberto Carducci has adopted a different approach. Building on the tradition
that Cataldo initially arrived in Taranto on his way back from Palestine,
Carducci has argued that the initial impetus for the 'hibernicization' of
Taranto's saint came from Bethlehem in Palestine, where *Catald'*, an abbre-
viated Latin form of the name of the saint is inscribed on a twelfth-century
enamelled painting honouring the saint in the church of the Nativity.[33]
According to Carducci, this form of the name might have been interpreted by
crusaders – contingents of whom from all over Christian Europe, including
Ireland, would have been present in Palestine at that time – as a version of
the Irish name Cathal, an opinion that subsequently found its way back to
Taranto. Carducci gives it to be understood that a 'simple suspicion' concerning the origin of the name, when brought back to Italy, was sufficient to
induce the clerical authorities in Taranto, perhaps influenced by the then current image of Ireland as an *insula sanctorum*, to invent an Irish origin for the
saint, piecing the details of his early life together from fragments of 'Celtic
hagiographical legends that were circulating in Italy'.[34]

Carducci's argument is, however, scarcely convincing; contingents of cru-
sading soldiers, including those from Ireland, are unlikely to have shown
much interest, either in onomastic investigation or in the question of a saint's

---

30 Hennig, 'Cataldus Rachau', p. 227; cf. *VSHP* ii, p. 336.   31 *BNÉ* i, p. 306 §26.
32 *AS* Maii ii, 577; Hennig, 'Cataldus Rachau', p. 243: 'a *vagus Hibernus* such as
Muiredach Mac Robartaig'.   33 Carducci, 'L'agiografia tarantina', p. 195.   34 Ibid., pp
195–6: *la biografia di san Cataldo ... è in realtà costituita da più frammenti, a volte ampi, di
alcune leggende agiographiche celtiche ... conservando gli stessi nomi ed avvenimenti.*
Interestingly, as far back as 1937, Patrick Power had suggested that Cataldo's Lives 'were
based on a Life of Carthage conflated with other material – some of it from the Life of
Declan': *Waterford and Lismore*, p. 218.

origins. Also, if we except the early seventh-century Life of Columbanus of Bobbio and the metrical Life of Brigid composed about 850 by Donatus of Fiesole, neither of which contains the names that occur in Cataldo's Life, there is no evidence for the circulation of Irish hagiographical texts in Italy by the middle of the twelfth century.[35]

As far as Carducci is concerned, further investigation of the saint's supposed Irish associations has now become superfluous, as it would serve only to illuminate the emergence on a local Irish level of the legendary elements that later, through borrowing, became part of the Tarantese history of the saint.[36] As against this view, though the Irish material in Cataldo's record consists of names of places and persons found frequently enough in Irish hagiographical texts, nowhere else is it to be found in a form that could have been readily borrowed in Taranto, either as a set piece or as a selection of such pieces. On the contrary, the section of Cataldo's Life that deals with his time in Ireland is not only unique to the saint; the manner in which it is pieced together presupposes some form of direct Irish influence on this part of the text.

Is nothing to be salvaged, then, from the explanations put forward by previous commentators? The view that the detail of Cataldo's origins was based in full or in part on information received from an Irish source, which is common to all previous assessments, is beyond question. Moreover, the Life composed shortly after 1100 for the Irishman Fursa, patron of the abbey of Lagny near Paris, a mere fifty or so years before the date now generally accepted for the composition of the Life of Cataldo, provides a pertinent basis for comparison.[37] Commissioned by the then abbot of Lagny, and written by a monk bearing a non-Irish name, Fursa's Life, like that of Cataldo, provides detailed information on the saint's Irish background, replete with onomastic detail, which, on examination, can be shown to have supplied by passing clerics from the west of Ireland, probably belonging to the powerful ecclesiastical family of Uí Dhubhthaigh.[38] This family provided bishops to several western sees from 1111, when Irish dioceses were first established, and this could well have given grounds for journeys to Rome during the years that led up to the establishment of dioceses.

35 Excepting the dossiers of Columbanus and Brigid, neither Kenney (*Sources*, pp 808–10) nor Plummer (*Miscellanea hagiographica Hibernica*, Subsidia Hagiographica 15 [Brussels, 1925], pp 234–54) cites an Italian manuscript earlier than 1200 that contains the Life of an Irish saint. This also holds true for Louis Gougaud, *Les saints irlandais hors d'Irlande* (Louvain and Oxford, 1936). The text of the *Navigatio Sancti Brendani abbatis*, of which a few pre-1200 Italian copies survive, likewise lacks the names contained in Cataldo's Life (Glyn S. Burgess and Clara Strijbosch, *The legend of St Brendan: a critical bibliography* [Dublin, 2000], p. 19). 36 Carducci, 'L'agiografia tarantina', p. 196. 37 Colgan, *Acta sanctorum*, pp 75–88. 38 Pádraig Ó Riain, 'Sanctity and politics in Connacht *c.*1100: the case of St Fursa', *CMCS*, 17 (1989), 1–14.

In Cataldo's case, no such considerations can be entertained. As far as can be judged, Taranto did not lie on an Irish pilgrim route. The assumption of contact, direct or indirect, between an Irish informant and the author of Cataldo's Life remains, nevertheless, the only credible means of explaining the detail of the saint's birth and upbringing. As it happens, a plausible case can be made for contact of this kind, involving high prelates of both Irish and Tarantese origin.

In the year 1138, Gerald, a man especially devoted to Cataldo, and later responsible for the final translation of the saint's remains in 1151, was elected archbishop of Taranto.[39] According to Ughelli, Gerald's predecessor Philip, demoted 'at a time of schism', made his way to Clairvaux in France, where he received the Cistercian habit from the hands of St Bernard. Twelve years later, in 1150, Philip was elected prior of Clairvaux, a position he retained until 1156.[40] Clearly a very highly regarded member of the community, Philip of Taranto would thus have been in Clairvaux when the abbey was twice visited by St Malachy, who resigned the archbishopric of Armagh in 1137 to look after the affairs of the diocese of Down. As is well documented, the Irish prelate's second visit, in 1148, led to his death there in the arms of St Bernard.[41] His first visit, in 1140, was, however, followed by the first Cistercian foundation in Ireland, at Mellifont in 1141–2, under an abbot named Christian Úa Conairche, whom Malachy had left behind in Clairvaux with some other companions to be trained in the rule.[42]

The significance of these circumstances is the opportunity they provided of close contact between two Irish prelates and a prominent Tarantese member of the community in Clairvaux. More importantly, both Irishmen had a close association with Lismore. As the Life written by Bernard for Malachy makes clear, the Irishman must have had a thorough knowledge of the area about Lismore, having studied there, exactly as Cataldo is said to have done, and having later chosen to spend some time in exile there.[43] It can be assumed, therefore, that Malachy would also have been familiar with Lismore's history, including perhaps the tradition that Mochuta had received the site of the monastery from a king named Máel Ochtraig.[44] As for Christian Úa Conairche, he accompanied the papal legate, Cardinal Paparo, to Ireland in 1151, having already been consecrated bishop of Lismore at Clairvaux, before also being appointed papal legate on the cardinal's departure.[45]

As can be seen from the appeal made to his witness by the author of *Libellus de ortu sancti Cuthberti*, who turned Cuthbert of Lindisfarne and

39 *AS* Maii ii, 571 §2; Ughelli, *Italia sacra*, viii, cols 130–1.   40 Ughelli, *Italia sacra*, viii, col. 130.   41 Hugh J. Lawlor, *St Bernard of Clairvaux's Life of St Malachy of Armagh*, Translations of Christian Literature, ser. 5 (London, 1920), pp 117–30; Pierre-Yves Emery (ed.), *Bernard de Clairvaux: Oeuvres complètes XXXI, Éloge de la Nouvelle Chevalerie; Vie de Saint Malachie*, SC 367 (Paris, 1990), pp 354–76.   42 Aubrey Gwynn and R. Neville Hadcock, *Medieval religious houses: Ireland* (London, 1970), pp 116, 139–40.

Durham into an Irishman, Malachy had an interest in tracing an Irish back-ground for saints that had otherwise no connection with the country.[46] Given these circumstances, therefore, involving the combined presence in Clairvaux of Malachy, Christian and an ex-archbishop of Taranto, we may easily imag-ine a situation in which, on being told of the Irish-sounding name of the patron of Taranto, provision was made by one or other of the Irishmen of all the background information, onomastic and otherwise, needed to fill in the story of Cataldo's birth and upbringing. Philip could then have transmitted the material to his earlier clerical colleagues in Taranto, to be incorporated into the new Life of the saint compiled on the occasion of the translation of the relics in 1151.

This is not to say that the authorities in Taranto might not already have propagated the view that Cataldo was of Irish origin – perhaps, as suggested by Carducci, under the influence of the medieval image of Ireland as an *insula sanctorum*; but the role played, either by Malachy or by Christian, would have been to provide convincing local Irish onomastic detail. So convincing was this information that, down to our own time, it has shaped the story of Taranto's patron saint, who may have arrived from no further away than northern Italy.

43 Lawlor, *St Bernard of Clairvaux's Life of St Malachy*, pp 18–24; Emery, *Vie de Saint Malachie*, pp 202–10.   44 *VSHP* i, p. 195 §57.   45 Gwynn and Hadcock, *Medieval religious houses: Ireland*, p. 91.   46 James Raine, *Miscellanea biographica*, Surtees Society 8 (1838), pp 63–87 at p. 64; Richard Sharpe, 'Were there Irish annals known to a twelfth-century Northumbrian writer?', *Peritia*, 2 (1983), 137–9 at 139.

Maidenhood, mourning, and Old English *meowle*

LISI OLIVER† AND ANDREA ADOLPH

An arguable position for Anglo-Saxon literature is that only three epic poems have survived the ravages of manuscript history: the secular *Beowulf* and the religious *Exodus* and *Judith*. The first two are united by the striking final image of a woman standing alone at the seashore. The woman in both poems is designated by the rare term *meowle*. The following discussion looks at all attestations of this word (one in a gloss and eleven in poetry), examining the range of meanings in both literary and historical contexts. We then propose semantic developments that account for the variety of uses specific to Old English, and particularly for the women who appear at the conclusions to *Beowulf* and *Exodus*.

In the *Thesaurus of Old English*, *meowle* is the only term to appear both under 'female person, woman' (02.03.01.02) and under 'unmarried state: a maiden, a virgin' (12.09.03). The former category lists, in addition to *meowle*, *cwēn* (with 100+ attestations), *cwene* (100+), *fǣmne* (100+), *frēo* (1), *frōwe* (1), *ides* (66) *wīf* (100+) and *wīfmann* (100+). The latter category lists *fǣmnhādes mann* (1),[1] *mǣgden* (52), *mǣgdenmann* (2), *mǣgþ* (100+), *mǣgþmann* (1).[2]

Etymology weighs in on the side of the second meaning. The term derives from a Proto-Germanic (henceforth PG) stem **maȝ-w-ī*, a feminine form with –ī suffix serving as counterpart to PG **maȝ-u-* 'boy, young man', cognate to Old English (henceforth OE) *magu*, m. 'son'. To the feminine stem is

During Máire's year at Harvard, she was a central figure in my quest to understand the intricacies of Old Irish. Two reasons guide my offering of this paper to Máire's *Festschrift*. First, this serves as a substantial revision of a project I had given to a graduate student, Andrea Adolph, and her research remains crucial to this essay. Any tribute to Máire would be incomplete without an acknowledgement that teaching remains one of the primary goals in our profession. Second, this work centres around the perception of women in early medieval England, in honour of Máire's brilliant studies on how the hagiography of Irish women saints expands our views of early medieval society. [LO]

We would like to thank Robbye Kees, David Porter and especially Katherine Willis for comments on previous drafts of this paper. All translations are our own except where otherwise noted.

1 The Brussels, RL 1650 manuscript of Aldhelm's *Prosa de virginitate* uses the compound *fǣmhadlices* twice: (1503) *virginalis materie* is glossed by *fǣmhadlices anwurce*, and (2240) *propter virginale propositum initium gradum* is glossed by *for femhadlicum ingehedum*. (See Richard L. Venezky and Antonette de Paolo Healey [eds], *A microfiche concordance to Old English* [Newark, 1980], s.v.).   2 For synonyms, see Jane Roberts and Christian Kay (eds), *A thesaurus of Old English*, 2 vols (London, 1995), i, pp 38, 593. For quantities, see Venezky and Healey, *Microfiche concordance*, s.v.

added an Indo-European diminutive suffix *-elo/-olo giving a doubly marked sense of 'young girl'. This formation can be dated back to Common Germanic: the Gothic equivalent is *mawilō* and the Old Icelandic *meyla / meyja*. In neither language, to the extent of our knowledge, does this meaning drift from the sense 'female child'.

The Old English umlaut of **aw** before a high front vowel is first **ew**, which can break to **eow** before the liquid l; apparently after the syncope of the middle glide the diphthong is lengthened to the attested **ēow**.[3] Hilding Bäck points out that 'the original sense is not recorded in OE, small girls not being treated in the poetry of that time'.[4] Indeed, the earliest recorded uses of the term in Old English demonstrate a shift in nuance from 'young female' to the associated concept of virginity.

In two manuscripts of Aldhelm's prose *De virginitate*, Brussels, RL 1650 and Oxford, Digby 146, *iuuencula pulcherrima* is immediately echoed by *uirgincula* ('young maiden'), which unambiguously supports the meaning of virginity or chastity. It is glossed by Old English *aenlicoste meowle* 'most incomparable *meowle*', but additionally by *scilcen / scylcen* and *faemne* '(bad) woman, woman' (both of which seem odd choices for *uirgincula*).[5]

If virginity plays an important part in the semantic makeup of *meowle* in Old English, we would expect this term to be applied to the Virgin herself. And indeed, two of the eleven non-glossarial instances refer to Mary.[6] *Christ II* begins with the birth of Christ and this testament to both Mary's holiness and her virginity:

> ... se ælmihtige
> accenned wearð þurh clænne had,
> siþþan he Marian, mægða weolman,
> mærre meowlan, mundheals geceas.[7]

3 See discussion in Hilding Bäck, *The synonyms for child, boy, girl in Old English: an etymological-semasiological investigation* (Lund, 1967), p. 227; also notes toward this etymology in Karl Brunner, *Altenglische Grammatik* (Tübingen, 1965), §159 n. 3, §213 n. 1; and Eduard Sievers, *An Old English grammar*, trans. Albert Cook (Boston, 1903), §73 n. 1, §174.3. Hildegard Stibbe, *'Herr' und 'Frau' und verwandte Begriffe in ihren altenglischen Äquivalenten* (Heidelberg, 1935), pp 93–4, without giving the morphological formation, similarly cites as the base form the root that gives Gothic *magaþs* and Old English *mæged* and *mægden*. See also Ferdinand Holthausen (ed.), *Altenglisches etymologisches Wörterbuch* (Heidelberg, 1974), s.v.   4 Bäck, *Synonyms*, p. 226.   5 Scott Gwara (ed.), *Aldhelmi Malmesbiriensis Prosa de virginitate cum glosa latina atque anglosaxonica*, CCSL 124, 124A, 2 vols (Turnhout, 2001), ii, p. 312, l. 61.   6 David Porter (pers. comm.) has suggested that Anglo-Saxon poetic practice dictates that one should not discount the similarities in consonantal frame between *Maria* and *meowle*, both of which have the form **m – liquid consonant**. 'Latin-English or Latin-Latin alliterating pairs were used as a general Latin-learning strategy, a bad strategy, since God wasn't thoughtful enough to provide alliterating semantic equivalents across language boundaries. The point is that it was a natural way of thinking for the Anglo-Saxons ... [T]here are many examples, starting with the Leiden Glossary: adtentus : attonitus'.   7 George Philip Krapp and Elliot van Kirk

... the Almighty was born in a state of purity, as he chose the protection of Mary, flower of women, illustrious *meowle*.

According to Mary Clayton, 'There was ... some controversy over Mary's virginity *in partu* and *post partum* as early as the third century, and insistence on her virginity became an important aspect within later Marian doctrine'.[8] Though Mary is present only in this brief phrase in *Christ II*, the importance of her virginity is emphasized both symbolically and literally: she is simultaneously a blossom and a virgin. The appositive phrases *mægða weolman* and *mærre meowlan* both glorify Mary and emphasise her holy chastity; the near-rhyme of *weolman* and *meowlan* intensifies the sense that the *meowle* represents the purity of a blossoming flower. (This anticipates the commonplace trope in medieval love poetry that associates flowers and virginity: to pluck the flower is to take the woman's virginity.)

In *Judgement day II*, the Virgin appears as a *meowle* at the end of the poem following the carnage of Doomsday, leading a throng of virgins in a procession to heaven:

> Þær þæra hwittra hwyrfð mædenheap,
> blostmum behangen, beorhtost weoreda,
> þe ealle læt ænlicu godes drut,
> seo frowe þe us frean acende,
> metod on moldan, meowle se clæne.
> Þæt is Maria, mædena selast ...[9]

There will wander a virgin troop of the pure, hung about with blossoms, brightest of companies, and God's excellent beloved will lead them, the woman who for us gave birth to the Lord, the Ruler on earth: the pure *meowle*. That is Mary, best of maidens ...

Mary is again linked to the freshness of blossoming flowers. Like the *Christ II* poet, the composer of *Judgement day II* uses two appositives in his description of Maria – *meowle se clæne* and *mædena selast* – both of which emphasise her chastity. The alliterating *meowle* both introduces *Maria* and links her to her son, our *Metod*. It is precisely this connection through Mary from virgin birth to (eventually) mourning mother which allows us to extend the connotations of *meowle*.

Mary Clayton's seminal study, *The cult of the Virgin Mary in Anglo-Saxon England*, examines the pervasiveness of Marian worship in early medieval

---

Dobbie (eds), *The Exeter Book* (New York, 1936), p. 15, ll 443–6.   8 Mary Clayton, *The cult of the Virgin Mary in Anglo-Saxon England* (Cambridge and New York, 1990), pp 5–6.   9 Elliott van Kirk Dobbie (ed.), *The Anglo-Saxon minor poems* (New York, 1942), p. 66, ll 290–5

England: to her offices are written, churches and nunneries are dedicated, and antiphons are sung. But the connection central to this argument is the relationship between Mary's conception of Christ and her role as mourning mother at the Crucifixion. This association is particularly clear in the carvings on the Ruthwell Cross. As Clayton points out:

> The placing of the Annunciation immediately above the Crucifixion panel is significant and is most probably intended to point to the coincidence of date of the two events, Christ's conception and death: 25 March was regarded as the 'historical' date of the Crucifixion, which was celebrated liturgically on the movable feast of Easter.[10]

In later Anglo-Saxon plastic arts, the Virgin is depicted in the Crucifixion either as witness or – as the cult of the Virgin progresses in early medieval England – as mourner:

> In some of the Crucifixion images she shares emotionally in the plight of her son on the cross, in a way which is new for the Middle Ages. She is celebrated to a much greater degree in her own right than was the case in the earlier period ... There are suggestions, too, of a more deliberate participation of the Virgin in the scheme of redemption.[11]

A good example of Mary as intercessor is provided in *Vercelli homily* xv:

> Then our beloved St Mary, Christ's mother, will see the wretched and sorrowful and sad troop and she will arise with a weeping voice and will fall to Christ's knees and to his feet and will say thus: 'My Lord, the Saviour Christ, you humbled yourself in order to dwell in my womb; never allow the devils to have power of such a great company of your handiwork'.[12]

This evolution in the roles of Mary during the Anglo-Saxon period may help elucidate uses of *meowle* which diverge from its etymological sense of 'virginal' to a sense of 'mourning mother'. The first example to be considered occurs in *The fortunes of men*. The beginning of this poem contains one of the darkest listings of unhappy fates in the English poetic repertoire. In a child's youth, *fergað swa ond feþað fæder ond modor, giefað ond gierwaþ* 'the father and mother foster and feed him; they give to him and adorn him' (ll 7–8).[13] And yet this early hope is often dashed, and a horrid death renders the mother's

---

10 Clayton, *Cult of the Virgin*, p. 150.   11 Ibid., p. 178.   12 From Paul E. Szarmach (ed.), *The Vercelli homilies* (Toronto, 1981), pp 37–8; cited in Clayton, *Cult of the Virgin*, p. 254.   13 Krapp, *Exeter Book*, p. 154.

mourning particularly poignant: *reoteð meowle, seo hyre bearn gesihþ brondas þeccan* 'a *meowle* weeps, who sees flames cover her child' (ll 42–3).[14] For S.A.J. Bradley, this death of a son by fire and the mother's response to it add a 'note of human compassion, mitigating the sometimes over-austere and world-contemptuous doctrines of AS Christian poetry'.[15] Within a Christian context, the mother of this poem recalls the Virgin Mary, whose own loss would be paradigmatic in Christian cultures. Though a religious follower might have occasion for joy at the death of Christ, which ensures life eternal for the true believer, a mother would have cause to mourn for the death of the human child, as depicted in later Anglo-Saxon iconography. Dolores Frese has commented that 'the most typical lamentory predicament of an Old English woman tends to involve the negative fate of a male child'.[16] But only *The fortunes of men* directly depicts a *meowle* lamenting for her son: the reason for this could lie in the generality of the reference. This is not a specific mother, but a woman representing the motherhood of all mankind. She is one of three *meowle*s that illustrate this role.

All three of the epics mentioned in our introduction – *Beowulf*, *Exodus* and *Judith* – have at least one instantiation of a *meowle* without virginal over-tones. Two echo *The fortunes of men* in depicting a *meowle* lamenting her off-spring or race; both appear in *Beowulf*, the first foreshadowing the second. In addition to the mourning woman who appears at the end, we also find an ear-lier *io-meowle*. This compound appears only in *Beowulf*, in the retelling of the Swedish dynastic wars, direly described by the herald who announces the death of Beowulf:

> Nē ic te Swēoðēode   sibbe oððe trēowe
> wihte ne wēne,   ac wæs wīde cūð,
> þætte Ongenðio   ealdre besnyðede
> Hæðcen Hrēþling   wið Hrefnawudu,
> þā for onmēdlan   ærest gesōhton
> Gēata lēode   Gūð-Scilfingas.
> Sōna him se frōda   fæder Ōhtheres,
> eald and egesfull   ondslyht āgeaf,
> ābrēot brimwīsan,   brȳd āhredde,
> gomela iomēowlan   golde berofene,
> Onelan mōdor   ond Ōhtheres;
> ond ðā folgode feorhgenīðlan,
> oð ðæt hī oðēodon   earfoðlīce
> in Hrefnesholt   hlāfordlēase.[17]

14 Ibid., p. 155. 15 Sid A.J. Bradley (ed. and trans.), *Anglo-Saxon poetry* (London, 1982), p. 341. 16 Dolores Warwick Frese, '*Wulf and Eadwacer*: the adulterous woman reconsid-ered', *Notre Dame English Journal*, 15, i (Winter 1983), 1–22 at 8. 17 Robert D. Fulk,

Nor do I expect the least friendship or loyalty from the Swedish nation; for it was widely known that Ongentheow took the life of Hæthcyn Hrethling near Ravenswood when the men of the Geats in their arrogance first went looking for the War-Scylfings. Straight away, Ohthere's wise father, old and terrible, struck a return blow, cut down the sea-king; he rescued the aged woman (*iomēowlan*), his wife of former years, the mother of Onela and Ohthere, stripped of gold; and then he pursued his mortal enemies until with difficulty they escaped into Ravenswood without their lord.[18]

For the meaning of *iomeowle*, L.L. Schücking offers 'eine Jungfrau, die vor alters lebte' ('a virgin, who lived long ago'), but this clearly cannot work for the wife of Ongenþeow. Better is Bäck's suggestion of 'old woman, wife';[19] we would add to this a connotative sense of 'mourning'. Although we know no more about this woman than what is mentioned here, we can piece together the story of her family from scattered references elsewhere in *Beowulf* and in various Scandinavian sources.[20]

Following the death of Hreðel, king of the Geats, a war of succession broke out between the Geats (family of Hreðel) and the Swedes (family of Ongenþeow). In an invasion by the Geats, Ongenþeow's wife was abducted. In a return raid, Ongenþeow regained his wife, but in a retaliatory battle at Ravenswood, he was killed by the Geatish warriors Eofor and Wulf. His son Ōhthere succeeded to the kingship. One legend has it that Ōhthere fell in a battle in Vendel, and his body was torn apart by carrion crows, giving him the name *Vendel-krāka* 'Vendel-crow'.[21] After Ōhthere's grisly end, his brother Onela seized the throne, forcing Ōhthere's sons Ēanmund and Ēadgils to flee to the Geatish realm. Eanmund was slain during the course of an invasion by Onela. Later Ēadgils mustered the aid of a Geatish force (including our eponymous hero in the Old English telling) against Onela, who himself was killed. Ēadgils ascended the throne.

To briefly sum up, then, our *iomeowle's* family history:

- she herself is abducted and robbed of her gold.
- although her husband rescues her, he is killed in a retaliatory action.

Robert E. Bjork and John D. Niles (eds), *Klaeber's Beowulf and the fight at Finnsburg* (4th ed.: Toronto, 2008), pp 99–100, ll 2922–35.   **18** Translation from Michael Swanton (ed. and trans.), *Beowulf* (Manchester, 1978), p. 179. Insertion in italics ours.   **19** See discussion in Bäck, *Synonyms*, p. 228, where Schücking's argument is also presented; also Tauno F. Mustanoja, 'The unnamed woman's song of mourning over Beowulf and the tradition of ritual lamentation', *Neuphilologische Mitteilungen*, 68 (1967), 1–27 at 3.   **20** See Raymond W.C. Chambers, *Beowulf: an introduction* (3rd ed.: Cambridge, 1921, 1959), p. 624, references to Onela and Ongenþeow; also Klaeber, *Beowulf and the fight at Finnsburg*, pp xlii–xlv and Fulk et al., *Klaeber's Beowulf*, p. lix.   **21** Other traditions associate this dismemberment with Ongenþeow. Chambers, *Beowulf*, p. 624.

- her eldest son is torn apart by carrion crows.
- her elder grandson is killed by her younger son.
- her younger son is killed by her younger grandson.

The Swedish dynasty begins with this family, but it is a succession baptized in the blood of kinsmen. Ongenþeow's wife is the matriarch of a family doomed from the start. Her role is not dissimilar to, simply more limited than, that of the *meowle* described in *The fortunes of men*. While the latter serves as a mother mourning for all mankind that suffers tragedy, Ongenþeow can be seen as the unfortunate mother who has cause to lament the house she herself has founded. Her mourning is predictive: she both allegorically and terminologically prefigures the other *meowle* who will shortly lament the death of the leader of her own people and the disintegration of the kingdom.

Much ink has been spilled over the enigmatic *meowle* who appears at the end of *Beowulf* (l. 3150). The text of BL Cotton MS Vitellius A. xv is both torn and difficult to read at points within this passage, so all interpretations are necessarily hypotheses. Julius Zupitza claims that for the now-illegible word preceding *meowle*, a later hand 'has freshened up at. But I think what the late scribe took to be **t** was originally the upper part of **g**; then follow traces of two letters which justify us I think in reading **eo**, so that we get *geo-meowle*'. This is the interpretation followed by Klaeber.[22] The previous use of *io-meowle* might argue for the reading of *geo-meowle* here. This argument is weakened, however, by the differences in spelling: although we might not be surprised by a difference of *io-* and *geo-* between the first and second scribes, both these sections are written by the second scribe.

John Pope restores the half line as *(Gē)at(isc) mēowle*, claiming that 'I am much more certain than the parentheses would suggest, because I can see traces of every letter – the tail of the **g**, a very black **i** which could once have been **e**, at unmistakable, **i**, high **s**, and **c** very faint but not hard to identify in the vestiges that remain'.[23] The alternative readings are thus either a *geo-* 'ancient' or *Geatisc* 'Geatish' woman whose lament can be heard on the head-land; the latter interpretation is now preferred by most scholars (including Fulk et al. in the fourth edition of Klaeber's *Beowulf*).[24] This figure predicts, just as both Mary in the Vercelli Homily and the wife of Ongenþeow actually see, the 'wretched and sorrowful troop' that will represent the doomed race of men. What do we know of this woman other than the illegibility of her modifier? Tauno F. Mustanoja summarizes the three main ways in which

---

22 Julius Zupitza (ed.), *Beowulf: reproduced in facsimile from the unique manuscript British Museum MS. Cotton Vitellius A. XV* (London / New York / Toronto, 1959), p. 144; Klaeber, *Beowulf and the fight at Finnsburg*, p. 118; see his reconstruction same page. 23 John Collins Pope, *The rhythm of Beowulf* (New Haven & London, 1942), pp 232–3. See also discussion in Robert D. Fulk, 'On argumentation in Old English philology', *Anglo-Saxon England*, 32 (2003), 1–26 at 14 and n. 25.   24 Fulk et al., *Klaeber's Beowulf*, p. 107.

critics have interpreted her appearance in the poem within the context of Beowulf's death:

> First, the interpretations arising from the assumption that the woman was Beowulf's widow. According to an elaboration of this view the woman was Hygd, Hygelac's widowed queen, who had married Beowulf. Second, the hypothesis that the woman was Hygd, who had not married Beowulf but lived as the queen dowager and, surviving Beowulf, was privileged to lead the funeral ceremonies. Third, the view that the woman was not Beowulf's widow and that she was not Hygd but just a (Geatish) woman.[25]

Mustanoja argues that the lack of textual evidence renders unlikely the idea of a married Beowulf, with his grieving widow or a bereaved dowager haunting the seashore. He has argued less persuasively, however, that the *meowle*'s role is that of a professional mourner. The personal elements of her lamentation and the political overtones that stem from her *(wīgen)des egesan, / hȳ[n]ðo (ond) h(æftnȳ)d* 'terror of warrior, / shame and captivity' (ll 3154–5)[26] seem to surpass the role of any merely paid mourner. John Pope's reading of the woman as *Geatisc meowle* gives her an archetypal quality: the mysterious mourning woman laments a race, a dynasty, the children that the future will never see. Just as the earlier *iomeowle* begat a family that plunged into bloodshed, this woman stands at the beginning of a period in which her own race will likely perish. She stands as a foreshadowing of the tragedy that will come to the Geats.

Another *meowle* appears similarly on the shore at the end of *Exodus* (l. 580). As the Israelites celebrate their passage through the waters thanking the Lord for his glorious deeds,

> þa wæs eðfynde   Afrisc meowle
> on geofones staðe   golde geweorðod. (ll 581–2)[27]

> Then was easy to find the African *meowle*
> on the seashore adorned with gold.

After this brief glance, the poet returns to the Israelites' celebration. No such woman appears at this point in the biblical *Exodus*, but Aaron's sister Miriam appears in the next chapter. The difficulty is that the modifier *Afrisc* 'African' would not apply to Miriam. Holthausen thus emends *Afrisc* to *ebrisc* 'Hebrew'.[28]

---

25 Mustanoja, 'The unnamed woman's song', 4.   26 Fulk et al., *Klaeber's Beowulf*, p. 107.
27 George Philip Krapp (ed.), *The Junius manuscript* (New York, 1931), p. 107, ll 581–2.
28 A different emendation was suggested by Gollancz (followed by Blackburn), who

As Krapp points out, however, *Afrisc* could refer to an Egyptian.[29] The woman who appears is not mentioned as a celebrant. Given the parallel in position and terminology, it is tempting to see her as serving the same purpose for the Egyptians that *Beowulf*'s *meowle* does for the Geats: functioning as a representative mourning mother for the many Egyptians who have perished. Attractive as this parallel is, two major inconsistencies would have to be addressed. First, if she was a member of the pursuing host, why would they have taken a woman with them? If she wasn't, then how did she get to this distant shore? Second, if she is lamenting the death of her people, why is she adorned with gold? The wife of Ongenþeow is, after all, specifically described as 'stripped of gold'. This descriptor, however, would be appropriate for one of Moses' followers: Exodus 12:35–6 tells us that the Egyptians had granted the departing tribes gold and silver to be rid of them and their plagues.[30]

Returning this *meowle* then to a position among the Israelites, some critics have viewed her as representing Moses' wife, an Ethiopian mentioned in the book of Numbers and who may or may not be identical to Zipporah whom he takes as wife in Exodus 2:21. This accounts for the African adjectival designation, but raises the problem of why the Anglo-Saxon poet adds her to the biblical narrative. Ellen Martin compromises by reading her as a conflation of Zipporah and of Miriam.[31] In the biblical account, Miriam appears soon after the Israelites arrive from their crossing of the Red Sea (Ex 15:20–1): 'Then the prophet Miriam, Aaron's sister, took a tambourine in her hand, and all the women went out after her with tambourines and with dancing'.[32] Compare this to the passage from *Judgement day II* cited above:

> There will wander a virgin troop of the pure, hung about with blossoms, brightest of companies, and God's excellent beloved will lead them, the woman who for us gave birth to the Lord, the Ruler on earth: the pure *meowle*.

The comparison of the biblical Exodus to *Judgement day II* seems far closer than that of the Old English *Exodus* to *Beowulf*. Like the Virgin Mary,

---

changed *meowle* to *neowle* 'prostrate', and took the clause as a reference to Exodus 14:30, 'Israel saw the Egyptians dead on the seashore'. This would, however, be an unlikely translation for the Vulgate *mortuus* (see Krapp, *Junius manuscript*, p. 217). For Exodus, see Bruce M. Metzger and Roland E. Murphy (eds), *The new Oxford annotated Bible* (New York, 1994), Old Testament, p. 88. **29** Krapp, *Junius manuscript*, p. 217. Krapp himself, allowing the possibility, discounts it as a probable interpretation, as 'there is no reason to suppose that the Egyptians have maidens with them in their army, and no reason for referring to them here if they had'. **30** Metzger and Murphy, *Oxford annotated Bible*, Old Testament, p. 84. **31** For previous analyses, together with her own, see Ellen E. Martin, 'Allegory and the African woman in the Old English *Exodus*', *Journal of English and Germanic Philology*, 81, i (1982), 1–15. **32** Metzger and Murphy, *Oxford annotated Bible*, Old Testament, p. 89.

Miriam appears following a scene of extensive death and carnage to lead a troop of women to glory. In a way, her march serves as an Old Testament prefiguration of Mary's New Testament parade to blessedness. This hypothesis makes something of a leap: it assumes both that the audience would have been familiar enough with the Bible to identify the woman on the seashore with Miriam, and that the term *meowle* has a strong enough Marian connotation that the parallel to *Judgement day II* would be apparent to those who knew both poems. In this regard we should remember Dorothy Whitelock's statement about the *Beowulf* poet:

> He was composing for Christians whose conversion was neither partial nor superficial ... He assumes their familiarity not merely with the biblical stor[ies], but with the interpretation in the commentaries – not, of course, necessarily at first hand, but through the teaching of the Church.[33]

Medieval exegesis substantiates this suggested connection between Miriam and Mary. In regard to the allegory of Miriam representing the Church, Zeno of Verona claims that:

> Maria, quae cum mulieribus tympanum quatit, typus Ecclesiae fuit; quae cum omnibus Ecclesiis, quas peperit, hymnum canens et pectoris verum tympanum quatiens, populum christianum ducit, non in eremum, sed ad caelum.

> Maria [Miriam], who beat the tambourine in accompaniment to the women, was a type of the Church; which, singing a hymn with all the Churches, which she had borne, and beating the true tambourine of the breast, leads the Christian people not into the desert but to heaven.[34]

Ambrose connects the figure of Miriam more directly to Mary:

> Talis enim fuit Maria... Quae pompa illa, quanta angelorum laetitia plaudentium, quod habitare meriatur in caelo, quae caelestem vitam vixit in saeculo! Tunc etiam Maria tympanum sumens choros virginales citabit cantantes Domino quod per mare saeculi sine saecularibus fluctibus transierunt.

> For such was Mary ... What pomp was that, what happiness of the applauding angels, because she deserves to dwell in heaven, who lived

33 Dorothy Whitelock, *The audience of Beowulf* (Oxford, 1951), p. 5. 34 Zeno of Verona, *Tractatus LIV, De Exodo, 1: In die Paschae* (*PL* 11, 510); translation from Martin, 'Allegory and the African woman', p. 12.

a heavenly life in the world! Thus also Maria [Miriam], taking up the tambourine, roused the troops of virgins singing to God because they had passed through the sea of this world without worldly vicissitudes.[35]

Both theologians use the form 'Maria' when speaking of Miriam: indeed, the two forms are variants of a single name. This correspondence provides the link between the Old and New Testament manifestations of the holy woman triumphantly leading a troop of virgins to glory. These two female figures are connected in early medieval Christian thought, as they are in OE poetry through their common designation as *meowle*.

The eponymous heroine of the poetic fragment *Judith* is the only figure to merit the designation of *meowle* twice within one poem. In the first instance, Holofernes' men take Judith to his tent so he can have his way with her:

> eoden þa stercedferhðe,
> hæleð heora hearran cyðan þæt wæs se halige meowle
> gebroht on his burgetelde.[36]

The warriors went then, troubled in heart,
to announce to their lord that the holy *meowle* had been
brought to his pavilion.

Judith escapes by beheading Holofernes and returns to gather the Hebrews for an attack on the Assyrians. Holofernes' men rush to warn him of the approaching battle, and one of the few truly entertaining scenes in Anglo-Saxon poetry ensues.

> Næs ðeah eorla nan
> þe þone wiggend aweccan dorste
> oððe gecunnian hu ðone cumbolwigan
> wið ða halgan mægð hæfde geworden,
> metodes meowlan.[37]

However there was not one of the lords who dared waken the warrior or find out how the fighter had fared with the holy maiden, the Lord's *meowle*.

The thwarted sexual encounter between Holofernes and Judith is framed by references to Judith as a *meowle*: first, when she is led to his tent, and second,

---

[35] Ambrose *De uirginibus* 2.2.17 (*PL* 16, 2222); translation from Martin, 'Allegory and the African woman', p. 11.   [36] Elliott van Kirk Dobbie (ed.), *Beowulf and Judith* (New York, 1953), p. 100, ll 54–7.   [37] Ibid., p. 106, ll 257–61.

when Holofernes' men are left outside a tent now empty except for the decapitated body of their leader, shuffling their feet and coughing loudly in a futile attempt to awaken him.

The description of Judith as a *meowle* on both sides of her heroic assassination of Holofernes emphasizes the chastity of Judith at this crucial moment. R.K. Gordon translates the term as 'virgin' in both instances,[38] but it is precisely the word *meowle* that calls for such a reading, rather than Judith's physiological state of virginity. Judith was the widow of Manasses (8:2–4)[39] and possibly had daughters by him (depending on how one reads the *puellis* of 8:5). The Hebrew Uzziah calls her *mulier sancta* 'holy woman' or possibly even 'holy wife' (7:29); and she herself begs the Lord to hear *mihi viduae* 'me, a widow' (9:3). In her disguise in the Assyrian camp, after *exuit enim vestimenta viduitatis* 'she put away her widow's clothing' (16.9), she is addressed by Holofernes' henchman Bagoas as *bona puella* 'good maiden' (12:4). No contradiction exists here: virginity is a state in which a person is born. Once relinquished, it can never be regained. Chastity, conversely, represents an abstention from sexual concourse; a woman may dedicate herself to this state at any time in her life.[40]

Nowhere in the Vulgate is Judith's sexual purity as linguistically central as in the Anglo-Saxon poem. Here the employment of the charged term *meowle* flanks on both sides the central scene in which Judith's chastity both resists and defeats Holofernes. And the emphasis is not on chastity alone, but on a sacred chastity: she is a *halig meowle* 'holy *meowle*', *Metodes meowl(e)* 'the Lord's *meowle*'. The similarity of the latter to the common description of Mary as *ancilla domini* is striking. As in the Marian references, the term *meowle* implies a chosen chastity specifically connected with holiness.

Another holy bride is indicated by the passing reference in *Genesis A* to a woman who is both *meowle* and mother. Fifth in the line of Seth is Mahalalel. *Him bryd sunu, / meowle to monnum brohte* (ll 1171–2)[41] 'to him a bride gave a son, a *meowle* [gave a son] to [his kins]men'. In the corresponding Vulgate biblical text (Gen 5:15), no mothers are mentioned; the passage that the *Genesis* poet has used as his inspiration is merely a series of Old Testament 'begats' that trace only patrilineage. The proximity of *bryd* implies the prior virginal status of the *meowle* who carries on the line of Adam; the child Jared is the first son of Mahalalel. Like Holofernes, Mahalalel might have done better to shun this uniquely mentioned *meowle*, as she seems to have shortened his life. He died in the blush of his 895th year, despite the fact that longevity seems to have run in his family: his father Kenan lived to 910, and

---

38 Robert K. Gordon (trans.), *Anglo-Saxon poetry* (London, 1926), pp 321, 324. 39 This and all subsequent references to the Vulgate are from Robert Weber (ed.), *Biblia sacra iuxta Vulgatam versionem* (rev. ed.: Stuttgart, 1994), *Liber Judith*, pp 691–711. 40 See Jane Tibbetts Schulenburg, *Forgetful of their sex: female sanctity and society, ca. 500–1100* (Chicago and London, 1998), pp 128–39. 41 Krapp, *Junius manuscript*, p. 37.

his son Jared, perhaps aided by the genes of his *meowle* mother, survived to a satisfying 962 years.[42]

Finally, the use of *meowle* in three of the Exeter Book riddles and in *Precepts* arguably plays deliberately on the connotation of a heightened sense of chastity. Two of the riddles present double entendres with distinct sexual allusions, and the third contains a likely sexual connotation. In Riddle 25, the object states:

> Ic eom wunderlicu wiht,   wifum on hyhte,
> neahbuendum nyt.   Nængum sceþþe
> burgsittendra,   nymþe bonan anum.
> Staþol min is steapheah;   stonde ic on bedde,
> neoþan ruh nathwær.   Neþeð hwilum
> ful cyrtenu   ceorles dohtor,
> modwlonc meowle,   þæt heo on mec gripeð.
> Reseð mec on reodne,   reafað min heafod,
> fegeð mec on fæsten.   Feleþ sona
> mines gemotes,   se þe mec nearwað,
> wif wundenlocc.   Wæt bið þæt eage.

> I am a wondrous creature, to the joy of women,
> useful to neighbours. I do not injure any
> of those who live in towns, excepting only my slayer.
> My position is high and steep; I stand in a bed;
> underneath I am shaggy. Sometimes
> a very handsome peasant's daughter,
> a good-looking girl (*modwlonc meowle*), will dare to grasp me.
> She seizes me in my redness, plunders my head,
> fixes on me firmly. She feels immediately
> my touch, she who draws near to me,
> a woman with curly hair. The eye is wet.[43]

The explicit answer is probably 'onion', but the sexual implication of the aroused penis is barely concealed. The bawdiness of the innuendo would thus be heightened by the virginal quality of the girl(s) grabbing hold. The same interpretation applies to the use of *meowle* in Riddle 61:

> Oft mec fæste bileac   freolicu meowle,
> ides on earce,   hwilum up ateah

---

42 See Metzger and Murphy, *New Oxford annotated Bible*, Old Testament, p. 8.   43 For original text, see Krapp, *Exeter Book*, p. 193; translation ours. For discussion of solutions, see Krapp, *Exeter Book*, p. 325; also Craig Williamson, *The Old English riddles of the Exeter Book* (Chapel Hill, 1977), pp 209–11; Moritz Trautmann, *Die altenglischen Rätsel* (Heidelberg, 1915), pp 86–7.

folmum sinum   ond frean sealde,
holdum þeodne,   swa hio haten wæs.
Siðþan me on hreþre   heafod sticade,
nioþan upweardne,   on nearo fegde.
Gif þæs ondfengan   ellen dohte,
mec frætwedne   fyllan sceolde
ruwes nathwæt.   Ræd hwæt ic mæne.

A lovely woman (*freolicu meowle*), a lady, often locked me
in a chest; at times she took me out
with her fingers, and gave me to her lord
and loyal master, just as he asked.
Then he poked his head inside me,
pushed it up until it fitted tightly.
I, adorned, was bound to be filled
with something rough if the loyal lord
could keep it up. Guess what I mean.[44]

The explicit meaning here is generally taken to be 'helmet' or 'shirt',[45] although it is accompanied by a strong innuendo of sexual encounter. The poet may have chosen *meowle*, with its connotations of chastity, to suggest to his audience one or both of two images to his audience. As in the poem above, this action could either be performed with serial virgins, or repeatedly with the same woman who is linguistically marked as chaste; either interpretation would be more ironic with the virginity implied by *meowle*.

Riddle 4, which contains the third use of *meowle* in the Riddles genre, has proven resistant to conclusive solution.

Ic sceal þragbysig   þegne minum,
hringum hæfted,   hyran georne,
min bed brecan,   breahtme cyþan
þæt me halswriþan   hlaford sealde.
Oft mec slæpwerigne   secg oðþe meowle
gretan eode;   ic him gromheortum
winterceald oncweþe.   Wearm lim
gebundenne bæg   hwilum bersteð;
se þeah biþ on þonce   þegne minum,
medwisum men,   me þæt sylfe,
þær with wite,   one wordum min
on sped mæge   spel gesecgan.

44 From Krapp, *Exeter Book*, p. 229; translation from Crossley-Holland, *Exeter Book riddles*, p. 65. 45 See Williamson, *Old English riddles*, pp 320–1; Trautmann, *Altenglischen Rätsel*, p. 120; Krapp, *Exeter Book*, p. 366.

Busy at times for my master,
bound with rings, I must eagerly obey,
break my rest, and loudly proclaim
that my guardian gave me a halter.
A man or a woman (*meowle*), weary and bleary,
has often called on me; winter-cold
I answer them, surly as they are. Sometimes
a warm limb looses the bound ring.
But it delights my master, a dull sort
of man, and satisfies me into the bargain,
if anyone can fathom and solve my riddle.[46]

The most generally accepted solutions seem to be either 'millstone' / 'hand mill' or 'bell', although neither of these seems to fully account for the clues, and Krapp admits that 'it may well be that the true solution has not yet been hit upon'.[47] Note, however, that the narrator speaks of a *wearm lim* 'warm limb' and speaks of an action that 'satisfies me into the bargain'. Likely this poem contains an underlying sexual double-entendre, typical for so many of the Exeter Book riddles. If so, this one, like the two more intelligible sexual jests, probably takes on a bawdier innuendo if the word *meowle* adds to the joke.

Similar irony may also underline the use of the word in *Precepts*, where it appears in a cautionary passage of paternal advice for a son. The father's words are didactic and smack of misogyny:

Forðon sceal æwiscmod   oft siþian,
se þe gewiteð   in wifes lufan,
fremdre meowlan.   Þær bið a firena wen,
laðlicre scome,   long nið wið god,
geotende gielp.

Therefore he must often wander ashamed
who turns towards the love of a woman,
an unknown *meowle*. One can always expect to find sin there,
hateful disgrace, long enmity against God,
and overflowing arrogance.[48]

---

46 From Krapp, *Exeter Book*, p. 183; translation from Crossley-Holland, *Exeter Book riddles*, p. 8, except for the first two lines, which we have rendered more literally. Crossley-Holland begins: 'Ring me, they ring me. I work long hours and must readily obey my master'.   47 Krapp, *Exeter Book*, p. 324. For possible solutions, see Williamson, *Old English riddles*, pp 141–5; Trautman, *Altenglischen Rätsel*, pp 68–9; Krapp, *Exeter Book*, pp 324–5.   48 Text from Krapp, *Exeter Book*, p. 141, ll 37–41. Translation from Thomas A. Shippey, *Poems of wisdom and learning in Old English* (Woodbridge, 1976), p. 49, except for first line, which we have emended.

If the word here carries the same connotations as in the riddles (and the sense of 'whore' certainly springs to mind), then *meowle* as a synonym for virgin would be used ironically and would imply a more spiteful overtone than might otherwise be inferred. This reading would amplify the 'sin' and 'disgrace' of such a liaison as that which the father foresees would bring. The *wif* of this passage is one seen in many literary texts, even through contemporary times: the woman who is the downfall of man, the eternal Eve, the bane of male purity. If mocked by virginal implications which imply conversely that she is not at all chaste, she can be seen as even more of a threat to the son.

In summation, we would offer the following semantic development of the term *meowle*. Its etymological sense of 'young girl' never appears in Old English, but the meaning was transferred to the pre-eminent characteristic of young girls: virginity or chastity (Aldhelm). Through connection with the icon of chaste women, the term came to be associated with the Virgin Mary (*Christ II*, *Judgement day II*), and perhaps her prefiguration in the person of Miriam in the Old Testament (*Exodus*). This use was extended to describe other women in a state of holy chastity or holy motherhood (*Judith*, *Genesis*). As plastic depictions of Mary expanded to take on the role of grieving mother, the connotations of *meowle* shifted accordingly (*The fortunes of men*, *Beowulf*). Finally, moving in another direction, the wags who composed the riddles of the Exeter Book and *Precepts* used this term so intimately connected with holy chastity in bawdy sexual contexts precisely for the shock value such a usage could provide.

Columba at Clonmacnoise

JENNIFER O'REILLY

Relatively few chapters on the monastic life in Adomnán's *Vita Columbae* (henceforth *VC*) quote Scripture or cite scriptural parallels directly; those that do provide such aids to interpretation often point beyond the literal letter of the biblical text or parallel to the traditions in which Scripture was understood in the early Insular world. What distinguishes the work is the skilful and often innovative way these insights are conveyed through narrative, yet not as allegory or parable. The present essay examines one such episode, in the light of examples from some of the exegetical, hagiographic and monastic traditions with which Adomnán was familiar. It is offered as a small tribute to a distinguished scholar and generous colleague whose foundational study on the monastic *familia* of Columba has done so much to extend our understanding of the contexts and significance of Adomnán's work.[1]

VC i, 3 begins with time and place:

> At one time, when for some months the blessed man remained in the midland district of Ireland, while by God's will founding the monastery that is called in Irish *Dairmag* [Durrow], it pleased him to visit the brothers who lived in the monastery of Clóin of Saint Céran [Clonmacnoise].[2]

Columba's arrival at this important monastic *ciuitas* beyond the Columban *familia* is described, however, not just as a fraternal visit but as a ceremonial entrance or *aduentus*. The abbot and the whole community went to meet him outside the *ualum monasterii*.[3] They acclaimed him, made obeisance, and led him in procession through the boundary to the church:

> When they heard of his approach all those that were in the fields near the monastery came from every side, and joined those that were within it, and with the utmost eagerness accompanying their abbot Alither they

1 Máire Herbert, *Iona, Kells, and Derry: the history and hagiography of the monastic* familia *of Columba* (Oxford, 1988). 2 *VC* i, 3: Alan O. Anderson and Marjorie O. Anderson (ed. and trans.), *Adomnán's Life of Columba* (2nd ed.: Oxford, 1991), pp 24–5. 3 For the suggestion that Adomnán's indication of a triple boundary system delineating areas of sacred space at Iona is an arrangement that 'can be seen in action' at Clonmacnoise in this account, see Aidan MacDonald, 'Aspects of the monastic landscape in Adomnán's *Life of Columba*' in J. Carey, M. Herbert and P. Ó Riain (eds), *Studies in Irish hagiography: saints and scholars* (Dublin, 2001), pp 15–30 at pp 19, 30.

passed outside the boundary-wall of the monastery, and with one accord went to meet Saint Columba, as if he had been an angel of the Lord. On seeing him they bowed their faces to the earth, and he was kissed by them with all reverence, and singing hymns and praises they led him with honour to the church. They bound together a kind of barrier of branches, and caused it to be carried about the saint as he walked, by four men keeping pace with him; lest the elder Saint Columba should be troubled by the thronging of that crowd of brothers.[4]

Adomnán's visionary evocation of Iona as a holy land in the *Vita Columbae*, with the monastery as the earthly city foreshadowing the heavenly Jerusalem, has a historical counterpart in the archaeological evidence of the symbolic imitation of Jerusalem in early Irish monastic sites, including Clonmacnoise.[5] Several circumstantial details in Adomnán's description of the procession at Clonmacnoise, however – the joining together of those who had come in from the fields, when they heard of Columba's approach, with those who came out from the monastery to meet him; their singing of hymns and praises; the carrying of branches around him; the multitude who accompanied him on the way into the monastery – have a more specific resonance. They serve not to replicate but to recall Christ's entry into Jerusalem. The Gospels recount that a great multitude in the city 'went forth to meet him', when they heard Jesus was coming to Jerusalem (Jn 12:12); some of the multitude 'cut boughs from the trees and strewed them in the way' and 'the crowds that went before and that followed' cried praises: 'Hosanna to the son of David. Blessed is he that comes in the name of the Lord. Hosanna in the highest' (Mt 21: 8–9).

The crowd's hymn of acclamation, *Benedictus qui uenturus est in nomine Domini*, from Psalm 117:26, is quoted in all four Gospel accounts and in the annual liturgical commemoration of the event through its ritual re-enactment. The abbot and community of Clonmacnoise received Columba 'as if he had been an angel of the Lord'. Adomnán later tells of how Columba visited his own monks unseen one harvest-time, as they returned wearily each evening from labouring in the fields (*VC* i, 37). Half-way home, they would experience a miraculous sensation of rest and refreshment (cf. Mt 28–30). Baíthéne explained that they received this solace through the coming of Columba to them in spirit. With great joy they knelt and 'worshipped Christ in the holy and blessed man' (*Christum in sancto uenerantur et beato uiro*). Columba is twice referred to by the epithet *uir beatus* in the chapter recounting his bodily visit to the monks of Clonmacnoise, where Adomnán also shows, by different

4 *Quandamque de lignis piramidem.* For the barrier or baldachino of branches, see Richard Sharpe (trans.), *Adomnán of Iona: Life of St Columba* (London, 1995), p. 261 n. 63.
5 Tomás Ó Carragáin, *Churches in early medieval Ireland: architecture, ritual and memory* (New Haven and London, 2010), pp 33–47, 57–9, 72–80.

literary means, that the blessed man came in the name of the Lord and that in their recognition and reception of him the community of Clonmacnoise honoured Christ. Columba's formal blessing of the community might be expected to follow, but events take a surprising turn.

In the course of the procession to the church, during which Columba was protected from the multitude of brothers by the four men around him carrying branches, a 'boy of the congregation' (*puer familiaris*) attempted to come up behind him out of sight in order that he might secretly touch but the hem of his cloak, 'without the knowledge or perception of the *uir beatus*'. Though Columba could not see this with his bodily eyes, he discerned it spiritually (*spiritalibus perspexit*), and suddenly stopped, reached back and brought the boy round to face him. Up to this point the incident recalls details from the synoptic Gospels' accounts of the woman with the issue of blood. When Christ was thronged by a great crowd of people she approached him from behind and secretly touched the hem of his garment (Lk 8:43–9).

The particular interest of Adomnán's story, however, lies in its departure from the familiar Gospel narrative, which leads the reader to reflect further on what, exactly, is the nature of the link being made between the two cases. Adomnán elsewhere testifies that Columba cured the ailments of many sick people, who received his blessing through various means, 'even by touching the hem of his cloak' (*VC* ii, 6), but the boy at Clonmacnoise is not described as sick. Rather, he was much looked down on for his countenance and demeanour; though accused of no particular sin, he was 'not yet approved by the elders'.[6] Those present did not want Columba to take any notice of 'this unlucky and mischievous boy' (*infelicem et iniuriosum ... puerum*), but Columba unexpectedly blessed the boy and publicly prophesied his growth in virtue, wisdom and renown.

The boy is finally identified by Adomnán as 'Ernéne, Crasén's son, famous afterwards among all the churches of Ireland, and very widely known' and 'the prophecy concerning himself' is formally authenticated as having been related by Ernéne to abbot Ségéne (623–52) in the presence of Adomnán's predecessor Faílbe. Adomnán adds, 'and from his disclosure I too have myself learned these same words that I have related'.[7]

The story is in some ways complementary to the previous chapter, which is set later in time, after the death of Columba. His successor, Baíthéne, reveals to the youthful Fintén, son of Tailchán, the prophecy privately made to him by Columba that Fintén had been chosen by God to remain in Ireland and become 'an abbot of monks, and a leader of souls to the heavenly kingdom'. Like Ernéne, Fintén was to be held in high repute among all the

---

6 *Eadem hora quidam ualde dispectus uultu et habitu puer familiaris, et necdum senioribus placens.* 7 On the transmission and recording of testimonies, see Herbert, *Iona, Kells, and Derry*, pp 134–6.

churches of the Irish, but the juxtaposed accounts of their early careers and reputations differ. Fintén had preserved 'from the age of boyhood' (*a puerili aetate*) integrity of body and soul and was devoted to studies of divine wisdom, meaning not only the acquisition of knowledge through study of the Scriptures, but the divinely inspired spiritual process of learning how to understand their underlying meaning in order to know God's will and, therefore, how to obey and love him. Encouraged by the guidance of a wise and venerable priest, Fintén while still in his youth had an eager desire to go to Columba and live in pilgrimage.

An early disposition to spiritual maturity is shared by the three universally revered saints whose Lives offered particular models for Insular hagiography, including the *Vita Columbae*. Gregory's *Life of Benedict* testifies, 'From the time he was a boy, he had the heart of an elder'.[8] From the earliest years of his holy childhood St Martin aspired to the service of God. Not long after the age of ten he was completely converted to the work of God.[9] St Antony had refused 'to join in the silly games of the other little children'; when he went to church 'he did not fool around as little children tend to nor did he show lack of respect as young boys often do'.[10] But precocious signs of sanctity could, as in the case of Antony, be compatible with the unfolding of stages in the saint's spiritual progress.

Other saints, moreover, were accorded some latitude in infancy, including St Cuthbert (*c.*635–87) in the anonymous Life produced at Lindisfarne, *c.*699–705, even though the same three early Lives, especially the Evagrian *Vita Antonii* and Sulpicius Severus' *Vita Martini*, were important influences, as were Irish traditions of hagiography.[11] As a high-spirited eight-year old, Cuthbert is pictured disporting himself with other youngsters in all manner of games and tomfoolery (*ioci uarietatem et scurilitatem agere ceperunt*) before he is summoned to his calling. This childhood is detailed further in Bede's reworking of the material in his prose *Vita Cuthberti*, *c.*720, but is also carefully annotated from Scripture to chronicle a stage in the working of heavenly grace in the saint's life: 'up to the eighth year of his age, which is the end of infancy and the beginning of boyhood (*usque ad octauum aetatis annum, qui post infantiam puericiae primus est*), he devoted his mind to nothing but the games and wantonness of children'; like the blessed Samuel, 'he did not yet know the Lord, neither was the word of the Lord yet revealed unto him' (1 Sam 3:7). Cuthbert's child-

---

8 *Dialogi* ii, 1: Adalbert de Vogüé (ed.), *Grégoire le Grand, Dialogues, II: livres I–III*, SC 260 (Paris, 1979), p. 129: *ab ipso pueritiae suae tempore cor gerens senile*. 9 *Vita Martini*, ii: Jacques Fontaine (ed.), *Sulpice Sévère, Vie de Saint Martin, I*, SC 133 (Paris, 1967), p. 254. 10 *Vita Antonii* i, 1; *PG* 26, 841; Carolinne White (trans.), *Early Christian lives* (Harmondsworth, 1998), p. 9. 11 *Vita Sancti Cuthberti auctore anonymo*, 2: Bertram Colgrave (ed. and trans.), *Two Lives of St Cuthbert* (Cambridge, 1940), p. 65; Alan Thacker, 'The social and continental background to early Anglo-Saxon hagiography' (D. Phil., University of Oxford, 1976), pp 87–100.

ish ways were checked by the Lord through the reproof and prophecy miraculously uttered by a three-year-old, prompting Bede to observe the truth spoken
by the Psalmist: 'out of the mouth of babes and sucklings you have perfected
praise' (Ps 8:3). From then onwards, that is, from the earliest years of his boyhood, heavenly grace urged Cuthbert 'little by little into the way of truth', so
that he might accomplish what was destined for him. He then 'put away child-
ish things' (1 Cor 13:11). While still a boy he was 'wholly given to the Lord'
and, conforming to Jeremiah's ideal (Lam 3:27, 28), submitted his neck from
early youth to the yoke of monastic discipline.[12]

In the case of Ernéne at Clonmacnoise, the wayward phase extended into
boyhood. His secret attempt to touch the hem of Columba's cloak, however,
gives some sign that his inner disposition may have been more favourable
than his unsatisfactory outward demeanour suggested. The reader is primed
to view the boy's action through the lens of the Gospel miracle, rather than
as a prank. The woman with the issue of blood had 'said within herself, "If I
touch but the hem of his garment, I shall be healed"' (Mt 9:21; Mk 5:28),
thereby recognizing the power of Christ. Knowing that someone had sought
the aid of his power (*uirtutem*), Christ asked, to the puzzlement of the crowd,
'Who touched me?'. The woman came trembling before him (*tremens uenit*)
and he reassured her, 'Daughter (*filia*), your faith has made you whole'.[13]
Similarly, the boy was trembling greatly when brought before the face of
Columba, who addressed him as '*O filii*', and in great trepidation he received
the saint's blessing (*ualde tremefactum ...cum ingenti tremore*).

The scriptural image of fear and trembling in the divine presence, or
before the Lord's chosen messenger, is a hagiographic motif used elsewhere
in the Life of Columba.[14] *VC* iii, 19–21, 23 in particular also shows familiarity with patristic and monastic traditions on *timor domini* as applied to the dif-
fering spiritual capacities of individuals and to different stages of spiritual
growth within the life of an individual. In Cassian's *Conlationes* 'the fear of
the Lord' can mean a negative fear of divine punishment in someone whose
spiritual understanding is elementary. Fear can also be seen as a more positive awe of God's power, leading to penitence, amendment of life and the
seeking of spiritual wisdom. The desert fathers and compilers of monastic
rules enigmatically taught that 'the fear of the Lord is the beginning of
wisdom' (Ps 110:10), describing a transformation from servile fear to the truly
filial kind of fear, which is fear only of being deficient in the love of God.[15]

---

12 *Bedae Vita Sancti Cuthberti*, 1: Colgrave, *Two Lives*, pp 154–7.   13 Lk 8:45–8, Mk
5:30–34, Mt 9:22.   14 *VC* second preface; i, 37; ii, 23; iii, 2, 19: Anderson and Anderson,
Adomnán's Life of Columba, pp 5, 71, 129, 185, 211.   15 Jennifer O'Reilly, 'The wisdom
of the scribe and the fear of the Lord' in D. Broun and T.O. Clancy (eds), *Spes Scotorum:
hope of Scots – Saint Columba, Iona and Scotland* (Edinburgh, 1999), pp 159–211 at pp
192–211.

Adomnán shows that Columba alone discerned Ernéne's secret and fearful action to be the beginning of gradual change, 'from this hour' (*ab hac hora*). He prophesied that the boy would grow in goodness of life and virtues of the soul (*bonisque moribus et animae uirtutibus*) by degrees from day to day; 'wisdom also with prudence will be increased in him more and more, from this day' (*sapientia quoque et prudentia magis ac magis in eo ab hac die adaugebitur*). The linking of *sapientia* and *prudentia* may recall their pairing in Christ's saying that the Father has hidden divine mysteries from the wise and revealed them to little ones: *quia abscondisti haec a sapientibus et prudentibus et reuelasti ea paruulis* (Mt 11:25). Christ was cautioning those who think themselves wise, rather than humbly acknowledge that wisdom comes from God. Columba's prophecy reveals the boy to be a recipient of divine grace, both as one of the 'little ones' in the Church whose understanding is still at a carnal level, and also as one who is to grow gradually in true *sapientia et prudentia* towards greater understanding of the spiritual and eternal.

In the Andersons' edition of the text, *prudentia* is interpreted as 'discretion'; this is not annotated but has the effect of indicating how *prudentia* had long since come to be understood in a monastic context.[16] In classical thought virtue had been defined as a disposition of the spirit (*habitus animae*) in harmony with the measure of nature and reason and consisting of four parts: *prudentia, iustitia, fortitutudo, temperantia*.[17] It was necessary to divide the four virtues from their contraries, but also to distinguish them from the extremes at their own borders, which misleadingly appear to be related to them but are not. *Prudentia*, 'the knowledge of what is good, what is bad, and what is neutral', therefore governed understanding of the other virtues.[18] In works on the monastic spiritual life, which probed intentions as well as actions and drew on scriptural traditions and a greatly increased vocabulary of the virtues, that sense of measured judgment was often expressed by the term *discretio* (discretion, discernment). In the rule of St Benedict, *prudentia* is among the qualities required of the abbot when correcting the brethren, but additional emphasis is given to its association with moderation and discernment: 'he should use prudence and avoid extremes', he should 'prune faults with prudence and love as he sees best for each individual', which required discernment of the individual's spiritual strengths and weaknesses; indeed, *discretio* is 'the mother of all virtues'.[19]

---

16 Anderson and Anderson, *Adomnán's Life of Columba*, p. 27: 'wisdom also with discretion will be increased in him more and more from this day'. Sharpe (*Adomnán of Iona: Life of St Columba*, p. 116) has: 'Wisdom and judgement will increase in him from today'. 17 Cicero, *De inuentione*, II, liii, 4–12: H.M. Hubbell (ed. and trans.), *Cicero, De inventione; De optimo genere oratorum; Topica* (Cambridge MA, 1949), p. 326. 18 Ibid.: *prudentia est rerum bonarum et malarum neutrarumque scientia*. 19 *Regula Benedicti*, 64: Adalbert de Vogüé (ed.), *La Règle de Saint Benoit, II*, SC 182 (Paris 1972), p. 652: *testimonia discretionis matris uirtutum sumens*; Timothy Fry (trans.), *The rule of St Benedict*

Columbanus, too, was familiar with the concept that 'virtues are placed in the mean between extremes' and taught that to avoid all excess, the virtues practised in the monastic life, 'grown to a huge forest of names', needed to be 'weighed in the balance of *discretio*'. It was not acquired by human effort alone; the monk was to pray humbly for the divine gift of true discernment, 'which opens the path to perfection'.[20] This emphasis on discernment in sixth-century monastic rules reflects the teaching of the desert fathers and was augmented by Gregory the Great's extensive practical advice in Book 3 of the *Regula pastoralis* on how the pastor was to weigh the disposition, temperaments and spiritual capacities of those in his charge and the means of appropriately admonishing or encouraging them.[21]

In Cassian's *Conlationes*, the conference devoted to discretion had cited the authoritative counsel of St Antony himself that '*discretio* is the begetter, guardian and moderator of all virtues'.[22] It is necessary for 'discerning the thoughts and intentions of the heart' (Heb 4:12), in oneself or in others; it is seen, moreover, as a gift of divine grace, requiring humility and purity of heart in order to be brought into effect, so that any admonishment or correction offered is not motivated by self-interest or spiritual pride. Discernment is regarded, not as milk for infants but as 'solid food for the fully grown, for those who through practice have their senses exercised for the discerning of good and evil' (Heb 5:14), though the fathers repeatedly warned that such spiritual maturity was not necessarily related to seniority of age or position. Abba Moses recounts the cautionary tale of an austere unnamed elder. His reproach of a junior monk troubled by mundane temptations was so harsh that the young man was on the point of leaving the monastic life in despair when he met Abba Apollos, who discerned the cause of his sorrow and gave him consolation. Then, laying bare the heart of the elder, he urged him to learn 'not to crush the bruised reed' (Mt 12:20) and to pray for that grace 'by which you yourself may be able to sing with assurance in deed and power: "The Lord has given me a learned tongue so that I might know how to sustain by a word the one who is weary"' (Is 50:4).[23] The 'learned tongue', instructed by wisdom, teaches and consoles others.

Much of the teaching of the desert fathers was conveyed through stories and case histories, characteristically less explicit than this example in pointing to a meaning to be drawn. They often simply present an image, an enigmatic episode or saying in the life of a father or a monk, requiring the reader

(Collegeville, 1980), p. 282.   20 Columbanus, *Regula monachorum*, 8: G.S.M. Walker (ed. and trans.), *Sancti Columbani opera*, SLH 2 (Dublin, 1970), pp 135, 137.   21 See Bruno Judic (ed.), *Grégoire le Grand, Règle pastorale, II: livres III et IV*, SC 382 (Paris, 1992). 22 *Conlationes* ii, 4: Eugène Pichery (ed.), *Cassien, Conférences I–VII*, SC 42 (Paris, 1955), p. 116: *Omnium namque uirtutum generatrix, custos moderatixque discretio est*; Boniface Ramsey (trans.), *John Cassian: the conferences*, Ancient Christian Writers 57 (New York, 1997), p. 97.   23 Pichery, *Conférences*, pp 26–9; Ramsey, *John Cassian*, pp 95–8 at p. 97.

to puzzle out its possible significance. It was a teaching device highly adaptable to different circumstances and literary genres.

Read in the light of monastic tradition on discernment, Columba's response to the boy at Clonmacnoise appears not as the arbitrary act of a wonder-worker but as a dramatic expression of the saint's insight into the boy's disposition and spiritual need and his discernment of the divine will for him. The particular power of Columba's spiritual insight proceeds from his closeness to God, 'the searcher of hearts and minds' (Ps 7:10), because, as Adomnán had earlier explained in the words of St Paul: 'he who clings to the Lord is one spirit' (1 Cor 6:17).[24] Those who witnessed Columba's response to a boy in whom they could see no promise, had urged the saint: 'Send him away! Why do you keep hold of this wretched and mischievous boy?'[25] On the contrary, 'the saint drew from his pure breast (*puro pectore depromit*) these prophetic words: "Let be, brothers, let be"' and blessed the boy. Specifically, he commanded the boy to open his mouth (*aperi os tuum*) and put out his tongue; the words are reiterated, 'the boy then opened his mouth as he was bidden and put out his tongue' and Columba earnestly blessed his tongue.

Monastic readers would be familiar with the psalm verse which begins the daily divine Office, 'O Lord, open thou my lips and my mouth shall declare thy praise': *Domine, labia mea aperies et os meum annuntiabit laudem tuam* (Ps 50:17). The psalms frequently speak of the calling of all people to praise the Lord, which commentators interpreted as meaning not only the literal singing of his praise, especially in the perpetual prayer represented by the daily round of the monastic Office, but the offering of praise through every aspect of a sanctified life, which builds up the Church. The formal blessing of Ernéne's tongue signals the final element of Columba's prophecy that he will grow in good deeds and inner virtues and will increasingly receive wisdom with discretion: 'His tongue also will receive from God eloquence, with healthful doctrine'. The words *lingua quoque eius salubri et doctrina eloquentia a deo donabitur* convey a sense of the saving power of the doctrine which the boy, grown to spiritual maturity, would one day teach others.[26]

Finally, the connection between the two parts of *VC* i, 3, the reception of Columba at Clonmacnoise and the incident with Ernéne during the procession into the monastery, receives oblique illumination from the account in the *Vita Martini* of the saint's entry into Tours and a curious incident on his arrival. Adomnán's story shares motifs with this story in a Life which was influential in the *Vita Columbae*, but handles them rather differently, and the nature of the differences helps identify further what is distinctive about his narrative. St

24 *VC* i, 1: Anderson and Anderson, *Adomnán's Life of Columba*, p. 18. 25 Ibid., pp 24–5: '*Dimitte, dimitte; quare hunc infelicem et iniuriosum retentes puerum?*'. 26 Sharpe (*Adomnán of Iona: Life of St Columba*, p. 116) translates the phrase as: 'God will endow his tongue with eloquence to teach the doctrine of salvation'; see p. 262 n. 65 on the terms *salubris* and *doctrina*.

Martin's triumphal progress into the cathedral city amidst tumultuous crowds
has an echo of Christ's *adventus* into Jerusalem, with the additional detail that
Martin was conducted to the city amidst the multitudes that lined the way
under a kind of guard: *sub quadam custodia ad civitatem usque deducitur.*[27] There
was one wish among those who had come out from the city and the crowds
who joined them from neighbouring cities that he should be bishop, except for
a few dissenters, among them some of the bishops who were assembled there
for the selection, and particularly one called Defensor. Their objection to
Martin was on the grounds of his contemptible appearance, clothing and
unkempt hair, which they thought unseemly for a bishop.[28]

When the lector was unable to get through the crush of people for the
appointed reading, an official took the Psalter and read aloud the first verse
he saw: 'Out of the mouth of babes and sucklings you have perfected praise
because of your enemies, that you might destroy the enemy and the
defender': *Ex ore infantium et lactantium perfecisti laudem propter inimicos tuos
ut destruas inimicum et defensorem* (Ps 8:3).[29] A great shout went up from the
people, and the opposition were confounded. Sulpicius Severus comments it
was believed this verse had been divinely chosen; it was prophetic because in
the case of Martin the praise of the Lord was perfected 'out of the mouth of
babes and sucklings', while 'the enemy and defender' (*defensorem* punning on
the name of Defensor) was pointed out and destroyed. The crowds in the
church, that is, although 'babes and sucklings', praised the Lord through their
acclamation of his servant Martin, while the bishops, particularly Defensor,
had failed to see beyond the unprepossessing appearance of Martin's humble
monastic clothing. Similarly, when Christ entered Jerusalem to the hosannas
of the crowd and then went into the temple, the chief priests and scribes
'were moved to indignation' and reproved him because even children in the
temple were singing his praises with the acclamation, 'Hosanna to the son of
David'. Christ, quoting Psalm 8:3, replied, 'Have you never read: "Out of the
mouth of infants and sucklings you have perfected praise"?' (Mt 21:15–16).

Augustine in his commentary on Psalm 8:3 cites Christ's quotation of the
verse, and then expounds the continuing significance of the psalm text for the
Church. He identifies the 'infants and sucklings' as people whom St Paul
protectively described as 'little ones in Christ' (*parvulos in Christo*), at a carnal
or elementary level of understanding God's word (1 Cor 3:1–2), in contrast
with 'the perfect', who are capable of receiving more substantial spiritual food
concerning the hidden mystery of the wisdom of God (1 Cor 2:6–7).[30]

---

27 *Vita Martini*, iv, 2: Fontaine, *Vie de Saint Martin*, i, p. 270. White, *Early Christian lives*,
pp 142–3. 28 Ibid., p. 272: *Impie repugnabant, dicentes scilicet, contemptibilem esse personam,
indignum esse episcopatu hominem vultu despicabilem, veste sordidum, crine deformem.* 29 This
is the version in the *Psalterium Romanum*. 30 E. Dekkers and J. Fraipont (eds), *Augustine,
Enarrationes in psalmos I–L*, CCSL 38 (Turnhout, 1956), pp 50–51.

Augustine stressed, however, that the Church is perfected in its praise of God not only by 'the perfect' but by 'infants and sucklings' who, though not yet capable of the knowledge of things spiritual and eternal, are called to salvation and drawn to Christ in faith. The 'enemy and defender' mentioned at the end of Psalm 8:3 represents, among others, people who count themselves as wise. Augustine cites Christ's warning that the Father has hidden divine mysteries from those who think they are wise and has revealed them to 'little ones' (cf. Mt 11:25: *quia abscondisti haec a sapientibus et prudentibus et revelasti ea parvulis*); this is so that wisdom might be seen to come from heaven, rather than from human effort alone. The paradox is enshrined in the wisdom tradition of Scripture, 'For wisdom opened the mouth of the dumb and made the tongues of infants eloquent': *quoniam sapientia aperuit os mutorum et linguas infantium fecit dissertas* (Wis 10:21).

Adomnán does not cite Psalm 8:3, which is central to the story of St Martin and Defensor, but some features of his narrative – the depiction of Ernéne as youthful in the faith, the opening of his mouth to eloquence, the importance of wisdom in Columba's prophecy – have more in common with the psalm text and related exegesis than with the way the psalm text is used in the Life of Martin. Ernéne and his community of Clonmacnoise are not inter-changeable with the polarized figures of St Martin and Defensor.

In *VC* i, 3 the allusion to the Gospel parallel in the narrative of Ernéne touching Columba's hem allows the reader to see what the community cannot discern and to share the implied reproof of them for seeing only the disreputable outward appearance and demeanour of the boy. But this does not lead to a general condemnation of Clonmacnoise. Columba's reaction gives the reader pause. Ernéne's community differs from Defensor and his fellow-bishops, for the credentials of their faith and practice have already been unmistakably presented in the way they honoured Christ in recognizing the sanctity of Columba, humbly bowing their faces to the earth. But they had failed to see that the boy's attempt to touch Columba's hem might similarly be an act of obeisance.

Stories in the *Vita Columbae* concerning the monastic formation of the saint's own spiritual sons on Iona, as well as figures such as Fintén and Ernéne who remained outside the Columban *familia*, present unexpected aspects or instances of precepts of the faith or monastic practice which are universally known, but whose understanding requires constant renewal and deepening, even by those advanced in the spiritual life. Columba taught the elders of Clonmacnoise through conferring his blessing on the boy they thought of little worth, but his fraternal correction of their lack of discernment in this case was measured: 'let no man despise him'. Columba remained as their guest in the monastery and did not use against them the revelation granted him, during those days, of the future dispute among the churches of Ireland over the dating of Easter. As he commended 'mutual and unfeigned charity, with peace' to his own community on the night of his death, so at the beginning of the book he is shown in concord with a great non-Columban Irish house. His prophecy was addressed not to the boy but to the community. He reassured them that they would recognize the boy's spiritual growth when they saw it and would be greatly pleased by it: 'in this community of yours he will be a man of great eminence'. The community would recognize the ideals of the monastic life in Columba's foretelling of Ernéne's spiritual growth in works and inner virtues and in receiving the gifts of wisdom with discretion and divine eloquence. Through this inspired prophecy Columba gave a blessing to Clonmacnoise.

Librán as monastic archetype

KATJA RITARI

The story of Librán in Adomnán's *Vita Columbae* (hereafter *VC*) ii, 39 is well-known and often commented on as an example of the transformative power of penance.[1] As one of the longest episodes in the Life, however, it merits to be dissected on its own in an attempt to analyse its message. In the introduction to their edition of the Life, the Andersons commented on the episode saying:

> A story set in the Iona period that deserves special mention is the tale of Librán of the Reed-bed, both on account of its length and elaborate structure, and because of the way Columba is integrated into that structure. It has two interlocking themes, a secular theme of retribution for crime and of social obligations, somewhat repetitious in the manner of oral story-telling, and a religious theme of penitence, penance, and absolution. Columba's part is not only that of seer and miracle-worker but that of priest and wise confessor.[2]

The aim of this contribution is to highlight the specifically religious themes in *VC* ii, 39 focusing especially on its vision of monastic life, thereby treating Librán as a paragon of conversion to true Christianity. Adomnán presents Librán as an example of repentance and describes his transformation into a monk in detail. Thus, the episode can be read as illustrating Adomnán's vision of monastic life and the requirements for entering into it.

The title of *VC* ii, 39 reads: *De Librano harundineti profetatio sancti uiri*,[3] thus presenting prophecy as the main topic of the episode. The episode is

---

1 Librán is mentioned as an exemplary penitent in, for example, Aidan MacDonald, 'Seeking the desert in Adomnán's *Vita Columbae*' in E. Mullins and D. Scully (eds), *Listen, O isles, unto me: studies in medieval word and image in honour of Jennifer O'Reilly* (Cork, 2011), pp 191–203 at p. 199; James E. Fraser, 'Adomnán and the morality of war' in J.M. Wooding (ed.), *Adomnán of Iona: theologian, lawmaker, peacemaker* (Dublin, 2010), pp 95–111 at p. 100; Katja Ritari, 'Holy souls and a holy community: the meaning of monastic life in Adomnán's *Vita Columbae*', *Journal of Medieval Religious Cultures*, 37 (2011), 129–46 at 137; eadem, *Saints and sinners in early Christian Ireland: moral theology in the Lives of Saints Brigit and Columba* (Turnhout, 2009), p. 138; Colmán Etchingham, *Church organisation in Ireland AD 650 to 1000* (Maynooth, 1999), p. 291; Clare Stancliffe, 'Red, white and blue martyrdom' in R. McKitterick and D. Dumville (eds), *Ireland in early medieval Europe: studies in memory of Kathleen Hughes* (Cambridge, 1982), pp 21–46 at pp 41–2. 2 Alan O. Anderson and Marjorie O. Anderson, 'Introduction' to *Adomnán's Life of Columba* (2nd ed.: Oxford, 1991), pp xv–lxxx at p. lxvii.

nevertheless located in Book 2 of *Vita Columbae* among the miraculous demonstrations of the saint's power, rather than in Book 1 dedicated to Columba's powers of prophecy.[4] In the prologue to Book 2, however, Adomnán states that the miracles of power are often accompanied by prophetic foreknowledge. The only miraculous thing in the episode though, apart from the miracle of turning winds into unfavourable ones and back again which only has a minor role in the story, is the prophetic knowledge of the saint concerning Librán's destiny. The last paragraph of the episode furthermore reinforces the image that the miracle at its centre is the saint's foreknowledge, since in his closing remark Adomnán states that what he has written about 'the true prophecies of Saint Columba concerning Librán' must be sufficient.[5]

The episode opens in Iona by relating how a layman (*plebeus*) who had only recently taken up the clerical habit came to the island. When the saint questioned him concerning his origins and the reasons for his journey, the man replied that he had come *ad delenda in perigrinationem peccamina*.[6] Librán seems to have come to Iona as a penitent ready to submit to the monastic discipline, but it is not clear whether it was his intention from the outset to eventually join the monastic community as a monk or only to serve the time of his penance in one of the penitential communities attached to the monastery.[7] The fact that he had assumed *clericatus habitu* may imply his intention of entering monastic life permanently. Columba replied immediately by setting out the harsh requirements of monastic life in order to test the newcomer's commitment to penance, which may be seen as the first step in the process of joining the monastery.[8]

The actions of Columba in questioning Librán's motivation and commitment are in line with the precepts of the *Institutes* of John Cassian who instructs that the newcomer's ardour in joining the monastic community should be tested by the trial of leaving them lying outside for days to be dis-

---

3 *VC* ii, 39: 'Prophecy of the holy man concerning Librán of the reed-plot'; translation by the Andersons. Librán is nicknamed *harundineti* because of his work on gathering reeds. 4 Thomas Charles-Edwards has also commented on the placement of this episode, concluding that Book 2 is less consistent in its materials than the other two books of *Vita Columbae*: 'The structure and purpose of Adomnán's *Vita Columbae*' in Wooding (ed.), *Adomnán of Iona*, pp 205–18 at p. 209.   5 *VC* ii, 39: *Has de Librano harundineti sancti ueridicas Columbae uaticinationes scripsise sufficiat.*   6 *VC* ii, 39: 'to wipe out his sins on pilgrimage'; translation by Richard Sharpe, *Adomnán of Iona: Life of St Columba* (London, 1995).   7 On the paramonastic penitential communities, see Etchingham, *Church organization*, pp 290–96; Sharpe, *Life of St Columba*, p. 282 n. 115.   8 Colmán Etchingham has discussed the status of the *athláech*, 'ex-layman', and quotes a legal passage which refers to the three stages of progression from a sinful layman into an 'ex-layman' in 'true unity with the church' through purgative penance. A similar process, in which the confessor's testimony concerning the aspiring monk's commitment has a central role, can be detected in the story of Librán. Etchingham, *Church organisation*, pp 296–7.

dained by the monks passing by.⁹ Columba's deeds are even closer to the
instructions in the Rule of Saint Benedict, in which it is stipulated that an
older brother should be chosen to ensure that the novice is really ready to
perform the work of God, to be obedient and to be treated in a humbling
manner. The novice should moreover be told about *omnia dura et aspera per
quae itur ad deum*.¹⁰ Librán's reply that he is ready to do whatever the saint
demands of him, *quamlibet durissima quamlibet indigna*,¹¹ echoes the same ideas
of total obedience, surrender to the superior's judgment and readiness to
undertake the demanding life of a monk. Columba's contemporary, the Irish
monk Columbanus, writes moreover in his monastic rule of obedience that
'nothing must be refused in their obedience by Christ's true disciples, *quamvis
durum et arduum sit*, but it must be seized with zeal, with gladness'.¹² All these
authors agree in stressing the hardships of the monastic path and the importance of obedience as a central virtue of monastic life. One possible source for
these ideas may be the words of the fifth-century author Salvian who writes
in his *De gubernatione Dei* that true Christians should happily bear all burdens
quamlibet dura quamlibet aspera, thus reflecting the same idea that the difficulties on the Christian path are trials on the road to heaven.¹³ In the context
of *VC* ii, 39, Librán's words underline his humility and commitment to submitting himself to the severe judgment of the saint and to the monastic discipline whatever hardships it entails.

Librán's use of the term *peregrinatio* for his stay in the monastery in order
to wipe out his sins agrees with the typical Irish usage in which pilgrimage is
a favourite metaphor for the journey of life to heaven, and especially for
monastic life.¹⁴ Another example of visitors coming to Iona as *peregrini*
involves the two brothers in *VC* i, 32 who came to the saint with the intention of staying in the monastery for a year. Against the expectations of the
monks of the community, Columba instead asked them to profess monastic

---

9 *Institutes* iv, 3. Boniface Ramsey (trans.), *The institutes* (New York, 2000), pp 79–80; *PL*
49, 53–476. 10 *The rule of St Benedict* §58: 'all the difficult and harsh things that he will
experience on the road to God'. Bruce L. Venarde (ed.), *The rule of St. Benedict*
(Cambridge, MA, 2011). The Rule also includes a separate chapter on obedience in which
the unhesitating obedience to the commands of the superiors is stressed: *The rule* §5.
11 *VC* ii, 39: 'however harsh, however degrading'; translation by Sharpe. 12 *Regula
monachorum* I, 'however hard and difficult'. G.S.M. Walker (ed. and trans.), *Sancti
Columbani opera*, SLH 2 (Dublin, 1957; repr. 1997), p. 125. 13 *De gubernatione Dei* i, 2:
'however difficult and harsh' ed. Franciscus Pauly, Corpus Scriptorum Ecclesiasticorum
Latinorum 8 (Wien, 1883). 14 For further discussion, see Jan Erik Rekdal, 'The Irish
ideal of pilgrimage as reflected in the tradition of Colum Cille' in A. Härdelin (ed.), *In
quest of the kingdom: ten papers on medieval monastic spirituality* (Stockholm, 1991), pp 9–
26; Thomas M. Charles-Edwards, 'The social background to Irish *peregrinatio*', *Celtica*, 11
(1976), 43–59; Kathleen Hughes, 'The changing theory and practice of Irish pilgrimage',
Journal of Ecclesiastical History, 11 (1960), 143–51; Katja Ritari, *Pilgrimage to heaven:
eschatology and monastic spirituality in early medieval Ireland* (Turnhout, forthcoming).

vows immediately, knowing that they would pass away within two weeks. By making the commitment to monastic life, the brothers were offering themselves as 'a living sacrifice to God' fulfilling in a short time long years of service as soldiers of Christ.[15] Thus they were able to secure the reward in the afterlife when they were taken to the Lord, thereby achieving the ultimate goal of monastic life. Librán's endeavours were directed towards the same lofty aim as later in the story when his younger brother pointed out that he had laboured in Britain with Saint Columba to obtain *salutem animae*.[16] The connection between penance and pilgrimage becomes clear when pilgrimage is understood as exile undertaken voluntarily in order to expiate sins or as an ascetic practice with penitential overtones.[17] In both cases, *peregrinatio* is more about leaving one's homeland and placing one's destiny into the hands of God than pilgrimage in the sense of visiting holy shrines.[18] The destination of the *peregrinus* is rather in heaven than some location on earth. The *peregrinatio* of both Librán and the pilgrim brothers is more about their stay on Iona rather than the journey there, and the goal of their purgative monastic sojourn is the heavenly kingdom.

Librán's purgative journey then began with his kneeling on the ground to confess all his sins, for which he was commanded by the saint to spend seven years in penance on Tiree.[19] Librán's process of freeing himself from sin and from earthly commitments then continued with him asking advice regarding an oath he had made to a wealthy relative of his after the said relative had rescued him from the punishment of death for manslaughter.[20] Librán had promised to serve his rescuer for the rest of his life but had soon come to

---

15 *VC* i, 32: *Hi duo proselyti uiuam deo se ipsos exhibentes hostiam, longaque in breui christianae tempora militiae conplentes.*   **16** *VC* ii, 39: 'the salvation of his soul'.   **17** For discussion of the connection between the status of an exile or an outlaw and that of the pilgrim, see Rekdal, 'The Irish ideal', pp 10–12; Charles-Edwards, 'The social background'. On penance as a form a martyrdom, see Stancliffe, 'Red, white and blue', pp 40–4.   **18** See Katja Ritari, '"Pilgrims in the world": monastic life as a quest for heaven in early medieval Ireland' in R. Hämäläinen, H. Pesonen, M. Rahkala and T. Sakaranaho (eds), *Pilgrimage of life: studies in honour of Professor René Gothóni* (Helsinki, 2010), pp 336–45.   **19** On the monastery of Mag Luinge on Tiree as a place of penance, see Sharpe, *Life of St Columba*, p. 303 n. 182.   **20** The *omnia peccata* confessed by Librán seem to exclude the false oath concerning which he asks Columba's guidance only after confessing 'all his sins'. Both Sharpe and the Andersons note the flaw in Adomnán's logic: that Librán begins to speak of the manslaughter and the oath resulting from it only after the confession. Curiously Librán raises the topic by asking what he should do about the false oath, while the manslaughter only comes up as the circumstances which led to swearing the oath. It seems that Librán must have already brought the killing up with the saint, especially since the seven years of penance would be appropriate atonement for manslaughter. Librán's words explaining that once when he still lived in his native land he killed a man, nevertheless, seem to suggest that the topic is introduced for the first time. See Anderson and Anderson, *Adomnán's Life of Columba*, p. 154 n. 180; Sharpe, *Life of St Columba*, p. 338 n. 311.

other thoughts, wishing to change his earthly master for a heavenly one and fleeing to Iona.[21] The legitimacy of Librán's decision is validated in Adomnán's eyes by the fact that the Lord had favoured his journey, apparently securing favourable winds for a swift and safe crossing.[22]

The *penitens perigrinus* was then shipped off to the monastery of Mag Luinge at Tiree to serve his seven-year sentence of penance, after which he was allowed to return to Iona and to approach the altar again as a purged man. Now that Librán had freed himself of the burden of past sins, it was his turn to liberate himself from worldly commitments before being able to enter monastic life. Columba gave Librán a preciously decorated sword and advised him to bring it to his earthly master in return for his freedom. With his divine foresight, the saint was able to predict how events would unfold, knowing that the master's virtuous wife would give her husband the sound advice of freeing Librán without payment. When Librán then went to his master, everything happened as predicted by the saint. The master's wife proved her prudence in advising her husband wisely and suggesting that Columba's blessing would be more valuable to them than the material gift of a sword.[23] She moreover seems to have recognized Librán's status as someone who served a higher master, since she told her husband that he should release 'the pious servant' to the saint without payment, thus suggesting that Librán's commitment to the service of God through the saint would override his earthly duties.[24]

After being freed from the bonds of servitude, Librán still had the filial duties of taking care of his elderly parents binding him to the world. The saint had, however, also foreseen this situation, knowing that Librán's father would soon pass away thus freeing Librán from the duty of looking after him, and that his younger brother would volunteer to take Librán's place in serving their mother. Like the virtuous wife of Librán's former master, his brother too recognized his higher calling, suggesting that they should let him go back to Britain where he had laboured for the salvation of his soul for the past seven years.[25]

On his way back to Iona, Librán had to turn to the saint for help when some sailors refused to take him into their boat for the crossing to Britain. Trusting in the saint's assistance, Librán addressed Columba, presenting him-

21 This episode includes very interesting references to early Irish legal practice. Richard Sharpe has discussed some of them in *Life of St Columba*, p. 338 n. 312. See also Fergus Kelly, *A guide to early Irish law* (Dublin, 1988), pp 215–16, 224. 22 *Vita Columbae* includes several stories in which the Lord controls the elements in order to help his faithful monks on their journeys. One is included further on in this episode, see also *VC* i, 4; ii, 12, 34, 42, 45. 23 On wise wives and the virtue of prudence in *Vita Columbae*, see Ritari, *Saints and sinners*, pp 71–3, 88–92. 24 *VC* ii, 39: *Liberetur ei pius hic gratis ministrator.* 25 Ibid.: *Nullo modo nos oportet fratrem in patria retentare qui per uii. annos apud sanctum Columbam in Britannia salutem exercuit animae.*

self as a *socius* of the saint and thus stressing the closeness of his connection with the holy man.[26] Although the saint was far away he was *spiritu presentem*, watching over Librán's journey in the same way as he accompanied his monks in spirit helping them in danger and refreshing them after a long day of working in the fields.[27] Librán's close relationship with the saint is brought up again when he replied to the sailors' invitation to join them in the boat and to change the contrary winds by stating that it is not he, but Columba whom he had obeyed for the past seven years, who could make the miracle happen. Librán moreover acknowledged that the power to do miracles did not emanate from the saint but ultimately from God, telling the sailors to hoist the sails in the name of the Almighty whose blameless servant Columba was.[28] Librán is here presented as an associate of Columba who could turn to the saint expecting to receive help thanks to his obedient subjection, just as the saint was protected and helped by God thanks to his dedication to the service of the Almighty.

After his adventures in Ireland, Librán finally returned to Iona where the saint renamed him as Librán to mark his liberty.[29] As Librán had freed himself of any worldly entanglements, he was now able to take the final step of taking the monastic vow. Columba then sent Librán back to the monastery of Mag Luinge with the prophetic words that he would reach old age but that his place of resurrection would not be in Britain but in Ireland. As Librán grieved when hearing this, the saint consoled him saying that he would die in one of Columba's monasteries and that his part in the kingdom would be with the elect monks of Columba. Everything then unfolded again as the saint had prophesied: after serving Columba obediently as a monk for many years, Librán was sent on some monastic business to Durrow where he died and was buried among the monks to rise again into eternal life. Librán's death in old age among the monks of Columba is one example of the paradigmatic good death in *Vita Columbae*, which happens in the fullness of years, peacefully and surrounded by friends.[30] Librán's burial among the elect monks in Durrow is another indicator of his destiny in the afterlife, since places of burial hold special significance for Adomnán as markers of one's destiny in heaven.[31]

---

26 Ibid.: '*Placetne tibi,*' ait, '*sancte Columba ut hi nautae qui me tuum non suscipiunt socium plenis uelis et secundis enauigent uentis?*', '"Does it please you, St Columba," he said, "that these sailors have full sails and a following wind for their voyage, though they refuse to take me, your friend, with them?"'; translation by Sharpe.   **27** See, for example, *VC* ii, 42 in which Columba helps the monk Cormac who is pestered by some small sea-creatures in the far north (*quamlibet longe absens corpore spiritu tamen praesens*), and *VC* i, 37 in which the saint goes in spirit to meet his monks returning from the fields. Sharpe, *Life of St Columba*, p. 254 n. 49 has pointed out that the source for these is 1 Cor 5:3, *Ego quidem absens corpore, praesens autem spiritu*.   **28** *VC* ii, 39: '*In nomine omnipotentis*', ait, '*cui sanctus Columba inculpabiliter seruit, tensis rudentibus leuate uelum*'.   **29** *VC* ii, 39: *Tu Libranus uocaberis, eo quod sis liber.*   **30** See, for example, *VC* i, 10, 13, 15; iii, 9. For discussion of good and bad deaths in *Vita Columbae*, see Ritari, *Saints and sinners*, pp 149–52.   **31** Thomas O'Loughlin,

The place of burial is also the place of resurrection for Adomnán, who writes of Librán that he would *in resurrectionem uitae de somno mortis euigelabis* with the elect monks of Columba among whom he is buried.[32] The image of death as sleep from which one wakes up at the end of time is biblical and comes from Job 14:12: *Sic homo, cum dormierit, non resurget, donec atteratur caelum, non euigilabit, nec consurget de somno suo.*[33] Gregory the Great furthermore uses the same phrase *somnus mortis* when commenting on the same passage from Job in his *Moralia in Iob* 3.12.8: *Liquet enim quia non resurget, scilicet donec atteratur coelum, quia nisi mundi huius finis aduenerit, humanum genus a somno mortis ad uitam non euigilabit.*[34] The bodies of the dead were thus expected to slumber in their graves while waiting for the Day of Judgement and the resurrection, when they would be reunited with their souls. Adomnán, however, seems also to have expected some kind of personal judgement at the moment of dying in addition to the final judgement; this emerges clearly from other episodes of *Vita Columbae*, in which souls are taken directly to heaven or hell at the hour of death.[35] Thus it was the bodies that stayed in the graves slumbering, while the souls were already deposited in heaven and hell for the interim before Judgement Day.

When the whole story is looked at structurally, it is possible to discern three sets of movement from one place to another which are complemented by analogous movements between different planes and statuses:

1. World (Ireland) – Iona – Tiree
2. Tiree – Iona – world (Ireland)
3. World (Ireland) – Iona – Tiree

In these itineraries, Iona (where the saint is located) plays the intermediate role of a place of guidance and spiritual counsel. In addition to the movement

---

'The tombs of the saints: their significance for Adomnán' in J. Carey, M. Herbert and P. Ó Riain (eds), *Studies in Irish hagiography: saints and scholars* (Dublin, 2001), pp 1–14: on Librán, see pp 7–8.   **32** *VC* ii, 39: 'from the sleep of death into the resurrection of life'.   **33** Job 14:12, 'so he lies down and does not rise; till the heavens are no more, people will not awake or be roused from their sleep'. The image is also used in Romans 13:11: *Et hoc scientes tempus: quia hora est jam nos de somno surgere. Nunc enim propior est nostra salus, quam cum credidimus* ('And do this, understanding the present time: The hour has already come for you to wake up from your slumber, because our salvation is nearer now than when we first believed'). Biblical translations from the New International Version.   **34** *Moralia in Iob* 3.12.8: 'For it is plain that they shall not rise again, that is, till the heavens be no more, in that except the end of the world come, the race of mankind shall not wake to life from the sleep of death': ed. M. Adriaen, CCSL 143, 143B, 2 vols (Turnhout, 1979–85).   **35** See, for example, *VC* i, 31; ii, 25; iii, 6–7, 9–14. On Adomnán's vision of the destinies of souls, see Ritari, *Saints and sinners*, pp 152–67; Nathalie Stalmans, 'Le jugement de l'âme dans la Vie de Columba' in Carey et al. (eds), *Studies in Irish hagiography*, pp 41–8.

happening horizontally on this plane, there is a fourth complementary axis of vertical movement between this and the other world.[36]

4. Tiree – Durrow (Ireland) – heaven

All these sets of movement consist of the place of origin from where the journey begins, the intermediate place of stopping, and the place of destination. The geographical movement between Ireland and Britain – the world and the monasteries of Iona and Mag Luinge – is matched by the movement between the statuses of layman, penitent and monk, with the intermediate state of preparation before taking the monastic vow.

1. World (Ireland) – Iona – Tiree (layman – penitent)
2. Tiree – Iona – world (Ireland) (penitent – preparation for entering monastic life)
3. World (Ireland) – Iona – Tiree (preparation for entering monastic life – monk)

To these three movements, between statuses, may be added a fourth which involves movement between the different planes of being.

4. Tiree – Durrow (Ireland) – heaven (monk – citizen of heaven)

Librán's journey from being a sinner and a layman through penance into becoming a monk and eventually a citizen of heaven is a paradigm of conversion from sinning to a truly Christian life. Before joining the monastery, he is required to shed his old self by the purifying process of penance and by freeing himself from any earthly entanglements. The whole story can be reduced to matching sets of geographical and social movement between the two planes of being and the different statuses:

1. The world – the monastery – heaven
2. Sinner – monk – citizen of heaven

In both cases, the monastic (as a space and a status) holds the intermediary place as the liminal stage in the process of transformation from human to angelic being. The monastery as a place can thus be understood as being set apart, halfway between earth and heaven. It is the holy ground frequented by

---

36 James Bruce has noted that the story of Librán demonstrates 'the idea of the three countries of earth, the kingdom of God on earth, and the kingdom of heaven' which he sees as central to the theological message of *Vita Columbae*: *Prophecy, miracles, and heavenly light? The eschatology, pneumatology, and missiology of Adomnán's Life of St Columba* (Carlisle, 2004), p. 210.

supernatural apparitions, and offers a glimpse of the heavenly life in the liturgical celebration of God.[37] Similarly, the monk holds a status closer to heaven than the rest of humanity. In his second preface, Adomnán confirms this when he says that Saint Columba showed himself to be ready for the life of heaven though placed on earth, since he was *aspectu angelicus* among his other virtues and saintly qualities.[38] As a saint, Columba has, of course, reached a level of perfection unattainable for most Christians, but nonetheless he is also presented as a model for his monks to emulate.[39] At the same time, the saint functions as a beacon who shows the way with his virtue as example and as proof of the soteriological promise of the rewards awaiting in the afterlife, since he is the person who has already gone to heaven and can intercede from there on behalf of the faithful. This promise is given to all Christians, but in monastic life it acquired particular emphasis as it came to determine the monk's relationship with this world and its way of life. The expectation of the afterlife gave meaning to monastic life on this side of the great divide, since in monasticism the monks (and nuns) dedicated their whole lives to reaching this goal.

Adomnán presents Librán as a paragon of transformation: first of a sinner into a monk and second of a monk into a citizen of heaven, thus reaching the ultimate goal of monastic life.[40] Librán is a model of repentance and obedience who merits a place in the heavenly kingdom. If the saint represents an unattainable model to be admired, Librán provides a more accessible example for emulation. The episode concerning Librán can be read as outlining Adomnán's programme for monastic life. Before being able to dedicate oneself to the search for the heavenly kingdom, the aspiring monk has to free himself from the burdens of the past, including the blemish of sin and any earthly commitments. Only then is he able to engage fully with monastic life, turning his back on this world and committing himself totally to the service of God. Obedience holds a central place in this vision as a sign of commit-

---

37 For further discussion, see, for example, David Jenkins, *'Holy, holier, holiest': the sacred topography of the early medieval Irish church* (Turnhout, 2010); Patricia M. Rumsey, *Sacred time in early Christian Ireland* (London, 2007). On the grave of the saint as the place which joins heaven and earth, see Peter Brown, *The cult of the saints: its rise and function in Latin Christianity* (Chicago, 1981), pp 1–22.   38 *VC* (2nd pref.): *quamuis in terra positus caelestibus se aptum moribus ostendebat.* Sharpe has pointed out that this and the following sentence which lists Columba's virtues, including being angelic in demeanour, is a quotation from *Actus S. Silvestri* (*Life of St Columba*, p. 248 n. 18).   39 On Columba leading a heavenly life on earth and as a model for his monks, see Ritari, *Saints and sinners*, pp 44–58.   40 Sara E. Ellis Nilsson has identified edification both for lay people and the monks as the main purpose of this episode: 'Miracle stories and the primary purpose of Adomnán's *Vita Columbae*', *Heroic Age*, 10 (2007) <http://www.heroicage.org/issues/10/nilsson.html>, see her appendix 'Miracle categorization in Adomnán's *VC*'. On the composition of *Vita Columbae*, see Máire Herbert, *Iona, Kells, and Derry: the history and hagiography of the monastic familia of Columba* (Oxford, 1988), pp 138–42.

ment and total subjugation of one's will to that of the superiors who represent God on earth. Librán's obedience is rewarded with the promise of rising again with the elect monks of Columba. A similar fate befalls the monk Cailtan, whose obedience in hastening to the saint at his command is praised and rewarded when he ends his life a few days later, going in peace to the Lord (*VC* i, 31). Both Librán and Cailtan were able to achieve the goal of monastic life at their deaths, having secured a place in heaven through their obedient commitment. Librán came to Iona *in peregrinatione*, which can be understood as including not only his penitential path to Iona and Tiree but his whole journey to heaven. His arrival on Iona was the first step on the road that would transform him from penitent to monk to citizen of heaven, and would take him from Ireland to Britain and back again until he reached his final destination of rising from the grave into everlasting life.

O'Friel's ghost

KATHARINE SIMMS

Quite some time ago, when I was a postgraduate working at my PhD on Gaelic Ulster in the later Middle Ages, I had the good fortune to share a flat with Máire, our honorand. I owe her a considerable debt of gratitude not only because she was a most accommodating companion over mundane house-keeping matters, but in order to assist my research she presented me with a copy of the Colum Cille poems from Bodleian Laud MS 615, that she had edited for her MA thesis.[1] Most of the poems concern the rights of the heads of the Columban shrines in Donegal and elsewhere, especially the churches of Kilmacrenan and Glencolumkille. He who violated the rights of one, was to be cursed by all. In particular the poem *Mairg mallaighter a port naoimh* vaunts the power of curses by the churchmen of Gartan, Derry, Glencolumkille and Kilmacrenan, as long as they are justified.[2] Excommunication, cursing and satire were the three parallel social sanctions exercised by ordained clergy, keepers of relics and bardic poets respectively,[3] and in late medieval Irish conditions, the same individual might be qualified to utter all three. In the case of poetic satire, we have written assurance that an unjust utterance would rebound to punish the poets.[4] It will be seen from what follows that the keepers of the relics of Colum Cille were also held to run a risk if they pronounced an unjust curse.

RIA MS C iv 2 (466) is a mid-sixteenth-century miscellany of medical and magical material, written by various scribes, Niall Ó Cuinn and Brian Mac Maol Tuile among them. Folio 1v, however, is distinguished from the other pages by a decorated border framing a set of verses attributed to returned spirits of the dead. As one verse was attributed to the spirit of 'Donnchadh Cairbreach', I originally imagined this to be a reference to Donnchadh Cairbreach Ó Briain (†1243), and took it as an indication that the verses came from different periods, and were collected together because of their alleged ghostly authorship. More recently I learned that Maghnus Ó Domhnaill, lord of Tír Conaill (†1563), who is criticized in the first three

---

1 Máire Herbert, 'Duanaire Choluim Cille i Laud 615: an téacs' (MA, NUI Galway, 1970). See also Anne O'Sullivan and Máire Herbert, 'The provenance of Laud Misc. 615', *Celtica*, 10 (1973), 174–92. 2 Oxford, Bodleian Library, Laud MS 615, p. 74 (Herbert, 'Duanaire Choluim Cille', p. 136). 3 See Tomás Ó Cathasaigh, 'Curse and satire', *Éigse*, 21 (1986), 10–15. 4 Rudolf Thurneysen, 'Mittelirische Verslehren: Text III', *IT* iii, 1 (1891), pp 67–105 at p. 97; Liam Breatnach, 'An aoir sa ré luath' in P. Ó Fiannachta (ed.), *Léachtaí Cholm Cille 18: An aoir* (Maigh Nuad, 1988), pp 11–19 at p. 14; *CIH* 1564.14.

verses, had two half-brothers called Donnchadh Cairbreach and Éigneachán, who were both slain by the forces of An Calbhach, the eldest son of Maghnus, in the course of 1545.[5] Clearly all the verses are thus related to each other, and to the bitter family disputes taking place among the Ó Domhnaill clan in the years 1545–8.

The overall message of the texts is to condemn Maghnus Ó Domhnaill 'high-king of Donegal' for opposing his good son An Calbhach, and to condemn three members of the Ó Firghil erenagh family of Kilmacrenan for yielding to Maghnus' request to fast and invoke the supernatural power of Colum Cille's relics to curse An Calbhach unjustly, a curse that has rebounded upon them, as they are now all dead, and their souls are damned. The soul of Maghnus' brother Éigneachán is also damned, since in life he plundered the church of Kilmacrenan and insulted the priests of Killydonnell, a Third Order Franciscan friary, associated with the Ó Domhnaill family in general and with An Calbhach in particular, as we find he was staying there, 'with a few soldiers, besides women and poets', when he was captured by Seaán Ó Néill in 1559.[6] Intriguingly, however, the soul of An Calbhach's other slain opponent, Donnchadh Cairbreach Ó Domhnaill, is said to be in heaven with the angels. Possibly he had been a generous benefactor of the friars of Killydonnell.

Tír Conaill about the year 1545 was experiencing a tangle of varied but interwoven tensions. There was a many-faceted religious dimension. On 6 August 1541, Maghnus Ó Domhnaill as one of his articles of submission negotiated with the Lord Deputy, Sir Anthony St Leger, repudiated the 'usurped authority' of the Pope. King Henry VIII's response to this news on 23 September was to urge that the Deputy press forward with the dissolution of religious houses, even in the territories

> of thothers, as Odoneyl, etc. dwelling in the remote partyes … And for the better alluring of those of the remote partyes, We shall not moche stick to let them have summe of the religious houses, which shalbe suppressed in their countreys, in ferme, at suche reasonable rentes as you shall thinke mete, so as We maye be in suretye to be aunswered of the rentes.[7]

This in itself might have caused those who sympathized with the Third Order Franciscans of Killydonnell to regard Maghnus Ó Domhnaill with suspicion. However, there was also tension over the bishopric of Raphoe. The

5 Darren Mac Eiteagáin, 'O'Donnell, Manus (Ó Domhnaill, Maghnas)' in J. McGuire and J. Quinn (eds), *Dictionary of Irish biography*, 9 vols (Cambridge, 2009), vii, pp 386–9; *AFM* 1545 (v, 1490–1).   6 *AFM* 1559 (v, 1564–7).   7 *State papers: King Henry VIII part III (contd.): correspondence between the governments of England and Ireland, 1538–46* (London, 1843), pp 318, 333–4.

death of Bishop Éamonn Ó Gallchobhair in 1543 reduced the number of rival claimants to this see from three to two: Cornelius Ó Catháin, who was supported by Henry VIII, and Art Ó Gallchobhair, who had been recommended to the Pope by King James V of Scotland, although Pope Paul III did not appoint him in opposition to the English king's candidate until after Henry VIII's death in 1547.[8] Between the death of Bishop Éamonn Ó Gallchobhair and the Pope's confirmation of Art Ó Gallchobhair as his successor, Maghnus' acceptance of Henry VIII's role as head of the church in Ireland as well as England tended to favour the absent claimant Cornelius Ó Catháin. During his initial submission to Anthony St Leger in 1541, Maghnus had petitioned the king to appoint his chaplain as bishop of Elphin, a request that was granted in 1544.[9]

From the mid-fifteenth century, the Uí Ghallchobhair had been acquiring an increasing stranglehold over leading church offices in Raphoe diocese, including the Cistercian abbey of Assaroe near Ballyshannon, and one branch of the family had extended their influence into Derry.[10] Their resulting wealth had also boosted their political importance. Tuathal Balbh Ó Gallchobhair, who died in 1541, is described in the annals as 'one of the most powerful of the sub-chieftains [or "nobles of the territorial council"] (*ar thend-maithibh oirechta*) of Tirconnell'.[11] They had loyally supported Maghnus Ó Domhnaill's right to inherit the chieftainship against a challenge from his brother Aodh Buidhe in 1537, developing a long-running feud with the Uí Bhaoighill, who had been supporting Aodh Buidhe at the time, and who had massacred a number of the descendants of the late Bishop Lochlainn Ó Gallchobhair.[12]

Aodh Buidhe himself died at Kilmacrenan in 1538. Maghnus faced a further challenge from two more brothers, Éigneachán and Donnchadh Cairbreach in 1540 but was in a sufficiently strong position to defeat and imprison them, until in 1543 the English administration stipulated that he release the pair as part of ongoing political negotiations. The reason for English interest in the matter seems traceable to the influence of Conn Ó Domhnaill, another brother of Maghnus, who had long been residing at the English court as a hostage, but who crossed to Dublin to oversee this release before returning to England.[13] In contrast to both Maghnus and Donnchadh Cairbreach, Conn was a full brother of Éigneachán and both were the sons of Sadhbh, daughter of Domhnall son of Henry Ó Néill, a former lord of Tír Eoghain (†1509), while Maghnus' own son Aodh (but not his eldest son An

---

8 Aubrey Gwynn, *The medieval province of Armagh* (Dundalk, 1946), pp 204–9. 9 *State papers: King Henry VIII part III (contd.)*, p. 320. 10 Pádraig Ó Gallachair, 'Muintir Ghallchobhair', *The Donegal Annual*, 10, iii (1973), 295–315; Gearóid Mac Niocaill, *Na manaigh liatha in Éirinn 1142–c.1600* (BÁC, 1959), p. 177. 11 *AFM* 1541 (v, 1462–3). My addition in square brackets. 12 Ibid., 1537 (v, 1436–7); 1540 (v, 1456–7). 13 Ibid., 1543 (v, 1478–9).

Calbhach), was son of Siobhán, daughter of Conn Mór Ó Néill, and thus a nephew of Conn Bacach Ó Néill (†1559), the newly-created Earl of Tyrone.[14] In 1543, the year Bishop Éamonn Ó Gallchobhair died, a number of the Uí Ghallchobhair seized Lifford castle and rebelled in support of Aodh son of Maghnus against his father and his elder brother An Calbhach. The newly-released Donnchadh Cairbreach Ó Domhnaill joined their revolt. The *Annals of the Four Masters* note that An Calbhach was particularly angry at this turn of events.[15] Since it was open to Maghnus to pacify his son Aodh by naming him as heir instead of An Calbhach, the latter had more to lose if the insurgents succeeded. The following year, An Calbhach brought an English army to besiege Lifford castle, whereupon the English killed a prominent Ó Gallchobhair hostage in a successful move to force the garrison to surrender. War then broke out between Ó Néill and Ó Domhnaill, provoked, it would seem, not only by Conn Bacach's support for his nephew Aodh son of Maghnus Ó Domhnaill, but by Maghnus' usurped authority over Ó Catháin, a vassal-chief within Tír Eoghain. The annals make clear that throughout 1544 Maghnus and his heir, An Calbhach, were fighting on the same side against Ó Néill and the internal dissenters in Tír Conaill.[16] However the verses in RIA MS C iv 2, f. 1v, imply that a rift occurred between Maghnus and An Calbhach in 1545, and that Maghnus induced the Uí Fhirghil of Kilmacrenan to fast against An Calbhach, and invoke the power of Colum Cille's relics against him – presumably because Maghnus did not feel strong enough to defeat his son by military might alone. The annals record that An Calbhach continued his fight against the insurgents and Éigneachán was killed by a party of An Calbhach's followers, just before Calbhach himself defeated his other rebellious uncles in the battle of Coill na gCuirridín (Killygordon, Co. Donegal) where Donnchadh Cairbreach Ó Domhnaill was slain.[17] The verses imply that three leading members of the Ó Firghil family[18] passed away about the same time, and unless one posits an unrecorded plague or Act of God, probability suggests that they too participated on the losing side of the battle of Coill na gCuirridín.

There is a possibility that some or all of the five 'disembodied spirits' were still alive when the verses were written, and that the poems were a kind of curse, foretelling their death, just as the poem *Theast aon diabhal na nGaoidheal* announcing the death of Ailéin son of Ruaidhrí Mac Domhnaill,

---

14 Paul Walsh, *Beatha Aodha Ruaidh Uí Dhomhnaill: The life of Aodh Ruadh O Domhnaill transcribed from the Book of Lughaidh Ó Clérigh*, ITS 42, 45, 2 vols (London, 1948–57), ii, pp 172–3. 15 *AFM* 1543 (v, 1478–81). 16 Ibid., 1544 (v, 1484–9). 17 Ibid., 1545 (v, 1490–1). 18 Although no surname is given for 'Toirdhealbhach Ballach', to whose disembodied spirit the second verse is ascribed, Dubhaltach Mac Fhirbhisigh's *Great book of Irish genealogies*, ed. Nollaig Ó Muraíle, 6 vols (Dublin, 2003), i, pp 350–1, §152.3 names a Toirdheabhach Ballach Ó Firghil as a coarb of Colum Cille at Kilmacrenan, along with a distantly related 'Toirdhealbhach the priest', one generation his junior.

chief of Clann Raghnaill, is considered by Watson to be a satire on a living man rather than a spiteful elegy.[19] Interestingly this chief is said by the poet to have 'died' from the curses of Colum Cille and Fionnán, whose shrines he had violated. However, since Éigneachán and Donnchadh Cairbreach Ó Domhnaill really did die within a short period of time in 1545, it seems more likely that the three Ó Firghil 'spirits' also represented actual deaths.

The six relics of Colum Cille enumerated in the verse attributed to the 'spirit of Toirdhealbhach Ballach' as two stones, two crosses, the *Cathach* and the saint's cowl, are mostly familiar from other sources. The *Cathach*, of course, is particularly well-known. A late sixth- or early seventh-century psalter, in the medieval period it was in the custody of the Mac Robhartaigh family of Ballymagrorty, parish of Drumhome, Co. Donegal.[20] The Mac or Ó Robhartaigh also seems to have been responsible for the Great Cross of St Colum Cille. In 1542, Brian Dorcha Mac Con Midhe is said to have died as a result of Ó Robhartaigh's curse, because he had struck and profaned the Great Cross some time before.[21] The poem *Éist rim a meic Cuanach* is presented as a dialogue between Baoithín and Colum Cille discussing the multiple coarbs of the saint and his various relics.[22] The prime relics of the saint are there identified as his Great Cross, his *Cathach* and his cowl. Two verses further on there is reference to his 'yellow flagstone' (*'gun leic buidhe*) where Colum Cille reposed and was resurrected at 'Doire', that is, almost certainly 'Doire Eithne' or Kilmacrenan. However there were a number of other 'stones of Colum Cille' in existence, including one on the outskirts of Derry,[23] and 'cursing flagstones' in Glencolmcille, mentioned in the poem *Mairg mallaighter a port naoimh*.[24] The reference by the 'spirit of Toirdhealbhach Ballach' to the 'two stones of Colum Cille' may point to Gartan, where there was both a hollowed stone and a red stone of Colum Cille, each associated with his birth. The red stone in particular was a portable relic, taken into battle like the *Cathach*.[25] This would leave a second 'holy cross' of Colum Cille to be accounted for. The miraculous bleeding cross of Raphoe springs to mind,[26] but this is merely speculation.

When thinking of possible authorship for these verses, one could bear in mind a family of poets who at this period developed a grudge against both

19 W.J. Watson, *Scottish verse from the Book of the Dean of Lismore* (Edinburgh, 1937), p. 285. **20** Raghnall Ó Floinn, 'Sandhills, silver and shrines: fine metalwork of the medieval period in county Donegal' in W. Nolan, L. Ronayne and M. Dunlevy (eds), *Donegal: history and society* (Dublin, 1995), pp 85–148 at pp 122–3. **21** *AFM* 1542 (v, 1466–7). **22** Laud MS 615, p. 58 (Herbert, 'Duanaire Choluim Cille', p. 106). **23** Brian Lacey, *Cenél Conaill and the Donegal kingdoms AD 500–800* (Dublin, 2006), pp 111–12. **24** Laud MS 615, p. 74 (Herbert, 'Duanaire Choluim Cille', p. 136), verse 5: *Eascaine Glinne na fert. dentar ar cert-lár a lec*. **25** See John O'Donovan, 'Ordnance survey miscellany', Dublin, RIA MS 14 B 7, p. 423; Andrew O'Kelleher and Gertrude Schoepperle (eds), *Betha Colaim Chille: Life of Columcille, compiled by Maghnas Ó Domhnaill in 1532* (Illinois, 1918; repr. Dublin, 1994), pp 38–9. **26** *AFM* 1411 (iv, 804–5).

Maghnus Ó Domhnaill and the Uí Ghallchobhair. A generation previously, Bishop Meanman Mac Carmacáin (1484–1514) had resisted the spreading power of the Uí Ghallchobhair within his diocese of Raphoe, and had replaced one branch of their family, who were erenaghs in the parish of Kilbarron, with the neighbouring Uí Chléirigh poets and historians.[27] The resulting ill-feeling between the Uí Ghallchobhuir and the Uí Chléirigh was to break out into a bitter quarrel in 1546 when another brother of Maghnus, Domhnall Ó Domhnaill, was killed while visiting Inis Samhaoir as a guest of Eoghan Ó Gallchobhair and his wife, although his safeconduct had been guaranteed by two poets, Gofraidh Mac an Bhaird and Cú Coigcríche Ó Cléirigh. Presumably Cú Coigcríche satirized the forsworn and murderous Eoghan Ó Gallchobhair, but the upshot was that the Ó Cléirigh family were dispossessed and driven out of Tír Conaill to seek refuge in Ó Briain's lordship of Thomond. Cú Coigcríche addressed four poems to Maghnus, seeking redress and upbraiding him for his failure to act against the Ó Gallchobhair tyranny.[28] He also addressed a poem to An Calbhach as a *mac ríogh*, seeking his assistance in the affair, and comparing his exile in Thomond with a trout swimming in milk, condemned to perish outside his natural environment.[29]

***

Could the verses appended below have been composed in 1546 by Cú Coigcríche himself or one of his kinsmen?[30]

(i)

Urlab*ra* na sp*i*rat an*n* so. Spirat i firg*il cecinit*.[31]
Mor nech do meall*ad* le maghn*us* . do lo*cht* cadhais 7 ceall
trosccad egoir air i*n* gcallbh*ach* . imdha a*n*mui*n* ris a ngeall
is mairce dhuinn do fuair ar n[d]a*m*nadh . *ar* com*u*rle *air*d*ri*gh dhui*n*
na ngall.

27 Ó Gallachair, 'Muintir Ghallchobhair', p. 300. 28 *Fada a gcairt ó Chloinn Dálaigh, Truagh gan Maghnus 'na mhac ríogh, Dligid file fagháil aissig, Tréan ríogh uaisligheas ollamh.* See Tomás Ó Cléirigh, 'A poem-book of the O'Donnells', *Éigse*, 1, i (1939), 51–61 at 58; texts in Damian McManus and Eoghan Ó Raghallaigh (eds), *A bardic miscellany* (Dublin, 2010), nos 216, 482, 177, 471 (sequence of poems follows that in the O'Donnell MS). 29 *Deacair iomlaoid chlann gConaill*: McManus and Ó Raghallaigh, *A bardic miscellany*, no. 154; extract in Eleanor Knott, *An introduction to Irish syllabic poetry*, 2nd edition (Dublin, 1957), pp 67–9. 30 I am very grateful to Damian McManus for advising me in my effort to transcribe and translate these texts, though, of course, I bear responsibility for any remaining errors. 31 In the manuscript, these lines occur in reverse order to that shown here.

The sayings of the ghosts here. The ghost of O'Friel sang:
Many of the people of churches and piety
were deceived by Maghnus.
Many a soul is forfeit through
an unjust fasting against the Calbhach.
Woe to us who received our damnation
on the advice of the high-king of Donegal.

(ii)

toird*heal*bh*ach* ball*ach cecinit*

An da cloic sa[n] da naomh chrois cochull is cathach na mbrigh .
si*n* is coluim na saorcheall . tuc saol g*err* dúin*n* ar dt*r*ir.

Toirdhealbhach Ballach sang:
The two stones and the two holy crosses,
the cowl and the powerful *Cathach*:
that and Columba (?) of the noble churches
shortened the lives of us three.

(iii)

clemint o firg*il cecinit*

Gidh be chluinfes an méit ran*n*sa . dighnaibh colui*m* cend na gcliar .
na denait trosgadh *no* escaoin . na haoraid m*a*c righ no t*r*iath .
co bfaict*er* cia dibh is ce[n]taighe . i*n* maor *no* mac righ na niath .

Clement O'Friel sang:
Whoever hears these verses
on the weapons (?) of Columba, head of the clergy:
let them not fast or curse,
let them not satirise a king's son or chieftain,
until it be seen which of them is the more guilty,
the steward [of relics] or the son of the king of the lands.

(iv)

don*n*chadh cairb*r*each *cecinit*

Ata don*n*ch*adh* a gcuirt na naing*eal* . is dó is daigh ní bec an brigh
Ata eiccneachan ag demhnaibh . uch is amhgar i*n* ní itchi.

Donnchadh Cairbreach sang:
Donnchadh is in the court of the angels;
hope [of salvation] is his, not small the significance.
Éigneachán is with the demons;
alas, misery is what he sees.

(v)

Siprat [sic] eign*e*chai*n*

Argai*n* mi*n*ic cild mic nenai*n* . tathaighe tulcha gacha laoi
masla tśagart chill o do*n*air . bual*adh* [bra?]thar mairg doní
Is e tuc man*am* ac dea*m*hnuibh . [uch?] is amhgar i*n* ní itchi
Atá eignechan a gl[as?]aibh isin caisil a taobh thall
cend na [o?]lli ... [lasair?] ... deacoir fana chenn.

Éigneachán's ghost:

Often plundering Kilmacrenan,
the frequenter of a mound[32] every day,
insulting the priests of Killydonnell,
striking [friars?]: alas for him who does it.
That is what caused my soul to be with demons.
Alas, misery is what it sees.
Éigneachán is in fetters in the castle beyond there.
The head of the ... [flame?] ... hard ... awaits him.

32 It is hard to see what sin is pilloried here. Maybe he is being accused of a kind of New Age paganism associated with the later medieval revival of *díberg* culture discussed in Katharine Simms, 'The barefoot kings: literary image and reality in later medieval Ireland', *PHCC*, 30 (2010), 1–21.

Leprechauns and Luperci, Aldhelm and Augustine

PATRICK SIMS-WILLIAMS

As convincingly argued by Jacopo Bisagni, leprechauns (*luprucáin*, etc.) take their name from the Luperci, bands of aristocratic youths who ran semi-naked through ancient Rome during the festival of Lupercalia on the 15 February.[1] The Romans seem to have discontinued the Lupercalia some time after the late fifth century, when Pope Gelasius I attacked it,[2] but a distorted memory of the Luperci lived on in early medieval scholarship, perhaps especially in Irish circles. Aldhelm, abbot of Malmesbury *c.*673–706, dissuading Wihtfrith from studying in Ireland, feared that he might 'expend energy by reading and studying the foul pollution of base Proserpina, which I shrink from mentioning in plain speech; or … record – in the heroic style of epic – the high priests of the *Luperci*, who revel in the fashion of those cultists that sacrifice to Priapus' (*Lupercorum bacchantum antistites ritu litantium Priapo parasitorum heroico stilo historiae caraxare*).[3] Aldhelm was well placed to know about Irish scholarship: he was in touch with people who had studied in Ireland; Malmesbury had been founded by an Irishman, Maíldub, perhaps the unnamed Irishman said to have 'nourished' Aldhelm; there was at least one other Irish foundation in the vicinity, Hanbury in Worcestershire, granted to

1 Jacopo Bisagni, '*Leprechaun*: a new etymology', *CMCS*, 64 (Winter, 2012), 47–84. The idea for my contribution to this Festschrift came to me when preparing a graduate seminar based on Dr Bisagni's article and the earlier articles in *CMCS* by Dr Rodway and Professor Clarke cited in n. 15 below. As well as these valuable studies, I should also like to acknowledge my long-standing debt to Professor Máire Herbert for her service on the Editorial Board of *CMCS* since it began in 1981 and for her many contributions as author and referee.   2 Gelasius is often said to have abolished it but the evidence is dubious; cf. William M. Green, 'The Lupercalia in the fifth century', *Classical Philology*, 26 (1931), 60–9; Neil McLynn, 'Crying wolf: the Pope and the Lupercalia', *Journal of Roman Studies*, 98 (2008), 161–75. It is sometimes speculated that later festivals, such as Shrove Tuesday, continued the Lupercalia: cf. T.P. Wiseman, 'The god of the Lupercal', *Journal of Roman Studies*, 85 (1995), 1–22 at 17; Christoph Schläublin, 'Lupercalien und Lichtmess', *Hermes*, 123 (1995), 117–25.   3 Rudolf Ehwald (ed.), *Aldhelmi opera omnia*, Monumenta Germaniae Historica, Auctores Antiquissimi 15 (Berlin, 1919), p. 479; Michael Lapidge and Michael Herren (trans.), *Aldhelm: the prose works* (Ipswich and Cambridge, 1979), pp 139 and 154. Cited by Bisagni, '*Leprechaun*: a new etymology', 74–5. Aldhelm's mention of Priapus seems a not unreasonable guess at the question posed by Wiseman, 'The god of the Lupercal', as to the identity of that god. He could have been aware of the pagan remains at nearby Bath; cf. Patrick Sims-Williams, 'St Wilfrid and two charters dated AD 676 and 680', *Journal of Ecclesiastical History*, 39 (1988), 163–83, repr. as Chapter V of idem, *Britain and early Christian Europe: studies in early medieval history and culture* (Aldershot, 1995). For another possibility, see below.

an abbot Colmán before 675; and Aldhelm himself had witnessed his learned
archbishop, Theodore of Tarsus, 'hemmed in by a mass of Irish students, like
a savage wild boar checked by a snarling pack of hounds'.[4]

Back in 1979, Michael Herren noted that 'Aldhelm's remarks are discom-
fiting to the sceptics (now in the majority) of the existence of classical learning in seventh-century Ireland'. More recently, however, these remarks have
been hailed as 'the medieval *locus classicus* for the reality of Irish classical
studies'.[5] However this may be, we should probably not assume that Aldhelm
is conveying specific information about what Irish scholars knew about the
Luperci; he may be elaborating on the topic simply to evoke and exemplify
pagan mythology in general, drawing on his own erudition.[6] (He would know
about 'the foul pollution of base Proserpina' from his own reading of
Claudian's *De raptu Proserpinae*).[7] In fact the key to Irish (mis)understanding
of the Luperci was not direct knowledge of classical mythology of the sort
deplored by Aldhelm, but a passage of St Augustine's *De ciuitate Dei* discussed by Bisagni and possibly, I shall argue, a further passage of *De ciuitate
Dei* to be quoted below.[8]

As Bisagni has shown, the main source for Hiberno-Latin understanding
of the Luperci was the following passage of *De ciuitate Dei* xviii, 17, where
Augustine mentions them towards the end of his attack on Varro's now lost
account of animal transformations:

> Hoc Varro ut astruat, commemorat alia non minus incredibilia de illa
> maga famosissima Circe, quae socios quoque Vlixis mutauit in bestias,
> et de Arcadibus, qui sorte ducti tranabant quoddam stagnum atque ibi
> conuertebantur in lupos et cum similibus feris per illius regionis
> deserta uiuebant. Si autem carne non uescerentur humana, rursus post

4 Patrick Sims-Williams, *Religion and literature in western England, 600–800* (Cambridge,
1990), pp 92, 105–9, and 274; Lapidge and Herren, *Aldhelm: the prose works*, pp 143–6 and
163. Cf. G.T. Dempsey, 'Aldhelm of Malmesbury and the Irish', *PRIA*, 99C (1999), 1–
22.   5 Lapidge and Herren, *Aldhelm: the prose works*, p. 140; Brent Miles, *Heroic saga and
classical epic in medieval Ireland* (Cambridge, 2011), p. 17.   6 'He set out to criticize the
study of mythology as a danger to the faith, but it would appear that he was more
interested in proving that he knew as much about matters mythological as any Irish
teacher' (Michael W. Herren, 'The transmission and reception of Graeco-Roman
mythology in Anglo-Saxon England, 670–800', *Anglo-Saxon England*, 27 [1998], 87–103 at
93). On English knowledge of Priapus, see ibid., pp 87 and 93.   7 Michael Lapidge, *The
Anglo-Saxon library* (Oxford, 2006), p. 180. Proserpina is also mentioned in some texts of
the *Liber monstrorum*, from Aldhelm's circle: Herren, 'Transmission and reception', 102;
Andy Orchard, *Pride and prodigies: studies in the monsters of the Beowulf-manuscript*
(Toronto, 2003), p. 278.   8 On second-hand knowledge of classical mythology via
Christian texts, see Michael W. Herren, 'Literary and glossarial evidence for the study of
Classical mythology in Ireland AD 600–800' in H. Conrad-O'Briain, A.-M. D'Arcy, and J.
Scattergood (eds), *Text and gloss: studies in insular learning and literature presented to Joseph
Donovan Pheifer* (Dublin, 1999), pp 49–67.

nouem annos eodem renatato stagno reformabantur in homines.
Denique etiam nominatim expressit quendam Demaenetum gustasse de
sacrificio, quod Arcades immolato puero deo suo Lycaeo facere
solerent, et in lupum fuisse mutatum et anno decimo in figuram
propriam restitutum pugilatum sese exercuisse et Olympiaco uicisse
certamine. Nec idem propter aliud arbitratur historicus in Arcadia tale
nomen adfictum Pani Lycaeo et Ioui Lycaeo nisi propter hanc in lupos
hominum mutationem, quod eam nisi ui diuina fieri non putarent.
Lupus enim Graece λύχος dicitur, unde Lycaei nomen apparet
inflexum. Romanos etiam Lupercos ex illorum mysteriorum ueluti
semine dicit exortos.

To bolster up this story [about the deification of Diomede, and the
transformation of his companions into birds] Varro adduces the equally
incredible tales about the notorious witch Circe, who transformed
Ulysses' companions into animals, and about the Arcadians who were
chosen by lot and swam across a certain lake and were changed into
wolves and lived in the desolate parts of that region in the company of
wild beasts like themselves. However, if they had not eaten human
flesh they used to swim back across the lake after nine years to be
turned back into human beings. To crown all, he expressly names a
certain Demaenetus, telling a story of how he tasted the sacrifice which
the Arcadians made to the god Lycaeus according to their custom,
with a boy as the victim, whereupon Demaenetus was transformed into
a wolf. Then in the tenth year he was restored to his proper shape; he
trained as a boxer and won a prize at the Olympic games. This same
historian also thinks that the reason for the surname Lycaeus, given to
Pan and to Jupiter in Arcadia, can only be this transformation of
human beings into wolves, which they supposed could only be effected
by divine power. For 'wolf' in Greek is *lykos*, and the name *Lycaeus* is
evidently derived from it. Varro also asserts that the Roman *Luperci*
took their origin from these mysteries, which were, we might say, the
seed from which they developed.[9]

---

9 Bernardus Dombart and Alphonsus Kalb (eds), *Sancti Aurelii Augustini De civitate Dei libri XI–XXII*, CCSL 48 (Turnhout, 1955), p. 607; Henry Bettenson (trans.), *St Augustine: concerning the city of God against the pagans* (Harmondsworth, 1972), pp 781–2. Quoted by Bisagni, '*Leprechaun*: a new etymology', 75–6, along with the similar account of the Arcadian werewolves in Pliny's *Natural History*, viii, 34. Pliny attributes this to an otherwise unknown Greek writer Euanthes. Probably Pliny and Augustine were both using Varro, who in turn had cited Euanthes (*recte* Neanthes?); see Dennis D. Hughes, *Human sacrifice in ancient Greece* (London, 1991), p. 99; and Jan N. Bremmer, 'Myth and ritual in Greek human sacrifice: Lykaon, Polyxena, and the case of the Rhodian criminal' in J.N. Bremmer (ed.), *The strange world of human sacrifice* (Leuven, 2007), pp 55–79 at p. 69.

Neither Varro nor Augustine supposed that the Luperci were werewolves, of course.[10] Neverthless, as Bisagni shows, readers of Augustine who knew nothing about the real Lupercalia could easily deduce that the Luperci had an aquatic nature and that they were a distinct 'race', two characteristics shared by the Luperci in early Hiberno-Latin texts[11] and the leprechauns in the Old Irish story of Fergus mac Leiti.[12] It is not a serious objection that leprechauns are never connected with wolves, because some of the medieval Latin texts also omit to mention the Luperci's lupine connection, possibly supposing it implicit in their name; for example:

> Luperci enim et Lurcones, duæ gentes sunt in Oriente, qui post immunditias totius anni lavabant corpora sua in quodam lacu qui inter illos est, et febricitabant, et sicut tradidit gentilitas tunc mutabant figuras.[13]

> The *Luperci* and the *Lurcones* are two peoples in the East who, after the impurities of the whole year, washed their bodies in a certain lake which is to be found among them, and had fever, and then, as the heathens recount, changed their appearances.[14]

An important difference between the Latin and vernacular Irish traditions, however, is that while both respectively regard the Luperci or leprechauns as a race, only the vernacular Irish texts trace this race back to biblical times. Thus, according to the Middle Irish 'Cain and Abel',

> do-sáraigh Día ar clainn Ádaim [MS *áaim*] cona derndaois clemnus nó cairdes re clainn Cáiin nó go críndis uili. Ambia ingen Cáiin .i. delb

10 The Arcadian connection was clearly suggested by the belief that the Lupercal sanctuary (where the she-wolf suckled Romulus and Remus) had been founded by Evander, who was from Arcadia, as Varro recorded elsewhere (cf. Ovid, *Fasti*, ii, 279). See Wiseman, 'The god of the Lupercal', p. 4. 11 References in Bisagni, '*Leprechaun*: a new etymology', 67–78. 12 D.A. Binchy, 'The saga of Fergus mac Léti', *Ériu*, 16 (1952), 33–48; discussed by idem, 'Echtra Fergusa maic Léti' in M. Dillon (ed.), *Irish sagas* (Cork, 1968), pp 40–52; Jacqueline Borsje, *From chaos to enemy: encounters with monsters in early Irish texts* (Turnhout, 1996), pp 17–91; and Neil McLeod, 'Fergus mac Léti and the law', *Ériu*, 61 (2011), 1–28. For his name, see Ruairí Ó hUiginn, 'Fergus, Russ and Rudraige: a brief biography of Fergus mac Róich', *Emania*, 11 (1993), 31–49 at 35–6 who regularizes as 'mac Leite'. The late medieval version, *Aidedh Ferghusa*, was edited and translated from London, BL MS Egerton 1782 by Standish H. O'Grady, *Silva gadelica*, 2 vols (London and Edinburgh, 1892), i, pp 238–52 and ii, pp 269–85 (translation reprinted in T.P. Cross and C.H. Slover [eds], *Ancient Irish tales* [London, 1936], pp 471–87). Note that O'Grady bowdlerized the translation; cf. Philip O'Leary, *The prose literature of the Gaelic revival 1881–1921* (University Park PA, 1994), p. 241. 13 Carolingian recension of the Irish *De diuisionibus temporum*, printed *PL* 90, 660. 14 Translation from Bisagni, '*Leprechaun*: a new etymology', 70, and discussed ibid., 81.

mná fuirri 7 eithre éisg lé; cuma ro-imdhegh-si muir 7 tír; co roibe
fecht ann ina codlud fon muir gur sgéth brec a iuchra ina bél gur ba
torrach de sin, co rug días ar .xx.it do clainn .i. días fa ro-mór méd 7
xx. do min-clainn in ingin (sic!) .i. Fomoir in fer 7 Ispela an ingen; is
[MS *i*] de ro-cét:

> Beg mac bric, builid a bunn,
> Mac is luga do-bí ann.
> Becnait, ba sí in rígan rán
> Ó táid líne luprucán.

God prevailed upon the children of Adam not to have relations or
friendship with the children of Cain or they would all wither. Ambia
daughter of Cain, i.e., she had the shape of a woman and the tail of a
fish; so she could travel the sea and the land; and she was once sleeping
under the sea and a trout squirted its spawn into her mouth so that she
became pregnant, and she gave birth to twenty-two children, i.e., two
who were of very great size and twenty small children of the girl, i.e.,
Fomoir was the man and Ispela the girl. It was sung concerning that:

> Bec son of a trout, ?fair his foot,
> The smallest boy there was.
> Becnait, she was the splendid queen
> From whom is the line of the leprechauns.[15]

Again, according to the Middle Irish *Sex aetates mundi*, §17, God forbade the
sons of Seth to consort with Cain's offspring:

> Tarmideochatar dano clanna Séth in forcital-sin 7 tucsat ingena clainni
> Caín, ar ba mór a caémi, 7 ro-clannaigset friu dar sárgud Dé. Conid
> de-sin ro-geinset torothuir in domuin .i. fomoraig 7 luchorpáin 7 cech
> n-écosc torotharda ndodelbda ro-buí for doínib. Ót-chonnairc Dia
> *hautem* tíctain dóib tar a thimna ro-chinnistar na doíni do huili-dil-
> genn, conid [d]ó tucad in díliu darsin domun, do bád[ud] clainni Caín.

The family of Seth, however, trangressed that instruction and they
took to themselves the daughters of the family of Cain – for they were
very beautiful – and they bore children by them in defiance of God.
So that it was through that that the monstrous creatures of the world
were born – i.e., *fomoraig* and *luchorpáin* and every monstrous form

---

15 Edition and translation (with minor changes) from Simon Rodway, 'Mermaids, leprechauns, and fomorians: a Middle Irish account of the descendants of Cain', *CMCS*, 59
(Summer, 2010), 1–17 at 2. For related material about Ambia and further verse, see
Michael Clarke, 'The lore of the monstrous races in the developing text of the Irish *Sex
aetates mundi*', *CMCS*, 63 (Summer, 2012), 15–49 at 31–2.

that was among mankind. After God had seen them contravene his commandment, however, he determined to destroy completely the human race; so that it was for that reason the Flood was sent over the earth, to drown the family of Cain.[16]

While *Sex aetates* does not state how the leprechauns survived the Flood, we are probably supposed to assume that they were aquatic, and that could apply to the fomorians as well, since 'sub-marine' was an obvious (folk-)etymology for their name.[17] It was known from Augustine that 'it was not necessary to preserve in the ark the creatures able to live in the waters' (*De ciuitate Dei* xv, 27),[18] so the leprechauns' independent survival was easy to explain. No doubt their aquatic nature was also a convenient explanation for their presence on the island of Ireland – insofar as an explanation was required, for as early as the mid-seventh century Irish scholars had anticipated the modern scientific opinion that some non-domesticated animals must have crossed to Ireland when the sea-level was lower.[19]

The doctrine of 'Cain and Abel' and of *Sex aetates mundi* §17 is rejected in §34 of the latter text (with which the associated poem *Rédig dam, a Dé, do nim* agrees).[20] Here the *luchorpáin*, *fomoraig*, goat- (or horse-) heads, and 'every other misshapen form that is among humanity besides' – note that non-aquatic monsters are specifically included now – descend from Noah's accursed son Cham (Ham):

> Conid hé-sin bunad na torothur 7 ní do síl Cháin dóib, amal ad-fiadat Goídil, ar níro-mair ní dia síl-side iar ndílinn, ar rop hé fochonn na dílenn do bádud clainni Caín.

> That, then, is the origin of the monsters and they are *not* of the race of Cain as the Irish say, for none of his line survived the deluge, because the very purpose of the deluge was to drown the race of Cain.[21]

16 Dáibhí Ó Cróinín (ed. and trans.), *The Irish Sex aetates mundi* (Dublin, 1983), pp 71 and 113; the above translation incorporates some modifications from Clarke, 'Lore of the monstrous races', 21.   17 Competing etymologies are discussed by Rodway, 'Mermaids, leprechauns, and fomorians', 16–17.   18 Bettenson's translation, pp 646–7.   19 See discussion of Augustinus Hibernicus, *De mirabilibus sacrae Scripturae* i, 7 (*PL* 35, 2158), by Marina Smyth, *Understanding the universe in seventh-century Ireland* (Woodbridge, 1996), pp 242–4, and Thomas Duddy, *A history of Irish thought* (London, 2002), p. 9. Cf. J.P. Mallory, *The origins of the Irish* (London, 2013), p. 42. For similar opinions from the Welsh side, see Patrick Sims-Williams, *Irish influence on medieval Welsh literature* (Oxford, 2011), p. 192. Augustine of Hippo had made heavy weather of the question 'Whether the remotest island received all kinds of animals from those preserved in the ark' (*De ciuitate Dei* xvi, 7, chapter heading from Bettenson's translation, p. 660).   20 On the relationship between the *Sex aetates* and *Rédig dam, a Dé, do nim* (ibid., §70, stanza 20/26), see Máire Herbert, 'The Irish Sex aetates mundi: first editions', *CMCS*, 11 (Summer, 1986), 97–112 at 106–7, and Clarke, 'Lore of the monstrous races', 18.   21 Ó Cróinín, *The Irish Sex*

Whether the origin of the leprechauns was antediluvian or immediately post-diluvian, they differ from the race of Luperci, who are never connected with Noah's Flood. The nearest any of the texts discussed by Bisagni comes to stating such a connection is *Pauca problesmata de enigmatibus ex tomis canonicis*, where typical products of the 'magic arts and incantations' preserved by Cham include 'the Arcades, swimming across a lake, who are turned into wolves';[22] the Luperci are not mentioned, however.

Indeed it was not really necessary to situate the origin of the Luperci in relation to the Flood, since, according to Augustine (*De ciuitate Dei* xvi, 8), monstrous races such as pygmies, 'shadow-feet', 'dogheads', hermaphrodites, etc., insofar as they really existed and were truly human, could all descend from Adam via Noah and have mutated at any historical period down to the present; it was common knowledge, he argued, that normal parents, at any period, might beget children with abnormalities.[23]

Why then were the leprechauns associated with Noah's Flood? While admitting that Irish scholars may have associated the Luperci and leprechauns with Cain or Cham simply because that was how they explained monstrous races in general, I would like to suggest that a thus far neglected passage in *De ciuitate Dei* may have provided a particular spur.

In Book xviii Chapter 10, Augustine alludes to Varro's dating of 'Deucalion's flood' to the reign of Cranaus, king of Athens, and notes that Eusebius and Jerome preferred to date it to the reign of his predecessor Cecrops. In Chapter 11, Augustine synchronizes this Cecrops with Moses. Then, in Chapter 12, he starts a lengthy discussion of the cults of false gods which were established by the kings of Greece in the time of Moses and Joshua:

> Per haec tempora, id est ab exitu Israel ex Aegypto usque ad mortem Iesu Naue, per quem populus idem terram promissionis accepit, sacra sunt instituta diis falsis a regibus Graeciae, quae memoriam diluuii et ab eo liberationis hominum uitaeque tunc aerumnosae modo ad alta, modo ad plana migrantium sollemni celebritate reuocarunt. Nam et Lupercorum per sacram uiam ascensum atque descensum sic interpretantur, ut ab eis significari dicant homines, qui propter aquae inundationem summa montium petiuerunt et rursus eadem residente ad ima redierunt ...[24]

---

aetates mundi, §34, discussed by Clarke, 'Lore of the monstrous races', 21–49. On the descent of monsters either from Cain before Noah's Flood or from Cham (= Ham) after the Flood, see Orchard, *Pride and prodigies*, pp 58–85.   **22** G. MacGinty (ed.), *Pauca problesmata de enigmatibus ex tomis canonicis*, CCCM 173 (Turnhout, 2000), p. 105; Bisagni, '*Leprechaun*: a new etymology', 73–4.   **23** See Bettenson's translation, pp 661–4, where the various races are identified in the footnotes (see also p. xxx).   **24** Dombart and Kalb, *De civitate Dei libri XI–XXII*, p. 602.

During this period, that is, from the departure of Israel from Egypt down to the death of Joshua, through whose agency that people were given the land of promise, ceremonies in honour of false gods were established by the kings of Greece. These cults recalled the memory of the deluge and the liberation of mankind from it, as well as the troubles of life at that time, when men first migrated to high ground and then returned to the plains. That, indeed, is the interpretation put upon the ascent and descent of the Luperci along the Sacred Way. It is said that they symbolize the men who made for the mountain tops because of the floods of water, and again returned to the lowlands when the floods subsided ...[25]

While it may be clear to us that Augustine is not referring to Noah's Flood, but is referring back to Deucalion's flood in Chapter 10 (a lesser deluge which 'did not reach Egypt and its adjacent lands'), that would not be obvious to someone exploring Chapter 12 out of context as a freestanding acount of pagan cults – perhaps one of the Irish scholars whom Aldhelm deplored. Such a reader might be mystified by Augustine's reference to the Via Sacra (the high street of ancient Rome) and other details.[26] What he might deduce, however, was that the Luperci were somehow involved in Noah's Flood and survived it and perhaps that they were distinct from normal *homines*, that is, a separate race.[27] Such a reading, taken together with the reference to the seemingly aquatic Luperci a little later in Book xviii (in Chapter 17, discussed above), may have been enough to establish the Luperci as survivors of Noah's Flood.

In this way Augustine may have provided Irish scholars with the term *luperc(án)* as a learned, latinate label for the native *abac* 'water sprite', a being equated with the leprechaun in the earliest Irish texts.[28] Evidently the

<hr/>

25 Bettenson's translation, p. 774.   26 Some scholars have assumed that Augustine also took this reference to the Luperci from Varro (e.g. Wiseman, 'The god of the Lupercal', p. 7). This is dismissed by McLynn, 'Crying wolf', p. 173, who speculates that Augustine, visiting Rome in February 384, heard from misinformed guides that 'the runners' course "up and down" the Via Sacra was interpreted as a replay of the Great Flood, a fabrication which cannot conceivably be foisted upon Varro'. Cf. J.A. North, 'Caesar at the Lupercalia', *Journal of Roman Studies*, 98 (2008), 144–60 at 155–6.   27 Strictly speaking it would be impossible to find a mountain top that rose above the level of Noah's Flood, other than the one on which Eden was believed to be situated (see Howard Rollin Patch, *The Other World according to descriptions in medieval literature* [Cambridge, MA, 1950], esp. pp 142, 145, 146, and 151 – I am grateful to Prof. Carey for this reference). Note however that Augustine speaks ambiguously of the saints at Judgment Day moving to 'higher regions to which the flames of that fire will not rise, in the same way as the waters of the Flood did not rise to that level' (*De ciuitate Dei*, xx, 18, trans. Bettenson, p. 931).   28 On the equation with *abac* (cognate with Welsh *afanc* 'water monster, beaver', from the stem *ab-* seen in Irish *abann*, Welsh *afon*, 'river'), see Rodway, 'Mermaids, leprechauns, and Fomorians', 15 with references, and Bisagni, '*Leprechaun*: a new etymology', 81–3. As

two were synonymous, or at least closely associated, and both evolved similarly into non-aquatic dwarves.

The Luperci as misunderstood in Ireland are a world away from Aldhelm's allusion to their priapic cult; the latter is much closer to the truth, for the ancient authors associate the Lupercalia with phallic fertility gods such as Pan, Inuus, Faunus, and Liber Pater (equated with Dionysus / Bacchus; cf. Aldhelm's *bacchantes*).[29] Aldhelm seems not to have had access to the main Latin sources used by modern scholars – Livy's *History*, Ovid's *Fasti*, and Justinus' *Epitome* of Pompeius Trogus – but Servius' commentary on *Aeneid* viii, 343–4 could have given him the gist of the Lupercalia, including its association with Pan and Liber Pater, the naked runners, and the promotion of fertility.[30] By contrast, according to Herren, it is 'not clear whether there was direct knowledge of Servius in Ireland before the ninth century'.[31] Aldhelm may invoke Priapus to underline how far the Irish had erred on the topic of the Luperci.

Another possibility is that Aldhelm learnt the true nature of the Lupercalia not from Servius but from his studies with Theodore at Canterbury. Early in his career 'Theodore had gone to Constantinople, perhaps as a refugee from Persian or Arab invasions of Syria and Cilicia'.[32] Now in tenth-century Constantinople a modified form of the Lupercalia was still celebrated under that name (abbreviated Λουπέρχ in the extant manuscript).[33] It is not impossible, then, that Theodore, noted for his antagonism

Bisagni notes, early Irish glossators may have tended to connect leprechauns with *lú* 'small thing' (p. 62) and certainly derived *abac* from *becc* 'small'. Presumably leprechauns derived their small size from the *abaic* or vice versa. On phonetic grounds, *abacus* glossed *corr* ('dwarf') in Paris, Bibliothèque Nationale Française lat. MS 10289 (s. ix) was presumably taken to be Irish *abac* rather than its Breton cognate (despite Antone Minard, 'Colorful monsters: the *afanc* in medieval Welsh narrative' in J.F. Nagy [ed.], *Myth in Celtic literatures*, CSANA Yearbook 6 [Dublin, 2007], pp 120–31 at p. 128, following Léon Fleuriot, *Dictionnaire des gloses en vieux breton* [Paris, 1964], pp 50–1, 60, and 119). The Irish word *abac* seems to have been loaned into Brittonic (+ *du* 'black') in Old Breton *amachdu* (ibid., p. 60) and Middle Welsh *Auacdu* (see Marged Haycock [ed. and trans.], *Legendary poems from the Book of Taliesin* [Aberystwyth, 2007], p. 322). **29** Wiseman, 'The god of the Lupercal', with *Testimonia* on pp 18–22. Priapus is never mentioned (apart from Aldhelm, who is ignored by the classicists), though Wiseman (p. 10 n. 76) speculates on a connection between a *Castrum Inui* between Antium and Ardea and a *villa Priapi in agro Ardeatino* attested in the tenth century. Inuus was the god of penetration (*inire*). **30** For Servius, see ibid., pp 10 and 18–19; for Aldhelm's reading, see Michael Lapidge, *Anglo-Latin literature 600–800* (London, 1996), p. 195 (Servius) and idem, *The Anglo-Saxon library*, pp 178–91. **31** Herren, 'Literary and glossarial evidence', p. 51 n. 12. Cf. idem, 'Transmission and reception', p. 91; Miles, *Heroic saga and Classical epic in medieval Ireland*, p. 25. **32** Michael Lapidge, 'The career of Archbishop Theodore' in idem (ed.), *Archbishop Theodore: commemorative studies on his life and influence* (Cambridge, 1995), pp 1–29 at p. 13. **33** *Constantine Porphyrogennetos: the book of ceremonies*, i, 73, trans. Ann Moffatt and Maxeme Tall with the Greek edition of the Corpus Scriptorum Historiae

towards Irish scholarship, and probably for his distaste for the pagan classics as well,[34] used first-hand knowledge of the traditions of the Lupercalia to mock Irish misunderstanding of the Luperci.

Byzantinae, vol. 1 (Canberra, 2012), pp 364–9. Cf. Y.-M. Duval, 'Des Lupercales de Constantinople aux Lupercales de Rome', *Revue des études latines*, 55 (1977), 222–70 at 226 n. 1; Wiseman, 'The god of the Lupercal', p. 17.   34 Jane Barbara Stevenson, 'Theodore and the *Laterculus Malalianus*' in Lapidge (ed.), *Archbishop Theodore*, pp 204–21 at p. 210; eadem, *The 'Laterculus Malalianus' and the school of Archbishop Theodore* (Cambridge, 1995), pp 73 and 177.

Tabula gratulatoria

Andrea Adolph
Anders Ahlqvist
Frank Allen
Christophe Archan
Terry Barry
Alexandra Bergholm
Edel Bhreathnach
Jacqueline Borsje
Cormac Bourke
Elizabeth Boyle
Liam Breatnach
Pádraig A. Breatnach
Mícheál Briody
Dauvit Broun
Andrew Byrne
Marc Caball
The Department of Anglo-Saxon, Norse and Celtic, University of Cambridge
Nicholas Canny
John Carey
Ann Mary Casey
T.M. Charles-Edwards
Thomas Owen Clancy
Anne Connon & Rick Graff
Patricia Coughlan
George Cunningham
Valerie Kelly Curtin
Seamus Darcy
Pádraig de Brún
Gearóid Denvir
Charles Doherty
Riona Doolan
Clodagh Downey
Clare Downham
Aidan Doyle
Seán Duffy
David Dumville
Carol A. Farr
Kelly Fitzgerald

Joseph J. Flahive
Marie Therese Flanagan
Roy Flechner
Hugh Fogarty
Maxim Fomin
Abbot and Community, Glenstal Abbey
Elizabeth A. Gray
Margo Griffin-Wilson
Anthony Harvey
Deborah Hayden
Philip Healy
Anne Herbert, Josephine Herbert & John Herbert
Michael W. Herren
Barbara Hillers
Peter Holzmann
Seán Hutton
Helen Imhoff
Colin Ireland
Karen Jankulak & Jonathan Wooding
Frank Johnson
Elva Johnston
Fergus Kelly
Patricia Kelly
Heather C. Key
Mary Kirby
John T. Koch
Ksenia Kudenko
Frédéric Kurzawa
Brian Lambkin
Margaret Lantry
Barry Lewis
Michael Linkletter
Martina Maher
Liam Mac Amhlaigh
Éanna Mac Cába
Pádraig Mac Cárthaigh
Máirtín Mac Conmara
Mícheál Mac Craith
Gearóid Mac Eoin
Donncha MacGabhann
Peadar Mac Gabhann
Catherine McKenna

Sarah McKibben
Neil McLeod
Wilson McLeod
Séamus Mac Mathúna
Michael Meckler
Michael Merrigan
Brent Miles
Jimmy P. Miller
Kay Muhr
Kevin Murray
Máire Ní Annracháin
Máire Ní Bháin
Emma Nic Cárthaigh
Próinséas Ní Chatháin
Aoibheann Nic Dhonnchadha
Máirín Ní Dhonnchadha
Máire Ní Íceadha
Máiréad Ní Loingsigh
Máire Ní Mhaonaigh
Deirdre Nic Mhathúna
Síle Ní Mhurchú
Máire Ní Neachtain
Meidhbhín Ní Úrdail & Jürgen Uhlich
Feargal Ó Béarra
Elizabeth O'Brien
Seán Ó Broin
Stiofán Ó Cadhla
Éamonn Ó Carragáin
Tomás Ó Carragáin
Gearóidín & Diarmaid Ó Catháin
Roibeard Ó Cathasaigh
Tomás Ó Cathasaigh
Pádraig Ó Céilleachair
Seán Ó Coileáin
Breandán Ó Conchúir
Josephine O'Connell
Donnchadh Ó Corráin
Dáibhí Ó Cróinín
Gearóid & Gay Ó Crualaoich
Caitríona Ó Dochartaigh
Liam Ó Dochartaigh
Ken Ó Donnchú

Pádraig Ó Fiannachta
Dónall Ó Fionnáin
Tony Ó Floinn
Mícheál Ó Geallabháin
Diarmuid Ó Giolláin
Cathal Ó Háinle
Donnchadh Ó hAodha
Tomás Ó hAodha
Ruairí Ó hUiginn
Roibeárd Ó hÚrdail
Aideen M. O'Leary
Pádraig Ó Macháin
Mícheál Ó Mainnín
Roibeard Ó Maolalaigh
Diarmuid Ó Mathúna
Nollaig Ó Muraíle
Liam P. Ó Murchú
Jennifer O'Reilly
Pádraig Ó Riain & Dagmar Ó Riain-Raedel
Tadhg Ó Síocháin
Lisi Oliver†
Oliver Padel
Andrea Palandri
Geraldine Parsons
Erich Poppe
Emer Purcell
Jan Erik Rekdal
Pádraigín Riggs
Katja Ritari
Jean Rittmueller
Royal Irish Academy Library
Paul Russell
Nathalie Schneider-O'Shea
Diarmuid Scully
David Sexton
Richard Sharpe
Katharine Simms
Patrick Sims-Williams & Marged Haycock
David Stifter
Cathy Swift
Simon Taylor
Marie-Luise Theuerkauf

Donna Thornton & Niall Ó Murchadha
Alan Titley
Gregory Toner
Ilona Tuomi
Emily Twomey
Seán Ua Súilleabháin
UCC Library
Mairéad Uí Fhlatharta
Nicole Volmering
Cameron Wachowich
Patrick Wadden
David Woods
Alex Woolf
Gerard Wrixon